Passions, Pedagogies,
and
21st Century Technologies

Passions, Pedagogies, and 21st Century Technologies

edited by

GAIL E. HAWISHER
CYNTHIA L. SELFE

UTAH STATE UNIVERSITY PRESS
Logan, Utah

NATIONAL COUNCIL OF TEACHERS OF ENGLISH
Urbana, Illinois

Utah State University Press
Logan, Utah 84322-7800

National Council of Teachers of English
Urbana, Illinois 61801-1096

Typography by WolfPack.

Cover design by Stephen Adams.
Cover photograph: "Mable" (detail), by Joseph Emery, a construction in cast bronze, concrete, plexiglass, with photographs, poem, pills, razor, glove.

The following chapters reprinted by permission.
    "Beyond next before you once again." Copyright © 1998 Michael Joyce.
    "Into the Next Room." Copyright © 1998 Carolyn Guyer, photographs copyright © 1996 Dianne Hagaman.
    "Technology's Strange, Familiar Voices" is based on an article first published in *College Composition and Communication* 48:3. Copyright © 1997 Janet Carey Eldred.
    "Liberal Individualism and Internet Policy" is based on a chapter first published in *Rhetorical Ethics and Internetworked Writing* by James Porter. Copyright © 1998 Ablex.

NCTE Stock Number 34971

Library of Congress Cataloging-in-Publication Data

Passions, pedagogies, and 21st century technologies / Gail E.
Hawisher, Cynthia L. Selfe, editors.
   p. cm.
   Includes bibliographical references (p.) and index.

   ISBN 0-87421-258-8

   1. English language—Rhetoric—Study and teaching—Technological
innovations. 2. English language—Rhetoric—Study and
teaching—Data processing. 3. English language—Composition and
exercises—Data processing. 4. Academic writing—Study and
teaching—Technological innovations. 5. Academic writing—Study and
teaching—Data processing. 6. Information technology. I. Hawisher,
Gail E. II. Selfe, Cynthia L., 1951-
PE1404 .P38 1999
808'.042'07—ddc21

        98-40118
        CIP

CONTENTS

The Passions that Mark Us
Teaching, Texts, and Technologies

Gail E. Hawisher
Cynthia L. Selfe

The American college wanted and revered men like Professor Fletcher O. Marsh, who in 1866 hauled manure all one day that the grounds of Denison College might in some way be made more beautiful; men of all work like John Smith of Dartmouth, whose appointment made him "Professor of English, Latin, Greek, Chaldee, etc., and such other languages as he shall have time for." What the American college wanted or needed was a man like Father William Stack Murphy of Fordham who in 1840s would, while shaving and gesticulating with his razor, listen to his students practice orations and then go off to conduct classes which were a wonder of charm, interest, and successful teaching.

Frederick Rudolph, *The American College and
University: A History*

I don't believe that many English teachers are lazy; rather the tension here is between the kind of work we see ourselves as doing and the kind society is most willing to pay us for. An explanation is required for the fact that English teachers don't claim more credit for the part of our work that society values and less for the part that society hardly knows of and would probably disapprove of if it knew more.

Richard Ohmann, *English in America: A Radical View
of the Profession*

It's a full-time job (and more) not only to keep pace with the inevitable changes in hardware and software, but also to stay current with the exponentially increasing body of theoretical and critical literature on everything cyber, virtual, hyper, and digital, and most importantly of all, to find ways in which to implement the technology so as to make a real difference in my classroom and in my scholarship.

Matthew G. Kirschenbaum, *Chronicle of Higher Education*
July 25, 1997: B11

POPULAR DISCOURSES RELATED TO TEACHING AND SCHOLARSHIP IN ENGLISH studies traditionally link life in the profession with the world of privilege and leisure in protected enclaves often associated with the upper classes—they seldom, if ever, mention technology. College English professors of both sexes tend to be represented as bookish types in tweeds and corduroys, wielding leaky pens, outfitted in the suitably subdued colors of navy and tan, and, more recently, in the pervasive all-black of those likely to take cultural studies as their field of study. And yet, all of this, one might argue, the pens, the books, and the attire, can be understood as technologies that are associated with language studies—even though the black of traditional academic robes has been afforded new authority with the ascendancy of postmodernism and the computer has assumed new importance in our study of discourses, communication, and language.

But these changes notwithstanding, as Richard Ohmann argues above, many in the public sphere continue to see English professors as occupying a station in life that requires less in the way of hourly, accounted-for-labor than that of their neighbors inhabiting worlds outside of academe. And, although we know that few citizens would cast English professors in the role of hauling manure to beautify the grounds of their college campuses, as Rudolf above describes Fletcher O. Marsh, few, also, we would argue, construct them as the erudite technology-wielding expert that English graduate student Matthew G. Kirschenbaum aspires to become through his work in the academy. Yet these various and contradictory renditions of English professors exist side-by-side in a world that is changing so fast that any commonplace understandings of what we're about as scholars and teachers in English studies are constantly being called into question—even our own. The passions that mark us—teaching, texts, the day-to-day work environs, the challenges of a changing society and sometimes the new technologies—descend from the scholarly deeds of those who have gone before us; yet they also mean that we enter the future transformed. Certainly the trajectories of our own lives—especially those portions that combine interests in the humanities and in the design, use, and study of computer technologies—escape easy classification and evade the stereotypes of English professors which continue to be kept alive in popular society.

As English professors who grew up in the 1950s and 1960s and entered the profession in the 1970s, neither of us started teaching with computers; we learned as we went. And what we learned convinced us that computers were becoming increasingly important in educational settings—not simply because they are tools for writing (they are not simply tools; they are, indeed, complex technological artifacts that embody and shape—and are shaped by—the ideological assumptions of an entire culture), but rather because these machines serve as powerful cultural and catalytic forces in the lives of teachers and students. Although the machines themselves mean little to us and to the authors of the essays we present here, the work they support and the connections they make possible mean a great deal.

It is through our own work with the new technologies, for example, that we continue to re-discover an essential truth about our profession—that teaching and research are inherently social and political activities, and that the human exchanges resting at the heart of our work take place not only among faculty members and students, but among faculty members themselves. As teacher-scholars, we do our best work when we can talk together, write together, and think together about what we do. Seldom have we been the lone, solitary writers of the garret. And even if current administrative structures of university teaching often serve to isolate instructors from one another—limiting collaborative teaching projects (as too expensive and not efficient) and restricting faculty members' travel to conferences and sites for scholarly research (by eliminating or reducing travel monies)—we have learned to use computers to re-establish connections with colleagues, share the important stories of teaching, reflect in critical ways on the work and profession that we share. Nonetheless, the changes supported by the new information technologies are not without complication, and they have their own price for English professors.

As the twentieth century draws to a close, we find ourselves very much in need of models that offer strategies for acting productively in the face of social change. Indeed, such change is so rapid and far-reaching that it sometimes threatens to paralyze us with fear and inaction. Our own classrooms, and those of most of our colleagues, seem to be populated by students who see little connection between traditional literacy education and the world problems that they currently face—the continuing destruction of global ecosystems, the epidemic spread of AIDS and other diseases, terrorism, racism, homophobia, the impotence of political leaders and the irrelevance of their parties. Faced with these challenges and with others of equal magnitude, many faculty teaching in English studies find themselves scrambling to re-think and re-design educational efforts within expanded ethical contexts that recognize vastly different global perspectives, learning how to function with an increasing sense of responsibility in new and taxing economic parameters, acknowledging and then addressing the need to learn a range of rapidly changing technologies that allow for an expanded network of communication and intellectual exchange.

Clearly these projects are complicated endeavors which require intelligence and passion, and an understanding of the underlying cultural formation and dynamics that link humans and their technologies in such robust ways. As scholar-teachers of English, we often find ourselves ill prepared for taking on many of the tasks involved in these efforts. Like the authors in this volume, most in the profession have come of age in a print generation and our thinking has both been shaped and limited by this fact. Few of us are equipped to function effectively and comfortably in virtual literacy environments. Indeed, like many citizens, college faculty are just beginning to learn what it means to work successfully within a society that is dependent on computer technology for literacy activities. We are only beginning to identify, for example, the complexity of the challenges posed by such a society, including the challenge of adapting to an increasingly rapid pace of change. Nor do we necessarily have the lived experiences that allow us to deal productively with this climate of change.

As a result, we often find ourselves casting about for effective ways to educate students for a world with which we, ourselves, are unfamiliar—and about which we remain uncertain. In her 1970 book *Culture and Commitment*, Margaret Mead describes the unsettling sense of functioning within such a cultural milieu. In this work, she calls cultures of this kind "prefigurative." The prefigurative learning culture occurs in a society where change is so rapid that adults are trying to prepare children for experiences the adults themselves have never had. The prefigurative cultural style, Mead argues, prevails in a world where the "past, the culture that had shaped [young adults'] understanding— their thoughts, their feelings, and their conceptions of the world—[is] no sure guide to the present. And the elders among them, bound to the past, [can] provide no models for the future" (70).

Mead traces these broad patterns of cultural change particularly in terms of American culture, all the while setting her analysis within a global context. She claims that the prefigurative culture characteristic of America in the 1960s and ensuing years—and, we maintain, in the new millennium—is symptomatic of a world changing so fast that it exists "without models and without precedent," a culture in which "neither parents nor teachers, lawyers, doctors, skilled workers, inventors, preachers, or prophets" (xx) can teach children what they need to know about the world. Mead notes that the immediate and dramatic needs our prefigurative culture faces—fueled by increasing world hunger, the continuing population explosion, the rapid explosion of technological knowledge, the threat of continued war, global communication—demand a new kind of social and educational response that privileges participatory input, ecological sensitivity, an appreciation for cultural diversity, and the intelligent use of technology, among other approaches.

In the prefiguratve society, Mead notes, students must—at least to some extent—learn important lessons from each other, helping each other find their way through an unfamiliar thicket of issues and situations about which the elder members of the society are uncertain. As teachers in such a culture, our education contributions must take a dramatic turn. Unlike previous generations of English professors, we cannot promise to provide students with a stable and unchanging body of knowledge—especially in connection with technology use. Indeed, we cannot even provide ourselves with such intellectual comforts.

The teachers and authors contributing to this volume add their passionate voices to the discussion of issues surrounding—and shaping—information technologies at the century's end. As a collection, the essays demonstrate the value of seeking understanding in unfamiliar and familiar places and of learning in new and old ways—of continuing to take risks in connection with the new technologies even when those risks produce results that are unsatisfactory in some way. Because we ourselves are uncertain of the directions that the English profession will take in the coming century, we believe that such an approach—as represented within this collection—offers a thoughtful look at the techno-cultural contexts with which all teacher-scholars must learn to contend.

The essays in this volume are grouped in four sections, each focused on one particular aspect of English professionals' lives as they struggle to bring the new technologies into their field of vision. The chapters in Part I, "Refiguring Notions of Literacy in an Electronic World," provide an historical overview of writing as a technology and move quickly to challenge—and sometimes defend—conventional and not so conventional notions of literacy within the context of the current wired world. In the first chapter, Dennis Baron discusses the development and spread of writing technologies from the invention of writing itself down to the present, with a focus on the pencil, the computer, and Henry David Thoreau, who contributed to the technology of pencils but scoffed at the invention of the telegraph. Baron argues that information technologies are invented for a limited purpose and are the property of a small group of initiates. As access increases across society, new functions are devised, costs decrease, and facility of use increases. Traditionally, Baron notes, such technologies proliferate by mimicking previous inventions, but often they are resisted by traditionalists. Once accepted, new technologies come into their own, as humans experiment with new—and previously undreamed of—modes of communication. Only at this stage, Baron contends, are previous technologies drawn under the sway of newer technologies. So goes the technological world of writing.

Technological development, however, does not always seem to advance the cause of literacy, as Douglas Hesse reminds us. Urging caution in chapter two, Hesse discusses what is lost if we too quickly celebrate the demise of essayistic literacy as we adapt to the cultural, and technological, context of postmodernism. In contrasting the essayistic tradition from Montaigne, developed as anti-methodical discourse, with the scientific tradition, he argues that commonly held misconceptions of the essay require more than just correcting a loose definition. His comparison allows us to see two very different critiques of the "essayistic" by those who promote new computer discourses. In affirming that there is a place for the essayistic, not as the model of discourse but as one important mode of discourse, Hesse's argument is part political/legalistic and cultural and part psychological, with implications for individual writers, readers, and teachers. Indeed, we might say that Hesse argues for an expanded understanding of the essay as a technology itself, and one that remains valuable for individuals within current cultural contexts. Like most technologies, he reminds us, the essay shapes our thinking and our understanding as well as our communication practices in ways that we need to continue to study, investigate, and appreciate.

In chapter three, Sarah Sloane focuses our attention on the writer, in this instance, a student writer. Based on a case study of J., a reluctant first-year writer in a computer-based writing classroom, Sloane's essay develops the critical term "genealogy" as a word that describes how memories and habits of other medial contexts affect the choices a student writer makes while composing at the computer. In a contribution that resonates with themes in both

Hesse's and Baron's work, Sloane argues that a writer's choice of composing tools and setting, as well as his or her choice of topic and form, are always informed by memory, or what she calls "medial hauntings" and "apparitional knowledge" of earlier writing experiences. The article first develops the critical category of "genealogy" (relying on Nietzsche and Foucault) and then applies the term to the experiences of J. as he chooses topic, tool, and setting in his first-year writing class. Sloane suggests that other practitioners of case study methodology pay more attention to how genealogy may inform their models of computer-based composing processes.

In chapter four, which also resonates with the other pieces in this section, Gunther Kress invites us to challenge current notions of literate activities which invariably, he argues, exclude considerations of the visual. He reminds us that the word "literacy" exists in English but has no precise counterpart in German or the romance languages where similar words denote a more literal facility with the technology of the alphabet, rather than encapsulating the wide range of abilities entangled in the English word "literate." He focuses on the changes that have occurred in the written form of the language by comparing the pages of newspapers and textbooks, and, in doing so, illustrates the need for changes in English curricula and pedagogy. Throughout his chapter, he emphasizes that the visual is not so much new in itself as new in the recent history of representation where display and arrangement are taking on new meaning and are often neglected in English courses of study. According to Kress, the latest relationships between text and image demand a new theory of meaning. Responding implicitly to Kress and to Hesse in the chapter that follows, Myka Vielstimmig, the collaborative author enacted by Michael Spooner and Kathleen Yancey, fashions an essay that experiments visually with the arrangement of text, but also touches on the shaping influences of technology. In explaining that the chapter is not an argument against the essay, Vielstimmig argues that it is itself an essay of "radically different identity politics," admitting many genres, and asks readers to experience the polyphonic visual and poetic patterns of coherence. Each chapter in this section presents an inkling of what is to come—the germ of an idea which is subsequently repeated and expanded upon throughout the chapters of the book.

Taken together, all five essays in this section prepare the way for Diana George and Diane Shoos's insightful response on the necessity for reconfiguring the role of the visual in literate societies in a postmodern age. As these authors note, to "get at some of the intertextual demands of a literacy that insists on the role of the visual (and the electronic) as well as the verbal," we have to learn to value the visual as a fundamental part of literacy. In order to accomplish this task, we have to look beyond a simplistic understanding of technology or medium—whether the information is presented in film, print, television and video images, web pages or print layouts, charts and other graphic illustrations of information, or the interplay of font and text—and focus on images as they embody meaning and force intertextual play at multiple levels and in multiple ways.

Part II, "Revisiting Notions of Teaching and Access in an Electronic World," foregrounds the difficult issues involved in the relationship between technological change and everyday teaching and work practices. In chapter seven, Lester Faigley reminds us that the relationship is not an easy one. He begins with four stories that highlight the promise and peril of the Internet and observes that his stories are only a few among the many that promote the Internet as purveyor of all things in the name of progress. But sometimes hidden in these stories, he argues, are huge inequities that teachers see every day. His essay ultimately asks: "What sort of future will children enter in the aftermath of the massive redistribution of wealth and disruption of patterns of employment that have occurred during the last two decades?"

In chapter eight, Marilyn Cooper turns to the challenges involved in developing a postmodern pedagogy that responds to some of the material conditions Faigley sets forth. For Cooper, postmodernism can provide opportunities to help us make sense of the changes we experience all around us—shifts in modes of transportation, in communication technologies, in the global economy, in ways of living. With these shifts, she argues, come changes in our responsibilities and practices as teachers. According to Cooper, we need to rethink assumptions about knowledge, language, and the self as they get played out in our everyday actions, if we are to use the new information technologies effectively in our teaching.

In chapter nine, James Sosnoski underscores the practical need for such reconsiderations by focusing on reading practices that attend electronic media. Just as we have come to understand writing as an activity enabled and extended by technology, Sosnoski would have us think of reading as an activity that is similarly shaped—and abetted—by technology. Without effective browsers, search engines, and indexing programs, we will be unable to manage the huge amount of information with which we are constantly deluged; even with them, some will understand the new reading—hyper-reading, if you will—as resulting in a loss of coherence and substance. Like Cooper, Sosnoski would have us undertake the teaching of hyper-reading as informed action, thoughtful action in which the pedagogical and postmodern connect rather than separate those of us who would teach English studies.

In chapter ten, Geoffrey Sirc demonstrates yet another way to view the changing and overlapping sites of teaching and writing and technology. Using Marcel Duchamp as a lens through which to view relevant issues, Sirc argues that we can begin to see how changes in conceptions of work accompany changes in technology. These changes, in turn, result in changes in the language about work or writing, and, eventually, changes in its function. All writing, for Sirc, has become screen writing—"the whole text double-exposed by images and sound-bites"—it is writing that never stops but is always in motion, home pages constantly updated, discussion lists ongoing, links connecting them all.

Thus he shows us how changes in writing practices—how changes in language, thought, and technology—shape one another and finally transform what we are about as teachers, students, scholars, writers.

Sometimes these changes, however, blind us to the realities of the material world that constitute our working lives. Charles Moran, in chapter eleven, insists that we pay more attention to issues of access that have been too long neglected. According to Moran, the field has a responsibility to address issues of access more directly than it now does. It could, and should, investigate not only high-end technology but low-end technology. It could, and should, encourage the widespread use of affordable technology as a teaching tool in our classrooms rather than moving so quickly to advocating high-end technologies. And when we do study the uses of high-end technology, we need to discover ways of foregrounding issues of access while we do so. Throughout his chapter, Moran argues convincingly that the field has for too long ignored what Kozol has termed "savage inequalities."

Bringing the chapters in this section together, Bertram Bruce gifts us with his insight: the authors in this section must swim against the current discourse surrounding the new technologies to talk about what is central to pedagogy. Although the issues they raise about income disparities, irregularity of employment, access issues, and moral responsibilities are ones that should not be ignored, they tend to fall outside acceptable academic discourse that seeks the neutral and analyzable, avoiding at all costs the passion so evident in these essays. When we as editors were asked which essay prompted us to lead off the title of this book with "passions," we had no ready answer. Many of the essays in this collection speak passionately about what should matter today—about the ethical dimensions of everyday teaching and living—and not a few are in this section.

The essays in Part III, "Ethical and Feminist Concerns in an Electronic World," are no less passionate in foregrounding issues that are too little written about in our profession. In chapter thirteen, James Porter invokes communitarian ethics to provide a heuristic through which cyberwriters can address some of the ethical dilemmas they face. Porter would have us ask how we situate ourselves ethically as writers and "publishers" of electronic discourse, as listowners and managers of discussion groups, as web authors, and as teachers in what he calls "Internetworked" writing classes. In certain cases, he believes, online communities need protection from individuals and that the field's current focus on the individual writer, student, and text endorses an ideology that precludes actions against individual online acts of violence. Throughout his chapter, he argues that liberal individualism as advocated by such groups as the Electronic Frontier Foundation will not bring about desired changes in fundamental online inequities anymore than it has offline. Instead of free speech on the networks, he fears that we will instead end up with increased commercial control, favoring society's same privileged groups that Moran describes as on the rich side of the "wealth gap."

Also interested in online equity issues and in the opportunities—or not—that the new media provide for women, Susan Romano, in chapter fourteen, turns to examining various subject positions that women take up in an online writing class. Using early archives of in-class synchronous writing, she finds that the online discursive environment has a history of both exclusionary and inclusionary practices. As "lurker historian," Romano looks at these practices framed by "pedagogies of the self," the means by which writing teachers encourage students to experiment with alternate identities. As they experiment, she argues, women must decide to position themselves as women or find other places to stand; even with their use of pseudonyms, she wonders how free the women are to say what they want or to occupy other subject positions. For Romano, the metaphors of freedom, open space, and frontiers that so frequently describe online life tend to mystify virtual social arrangements and may have little value in opening up new subjectivities for women.

Following fast upon Romano's inquiry, in chapter fifteen, Hawisher and Sullivan look to the World Wide Web and its representation of women. In scrutinizing how women visually represent themselves on home pages and how they get represented, the authors begin to describe how women write, authorize, and control the electronic spaces of the Web pages. Their overarching argument is that although feminists in computers and composition have focused almost exclusively on the textual environments of computer-mediated communication, the heightened possibilities for self-representation brought about by the Web suggest that a simple transfer of arguments about women's verbal online lives is inadequate as a strategy for exploring visual representations. In an effort to complicate electronic discourse theories, they analyze online visual representations of women in a variety of discursive settings.

This scrutiny of the visual, especially within the context of a technological culture, continues in chapter sixteen, authored by Cynthia Selfe, and focuses on commercial advertisements about technology that appear in print magazines. The visual representations used to sell computers and other information technologies, Selfe tells us, are often shot through with the same old traditional narratives of our culture where women are represented as beauties or seductresses and men as bikers and techno-geeks. These conventional stories told yet again in the context of new technologies, she argues, should remind us of our ethical responsibilities to work as college English teachers toward productive change, however slow or difficult that change may be.

A related focus on narratives also informs chapter seventeen, in which Carolyn Guyer and Dianne Hagaman acknowledge the "impulse to narrative" and present us with Carolyn Heilbrun's notion that we have no choice but to use the stories we have read or heard to make new narratives. These are what we must build on. In moving from the material enclosures of rooms to the virtual textual spaces of MOOs to the visual settings of the World Wide Web, Guyer would have us see neither word nor image as dominating. She believes that the electronic meeting places of the Internet—where people from all over the world mingle and cross boundaries—just might enable us to construct new stories, to construct ourselves anew, to move into the next room. In Guyer and Hagaman's chapter, there are no images of the electronic frontier with its requisite console cowboys; instead we see and read Hagaman's evocative photographs of a mission room, a San Francisco kitchen, a dining room, a memorial service room, and other meeting rooms, one furnished with "sun chairs."

In the response chapter that closes this section and that speaks to the issues raised in all five of the previous chapters, Cynthia Haynes seeks to expose the hidden connections among the contributions and, in doing so, regards herself as a "co-respondent" who prefers being understood as permeating and being permeated by the "running exchange" of the authors in this section.

Part IV, "Searching for Notions of Our Postmodern Literate Selves in an Electronic World," picks up again the theme of literacy and explores its many facets. In chapter nineteen, Anne Wysocki and Johndan Johnson-Eilola ask why our culture tends to use the metaphor of literacy "for everything else?" By continuing to use "literacy" to explain what we and our students will achieve with new technologies, the authors argue, we continue to reproduce the idea that our relationship with technologies should be the same as that which we have with words—relationship which for most people is thought to be built step-by-step upon skills that are basic, neutral, visual, and disconnected from other practices. For Wysocki and Johnson-Eilola, hypermedia and synchronous conferencing are technologies that demand a re-thinking of the relationship of literacy and the technologies of writing. For them, such technologies are implicated in radical shifts in stability, identity, temporality, and spatial relations, all of which defy traditional analyses.

To illustrate some of the complications tied up in the god-term "literacy," Joe Amato then turns in chapter twenty from the academic to the autobiographical. In approaching the question of literacy, he deals with notions of socio-economic class, online technologies, and the teaching of writing but does so from the perspective of growing up mostly poor as an Italian-French-American in Syracuse, New York. He too sees "literacy" as a "powerfully fuzzy word" and writes, in part, about his father who possessed all those supposed basic literate skills mentioned by Wysocki and Johnson-Eilola but who struggled mightily to write the required words on welfare forms.

Continuing the autobiographical thread, Janet Carey Eldred, in chapter twenty-one, gives us stories and photographs depicting her relationship with her mother and writes of the technologies that connected and separated them. As a teenager, she was sometimes able to make herself heard by writing long impassioned letters to her mother; her spoken words were less powerful. In her mother's final days, Eldred turns to another writing technology—email—to put off hearing her mother's failed speech now replaced by the strange operator's voice of the T.D.D. phone. She wants to hear her mother's old voice, the written one if necessary, and this can be achieved through email: her mother's fingers, unlike her voice, can still make her voice ring loud and true. For Eldred, technology's inflections will always be heard in any discussion of voice.

In chapter twenty-two, Michael Joyce refocuses the discussion on the future and asks "what next?" He asks his question not in the sense of wanting to know which new technology will follow upon the World Wide Web but rather in the sense of reviewing, and ultimately renewing, our relations of being in the world. He follows the open question with a series of more specific queries: "What next literacy, what next community, what next perception, what next embodiment, what next hope?" For Joyce, we are always living in the shadow of what comes next. While remembering his old teacher and mentor, he tells us that the electronic culture might well return us inevitably once again to prizing "human communities as sources of value, identity, and locality."

Finally, Stuart Moulthrop, in the last essay of the volume, responds to the chapters in this section and adds his own story to the collection. As a recent guest editor of a special issue on writing in and about hypertext for the online journal *Postmodern Culture*, Moulthrop must heed the copyright laws designed for print contexts. He must suppress a publication that its authors expected to be published because of his responsibilities to the academic press that publishes the journal. His actions, to himself, seem incongruent—they fly in the face of the optimism and hype that continue to accompany the new technologies as they enter the academic publishing world. There should, he argues, be "rules of intellectual property more appropriate to its fluid, promiscuous information space." As writer-teacher-editor, Moulthrop, like the other authors of this volume, must grapple directly with these legal and ethical issues as he negotiates the use of communication technologies in his everyday work.

Faced with these challenges and with others of equal magnitude, the authors in this collection find themselves scrambling to re-think and re-design educational and professional efforts within expanded ethical contexts. Like others in English studies, they must learn how to function with an increasing sense of responsibility in new and taxing economic, political, and cultural contexts, all the while acknowledging and then addressing the need to learn a range of rapidly changing technologies that allows for an expanded network of teaching, communication, and intellectual exchange. Their essays present a remarkable set of insights. The passions and pedagogies that mark them enrich our understanding and enlarge our appreciation of our present place in society, and they expand our understanding of how others might see us as English studies teachers, writers, and scholars.

In some ways, then, we have not changed our approach to teaching and scholarship so radically since the days when Professor Fletcher O. Marsh contributed to his college by offering manual labor in the service of beauty. We still offer labor—albeit in a different and sometimes more intellectual guise—to the service of learning and knowledge to the institutions and the students for whom we work. Nor have we really made such radical changes in our academic apparel, if we are judged by the fact that black is yet again our preferred color, or by the fact that we still depend on technologies to teach, study, and communicate with one another (although far fewer of us gesticulate while shaving as we teach!). But in other ways the changes we face as we enter the next century couldn't be more dramatic and more deserving of passionate investigation and consideration. If we still depend on technologies to communicate with one another, for example, the specific technologies we now use have changed the world in ways that we have yet to identify or appreciate fully. And if we still concern ourselves with the study of language and the nature of literate exchanges, our understanding of the terms *literacy*, *text*, and *visual*, among others, have changed beyond recognition, challenging even our capacity to articulate them to the public and to one another in ways that will make productive differences in our lives and in the lives of others. In identifying these challenges and in trying to articulate their importance, the authors in this volume find themselves engaged in the messy, contradictory, and fascinating work of understanding how to live in a new world and a new century. As editors of this volume, we take great pleasure and pride in recommending these essays to you our readers. Not a little passion has gone into them.

PART ONE

---

*Refiguring Notions of Literacy
in an Electronic World*

CHAPTER ONE

From Pencils to Pixels
The Stages of Literacy Technologies

Dennis Baron

THE COMPUTER, THE LATEST DEVELOPMENT IN WRITING TECHNOLOGY, promises, or threatens, to change literacy practices for better or worse, depending on your point of view. For many of us, the computer revolution came long ago, and it has left its mark on the way we do things with words. We take word processing as a given. We don't have typewriters in our offices anymore, or pencil sharpeners, or even printers with resolutions less than 300 dpi. We scour *MacUser* and *PC World* for the next software upgrade, cheaper RAM, faster chips, and the latest in connectivity. We can't wait for the next paradigm shift. Computerspeak enters ordinary English at a rapid pace. In 1993, "the information superhighway" was voted the word—actually the phrase—of the year. In 1995, the word of the year was "the World Wide Web," with "morph" a close runner-up. The computer is also touted as a gateway to literacy. The Speaker of the House of Representatives suggested that inner-city school children should try laptops to improve their performance. The Governor of Illinois thinks that hooking up every school classroom to the Web will eliminate illiteracy. In his second-term victory speech, President Clinton promised to have every eight-year-old reading, and to connect every twelve-year-old to the National Information Infrastructure. Futurologists write books predicting that computers will replace books. Newspapers rush to hook online subscribers. The *New York Times* will download the Sunday crossword puzzle, time me as I fill in the answers from my keyboard, even score my results. They'll worry later about how to get me to pay for this service.

I will not join in the hyperbole of predictions about what the computer will or will not do for literacy, though I will be the first to praise computers, to acknowledge the importance of the computer in the last fifteen years of my own career as a writer, and to predict that in the future the computer will be put to communication uses we cannot now even begin to imagine, something quite beyond the word processing I'm now using to produce a fairly conventional text, a book chapter.

I readily admit my dependence on the new technology of writing. Once, called away to a meeting whose substance did not command my unalloyed attention, I began drafting on my conference pad a memo I needed to get out to my staff by lunchtime. I found that I had become so used to composing virtual prose at the keyboard I could no longer draft anything coherent directly onto a piece of paper. It wasn't so much that I couldn't think of the words, but the physical effort of handwriting, crossing out, revising, cutting and pasting (which I couldn't very well do at a meeting without giving away my inattention), in short, the writing practices I had been engaged in regularly since the age of four, now seemed to overwhelm and constrict me, and I longed for the flexibility of digitized text.

When we write with cutting-edge tools, it is easy to forget that whether it consists of energized particles on a screen or ink embedded in paper or lines gouged into clay tablets, writing itself is always first and foremost a technology, a way of engineering materials in order to accomplish an end. Tied up as it is with value-laden notions of literacy, art, and science, of history and psychology, of education, of theory, and of practicality, we often lose sight of writing as technology, until, that is, a new technology like the computer comes along and we are thrown into excitement and confusion as we try it on, try it out, reject it, and then adapt it to our lives—and of course, adapt our lives to it.

New communications technologies, if they catch on, go through a number of strikingly similar stages. After their invention, their spread depends on accessibility, function, and authentication. Let me first summarize what I mean, and then I'll present some more detailed examples from the history of writing or literacy technologies to illustrate.

THE STAGES OF LITERACY TECHNOLOGIES

Each new literacy technology begins with a restricted communication function and is available only to a small number of initiates. Because of the high cost of the technology and general ignorance about it, practitioners keep it to themselves at first—either on purpose or because nobody else has any use for it—and then, gradually, they begin to mediate the technology for the general public. The technology expands beyond this "priestly" class when it is adapted to familiar functions often associated with an older, accepted form of communication. As costs decrease and the technology becomes better able to mimic more ordinary or familiar communications, a new literacy spreads across a population. Only then does the technology come into its own, no longer imitating the previous forms given us by the earlier communication technology, but creating new forms and new possibilities for communication. Moreover, in a kind of backward wave, the new technology begins to affect older technologies as well.

While brave new literacy technologies offer new opportunities for producing and manipulating text, they also present new opportunities for fraud. And as the technology spreads, so do reactions against it from supporters of what are purported to be older, simpler, better, or more honest ways of writing. Not only must the new technology be accessible and useful, it must demonstrate its trustworthiness as well. So procedures for authentication and reliability must be developed before the new technology becomes fully accepted. One of the greatest concerns about computer communications today involves their authentication and their potential for fraud.

My contention in this essay is a modest one: the computer is simply the latest step in a long line of writing technologies. In many ways its development parallels that of the pencil—hence my title—though the computer seems more complex and is undoubtedly more expensive. The authenticity of pencil writing is still frequently questioned: we prefer that signatures and other permanent or validating documents be in ink. Although I'm not aware that anyone actually opposed the use of pencils when they began to be used for writing, other literacy technologies, including writing itself, were initially met with suspicion as well as enthusiasm.

HUMANISTS AND TECHNOLOGY

In attacking society's growing dependence on communication technology, the Unabomber (1996) targeted computer scientists for elimination. But to my chagrin he excluded humanists from his list of sinister technocrats because he found them to be harmless. While I was glad not to be a direct target of this mad bomber, I admit that I felt left out. I asked myself, if humanists aren't harmful, then what's the point of being one? But I was afraid to say anything out loud, at least until a plausible suspect was in custody.

Humanists have long been considered out of the technology loop. They use technology, to be sure, but they are not generally seen as pushing the envelope. Most people think of writers as rejecting technological innovations like the computer and the information superhighway, preferring instead to bang away at manual typewriters when they are not busy whittling new points on their no. 2 quill pens.

And it is true that some well-known writers have rejected new-fangleness. Writing in the *New York Times*, Bill Henderson (1994) reminds us that in 1849 Henry David Thoreau disparaged the information superhighway of his day, a telegraph connection from Maine to Texas. As Thoreau put it, "Maine and Texas, it may be, have nothing important to communicate." Henderson, who is a director of the Lead Pencil Club, a group opposed to computers and convinced that the old ways are better, further boasts that Thoreau wrote his anti-technology remarks with a pencil that he made himself. Apparently Samuel Morse, the developer of the telegraph, was lucky that the only letter bombs Thoreau made were literary ones.

In any case, Thoreau was not the complete Luddite that Henderson would have us believe. He was, in fact, an engineer, and he didn't make pencils for the same reason he went to live at Walden Pond, to get back to basics. Rather, he designed them for a living. Instead of waxing nostalgic about the good old days of hand-made pencils, Thoreau sought to improve the process by developing a cutting-edge manufacturing technology of his own.

The pencil may be old, but like the computer today and the telegraph in 1849, it is an indisputable example of a communication technology. Henderson unwittingly concedes as much when he adds that Thoreau's father founded "the first quality pencil [factory] in America." In Thoreau's day, a good pencil was hard to find, and until Thoreau's father and uncle began making pencils in the New World, the best ones were imported from Europe. The family fortune was built on the earnings of the Thoreau Pencil Company, and Henry Thoreau not only supported his sojourn at Walden Pond and his trip to the Maine woods with pencil profits, he himself perfected some of the techniques of pencil-making that made Thoreau pencils so desirable.

The pencil may seem a simple device in contrast to the computer, but although it has fewer parts, it too is an advanced technology. The engineer Henry Petroski (1990) portrays the development of the wood-cased pencil as a paradigm of the engineering process, hinging on the solution of two essential problems: finding the correct blend of graphite and clay so that the "lead" is not too soft or too brittle; and getting the lead into the cedar wood case so that it doesn't break when the point is sharpened or when pressure is applied during use. Pencil technologies involve advanced design techniques, the preparation and purification of graphite, the mixing of graphite with various clays, the baking and curing of the lead mixture, its extrusion into leads, and the preparation and finishing of the wood casings. Petroski observes that pencil making also involves a knowledge of dyes, shellacs, resins, clamps, solvents, paints, woods, rubber, glue, printing ink, waxes, lacquer, cotton, drying equipment, impregnating processes, high-temperature furnaces, abrasives, and mixing (Petroski 12). These are no simple matters. A hobbyist cannot decide to make a wood-cased pencil at home and go out to the craft shop for a set of instructions. Pencil-making processes were from the outset proprietary secrets as closely guarded as any Macintosh code.

The development of the pencil is also a paradigm of the development of literacy. In the two hundred fifty years between its invention, in the 1560s, and its perfection at John Thoreau and Company, as well as in the factories of Conté in France, and Staedtler and Faber in Germany, the humble wood pencil underwent several changes in form, greatly expanded its functions, and developed from a curiosity of use to cabinet-makers, artists and note-takers into a tool so universally employed for writing that we seldom give it any thought.

THE TECHNOLOGY OF WRITING

Of course the first writing technology was writing itself. Just like the telegraph and the computer, writing itself was once an innovation strongly resisted by traditionalists because it was unnatural and untrustworthy. Plato was one leading thinker who spoke out strongly against writing, fearing that it would weaken our memories. Pessimistic complaints about new literacy technologies, like those made by Plato, by Bill Henderson, and by Henderson's idol, Henry David Thoreau, are balanced by inflated predictions of how technologies will change our lives for the better. According to one school of anthropology, the invention of writing triggered a cognitive revolution in human development (for a critique of this so-called Great Divide theory of writing, see Street 1984). Historians of print are fond of pointing to the invention of the printing press in Europe as the second great cognitive revolution (Eisenstein 1979). The spread of electric power, the invention of radio, and later television, all promised similar bio-cultural progress. Now, the influence of computers on more and more aspects of our existence has led futurologists to proclaim that another technological threshold is at hand. Computer gurus offer us a brave new world of communications where we will experience cognitive changes of a magnitude never before known. Of course, the Unabomber and the Lead Pencil Club think otherwise.

Both the supporters and the critics of new communication technologies like to compare them to the good, or bad, old days. Jay Bolter disparages the typewriter as nothing more than a machine for duplicating texts—and as such, he argues, it has not changed writing at all. In contrast, Bolter characterizes the computer as offering a paradigm shift not seen since the invention of the printing press, or for that matter, since the invention of writing itself. But when the typewriter first began to sweep across America's offices, it too promised to change writing radically, in ways never before imagined. So threatening was the typewriter to the traditional literatus that in 1938 the *New York Times* editorialized against the machine that depersonalized writing, usurping the place of "writing with one's own hand."

The development of writing itself illustrates the stages of technological spread. We normally assume that writing was invented to transcribe speech, but that is not strictly correct. The earliest Sumerian inscriptions, dating from ca. 3500 BCE, record not conversations, incantations, or other sorts of oral utterances, but land sales, business transactions, and tax accounts (Crystal 1987). Clay tokens bearing similar marks appear for several thousand years before these first inscriptions. It is often difficult to tell when we are dealing with writing and when with art (the recent discovery of 10,000-year-old stone carvings in Syria has been touted as a possible missing link in the art-to-writing chain), but the tokens seem to have been used as a system of accounting from at least the 9th millennium BCE. They are often regarded as the first examples of writing, and it is clear that they are only distantly related to actual speech (see figure 1).

We cannot be exactly sure why writing was invented, but just as the gurus of today's technology are called computer geeks, it's possible that the first writers also seemed like a bunch of oddballs to the early Sumerians, who might have called them cuneiform geeks. Surely they walked around all day with a bunch of sharp styluses sticking out of their pocket protectors, and talked of nothing but new ways of making marks on stones. Anyway, so far as we know, writing itself begins not as speech transcription but as a relatively restricted and obscure record-keeping shorthand.

Figure 1
Clay Tokens and Sumerian Inscriptions

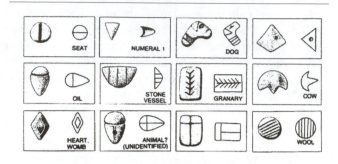

Clay tokens. Some of the commonest shapes are here compared
with the incised characters in the earliest Sumerian incriptions
(only some of which have been interpreted) (Crystal 1987, 196).

As innovative uses for the literacy technology are tried out, practitioners may
also adapt it to older, more familiar forms in order to gain acceptance from a
wider group. Although writing began as a tool of the bean counters, it eventually added a second, magical/religious function, also restricted and obscure as a
tool of priests. For writing to spread into a more general population in the
ancient world, it had first to gain acceptance by approximating spoken language. Once writers—in a more "modern" sense of the word—discovered what
writing could do, there was no turning back. But even today, most written text
does not transcribe spoken language: the comparison of script and transcript in
figure 2 makes this abundantly clear.

Of course writing never spread very greatly in the ancient world. William
Harris (1989) argues convincingly that no more than ten percent of the classical Greek or Roman populations could have been literate. One reason for this
must be that writing technology remained both cumbersome and expensive:
writing instruments, paints, and inks had to be hand made, and writing surfaces like clay tablets, wax tablets, and papyrus had to be laboriously prepared.
Writing therefore remained exclusive, until cheap paper became available, and
the printing press made mass production of written texts more affordable and
less labor-intensive.

WHAT WRITING DOES DIFFERENTLY

As a literacy technology like writing begins to become established, it also
goes beyond the previous technology in innovative, often compelling ways. For
example, while writing cannot replace many speech functions, it allows us to
communicate in ways that speech does not. Writing lacks such tonal cues of
the human voice as pitch and stress, not to mention the physical cues that

Figure 2
Script and Transcript

Scripted dialogue:

Thersites: The common curse of mankind, folly and ignorance, be thine in great revenue! heaven bless thee from a tutor, and discipline come not near thee! Let thy blood be thy direction till thy death! then, if she that lays thee out says thou art a fair corpse, I'll be sworn and sworn upon t she never shrouded any but lazars. Amen.

Shakespeare, *Troilus and Cressida*, II, iii, 30.

Unscripted dialogue (ostensibly):

Lt. Col. North: I do not recall a specific discussion. But, I mean. It was widely known within the CIA. I mean we were tracking that sensitive intelligence. I—I honestly don't recall, Mr. Van Cleve. I mean it—it didn't seem to me, at the time, that it was something that I was trying to hide from anybody. I was not engaged in it. And one of the purposes that I thought we had that finding for was to go back and ratify that earlier action, and to get on with replenishing. I mean, that was one—what I understood one of the purposes of the draft to be.

from *Taking the Stand: The Testimony of Lt.Col.Oliver North*, 15

---

accompany face to face communication, but it also permits new ways of bridging time and space. Conversations become letters. Sagas become novels. Customs become legal codes. The written language takes on a life of its own, and it even begins to influence how the spoken language is used. To cite an obvious example, people begin to reject traditional pronunciations in favor of those that reflect a word's spelling: the pronunciation of the "l" in falcon (compare the l-less pronunciation of the cognate name Faulkner) and the "h" in such "th" combinations as *Anthony* and *Elizabeth* (compare the nicknames *Tony* and *Betty*, which reflect the earlier, h-less pronunciation).

In order to gain acceptance, a new literacy technology must also develop a means of authenticating itself. Michael Clanchy (1993) reports that when writing was introduced as a means of recording land transfer in 11th-century England, it was initially perceived (and often rightly so) as a nasty Norman trick for stealing Saxon land.

As Clanchy notes, spoken language was easily corroborated: human witnesses were interactive. They could be called to attest whether or not a property transfer had taken place. Doubters could question witnesses, watch their eyes, see whether witnesses sank when thrown bound into a lake. Written documents did not respond to questions—they were not interactive. So the writers and users of documents had to develop their own means of authentication. At first, seals, knives, and other symbolic bits of property were attached to documents in an attempt to give them credibility. Medieval English land transfers also adopted the format of texts already established as trustworthy, the Bible or the prayer book, complete with illuminations, in order to convince readers of their validity.

Questions of validity came up because writing was indeed being used to perpetrate fraud. Monks, who controlled writing technology in England at the time, were also responsible for some notorious forgeries used to snatch land from private owners. As writing technology developed over the centuries, additional ways of authenticating text came into use. Individualistic signatures eventually replaced seals to the extent that today, many people's signatures differ significantly from the rest of their handwriting. Watermarks identified the provenance of paper; dates and serial numbers further certify documents, and in the absence of other authenticators, stylistic analysis may allow us to guess at authorship on the basis of comparative and internal textual evidence. In the digital age, we are faced with the interesting task of reinventing appropriate ways to validate cybertext.

THE PENCIL AS TECHNOLOGY

Just as writing was not designed initially as a way of recording speech, the pencil was not invented to be a writing device. The ancient lead-pointed stylus was used to scribe lines—the lead made a faint pencil-like mark on a surface, suitable for marking off measurements but not for writing. The modern pencil, which holds not lead but a piece of graphite encased in a wooden handle, doesn't come on the scene until the 1560s.

The 16th-century pencil consists of a piece of graphite snapped or shaved from a larger block, then fastened to a handle for ease of use. The first pencils were made by joiners, woodworkers specializing in making furniture, to scribe measurements in wood. Unlike the traditional metal-pointed scribing tools, pencils didn't leave a permanent dent in the wood. By the time Gesner observed the pencil, it had been adopted as a tool by note-takers, natural scientists or others who needed to write, sketch, or take measurements in the field. Carrying pens and ink pots outdoors was cumbersome. Early pencils had knobs at one end so that they could be fastened with string or chain to a notebook, creating the precursor to the laptop computer.

Pencils were also of use to artists. In fact the word pencil means "little tail," and refers not only to the modern wood-cased pencil but to the artist's brush. Ink and paint are difficult to erase: they must be scraped off a surface with a knife, or painted over. But graphite pencil marks were more easily erased by using bread crumbs, and of course later by erasers made of rubber—in fact the eraser substance (caoutchouc, the milky juice of tropical plants such as ficus) was called rubber because it was used to rub out pencil marks.

THOREAU AND PENCIL TECHNOLOGY

It is true that Thoreau rejected modern improvements like the telegraph as worthless illusions. In *Walden* he says, "They are but improved means to an unimproved end." Thoreau did not write much of pencils. He even omitted the pencil in his list of items to take into the Maine woods, though like naturalists before him, he certainly carried one on his twelve-day excursion in order to

Figure 3
De Figuris Lapidum

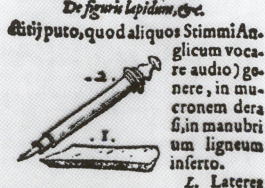

De figuris lapidum, &c.

Ætij puto, quod aliquos Stimmi An-
glicum voca-
re audio) ge-
nere, in mu-
cronem dera
fi, in manubri
um ligneum
inferto.

L. Lateres
è luto finguntur & coquunt, ad ædi-
ficiorum parietes, pauimenta, cami-
nos: item ad furnos, aliosq́ vfus.

Lithoftrota dicuntur loca lapidibus ftrata: vt apud Varronem pauimenta nobilia lithoftrota. fiebant au-
tem è cruftis paruis, marmoreis præ-
cipuè, quibus folum pauiméti incru-
ftabatur. Vide Agricolam libro 7. de
nat. foffilium.

M. Menfæ fiunt nó folùm è ligno:
fed etiam lapidibus & marmore, fiue
folidæ: fiue marmore aut lapide fifsili
incruftatæ duntaxat.

Molaris lapidis icon pofita eft Ca-
pite

Translation: "The stylus. . . is made . . . from a sort of lead (which I
have heard some call English antimony), shaved to a point and
inserted in a wooden handle." From *De rerum fossilium lapidum et
gemmarum maxime, figuris et similitudinibus liber,* a book on the
shapes and images of fossils, esp. those in stone and rock. Gesner
wrote a Greek-Latin dictionary, was a doctor, lectured on physics,
and, obviously, was a rock hound.

record his thoughts. Despite this silence, Thoreau devoted ten years of his life to improving pencil technology at his family's pencil factory. It was this pencil technology, not inherited wealth or publication royalties, that provided the income for one of the greatest writers of the American renaissance.

As Petroski tells it, the pencil industry in the eighteenth century was buffeted by such vagaries as the unpredictable supply of graphite, dwindling cedar forests, protective tariffs, and, for much of its history, an international consumer preference for British-made pencils. All of this affected John Thoreau and Co., manufacturers of pencils. Until the nineteenth century, the best pencil graphite (or plumbago, as it was often called), came from Borrowdale, in England. There were other graphite deposits around the world, but their ore was not particularly pure. Impure ore crumbled or produced a scratchy line. In the later eighteenth century, the Borrowdale deposits began to run low, and exports were curtailed. After the French Revolution, with his supply of English graphite permanently embargoed, the French pencil-maker Nicholas-Jacques Conté learned to produce a workable writing medium by grinding the local graphite, mixing it with clay and water, and forcing the mixture into wooden casings.

This process allowed the French to produce their own pencils, and it also permitted manufacturers to control the hardness of the lead, which in turn controlled the darkness of the mark made by the pencil. (The more clay, the harder the lead, and the lighter and crisper the mark; less clay gives a darker, grainier mark). So successful was Conté's process that Conté became synonymous with pencil, and Conté crayons are still valued by artists. In Nuremberg, Staedtler learned to mix ground graphite with sulfur. He and his rival, Faber, founded German pencil dynasties that also survive to this day.

The superiority of Borrowdale English graphite was evident to American consumers as well, and they regularly preferred imports to domestic brands. American pencil manufacturers had a hard time convincing the public that they could make a good native pencil. In 1821 Charles Dunbar discovered a deposit of plumbago in Bristol, New Hampshire, and he and his brother-in-law, John Thoreau, went into the pencil business. By 1824 Thoreau pencils were winning recognition. Their graphite, however, was not as pure as Borrowdale, and since the Conté process was unknown in the United States, American pencils, though cheaper than imports, remained inferior.

Henry Thoreau set about to improve his father's pencil. According to Petroski, Thoreau began his research in the Harvard Library. But then, as now, there was little written on pencil manufacture. Somehow, Thoreau learned to grind graphite more finely than had been done before and to mix it with clay in just the right proportion, for his improvements on the pencil-making process, combined with the high import duty imposed on British pencils after the War of 1812, led to great demand for Thoreau pencils.

Thoreau did not ascribe transcendent value to pencils. As Petroski sees it, Thoreau's purpose was simply to make money. Once he developed the best pencil of the day, Thoreau saw no sense in trying to improve on his design. His pencils sold for seventy-five cents a dozen, higher than other brands, a fact which Emerson remarked on, though he still recommended Thoreau pencils to his friends. It is easy for us to think of Thoreau only as a romantic who lived deliberately, disobeyed civil authority, and turned Walden Pond into a national historic site. But to do these things, he was also an engineer and marketing expert. When pencil competition grew, shaving his profit margin, Thoreau stopped pushing pencils and sold his graphite wholesale to electrotypers because this proved more lucrative (Petroski 122).

Perhaps, then, Thoreau, despite his technological expertise, opposed Morse's telegraph just to protect the family business. It is more likely, though, from the absence of references to pencil-making in any of his writings, that Thoreau honestly thought pencils were better for writing than electrical impulses, and he simply kept his business life and his intellectual life in separate compartments. In any case, Thoreau's resistance to the telegraph didn't stop the project.

THE TELEPHONE

The introduction of the telephone shows us once again how the pattern of communications technology takes shape. The telephone was initially received as an interesting but impractical device for communicating across distance. Although as Thoreau feared, the telegraph eventually did permit Maine and Texas and just about everywhere else to say nothing to one another, Samuel F. B. Morse, who patented the telegraph and invented its code, saw no use for Alexander Graham Bell's even newer device, the telephone. Morse refused Bell's offer to sell him the rights to the telephone patent. He was convinced that no one would want the telephone because it was unable to provide any permanent record of a conversation.

Indeed, although we now consider it indispensable, like writing, the uses of the telephone were not immediately apparent to many people. Telephone communication combined aspects of speaking and writing situations in new ways, and it took a while to figure out what the telephone could and couldn't do. Once they became established, telephones were sometimes viewed as replacements for earlier technologies. In some cities, news and sports broadcasts were delivered over the telephone, competing with the radio (Marvin 1988). Futurologists predicted that the telephone would replace the school or library as a transmitter of knowledge and information, that medical therapy (including hypnosis) could be delivered and criminals punished over the phone through the use of electrical impulses. The telephone even competed with the clock and the thermometer: when I was growing up in New York in the 1950s, my family regularly called MEridian 6-1212 to find out the time, and WEather 7-1212 for the temperature and forecast.

Of course the telephone was not only a source of information. It also threatened our privacy. One early fear of putting telephones in people's homes was that strangers could call up uninvited; people could talk to us on the phone whom we would never wish to converse with in person—and no one predicted then that people selling useless products would invariably call at dinner time. Today, as our email addresses circulate through the ether, we find in our electronic mailboxes not just surprise communications from long-lost acquaintances who have tracked us down using Gopher and other Web browsers, but also unwelcome communiqués from intruders offering get-rich-quick schemes, questionable deals, and shoddy merchandise. Even unsolicited religious messages are now circulating freely on net news groups.

The introduction of the telephone for social communication also required considerable adaptation of the ways we talk, a fact we tend to forget because we think of the modern telephone as a reliable and flexible instrument. People had to learn how to converse on the telephone: its sound reproduction was poor; callers had to speak loudly and repeat themselves to be understood, a situation hardly conducive to natural conversation. Telephones were located centrally and publicly in houses, which meant that conversations were never private. Telephones emulated face-to-face communication, but they could not transmit the visible cues and physical gestures that allow face-to-face conversation to proceed smoothly, and this deficiency had to be overcome. Many people still accompany phone conversations with hand and facial gestures; very young children often nod into phone instead of saying "Yes" or "No," as if their interlocutor could see them.

Initially, people were unsure of the appropriate ways to begin or end phone conversations, and lively debates ensued. The terms "hello" and "good-bye" quickly became standard, despite objections from purists who maintained that "hello" was not a greeting but an expression of surprise, and that "good-bye," coming from "God be with you," was too high-toned and serious a phrase to be used for something so trivial as telephone talk. As people discovered that telephones could further romantic liaisons, guardians of the public morality voiced concern or disgust that sweethearts were actually making kissing noises over the phone. Appropriate language during conversation was also an issue, and phone companies would cut off customers for swearing (like today's computer Systems Operators, or Sysops, the telephone operators, or "hello girls" as they were called in the early days, frequently listened in on conversations and had the authority to interrupt or disconnect calls).

While the telephone company routinely monitored the contents of telephone calls, when transcripts of telephone conversations were first introduced as evidence in trials, phone companies argued that these communications were just as private and privileged as doctor-patient exchanges (Marvin 68). Phone companies also tried to limit telephone access solely to the subscriber, threatening hotels and other businesses with loss of phone service if they allowed guests or customers to make calls. Telephone companies backed down from their demand that phones only be used by their registered owners once another technological development, the pay telephone, was introduced, and their continued profits were assured (this situation is analogous to the discussions of copy protection and site licensing for computer software today).

THE COMPUTER AND THE PATTERN OF LITERACY TECHNOLOGY

Writing was not initially speech transcription, and pencils were first made for woodworkers, not writers. Similarly, the mainframe computer when it was introduced was intended to perform numerical calculations too tedious or complex to do by hand. Personal computers were not initially meant for word processing either, though that has since become one of their primary functions.

Mainframe line editors were so cumbersome that even computer programmers preferred to write their code with pencil and paper. Computer operators actually scorned the thought of using their powerful number-crunchers to process mere words. Those who braved the clumsy technology to type text were condemned to using a system that seemed diabolically designed to slow a writer down well below anything that could be done on an IBM Selectric, or even with a pencil. (Interestingly, when the typewriter was developed, the keyboard was designed to slow down writers, whose typing was faster than the machine could handle; initially computers too were slow to respond to keystrokes, and until type-ahead capability was developed, typists were frustrated by loud beeps indicating they had exceeded the machine's capacity to remember what to do.)

Early word-processing software for personal computers did little to improve the situation. At last, in the early 1980s, programs like Wordstar began to produce text that looked more like the typing that many writers had become used to. Even so, writers had to put up with screens cluttered with formatting characters. Word wrap was not automatic, so paragraphs had to be reformatted every time they were revised. Furthermore, printed versions of text seldom matched what was on the computer screen, turning page design into a laborious trial-and-error session. Adding to the writer's problems was the fact that the screen itself looked nothing like the piece of paper the text would ultimately be printed on. The first PC screens were grayish-black with green phosphor letters, displaying considerably less than a full page of text. When it came along, the amber screen offered what was seen as a major improvement, reducing eye strain for many people. Today we expect displays not only with black on white, just like real paper, and high resolution text characters, but also with color, which takes us a step beyond what we could do with ordinary typing paper.

If the initial technical obstacles to word processing on a PC weren't enough to keep writers away from the new technology, they still had to come up with the requisite $5,000 or more in start-up funds for an entry-level personal computer. Only die-hards and visionaries considered computer word processing worth pursuing, and even they held on to their Selectrics and their Bics just in case.

Figure 4
Instructions from a Wordstar manual

If you type this:

^BCombining Special Effects^B. To combine special effects, simply insert one control character after another. For example, your ^BWordstar^B^VTM^V cursor may look like this: H^HI^HN^HZ.

|^Ba^B| = /(a^Vx^V^T2^T + a^Vy^V^T2^T + a^Vz^V^T2^T)

You (might) get this:

Combining Special Effects. To combine special effects, simply insert one control character after another. For example, your **Wordstar**™ cursor may look like this: ■.

| **a** | = / $(a_x^2 + a_y^2 + a_z^2)$

The next generation of word-processing computers gave us WYSIWIG: "what you see is what you get," and that helped less-adventurous writers make the jump to computers. Only when Macintosh and Windows operating systems allowed users to create on-screen documents that looked and felt like the old, familiar documents they were used to creating on electric typewriters did word processing really become popular. At the same time, start-up costs decreased significantly and with new, affordable hardware, computer writing technology quickly moved from the imitation of typing to the inclusion of graphics.

Of course that, too, was not an innovation in text production. We'd been pasting up text and graphics for ages. The decorated medieval charters of eleventh-century England are a perfect parallel to our computerized graphics a millennium later. But just as writing in the middle ages was able to move beyond earlier limitations, computer word processing has now moved beyond the texts made possible by earlier technologies by adding not just graphics, but animation, video, and sound to documents. In addition, Hypertext and HTML allow us to create links between documents or paths within them, both of which offer restructured alternatives to linear reading.

The new technology also raises the specter of digital fraud, and the latest literacy technology is now faced with the task of developing new methods of authentication to ensure confidence and trust in its audience (see figure 5).

Over the years, we have developed a number of safeguards for preventing or detecting fraud in conventionally produced texts. The fact that counterfeit currency still gets passed, and that document forgeries such as the *Hitler Diaries* or hoaxes like the physicist Alan Sokal's spoof of deconstruction, "Transgressing the Boundaries: Toward a Transformational Hermeneutics of

Figure 5
Example of Digital Fraud

From Feb. 1994 *Scientific American*, William J. Mitchell, "When is seeing believing?" (68-73). Mitchell explains the process used to create this photograph of Marilyn Monroe and Abraham Lincoln that never existed in the original. The final result can be so seamless that the forgery is undetectable. Examples of the intrusion of such false images include an ABC News broadcast in which correspondent Nina Totenberg was shown on camera with the White House in the background. In actuality, she was miles away in a studio and the montage gave the impression she was reporting from the field. Needless to say, fraudulent computer text is even easier to compose and promulgate across the bandwidth.

Quantum Gravity," come to light from time to time shows that the safeguards, while strong, are not necessarily foolproof. The average reader is not equipped to detect many kinds document falsification, and a lot of text is still accepted on trust. A writer's reputation, or that of a publisher, predisposes readers to accept certain texts as authoritative, and to reject others. Provenance, in the world of conventional documents, is everything. We have learned to trust writing that leaves a paper trail.

Things are not so black and white in the world of digital text. Of course, as more and more people do business on the Internet, the security of transactions, of passwords, credit card numbers, and bank accounts becomes vital. But the security and authenticity of "ordinary" texts is a major concern as well. Anyone with a computer and a modem can put information into cyberspace. As we see from figure 5, digitized graphics are easy to alter. Someone intent on committing more serious deception can with not too much trouble alter text, sound, graphics, and video files. Recently several former Columbia University students were arrested for passing fake twenty-dollar bills that they had duplicated on one of Columbia's high-end color printers. The Treasury Department reported that while these counterfeits were easy for a non-expert to spot, some $8,000 to $9,000 of the bad money had been spent before the counterfeiters attracted any attention. Security experts, well aware of the problems of digital fraud, are developing scramblers, electronic watermarks and invisible tagging devices to protect the integrity of digital files, and hackers are probably working just as hard to defeat the new safeguards. Nonetheless, once a file has been converted to hard copy, it is not clear how it could be authenticated.

Digitized text is even easier to corrupt accidentally, or to fiddle with on purpose. Errors can be inadvertently introduced when print documents are scanned. With electronic text, it may be difficult to recover other indicators that we expect easy access to when we deal with print: the date of publication, the edition (sometimes critical when dealing with newspapers or literary texts), editorial changes or formatting introduced during the digitization process, changes in accompanying graphics (for example, online versions of the *Washington Post* and the *New York Times* use color illustrations not found in the paper editions). And of course digital text can be corrupted on purpose in ways that will not be apparent to unsuspecting readers.

Electronic texts also present some challenges to the ways we attribute expertise to authors. When I read newsgroups and electronic discussion lists, I must develop new means for establishing the expertise or authority of a poster. I recently tried following a technical discussion on a bicycle newsgroup about the relative advantages of butyl and latex innertubes. I can accept the advice of a bicycle mechanic I know, because we have a history, but posters to a newsgroup are all strangers to me. They may be experts, novices, cranks, or some combination of the three, and in the case of the two kinds of tire tubes, I had difficulty evaluating the often conflicting recommendations I received. After reading the newsgroup for a while, becoming familiar with those who post regularly, and getting a sense of the kinds of advice they gave and their attitudes toward the subject, I began to develop a nose for what was credible. My difficulty was compounded, though, because the most authoritative-sounding poster, in the conventional sense of authoritative—someone who evoked principles of physics and engineering to demonstrate that flats were no more common or disastrous with latex than butyl tubes, and who claimed to have written books on bicycle repair—was clearly outshouted by posters attesting the frequency and danger of rupturing latex inner tubes. In the end I chose to stay with butyl, since everyone seemed to agree that, though heavier than latex, it was certainly not the worst thing in the world to ride on.

My example may seem trivial, but as more and more people turn to the World Wide Web for information, and as students begin relying on it for their research papers, verifying the reliability and authenticity of that information becomes increasingly important, as does revisiting it later to check quotations or gather more information. As anyone knows who's lost a file or tried to revisit a website, electronic texts have a greater tendency to disappear than conventional print resources.

CONCLUSION

As the old technologies become automatic and invisible, we find ourselves more concerned with fighting or embracing what's new. Ten years ago, math teachers worried that if students were allowed to use calculators, they wouldn't learn their arithmetic tables. Regardless of the value parents and teachers still place on knowing math facts, calculators are now indispensable in math class. When we began to use computers in university writing classes, instructors didn't tell students about the spell-check programs on their word processors, fearing the students would forget how to spell. The hackers found the spelling checkers anyway, and now teachers complain if their students don't run the spell check before they turn their papers in.

Even the pencil itself didn't escape the wrath of educators. One of the major technological advances in pencil-making occurred in the early twentieth century, when manufacturers learned to attach rubber tips to inexpensive wood pencils by means of a brass clamp. But American schools allowed no crossing out. Teachers preferred pencils without erasers, arguing that students would do better, more premeditated work if they didn't have the option of revising. The students won this one, too: eraserless pencils are now extremely rare. Artists use them, because artists need special erasers in their work; golfers too use pencils without erasers, perhaps to keep themselves honest. As for the no-crossing-out rule, writing teachers now routinely warn students that writers never get it right the first time, and we expect them to revise their work endlessly until it is polished to perfection.

The computer has indeed changed the ways some of us do things with words, and the rapid changes in technological development suggest that it will continue to do so in ways we cannot yet foresee. Whether this will result in a massive change in world literacy rates and practices is a question even more difficult to answer. Although the cost of computers has come down significantly enough for them to have made strong inroads into the American office and education environment, as well as in the American middle class home, it is still the case that not every office or every school can afford to computerize, let alone connect to the World Wide Web. And it is likely that many newly-computerized environments will not have sufficient control over the technology to do more than use it to replicate the old ways.

After more than a decade of study, we still know relatively little about how people are using computers to read and write, and the number of people online, when viewed in the perspective of the total population of the United States, or of the world—the majority of whose residents are still illiterate—is still quite small. Literacy has always functioned to divide haves from have nots, and the problem of access to computers will not be easy to solve (see Moran, this volume).

In addition, researchers tend to look at the cutting edge when they examine how technology affects literacy. But technology has a trailing edge as well as a down side, and studying how computers are put to use raises serious issues in the politics of work and mechanisms of social control. Andrew Sledd (1988) pessimistically views the computer as actually reducing the amount of literacy needed for the low end of the workplace: "As for ordinary kids, they will get jobs at Jewel, dragging computerized Cheerios boxes across computerized check-out counters."

Despite Sledd's legitimate fear that in the information age computers will increase the gap between active text production and routine, alienating, assembly-line text processing, in the United States we live in an environment that is increasingly surrounded by text. Our cereal boxes and our soft drink cans are covered with the printed word. Our televisions, films, and computer screens also abound with text. We wear clothing designed to be read. The new computer communications technology does have ability to increase text exposure even more than it already has in positive, productive ways. The simplest one-word Web search returns pages of documents which themselves link to the expanding universe of text in cyberspace.

Computer communications are not going to go away. How the computer will eventually alter literacy practices remains to be seen. The effects of writing took thousands of years to spread; the printing press took several hundred years to change how we do things with words. Although the rate of change of computer development is significantly faster, it is still too early to do significant speculating.

We have a way of getting so used to writing technologies that we come to think of them as natural rather than technological. We assume that pencils are a natural way to write because they are old—or at least because we have come to think of them as being old. We form Lead Pencil Clubs and romanticize do-it-yourselfers who make their own writing equipment, because home-made has come to mean "superior to store-bought."

But pencil technology has advanced to the point where the ubiquitous no. 2 wood-cased pencil can be manufactured for a unit cost of a few pennies. One pencil historian has estimated that a pencil made at home in 1950 by a hobbyist or an eccentric would have cost about $50. It would cost significantly more nowadays. There's clearly no percentage in home pencil-making. Whether the computer will one day be as taken-for-granted as the pencil is an intriguing question. One thing is clear: were Thoreau alive today he would not be writing with a pencil of his own manufacture. He had better business sense than that. More likely, he would be keyboarding his complaints about the information superhighway on a personal computer that he assembled from spare parts in his garage.

In the brave new world virtual text, if you chain an infinite number of monkeys to an infinite number of computers, you will eventually get, not Hamlet, but Hamlet BASIC.

CHAPTER TWO

Saving a Place for Essayistic Literacy

Douglas Hesse

LESTER FAIGLEY AND SUSAN ROMANO RECENTLY ENCAPSULATED THE ONGOING argument that computer networks disrupt traditional assumptions about advanced literacy. Following anthropologists Ron and Suzanne Scollon, they refer to the old framework as essayistic literacy, writing practices characterized by texts of a certain length, complexity, and expected integrity. Essayistic literacy supports process pedagogies that have been ascendant in the past thirty years and thus is conserved by familiar and dominant teaching strategies, perhaps out of proportion to its value. In contrast, writing common to computer networks is terse, mostly single-draft, often composed in immediate response and not repose, dependent on pathos and humor to a much greater extent than usually sanctioned by essayist literacy. Students frequently find it more familiar and worthy of pursuit, and Faigley and Romano urge writing programs to take seriously students' demands for "an education they perceive as relevant to the twenty-first century and not the nineteenth" (57). They stop short of saying that network literacy should define literacy, but they advocate its broader place in the curriculum.

By calling the old tradition essayistic literacy, Faigley and Romano perpetuate a definitional confusion at least a century old. As Robert Scholes and Carl Klaus observed nearly 30 years ago, "essay" has "come to be used as a catch-all term for non-fictional prose works of limited length" (46). There's no doubting the term's prevalence on campuses, where students perceive everything they write as an "essay" or "paper." Although faculty in certain disciplines or courses may have students write reports, memos, or other genres, they typically do not have undergraduates write articles—or at least don't call them that. But "articles" would more appropriately be the object of concern, and complaints would more accurately be against "article-istic" literacy.

My argument is occasioned at least partially by a desire to wrestle back for the "essay" its history. I'll confess selfish interest in this goal because the genre has been an object of my professional publication. I sympathize with Carl Klaus's quite serious proposal at a gathering of essayists and essay apologists that we agree each to use Montaigne's original French, *essai*, and forfeit the corrupted "essay." However, I'm realistic enough to know that Kleenex and

Xerox both failed to control names used in the popular sphere. Besides, the issue is more than definitional quibbling. We occlude important literacy issues if we misunderstand what might be meant by essayistic literacy.

Faigley and Romano acknowledge the breadth of the term when they make a definitional partition—but then define the whole from the part:

> In essayist literacy, "good" writing is defined by those characteristics most prized in an academic essay. In a "good" piece of writing, logical relations are signaled, references to sources carefully documented, and statements of bias either absent or well-controlled. The presence of these features signals to readers that the author is truthful and that what he or she writes may legitimately pass for knowledge. Appeals to pathos as conventionally understood, unless carefully managed are apt to discount author credibility. Both writer and readers are imagined as rational and informed people not inclined to excessive passion, fragmented reasoning, or posturing. (47)

By this definition, in which essayist literacy is defined by the academic essay, Montaigne, the very father of the genre, did not possess essayist literacy. After all, his writings frequently fail to signal logical relations, and his biases are foregrounded like his famous moustache. As "academic essays," his explorations of smells and cannibalism would fail undergraduate biology or anthropology courses. I'm not objecting to Faigley and Romano's depiction of the kind of writing deemed most appropriate for the academy; I'm fairly certain that professors who assign writing mostly do expect these qualities. Rather, I'm saying that these qualities do not define essays.

The confusion about "essayistic" literacy is perhaps best sorted by considering lines of thinking since the mid-1980s in three scholarly fields: the essay as genre, social constructivist theory, and network literacy theory. Scholars working in each of these fields have tended to regard the others primarily as sources of ideas to oppose. For example, apologists for the essay have tended to promote the genre to resist what they perceive as the dehumanizing effect of social constructivism. Simultaneously social theorists have scorned what they perceive as the untheorized romanticism of the essayists. Theorists of network literacy, by which I mean reading and writing not continuous and "self-contained" linear texts but rather distributed, context-embedded, spatial texts, similarly repudiate the essayistic. They fear that the genre manifests theoretically suspect assumptions of stable knowledge and pragmatically naive assumptions about the kind of writing that college graduates will actually need to do. And yet all these fields aspire to relatively similar characteristics of student writings, whether they can acknowledge it our not.

WHAT IS AN ESSAY?

Within the academy the term "essay" has evolved into a generic term for all works of prose nonfiction short enough to be read in a single sitting. But the genre's history and the qualities of its defining texts make clear that essays are a specific kind of nonfiction, one defined in opposition to more formal and explicitly conventional genres—the scientific article or report, for example, or the history, or the philosophical argument. Whereas these latter genres have aspired to objective truths through the constraints of method, enacting the Lockean dream of language beyond the idols of language, essayists have pursued conditional representations of the world as the essayist experiences it. Some might critique this stance as solipsistic romanticism. But it can alternatively be viewed as an ultimate rejection of knowledge as objective and truth as independent of context and experience. Social constructivism shares this position. Essayists declare the contingency of their claims about the world by rejecting method and the self-effacement of form. Instead they constantly figure themselves as the makers of that knowledge. Edward Hoaglund's formulation that the essay exists on a line between "what I think and what I am" is revealing for what it does not declare, namely, that the essay does not say "what the world is."

This is perhaps too abstract, so let me take another run at it. By essay, I mean that tradition of works initiated by Montaigne, begun in English by Bacon, continued through Cowley, Addison and Steele, Johnson in *The Rambler*, Goldsmith in *The Bee*, Ben Franklin, Lamb and Hazlitt, Emerson and Thoreau, Woolf, Orwell, E.B. White, Didion, Dillard, Hoaglund, Scott Sanders, and so on. Constructing any such partial list invites charges of canon-making and promotes the genre as celebrating a literary aesthetic. I'm just trying to clarify the kinds of works I mean. The essayistic can be located today in much journalism, Ellen Goodman's or Anna Quindlen's columns, for example, or the works of science popularizers or naturalists like Stephen Jay Gould or David Quammen. For all these pieces, the author's experience and consciousness in pursuit of an idea determines the content and form of the essay, not some external "topic" or "method." So it is that in "Reflections in Westminster Abbey," Addison can "digress" about the quality of Dutch monuments to dead admirals or that in "Human Equality is a Contingent Fact of History" Gould can discuss how the Spirit of St. Louis ought to be represented for blind visitors to the Smithsonian.

In fact, one characteristic quality of contemporary essays is the attempt to cast the widest net of associations possible, then struggle to bring the gathered ideas into some meaningful relation. Annie Dillard's "Expedition to the Pole" intricately weaves an autobiographical strand, her experience attending a folk service at a Catholic church, with an informational strand, accounts of preparations for various arctic and antarctic expeditions, to create a metaphor for how we ought and ought not encounter the sacred and the strange. Joan Didion's "The White Album" consists of several apparently disconnected snippets of California life in the late 1960s. Didion famously asserts that "We live entirely, especially if we are writers, by the imposition of a narrative line upon disparate images" (11). It is that narrativizing of experience, information, and idea—the imposition and making plausible of a certain sequence of textual moves—that characterizes the essay.

My term "narrativizing" may seem an odd one, especially when so many essays don't consist of what we traditionally might call narratives, the representation of events as they happened or might happen in the world. Yet, as I've argued previously ("Time"), essays are emplotments of their author's experiences, ideas, readings, and so on. A venerable way of talking about essays is to say that they render the shape of thinking, not of thought. Form in an essay is not dictated by conventions of deductive logic or formal convention but rather by the author's attempt to create a satisfying and finished verbal artifact out of the materials at hand. This is not to say that essays are inherently more natural than other forms of writing; as I've also argued previously ("Recent"), our perception of an essay as a "satisfying and finished verbal artifact" is due to our socially constructed expectations as readers. While it has been common to talk about essays as "unmethodical" discourse, as does Lane Kaufmann, in fact they are certainly methodical, just as bound by discourse conventions as other genres. It's just that the conventions are those of essaying.

The rhetoric of the essay depends on consoling the reader that the world can be made abundantly complex and strange and yet still be shown as yielding to ordering, if not order. In genres like the scientific report, narrativity precedes the content matter, embodied in prescribed elements like the methods, results, and discussion sections; in the essay, the narrative must be constructed out of the subject matter, giving rise to notions of "organic" form. It is telling that the essay's rise paralleled the rise of the scientific method in the late Renaissance and early Enlightenment and that Francis Bacon, author of "The Advancement of Learning," should be its first prominent English practitioner. It is as if Bacon himself recognized the limitations of a single method and sought to establish a counter method, one that later essayists would call anti-methodical. His own essays, aphoristic, propositional, and declarative, hardly seem to demonstrate the narrative qualities I've attributed to the genre. And yet the movement between his assertions is tentative and exploratory. An essay like "Of Marriage and Single Life" can begin with the claim that "He that hath Wife and Children, hath given Hostages to Fortune" only later to acknowledge the benefits of marriage, so that the whole work narrates an idea evolving.

So far I have been trying to argue that the essay is a sub-genre of short prose, modest and self-limiting in its truth claims, contingent on the perspective of its author, wearing that contingency on its sleeve, constrained not by topic but by the author's thought process and by conventions of satisfying form—in Kenneth Burke's most basic definition of form as the arousal and fulfillment of desire—associative, exploratory, essentially narrative rather than hierarchical in its logic. What I have not yet argued is the value of the essay. What is the worth of the genre at a time when computer networks allow, even invite, texts to exist as units approachable from many directions, able to be employed in multiple contexts, digital, malleable, transportable, reproducible? What can essays and essaying do that really needs to be done and can't happen another way? Could it be that essaying, after hypertextual technology, can go the way of *memoratio* after wide alphabetic literacy? Perhaps we might agree on a precise definition of essays and, thus, essayistic literacy. Yet we may still determine that such a literacy is pedagogically, theoretically, or politically undesirable.

Several composition theorists have argued just the opposite in recent years. As I noted above, some of this has come in response to 1980s pedagogies of academic discourse, as with many of Jim Corder or Peter Elbow's concerns. Kurt Spellmeyer has been perhaps the most eloquent and rigorous in the articulation of this position. Spellmeyer characterizes pedagogies of discourse-specific analysis and emulation as preventing the kind of inquiry that represents and motivates learning. Worse, it disempowers students by limiting content and form to existing disciplinary conversations to which they must by definition be outsiders, and by excluding the resources of students' own experiences. Spellmeyer contends that

> By reifying discourse communities as teachers reified texts a generation ago, we disempower our students in yet another way; whereas before they were expected only to look to an author's language, their task now is more complicated and more intimidating, to speak about such language in terms of extratextual conventions with which they are almost always unfamiliar. And poststructuralist teachers, enabled by a knowledge of these invisible conventions, wield an authority that would probably have embarrassed their New Critical forerunners. The alternative, I believe, is to permit our students to bring their extratextual knowledge to bear upon every text we give them, and to provide them with strategies for using this knowledge to undertake a conversation that belongs to us all. (119)

For reasons both pedagogical and political, then, Spellmeyer nominates the essay as that genre best suited to promote writing and thinking. Panegyrically, Paul Heilker takes Spellmeyer's position a step further. Deciding, finally, that the essay is nothing less than "transgressive symbolic movement," Heilker asserts that "what the essay highlights is that thought and language resist domestication" (181), that as "kineticism incarnate," the essay is necessarily "an intellectual activity on par with dialectical speech in that it, too, can lead us to wisdom and truth, can allow us to move toward transcendence," the very genre reminding us that "writing is a form of sociopolitical action undertaken to make ourselves better, wiser people and make the world a better, wiser place in which to live" (183).

I'm leery of these aspirations to transcendence and of representations of the essay as pure movement. The essayist's ultimate goal is to create an artifact, an artifact that may figure movement through its narrativity, but an artifact nonetheless, in the way that a film is an artifact, bounded by beginning and end. Movement, the transition from "this" to "that," is only half the essay's mode of being, the other half consisting of the writer's constructing a well-made whole, transforming narrative to story or mere movement to action. Further, as Joel Haefner has pointed out, claims of the essay's inherently democratic status ignore the fact that it, like every genre, has a history. Any essay—especially a student one—is read against the essay tradition in which certain rhetorical moves are deemed more appropriate than others.

And yet, even though they might vehemently reject the neoplatonist rationales that I've cited above, many social theorists embrace the essay. There are two broad manifestations of social constructivism in composition studies. One is an accommodationist pedagogy in which students analyze target discourses with the goal of reproducing them, critique coming through—and after—understanding the discourse from "within." Charles Bazerman's *The Informed Writer* enacts such a pedagogy. The other is a resistance pedagogy in which critique drives analysis and serves to expose ways that conventional discourses conceal class, gender, or local circumstance. Proponents of such pedagogies, grounded in feminist theories, for example, have promoted and published scholarly work that more explicitly foregrounds the experience and perspective of the writer. The stance has always been the essayist's.

Lester Faigley's own position in *Fragments of Rationality* is interesting in this vein—and inconsistent with his and Romano's later critique of essayistic literacy. Faigley summarizes postmodernist dismantlings of the possibilities of unified individual consciousness and grand narratives. Vestiges of both these assumptions within composition classes can be seen in the way teachers tend to privilege confessional narratives, in which honesty and truthfulness derive from revealing embarrassing or potentially damaging events. Teachers might more appropriately have their students write what Faigley calls local narratives or microethnographies. In such works, students must observe, record, analyze, and interpret information, but Faigley deems as most valuable "the opportunity for students to explore their own locations within their culture" (223). What he calls microethnography, I would call essay. The confessional narratives that Faigley criticizes have some roots in some essayistic practices: Montaigne's confession in "On Smells," for example, that he likes the way food and perfume stick to his mustache so he can savor the smells longer, or Orwell's confession that he shot an elephant he did not need to shoot. But in the essay tradition, occasional confessions almost always serve writers exploring their locations within cultures, as does Orwell's shooting the elephant. A critique of "the confessional" is not necessarily a valid critique of the essay, as confession is but one trope practiced in some essays.

I'm not the first to point out that the term essayistic literacy stands defining features of essayism on their head. John Trimbur notes that the former term, coming out of literacy studies rather than literary history and composition studies, "has little to do with the self-revelatory stance, flexible style and conversational tone we find in literary essayists such as Montaigne, Addison, or E.B. White" (72). In fact, Trimbur summarizes David Olson's history of essayistic literacy—the rise of a plain, impersonal style, transparent, the meaning of texts presented literally in words on the page, all texts self-contained, the world objectively mapped in words—as grounded explicitly in a break with the figurative language and self-revelatory features of writers like Montaigne (76). It strikes me as nearly perverse for scholars like Olson to name the stylistic project of the Port Royal logicians and 17th Century Royal Society after a genre whose practitioners would resist that project. Perverse is probably less appropriately the word than beguiled, in the way that many of us have been beguiled by the convenience of essay as a catch-all term. In any case, trying now to change the label is like being a salmon swimming up the well-dammed Columbia River. Rather, as essayistic literacy is that which computers and computer networks, abetted by postmodern theory, are time and again supposed to challenge, then let's be careful what gets swept under the term. Some of the very qualities associated with literacy online—specifically, movement and exploration in a method more provisional and contextual than methodical—have been true of the essay since its inception.

NETWORK LITERACY AND ANTI-ESSAYISM

In *The Electronic Word*, Richard Lanham sounds a theme that Bolter and Landow before him have sounded and many others have since: reading will—and should—migrate beyond linearly following extended print texts, and writing should accommodate this change. Thus, "the essay will no longer be the basic unit of writing instruction" (127). Computers and, more importantly, computer networks permit and invite writing to come in smaller chunks never designed to be free-standing in the way that articles and essays have been for the past four centuries. This is clearest in works authored as hypertexts or works authored to be housed in hypertextual spaces like the World Wide Web, where perhaps even more salient than what a text says is how it connects. Bolter's pronouncements about hypertext (a prehistoric six years ago, as I am writing), underestimated the direction that hypertextuality has tended. Bolter took as his exemplars large, single authored (at least in origin) hypertexts such as Michael Joyce's "Afternoon." In fact, through the World Wide Web, we have passed over the bother of creating a generation of texts like "Afternoon." Rather than large and complex texts initiating their own revision and evolution in hyperspace, network discourse evolves from more modest writings: brief intact texts that exist explicitly in relation to other texts, not parts of themselves, posed questions, for example, or comments on an event. Bolter and Lanham imagined a reading and writing world of glosses, in which readers interactively modified and constructed texts by direct reference. In fact, the Web evolves by accretion, not substitution or critique.

In practice, web pages and the documents they organize do not comment on other documents except by connecting to them; web documents rarely contain analyses, syntheses, or critiques of other web documents. Instead, they contain recommended URLs. A common feature now of celebrity profiles as published in magazines like Esquire is a list of the celebrity's favorite bookmarks or websites, which are always presented without explanation.

Here is a difference between essay literacy, as I would have us understand the term, and current practices of network literacy. The earliest essays, Montaigne's for example, consist largely of glosses of the author's reading, her or his bookmarks, if you will. The tradition continued through Virginia Woolfe's *Common Reader* series, transformed into book reviews, the review essay, and the common device of using a reading as a point of departure for some more discursive exploration. It falls on the essayist to explain why he or she had referred to those texts, to narrate the relation of those writings to one another or to the essayist's experience or to the ideas being developed, and these explanations have taken the form of writing explicitly about the connections. Internet writers, in contrast, connect through juxtaposition, not commentary.

Bolter and Lanham have embraced the sufficiency of reading as juxtaposition and writing as addition primarily because such a conception enacts some postmodern positions. If the stability of knowledge is a fiction perpetuated diffusely and even unconsciously by discourse communities whose interest that fiction serves, then forms of communication that expose or refuse that stability have a theoretical purity. The danger, as critics particularly of Baudrillard have noted, is that a landscape leavened by the ultimate equality of all texts offers no fulcrum for advocacy or change. Lanham and Bolter might contend—and I might agree—that a textual space that encourages addition and discourages critique holds open possibilities for change that apparently self-containing texts do not. The difference is that the essay allows the writer to incorporate other texts into her or his own, representing and discussing them in explicit relation to the writer's own ideas and experiences. This is a different kind of agency than merely having one's texts available in the same space as another. Of course, in explicitly representing and embedding others' writings, there is always the possibility of misrepresenting or domesticating, as perhaps I have done with my appropriations of Lanham and Bolter.

HOME PAGE AS ESSAY?

The difference between summarizing and discussing versus presenting and linking is the difference between electronic texts being essayistic or not. Obviously, it's possible and common to publish essays on the Internet, in a form and format similar to mere print. As a journal editor who occasionally has to accommodate requests for back issues, I recognize the potential archival salvations of the Internet. The kind of piece you're reading now exists via home pages up and down the Internet, not only in electronic journals but also in the home pages of individuals who make available copies of conference papers and printed articles. (See, for example, Doug Brent's "Articles on Communications, Information Technology, and Rhetoric.") One could imagine an E.B. White home page containing the "The Death of a Pig," "The Ring of Time," "Once More to the Lake" and so on, that home page linked to essays by other writers, other home pages, and so on.

But when writers like Faigley and Romano call for alternatives to essayistic literacy and imagine appropriate pedagogies and target discourses for students, they are not imagining the essay merely transported onto a file server. One can publish sonnets in hyperspace, too, but there are relatively few arguments these days that the sonnet should be a featured genre in first-year composition. There are two orders of issues at stake, existing in a particle/field relationship. One is the nature of individual texts, some of them certainly essays, in the Internet. The other is the nature of those texts or structures that connect or organize others.

This latter issue can be explored by asking, "When is a home page an essay?" The question is perhaps both more and less odd than it seems, as the home page is an interesting hybrid genre. Like essays, home pages have the function of organizing and presenting a view of something (in this case, other documents, sites or images), and like essays they are developed and managed by a single author (or authorial entity), which distinguishes them from other types of electronic discourse, such as listservs, which I discuss below. Above I tried to suggest that a typical essay gambit is to bring into some meaningful relationship a set of ideas, events, and references that are perhaps not automatically associated with one another, the author's goal being to constellate them in a meaningful structure. Certainly, there are home pages with some of these features, especially those devised by individuals rather than organizations.

One test of a home page as an essay would be to read it as printed out or with its links disabled. Think first of home pages that have the status of directories, consisting of a few sentences of explanatory text but mainly providing buttons or links to other information or documents, an academic department's home page, for example, or a corporation's. Such sites are no more essays than tables of contents are essays. Some principles of inclusion exist and the page can be read in terms of choices made. As with elements included in an essay, things included even in a directory home page "say something" about its author. That Nancy Kaplan's home page, for example, includes a link to the "Compact for Responsive Electronic Writing," along with links to University of Baltimore pages, to "Current and Recent Course Materials," "A Sampler of Projects," "Essays, and Other Stuff," and to "Websites Worth the Whistle" tells much about her activities and interests but little about the connections among the various things represented other than that they are here juxtaposed.

Looking at such home pages is like looking at catalogs of a personal library put up for estate auction. One is left to infer the consciousness that assembled such a library. Kaplan and other "directory page" authors make no claims about the meaning or significance of what is there beyond, perhaps, that "you might find this useful" and "you might find this interesting; I do." Of course, the rhetoric of even directory home pages can be extremely complex in the play among organizational and graphical elements. My point is writers of directory home pages don't explicitly present an interpretation of the page in terms of the relationships among the elements that comprise the whole, at least not in the way that an essayist articulates (but obviously never completely or exclusively) the relationship between elements of a text.

Now, some essays do rely extensively on pointing and juxtaposition. E.B. White's "Spring" consists of twelve short segments, each separated by white space, the first of them simply announcing "Notes on springtime and on anything else of an intoxicating nature that comes to mind" (186). The chunks present disconnected clips of life on White's farm, the longest of them a narrative of a stubborn brooder stove in his hen house, along with references to events in Europe. However disjointed, "Spring" invites readers to perceive or supply a larger theme holding the pieces together—to hear in the final section on the 1941 Nazi Frühling White's reference to Superman in the second section, and to reinterpret that reference, for example. Perhaps this is largely because of our reading conventions and faith in the author. But White has plotted this reading experience for it. The plotting may be tyrannically linear, tainted with modernist and romantic assumptions about the desirability of our apprehending a theme, enslaved to mere print. Even then, we aren't helplessly stuck with White's theme or point; reader response theory demonstrated the reader's role in constituting texts long before hypertexts did.

Other home pages are more essayistic in that they either embed directory information or links in extended prose or they juxtapose the two. A modest example of the former is Kathleen McHugh's home page, which in 1997 consisted of a large image of an early twentieth-century costumed woman on the left of the screen, the text below on the right and beneath that text a button for Free Speech Online:

> *Kathleen McHugh's*
> *Web Extravaganza*
>
> Who is this <u>"Kathleen McHugh"</u> anyway? And why is she so fascinating?
> <u>The Many Rachels (and others) I Know.</u> Despite the fact that none of The Many
>   Rachels She Knows currently have home pages, Kathleen has named her
>   Page of People She Knows With Web Pages after them.
> Kathleen has also been known to wildly invite the people she knows over for
>   bacchanals. Check out the invitation which led to the <u>Halloween Party.</u>
> Who cares about Kathleen's life and friends? We want to see <u>zany articles</u> from
>   the early part of the century.
>   (darkwing.uoregon.edu/~kmchugh/index.html)

Brooks Landon's home page (as of September 1998) is a modest example of a home page that juxtaposes links and extended texts (in the form of quotations, a "Credo, sort of. . ." and "Musings on Multimedia"). Both McHugh's and Landon's home pages glance in the direction of the essayistic by starting to suggest connections among their linked elements. And yet Landon's observation reveals much about what I consider the ultimately anti-essayistic impulse of the home page. Landon writes, "I hope to make this page a place where I can point to some of the issues and opportunities raised by the Web. I also hope to make it a place where I can just point to things I find interesting."

One of the main responsibilities of the essayist is to point—at books, ideas, experiences, people, and so on. But essayists interpret their pointing. They narrate reasons why their metaphorical fingers and our metaphorical glances move from this object of attention to that. Some might find home pages ultimately liberating for readers who are "free" to narrate their own interpretations of linkages, the possible whys of the pointings. Of course, such freedom has the cost of intellectual work—unless, of course, one is willing to swap the synchronic or interpretive dimension of reading for the merely diachronic or successive, this screen of images pointing to some next because it is "interesting" in some undefined way or because one is motivated by the drive of finding information. Similarly freed is the author, whose only burden is to point, to find or make links. It's telling that home pages are yet judged primarily by two criteria: 1) their graphic design, clarity, and seductiveness and 2) the richness of the resources they organize—as constrained by criterion one. Perhaps because of their relative novelty we haven't yet developed a criterion something like "the quality of thought or analysis" in home pages.

LISTSERV AS ESSAY?

What most theorists celebrate as network literacy is not the ability to write linkable individual essays but rather the ability to negotiate terser data fields. Home pages may serve as gateways for essays stored electronically, but they mainly function now to channel information rather than to convey extended arguments. A clearer sense of the network literacy imperative can be seen in email driven media like listservs or Internet relay chats or Daedalus interchanges, all of which exist because of the interdependency of writings that constitute them. The necessity of interdependency is demonstrated by the dislocation one feels in setting a list on no mail for a period of time, then returning to read messages in stream whose banks are strange and disorienting. After reading awhile, we get a sense of the new geography and perhaps even wade in. Or, more likely, new streams originate, and we follow a discussion from the mouth.

To some extent it's possible to think of threads on listservs as essays. Heilker has summarized the longstanding depictions of the essay as wandering, exploratory, and unmethodical, with topics or ideas triggered associatively by previous topics or ideas. Certainly all these apply to most listserv threads. A thread begins at one point and moves, if the interest is there, to others until, frequently, someone is inclined to change the subject line because the original one no longer pertains. Rather than associations being driven by the multiple subject positions and experiences of a single author, of course, the listserv distributes associativity among members participating in a thread. But the analogy ultimately breaks down when one compares the finished "product" of a listserv thread with a finished essay. In some ways, threads are clearly finished when a subject line no longer appears on the list; in other ways, the very notion of a thread being finished runs counter to the spirit of the list that preceded and endured any particular thread. When I grew up in eastern Iowa, we used to go fishing on backwaters and oxbows of the Mississippi, channels of the river and yet not quite the river.

Imagine an experiment in which one takes a discussion thread and, with minimal editing, presents it as an essay. The editing can consist only of removing the summative contextualizing materials, the transitions that become unnecessary and intrusive when messages are presented contiguously with one another; the addition of an introduction or conclusion or a voice-over narrative isn't permitted. Would the result be recognizable as an essay? Even suspending the interesting issues of style and voice, the main quality that threads-as-essays lack is shape and closure.

To illustrate this, I'll discuss an example from a listserv to which I belong, WPA-L. Members of this list are primarily writing program administrators (directors of first-year writing programs and writing centers, for example, or WAC programs) and others interested in program administration. Throughout the fall of 1996 there was a heated and extensive discussion about a situation at a large state university whose prominent writing program director was fired, seemingly out of the blue and seemingly for political rather than professional reasons. Participants on the list wanted to know the facts of the case and, knowing them, wanted to consider reasonable responses. For many, the case involved professional issues about perceptions of what constituted expertise in administering writing courses. Beyond whatever personal regard they had for the WPA and institution involved, their stake was "what happened here might happen here." Many saw this as a defining moment for the Council of Writing Program Administrators, the professional organization informally affiliated with the listserv. Participants in the discussion debated courses of action as well as philosophical and structural issues regarding who had standing in the matter and what standing meant. At one point, a few members argued that the president and vice president of WPA should undertake a fact finding mission to the institution involved, and some even offered to contribute amounts ranging from $50 to $100 to pay the way. More discussion. In the end, the members of the list agreed on nothing, nor—and this is my point—could they have, since the genre they were employing resists such agreement. The "essay" of this thread remained a fragment, a very long one, but with none of the shape and form that a "real" essay would have. There was a kind of Freytagian climax. In November, a participant in the discussion visited the institution in question as part of an unrelated invitation, and he reported some extensive and unofficial observations about the situation he discovered. This report was rejoined by a stinging rebuttal, which itself was followed by an even more stinging rebuke by a third discussant. And that was it. It's never certain why threads end. Perhaps WPA-L members had become tired of the issue. Perhaps it was irresolvable. Perhaps they felt catharsis in the final exchange. But the essay of this thread has no consolation of good form. What the event ultimately meant or what one should think about it was never determined.

I hope this example resonates in a couple of rich frequencies. The exchanges that constitute the thread illustrate dramatically the best of what Faigley and Romano and others might imagine of network literacy. The issues under discussion were scrutinized from several perspectives, and new contingencies continually destabilized hegemonic positions. A variety of writers not only chose but were able to participate. The rhetoric of explicit analysis and argument from principles was complicated and sometimes even trumped by the rhetoric of the bon mot, the rhetoric of passion. And yet the very openness of network literacy, the purity of its enacting postmodern resistances to closure, is ultimately its limitation. Had these issues been rendered through an essay rather than a listserv—and I can virtually guarantee that they will be, just as Linda Brodkey and others essayed the fate of English 306 at Texas—the essay would itself have enacted these resistances. After all, it's in the nature of the genre (the genre "essay" and not the construction "essayistic literacy") to do so.

But an essay would have done something more. It would have "finished" the issues, not in the sense of resolving them once and for all, having the last authoritative word, but in the sense of providing a possible interpretation through the figure of the essay narrator who says, both explicitly and formally through an imposed narrative line, "this is what all of it means to me, now, writing from this position." Interestingly, some of the longer posts in this thread are themselves essays, their writers characterizing issues in the preceding discussion and using them to occasion an extended discussion. Important explorations remain to be done of essayistic messages in listserv threads: under what conditions do they occur? What is their rhetorical effect? Their structural import?

In the main, however, listserv discussions demonstrate "kineticism incarnate" far more thoroughly than do essays. Essays are ultimately constrained by an impetus to form. That's why I consider Heilker's definition of the essay incomplete and why I must concede one point to those who contest essayistic literacy. Yes, the essayist does aspire to create a text that is "self-sufficent." But essays (again, I'm talking about essays, not necessarily articles or reports or other prose forms) convey the strain of their self-sufficiency in ways compatible with social and postmodern theory.

BUT WHY ESSAYISTIC LITERACY IN AN ELECTRONIC AGE?

John Trimbur notes that students tend to read self-reflexive personal essays with the same "deproductive" lens that they read all prose. They regard a fact in an Annie Dillard essay as having the same status as a fact in an encyclopedia article. Part of this, Trimbur notes, may be due to some prose conventions the two genres share. But the reason that students domesticate texts has less to do with the texts themselves than the way they've been taught to read and view reading. The same might be said of reasons for dismissing essayistic literacy.

I have been trying to suggest the role that essay writing should have in the undergraduate curriculum and the larger culture. There is an important value to reading and writing extended, connected texts whose authors manage the double pulls of complexity and order, producing works that convey their status as products of a certain experiential and intellectual nexus, not as objective truth. I believe such writing is consistent with current theoretical tenets, and that any perceived inconsistency comes from assuming that all extended, connected prose is of a piece, driven by early modern goals of perspicuity and unfortunately labeled as essayistic literacy. The personal essay originates and inhabits a very different set of goals. Please note, further, that I'm emphatically not arguing the essay as the sole or even main genre for writing instruction. I'm arguing that it needs to be in the mix.

Theoretical challenges to essay writing are only a part of the issue, and what remains to be answered are pragmatic ones. Faigley and Romano note that many students come to writing classes already experienced in transacting computer networks. Cindy Selfe underscores the voluntary aspect of email, a literate practice that increasing numbers of students and citizens alike elect to perform, a practice that might even be threatened by organized education's disciplining it (281). Various writers in Patricia Sullivan's and Jennie Dautermann's *Electronic Literacies in the Workplace* take as a point of departure the observation that work less and less depends on extended writings by single authors. In light of all this, writers may desire and more clearly need certain literacy skills. Even if theoretically redeemed, the essay may be a relic of a certain conception of liberal education, its dynamic of complication, reflection, and form incommensurate to an age when more pragmatic needs must first be met. Montaigne and Bacon and White, after all, were writing in comparative leisure—though Samuel Johnson was certainly not. In terms of Maslow's hierarchy of needs, the need to be a skilled writer of email may precede the need to write essays. Spellmeyer and Heilker's calls for the essay as a fundamental genre for education—or even Faigley's calls for microethnographies—may miss the reality of where writers are psychologically and materially.

It's conveniently beyond the scope of my essay to explore the issues of vocationalism versus liberal education that I've invoked or the related issues of education for work and education for citizenship. Many values of the essay as genre overlap the values of liberal education, especially those embracing what Coleridge called the "two conflicting principles of free life and the confining form" (24), with free life understood not as unfettered and transcendent agency but as resistance to closure and the bounds of topic and method.

Instead, I offer a small observation, appropriately tinged with Coleridgian romanticism but surprisingly coming via Fredric Jameson. Selfe summarizes Jameson's observations that the fragmentation propagated by computer networks, with their insistent reminder that there are ever more selves and ideas "out there," may actually prevent individuals or groups from "acting effectively with a sense of personal agency" (284)—as happened to some small extent with the WPA-L list that I characterized above. The boundless expanse of the Internet, fueled by an additive logic that directly confronts the individual writer with how much there is and is to come, has a paradoxically paralytic effect. In the face of such verdant complexity, writers may, I fear, be cornered into ever-smaller—though admittedly more frequent—forays into the network, developing an online consciousness that offers no psychic or political resting places. The essay offers such places, though they are hard to win and never permanent. Essays remain places with rhetorical power, as readers are consoled by writers who can organize corners of chaos, not just by gathering, arranging, and exchanging but by venturing to say what a part might mean. It's ultimately debilitating to ignore the variety of genres that constitute network discourse, to imagine that all texts are like emails, for example, and all emails alike, debilitating to prize linkage over that which is linked. Essays and patches of the essayistic can and should populate the Internet, like raisins in the cake of the expanding electronic universe, to recall my favorite seventh grade cosmological figure. Essays resist the entropic forces of discourse, perhaps naively and perhaps to conservative ends. Perhaps in some near future we will stop worrying and love the entropic, and essays will be historically interesting texts that we thought we once needed but found we can do better without. But for now and until then, for reasons rhetorical, intellectual, political, and psychological, we ought to save a place for essayistic literacy, in our writing and our teaching.

CHAPTER THREE

The Haunting Story of J
Genealogy as a Critical Category in Understanding How a Writer Composes

Sarah J. Sloane

Sitting Bull, too, met the instrument. He was hooked up to a Mrs. Parkin, who was twenty-five miles away at Cannonball River. She was a mixed-blood who spoke fluent Sioux, but Sitting Bull reasoned that the telephone understood only English, so when Mrs. Parkin answered the call he exclaimed, 'Hello, hello! You bet, you bet!' which exhausted most of his English. And when he realized that he could speak Dakota with this woman such a long way off he, like his contemporaries, was gravely shocked.

Cornell, E., Son of the Morning Star.
Meeting the Instrument

WHEN SITTING BULL SPOKE INTO A TELEPHONE FOR THE FIRST TIME, HE approached that new communicative technology with reasoning based on his experience: he relied on his memories about technology, people, and language to guide his choice of what to say. His prior experiences led him to assume that a telephone invented by a Scotsman could transmit English words only, and he framed his conversational gambit to Mrs. Parkin accordingly. As Evan S. Cornell recounts in the selection above, when Sitting Bull realized the telephone could transmit his own Dakota language, he was "gravely shocked." That shock was in part cultural, of course, and Sitting Bull's conversation was galvanized by the knowledge that this instrument could do something unexpected. Sitting Bull's assumptions about the telephone were, of course, perfectly reasonable when placed in their own historical context: when we listen to Sitting Bull's first words spoken into the waiting instrument, we can hear the fraught echo of a larger dissonance in Native American and European conversations, a conversation haunted by earlier encounters between Native Americans and English-speaking outsiders, words steeped in a cultural brew of suspicion, misunderstanding, and the rhetoric of genocide.

In our professional writings to date about computer-mediated communication, we often forget to note the echoes of personal experience that reverberate in the ways we approach writing. We need to be more critically aware that our encounters with new communicative technologies are always colored by memory, informed by learned response, and haunted by earlier experiences with writing, reading, and communicative technologies.[1] Further, our technologies themselves are always haunted by their own individual and cultural genealogies. When researchers in computer-based writings explore the relations among readers, writers, texts, and technologies, a close analysis of the genealogies of each of these components is crucial.

When voices and messages are transposed into a new medium, writers and readers retain habits of communication learned over other media. These new patterns of communication are themselves inscribed by medial hauntings which both constrain and enable writers and readers using the new technology. Exploring how to read these ghosts, the vestigial remnants of earlier experiences with writing and technology, as they are realized in a particular case history, is one purpose of this article. The other, larger purpose, however, is to posit that the critical term genealogy, and its realization within scribal cultures as apparitional knowledge and medial hauntings, needs itself to be resurrected as a useful entry into our growing understanding of how writers use computers today.

In this article, I propose the critical terms of apparitional knowledge, medial hauntings, and genealogy as a way into understanding how a writer's past writing experiences inform his present choices in constructing the scene of his writing: how a writer's memories inform what topic he chooses to write about, what tools he uses to write with, where he chooses to write, and what writing community he chooses to join. After developing these terms below, I test their usefulness by applying them to the case history of J., a freshman writer at a large public university. In particular, I develop the critical term genealogy as a lens through which to interpret how histories of computers, users, and the scenes of writing complicate contemporary patterns and choices of toll, setting, and self-revelation in text. By testing the usefulness of this critical term and the position it permits by applying it to the case study of J., a reluctant keyboarder, I hope to rehearse how we might explore genealogies of the writing scene when the act of composing takes place on the Internet. From observations of character interaction in MUDs to our analyses of the design and use of home pages, from our observations of how designers configure computer games to our descriptions of computer hardware, we need to pay more attention to how the language we use to name the parts reflects personal and cultural histories of people who read and write on the machine.

I anticipate that readers might protest that my development of the critical terminology and apparatus overshadows my case study of J. Let me explain that I allow this imbalance because the intent of this article is to introduce a new perspective, a new line of vision, on our case studies of writers, in general. I hope the work I do in this article, developing the terms necessary to improve our qualitative analyses of descriptive methodologies such as the case study, will be useful to other readers interested in exploring why writers choose the instruments, settings, and topics they do.

To return to my opening example, Sitting Bull's first encounter with the telephone suggests a new category we must consider to understand writers' encounters with the personal computer as a writing instrument: the category of memory (and its native activities of reconstruction and reconstitution) and a concomitant consideration of how memory informs the contemporary writer's choices. If we are serious about understanding the dynamics of the composing process, we must analyze how encounters with today's writing technologies, especially computers, are themselves haunted by earlier versions of textuality, speaking, authoring, and reading. We must explore how subjects, their writing instruments, and the scenes in which they compose are always determined in part by personal and cultural histories. When we researchers in composition explore how writers compose at the computer, we must consider the role of genealogies and uncover the historical motivation for the choices a writer makes as she or he composes in real-time. That is, we researchers need to remember that writing processes are not only synchronic but that potent diachronic traces undergird every gesture a writer makes, as well.

AN INTRODUCTION TO GENEALOGY

> *"I did this," says my Memory. "I cannot have done this," says my
> Pride and remains inexorable. In the end—Memory yields.*
>   Freud's "Rat Man," quoted in Gay, 129

Embedded in most writers' encounters with digital technology are the visible traces of conventions, structures, and styles of communicating over paper. (Embedded as well, of course, are the invisible traces of memory, such as the ways a mother's attitude towards computers or a father's occupation can be embedded in a young man's attitude towards word processing, as we will soon see.) Because paper was until very recently an almost ubiquitous medium for communicating ideas, the dynamics of how that medium structures discourse, how it locates important points, and how it favors particular styles, are conventions largely invisible to today's casual user—and, sometimes, to the composition researcher. By introducing the category of apparitional knowledge to our studies of writers using computers, we can focus more narrowly on how a familiar medium like paper haunts our encounters with a less familiar medium, the digitized, bit-mapped, two- and three-dimensional texts we encounter on a computer screen with the help of a mouse, keyboard, joystick, or helmet and glove.

By offering the notion of medial hauntings as a form of apparational knowledge that haunts all our reading and writing activities, I wish to remind readers of the importance of memory in all our lettered transactions, to remind readers of the Derridean notion that writing is always prior to speaking,[2] that all our choices as writers are informed by past experiences with writing. In some ways a counterpart to the Ongian hypothesis[3] that writing transforms consciousness, I wish to argue here that our experiences with paper-based textual artifacts haunt our contemporary awareness of what computer writing technologies can do. Paper-based literacies are transmitted and transmuted in our contemporary lettered exchanges.

Not only are computer writing technologies steeped in the powerful brew of prior experiences with paper texts, pens, pencils, and office settings, however. The writers who use computers are haunted by prior versions of writing, writing instruments, writing situations, and themselves. To account for the comprehensive effect of genealogy on writers and writing, as well as to understand precisely how the memory of paper comes to be realized across a computer screen,[4] we must understand composing as a process both haunted and iterative not only within the visible processes of writing but within the imagination of the writer as well. In other words, writing is an iterative process not only in a single user's cycling through different stages of invention, writing, and revision; writing is also an intellectual and emotional activity of splicing together prior selves, understandings, and experiences.

As we construct theories about how computers affect writing processes and products, as we start to explore the consequences of contemporary medial hauntings, we must examine the genealogies of users, texts, machines, situations, and readers, exploring how earlier incarnations of each partner in the writing process haunts its subsequent incarnation in discursive transactions. Although recent work by Selfe and Selfe (1994) offers a valuable perspective on how existing power structures are realized and reified in computer documents, I venture here the importance of local and idiosyncratic traces of memory (memory not only of the powerful contexts that shape discursive structures, but memory of familiar settings, instruments, people, and our half-conscious efforts to resurrect them) in our reconstructions of individual writers' responses to a relatively new, even if ubiquitous, writing technology: the computer.

GENEALOGY AS CRITICAL TERM

I use the term genealogy here in a different sense from both Nietszche and Foucault, although I am relying on Foucault's excavations (and extrapolations) of Nietszche's term. In *Power/Knowledge* (1980), Foucault largely reconstructs the term genealogy as Nietszche (1956) uses it in his important work, *The Genealogy of Morals* (a work in which Nietszche outlines "the provenance of our moral prejudices" (150) and discusses moral genealogies as though they represented universal originary patterns). Foucault uses the term genealogy, in contrast, not to ascribe origin (especially not in any universal sense) but to describe "the union of erudite knowledge and local memories which allows us to establish a historical knowledge of struggles and to make use of this knowledge tactically today" (During 195). In other words, in my reading, Foucault is using the term genealogy to describe a lineage or pedigree, rather than to describe a search for an originary point or the germane moment in some universal pattern of evolution. I find this Foucauldian analysis of how genealogy informs action and event relevant to my own work on the influences of memory on writing at the computer.

Foucault's notion of the importance of local memory in the reconstruction of genealogies is the notion I wish to explore most closely here, in the context of my discussion of the case study of J. Foucault's discussion of the importance of identifying and tracing genealogies draws our attention away from the Nietzschean idea of universal provenance and towards a focus on the local or particular pattern of how a subject constructs itself, to ". . . the way in which the body is historically, culturally, and socially 'imprinted' (by housing, training, diet, manners, and so on) and the way in which the constantly shifting distinction between the self and the body is organized at particular historical moments" (During, 126). By reading the following case study through an extension of the critical apparatus and definition of genealogy offered by Foucault, we can see better the importance of memory and history, of apparational knowledge, in our reconstructions of the composing process as it progresses at a computer keyboard.

In Simon During's intelligent tracing of Foucault's use of the term genealogy, he explains that, in contrast to Nietzsche, "[Foucault's] genealogy has affinities with archeology: it is against totality, it is against the received unities, it does not operate in terms of deep structures, it does not work in terms of essences or origins or finalities" (126). By extending Foucault's notion of genealogy, we too can analyze writing situations in a new way, in a way that recognizes explicitly the importance of memory in our understandings and reconstructions of particular writers, their documents, and their composing processes.

In short, a rhetorical analysis based on a Foucauldian understanding of genealogy grants us rhetoricians new perspective on how the local memories of a single computer user cohere with the "erudite knowledge" of his immediate academic discourse community to create an idiosyncratic composing style, a style haunted by that user's past experiences with family, school, computer, and writing, as well as by his self-concept as a writer and his received evaluations of his writing. A rhetorical analysis that emphasizes the importance of medial hauntings nudges us to look more deeply at how memory inheres in discursive choices made by a composer at a computer—and in his choice to compose at a computer at all.

My use of the word genealogy here—and my search for a real-time palimpsest, the visibly inscribed echoes of past writerly selves, writing contexts, and writerly tools and media in an analysis of any individual writer—deliberately echoes and extends Foucault's use of the term. By looking to the genealogies of writers, writing contexts, and writing tools, and by identifying their echoes in particular writing situations, like Foucault I wish to emphasize the importance of building more comprehensive records of event, records that rely on personal and institutional memory and that recognize their own fallibility even as they trace and account for it.

In my analysis of a case study of J. offered below, I am looking to extend my genealogical investigation of the writer beyond the simple acknowledgment of the local memories of a single user; I am searching also for those important apparitional traces we can identify in the contexts of J.'s writing habits and products. Within the remarks, rough drafts, and writing spaces of J., I am looking for the ghosts of paper-based habits of reading and writing, for the recurrent voices of family, for the visible traces of earlier encounters with writing instruments. The metaphor of the visible apparition, as it is realized in the flickering box of today's computer on a desk, and the invisible apparitional knowledge that is its user's counterpart, helps us focus on the genealogies of writers. As writers construct texts on computers, we can see better how their attitudes and assumptions about computers and writing are deeply haunted by their prior experiences with writing and writing instruments. Although my case study of J. details the effects of genealogy on only one student writer's contact with word-processing in a first-year writing class, I trust that genealogy is a useful critical term to bring to bear on many examples of computer-mediated communication. Whether we are studying the designs and designers of interactive fictions or the soporific motions many first-time users make as they swim through virtual spaces, we need to examine how those notions and motions are determined by the past.

To demonstrate how the metaphor of apparitional knowledge provides a useful terministic screen for understanding the writing of today's computer composers, I offer below a focused description of a particular writer that I studied over the course of a semester at a large state university not long ago. I discuss the student's background (or how he is grounded in what lies in back of him), his attitudes towards writing in general, and his attitudes towards writing on a computer. I make an effort to link his remarks, his unremarked genealogies, and his statements about his past to his present attitudes and abilities as a writer. By meeting J. and listening to his own descriptions of his abilities and feelings, the importance of applying the new category of genealogy, and its revelations of medial hauntings and apparitional knowledge, to capture the experiences of writers composing at the computer, grows more obvious. It is this author's hope, obviously, that this article itself will become a substantive moment in the genealogy of research in computer-mediated communication, in general.

GENEALOGY OF THE CASE STUDY

In an effort to trace out these metaphors and to assemble a particular and coherent example, I recently spent a semester studying the composing processes of one novice writer, a writer whom I will call J. At the time of my study, J., a student writer in a large computer-based freshman writing program at a public land-grant university located in the United States, was an eighteen-year-old white male from a middle-class home who was considering a major in law. J. lived in a dorm on campus while he undertook his first semester of study at the institution, played basketball in his spare time, and took classes which he said boosted his continuing enjoyment in writing. I chose to study J. in part because his diagnostic essay (composed by hand) was among the most polished in the class, and because in the first week of the course, I noticed that he was articulate, affable, mature, and self-aware. When I asked J. if I might follow his writing as it evolved over the semester, supplementing my study of his drafts with open-ended and discourse-based interviews, J. accepted happily. J. said he agreed to be part of my case study because he liked to write and would enjoy the opportunity to "think more about what [he does] when [he writes]."[5] Over the course of the study, J. was a willing participant, in general flattered to be selected and eager to explain his particular processes of writing.

As his freshman writing teacher, I observed J. writing in a class that met three hours a week for fourteen weeks. I collected at least three drafts of each of the six essays he wrote for my class, and I interviewed him formally three times (for about two hours each time) during the course of the semester, asking a combination of open-ended questions and discourse-based questions about his background, writing history, and composing process in general and as it related to his essays-in-progress. I had been teaching writing for four years at the time of this study, two of those years in this computer writing lab in which J. was a student.

J.'s writing class of twenty students met in a computer writing laboratory stocked with Leading Edge computers and printers available to each student, arranged in rows of four. Teachers in this classroom typically rolled around the class on their chairs, pointing at individual screens during drafting sessions and offering what they hoped was constructive advice. Freshmen in general in this large writing program were expected to write six essays of three-to-five pages, each essay to go through at least three distinct drafts. The majority of class time was devoted to actually writing.

I also chose to study J. in part because the parts of his writing process that were visible to me as his instructor were not representative of the other students in his class nor of the other students I had recently taught in that room. In J.'s class, during a typical session devoted to drafting an essay, nineteen students would huddle over their computer keyboards and watch the green words appear on the screen, while J. would push his keyboard to the side of his desk and sit writing with a pen in a spiral-bound notebook. Between the clicks and beeps of the computer keyboards, his ball-point pen would loop silently over his white notebook page, sometimes pausing to scratch out what he had already composed. During the whole semester, J. consistently used the computer less than anyone else in his section of this computer-based freshman-writing class. He used his blue Bic pen for first drafts, subsequent drafts, and revisions—in fact, for almost everything except his final versions of his drafts, which he laboriously typed at the computer.

Sailing, Sailing, Over the Bounding Main

J.'s first essay for the class, written in response to an assignment to write about a personal experience that changed him, was called "Sailing," and addressed the experience of sailing with his three best friends for 26 hours through the Chesapeake Bay. I asked the class to freewrite about the assignment for ten minutes, and J. did so, uncharacteristically at the keyboard, writing about an apparently unrelated topic, the death of a close friend's mother and brother in a car accident. After ten minutes, J. left the keyboard and opened his spiral notebook to continue writing his rough draft, but as he switched medium, he switched topic, as well. He began writing in his notebook about his sailing adventure. As I walked through the class, I noted J. had switched topics and I asked him why he had left the keyboard to write in his notebook. "I can think better [writing with pen]" he said. He finished a first draft of "Sailing" in his notebook.

Before the next class, J. typed a draft of his essay on the computer, changing only single words or short phrases as he copied from his notebook onto the computer. J. put the essay through three more drafts, doing almost all of his revising by hand, and doing his most substantive revising between his next-to-last draft and his last one. He crammed additional information into every margin of his penultimate print-out, rewrote his opening paragraph three times over the printed version, and wrote notes to himself on every page of the draft. J.'s final draft incorporated all of his handwritten changes and nothing more.

Higher Education

J. wrote a comparison/contrast paper for his second essay. He called the essay "Harvard vs. Public Education: Is it Worth It?", an essay in which J. compared the costs and benefits of private and public universities. He wrote his first draft outside of class, by hand in his customary spiral bound notebook. He wrote his second draft in the computer writing lab, and that draft, characteristically, was an almost exact copy of his handwritten one. J. told me the changes he had made were only those that would clarify his original meaning or that would help him avoid repetitions. (An example of J.'s attempt to clarify meaning is his revision of the phrase 'burdensome decision' to 'awesome decision.' J. told me he thought 'awesome decision' was clearer because it underscored the 'huge financial considerations' that are part of the decision whether or not to attend Harvard.) J. added just one sentence to his second draft, a sentence at the beginning of a paragraph; he said he added that sentence because he needed a transition.

In contrast, the revisions J. made between his second and third drafts were more sweeping and involved rewriting the ending and adding new material. J. made these revisions with a pen. He crossed out material by hand and circled sentences in several paragraphs "to see if they had a main idea." J. went back to the keyboard to write his next draft, which again was essentially a typed version of these handwritten changes. His final draft was virtually identical to this penultimate one; J. repaired only a few typographical and spelling errors.

Work

The third piece of writing J. undertook for the class was an essay exploring his recent work experiences. As the assignment asked him to do, J. first wrote two paragraphs about recent jobs he had held, and he then developed an arguable proposition about work in general. J. began the assignment at the keyboard and in ten minutes had written two paragraphs about two different jobs. He then made a hard copy of these two paragraphs and developed his propositions about work in pen at the bottom of this hard copy. J. submitted this combination of handwritten and typed material to me at the end of class.

GENEALOGY OF THE SUBJECT: SCREEN MEMORIES

> *It is not just as though we have something called factual knowl-edge which may then be distorted by particular interests and judg-ments, although this is certainly possible; it is also that without particular interests we would have no knowledge at all, because we would not see the point of bothering to get to know anything. Interests are constitutive of our knowledge, not merely prejudices which imperil it.*
>
> Eagleton

J. is a student who elected the word-processing section of College Writing but who came to this computer-based writing lab suspecting that computer-based word processing would hinder his writing and transform his message, making his writing "indirect and impersonal." For J., adapting to using computers as writing tools entailed not only a change of habit—switching from his preferred writing tool of a blue Bic pen to a computer keyboard—but entailed a change in the way he looked at what we do when we write.

Although J. elected to take this word processing section of College Writing, he entered the class with a strong prejudice against all computers, and he clearly saw word processing as related to computers. J.'s attitude towards computers is an echo of his mother's, he explained in one of his interviews. His mother, a nurse and a teacher of nursing, held different attitudes towards computers than did J.'s father, an engineer who worked with computers every day. J. explained, "He [his father] always thought I should learn how to use [a com-puter] . . . She [his mother] hates them . . . just because they're so impersonal. She never really was hooked on computers like he was."

J. seems more his mother's son than his father's in regard to how he feels about computers. He described the people who work for his father:

> I worked in my father's company last summer and there are guys who just sit there in front of a computer screen . . . for ten hours a day. And you get them in

the cafeteria and they're like social idiots. You know, they don't know how to communicate with people. They just—it's sad. They get in a social scene and they don't know what to do.

By the end of the semester, J. was differentiating between computers equipped with word-processing software and all other computers. He said, "This is just writing. On the computer, I think about sitting down and doing a program so it'll do something for you. This is just totally different. It's helping me with something I want to do, so that's—appealing." In general, J. identifies himself as bored by computers. In both interviews he volunteered that he "hates" both math and science; a pre-law student, J.'s favorite courses, he says, are classes in writing and political science.

J. takes great pleasure in writing well; in fact, he claims "writing well is one of the best things I can do." But J.'s initial perception of word processing as a computer-based activity that hinders personal communication, transforms directness into indirectness, and frustrates thinking, slowed his integration of the computer into his writing process. According to J., he prefers his particular combination of pen and computerfor two main reasons: he is hindered by the physical constraints of the word-processing software and computer writing lab, and, in his own words, he has trouble with "writing at the keyboard and thinking at the same time." J. made this last point in virtually every conversation we had about his writing during the first half of the semester.

However, by the end of the semester, problems with knowing the keyboard no longer inhibited J.'s use of word processing. In our last interview, I reminded J. that he had referred to the computer as "a glorified typewriter," in our first interview, and I asked him what he thought now. He replied, "It's still that [a glorified typewriter], because if you had to type something in, it's so much easier. But now it's more than a typewriter because I could never just start writing at a typewriter. I can't type that well and I'd be making mistakes all over the place and it would look terrible. And [now] I can write or create a story right on the word processor. It used to be just a fancy typewriter and now it's something I can actually create on." Later in our last interview, J. referred to learning to write on the computer as "learning a new way to communicate." However, I noted that in his class work, Jay was still relying more on his pen to generate and revise than any other student currently in the room.

J. encountered problems "thinking" at the keyboard that he didn't encounter when writing with a pen, most markedly at the beginning of the semester. The computer didn't lend itself to J.'s habitual use of visual cues such as circles and arrows. But by the end of the semester, J. was using the word processor in earlier drafts and for more extensive revisions. "I'm a lot more comfortable," he reported. "I can get the ideas and get them down. At the beginning, sitting there with all those people . . . [Now I can] just concentrate on the essay."

So, in addition to the obvious traces of memory in his selections of topic for his first three essays in the class, J.'s choice of writing space was informed by memories of his mother's words and his father's workplace; his shifting between pen and keyboard was prompted by learned responses, by habits learned in one medium haunting another. When J. chose to write about sailing, he wasn't remembering only the joys of seeing dolphins cut the water around his boat; he was remembering a composing process learned on paper. When J. chose to write about Harvard vs. public institutions of learning, he was not only remembering his own choice of a state school; he was remembering how to frame an argument on paper, how to make every sentence "have a main idea," how to create paragraphs that led a reader to the same conclusion he reached. Further, as he revised his second paper, J. was remembering his own genealogy as a writer; he remembered how to develop an argument and to indicate his revisions with arrows, circles, lines—habits, again, learned by hand on paper. Finally, when J. wrote about his experiences of work, he was remembering not only a general impression of workplaces; he was remembering a specific work experience at his father's company. And in his recounted memories of writing programs he gave evidence of an apparitional knowledge infusing his choices of topic, of writing space, and, ultimately, of his claims about how his work affected his identity today. Like the screen memories that Freud says we construct to cover up an uncomfortable past, like the "interests" that Eagleton says are constitutive of knowledge, genealogies of where and with what tools we learned to inscribe our world affect how we approach a new set of tools with which to write.

GENEALOGIES OF SETTING

> . . . *there is nothing modern in the furnishings of Mr. [Laurence] Hutton's house. Tables, chairs, clocks, divans, sideboards, beds, the thousand and one things we have for daily use, are old in the historic sense. With each thing here there is some fact, fancy, place, or person coupled. . .[For example,] there is a portrait, or rather caricature, of Thackeray drawn by himself . . . Underneath is written in Thackeray's hand, "There is a skeleton in every man's house."*
>
> Halsey

> *Even in the house of words, sometimes you still have to go out and buy milk.*
>
> Rachel Brumbaugh, undergraduate writer.

In 1902, a compilation of "sketches" of American authors originally published in *The New York Times Saturday Review of Books* appeared under the title *Authors of our Day in their Homes* (Whiting). Lightweight and charming, each verbal portrait of an author was preceded by a photograph of his work space, typically an elegant book-lined study captured in a grainy black-and-white view snapped by a "kodak fiend." Many of these sketches of the settings in which authors composed include wide fireplaces with oak mantels and brass inscriptions of favorite sayings. Mark Twain's mantel (brought from a house in Scotland), for example, is inscribed with the lines, "The ornament of a house is the friends who frequent it" (126) while Goldwin Smith's overmantel "richly carved in oak" has an inscription from Cicero: *Magna vis veritatis qui facile se per se ipsa defendat* (104).⁶ The settings in which writers compose, the rooms in which they think and write, are themselves cultural constructs, of course, as well as compilations, loose aggregates, of past scenes of writing and writers' imaginings about the ideal scene for their own writing. The sketches in this book are an entertaining rendering of how fin de siècle writers composed the studies and dens, the living rooms, in which they wrote.

At the beginning of the semester, J. said he felt distracted by the noise in the computer-based writing lab—primarily the noise of the printers. According to his own account, by the end of the semester, J. was less bothered. In his words, "It's definitely easier to write alone—without the printers and everything else. But that's affected me less and less. I just block it out . . . I'm just using [the computer] more and more." The physical constraints of the word processor bothered J. most at the beginning of the semester. He experienced problems using word processing similar to ones noted in studies by Lillian Bridwell-Bowles, Donald Case, and Christina Haas, among others. Some of his habits of composing by pen clearly did not translate well to the medium; in addition, however, the space in which he composed was unfamiliar and occasionally rattled him.

As the semester progressed, J. grew accustomed to some physical constraints of the computer and the setting of his computer-based writing, such as his need to learn keyboard commands and block out the noise, but he reported other environmental constraints that bothered him. He said he didn't like not being able to drink a soda while he worked, and he didn't like not being able to listen to the radio in our computer lab. But the constraint that J. mentioned most often—and most vehemently—was the difficulty of access to the computer lab. J.'s dormitory was almost a mile from the computer-based writing lab. Because J. did not own a computer, he was able to write only with pen and paper in his dorm room. There were many evenings, according to J., when it was just easier—and more comfortable—not to brave the elements but to stay at home and write a draft there by hand.

In our final interview, I asked J. what would be the most comfortable way to integrate word processing into his writing habits, and he described this setting: "Have it in my room. Turn off all the lights but the one I'm working under. Have something to drink. Even having a phone there is good, so if you're expecting a call you don't miss it. It [would have] to be an environment where you feel at home and you can do writing and nothing else." In other words, the computer-based writing lab as writing scene fell short of J.'s expectations, expectations built on past experiences with place, with what it feels like to be "home." Interestingly, one piece of technology, voice mail, might have supplied a palliative for the demands another piece of technology put on him—going to the lab to find the tools with which to write.

J. said he had to struggle to achieve the necessary level of concentration in the computer lab. He had to discipline himself "not to look around and see what's going on, who's coming in, who's going. I have to just start to work and not think about anything else." J. reported growing ease with the computer, an ease that was related to his evolving sense that the machine wouldn't "take away from [his] essay." "Over the course of the semester," he reported, "just using [the computer] over and over, and getting used to it and getting more comfortable, made me feel right at home at using it in my writing." Recreating that sense of "being at home" was an important element in J.'s adjustment to composing in the computer lab.

GENEALOGIES OF THE COMPUTER

> *The end of the codex will signify the loss of acts and representa-*
> *tions indissolubly linked to the book as we now know it. If the*
> *object that has furnished the matrix of this repertory of images*
> *(poetic, philosophical, scientific) should disappear, the references*
> *and the procedures that organize the 'readability of the physical*
> *world, equated with a book in codex form, would be profoundly*
> *upset as well.*
>
> Chartier

"I find it a lot easier to free-write with my own handwriting," J. said in our first interview. "Because I'll think of something and then I can't type fast enough to get it, but I can scribble it down." At first, as well as typing slower than he wished, J. found using the word processor's special functions too slow. In his words,

> I think I [switch from writing with the keyboard to writing with a pen] because if I want to change something I can put a line through it when I want. I don't have to do the arrows and then delete. Because then I'll, you know, put spaces in and then I'll be, all right, What do I want to say? (Laugh.) I forgot. I find it a lot easier just to write something in or cross it out.

J. used "the machine" more often late in the semester, once he realized that composing at the screen did not "take away from" the essay for him. He commented on his more frequent use: "The way I used to think [at the beginning of the semester] was it's kind of like—you—the thought would be going, you know, just right through you and then right through the pen and on the paper, and now it's kind of going from you, through the machine, and then on the paper. It seemed like it would be more indirect and wouldn't be the same, but now I can see what comes out is okay."

J. initially worried that writing on the computer would make his writing more impersonal:

> Before the course I'd always looked at computers as being impersonal—and, from my writing, some of it gets really personal. And I'm just thinking, I'll just write and then I'll type it into the word processor. As I've gotten more comfortable I can see that I can write [on the word processor] the same way as I can by hand and get the same effect.

J.'s writing process at the computer was haunted by his prior successes with Bic pens and notebook paper. As I watched J. compose these three essays, it became clear to me that J. used his pen when he had a more sophisticated logical task to perform, when he felt his subject matter was personal, and when he undertook global revisions. I hypothesize that the very familiarity of the writing instrument allowed J. to undertake these more difficult writing tasks when the unfamiliarity of the computer would have interceded too visibly or obstructively in his composing process. Parallel to how contemporary readings are invisibly informed by habits learned by the eye's endless boustrophedon over the pages of a codex, contemporary writings are haunted by the apparition of a hand reaching for paper and pen, a medial haunting that reveals itself in the reinvention of paper-based composing habits on a computer platform.

However, the primary metaphor is metamorphic, not sedimentary; an active agent within the layers, underlying the whole palimpsest, is a metamorphic dynamic, a conversation among the apparitions of past selves, past places, past beliefs, and past settings of composition that are revealed in J.'s current choice of materials and locations with and in which to write. When J. shifts from keyboard to pen, he shifts from the unfamiliar to the familiar, from his father's work world to his mother's writing space, from a virtual writing surface to a tangible one, from a treacherous medium to a reliable one. He sees in the computer both possibility and problem, and he leaps from its dynamic surfaces to the habit and memory of using paper and ink in a familiar surrounding.

DISCUSSION

> *From this Foucault draws a quasi-archeological conclusion: the intelligibility of history is not to be found in its documents. Behind documents exists the non-discursive condition—the power network—which allows the subject to speak (and act).*
>
> During

> *What matter who's speaking?*
>
> Foucault

This case study of J. ultimately describes the composing style of one freshman writer, a writer who integrated the computer into his writing process less quickly and thoroughly than other members of one section of College Writing.

When we listen to J.Os own words as recorded in his essays, logs, and during interviews, and we observe J. at work at the lab, three attitudes towards composing at the computer become obvious. J. assumes that word processing is impersonal, that it hinders his thinking, and that it is an object that has the capacity to randomly transform his messages. We can see the roots of J.'s frustration with word processing in his memories of paper and ink, his learned responses to place, his work habits, his family, and his self-definition—in short, the genealogies, personal and cultural histories, that grant depth to each of these dimensions.

The student writer of today, who learned to write with pen or pencil in hand, may not be the student writer of tomorrow, who will have learned to write on a keyboard and may well have a familiarity with computers that far outpaces our own. However, as students enter our classes with greater experience with computers, we need to pay attention to how their memories and their genealogies affect the integration of computers into their writing processes. While the precise set of memories of place, tool, and self a writer brings to a computer-based writing space will no doubt differ, the general category of genealogy remains a stable construct for interpreting the traces of memory in the choices a writer makes as she or he shifts from one communicative technology to another.

Every writing technology bears visible traces of earlier writing technologies in its design and in how writers use it; typically, it also belies traces of the assumptions bound to earlier technologies and to historical world views that may no longer apply. In the introduction of many writing instruments, in the ways we use those instruments, in the assumptions we make about readers and writers, in the genres that evolve, even in the particular textual innovations (the table of contents, the appendix, the home page) that we subsequently realize, we are always mirroring, echoing, or resisting the technologies that came before. We can never conceive of nor create a communicative technology that is not saturated by the prior technologies and communities within which it is embedded. Why shape a computer screen as a square? Why put a computer on a desk at all? How are paper and ink haunting our every imagining of post-print culture? Is every writing technology in some sense vestigial?

When I hold meetings at the Human Interface Technology Laboratory at University of Washington to discuss how interactive stories might work in virtual reality, I find myself relying heavily on my own experiences with paper-based stories. Yesterday, at a meeting of our Scripts and Narrative Group at the lab, I was asked to explain what a story is in terms that anyone could understand. I found myself in front of a white board holding a green magic marker and drawing triangles, talking about Aristotle, scrawling the word *catharsis* on the board. A few minutes later, a graduate student in our group was arranging a demonstration of a Nintendo 64 so that we might see how a game company was handling questions of plot and character in an interactive medium. In other words, as researchers in virtual reality think ahead to the consequences of interactivity for narrative, as we work towards designing the narrative tools which will help users make shifts in time and location, we are relying implicitly on stories and ideas about narrative that were realized first in speech and later in paper and ink. Whether we choose to call the evolving informality of email an example of litteraturizazzione, or to outfit our character in a MUD in clothing and weapons reminiscent of a Tolkien novel, we are creating stories and spinning theories which themselves are steeped in a cultural stew of prior images and words. Genealogies of self, setting, task, and tool will reveal that the current activities of writers and readers are based on prior experience more than we ordinarily see. Our media and our scribal gestures are haunted by the past in powerful revelations of apparitional knowledge. Lest I sound too much like my neighbor in Yelm, the woman who channels Ramtha, let me hasten to add that this haunting is not so much a literal engagement of the past as it is the gauzy imposition of habit, idea, and places from the past, a half-visible, vestigial presence apparent in our writing tools and composing processes.

DEJA VU ALL OVER AGAIN: THE ACT OF REMEMBERING

Our current communication habits and instruments are overwhelmingly haunted by earlier ones. This statement may seem too obvious for words, yet, in fact, our research methods do not often enough consider the influences that shape writers' choices of everything from revision strategy to writing implement, from how much they like to talk about drafts-in-progress to when and how the computer enters their composing process.[7] However, one value of new communicative technologies is that they throw old rhetorics, messages, genres, forms, and the models of reading and writing they inform, into sharp relief; they make newly visible the materials, habits, and contexts of paper-based composing processes. But our current research into computer-based communication does not, initially anyway, transform larger notions of how writing works nor what a written document might be composed of, nor even sufficiently decontextualize the notion of "document" itself. It is in addressing this myopia that the Foucauldian insight about genealogy may be useful.

If we wish to understand the evolution of literacies as they evolve across different medial planes, we need to make visible the traces of earlier technologies, contexts, and composing processes as they are realized in contemporary reading and writing practices and apparatuses. When we examine the genealogies of subject, setting, and technology, we can better construct interpretations of how a writer uses technology to express herself. When we teach our students how to write with, in, and on computers, we need to acknowledge the apparitional knowledge, the medial hauntings and dissonance, the genealogies that infuse our students' and our own knowledge of composing processes and our judgments about the places from which we compose.

NOTES

1. A person's first encounter with any new communicative technology is always haunted by her prior experiences with technology. Just listen to how we use voicemail today: older users often leave messages on voicemail in the form of paper-based letters, sometimes with elaborately contrived salutations and exit remarks. Or look at the evolving discourse conventions of email: Our email today looks and sounds like informal memoranda, like paper-based office discourse with an edge. The opening and closing remarks of email authored by novices are often suited better to a paper-based epistolary culture than to our information spaces etched today by voicemail, email, cellular telephone calls, and the fine traceries of the World Wide Web.

2. See Jasper Neel's discussion of this point in *Plato, Derrida, and Writing*, pages 112-117, as well as all of Jacques Derrida's *Speech and Phenomena*.

3. Ong persuasively argues that scribal cultures are cultures which have experienced a shift in human consciousness; he sees writing as having fostered a shift from aggregative, associative thinking to analytical, hierarchical, and logical thinking. He notes the development of forms such as tables of contents and indices as being tied particularly to writing technologies and to the visible inscriptions of writers. See Walter J. Ong, *Orality and Literacy*, 78-116, for a richer discussion.

4. I see this imposition onto the computer screen of paper-based conventions, memories, and habits as a kind of "screen memory." (As most readers will remember, Freud called screen memories those images that stood in place of real memories but that retained some traces of that which was repressed. See Peter Gay's biography of Freud for a good discussion of this point.)

5. This remark, and all subsequent remarks quoted, are reported verbatim from three tape-recorded interviews with J. undertaken in 1986 and 1987.

6. "Great is the strength of Truth, who is easily her own best defender."

7. Not only do our habitual ways of communicating inform our compositions and conversations across new media, our habits of talking and writing (these familiar ghosts of ourselves) haunt also our design of new communicative technologies. We can see traces of the Roman diptych and late Greek papyri (with words blocked into pages within a long manuscript scroll) in our paperback books of today. We design our computer monitors to echo the look and shape of paper pages, we model our computer keyboards after manual typewriters, and the black pixeled fonts realized on a Powerbook computer screen (on which I write this essay) mirror the calligraphy of a black fountain pen—itself a more recent embodiment of the carbon and gum into which a stylus might dip. Not only do we constantly reinvent the wheel, we never consider alternative modes of transportation.

CHAPTER FOUR

"English" at the Crossroads
Rethinking Curricula of Communication in the Context of the Turn to the Visual

Gunther Kress

NEW QUESTIONS FOR ENGLISH

MY PRESENT JOB REQUIRES ME TO THINK ABOUT THE ENGLISH CURRICULUM in the upper years of schooling in England. I can't think about this without also thinking about the subject in the earlier years of schooling. Nor can I think about it other than in the context of the vast political, social, economic and technological changes which characterize the present, and which will, if anything, become more intense over the coming decades. These lead me to the conclusion that the purposes of the curriculum need to be questioned. If in the past, the curriculum had been (seen as) the site of the reproduction of young people in the image of their society and of its values, that view clearly is no longer tenable. There are no stable values, no reliable or agreed structures. All we can know is that tomorrow will not be like today, let alone like yesterday. The idea therefore of making the young in the image of what we know today, which is itself a version of what has been handed down to us from yesterday, will no longer do. Curriculum now needs to be focused on the future: its task is to provide young people with dispositions, knowledges and skills which they will need in their future social lives. So one urgent task is to try to understand what skills, aptitudes, knowledges, dispositions concerned with representation and communication young people will need in the world of the next two decades or three, in order to be able to live productive, fulfilling lives.

What will the subject English need to become in order to function as an essential part of the education of young people? What does it need to focus on? What questions, issues, concerns, knowledges need to be central? At the moment the prevailing commonsense is that English is a language-based enterprise; the debate is whether the emphasis should be on practical issues such as spelling, syntax, or proper forms of speech, in other words, English as communication; or whether it should focus on questions of value, on aesthetic and ethical issues, in other words English as the curriculum of 'culture'. In practice, and unsurprisingly, in its different versions it becomes a quite variable mixture of both, depending on many factors, of which the characteristics of the community around the school and of the community in the school and in classrooms may be the most significant. In the meantime, however, the landscape of communication is changing fundamentally. This can't be ignored in the school-curriculum. If English is to remain relevant as the subject which provides access to participation in public forms of communication, as well as remaining capable of providing understandings of and the abilities to produce culturally valued texts, then an emphasis on language alone simply will no longer do. English will need to change.

This issue is addressed in this chapter in two parts. On the one hand, I suggest that the visual is becoming prominent in the landscape of public communication, and that this cannot be ignored by school-curricula. On the other hand, I suggest that our present theories of language and meaning are simply inadequate and inappropriate for the task which English will need to perform. Our present theories of semiosis are theories founded on convention and on use. Consequently, creativity is regarded as unusual, as rare and therefore most prized. This theory of semiosis is not adequate to what actually is the case: it is implausible as a theory. An apt, plausible theory will be founded on innovation, on constant transformation and change, brought about by individuals. In that theory creativity is usual, and conventionality, in its strong form of "doing things as they have always been done," will be unusual. That new theory is required by the demands made of a curriculum focused on the needs of the future.

The newer technologies of representation and of communication in any case suggest the second of the two theories as appropriate: 'conventionality' does not provide a means of understanding or using these new media. This is not to say that countervailing forces—discernible even now—will not become active and powerful. Control over communication and over the means of representation is, as always, a field in which power is exercised. We know that the economies of the postindustrial societies will be information and knowledge-based economies, in which the capacity for innovation will be the required and the most highly prized commodity. A curriculum based on theories of semiosis of convention and use cannot hope to produce human dispositions deeply at ease with change, difference, and constantly transformative action. There is therefore a coming together of developments—economic, technological, social, political—which requires a rethinking of the processes and the means for representing ourselves and our values and meanings, broadly the set of things named in anglo-phone countries by the word "literacy".

Representation and Literacy

One issue which arises in sharp form in any rethinking of modes of representation and forms of communication in the context of deep technological changes, is that of the concept of literacy itself. The word does not occur in romance languages, nor in German. Those languages have a more specific term, focused on control of the alphabet: *alphabetisme, Alphabetismus,* etc. The English word collects together a vast and quite disparate range of skills, aptitudes, processes, dispositions: and it presents them as though they were all of one kind. These range from competence in handling letter-sound correspondence, via the competence of producing grammatically and textually well-formed texts, to the competence of subtle understandings of complex text, to the production of 'sensitive' responses to aesthetically valued texts. As a noun, the word "literacy" presents this most diverse range of phenomena as one reified thing. The possibilities offered by electronic technologies of communication raise this question of the constant metaphoric extension of the term literacy sharply. My own preference is for a disentangling of all these diverse processes and phenomena covered by the cloak of the term "literacy", and discussing them separately, evaluating each for its uses and potentials. I am extremely reluctant, at a time when deeply transformative processes are remaking the means of representing and communicating to stretch this cloak even further by further metaphoric extensions of the term literacy.

Let me mention just some of these processes, to indicate the range and direction of these changes. The visual is becoming more prominent in many domains of public communication. From a different perspective, this is to realize that written language is being displaced from its hitherto unchallenged central position in the semiotic landscape, and that the visual is taking over many of the functions of written language. This shift is, from yet another perspective, a shift from the temporal-sequential logic of spoken (and to a somewhat lesser extent written) language to the spatial-simultaneous logic of the visual. This shift may lead to a fundamental challenge to the form which is perhaps most typical of speech, namely narrative, and its replacement by the visual/spatial display. I discuss this at some length below. These are at the same time challenges to conventional notions of text, and of its limits. Contemporary semiotic processes—based only in part on the "affordances" of electronic media—seem to signal a shift from text as a cohesively and coherently organized representation of the world to be read, to the notion of unorganized semiotic resources to be used. This parallels and reinforces the move away from narrative. Neither hypertext nor the contemporary rock-video are organized through narrative structures. In all this the status of the book is also coming into crisis. The school text-book may serve as an example. It is no longer a semiotic object defined by language: not units of knowledge coherently organized around the chapter, but resource materials organized by the unit of work (presenting a set of tasks to be performed). Whereas textbooks even in my own period of schooling were texts to be read from beginning to end, contemporary textbooks are collections of resource materials to be used in relation to specific tasks. Their emphasis is less on reading than on doing.

The Change in the Landscape of Communication

The last two decades have seen a far-reaching change in media and in modes of communication. On the one hand this change has attracted widespread comment and yet, on the other, it has not been fully acknowledged or understood. A comparison of texts from any of the major media across the last 30 years or so clearly reveals the differences. In newspapers, the pages of the 1960s are black and white, and covered in print; in the 1990s by contrast there is color, there are images; and in many contemporary newspapers in 'the west' print has very nearly been pushed off the page. If we look at television of the 1960s, at a news program let us say, the screen is dominated by the figure of the newsreader: usually in a medium shot, showing the person from about chest up. It is noteworthy that then, and to some extent even now in Great Britain, the term in use was 'newsreader': the news was a linguistic event by and large, even on television. Now of course the term presenter is coming to be used: the news still has verbal (written-to-be-spoken) elements, but the task of the 'mediator' has shifted from 'reading' much more to that of 'presentation'.

What is presented in TV news is information predominantly in the form of images, though the film and video footage which make up so much of the television news do have sound as an important element. But now speech is used to do the "presenting"; it frames and points to the central elements of information, which are visually mediated. There is a similar shift in terminology as far as newspapers are concerned in the word 'correspondent'—as in 'our foreign correspondent', as someone who wrote to the paper. The landscape of communication of the 1990s is an irrefutably multi-semiotic one; and the visual mode in particular has already taken a central position in many regions of this landscape. Other modes are also becoming more significant than they have been in the more recent past. Sound, as I mentioned, whether in the form of "soundtrack", or "music", or "background-noise", is one of these. And the body is coming to be used as a medium of representation and communication: even a brief look at a contemporary rock video will illustrate this clearly enough, and so do the 'industries' of aerobics, jogging, roller-blading, and the televisual entertainments developed out of these.

These changes are not in themselves new: the body has been used in many cultures and in many periods as a medium of communication; the visual has had a central place in other periods, even in 'the West'. The point is rather this: that after a period of some two-to-three hundred years of the dominance of writing as the means of communication and representation, there is now, yet again, a deep shift taking place in this system, and in the valuation of elements of this system. The change is of great significance in its social and political ramifications. To call it a 'tectonic shift' may not be an exaggeration because the semiotic landscape is indeed being remade. Where before there was the single, central mountain-range of written language, now another alpine system is being thrust up by forces of a complex kind: in part, social, political, technological, and, as yet less recognized, by economic forces as well.

I will say something about the newer relations of language and image; about changes to writing which may be a consequence of this; and about a new theory of meaning, which is, I believe, essential in the light of these developments. I will say very little about causes, though some few comments about the interrelation of technological change and the possibilities which it affords are essential. I will conclude with some programmatic statements from the point of view of a wider conception of curriculum: a broad, social, economic, cultural curriculum of representation and communication, active in many social sites and not just in institutional education.

Language and Image

Even though writing has been the most valued means of communication over the last few centuries—the means which has regulated access to social power in western societies—other means have of course always existed together with writing. Even the densely printed page of novels, or of older textbooks, as of governmental reports, had layout, used typefaces of a certain kind, had paragraphing, all of them visual elements. The fact that the layout of the book adhered strictly to the observance of regular margins around the text, therefore displaying writing as a block of print, both obscured this fact of laying-out by making it invisible through its usualness, its "naturalness," and at the same time intensified the meaning of regulation, much as did the stiff collar worn by the military and the white-collar worker alike. Of course, speech has always been there—except for the members of speech-impaired communities—and it has always accompanied all other modes.

Communication has always been multi-semiotic. What is happening at the moment is not in itself new; and yet it is a significant change. The cultural and political dominance of writing over the last few centuries had led to an unquestionable acceptance of that as being the case; it made the always existing facts of multi-modality invisible. The recent powerful re-emergence of the visual has, then, to be understood in that context: not as new in itself, but as new in the light of the recent history of representation, and of a nearly unshakeable commonsense which had developed around that. As a mildly critical note one might comment that the sustained attacks on this "logocentrism" from post-structuralist quarters have used written language in its most formal mode, without much evidence of self-consciousness or irony.

My focus from here on will not be on language-as-such (a theoretical fiction in any case), but on language in its written form, and on actual changes in its new relation with the visual. A simple means of illustrating the shift from the previous situation to the present one is to compare the front-pages of newspapers—either of one contemporary newspaper with a copy from, say, twenty/thirty years ago; or, to compare one of the few remaining papers which adhere to the older mode and one which exemplifies the contemporary situation. Figures 1 and 2 are an instance of the second.

The metaphor of 'writing being pushed to the margin' can be seen, literally, to be the case in figure 2. That is characteristic of many forms of public communication—whether publicity materials, brochures, advertising texts, and so on. Here I will explore a different instance of this changed relation,

Figure 1
Frankfurter Allgemeine

Frankfurter Allgemeine

ZEITUNG FÜR DEUTSCHLAND

200 Menschen in Peru als Geiseln in der Hand von Guerrilleros

Überfall auf die japanische Botschaft / Vermittlungsversuche des Roten Kreuzes / Kinkel bietet Hilfe an

Zum Schnuppern

„Netanjahu verhindert Klärung des Schicksals von Ron Arad"

Schmidbauer: Ich gebe die Hoffnung nicht auf / Vorwürfe aus Teheran / Der Schlüssel bei den Syrern?

Parteienlandschaft Ost

Von Friedrich Karl Fromme

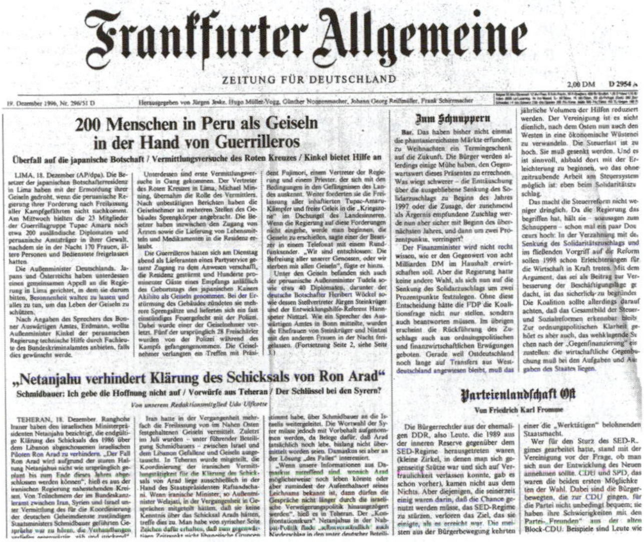

Figure 2
National Examiner

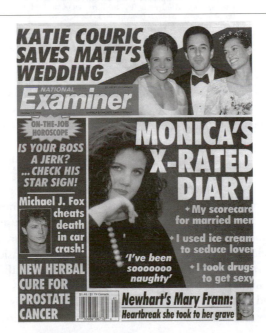

Figure 3
1936 Science Textbook

76   MAGNETISM AND ELECTRICITY

the magnetic poles. Fig. 62(c) shows the combined field of (a) and (b) when the wire is placed between the poles.

Note that, in Fig. 62(a) and (b), the lines of force on the left of the wire are in the same direction as those of the external field, while those on the right of the wire are in the opposite direction. Consequently in the combined field of Fig. 62(c) the field to the left of the wire is strong—there are a large number of lines, while the field to the right is weak.

If we assume, with Faraday, that the lines of force are in tension and trying to shorten (see p. 18), we should expect the wire to be urged to the right. This is precisely what we find by experiment.

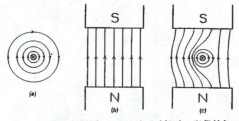

Fig. 62. (a) Magnetic field due to current in straight wire. (b) Field due to magnetic poles. (c) Combined field of (a) and (b).

The principle of the electric motor.

The simple electric motor consists of a coil pivoted between the poles of a permanent magnet (see Fig. 63). When a current is passed through the coil in the direction indicated in the figure we can show, by applying Fleming's left-hand rule, that the left-hand side of the coil will tend to move down and the right-hand side to move up. (Remember that the direction of the field due to the permanent magnet is from the N. to the S. pole.) Thus the coil will rotate in a counter-clockwise direction to a vertical position.

which I want to characterize, among other things, as 'specialization'. My hypothesis is that in the newer visual-verbal texts the two modes take on specialized tasks, each task being more appropriate to the inherent characteristics of the visual and the written mode. My example consists of two science textbook pages: one from 1936, and one from 1988. Both are aimed at students of about 14 years of age.

In figure 3 language as writing is dominant. In terms of space on the page, the image here takes a little more than one third of the page; most of the pages in this book are more usually given over wholly to print, or use smaller illustrations. Writing is the vehicle for providing all the information which is judged to be relevant. Language (in the written form) is considered as a full medium of representation and communication: everything that needs to be said is said in language; conversely, the implicit assumption is that everything that can be said can only be said in language. The syntax is that which we might even now associate with scientific writing (or with "formal" writing in any context). Its central unit is that of the (complex) sentence. The structure of the sentences here is itself indicative of the deeper logic of this form of writing. Take as an example the following:

> When a current is passed through the coil in the direction indicated in the figure, we can show, by applying Fleming's left-hand rule, that the left hand side of the coil will tend to move down and the right hand side to move up.

This sentence consists of between six and eight clauses (depending on your mode of parsing and its theory of syntax); 1) a current is passed (by someone) through the coil; 2) the direction is indicated (by someone); 3) we can show; 4) (someone) applies Fleming's left-hand rule; 5) the left-hand side tends 6) to move down; 7) the right-hand side tends 8) to move up. The clauses are in an hierarchical arrangement in which the position of the clause in the hierarchy is an indication of its ontological, representational and communicational significance. Here "we can show" is the main clause, so that what is at issue in the first instance is the (generic) scientist ("we") as demonstrator of truth. The clause "by applying Fleming's left-hand rule" is directly subordinate to the main clause syntactically and conceptually: it is the means by which "we can show." The two clauses which contain the substance of the demonstration "the left hand side. . . the right-hand side "are also subordinated syntactically and conceptually to the main clause though "by applying Fleming's" has as its deleted agent the "we" of "we can show." Its immediate proximity to the main clause mimetically indicates the closer connection. Hierarchical syntax serves the expression of the hierarchy of conceptual organization.

The use of agentless passives ("when a current is passed", "the direction indicated") puts into the background, to the point of disappearance, the figure and the action of the scientist/technician. This de-personalization is also present in the "we", which subsumes the writer's persona to the collective "we." Another meaning of this kind is shown by the "will tend"—the careful nuance and hedging of the experimenter/scientist, who is dealing, after all, with nature. But the major meaning in this textual example is that carried, more or less, by the words and their syntactic arrangement—what will happen to a coil when a current is applied in a particular way. The emphasis on place and space, "the direction indicated in the figure", "we can show", "left-hand side", "down", etc, show that spatial, locative meanings, are here expressed through language; on the face of it, they could be more easily shown visually. But here language is the means for carrying all information.

When language has the role, as here, of expressing all the essential information, images (are assumed to) have the function of 'illustration'. Some meaning is expressed fully by written language, and the image is assumed to be repeating that information. Nothing new is assumed to be added which is independent of or not subordinate to the written part of the message. There is one direct link here between written text and visual illustration; in the clause "in the direction indicated in the figure." Language is used to point. Clearly it is easier in this instance to make use of the spatial potentials of the image; which is the point I made just above about the continuity of the multi-semiotic land-scape. The means for doing so existed then, in 1936, and could be used. The question arises as to what the function of images actually is in this context. In other words is this really an illustration, or just what is 'illustration'? (see Barthes 1976) The author of this textbook was praised by reviewers of the book for his "enlivening use" of images. This points in the direction of plea-sure; and through pleasure perhaps to an increased possibility for learning and remembering. But beyond that lies even here, even if implicitly, an assumption that certain forms of information may be better represented and communi-cated by visual rather than by verbal means.

The page from the textbook of the 1980s (figure 4) functions very differ-ently. Here writing is not dominant. In terms of the amount of space taken up by language and image on the page the proportions are now reversed—about one third is writing, two thirds is given over to image—though that alone is not the major indicator of the changed relation. Rather it is the fact that now writing is not the vehicle for conveying all the information which is judged to be relevant. Here language is implicitly seen as a medium which is only in part able to express and represent what needs to be represented. Everything that needs to be communicated is now not judged to be communicable in the writ-ten mode alone; the assumption is that some things are best done by using writing, and others are best done by using images. The two modes have become specialized to particular tasks.

The syntax is fundamentally different from that of the earlier text: both for-mally and in its content and function. Take as an example the first paragraph:

Circuits
In your first circuits you used torch bulbs joined with wires. Modern electri-cal equipment uses the same basic ideas. But if you look inside a computer there are not many wires or torch bulbs. The wires and bulbs have been replaced by electronic devices like transistors, chips and light-emitting diodes.

Here the sentences are not only shorter, they are syntactically simpler. Sentence 1 consists of two clauses; sentence 2 of one clause; sentence 3 of two clauses; sentence 4 (the longest) consists of one clause.

In fact this much simpler syntax is also much closer to the grammatical/tex-tual organization of (informal) spoken language (see Halliday 1989; Kress 1994). This gives another clue to causes for the changed relation: the informal-ity of spoken language brings with it a suggestion of a less formal social rela-tion. The relation of the maker of the text to the audience has changed, (secondary school education had become, well before the 1980s, a mass-com-modity, whereas that was not so in the 1930s), and in part because there have, in the fifty years between the two examples, been far-reaching social changes which have deeply altered relations of power. Gender is no doubt imbricated in this: the author of the late 1930s book could declare in his Preface that his

Figure 4
1988 Science Textbook

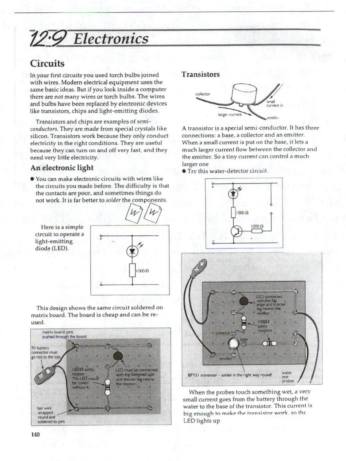

book would be "easy to read for the boy." The authors of the 1980s book have no doubt made strenuous efforts to make their books appealing to student of both genders: professionals concerned with science have been very conscious of the absence of young women from this subject.

Whereas the logic and order of hierarchy typifies the writing (the sentence) of the 1930s text, now there is the logic and order of sequence, often a sequence of events: First you did this, then you did that, then (if) you do that . . . The new formal arrangement expresses a change in the ontology/epistemology of the (presentation of the) subject (see Halliday 1989; Kress 1994).Along with this, the language is more informal, more personal, more (reader-) friendly. The reader is addressed directly, personally, as "you"; agentless passives are fewer; the hedging has lessened. And whereas in the first sample the major meaning was carried by language alone (or that at least was the ostensible assumption), now it might be said that the major meaning, the core meaning, is carried by the images. Take as an example the relation between the writing and the image under the heading An Electronic Circuit. The writing says: "Here is a simple circuit"; but it is the image which provides the information of what a circuit is like. The image carries the main information.

This is not the relation of illustration, where the written text is assumed to carry all the information, so that the image merely 'repeats' that information, for whatever reason. Now both writing and image are informative. However, they are not informative in the same way or about the same things. A specialization has occurred, which it is essential to note. Language has—here at least—the functions of narrating (you did this, then you did that, (if) you do that), of pointing ("Here is a simple circuit"); and still, of describing/classifying ("Transistors are examples", "they are made from", "they are useful"). But perhaps the central aspects of information—what a circuit is like, how it works, what its components are—are now communicated by an image. Writing is oriented towards action and event, broadly; and the visual is oriented towards the display of elements and their relations.

This example seems to show an instance of a new code of writing-and-image, in which information is carried differentially by the two modes. Information which displays what the world is like is carried by the image; information which orients the reader in relation to that information is carried by language. The functional load of each mode is different.

The simpler syntax does not mean that the text—the verbal and visual elements together—is less complex than the 1936 example. The diagrams have taken over certain of the functions carried in the earlier text by language. The diagram just discussed is a highly abstract representation of a circuit; it is a topological representation, which focuses on relations abstractly rather than 'realistically'. In other words, abstraction and generalization are not absent from this page, and the cognitive demand made of the reader/viewer is as great (though different in character) as in abstractions made in verbal language. Equally, the communicational and representational power of the diagram is such as to cope easily with that demand. If we follow a top to bottom reading direction the abstract, topological diagram is followed by a realist representation, a topographical diagram. It is realistic and specific enough to enable someone to produce an actual circuit from this model. This is then followed by two abstract diagrams; and the page concludes with a further realist, topographical representation. Reading the page demands from the reader a constant switching from abstract to realist forms of representation. This new representational and communicational situation is not one of lesser complexity, or of lesser cognitive demand: it is one of a different kind of complexity, and of different cognitive demand.

The order in which the elements in this verbal and visual text are read is significant: as far as the diagrams alone are concerned, if we follow the conventional reading direction of the printed page, (left to right, from top down to bottom) then the abstract, generalized representation precedes the realist, specific one. In other words, as a pedagogic strategy, in one form of reading the text offers the abstract version first and follows that with the specific. However, this page can also be 'read' as a visual unit, that is, as a 'picture'. In that case a different relational order obtains, one in which the realist images occupy the lower part of the page/image, and the abstract images occupy the upper part of the page/image. That leads to a different reading—of empirical reality as both the anchoring and the grounding of the abstract, theoretical. (see Kress and van Leeuwen 1996). I make this point because it might be thought that visual representations do not lend themselves to abstract thinking, or to teaching practices which move from the abstract to the concrete or vice-versa. That is not the case.

For the age of print, in the period of the high valuation of writing, the book may be thought to be the criterial, the defining medium of dissemination. The book with its densely printed pages is the particular achievement of the era of print-literacy; and the book also stood in specific relation with conceptions of knowledge. Whether as novel or as scientific treatise, the book presents an integral, coherent account of a world. It does not matter from that point of view, whether that world is factive or fictive. In the book, authority and knowledge are inextricably intertwined: the book presents a coherent, cohesive, internally consistent account of (a part of) the world. The book was, in the last resort—other, beyond and above the author's name—the guarantor of knowledge. The contemporary science text-book is no longer a book in that sense at all; it functions as a packaged resource kit. The relevant element is no longer the book itself, nor its chapters. In the newer science textbook (as of those of geography, history,) the relevant element is the 'unit of work'. Whereas the old-fashioned book was read from beginning to end, this new book is not read at all, it is used. The shift is from an older organization of text to a newer organization of resource; from an older concern with knowledge to a newer concern with the marshalling of information for the management of a task, related to, work. The book now makes available resources. It is not read but used: the "work" in 'unit of work' has to be taken seriously; it signals the deep shift from the inwardly focused, contemplative activity of 'reading', to outwardly focused action, both physical and cognitive.

In this, the newer book is in line with other organizations of semiotic materials in which the boundaries of the 'text' are dissolving, and reading and use become both blurred and fused.

Is Language Changing?

One of the new buzzwords in information technology circles is "visualization," (see Brown et al. 1995; Lanham 1994; Tufte 1990). This names the trend towards the visual representation of information which was formerly coded solely in language. With the increasing availability of "bandwidth," visualization is now a possibility, and will become more so in the near future. "Visualization" in this sense proposes one answer to the question whether language and image are "doing the same thing": it says, yes, they are; it is merely a matter of translating between the two modes. Just as it is possible, so the argument goes, to translate from one language to the next, so it is possible to translate from one semiotic mode to another. Of course this bald formulation leaves out of account why anyone would want to engage in this translation if both modes convey "the same" information, in the same way, with the same effects. If, as I have suggested, the visual and the verbal provide fundamentally distinct possibilities for engagement with the world then the translation from one mode to another has to be seen in the more radical sense of "translation as transformation." In such transformations, the figure of the translator, as a socially formed and located person with his or her own interest, has as always to be taken into account. But that apart, the "affordances"—what any semiotic system makes possible or rules out—are the starting point for any serious attempt to understand this process of translation/transformation. Are language and image doing the same? Can they ever do the same? must be the early questions, rather than left as unproblematic.

A second set of questions concerns the interaction/interrelation of any two languages or semiotic modes between which translation takes place. Do they merely co-exist? Or do they interact? To what degree do they interact? If language and image do not merely co-exist, but interact, what are the consequences? If they have different potentials, will they come to serve different functions, and will they then inevitably become specialized, both representationally and communicationally? There is a third set of questions which I will not engage with here, namely: is the visual as a mode of representation systematic, rule-governed, an effect of the values of the culture in which it is used? I will simply assert that it is, and that the patently obvious cultural differences in visual forms and in their modes of use point precisely in that direction. (See Kress and van Leeuwen 1996)

To answer the first set of questions requires a departure from usual ways of thinking about and theorizing language, that is, it requires a focus on the material and formal aspects of language in ways which are not a part of the theoretical mainstream. Within that, language has been treated in a quite abstracted way, as an "immaterial" phenomenon—in conceptions such as Saussure's "langue," Chomsky's "competence" (see Chomsky 1965), and the many transmogrifications of that term; and indeed in much discussion whether in linguistics or in psychology. But to understand the semiotic potentials of language, we need to engage with it as material, and as substance, whether as speech—in its physicality and materiality as sound, as well as in its more abstract grammatical/syntactic/textual organization; or as writing—in its physicality and materiality as graphic (and visual) substance, as well as in its more abstract grammatical/syntactic/textual organization.

Of course, in certain linguistic and literary approaches to language such aspects have always been included: the study of poetry has dealt in detail with aspects such as pace, rhythm, sound-shapes, whether used in rhyme, assonance, alliteration, or in phonaesthetic considerations. Similarly, with certain forms of poetry—and advertising!—in written/printed form. In linguistics— in phonetics as well as in some grammatical theories, certain suprasegmental features have had much attention (e.g., Firth 1957 ; Crystal and Quirk 1964; Halliday 1989). Nevertheless, these concerns have not entered the mainstream of linguistic theorizing, but have always appeared on the margin, in stylistics perhaps, or in certain forms of applied linguistics, often even more marginally as paralinguistic, or extralinguistic, concerns. They have not led to a radical revision of notions of language.

At the point where language is used in a radically new medium—in elec- tronically mediated communication—the issue of what language is needs the most serious rethinking.

From a more radically material point of view, language has to be thought about as either speech or writing, and each of these has then to be further described in terms of its multiple material aspects. Writing, for instance, is not only distinctive in terms of its characteristic syntax but also in material terms such as its multiple forms of visual display, on multiple forms of surface. From this perspective speech and writing are deeply different. Speech is necessarily a temporally, sequentially organized mode, using the medium of air and the mode of sound, depending on sets of physiological characteristics of the so-called speech-organs, and the organs of hearing. Its temporality and sequentiality leads to an underlying logic of sequence in time: the logic of the iteration of one thing after another. This logic lends itself readily to the repre- sentation of (sequentially conceived) events in the world—sequences of actions, sequences of events. These can readily be turned into the textual form of narrative. Speech is oriented to action and event. The implicit and founda- tional question posed by the organization of speech is what are the salient events, and in what sequence do they occur?

The visual by contrast is a spatially and simultaneously organized mode, using the medium of light, and the materiality of certain kinds of surfaces, in the mode of graphic substance. It too relies on physiological, bodily character- istics. Its spatiality and simultaneity leads to a different underlying logic, namely the logic of simultaneous presence of a number of elements and their (spatial) relation. This logic can, of course, be turned into sequences of images following another; but its inherent characteristics are those of display: showing what the salient elements in the world are and what the spatial relations between them. Display and arrangement are the fundamental features of the logic of the visual. The implicit and foundational question posed by the organ- isation of a visual representation is: what are the salient elements, and in what spatial relation do they stand to each other.

Of course aspects of sequentiality—such as anteriority and posteriority, before and after, can be used metaphorically to signal other meanings: "before" can become "cause," and "after" can become "result"; or, "first in the sequence" can become "most important". Similarly, spatial relations can be used in

Figure 5
My Visit to the Toy Museum

metaphors of various kinds: "above" can become "more important"; "next to" can become "closely related"; and so on. The technology of film and video sequentializes and temporalizes visual images. But their initial logic remains, and their metaphoric developments are just that: developments of a particular orientation towards and engagement with the world. Here, as an illustration, is a child's recollection through the visual mode of an event, a school-outing to a toy museum.

Interestingly, the teacher's demand had been "to draw a story", mixing the categories of "narrative" and "display" in her request. The child's drawing is a recollection; a reordering, and a reconstitution of a complex event, (taking place during a visit of about one and a half hours): a representation of salient elements in a particular order. It is not a drawing of a particular shelf or display-case in the museum: it is a mental remaking, and a visual representation of that internal remaking. It shows salient elements; in a particular arrangement—in a line, suggesting similarity; and ordered by size, suggesting difference; and in a particular relation to the maker of this representation. It needs to be stressed that this is a cognitive act of reshaping an event that happened, from one point of view, out of the interest of this maker of the representation. Images are ideological constructs, just as much as are verbal textual objects.

Had the teacher requested a written story, or a spoken account of the visit, the resulting semiotic object would have been entirely different: not the classification of elements as here, but the recounting of events in sequence: 'first we did this, then we did that, then Lucy lost her bag, then we saw the dolls house', etc etc. In other words, the inherently distinct possibilities of speech and of the visual would have led to different cognitive action, to different representations, to the construction of a different world, with a different order. As we face the new era of the world mediated everywhere on the visual space of the screen, this is a fact of fundamental importance. The shift from page to screen is having its effects on the modes of communication—writing and the visual—as much as it is having effects on the media, such as book, page, and screen.

Speech-based cultures, oriented to the world through the deep logic of speech, are thus likely to be distinctly different from image-based cultures: their engagement with the world is different, their habitual modes of representing the order of that world are different; and these differences become, over time, normal and then 'natural'. Writing-based cultures are similarly likely to feel the effects of the shift from representation through language in written form to representation in visual form.

The logic of writing participates in the logic of the visual (writing is a visual mode) and in the logic of speech (writing, even in highly literate societies still stands in a complex dynamic and close interrelation with speech). As I pointed out earlier, hierarchy—a metaphoric spatiality with 'higher' and 'lower' expressed via the syntactic means of embedding as well as of other forms of subordination—is a feature of many forms of writing in the public domain. In addition, there is the actual spatiality of the graphic material of the surface on which writing is displayed. Not only does this permit, as has been pointed out frequently, a going back over written text, a visual reassembly, it also affords other possibilities of the visual through the multiplicity of means of layout: paragraphing; spacing of lines and of letters; indenting; the use of 'bullet points'; size and shape of letters; and so on. The syntactic hierarchy of clauses can in this way be further amplified, underscored, or counteracted through directly visual means. Writing is thus doubly spatial: once metaphorical, through the order of syntactic hierarchy, and once actual, through the visual display on a surface.

In pages such as those discussed earlier (figure 4), blocks of writing come close to becoming one element in the set of elements of the now visual rather than verbal unit of the page. In contemporary usages pages differ in the extent to which they are either 'written text' as such, or a 'block of text', a visual element in a visual unit. As I mentioned earlier, language in its written form is becoming specialized, as in the instance of figure 4, which is not at all an unusual example. In this new specialization, written language tends syntactically in the direction of speech, and tends semantically in the direction of the inherent logic of speech—the reporting/recording of actions and events, and of the use of language in issuing commands, i.e., actions to be undertaken.

These often have a deictic function in relation to the images: look at this, copy this drawing, follow this line, etc. In this new specialization written language is getting closer to speech-like forms than to what are still considered (formal) writing-like forms.

Images are, on pages such as that of figure 4, taking on certain functions formerly carried by language. Again, these functions tend in the direction of the inherent logic of spatial display: showing the salient elements, and their relations. Whereas, in the former situation, all these tasks were performed by writing, now a separation is evident: the functional load of the two modes is becoming distinct. And so the answers to my earlier questions are: No, the two modes are not doing the same; and no, they are not merely co-existing; and yes, there is, it seems, strong interaction between the two which could, over time, have real effects on language in the written mode.

Both modes produce semiotic objects—messages, textual forms. If texts are metaphors of the organization of the world, then the two modes produce quite distinctly different takes on the world, different images of that world, and different dispositions by their users—whether as text-producers or as text-consumers—towards the world. The shift which I have described here is one which could be characterized, in perhaps oversimplified form, as a move from narrative to display (to use two foundational categories to name the essence of that shift). Narrative and display as ways of organizing representations of the world each have the most fundamental consequences for an individual's or a culture's orientation in the world, so that this shift is bound to have equally fundamental repercussions in social, cultural and economic practices, and in the subjectivities of individuals. This is a story which is still in the process of being told, and a display still in the process of being sketched.

From the point of view of the focus of this book, the issue I have been discussing connects directly: the 'screen' is the new space of representation. How it will be organized—whether as a largely visual entity or as a largely linguistic entity will have far-reaching repercussions. It is too early to know, though my money is on the visual. In either case, the effects on representation through writing will be far reaching, though deeply different in each case.

New Theories of Representation

The semiotic changes which characterize the present and which are likely to characterize the near future cannot be adequately described and understood with presently existing linguistic theories. Most obviously, if language is no longer the central semiotic mode, then theories of language can at best offer explanations for a part of the communicational landscape only. Moreover, theories of language will not serve to explain the other semiotic modes, unless one assumes, counterfactually, that they are, in every significant way like language; nor will theories of language explain and describe the interrelations between the different modes, language included, which are characteristically used in the multi-modal semiotic objects—'texts'—of the contemporary period.

In other words, and as a first requirement, multimodal texts/messages need a theory which deals adequately with the processes of integration/composition of the various modes in these texts: both in production/making, and in consumption/reading. This, in turn, presupposes adequate understandings of the semiotic characteristics of the various modes which are brought together in multimodal compositions. At this level, a semiotic theory which is too much tied to and derived from one particular mode—for instance, our conventional language-based theories of communication and meaning—will permit neither an adequate nor an integrated description of multi-modal textual objects, nor of multi-media production. In other words, an adequate theory for contemporary multi-modal textual forms needs to be formulated so as to permit both the description of the specific characteristics of a particular mode, and of its more general semiotic properties which allow it to be related plausibly to other semiotic modes. Take as an instance the need for all semiotic modes to be able to express the meaning 'social distance'. This is done in specific ways in language, for instance through the use of the pronoun 'we' rather than the pronoun 'I', or through the use of the 'past tense' as in 'I wanted to ask you for a loan of your car' rather than the 'present tense' as in 'I want to ask you for a loan of your car'. This meaning is expressed in quite other ways, necessarily, in images: for instance by the distance of viewer from object—not close and friendly, but distant and formal; or by the vertical angle: 'looking up to an object or person of power' or 'looking down on a person or object of lesser power'. Both the relatedness of the means through which this is expressed (e.g., 'distance' in both cases: temporal distance in one case and spatial distance in the other), and the differences in expression between two given modes need to be readily describable in an adequate theory of meaning.

A second issue is that contemporary, and in particular mainstream, theories of semiosis are theories of use rather than of remaking and transformation. That is, individuals are seen as users, more or less competently, of an existing, stable, static system of elements and rules. This view has historic as well as contemporary social and political-ideological causes. One of these has, as an unacknowledged consequence, the widely entrenched commonsense about the arbitrary relation in the sign between signifier and signified. That relation is seen to be both established and sustained by convention. Yet all the examples which I have discussed here speak of change: changes in forms of text, in uses of language, in communication and representational potentials. Indeed change is the whole point of this chapter. But change and conventionality are not easy bedfellows: the common understanding is that convention impedes change, that convention is a force for the maintenance of stability. If change and convention are not to be treated as mutually exclusive terms, then the question still remains, forcefully, how we are to account for change.

My argument is that the semiotic landscape is changing in fundamental ways, and that this change relates to others in social, cultural, economic and technological domains. While a semiotic theory which could not easily account for change was never adequate to the facts of semiosis, it may have been sustainable in periods where change was less intense than it is at the moment. A semiotic theory which does not have an account of change at its core is both simply inadequate and implausible in the present period.

Dominant theories of semiosis—in linguistics by and large—are theories of use in which language is seen as a stable (and largely autonomous) system of elements, categories, and rules of combination. All the examples in this chapter demonstrate changes in the use, extension, and function of both the categories and the rules. In other words, they show a quite different situation to that portrayed—largely implicitly—in current theory. The other point demonstrated by the examples is equally important: the changes in use, form and system arise as a result of the interested actions of individuals. It is the need by individual makers of texts which leads them to stretch, change, adapt, modify the elements, and thereby the whole set of representational resources with its internal relations.

An adequate theory of semiosis will be founded on a recognition of the "interested action" of socially located, culturally and historically formed individuals, as the remakers, the transformers, and the re-shapers of the representational resources available to them. Notions of language use—that is, deployment of existing resources without changing them—will need to be replaced by notions of the constant re-making of the resources in the process of their use, in action and in interaction. The remaking of the resources is an effect both of the demands of particular occasions of interaction, and of the social and cultural characteristics of the individual maker of signs. Both together account for the sign-maker's interest in representing a phenomenon in a particular way, and in communicating it in certain media. This interest is personal, affective and social and it shapes the 'direction' of the remaking of the resources. In this way the remaking on the one hand reflects individual interest, and on the other, due to the social history and the present social location of the individual also reflects broad socio-cultural trends. Semiotic change is thus shaped and guided by the characteristics of broad social factors, which are individually inflected and shaped.

The interested action of those engaged in semiosis is the crucial matter in attempts to get beyond a theory of use. It defines one central aspect of the process of semiosis: the sign is the expression of the maker's interest through the motivated expression in apt form of the meaning of the sign-maker. This action is transformative rather than totally creative: that is, it is action on and with existing semiotic (cultural) resources. The more the sign-maker is in the culture, the more he or she is 'socialized,' the more the shapedness of the social and cultural resources will be in the foreground; but the transformative, re-shaping action is always seemingly present, however invisible.

With this approach use is replaced by transformation and remaking. In present semiotic (-linguistic) theories, the action of the individual is use, the implementation of an existing system; in a semiotic (-linguistic) theory of transformation and remaking, the action of the individual is that of the changing of the resources: using existing resources in the guiding frame of the maker's interest. If competence in the use of the possibilities of an existing stable system is the goal of present theories, the capacity of design through the (re)shaping of the potentials of existing resources is the goal of the latter. The two approaches assume very different notions of individual action and of individual responsibility. Consequently the two approaches have deeply differing potentials and implications for applied areas—whether in language use and language learning, or in education more generally. I will return to this in the final section of the chapter.

Semiotic systems, language included, are then seen as sets of resources, which are given their regularities by larger cultural values and social contingencies, and deployed and remade innovatively in the making of always novel signs by individuals in social interactions. Use is replaced by remaking, which is transformation; and the notion of the semiotic system is now replaced by that of a dynamic, constantly remade and re-organized set of semiotic resources.

The focus on language alone has meant a neglect, an overlooking, even suppression of the potentials of representational and communicational modes in particular cultures; an often repressive and always systematic neglect of human potentials in many of these areas; and a neglect equally, as a consequence, of the development of theoretical understandings of such modes. Semiotic modes have different potentials, so that they afford different kinds of possibilities of human expression and engagement with the world, and through this differential engagement with the world, make possible differential possibilities of development: bodily, cognitively, affectively. Or, to put it provocatively: the single, exclusive and intensive focus on written language has dampened the full development of all kinds of human potentials, through all the sensorial possibilities of human bodies, in all kinds of respects, cognitively and affectively, in two and three dimensional representation.

Just at the point where 'literacy'—socially made forms of representing and communicating—is undergoing radical changes in the context of the deeply revolutionary effects of the 'Electronic Age', it is essential to ask this question about the adequacy of present theories of semiosis and their effects. The fast developing technologies of virtuality are promising and threatening a new and more intense distancing—a new alienation of ourselves from our bodies. This demands the most serious rethinking at this point. If we do not take this opportunity, we deny ourselves not only the possibility of actively participating in the shaping of this 'age', but we may unwittingly collude in a new diminution of the potentials of being human.

Synaesthesia

This newer theory of representation may prove adequate to the demands of several urgent tasks posed by the electronic technologies: the needs for dealing with constant change; the need to treat individuals as agentive in relation not only to the production of their textual objects, but also in relation to their constant re-making of their community's representational resources; the interaction of many semiotic modes in a text; and to do so both from the maker's and the reader's point of view. The interaction of different modes and of different possibilities of expression in multi-modal texts and multi-media production poses questions not only at the level of text, but also at the level of cognitive processing: new demands are made cognitively (and no doubt affectively) by the new technologies and by their textual forms. A new theory of semiosis will need to acknowledge and account for the processes of synaesthesia, the transduction of meaning from one semiotic mode in meaning to another semiotic mode, an activity constantly performed by the brain. In other words, a theory of semiosis which incorporates the facts of multimodality also needs to be a theory in which synaesthesia is seen as an entirely usual and productive process, essential equally for the understanding of semiosis in a multimodal semiotic landscape as for the possibilities of real innovation, rather than as too often now seen as a pathology to be remedied.

In the most immediate past, as in our present, synaesthetic activity has been suppressed in institutionalized education, due to the social and cultural dominance of language in the written mode in the public domain. Culture affects and even structures, through privileged and thereby habituated usages, which semiotic modes are available or not, which are made focal and valued, made useable or not, and which are ruled out of or into the public landscape of communication. Social and cultural forces thus determine which modes are 'there' for humans to use in particular domains; they affect the manner in which they are used. The school, in Western societies, says that writing is serious and most highly valued; music is for the aesthetic development of the individual, as is visual art. These structures, pressures, and actions have not only shaped the representational landscape, but also the cognitive and affective potentials of individuals. A more developed understanding of these processes is essential to open up full and productive access to the multiplicity of representational and communicational potentials, which will be essential for competent practice in the electronic age, in the socialities and economies of the near future. At the moment our theories of meaning (hence our dominent theories of cognition) are entirely shaped by and derived from theories of language. Meaning is in fact identified with 'meaning in language'. this constitutes a major impediment to an understanding of the semiotic potentials of, among other modes, the visual and of its role in cognition, representation, and communication.

From Critique to Design: The New Curricula of Communication.

In a theory of use the task of the individual is to understand and have competent control of the representational system and its capacities. Although the potentials of the system make possible a vast—even infinite—range of textual forms, their scope remains relatively circumscribed by convention: hence the valuation of 'creativity' as 'rare' in such a theory. In that theory, change, other than as that rare event of creativity, is produced via critique: that is, existing forms, and the social relations of which they are manifestations, are subjected to a distanced, analytical scrutiny to reveal the rules of their constitution. It is now essential to offer a critique of critique, by showing it to be a response to particular circumstances in a particular period, showing it as a historical phenomenon and not as naturally there. In periods of relative social stability, critique has the function of introducing a dynamic into the system. In a situation of intense social change, the rules of constitution both of texts and of social arrangements are in crisis: they are not settled, but in process of change. In the new theory of representation, in the context of the multi-modal, multi-media modes of textual production in the era of electronic technologies, the task of text-makers is that of complex orchestration. Further, individuals are now seen as the remakers, transformers, of sets of representational resources—rather than as users of stable systems, in a situation where a multiplicity of representational modes are brought into textual compositions. All these circumstances call for a new goal in textual (and perhaps other) practice: not of critique, but of design. Design takes for granted competence in the use of resources, but beyond that it requires the orchestration and remaking of these resources in the service of frameworks and models expressive of the maker's intentions in shaping the social and cultural environment. (see Buchanan and Margolin 1995) While critique looks at the present through the means of past production, design shapes the future through deliberate deployment of representational resources in the designer's interest. Design is the essential textual principle for periods characterized by intense and far-reaching change.

Design rests on a chain of processes of which critique—as distanced analytic understanding—is one: it can, however, no longer be the focal one, or be the major goal of textual practices. Critique leaves the initial definition of the domain of analysis to the past, to the past production of those whose processes are to be subjected to critique. It leaves the definition of the agenda to those whose purposes are to be the subject of critique, and are not mine. The task of the critic is to perform analysis on an agenda of someone else's construction. As a result a considerable degree of inertia is built into this process. The idea of the intellectual as critic corresponds to social arrangements and distributions of power, rights and responsibilities of certain social arrangements and of certain historical periods: namely arrangements in which some individuals and groups set the agenda and others either follow or object. Design takes the results of past production as the resource for new shaping, and for remaking. Design sets aside past agendas, and treats them and their products as resources in setting an agenda of future aims, and of assembling means and resources for implementing that. The social and political task and effect of the designer is fundamentally different from that of the critic.

It is here that I wish to make two brief points about curriculum. Curriculum is a design for the future (see Kress 1995). The contents and processes put forward in curriculum and in its associated pedagogy constitute the design for future human dispositions. They provide one set of important means and resources for the individual's transformative, shaping action in making herself or himself as social humans. That is one point. The other is that the sites of education are now also in question, as are their aims. The state's threatened withdrawal from institutionalized education with its aim of producing citizens, in favor of the market with its aim of producing consumers, is one strand in that. In that shift, new (and also very ancient) sites of education are coming back into the foreground: the workplace prominently (as in the ancient guild system), and now also the multiplicity of modes of mediated communication. These are not only or no longer just the 'mass-media', but quite new media, as yet only hazily knowable in their effects—with the Internet of course the dominant metaphor at the moment—and their educational aims and effects. All these pose entirely new questions for 'curriculum'. In all of these, the category of design is foundational.

Critique and design imply deeply differing positions and possibilities for human social action; and deeply differing potentials for human subjectivities in social and economic life. The likely shape of the near future is such that the facilities of design rather than those of critique will be essential for equitable participation in social, economic and cultural life. It would be an unforgivable dereliction of the responsibilities of intellectuals if the potentials of representation and communication—of literacy in a very broad and metaphoric sense—offered by current developments were not fully explored, and a concerted attempt made to shape their direction to bring about at least some of the much talked about utopian visions of communication in the electronic age.

Petals on a Wet Black Bough
Textuality, Collaboration, and the New Essay

Myka Vielstimmig[1]

[W]orking on email—constructing the messages within a pre-genre that is still being shaped itself—is constructing us, too.
<kbyancey>

DOUBLECLICK[2]: MULTIPLICITY MON AMOUR

Gregory Ulmer suggests that there are three general ways of constructing information: narrative, exposition, and pattern. In traditional academic texts, exposition has been the privileged mode. But as writers move between print-based alphabetic literacy and electronic literacy, we will see a shift in how we represent what we know.

`[M]ultivocal texts are emerging as a new force in composition studies. (Kirsch 192)`

When you place Ulmer next to Moffett, you begin to apprehend the change that Ulmer is constructing. Moffett's is a universe of print discourse that is univocal; Ulmer's is a universe of electronic discourse that is multi-vocal. The anchors in Moffett's universe—the text, the audience, the author—have disappeared in Ulmer's, almost while no one noticed. The text isn't your mother's text anymore; the audience is some shifting polyglot "out there"; and the author—well, speak to Barthes about the author.

Tornow finds the influence of a fragmented "quantum world view" in the online writing of students, and it's obvious too in many dimensions of popular culture—from body-piercing to beer commercials to the heroin-chic ennui of the fashion world.

In a Station of the Metro[3]

In Wendy Bishop's "If Winston Weathers Would Just Write to Me on Email," we see the narrative of her responding to her students' work. We see Bishop differ and agree with other scholars—exposition. And right in the middle of the piece we have a poem. Bishop's may be an example of what Gesa Kirsch identifies as a "new force," and what the field may soon want to call the "new essay," a place where multiple ways of knowing are combined, collage-like: a site where alternatives are at least as valuable as single-voiced, hierarchically-argued, master narratives.

The apparition of these faces in the crowd.

I think there *is* a narrative in Bishop's article, but it's subtle, it's multiple—perhaps that's it: it's narratives.

Wittig's fond prophecy of "surrealism triumphant" offers the same opinion from the point of view of the creative writer/artist. We're learning to love the, oh . . .

The intuitive leap?

The juxtaposition.

The unarticulated predication.

Petals on a wet, black bough.

The new essay seems to have its own logic: intuitive, associative, emergent, dialogic, multiple—one grounded in working together and in re/presenting that working together.

At the same time, it offers an aesthetic that gives writers permission to expose and explore the disconnects as they develop the plot of a given piece of writing— and permission to dramatize those disconnects, this process, in the concrete formatting choices they make (e.g., multiple fonts, shifting margins, etc.).

> Isn't it possible that the singular state an intent channel flipper falls into is not, as it is often described, evidence of a "short attention span," but, rather, of a new kind of attention? The qualities of this new attention would include irreverence, quick decision making, ability to identify the whole from the fragment, and an exquisite taste for juxtaposition. Not a bad starting list of skills if one happened to be faced, on a daily basis, with an overwhelming onslaught of information. (Wittig, 91)

Even the plots—plural? I think that's part of the point of multi-vocality: when a piece is sufficiently multi-vocal, it invites readers to invent the plots articulated by the voices. Kirsch is making a related point when she criticizes the *semblance* of multi-vocality for its potential to re-enact "forms of domination and colonization" (199) under the controlling hand of the authors, in spite of themselves. But I think the new essay works toward genuine multi-vocality, which means that the piece will stop, start, branch right and left, resisting a master narrative as it represents narratives.

This is not an argument against The Essay or against "print classic" or conventional logic. It is an argument toward another kind of essay: a text that accommodates narrative and exposition and pattern, all three. It allows for differentiation without exclusion, such that it resists becoming unified in a community of shared final ends, to borrow from Susan Miller. It is an essay of radically different identity politics, of radically different mentality.

It is an essay the academy is learning to write.

> DoubleClick: Wrinkles on the Interface

It is interesting that so many of those who experiment with form in the academic essay are not only online writers, but are also group writers. Kirsch (rightly, I think) divines that these writers believe the form of their writing to be an expression of the collaborative ethic, as well as of "the interactive, dialogic nature of writing and research processes, . . . [and that they] expose the multiple subject positions writers and readers often occupy" (193). Whether many collaborators simply work online for their own reasons, or online writers simply find it convenient to collaborate, there seems a tacit connection between the two. The emerging e-journals in composition and rhetoric, the experiments in form within established print journals, even stand-alone websites that offer work in progress—it seems a majority of these efforts conceive of the online publication as a place of interaction. The texts usually have multiple authors, they're hyperlinked to other sites, they invite readers to contribute, and so on. Their tacit theory seems to be that the ethos of the net is a "collaborative" one, broadly understood.

So far in these texts, though, not many writers are looking at how such different voices—the ones nominally so important in collaboration of whatever variety— might be represented textually. The assumption seems pretty much conventional and universal: that writing will continue to be writing: the old genres will suffice to contain it. That's part of the problem: the old genres contain it. In other words, it seems pretty obvious that if we want traces and resonances of these collaborative processes—this collective intelligence?—represented textually, we might have to invent new genres that wouldn't contain it, might have to refigure old genres so that they couldn't contain.

Still, I enjoyed Kirsch's critique because it calls to account the writers of multivocal pieces, before we get carried away with ourselves. The truth is that, as much as we'd like to, we can't afford the stance of those literary writers who (claim to) answer for their sullen craft only to the muse.

Speak for yourself, pal.
Kirsch is surely right that we need to be conscious of how we represent ourselves, of the potential to misappropriate other voices, and of the interpretive troubles we may be creating for readers. "Experimental" writing too easily becomes obscure writing. Or: the "old" genres may still offer some usefulness.

Another concern is what to do with this stuff in the classroom. As the editors of this volume asked in their response to a draft of this paper,

```
in what ways would [new approaches to genre and
authorship] force us to re-think the rhetorical advice
we currently provide students? How does this new voice
(and the new genres it supports) speak to students?
<hawisher>
```

DoubleClick: Assaying the Essay

Some will say that our characterization of the essay as a confinement is untenable; that we fail to credit it with the place it offers writers; that the essay is indeed, as John Trimbur put it, wonderfully mobile; that as genre, it in fact does offer exactly the kind of flexibility we are suggesting is absent.

A quick look at the history of the essay does make this complaint seem valid. Kurt Spellmeyer, for instance, locates the historical genesis of the essay with Montaigne, the epistemological genesis of any essay with the self:

```
The essay serves to dramatize the situation of the
writer who moves beyond the familiar to bring language
into closer accord with life. Against the systematic
impersonality of the scholastic tradition, Montaigne
defends the central position of the author-as-speaker,
at once subject and object in discourse. . . . For
Montaigne, convention was literally con-vention, a
"coming together" of dissonant perspectives in order
to restore the lived world, at the risk of imprecision
and incongruity. (263)
```

Michael Prince, in "Literacy and Genre: Towards a Pedagogy of Mediation" makes much the same point. Although he too cites the contribution of Montaigne to the essay as a place for tentative reflections, Prince details the role that Shaftsbury, Addison, and Hume played in defining the essay as a mediating genre: a "position between systematic, often technical arguments and the aimless repetition" of gossip and stories (735). Interestingly, Prince makes of Shaftesbury a postmodern hero in this regard:

Shaftesbury urged instructors to remain suspicious of their own authority: by dividing a unified sense of self into a dialogue of oppositional forces, teachers might ensure that they remain both authority and questioner, teacher and student, and thus make not only their knowledge, but also their way of coming about it available to those they instructed . . . .

(Internal dialogue, interaction, performance, ex/tensive identity.)

 Perhaps more fundamentally, the writing of interac-
tive genres such as the letter affirmed Shaftesbury's view of the social nature of identity.(734)

As described here, the essay seems, at least in part, what we are arguing for when we talk about new/text or new/essay.

Yes. In fact, though I hate to drag my feet, I think there's some truth in the idea that the essay as genre is mobile and flexible enough to accommo-
date the new influences that electronic writing now offers. Insofar as the traditional essay is a space where exploration of the self as both subject and object (and the self's interaction with the social, and all the rest) is sanctioned, I would think it offers a great deal of room for the net/essay to move. Virtuality is fascinated with itself as subject and object.

Only if we suspend the rather rigid con-
ventions that often define the "postmod-
ern" academic essay—the ones that call
for unity, single voice, and the prevailing
view.

But the fact that current convention may have narrowed the essay tradi-
tion, e.g., in regard to how voice or collaboration might be represented, doesn't argue that we must create a newly theorized essay. You're antici-
pating here, but I do wonder why it isn't fair to say that what we're call-
ing for isn't a *regeneration* of the essay instead of a new essay altogether.

Ironically, both Spellmeyer's and Prince's purpose in reminding us of the essay's history is to restore it to its prior position: as a place for exploration not governed by the scholastic. They are prompted to do so, of course, by what they see as the frozen, non-personal, entirely scholastic nature of the current essay, particularly the essay we academics know best: the academic essay. Its domination of the essay model provides, for Spellmeyer and Prince, the exigence for a return to the past, but for us a move to the future, to new essay.

*A call, then, for a new essay that is wonderfully mobile seems legitimate. It may be that we too are asking for a return to once was, though I doubt it. Returning to once was isn't possible, and isn't desirable either. Still, some of the traces and con-
ventions of old essay as defined by Spellmeyer, Prince, and others—especially*

*those that emphasize "a lowering of high forms through mixture with conversa-
tional modes, and the heightening of low forms through the inclusion of elevated
intellectual content" (Prince, 736)—are what we hope for in new essay.*

But *please*. I don't see a revolution, either. I don't see how the rhetorical
project here is essentially any differ-
ent from Montaigne's. I take especially the congeniality of (if you
must) the "old" essay toward "the
low," and "the informal" as evidence
that it is a welcoming genre for the
impulsive, irreverent, and eclectic
tropes of the net.

As important, however, we are talking
about more than a re-vitalizing of the
old: given multiple authorships, visual
or poetic patterns of coherence, new
media for creating this essay, multiple
literacies, we aren't talking a return to
the past.

*Low and high are simply registers, and the range here of low to high is fairly
restricted: it almost calls the terms "low" and "high" into question.*

But Montaigne already called them into question.

*We are talking about more than a mix. Plug in Batson: different modes of
thinking—modes that surely operated in Montaigne's day but that were not represented in those essays—voices that
must have spoken but that didn't find a
place in those essays. Like women's
voices.*

This isn't just the marginal either,
the impulsive, irreverent, and
eclectic tropes: this is another way
of being, represented textually,
one that online seems hospitable
to and that could migrate offline to
the essay. So different media are
involved; and the mix of media
seems another key difference.

Multiple authorship still implies an
Author; shifting ideas about coherence still imply coherence; changing
media for writing still imply writing.
If we see genre as interpretation of
writings (i.e., something the reader
does) instead of prescription, I think
we're merely asking whether this extant genre, The Essay, can explain the alternatives in writing online.

*Well, of course of course of course of course. But the generalizations are so
broad that even I can hardly quarrel with them.*

*All authorship isn't alike; if we thought it were, we wouldn't have gone to the
trouble of theorizing kinds of authorship (e.g. "Single Good Mind"). All coherence isn't alike, and in fact difference in forms of coherence often marks differences in genre. Differences in media will produce different kinds of writing and
different reading processes—hence hypertext and even the reaction we got to
"Postings on a Genre of Email." At what point does the stretch and strain begin
to break?*

DoubleClick: I am Legion

Middle class composition teachers, ever Emersonian in spirit, stress the importance of self-reliance ('Your work must be your own'), even in nominally collaborative classrooms.

Lynn Z. Bloom

The concept of group solidarity is much stranger in Western cultures than it is elsewhere, and I imagine that our unfamiliarity with it—our cultural reverence is for the individual—accounts for how difficult is our relation to collaboration. Our cultural honor code depends on individuals (students, colleagues, citizens) "doing their own work" when it counts, instead of on a sense of accountability for each other. Americans (and others of the West) have trouble making sense of the radical family/community/collective orientation of other cultures. Fox relates an introduction to this idea from an international development workers' manual.

Even for those of us who engage in it regularly. It's like taking on a new identity; issues you hadn't foreseen arise. It's easier not to sail to the new land.

[In the drawing,] the government census taker in a collectivist culture is asking a group of local people, "How many of you are there?" The villagers are lined up, linked arm in arm: the old man, the child, the man with the hoe, the adolescent, the woman with baby in arms. "We are one," they answer. (32)

This thinking proceeds from a logic that the West usually can't see. Postmodern theory, in one sense, is quintessentially Western; its project is to disintegrate by analysis, to find ever-smaller constituents where once there were wholes. But, ironically, in dismantling the Western self, postmodern theory at the same time integrates it within a vast network of other (non)selves. And collaboration enhances this effect, since it heightens the sense of connection among collaborators: the individual disintegrates as the writing group integrates, and you begin to see, in small, the large constructivist vision of interconnection.

Dear Editor:
We have a revision to make in the chapter you've accepted. We want to change our names.
Well, not in some ways, perhaps (I'm up for P&T this year).
This is not virtual cross dressing. It's really just an acknowledgment, a formality.
In one sense, this grows out of the conversation you

This is more a problem, if problem it be, for us; my students seem to understand this implicitly.

and we had about "signing" the different sections of the paper to help the reader keep the two voices and arguments as/sign/ed to the "right" one of us.
As you may recall, our trouble with doing this was that we felt we had both contributed to both of the voices. Some of the text we would have assigned to one of us was written by the other, and vice versa.
Assigning authorship to "Writer X" and "Writer Y" didn't fit the spirit of this collaboration. The two voices had become *characters* in a narrative that was jointly written.
Now. The more we think about this, the clearer it becomes that even the author *of that narrative is a joint creation.*
The process itself created a collaborated authorial persona, who began to seem a more integrated persona than can be represented by signing two names in the conventional way.
That is, one could say the piece isn't written by two individuals, but by this third persona—this author—created by the process of collaboration.
But don't worry; we're not getting mystical on you. You could say that we are asking for a kind of Emersonian hobgoblin of consistency here: the text, we think, is different, and so, we speculate, was the authorship. We'd

I think students understand disintegration but not re-integration—the flip side of the postmodern coin. This is closer to a non-Western, communitarian self for which we are not culturally prepared, and there, perhaps is some of the difficulty.

Difficulty for whom?

For (American) students—who, by and large, resist collaboration; for teachers—who, largely, under-conceptualize it; even for scholars writing "collaboratively"—who, in the face of institutional resistance, are unable to claim or reveal the real extent of collaboration in their work: the collective identity, the "We are One" or the "I am Legion" effect. Ede and Lunsford make a now-famous remark on this.

We have even considered publishing major projects . . . under coined neologisms, such as Annalisa Edesford . . . Our ultimate recognition of the problems this practice might cause . . . forced us to abandon this plan. (Ede and Lunsford, x)

Susan Miller points out the paradox through which even collaborativist pedagogy "began in, and still ambivalently reproduces, bourgeois visions of individuality" (296). Miller suggests that her students avoided her encouragement to identify as a (writing group) community, and "chose instead to identify themselves as being in [impersonal] secondary relationships" (297) of the sort associated with urban society. One would guess that resistance to collaboration among Americans—whether the like the attribution to so indicate.

This was interesting to learn, just as a meta-collaborative exercise, but it also seemed important as a stray bit of theory that we hadn't taken into account at first. It is congruent with what is taken for granted in literature, of course: the narrator is never utterly identified with the writer.

Or: whereas Murray says that all writing is autobiographical, one could also say that all writing is pseudonymous.

Literary collaborators acknowledge this kind of thing frequently, but you don't see it among academic writers—even those who study collaboration.

Lunsford and Ede did consider the idea, but decided against it.

They did Singular Texts/ Plural Authors. We may be doing pluralistic texts/ collaborated authors.

So here's what we'd like you to do. Take off "Kathleen and Michael." Use "Myka Vielstimmig" in-stead.

Think of us as a writing group with tee shirts, ballcaps, a mascot—and a team name:

Myka V. The author(s) of this [chapter].

unconscious paradoxical sort or the conscious demurral—is related to our cultural discomfort with group solidarity and the shared, decentered self.

I don't know about this. We certainly accept it in certain contexts: think of the jazz quartet. Think of a student fraternity. A cheerleading squad. The resistance to collaboration seems linked to invention. The jazz quartet plays: it doesn't compose. We expect the self to compose. We want the grades we earn ourselves. If this is right, then the project would be to help co-authors see themselves-as-self.

Not just see: invent.

I think co-authors see this, or at least a glimmer of it. (There are examples of co-writers of fiction—"inventive" folks, you'll agree—who publish under a single pseudonym.) But those in academe are resisted within and without by the deep influence of the myth of the individual. Clearly, in the West, whole socioeconomic systems are built on premises of individual property, accountability, and reward.

However, the point here is not political. It's just that a close look at collaboration reveals an "our/self," a collective Authorial identity, that is established in the process of writing together. As co-writers explore their own processes of collaboration, it may be the our/self that they have to discover and acknowledge, because this collective persona is the dynamic, integrated and reciprocating intelligence that guides the creation of the collaborated work.

Like collaboration: understood this way, the digital venue welcomes collective personae.

So, in a sense, collaborative writing widens the distance between Author/narrator and individual writer(s).

We take it for granted in reading a literary work that it is a mistake of naive realism to identify the narrative voice with the "real" voice of the writer. Beware the "I" in a Browning monologue, an O'Connor short story, and so on. Since the authorial voice of a *collaborated* work is even more obviously a constructed one (i.e., of two or more writers), the "I" or "we" of the Author is at an even further remove from the individual writers. Thus, the narrative voice of a collaborated academic essay is an artifice just as much as any narrative persona created by a writer of fiction. We should beware the "we" of Hawisher/Selfe—at least beware the impulse to identify that "we" with the "I" and the "I" of Hawisher and of Selfe. The reader needs to think about this.

I don't buy it. Yes, the persona is personae—or can be. But the twosome (or more) doesn't per sé increase the distance. The reverse, actually, could happen if the reader is able to connect with at least one of the personae, particularly if the personae are specified, as they are in a dialogue/essay. If they don't connect with Voice A, perhaps B will do. I think you are right that the collaborated Author is artifice, but in the same way—within the same parameters—as the single Author is artifice. That is, some writers work pretty hard to shrink the distance between themselves and a reader (I'm thinking of Lynn Bloom here, for instance), while others "portray." There must be a spectrum, and I think those who portray are more committed to embodying the poetic in their rhetoric, hence the artifice of persona.

But you can connect with Ishmael and never know Melville. I'm just saying that readers need to theorize the Author and Narrator of expository work—especially collaborative work, more especially stylized or "portraying" work—in much the same way they theorize the Author and/or Narrator of literary work.

Yes. Which gets us back to Kirsch and interpretive strategies. Only: if we saw these narrators as on a spectrum, then any reader would always be reading to discern such authors or narrators. Isn't that what reading is?

I'm with you, if by "discern" you mean "understand the stance and functions of." But when they come to an expository text, many readers do the equivalent of identifying the narrator Childe Roland with the author Browning. In "Postings," for example, we formatted the dialogue into two main voices (with interruptions from others). It would be natural by innocent logic for the expository reader to assign the left voice to one of us and the right voice to the other. As many readers did, evidently.

"Natural" is such a misleading word in this context. It might have been an ordinary interpretive strategy, but then we saw in the published responses

(Holdstein, Miller, Sosnoski) that the ordinary did not prevail: neither of the voices was assigned.

They were coached. And don't forget that, in fact, some readers of a late draft suggested even "signing" each segment of the dialogue, precisely in order to clarify *who* was saying *what*. And since publication, each of us has heard "I agreed with *you*, if you were the one saying *x, y, z*."

My concern is that authors of multi-vocal texts will do less interpretive work for readers when they focus on presenting, quoting, and highlighting the voices of others. (Kirsch, 8)

(My concern is how we got *three* voices in this one.)

We didn't sign the voices, because we felt this would encourage a false reading of the piece; because the two voices did not represent pure versions of individual narratives. Instead, they were both creations of a creation: a collaborated Author, an our/self, who projected from itself two characters in a manner not unlike the projection of characters in a fiction. The pragmatic point is we both had a hand in writing both voices. Other collaborators make the same sort of claim (e.g., Ede and Lunsford), *though they may not choose a multivocal style.* On the other hand, some collaborators "take turns" and do sign individual sections of a collaborative work (e.g., Monseau, et al.). Even there, however, what is written grows out of the collective intelligence, and it reflects the dynamic exchange between individual knowledge and shared knowledge. So the naive readerly stance (voice A is you; voice B is me) still neglects an important theoretical dimension of reading as well as of writing.

Well, yes. Collective intelligence and all that. But a different aesthetic, a different rhetoric, methinks.

In any case, assumptions of "she said / he said" are complicated in this kind of work. Of course, this should be no surprise to postmodern readers, should it? I mean, if you're going to declare the Author dead, then why should Whoever's Left make it easy for you? But all writing is artifice; we know this (though it's easy to forget). "New essay" writers call upon this critical awareness constantly, since they do not hide the artifice: they deliberately make constructing and constructed-ness visible. A reader need only turn around to see the authorial hand at work.

DOUBLECLICK: IN/COHERENCE

In some critiques of "experimental" academic works (like this one?), there's a fundamental question about what counts as coherence, cohesion, and other interpretive conventions. I think what's happening in the field is not that writers are abandoning these, but that they are offering new forms of them.

Yes, but then Kirsch is correct on this point: we need to theorize it. Louise Phelps and Richard Haswell can provide us with a start. Phelps takes the foundational Witte and Faigley distinction between cohesion and coherence one additional step by placing both product and process under a phenomenological umbrella:

> Before, "process" referred to the writers' act of com-
> posing written thought and "product" to the text
> encapsulating that meaning. Now, the overarching
> "process" is the cooperative enterprise whereby writ-
> ers and readers construct meanings together, through
> the dialectical tension between their interactive and
> interdependent processes. The text is the mediating
> instrument for that joint effort, and the resulting
> product is the set of meanings so constructed and
> attributed by readers to a writer and a text. (14)

In "Textual Research and Coherence: Findings, Intuition, Application," Haswell comes to a situated notion of coherence in another way. Like Phelps, he claims that our understanding of coherence is framed and thus limited by handbooks whose admonitions fail to accord with the actual practices we see in writers with varying levels of expertise. Haswell tests his theory by asking adults and students to write essays responding to the same prompt. He then "is startled to find" "results . . . unexpected in terms of the Harbrace precept": the papers scored as superior included

Re-thinking text as multi-pathed and multi-voiced leads us to alternate strategies for finding coherence, or even re-defining coherence. (Batson)

"fewer" of the four transitional devices recommended by Harbrace" (308). After considering the significance of this finding, Haswell offers the concept of cohesive efficiency or elegance:

> It occurred to me that with such a supply of ways to
> help discourse flow, better writers may have a lower
> rate of a certain device simply because they are
> inclined toward variety. They may be disinclined
> toward the orthodox devices of pronouns, repeated
> words, synonyms, and logical transitions because
> these means are explicit, stated, whereas other means
> are tacit, operating in invisible chunks around the
> words and thereby quickening pace and reducing
> short-term memory load. (309)

In other words, coherence isn't universal, but situated, varying according to the choices and sophistication of the writer, but not in ways suggested by the collected lore of handbooks.

And I want to take this notion of situatedness one additional step: to a rhetoricity of coherence. What I mean by this is that the coherence any reader will create in a piece is, as Phelps suggests, set in motion by an author, but it is re-created by the reader; thus, it is a joint creation. It will vary according to the genre of the text, the authorship, the readership. It is, in a word, rhetorical. In "Postings," where the authorship is multiple, where the reader is presumed to be sophisticated, where the text is iconic, coherence becomes a function of surprise: of the non-fictional plots that structure it; of the voices that develop those plots; of the voices that take issue with the plots; of the multi-logue itself.

I think the text is iconic of process and multiplicity, most of all. But to what purpose does a work foreground multiplicity? Or how do concrete modes like collage/montage hang together? The answer may be that in making the multiplicity of process more visible, authors suggest the role of synthesis in their effort. We shouldn't forget that this is not a random multiplicity; it is an orchestrated or simulated one. Thus we have both part and whole, particle and wave, in a work whose reading recapitulates (a fictionalized version of) its writing.

The coherence here is performative.

DOUBLECLICK: MUTUAL MIGRATIONS

```
This is a living document . . . I invite those who
would like to add to this document to do so by either
providing me links to other URLs or by simply sending
me email text to link myself. (Kemp)
```

The interaction between "print classic" and "print digital" is the subject of a number of website convocations. In "Evolving Past the Essay-a-saurus," a SnapShot on *RhetNet*, Beth Baldwin advocates teaching students to write "textual conversations" instead of the traditional academic essay. The online world has changed the classroom, she says, to the extent that the essay has become a dinosaur.

At the same time, we see the influence of online discourse migrating offline into the scholarly journals. It seems rare anymore that an issue goes by without at least one unorthodox "essay." I'm thinking of experiments with dialogues (e.g. Elbow/Yancey); with crots and/or lists (Bishop 1995a); hypertexts (Purves); even prose/dialogue/language-poetry collages (Paley and Jipson). Most of these migrations deliberately carry the traces of online textual treatments to their offline venue.

Well, it's early. Besides, even when multivocality and all the rest become common, they won't necessarily be appropriate for everything published online. (It's too much work, for one thing.)

It is disappointing, though, how much influence is moving the other direction: that is, too many *online* essays merely reproduce *offline* textual conventions. Although a great deal of academic prose is created and published online, most of it doesn't explore the unique possibilities of online discourse, doesn't acknowledge the multivocal, collaborative subtext of the online world. Most *scholarly* texts online show very little digital panache; textually, they're almost indistinguishable from the print classic academic essay.

It's print uploaded. Which perhaps is to be expected. After all, they're not writing for the screen; they're simply posting it there.

Online discourse varies, no question, and I don't want to argue that all web pages, for instance, have to embody new essay. The purpose of a page like the Alliance for Computers and Writing, for instance, is simply to outline and then link to multiple sources of information, and it's relying on a clean, linear, crisp list. It's useful. Other venues provide other kinds of discourse: Rhetnet with its snapshots and email responses pulls together listserv discussions with print-like text to provide another kind of resource. Again, great.

So why is that "great" so tepid? Because I had hoped to see something online that was more crafted or composed or sympathetic and responsive to the medium, and that's not what I see.

There's more of archive than of art about most online publications. With all its expressive potential, the computer serves often only as a workhorse database.

In other words, I think Negroponte is right about there being a logic of the medium itself, and I don't think we explore this as we might. Wasn't this McLuhan's point? Isn't Birkert's point in The Gutenberg Elegies *that the logic of the printing press is being displaced by another logic, one that displaces him as well?*

Sometimes, emailed statements are simply linked together in a chronological structure; sometimes a thread from a listserv is compiled and offered as "text." These make interesting reading, indeed, but they're surely not coherent compositions. I get the feeling that we're not distinguishing well between scholarly composition and scholarly conversation.

When I look at online I see lots of discussion about new text, and much of that is framed in dichotomous terms, even when the intent is to create new ground:

```
Once in print, digital dialogue is little more than
paper transcript—the living text destroyed, leaving
only skeletal remains. (Salvo)
```

And even when online discourse is talked about as new discourse, the discussion is too often preoccupied with how to include markers of navigation—where they should be placed and what they should refer to. I don't see text representing/

expressing/articulating the new identities or collaborations alleged to characterize the place.

```
But we prefer, in this type of writing, as much help
as the writer can give so we can navigate the text as
well as the argument. Icons, subheads, links, smaller
units to fit the screen, transitions, summaries, topi-
cal organization. (Gresham and Jackman)
```

Perhaps that's because we brought with us too much baggage from offline. In online academic discourse, many of the processes that we are using, it turns out, are offline:

```
Although  we  also  worked  alone  or  corresponded  by
email, we mostly sat side by side in front of the com-
puter  and  talked,  transcribed,  coded,  typed,  ate,
drank  and  listened  to  light  jazz  FM.  (Gresham  and
Jackman)
```

When we migrate online, maybe we bring so much offline with us that we can't get to online, can't get to that sympathy, are so locked in by our Burkean terministic screens that we can't see the online screen. This is true for non-academics, too, I might add. Take a look at Michael Kinsley's Slate, *which is supposed to be one of the hippest zines around since* HotWired *(hear echoes of Andy Warhol, do you?) The toons are right out of* Time *magazine and not as good,* Time *itself is synopsized, and when you are ready for something new, feel free to navigate yourself to the "Back of the Book." If we frame the new so completely in terms of the old, however can the new deliver on its promise?*

> Wait wait wait. What happened to *"I don't want to argue that all web pages, for instance, have to embody new essay"*? Sounds like that is precisely what you argue. But why should you be disappointed that today's technology is hospitable to yesterday's text? It would be more alarming, one would think, if yesterday's text were *impossible* online.
>
> And since when does the process of creating discourse belong to one or the other? Invention is always virtual, but it always begins in the brain. Even when it reeks of online process, it is equally a work of the *body*.

DoubleClick: the Romantic Postmodern

> There's a sense in which, as Hawisher and Selfe, Selfe and Selfe, and others argue, we should see the computer (or whatever technology is used) as a partner in collaboration—more than a recording device. Personally, I would find it a stretch to say that a computer *generates* knowledge, as some suggest (information, yes, but knowledge, I don't know); but there is no denying that the computer plays an important role when it comes to the organization of knowledge in the conceptual artifact we create. For a practical example, the computer's facility with hyperlinking and

multi-tasking has made convenient a more multilinear, associative approach to presenting text—especially online—than has previously convenient heretofore.

But let's remember the larger context, the Burkean context: associative thinking is being valorised elsewhere, so the computer's timing is pretty good. This matters. Otherwise, folks would take the associative off the computer and re-arrange it in a tidy, familiar, linear, hierarchically arranged text whose traces of invention would be lost.

(Which some folks do: there was a discussion to this effect on the online 1996 Computers & Writing Conference where people were arguing for email as invention but not prose. What does that tell you? Many online texts are as chronological as they are associative, and there is no leap to composing them. To: composition.)

But has the computer affected the way we think? Made us more "associative"? I doubt it, substantially, anyway.

Well, maybe it has, but indirectly; that is, the computer does make it easier to work associatively and implicitly, and certain forms of electronic communication behave as though they are situated, with respondents ready to ask for clarification, to print back what was earlier said, to explore—as in an oral situation. What's interesting is that if this mode of thinking makes it to print—to mainstream—then such thinking is represented as legitimate. In the aggregate, efforts like that change thinking.

On the other hand, presumably, it also closes the door to certain other ways of presenting text (and thinking, if you believe that).

But what interests me more is that it has encouraged an aesthetic in composing via computer that approves formatting conventions in text that were not approved before. What has become convention/al now, in turn, has an effect on the course of conceptual development. New understandings occur to us as we perceive new potential links among blocks of knowledge we had thought were independent. It is the facility of the computer in cre-ating and representing links that suggest both new, unpredictable, conceptual links to us in our own project, and also new ways to represent those links on the page. The expressivity of the medium makes representing the process in the product viable.

But it's not just that writers can do this now; it's that it makes print. Don't forget this. Without that, we are only authors in our virtual garrets, amusing ourselves, but not to text.

And the coherence borrows from aesthetics, from poetry, really, more than from nonfiction prose.

Well, from "pattern," the visual coherence, a more concrete mode of thinking. *Some* poets write this way; others (Milton, Millay) do not. But yes, more conventional in poetry than in prose.

And a shared appreciation for the concrete and visual capacities of the computer, or what Turkle might call the "aesthetics of simulation," may be what makes our personal approaches to writing compatible, in spite of frequent differences of opinion. The role of the computer in fostering new essay is central.

Turkle suggests that the rise of the personal computer in the 1980s—one could say the personalizing of the computer—began to encourage users to "experience the computer as an expressive medium" (54, emphasis added). By these late 1990s, this personal/expressive dimension of computer use is well-established, even taken for granted, even pandered to by software makers. I don't think we have theorized it as such, but the medium's potential for expressivity is surely encouraging the experimenting in classroom, online, and academic writing that seems to be unfolding geometrically here at century's end. Turkle connects this expressivity with new acceptance of concrete modes of symbolizing and thinking—modes that traditionally have been out of favor—in both the computer user's approach to the machine and in the aesthetics of software design.

> The new software design aesthetic effectively says that computer users shouldn't have to work with syntax; they should be able to play with shape, form, color, and sound. . . . [T]hey should be given virtual objects that can be manipulated in as direct a way as possible. . . . [A]s computing shifts away from a culture of calculation, bricolage has been given more room to flourish. (60)

Without rehearsing her complete exposition, we should note those three elements of current "life on the screen": expressivity, concrete modes of thinking, and aesthetics. And then, in what I nominate as the oxymoron of the age, Turkle says that we now have room for a "romantic postmodern" vision of computer intelligence (63). Hear hear.

I read something recently—on an email I've since lost—about writing for the screen. It didn't add anything more than this phrase, but that's enough to locate the issue here: new essay involves writing for the screen—the screen of email, the screen of email going to print, the screen of hypertext, the screen of the Web. More to the point, and my most inflated claim: writing for the screen is a new rhetorical act. As Negroponte and Turkle, Lanham and Landow, suggest, the thinking in this rhetoric is associative, expressive, disjunctive, dialogic, often dialectical. It involves multiple kinds of literacy—from that of the page to the screen to the personal. It's surprisingly collaborative; when authors compose together, new identities can be formed; new readership is assumed; and new processing, as Fisher and Watkins and Takayoshi demonstrate, is being developed and (only recently) articulated.

DOUBLECLICK: THINKING AS WE MAY

Discussions of net discourse often invoke Vannavar Bush's essay "As We May Think," in which he develops the idea of a machine like a magic microfiche reader (he calls it a "memex") that could store and recover user-designated "associations" and trails among texts that would be impractical for the user to recover alone. Rereading him from the present day, it is tempting to believe, as many seem to do, that Bush envisioned electronic hypertext, if not the World Wide Web, fifty years ahead of its time. What Bush describes was an astonishing scenario in the 1940s, and I don't take his vision lightly, but let's remember that it was a vision of a mechanical device combining dry photography and something like punch cards (remember those?). More important, "association," to Bush, was essentially an Enlightenment concept, a rational and linear sequence of ideas, methodically projected by a knowable mind. As striking as his idea was in its day, to appreciate the exponential difference between the "memex" and the postmodern world of the Web, we need to leap far beyond any mechanical sense of the term "association."

Association you can get in print classic, actually, whereas multi-linear is supposed be in hypertext. Though as you and I have traded notes, we have learned that we read hypertextually—from the dipping into chapters in an edited collection to the locating a source in a reference to reading the last chapter first in a mystery. Hypertextual reading isn't all that new. Our awareness of it, our deliberately structuring text to produce this kind of role: those are.

Most hypertext I have seen is multi-linear, but it is still linear. That is, the hyperlink offers a new branch of exposition that contributes as a tangent to the "main" text.

At the gateway to the beast[4] your arms brim with dead leaves. Words, not fate, put you here.

So, as long as we can identify a "main" text, we're offline, regardless of megahertz?

And in theory we have two sets—at least—of associations that undergird these choices: we have, on the one hand, those that the writer relied on to create the links, and on the other hand we have those that the reader relies on. Also, the branch often becomes the main text, so that "main" is a bit anachronistic here.

That's fine; I like it. But I mean that in much of scholarly hypertext, the relation between the main and the branch tangent is an *expository* relation—i.e. a linear (deductive, abductive, conjunctive) one. I'd rather distinguish association as an intuitive mode, from exposition, which is an analytic one. For example, a footnote is a (print) hyperlink; thus, to me, merely hyperlinking a text is not enough to make it associative. What matters is the *kind* of hyperlink.

> The *mind* of the hyperlink.

Yes, we agree on this: that the promise of hypertext—to promote and to bring about new discourse—is not being realized. It is linear, migrated to a new medium.

Sweet breath of the beast wets this fall air. That wrist of sunlight snagged in the weeds

The relation represented by an associative hyperlink would be more "poetic," more like Weathers's Grammar B crots. You get at the relation between crots in a wholistic and intuitive way: not inductive, deductive, abductive.

It is a kind of coherence that comes not from the mediated ties of Halliday and Hasan, but from inferred ties, if any ties at all—from ties of the reader's making ultimately. But as in this piece, there are structural signals—making the associations conform in structure to an expository convention, making it interesting to process—a juxtaposition in expository form.

But I don't think associative thinking would conform to an expository convention. If we use Ulmer's terms, I'd think that multilinear text is "exposition," while associational text is "pattern." I take "associational" to mean something more like poets' juxtaposition without predication.

Feel the pulse, yes the beast feels it, too.

Bury your face in the leaves, breathe; prepare to teach the beast: these.

Yes, that's a good starting place—with predication at one end of the continuum, and juxtaposition down left. But I think those ends end up being circular, with writers *and* readers using one in service of the other.

Part of my trouble is that I'm not ready to agree that they're on a continuum. I think of them as different in kind. So the nudge I'd give the discussion would be toward a refinement on this. I'd argue that "true" associational thinking is *very* different from what we're trained to do in academic life.

As thinking processes, yes, I agree: different in kind. But what happens when we move into text—of whatever variety? I think that simply to get associative thinking into published form often requires, particularly in the more prestigious venues, a kind of expository textual packaging, which is what we see in Bishop's article—and as you say, in the texts we see online. And "true" associational thinking? You mean, as opposed to untrue?

I mean as opposed to the more generic, more Enlightenment, use of the term. As Turkle argues, the computer is now an expressive medium that encourages concrete as well as abstract modes of symbolizing; in its expressive facility, it now rivals the camera, the poem, and the pallette (all at once, in fact). Don't we have to see the "associations" of which it is capable in terms of concrete and expressive modes of symbolizing? As you have said somewhere, academics are trained to analyze—which I would spin: to ex/posit or to predicate. Associational thinking may be another, more concrete and synthesizing, intelligence altogether.

Words put you here, not stars.

I'm not sure about this: Gardner notwithstanding, "intelligence" sounds essentialist on a good day, and deterministic on a bad. But yes, there are different ways of knowing, and yes, the visual is different from the verbal from the personal and so on. But they aren't, ultimately, independent constructs or domains: the football player who is kinesthetically inclined is also spatially inclined. So while I think it is important to distinguish between these different ways of knowing—so as to try to identify them, to learn what they have to teach us—I also think that in our lived experience, we bring them together.

Yes, but Gardner doesn't imply that they're exclusive, but clearly individuals don't have equal portions of each. And individuals (and cultures) attend more to some intelligences while others are neglected. Even if you're skeptical of multiple intelligence theory, we can use it as a metaphor for intellectual diversity. Can we view these diverse intellectual strengths as circles in a Venn diagram? The circles are of different sizes and they overlap each other to some degree.

OK: some tentative agreement. A Venn diagram gets at both difference and relationship: the sense that the modes/intelligences have some definition, but that the construct somehow slides into and works with other related constructs.

Listen to its supple flex across the weeds, that cupped palm of sunlight.

What we notice from this vantage is that the traditions of written discourse in academe valorize the modes of intelligence that depend on the verbal and rational and deductive. The facility to ex/posit, one could say. This is not news. But elements like multivocality, association, dis-

```
. . . volatility, interactiv-
ity, easy scaling changes, a
self-conscious typography, col-
lage techniques of invention
and arrangement (Lanham xiv)
```

Words, not God.

ruption, the unpredicated assertion, not to mention the graphical high jinks now available to writers, require academic readers to apprehend by a more wholistic, more intuitive logic. They need to draw on something more than the verbal intelligence that is their gift. They need a bit of the visual artist's instinct for pattern, contrast, unity, and balance, and a bit of the poet's ability to posit and to juxta/pose. Wouldn't this explain why, on the one hand, academic readers resist the new essay, and on the other, academic writers *even on the net* produce it so unevenly? We're not naturals at this stuff. Juxtaposition without predication challenges conventional readerly expectations, perhaps especially in academic writing.

But we do enjoy it. While the academy does privilege one, it doesn't entirely ignore the other: most of us were trained also to identify the associations in the work of the other (artist), to link them. If there is a difference between consumption and production, my suggestion is that we are "trained" associatively in consumption—we are trained to read poetry and fiction. Maybe what you also mean by associative is a kind of composing as well as thinking, a holistic way of apprehending, that the writer attempts to reproduce textually?

So it's not like such texts are strange to read. They are strange to write.

Words.

DoubleClick: F2F with the Classroom

In some ways, writing with electronics in the way we're describing became an issue of practice before it became an issue of theory. In 1989 (that is: before the World Wide Web, even before the Internet was much in request), Cynthia Selfe notices this about her students writing on computers:

```
Using different fonts, font sizes, symbols, high-
lighting, and graphic elements, [students] have not
only adjusted their writing to the conventions of the
screen and the computers, but have also reconceptual-
ized the content of their assignments in terms of
these conventions. (1989, 13)
```

Joan Tornow reports that the students she studied in an early networked classroom were prepared for the "link/age" by the intellectual values of youth/pop culture.

```
[They] grew up with the mature medium of television bring-
ing them amazing windows into world events—and also bring-
ing mind-numbing trivia.
     Meanwhile, even as our students are coming of age, a new
medium is coming of age along with them—the medium of com-
puter networks. It's no wonder that students think of this
medium as theirs—a space where they can bring their own
```

```
language and concerns. . . . On computer networks, whether
local or wide, students pursue learning on their own
terms. (1997, 222)
```

To some extent, then, *teaching* New (or Net) Essay will be preaching to the choir.

I'm not convinced there is a choir, which is part of the point of this text. Even if a choir exists, it's small, and its musical compositions aren't written yet—much less performed.

The larger task may be to encourage teachers themselves to accommodate the experimentation with multivocality, typography, even with pictures and sound, that will come with the new forms. Will the first-year composition course include a homepage assignment? Will it reward collage and montage techniques of presentation? Will it encourage the synthetic as well as the analytic?

Which do you suppose comes first: the multi-vocality, or the forms?

What about the disjunctive: will *this* be valued?

Without an assessment that's congruent with the pedagogy, we give only lip service to new pedagogy. A pretty good example of this we see in collaboration. We require students to work together, then we ask them to parse out who did what (because we don't trust them, and they don't trust each other), and then we ask each student to submit his or her own document. We assign collaboration: we assess individuation. And students know it; no wonder they don't want to collaborate.

So maxim/principle one: the assessment has to fit the pedagogy.

Maxim/principle two: the pedagogy has to fit the textuality.

If what we are going to value is the essay proper—whether it's Bartholomae's or Elbow's—then by all means, let's turn the Internet off. (Let 'em word process; that won't threaten anything.) However, if we are going to embrace the "readymade" as Geoffrey Sirc suggests (in this volume); if we are going to talk about what we value in the readymade and ask students to theorize it in some way—well, then, why sure, let's turn the Internet on. But this is what we are facing: a conception of literacy

Texts in such a class would range from "standard" single-authored print to collaboratve online to online composed to web page creation to a rhetorically/poetically based presentation package guiding in-class investigation of readymade. Disjunction among textualities would provide the focal point of the class, as well as points of critique. To exit the class, students answer: "So what? What/how do these textualities/voices/poetic rhetorics mean?" And: "how do they construct us?"

that is democratic in the fullest sense of the word: something we create together. Furthermore, we don't know this textuality, haven't necessarily "done" it ourselves, so we can't very well assume any expertise here.

Insofar as multiplicity (of voice, of content, of genre) becomes an issue in the classroom, I think we do know at least *something* about this textuality. At least some folks have done it in the writing classroom.

In this connection, the novelty of the net is overstated. Multiplicity, multivocality, genre-crosssing and how to manage such things in the mainstream classroom was the subject of Winston Weathers's composition textbooks published in the sixties and seventies. Donald Murray has frequently embedded (for example) poetry within academic articles, advocated a permissive teacherly stance toward voice in student compositions. Wendy Bishop explicitly addresses these same issues in both her textbooks and her theorizing; her essay "Teaching 'Grammar for Teachers' Means Teaching Writing as Writers" is a virtuoso performance. Hans Ostrom, Tom Romano, and others take up the same concerns. Even Sirc's interest in Duchamp (this volume) puts the "anything-whatever," the "readymade" of net textuality in an era long before the era of the computer. The commonality here is art, not archive; poetics, not electronics. Therefore, I think it's the creative writers, the postmodern romantics, who can teach us how to approach the expressivity of the computer and the concrete modes it enables.

Suppose we asked students to do *this*: to navigate among all these textualities—not just in print and online, but in talk as well—and in bringing them together, to invoke/create a new readymade based, in part, on what Tornow rightly sees as a kind of readymade intelligence of their own.

Of course, all this is quite apart from the genuine concerns about the impact of such textuality expressed by scholars (of electronic discourse even) like Myron Tuman. Like Ong, he seems to make the argument that mental structures will be shaped by the kind of literacy we value and develop; his concern (put reductively) is that info-bits will produce cognitive bits that don't compose. No one knows if this prediction is true. Still.

I think Sirc is right about new forms of textuality being written and read right behind our eyes; we ought to turn around. And unlike Tuman, we seem to think that there are principles governing these texts—as do Sirc and Wysocki and Johnson-Eilola—that are even-as-we-email being articulated.

In other words, conditions indicate (1) a readiness for a new textuality in the classroom since it's already in motion offschool; (2) we can frame the task—understanding such textuality—using this understanding to inform a new assessment.

Maxim/Principle 3: Can changes in pedagogy *not* be far behind?

DoubleClick: Writing for the Screen

Is the new essay, then, a kind of Bakhtinian pre-generic phenomenon? That is, it's not a concerted or managed effort, but a number of writers—and editors and publishers—are moving in the same direction—away from single-authored, highly conventionalized prose.

Sooner or later, don't we have to ask what makes a publication "electronic" enough to be a new/essay? If one of the "Snapshots" on *Rhetnet* isn't, then why not? It does explore some purely online facilities—hyperlinking and reader interaction, primarily. But we're saying that isn't enough.

```
Once we've allowed ourselves the luxury of many voices
in our writing, we just might find it tolerable . . .
to accept the many voices in a joint collaborative
text, even if these voices seem conflicting, confusing,
or chaotic at first. (Batson)
```

The trouble with many online texts is that they're like home videos: the film is running, but this ain't no movie. You have to exploit (fulfill? master? indwell?) the technology, not just use it. And you're saying something like they don't exploit the technology because they don't know cinematography.

Well, who did before cinematography became *cinematography*?

A movie is *composed*. Still, doesn't this put us in the position of saying just "I know it when I see it"? What is the proper number and balance of "new" conventions to cross the line into something truly new? How big does the critical mass have to get?

I want to go back and think in terms of the sensibility *that online is alleged to welcome. And then think in terms of whether or not we actually see evidences/traces of this in the text in question. So I'm working from the virtual ground up.*

- *Ulmer's relevant points here: the various kinds of discourse—narration, exposition, and pattern—that themselves compose a kind of electronic universe of discourse. Do we see these modes of discourse? Do we see them working cross-genre, which is what we'd expect in a medium that is fluid? More particularly, do we see (much of) the poetic here at all?*
- *Batson connects nicely with the poetic here, since he emphasizes what he calls online ways of knowing that we traditionally have thought of as poetic: e.g., the associative, the multi-vocal. (This entails, imho, distributed authorship.) Do we see evidence of this?*
- *And then I'd be looking for writing for the screen, not for the page. This eliminates print uploaded, for instance. I'd be looking for use of the screen, working off of what we find on the online screen that we don't* associate *with the page—* cutting *and* pasting, *responding and circling back.*

- *Do we see evidences of the processing in the text, as Negroponte and Lanham suggest?*

```
. . . a new kind of self-consciousness about the "pub-
lication" and the "publicity" that lies at the end of
expression. (Lanham, xiv)
```

I can think of print texts that have no apparent connection to online that exhibit some of these features: Miller's article written with students, Kirsch and Ritchie on the personal. I can think of print texts that were produced online in part and that exhibit some features: the Nedra Reynolds interview, the Elbow / Yancey dialogue. (Even the conclusion for *Voices on Voice* that you and I did.) And I can think of some online texts that, again, embody some of the features listed here: some of what we see in *Kairos*, for instance; some of the CMC pieces.

They're not uncommon outside the realm of the academic essay. In fact, the tradition is quite long. We can reread *Tristram Shandy* as a hypertext; Blake wrote in crots; Mallarmé in collage; then there's Pound, Joyce, the concrete poets, the language poets, mainstreamers like May Swenson and William Gass, even compositionists (wow)—especially those with an interest in creative writing. For creative writers this stuff is well known. And really, why not? Creative writing is always writing virtually.

```
The work of art has always
been to demonstrate and cele-
brate the interconnectedness:
not to make everything "one"
but to make the "many"
authentic.
                    Snyder (90)
```

But writing this way in academic texts is a stylistic choice to represent synthesis and process; it jars the reader away from the analytical habit of Grammar A, the academic custom. Still, that doesn't make it inarticulate or incoherent—or even unfamiliar. Given its tradition, some would say it isn't even experimental—it's alternate.

I'm wondering, given our own history, if there isn't a move in this direction that one would make. Think about it this way: when we wrote "Concluding the Text" we put it in a format that more or less represented the dialogue we had experienced. We did not move to transform it into another kind of text. But in "Postings" given the substance under discussion, or perhaps because we wanted narration/vignettes, exposition, and poetry, or perhaps because we wanted it to feel online, with all the short circuits and forays and interruptions—we chose to write a text that was different, that spanned the divide between print and online, that worked epistemically in both places, that invited even the most technophobic readers to participate.

Maybe that's what *you* were doing . . .

It seems to me that in new essay (call it what you will) we are arguing for a hybrid textuality that crosses genres in two ways. First, it includes poetic and rhetoric, privileging neither, invoking each that they might

New Essay
Net Essay
Alternate Essay
Digital
Experimental
Constructed

t o g e t h e r express what cannot be *represented without the other.*

Suppose we didn't think rhetoric *or* poetic. Suppose we thought rhetoric *and* poetic. Suppose we thought rhetoric *and* poetic *and* electronic. Multiple ways of embodying text: multiple textualities.

Such an essay mixes the conventions governing narrative, exposition, and pattern, in its effort to invite multiple readings: aesthetic ones as well as efferent.

Second, we see a link between online and off; such linkage isn't required, but fruitful. Like the crossing of scripts articulated by Koestler, the crossing of these media invites what Lanham has identified as playfulness, eloquence, and self-dramatization. Such crossings, then, invite another authorial identity.

And especially invite this when the work is done in collaboration, which brings its own identity complications already.

In short, we find ourselves in process, struggling to articulate a process that is articulating us, too. As you always say.

I thought that was you.

DoubleClick: Notes

1. "Vielstimmig" is German for "many-voiced." There is plenty to say about multivocal, collaborated authorship and what it implies for ideas about writer identity; some of that is explored in this chapter, and some in other places by those who theorize collaboration in writing. On occasion, Myka Vielstimmig includes other members, but in this text the group is the ~~Author~~ projected by the electronic writing partnership of Michael Spooner, of Utah State University, and Kathleen Blake Yancey, of the University of North Carolina—Charlotte (in reverse alphabetical order by institution).

2. For the idea of "DoubleClick," we are indebted to Deborah Holdstein, who used a very similar trope to link sections of her keynote address at the 1996 Computers & Writing Conference, and later in the print version of that address.

3. The poem "In a Station of the Metro," by Ezra Pound, was originally published in *Personae.* New York: New Directions Publishing 1928.

4. The poem "Instruction at the Gate," by Bill Ransom, was originally published in *The Single Man Looks at Winter.* Port Townsend: Empty Bowl Press 1983.

CHAPTER SIX

Dropping Bread Crumbs in the Intertextual Forest
Critical Literacy in a Postmodern Age
or: We Should Have Brought a Compass

Diana George
Diane Shoos

So one urgent task is to try to understand what skills, aptitudes, knowledges, dispositions, concerned with representation and communication young people will need in the world of the next two decades or three, in order to be able to live productive, fulfilling lives. What will the subject English need to become in order to function as an essential part of the education of young people? what does it need to focus on? What questions, issues, concerns, knowledges need to be central?

Gunther Kress

ONE WAY TO ADDRESS THE LARGE QUESTIONS KRESS POSES IS TO TURN TO cultural theorist bell hooks who insists that we "can't overvalue the importance of literacy to a culture that is deeply visual. . . . Rather than seeing literacy and the visual (and our pleasure of the visual) as oppositional to one another, we have to see them as compatible with one another" (*Cultural Criticism*). Certainly, Kress would agree, and while we will not concentrate on Kress's discussion alone, it is a good one to open with because it does center our concern for reconfigurations of literacy on the overwhelming role the media and corresponding changing technologies play in the ways we must talk about literacy education.

The image is at issue in so very much of this discussion whether it is film, print, television and video images, or web pages, print layouts, charts and other graphic illustrations of information, or the play of font and text as we see in the work of Myka Vielstimmig (a.k.a., Kathleen Yancey and Michael Spooner). To get very briefly at some of the intertextual demands of a literacy that insists on the role of the visual (and the electronic) as well as the verbal, we begin with three images.

Figure 1

Figure 2

Figure 3

The first, a publicity poster for the British film *Trainspotting*, might easily be compared to or at least put in juxtaposition with the second, portion of a popular Calvin Klein print ad for *Be* cologne. The two are so easily juxtaposed not because the two products are alike. Instead, it is the similarity of the images themselves that make possible a comparison—even a new conversation entirely—in the ways they call upon each other, perhaps even comment upon one another (figures 1 and 2). To make that comparison even sharper, we could take away the language of the poster, as we do in the third illustration, and view the Trainspotting group horizontally rather than vertically, thus much more literally calling forth the way the two images seem to be one, about one thing, sprung from the same lens and attitude and conversation (figure 3).

And, what is that conversation? Well, it is partially about style—in this case, something called "streetwise" or "heroin chic"—about a youth culture determined to be on its own and separate from the overculture of institutional employment and the drone of everyday responsibility. "Choose life. Choose a job. Choose a starter home. Choose dental insurance, leisure wear and matching luggage. Choose your future. But why would anyone want to do a thing like that?" the poster shouts. It's an accusing or taunting challenge that calls for choosing anything but a mundane existence in which dental insurance is as important as matching luggage and life itself. And even without the *Trainspotting* poster next to it, the Calvin Klein ad says much the same: "Just Be." And, yet, as contemporary as this image looks, the call to "Just Be" echoes earlier youth rebellions: "Tune in. Turn on. Drop out." "Do your own thing."

But there is more: The heroin chic style in the Calvin ad next to the poster of actors playing burnt-out but likable heroin addicts in a funny/tragic film calls up something of the tenor of both images. The tough girl looks of the ad match the tough girl sneering at the camera for *Trainspotting*. The *Trainspotting* actor wearing a peace dove on his shirt calls up Sixties youth. And the androgynous young woman crouched in the foreground of the Calvin ad wears the tattoo of an ex-marine or an auto mechanic addicted to those old girlie calendars. The mocking, "Choose life." of the poster accuses conformists of being sedate, over-protective, conservative, and perhaps fundamentalist in issues of sexual or bio-logical freedom. The young women in both images look anything but conservative or safe. They are images about transgression, but as bell hooks reminds us to ask, "Transgression in the service of what?" That question isn't at all easy to answer given the fact that one image is an ad for a not-exactly-cheap cologne, and the other is Miramax's publicity for a hit movie.

The many ways these two images call upon each other and the multiple texts we do not see that readers draw upon to read either or both images is a part of the complex of literacy. And, of course, we have put these images side-by-side. They weren't placed in juxtaposition for us. It would be by sheer coincidence to see the two together in a public setting. Yet, in looking at a poster like the one for *Trainspotting*, a critical literacy demands that readers recall where else they have seen such an image, what it is like, what it reminds them of, in what contexts it occurs, and more. It is something like what Sarah Sloane suggests with the wonderful concept of medial hauntings, but not quite.

New communication technologies, it is frequently argued, have the poten-tial to give us access to more and different kinds of texts. They thus by their nature, we could argue, generate a kind of intertextuality: the term intertextu-ality itself has a rich history beginning in literary theory, specifically in Mikhail Bakhtin's concept of dialogism, which he defines as "the necessary relation of any utterance to other utterances." For Bahktin, as Stam, Burgoyne, and Flitterman-Lewis note,

> All texts are tissues of anonymous formulae, conscious and unconscious quota-tions, conflations and inversions of other texts. In the broadest sense, intertex-tual dialogism refers to the infinite and open-ended possibilities generated by all the discursive practices of a culture, the entire matrix of communicative utterances within which the artistic text is situated, and which reach the text not only through the recognizable influences but through a subtle process of dis-semination. (Stam 204)

Such a notion of intertextuality is perhaps even more significant in a post-modern age where cultural artifacts are often steeped in ambiguity and nuance. The Calvin ad, for instance, is deliberately vague, combining some facial and body cues which imply "natural" personal interaction or narrative with the flat white background and staged poses of traditional high fashion ads. Such contradictions invite interpretation, demand that the spectator par-ticipate in the process of making meaning. Again, the idea of intertextuality suggests that the references and resources for such a process are more representational than real—part of a cultural matrix.

So, then, to go back to those large questions Kress poses—what "questions, issues, concerns, knowledges need to be central" to a literacy education that can prepare students for the next few decades—our first response would be one suggested by the reading we have just begun on the images reprinted here. Literacy itself makes intertextual demands of the reader. What's more, changing technologies make those intertextual demands increasingly more multiple, widespread, and intricate than they were even thirty years ago. Let's take, for example, Dennis Baron's comments on the implications of web technologies. As Baron notes, "in a kind of backward wave, the new technology begins to affect older technologies, as well."

With respect to our illustrations, then, the matrix of technologies informing our reading of both the poster and the ad includes television commercials for *Be* cologne, music videos sporting heroin-chic styles, a giant Times Square billboard featuring Kate Moss, Richard Avedon's preference for shooting ads and posters like these with a large format camera, several Calvin Klein websites including one calling for a boycott of the heroin chic look,[1] *Trainspotting* websites, style programming shown on videos in clothing sections of major department stores, the film *Trainspotting*, news broadcasts of the Dole campaign lambasting that film for making heroin addiction "attractive," and more.[2] How all of these communication technologies interact, affect the reading of and change each other is what may be at issue here. Any attempt to pin down all of the possible connections and effects would certainly be pointless. We won't even try.

Instead of drawing an intertextual treasure map we offer more questions, more concerns, again in response to Kress's demand for a new way of thinking through the issues of literacy education. One concern that Dennis Baron raises, for example, is that of reliability: "Not only must the new technology be accessible and useful," Baron writes, "it must demonstrate its trustworthiness as well. So procedures for authentication and reliability must be developed before the new technology becomes fully accepted." That is true, of course, but it is even more complicated than just developing "procedures for authentication and reliability." Such procedures are already in place in the ways we read the word and the world. They simply aren't quite as reliable as we would like them to be. In fact, we might argue that searching for ways of assuring reliability of information could lead to just another dead end. It won't get us anywhere because the concepts of authenticity and reliability are much too slippery.

IT LOOKED REAL ENOUGH TO ME

On December 14, 1996, NBC broadcast the episode "We Shall Overcome" of a program that, as of this writing, appears to have been canceled after one short season. "Dark Skies", we are told by co-creator Bryce Zabel whose words appear on the official NBC website for this program, "isn't just a TV series; it's a blend of fact, informed speculation and dramatic license. The series premise is simply this: our future's happening in our past." Executive producer James D. Parriott makes the show's premise even clearer: "This is being presented as alternative history. Everyone has their favorite conspiracies, but we will challenge and expand on those by building a framework that adds consistency to the alien-awareness theories."[3]

Yes. Everyone has their favorite conspiracies, but let's take a look at this particular conspiracy. This episode written by Zabel and Brent V. Friedman opens with black and white film footage of Martin Luther King, Jr. giving his "I Have a Dream" speech then cuts to news clips (still in black and white) of civil rights organizers clashing with police. These, too, are familiar images: children being thrown up against buildings by the force of high pressure fire hoses; men and women beaten and dragged through the streets; angry white protesters threatening black demonstrators. What's more, this is actual news film footage; it is not a re-enactment of events. Eventually, we see a newspaper headline: three civil rights workers in Mississippi are missing. There is no mention of Schwerner, Chaney, and Goodman (the three civil rights workers murdered in Mississippi during this period), but this plot is a clear reference to that event.

As the episode continues, we discover that the missing civil rights workers were indeed murdered and that, contrary to popular opinion, it was not uncontrolled racism that led to these deaths but space aliens who "manipulated racial strife" to plant their pods in a local church. For its plot, the episode draws upon not only the murder of these three young men but also at least an implied reference to King's murder and the torching of a Black church, suggesting perhaps that all of it—King's assassination, the deaths of Schwerner, Chaney, and Goodman, the brutality of police against pacifist demonstrators, recent church burnings, and more—can be blamed on something over which we have no control: space aliens.

These documentary moments inserted into the fiction serve to validate the fiction. In the case of "Dark Skies," we might argue, these moments insult the historical moment by suggesting that none of us has control over racial clashes. We are the dupes of alien forms. And, what's more, in a political climate of paranoia over undocumented workers coming into the US from Mexico, the very term alien takes on meaning well beyond ET.

Certainly, "Dark Skies" is just one of many venues taking advantage of new technologies that allow Tom Hanks as Forest Gump to stand next to Nixon or (to use Baron's example) Marilyn Monroe to flash Lincoln. In that sense, the program is a technological delight through which viewers slip in and out of history by way of old news footage intertwined with new stories. In this context, however, it is well to remember what the creators of this show claim: "This is being presented as alternative history."

The literacy education, then, that becomes necessary for reading a program like this is one not only cognizant of the technological advances making such "digital frauds" possible, but a critical literacy that questions the reasons for and effects of digital prestidigitation. The medial hauntings or intertexts that come into play here range all the way from original broadcasts of these events in the civil rights movement to any number of documentaries that replay these same moments to more recent television re-enactments of these moments (as in the series "I'll Fly Away"), to stories of recent church burnings, to the passage of California Proposition 209 which attempts to strip away affirmative action legislation won through civil rights struggles, and more. What we are suggesting is that the literacy it takes to "read" a program like "Dark Skies" is no simple skill.

We might pause here to focus on documentary partially because it is through documentary insertions that a program like "Dark Skies" attempts to achieve credibility, and because documentary is one of those genres viewers seem to think must stand up to tests of reliability and authenticity. Besides, the documentary appears, at least to many of our students, like a form that ought to be straightforward, factual, and beyond interpretation, and yet the documentary is hardly that. Instead, it takes on a number of forms and functions, from Ken Burn's attempt to re-enact history in "Civil War" to Michael Moore's funny and biting satire on the auto industry in *Roger and Me.*

Film scholar Michael Renov reminds us that documentary has been called "the film of fact," 'nonfiction,' the realm of information and exposition rather than diegetic employment or imagination—in short, at a remove from the creative core of the cinematic art" (13). It is typical for viewers to think of documentary as a form that "reveals truth." The common definition reasserts that understanding of documentary:

> 1. Consisting of, concerning, or based upon documents. 2. Presenting facts objectively without editorializing or inserting fictional matter, as in a book, newspaper account, or film. n. A television or motion-picture presentation of factual, political, social, or historical events or circumstances, often consisting of actual news films accompanied by narration. (American Heritage Dictionary)

The popular definition clearly links documentary to unbiased reporting, but the history of this genre places it far from unbiased reporting. As early as 1932, John Grierson distinguished documentary from what he considered a "lower order" of film (travelogues, newsreels, etc.). For Grierson, already in 1932, documentary was the place where nonfiction film entered the world of art. In designating documentary as art, Grierson acknowledged its status as a carefully constructed form rather than a window to the real.

Renov, of course, rejects the oversimplified notion of documentary as "fact" and argues that film documentary has at least four specific textual functions, any combination of which might be present in a given text. If you view these separate functions as overlapping layers of a film rather than rigid, prescriptive elements, they can give us some insight into the complexity of the documentary text:

1) to record, reveal, or preserve (realism)
2) to persuade or promote (argument)
3) to analyze or interrogate (discover meaning)
4) to express (Renov describes this function as "aesthetic," the emotive function)

The last three of these functions already take us beyond that dictionary definition. The impulse to record, reveal, or preserve—as crucial as it may be for the documentary moment—is clearly only the initial impulse of much documentary film. By contrast expression is, perhaps, the least apparent function of the documentary, and it is probably the function students are least likely to identify as documentary. Indeed, they might argue that a film with a strong emotive function is not a documentary at all. That split—between the real and the expressive—is of course a false one. Photographs and journals do not capture the real any better than satire and parody. And, all of these films are constructions. All are parts of larger conversations.

WHAT'S SO REAL ABOUT FICTION?

At this point, it will be useful to turn to another example of the sort of text that makes tests of reliability and authenticity seem maddeningly difficult to design. The film *Dead Man Walking* was suggested by the 1993 memoir which chronicles Sister Helen Prejean's ministry to death row inmates in Angola prison, an experience which solidified her opposition to the death penalty and led her to become an activist against it. Tim Robbins wrote and directed the feature film of the same name; Sean Penn plays the role of death row inmate Matthew Poncelet, and Susan Sarandon won the Academy Award in 1996 for her performance as Sister Prejean. PBS's *Frontline* has done a story on Sister Prejean crediting her with bringing the issue of the death penalty back into public debate in the US. As well, PBS maintains an official *Dead Man Walking* web page through which readers can access interviews with Sister Prejean, with Tim Robbins, and with Susan Sarandon. The page is also linked to other discussions of the death penalty.[4] Already, the medial hauntings are many.

The death penalty is one of those issues which is certainly likely to come up in the English classroom but which teachers often dread putting before their students precisely because it evokes such strong emotional responses. Like the issue of abortion in the U.S., discussions of the death penalty tend to elicit polarized responses rooted in moral or religious beliefs that appear to be beyond reconciliation. One step in the process of teaching students to read the terrain of a discussion like this one is to help them to see that debates like the one on the death penalty exist, as John Trimbur has suggested, within a continuum of discourse.[5] And one way to help students see a film representation not as an isolated event but as one text in a larger conversation is to introduce some of those other texts into the classroom. In the case of *Dead Man Walking*, this might mean, for instance, discussing parts of Prejean's book, reading accounts by death row inmates and victims' rights advocates, calling up the

PBS website and following the links it provides, and watching a segment from the *Frontline* episode. The rationale behind such an approach is not to present one text as primary and the others as "support," but to consider how each helps create a context for understanding the others. All of this is to remind us of what we already know: students are much less likely to blindly accept or reject certain texts as "real" if we don't set them up to do so by neglecting to provide them with resources to help situate the discussion. Equally, the point of this approach is not to engage in a search for "truth" or reliability as a sequence of events that can be observed and recorded but instead to pursue a fuller, much more complicated reality.

Certainly Tim Robbins's film is a powerful portrayal of that kind of complicated reality. Although sometimes credited for its evenhandedness in dealing with the death penalty, it is a film that does take a position, one that is in line with Sister Prejean's opposition to capital punishment. What we believe is unusual about this film, however, is that it humanizes the death row inmate and in so doing makes real the consequences of the death penalty at the same time that it acknowledges the equally real pain and suffering of the victims and their families. It is a film which very directly and intentionally plays to our emotions not to cloud our understanding of the issue at hand but to make our understanding more acute. From this perspective *Dead Man Walking* is clearly docu-drama rather than documentary in that it privileges the expressive rather than the recording function. One way Robbins makes this clear is through the disclaimer from the film credits:

> This film is inspired by the events in the life of Sister Helen Prejean, C.S.J. which she describes in her book, *Dead Man Walking*. As a dramatization, composite and fictional characters and incidents have been used. Therefore, no inference should be drawn from the events and characters presented here about any of the real persons connected with the life of Sister Helen Prejean, C.S.J.

What this disclaimer means is that the character of Matthew Poncelet does not exist in real life because he is a composite and thereby a fiction. As well, the families we see portrayed are composites. And yet, all of the incidents portrayed, including much of the dialogue, come directly from Sister Helen's experience as she describes it in her book.

Of course for some viewers this can pose a problem. If Matthew Poncelet is neither Pat Sonnier nor Robert Lee Willie (the two death row inmates of the memoir), and if the Percys don't exist, then why watch this movie at all? If it isn't real, then what good is it? What the film provides, then, is not the documentation of particular murders but a fuller context which enables the audience to see all of the characters involved as human beings—including so-called "animals" like Matthew Poncelet. The kinds of literacy skills students must call on to understand this continuum of discourse are rarely taught but they certainly include an understanding of intertextuality, a validation of many kinds of texts, and an ability to sort through positions on a topic like the death penalty—positions that are often contradictory or that seem to form and reform themselves as the discussion progresses.

ESSAYIST LITERACY AND THE SEARCH FOR A CENTER

All this talk of multiple texts that take all forms each posing its own problems of reliability must make Doug Hesse's concern for the recovery of essayistic literacy seem an old fashioned one, at best. And, yet, it seems to us that Hesse's real concern is at the heart of critical literacy in a postmodern age. When we speak of the importance of intertextuality for a discussion of literacy and technology, we are speaking not of easy access to an ever-growing number of texts, but, like Hesse, of a process of reading. This process is one of discerning the relationship(s) of texts to one another and to their multiple contexts. It demands that readers pose questions about origin, voice, and, ultimately, reception: that they ask not only where texts are generated from, but also more precisely who is speaking, and for and to whom. Thus, in a discussion of a film like *Dead Man Walking* a consideration of our own attitudes about murder or religion or the death penalty are not peripheral but central to a consideration of the text's "meaning." To paraphrase Hesse, for us an important part of the process of reading involves readers constantly figuring themselves as the makers of knowledge.

Although the notion of process may be in danger of becoming a critical and pedagogical cliché, we emphasize literacy as a process for two reasons: first and most obviously, if literacy is henceforth linked to technology, it is by definition changing and changeable as technologies evolve. More importantly for our discussion, however, if literacy is intimately connected to intertextuality as an awareness and understanding of the relationships among texts and between texts and readers, then literacy is never fixed or finished. Instead, it entails an ongoing re-evaluation and reformulation of the cultural and textual terrain as that terrain itself, including the positions of readers, shifts.

Defining critical literacy as a process of reading in which readers themselves are central to meaning-making leads to the question of whether that role and process shift with different kinds of texts. Although on the one hand we might want to argue that, in a postmodern technological age, the basic parameters of this process hold for all texts, it has nonetheless been a familiar critical claim that postmodern texts make different demands and construct diverse roles for readers. The multi-vocal, multi-font, multi-directional character of the Vielstimmig essay, for instance, suggests a kind of freedom enabling both writer(s) and reader(s) to dive straight into the play of text and idea. Myka Vielstimmig is, of course, not simply a combined person/a or collaboration but a position being staked out in academic rhetoric. It is a position that openly demands that its readers make connections not being made for them, that they treat this text as hypertext, and that they know how to read hypertext.

What remains problematic from our point of view is the extent to which postmodern play threatens to abandon responsibility for the way these ideas will be linked. Hesse's warning that "a landscape leavened by the ultimate equality of all texts offers no fulcrum for advocacy or change" is one we take very seriously because of the way certain kinds of texts (like the listserv Hesse writes of) can appear to be all-inclusive and interactive and yet lead to no action at all—they simply take on more voices, more length. Although the links we find in web pages are intriguing to follow, but they are often arbitrary links. They don't necessarily make an argument, present a position, or offer options, and (though this may be the information superhighway) they also will not lead us to all information available on a given subject, as some novice Internet explorers believe.[6]

Most likely, Vielstimmig would say that responsibility remains with the reader—it is the reader and not the writer who will make meaning here—yet we are not at all sanguine about the writer's hidden role in all of this. Critical literacy must call equal attention to the production as well as the reception of texts. In her discussion of using film and video texts in the classroom, bell hooks reminds us that viewers often do not want to believe that these images and their stories are constructions. They want to preserve, for movies at least, the sense of magic. And, it is when the technology is very good at hiding that process of selection and construction that the process is mystified—the ideas being presented seem real or natural. They don't seem to come from anyone at all but rather to exist out there, ready to be represented.

We aren't arguing here for a return to the notion of a unified subject who constructs a single meaning for a text. We do know and accept that the center is not always there or that there are many centers possible. What we are concerned about is the potential for abandoning the responsibility writers, filmmakers, and other cultural producers must take for the ideas they put before us. Representation is never innocent. It has real effects and repercussions. This is a very serious business in a world in which racism, hatred, poverty, violence, hunger, and fear play no small part in the ways we live our lives and the decisions we make about our communities. What that means is that the burden is equally on the producer as it is the reader of these texts to understand the sometimes contradictory roles they can play in a larger system.

Kress asks us to identify, "What skills, aptitudes, knowledges, dispositions, concerned with representation and communication young people will need in the world of the next two decades or three, in order to be able to live productive, fulfilling lives." We would answer simply that the one skill most necessary for a critical literacy in a postmodern age is the ability to take on that responsibility for ideas and for action both as a producer of texts and as a reader. We fail if we only either encourage our students to pursue or warn them away from the fragmented, ever-growing information on the Internet. Or, if we teach them to deconstruct advertising images but do not give them the critical skills to produce something in their place, we fail just the same.

We would argue that real change can only happen when we combine an awareness of the world around us and how that world functions with a language by which to communicate that awareness. That language can take many forms, but the form it does take we believe must be taken consciously. Critical literacy in a postmodern age demands that we acknowledge our role in and take responsibility for language and form and image and communication systems in a way that not only critiques but envisions new possibilities. It does, at times, seem like we are marking our way by dropping bread crumbs in an intertextual forest, only to look behind us and see that they have disappeared. We wish we could have brought a compass. There just isn't one that points in all of those directions at once.

NOTES

1. We found a number of sites simply by entering the words Calvin Klein or *Trainspotting* in the search engine. The heroin chic boycott site currently resides at http://www.emory.edu/NFIA/NEW/HEROINCHIC/ck.html. Of course, websites are ephemeral things. This one may or may not exist by the time you read this.

2. We might add here that our own reading of *Trainspotting* does not agree with the Dole campaign's. It isn't the film—certainly not the events or plot of the film—that might make heroin addiction seem attractive. What makes heroin addiction (or at least the characters in this film) attractive is the way they mirror hip, streetwise styles and thus epitomize a certain contemporary youth culture look.

3. With the cancellation of "Dark Skies," the Website seems to have disappeared as well, but during the 1996 season, the site was open and accessed through NBC's official site.

4. As of this writing, the *Dead Man Walking* page can be found at http://www2.pbs. org/wgbh/pages/frontline/angel/walking/index.html It includes information from the *Frontline* episode "Angel on Death Row" as well as links to other kinds of information that might be related to the issue of the death penalty or the people involved in the making of the Robbins film.

5. We don't know that John would expect or even want to be credited here, but his comments came in a conversation we had with him while we were working on a very early version of our discussion of *Dead Man Walking*, and they helped us clarify what we could see as potential problems with bringing documentary and docu-drama into a classroom discussion of a serious issue like the death penalty.

6. America Online's current television spot on how the Web can help you do your child's homework late on Sunday night is a good representation of what many new users think the Internet can do. There is always, claims the commercial, a teacher online waiting to help.

PART TWO

Revisiting Notions of Teaching and Access in an Electronic World

CHAPTER SEVEN

Beyond Imagination
The Internet and
Global Digital Literacy

Lester Faigley

*I*BEGIN WITH FOUR NEWS STORIES THAT APPEARED IN NEWSPAPERS IN THE United Kingdom and Ireland during late March and early April 1996. The first story from the *Irish Times* describes a class in an isolated rural school in County Donegal that in the words of the article has "caught Internet fever" ("Drawn into the Net"). Even though the school has no computers, a first and second grade teacher, Michael McMullin, came up with the idea of teaching a unit on weather by connecting children on different continents using his home computer. McMullin identified partner schools in Alaska and Tasmania where elementary teachers had children collect weather data, and their observations were exchanged daily. Soon the children began to ask other questions. The children in Alaska wanted to know whether the water swirls down the toilet in the same direction all over the world. By comparing observations with children in Tasmania and Ireland, the children in Alaska discovered that water swirls in different directions in the Northern and Southern hemispheres. It was not long before the children began writing about other subjects, including their favorite television shows. The story ends with the teacher commenting that the project has been a good start, but the situation is far from ideal because the children are not getting hands-on experience and the school lacks funds for purchasing equipment.

The second story from *Computer Weekly* runs with the headline, "UK: A Battle for Young Hearts and Minds." It describes a large-scale give-away package to British schools from Microsoft that includes software and Internet access. Mark East, a manager for Microsoft, is quoted as saying: "Microsoft does not see education as a revenue stream. We want to give children access to our products as early as possible." Until recently schools in Britain have been dominated by Acorn and Apple platforms, but the Microsoft offer is likely to direct future purchases to Intel-based computers. The article summarizes Microsoft's goals with an adaptation of the Jesuit maxim, "Give me a child of seven and I will give you a Microsoft user for life."

The third story from the *Evening Standard* concerns a television ad campaign for British Telecom office products that include Internet connections and videoconferencing (Bradshaw). The campaign runs with the slogan "Work smarter, not just harder." One of the ads depicts a bumbling male manager attempting to persuade a female secretary to stay late and type letters for a mass mailing. His inducement is an offer of cups of tea. She gently explains to him that they have a database program that can produce the letters with a simple command, and thus the commercial ends with smiles all around.

The fourth story from *The Scotsman* with the headline, "Fears of Financial Jobs Axe" begins: "Job losses in the financial services sector will rise sharply in the next three months, according to the latest survey of the sector by the Confederation of British Industry" (Stokes). It goes on to mention that huge job cuts have been announced by companies such as Barclays Bank. The results of the survey anticipate even larger cuts during the second quarter of 1996. The associate director of economic analysis for the Confederation of British Industry, Sudhir Junankar, is quoted as saying: "Firms seem determined to ease the pressure on profit margins in the current highly competitive market, and are planning to cut their costs by cutting employment and investing more heavily in information technology."

At this point you likely are thinking you have heard all these stories before set in different locations among the advanced nations of Europe, North America, and the Pacific Rim. Hundreds of articles have appeared recently about children around the world who are now connecting with other children on the Internet. Many of these articles are framed with sweeping pronouncements claiming that the Internet has become the best opportunity for improving education since the printing press (Ellsworth xxii) or even in the history of the world (Dyrli and Kinnaman 79). In spite of the hyperbole, these claims do have some justification, at least within the span of our lifetimes. According to the National Center for Education Statistics, the percentage of public schools in the United States with Internet access rose from 37% in fall 1994 to 78% in fall 1997. Schools with five or more instructional rooms increased from 25% in 1996 to 43% in 1997. And while poor and rural schools lag behind in these categories, they too have made substantial gains in connectivity. Furthermore, a little noticed provision of the Telecommunications Act of 1996 requires telephone companies to pay for wiring all schools and libraries in the United States to the Internet. By spring 1998, the Federal Communications Commission had collected $625 million to hook up American schools and libraries with the eventual price tag expected to run much higher (Tumulty and Dickerson). If phone companies are allowed to raise rates to fund this initiative (which may be a big "if" when consumers see higher phone bills), the promise of President Clinton's Technology Literacy Challenge to connect all U.S. public schools and every instructional room (classrooms, computer labs, libraries, and media centers) to the Internet seems not only possible but inevitable.

The curiosity of the first and second graders in Michael McMullin's classroom in County Donegal suggest the potential for students creating local content and communicating worldwide. Furthermore, children connected to the

Internet can use library resources on a scale that is almost beyond comprehension. Massive data bases like Lexis/Nexis offer access to thousands of periodicals, and the search tools for using these data bases are becoming increasingly easier to use. In President Clinton's words, "This phenomenon has absolutely staggering possibilities to democratize, to empower people all over the world. It could make it possible for every child with access to a computer to stretch a hand across a keyboard, to reach every book every written, every painting ever painted, every symphony ever composed." It raises the question: How does education change for a child who begins school with the potential to communicate with millions of other children and adults, to publish globally, and to explore the largest library ever assembled?

Sometimes hidden in these stories and statistics about the incredible potential of the Internet are hard facts that classroom teachers know all too well. Even though the student-to-computer ratio in American schools has risen to about 9-to-1, over half of those machines are so obsolete that they cannot be connected to the Internet. Cheap Internet access does little to help classrooms still equipped with XTs, Apple IIs, and Commodore 64s. Nearly everywhere else the situation is worse. Even in Germany, one the most technologically advanced nations in the world, the Research and Technology Minister, Juergen Ruettgers, bemoaned the fact that of the 43,000 German schools, only 500 were connected to the Internet in 1996 and only two percent of students had access to a computer in school (Boston). The ending of the County Donegal story that the school lacks funds for purchasing equipment is unfortunately the often repeated downside of children's enthusiasm for the Internet.

In rich and poor nations alike, educators are looking to the private sector to provide information networks and computers for schools. Microsoft, which now controls over eighty percent of software business worldwide, is pouring tens of millions of dollars into education. The motives of Microsoft are perhaps most clear in China, a nation that sanctions software piracy on a massive scale. Pirated copies of the latest Chinese version of Windows are sold for about five dollars before they are even announced. Nevertheless, Microsoft is spending two million dollars a year to train Chinese technicians and programmers and giving away millions more to government ministries and universities. The great irony of the massive piracy of Microsoft is that it makes Microsoft the standard with a huge base of installed customers. Microsoft figures that it will make the money back in the long run with sales of upgrades, applications, and service contracts (Engardio 1996).

The second question I want to pose is raised by the Microsoft example and its adapted slogan: "Give me a child of seven and I will give you a Microsoft user for life." Technology has brought corporate involvement in education to an extent never before seen. At a time when the level of public expenditure on education in many nations continues to decline, schools have little choice but to accept corporate support for expensive technology. Microsoft might well be commended for its largess, but the dependence on corporations to provide technology for schools is a large step toward the privatization of education. Thus my second question is: how will education be affected by the increasing presence of large corporations in making decisions about how children and adults will learn?

Finally, I want to examine the question implicit in the third and fourth news articles—the story about the ad campaign promoting the coming of digital technologies and one about corporate downsizing. Let's begin with the brutally obvious. The manager and secretary story does not have a happy ending. They are fodder for the next volley of layoffs. "Working smarter" really means cutting salaries and increasing profits. The technologically savvy secretary might be able to retrain herself, but the manager is a hopeless case. Any bean counter would identify him as a prime candidate for redundancy. The manager will be lucky to have a job drawing pints in a pub a few months from now. The question these stories present is: what sort of future will children enter in the aftermath of the massive redistribution of wealth and disruption of patterns of employment that have occurred during the last two decades?

Clearly these questions are of a scope much greater than I can address in this chapter, but I will argue that we as teachers must address them if we are to have any influence over how technology will reshape education. Times of major transition offer many possibilities as well as pitfalls, and those who can assess the terrain will be in the best positions to make convincing arguments about what roads to take. I begin with the unprecedented opportunities for education made possible by the Internet and for the moment put aside the limitations of access to equipment and willingness of teachers to enter new environments. To date there have been four primary educational functions of the Internet: communicating one-to-one, communicating in groups, publishing globally, and finding information globally.

Person-to-person communication is the most common use of computer networks big and small. The example of County Donegal is quite typical use where children exchange local information. Children learn a great deal about other countries and other cultures by communicating directly. One teacher in the United States observed: "You can't imagine how powerful it is for my kids to learn that their Malaysian counterparts speak three language, are members of a religion they never heard of, and live in a community with six racial groups" (Dyrli and Kinnaman 79). Even more dramatic instances of one-to-one communication have occurred following natural disasters like the 1995 earthquake in Kobe, Japan, where the Internet stayed up when other lines of communications went down and the first reports came from eyewitnesses. Other major world events (e.g., the Gulf War and the fall of the Berlin Wall) have also produced vivid accounts by those on the scene.

In addition to their peers, students can communicate with members of government, professionals in various fields, and online mentors. On my campus, staff members at the Undergraduate Writing Center have been working online with students in Roma, Texas. Roma is a town with a population of about

8,500 located in the Rio Grande Valley in one of the poorest areas of the country. As part of an outreach project to introduce high school students to the expectations of college-level work, students in Roma work with consultants in the writing center who provide the students with regular online commentary on their drafts. The computers were donated to the school as part of a technology transfer program, and they are connected on a statewide network. The Roma students are enthusiastic about their online instruction and find it one of the most successful aspects of the outreach program.

The easiest and most popular way to get students started communicating online is to have them join a discussion group. Thousands of these groups exist on the Internet and on all major commercial online services. Many are specifically for children, and several others are addressed to educational and curricular issues. Besides facilitating ongoing conversions that new voices can join, network discussion groups also give many possibilities for one-to-one communication. Because individual addresses of those who post messages to discussion groups are included in the message, these individuals can be contacted one-to-one. To give one example of how students can benefit from contacting individuals, a writing instructor at Texas had his students write to individuals posting in a discussion group concerning South Africa at the time of the elections that brought Nelson Mandela to power. They were able to ask questions and obtain first-hand reports from people in South Africa.

With the development of the World Wide Web, students can now publish their work online and make it potentially available to millions of people worldwide. A typical example is Smoky Hill High in metropolitan Denver, where students have placed a virtual school on the Web. Visitors can click on click-on pictures of teachers, read the parent newsletter and student newspaper, find email addresses and browse student projects. The students have also created a virtual mall where online shoppers can buy products from the student store (Bingham). There's no doubt that these and other students across the nation have put an enormous amount of effort into creating Web pages. As teachers who encourage students to publish work in print formats have found, publication itself is a strong motivating factor. Friends and parents now regularly read the work of students at all levels of education. Many of these student Websites are quite innovative in combining graphics, text, and even audio and video, taking full advantage of the multimedia capabilities of the Web.

Finally and perhaps most important, the World Wide Web already contains vast information resources. The printing press led to the widespread distribution of information, and the Web is extending that democratization, allowing anyone with an account on a Web server to become a publisher. Companies, government agencies, non-profit organizations, and individuals have been quick to publish on websites. Large libraries like those at the University of Texas have effectively put the entire reference room online along with hundreds of periodicals with full-text articles. Much information produced by the U.S. Government is available through FedWorld, extensive scientific information is on the Fisher Scientific Internet Catalog, and economic data is available on EDGAR. Conventional print publishers have also joined the rush to the Web.

Quite extraordinary kinds of learning facilitated by the Internet are happening now and no doubt will become more common in the near future. But we should remember that similar pronouncements were issued by advocates of cable television in the late 1960s and early 1970s. They envisioned two-way interactive systems that would facilitate political participation, improve education, and overcome social isolation. Seldom-viewed community-access channels are a legacy of this optimism. But as we all know the major result of cable television has been much more of the same. The Internet provides resources and opportunities for communication of a far greater magnitude than the most ambitious scheme for cable television, and therein lies the rub. Finding information on the World Wide Web has been compared to drinking from a fire hose. The quantity is overwhelming, even to experienced researchers. Finding information the World Wide Web is not magic. For those new to the Web, it is like a vast library with the card catalog scattered on the floor. You can spend hours wandering serendipitously on the Web just as you can spend hours browsing in a large library. But when you want to make a sustained inquiry, you need assistance. Libraries have very well developed tools to guide researchers. There are also powerful tools for searching the Internet, and if you want a specific piece of information such as a telephone number, a stock quote, or a train schedule, you can pull it up very fast.

But if you're looking for information that isn't so specific, such as the causes of the Cold War or the questions I began with, you will not find existing search tools nearly so helpful. Even if you can narrow down the search, you still will pull up much that isn't useful. One of the biggest problems with the Internet from a teacher's perspective is that it's not just the amount of information that is daunting to students; it's also the extreme variety. Pornography has been represented as the great danger to children who use the Internet, but a far greater danger is the amount of misinformation on the Internet. Misinformation even confounds the most literate users. Highly educated people swear to the validity of Internet-circulated urban folklore like the story of the scuba diver who was scooped out of the ocean in the water bucket of a fire-fighting helicopter and then dropped alive onto a forest fire in California.

Misinformation, of course, is a problem with print literacy also. The elaborate classification schemes of libraries, however, give many clues about the origins and reliability of information. Academic periodicals are often shelved in locations apart from popular periodicals, but such differences on the Internet are often hidden. Many discussion groups and websites purport to offer factual, neutral information but in fact contain highly biased and false information. There are Web pages that deny the Holocaust with seemingly credible references and statistics. Images likewise can be deceiving because they can be easily altered. In the past teachers have managed the information students receive by limiting the number and variety of sources. Of course, they can still impose such limitations, but at some point students need to learn how to access the vast information on the Internet and how to assess its value. Usually access is described in terms of equipment and technical skills, but information literacy will require a great deal more on the part of teachers and students. The Internet is sometimes described as a tangled information jungle, but perhaps a better metaphor is a metropolis of tribes, each with a different view of reality. Perhaps the hardest task of all is leading students to understand why the different tribes interpret reality differently.

At this point I would like to return to the issues of access I raised with my second and third questions. For those who foresee the coming the coming of a techno-utopia via the Internet, access is simply a matter of bandwidth. Expand the bandwidth by going from wires to wireless and all can communicate to their hearts' content. This vision continues a deeply embedded libertarian ideology that dates to the origins of the Internet as a Cold War project designed to maintain communications in the aftermath of a nuclear war. The ingenious solution was to flatten the lines of communication so that every node was an independent sender or receiver and messages could take any route to their destination. All that was necessary to hook up a computer to the system was a small robust set of protocols. This ease of access was celebrated in slogans like "Information wants to be free."

In fact, this vision of the Internet depended on a government-supplied communications backbone funded first by the United States Department of Defense and later by the National Science Foundation. The end of this libertarian vision of the Internet came on April 30, 1995, when the National Science Foundation unplugged its backbone and the Internet became privatized. In February 1996, the signing into law of the Telecommunications Reform Act set off a frenzy of mergers and partnerships among corporations involved in computing, communications, publishing, and entertainment—mergers that perhaps are only the beginnings of consolidation of power as the giants buy up the technology to control how we work, how we get information, how we shop, how we relax, and how we communicate with other people. The supporters of the Telecommunications Act of 1996 claimed deregulated airwaves would bring increased competition and lower prices, but to date, just the opposite has happened. The big players recognized that the biggest profits would come from the biggest market shares, and they have consolidated by merging rather than engaging in a competitive free-for-all. Prices for customers often have gone up. In November 1996 AT&T raised long-distance rates 6% for its 80 million residential customers, and some of the Baby Bells including PacTel and Bell South increased prices for high-speed ISDN Internet access.

The corporate giants are also influencing ambitious plans for higher education. Large companies such as Federal Express, Motorola, IBM, and Xerox have extensive online education programs, and state governors are looking to corporate education for models of alternatives to traditional higher education. The leaders in this movement have been Mike Leavitt, Governor of Utah, and

Roy Romer, former Governor of Colorado, who have been the chief proponents of Western Governors University, that takes its name from the
Denver-based Western Governors Association. Sixteen of the eighteen states in
the Western Governors Association, along with Indiana, have signed on. South
Dakota and California are not part of the consortium, but Pete Wilson, when
he was governor, announced a similar plan for California.

Western Governors University is designed to be a virtual university without
a traditional campus. Students will in enroll in courses and receive instruction
online. The governors endorsed the following criteria for Western Governors
University. It is to be:

- market driven, focusing on the needs of employers rather than a
  faculty-defined curriculum;
- degree granting, going into direct competition with community colleges,
  4-year colleges and universities;
- competency-based, grounding certification on the demonstration of
  employer-defined competencies rather than credit hours;
- non-teaching, thus not providing direct instruction;
- cost effective, meaning that without campuses to build and maintain and
  large faculties to pay, it is far cheaper than traditional education;
- regional, allowing students to enroll in online courses offered at colleges and
  universities in any of the other states or courses offered by businesses; and
- quickly initiated, with the first associate degrees awarded in 1998.

Western Governors University is designed from an employers' perspective.
Degrees from WGU are certifications of particular skills, thus in theory guar-
anteeing the employer that a trained worker is being hired. Companies that
have contributed to WGU and sit on its Advisory Board include 3Com
Corporation, AT&T, Educational Management Group (a unit of Simon and
Schuster), IBM, International Thomson Publishing, MCI, and Sun
Microsystems Inc. (Fahys).

One of the goals is to expand access to postsecondary education for citizens
of Western states. There's no question that extensive content can be delivered
by digital technologies and that it is absolutely essential for professionals in
fields such as medicine, pharmacy, and engineering to have access to continuing education. But the motives of the Western governors are not solely based
on expanding access. They are worried about how they will meet increasing
demand for higher education when the "baby-boom echo" generation expands
the traditional college age group by fifteen percent by 2008 and more adults
are returning to college. This boom has been called "Tidal Wave 2," with most
of the impact coming in the Western states which will see a 60% growth by
2008, in contrast to 10% in the Midwest, 21% in the Northeast, and 22% in the
South (Honan).

In the late 1960s and early 1970s, in response to the surge of baby boomers,
California built 42 new community colleges, 4 state colleges, and three new UC

campuses. Want to bet that it will happen again? Spending on education in the Western states and especially Washington, Oregon, California, Idaho, and Nevada, is limited by voter-led tax initiatives, and elementary and secondary education is first in line for what money is available for education. In Oregon the spending on higher education has been cut by almost half in actual dollars since 1990.

The primary motive driving Western Governors University is providing higher education on the cheap. The logic is economy of scale. What can be taught to 10 can be taught to 100. What can be taught to 100 can be taught to 1,000. What can be taught to 1,000 can be taught to an infinite number.

With budgets already strained, governors and legislators are looking for cheap solutions. Online courses offered from virtual universities that do not require new buildings or faculty are going to be very popular with state legislators who want to slash faculty payrolls and abolish tenure. But if the primary motive driving distance learning is to cut costs, distance learning will be inferior learning. We've seen ambitious schemes for distance education based on economy of scale before, and they've produced a list of disappointments. You may remember Sunrise Semester, Continental Classroom, and University of Mid-America.

Not every administrator is enthusiastic about eliminating the faculty's role in teaching and defining the curriculum. Kenneth Ashworth, former Commissioner of the Texas Higher Education Board, says that Western Governors University "has enormous possibilities of harming higher education as we know it, particularly if it is largely controlled and organized to meet the demands of employers." His voice, however, is not the one of the majority.

The most immediate question for us as college teachers and administrators is how do we respond. Denial is not an option.

First, we have to keep the focus on learning and not on technology, and to do that we have to ask: What do we want students to learn? I believe we have good answers to this question. We want students to recognize and value the breadth of information available and to evaluate, analyze, and synthesize that information. We want students to construct new meaning and knowledge with technology. We want students to be able to communicate in a variety of media for different audiences and purposes. And we want students to become responsible citizens and community members. We want them to understand the ethical, cultural, environmental and societal implications of technology and telecommunications, and develop a sense of stewardship and responsibility regarding the use of technology.

The next question is how to create the best possible environment for learning, and to answer that question, we need to query our assumptions about how people learn best. I believe that most learning is not "self-taught," most learning is not a solitary experience, and that people learn best learning with other people. From research I have read, from my experience administering a large computer-based writing program, and from ten years of teaching in networked classrooms, I offer you the following characteristics for the best possible learning environment with technology:

First, students trained in collaborative learning have higher achievement and self esteem. Even though the value of collaborative learning has been well established, many faculty still remain resistant to collaborative learning.

Second, introducing technology has made learning more student-centered, encouraged collaboration, and increased student-teacher interaction. Students who would probably not make a special trip to an instructor's office hour for a simple question will pose that question in an email message. Students likewise can work collaboratively without having to meet always face-to-face.

Third, students who use telecommunications across different geographic locations are more motivated and learn more. For one example, Wallace Fowler, professor of aerospace engineering at Texas, administers a project that joins students from historically African-American and predominantly Mexican-American colleges with students at Texas in designing actual spacecraft. He said when the project started, he feared the educational differences would be too extreme for successful collaboration, but by the end of the first year, the performance levels across institutions were comparable.

Fourth, exemplary computer-using teachers typically enjoy smaller classes and more technical support than other teachers. At Texas we have never pretended that our computer-assisted courses are cheaper than traditional courses. Instead, we have argued that our computer-assisted courses offer students opportunities that are not available from traditional courses.

Fifth, teachers are more effective with training and support for integrating technology into the curriculum. While this statement seems beyond the obvious, of all the professionals who use technology, teachers are probably the most poorly supported. Training reduces anxiety and increases understanding in how to use technology.

Sixth, major change does not come overnight. I would like to end by briefly talking about my own experience. I began using mainframe computers for statistical and linguistic analyses in the mid-1970s and for word processing by the end of the 1970s. When microcomputers came on the scene in the 1980s, I like most writing teachers advocated their use because they facilitated revision. In spring 1988 I began teaching in classrooms where computers were connected in local networks. I and others have written about how these local networks led to significant changes in patterns of classroom interaction, but most of the work of students in these classes remained discussing topics which I had selected and producing essays in multiple drafts with peer reviews. If I had to plot my trajectory as a college writing teacher from my first course as a graduate assistant in 1970, I would note incremental change up to spring 1996 when I began teaching a lower-division elective course designed to give students opportunities to publish on the Internet. I had just finished teaching a practicum for new graduate student instructors, and I found myself in desperate need of a similar course. Even though I adapted most of my materials from other instructors who had taught the course before, I still spent a great deal of time preparing for the course.

Part of my difficulty was caused by shifting from essays to multimedia websites as the students' main products. I dug out books on graphic design that I had used as an undergraduate studying architecture. I went to Web publishing classes offered by my university and did independent tutorials in Photoshop. But that was only the beginning. I had to find teaching materials and figure out how to sequence activities. The biggest problem I had, however, was adjusting to a very different classroom space. We had a sense of community and we worked together well, but at the same time everything that we did involved interacting with the big world. We had throughout the semester virtual visitors from around the world who would comment on what we were doing and occasionally engage us in discussion. What I was teaching was not preparatory to interacting with the world. We were doing it from the get go.

I'm struck by the mismatch between my experience teaching with technology and visions of the future of education set out in the public media and by government officials. I find the following statement nothing short of astounding:

> Academic technophobes, of course, insist that nothing will ever replace the good teacher. But even the best teacher cannot match the flexibility, the richness of resources and the ease in mastering a body of knowledge made possible by top-quality instructional software, especially for a generation often more at home on the Internet than with a textbook. (Elfin)

This quotation appeared in the lead article for *U.S. News & Word Report's* annual "Best Colleges" issue, one of the most widely read statements on higher education. I do not discount the facts that there are many academic technophobes and that many students have learned a great deal on their own by using technology. But I do not see top-quality software providing the answers for the questions I have raised nor do I see top-quality software preparing students to take active roles in public life.

Indeed, I see teachers needed more than ever before because the demands of digital literacy are greater cognitively and socially than those of print literacy. Because we have a great deal of convincing to do, I believe that teachers have to enter policy debates, even when they are not invited. We have to convince those in corporations and government and the public at large that teachers should still be allowed to determine the curriculum and be granted leadership roles in educational policy. So the downside is that we're going to have to learn a lot more and do a lot more and speak out a lot more, and we're probably not going to be directly rewarded for doing it. But if we're underappreciated, under-loved, and underpaid, at least we're not irrelevant. And that's our big advantage in the long run.

CHAPTER EIGHT

Postmodern Possibilities in Electronic Conversations

Marilyn M. Cooper

AT THE END OF HIS 1992 CHAPTER ON "THE ACHIEVED UTOPIA OF THE Networked Classroom," Lester Faigley invites us to think more about the pedagogy that arises from the use of electronic discussions in writing classrooms, "to theorize at greater depth and to take into account the richness of the classroom context" (Faigley 199), and he suggests, here and elsewhere in *Fragments of Rationality*, that such a pedagogy is or will be a postmodern pedagogy. Postmodern theory is most often connected with nihilism: the loss of the centered self, the loss of truth and certainty, the loss of values and responsibility, the loss of the Enlightenment dream of a good society and the programs designed to achieve it. But postmodernist theory has a positive, progressive face—possibilities that open up when we jettison those things that are "lost"— and it is those possibilities that I want to examine as they emerge in a pedagogy that employs electronic conversations.

The use of electronic conversations in writing classrooms—both synchronous and asynchronous, in-class and out of class—has become widespread and much discussed: experiences of them are at the same time reported to be exciting and distressing, promising and depressingly familiar. Faigley's response to an especially rowdy electronic class discussion captures the feelings that many teachers undoubtedly felt early in their experimentation with electronic pedagogy:

> The messages seemed like they were coming from outer space: that beyond the giggly, junior-high-school-bus level of the discussion of sexuality, it had a ghostly quality, an image of the dance of death on the graves of the old narratives of moral order. (196)

Partly this response comes from the emergence of some aspects of student "underlife" into "official" classroom discourse: teachers are simply startled by the intermingling of post-adolescent posturing and off-topic joking with the more familiar earnest comments on teacher-initiated topics. But such responses also indicate that electronic conversations do make significant changes in classroom dynamics.

At first, some of these changes were seen as welcome and even utopian, as Faigley also suggests: the student-centered nature of such discussions was hailed as liberating students from many of the constraints of face-to-face traditional classrooms (cf. Cooper and Selfe) and, more broadly, as leading to "egalitarian classrooms" (Selfe and Meyer 165). More experience with and closer analysis of electronic conversations led to a more sober evaluation that electronic pedagogies deserve our interrogation. The cavalier equation of "decentered/networked" and "egalitarian" results in a failure to acknowledge the strength and pervasiveness of dominant discourse spoken both by students and by instructors. (Romano 21)

Trent Batson best captures the ambivalence most teachers feel, asking whether electronic conversation is "the best friend a teacher ever had or the worst nightmare" (quoted in Sirc 265).

At the same time, as Batson and Geoff Sirc point out, the nightmarish qualities of electronic conversations may also simply represent contemporary changes in writing that may bring new possibilities; Sirc works to uncover "the opportunities for the transformation of our textual strategies available through this retrojective moment in networked technology" (266). That electronic writing differs from printed writing is indisputable, but the nature of the differences and their causes and effects are not as clear. I tend to agree with Michael Spooner and Kathleen Yancey (1996) and Carolyn Miller (1996) in seeing the differences as similar in kind to the differences attending other shifts in medium or technology: the shift from orality to literacy, from face-to-face conversations to telephone conversations, from handwritten to printed texts. Like all writing (and language use), electronic writing responds to cultural changes, including the specific ways that communication technology has been developed: writing online sets up a different rhetorical situation and encourages different writing strategies than writing for print technology does (see also Hawisher and Moran 631). From this point of view, it should not be surprising that electronic writing—and electronic conversation in particular—reflects the postmodern condition of contemporary culture.

Spooner comments:

> maybe we should acknowledge that in the postmodern age, the reader, not the writer, is the real tyrant: multi-tasking, channel-surfing, capricious and fickle, free to interpret, misread, manipulate, and (horrors) apply. We're all guilty; we start at the end, in the middle, we don't finish, we joyously juxtapose bits of what we read with other readings, other experiences. But the point is that this is our most natural process. Both reader and writer are engaged constantly in making knowledge from a very random world. (274)

And Yancey adds: "Through the technology, we can more easily than ever make the multilayered 'postmodern' dimension of writing evident" (274).

Sirc's analysis of "ENFI-Null" writing delineates some of the characteristics that make it postmodern. He cites Bill Coles's choice of a student paper to include in *What Makes Writing Good* as a "highly ENFI-Null piece of writing: drifting paratactically, weaving in dialogue from other speakers, it moves through a series of almost-definitions of the university to arrive at nothing but a more intense sense of being" (274). Postmodernism is, above all, a response to our increased awareness of the great diversity in human cultures, a diversity that calls into question the possibility of any "universal" or "privileged" perspective and that thus values the juxtaposition of different perspectives and different voices and the contemplation of connections rather than a subordinated structure of ideas that achieves a unified voice and a conclusive perspective.

It is just the "unresolved nature of ENFI-Null writing" (Sirc 274), its paratactic rather than hypotactic structure, and the identity-diffusion or loss of authorial authority and responsibility that results from the interweaving of other voices that causes many writing teachers to look askance at what goes on in electronic conferences, to see them as superficial, irresponsible skating across the surface of important issues rather than the in-depth exploration and critique of issues that classroom discussion—and academic discourse—is supposed to achieve. Writing teachers are not alone in fearing the loss of complexity in thought and in the use of language that such communicative strategies seem to demonstrate (cf. Lanham, 227-54). Despite the changes, however, it is not clear that anything of importance has been lost in the move to electronic conversations in writing classes, just as despite claims that it was print technology that made analytic thought possible, researchers have found no evidence that literate people think more complexly than illiterate people (cf. Scribner and Cole). And, in any case, as Richard Lanham suggests, for the time being we are in a period in which the two modes—electronic/hypertextual/postmodern and print literate/modern—alternate, in which we oscillate between them (Lanham, 260), and, perhaps, use both in different ways to make sense of a very mixed culture.

What has been called the postmodern condition is a messy and partial transition that we are still in the midst of from old modernist ways of thinking and acting to new postmodern ways. The new ways of thinking and acting that are called postmodern arise out of the changed circumstances of our lives and are adaptations to these new circumstances—the global capitalist economy that is a result of new corporate strategies and trade policies, the global village that is a result of the desire for and development of new communication and transportation technologies. The postmodern condition does not necessarily represent progress, but it is certainly real (not only virtual; cf. Eagleton, ix) and it certainly requires new strategies if we are to work effectively within the new systems that structure many of our everyday experiences.

In this essay, I suggest that to understand what's happening in electronic conversations in writing classrooms we need to understand some transitions in assumptions involved in the shift from modernism to postmodernism. As applied to the practices of teaching writing, the postmodern condition involves a transition in assumptions in at least four areas: a transition in assumptions about knowledge, language, and the self, a transition in assumptions about power, a transition in assumptions about responsibility, and a transition in assumptions about the teacher's role in the classroom.

The transition in assumptions about knowledge, language, and the self has received the most attention in discussions of postmodernism, even though the theoretical work was largely accomplished in the poststructuralist theories of language that presaged postmodernism. Most simply put, the transition involves a shift from the notion of knowledge as the apprehension of universal truth and its transparent representation in language by rational and unified individuals to the notion of knowledge as the construction in language of partial and temporary truths by multiple and internally contradictory individuals. In composition circles, postmodernism became attractive primarily because of its critique of "the tradition of epistemological inquiry founded by Locke and Descartes" (Schilb, 85). John Schilb notes, "it encourages interest in rhetoric, including rhetoric-as-persuasion. . . . For postmodernists, knowledge is always the product of persuasion, and truth-claims inevitably reflect the human exchanges in which they occur" (86). Earlier, Thomas Barker and Fred Kemp also focused on the "maturing epistemology" suggested by postmodernism to develop computer-aided writing "instruction that emphasizes the communal aspect of knowledge making" (2). With knowledge seen as rhetorical, or socially constructed, the collaborative aspects of writing became foregrounded, and any technology that enabled more effective collaborative practices in writing became attractive. Summing up a lot of work that built on this insight, Gail Hawisher and Charles Moran say, "we believe that a pedagogy that includes email will be inevitably collaborative. Our profession is increasingly interested in collaborative writing; email and the virtual 'space' of a network make collaboration easier by dissolving the temporal and spatial boundaries of the conventional classroom" (633).

But more than temporal and spatial boundaries are dissolved, as Faigley suggests; by bringing writing into a public space, electronic conversations also dissolve the romantic illusion that individuals develop a unified identity through aligning themselves with universal truth in the process of contemplation. One of the modernist practices that electronic conversations undermine is that of "classroom acts of writing, especially writing about the self, as part of a much longer process of intellectual self-realization" (Faigley 191). Intellectual self-realization, in the tradition that stretches from Plato to Wordsworth to Peter Elbow, is a process that results in the discovery of the universal forms of truth that define knowledge, and that relies on developing the thought processes of the individual in line with these universal forms. In contrast, in electronic conversations, the individual thinker moves in the opposite direction, into the multiplicity and diversity of the social world, and in social interaction tries out many roles and positions. As Schilb notes, "Modern epistemology . . . also presupposes a human subject who is more or less stable and coherent. . . . On the other hand, postmodern theory evokes a self who may occupy multiple positions, form various allegiances, and teem with conflicting ideas" (87-88). David Bartholomae comments on the postmodernist selves displayed by students in an electronic conversation that took place in a classroom at New York Institute of Technology:

> In a sense, this reads like dialogue in an experimental novel. There are two discussions going on simultaneously—one about rock and roll, one directed at the assigned material. . . . It is important to note that this is not a matter of a few students who want to stay on track struggling with those who want to goof around. Individual speakers (like 1935) produce both tracks simultaneously. Read with some detachment—as the Song of Schooling, for example—the transcript is a striking representation of the competing discourses that inhabit (or, according to some theorists, construct) the sensibility of late adolescence in the nineties. (255)

In this most familiar of shifts in assumptions associated with postmodernism, both knowledge and the self are seen as socially constructed in language and thus multiple, contradictory, divided. The shift was caused primarily by changes in social structures, but it was emphasized and furthered by the particular ways people chose to converse in electronic media.

It is this shift from the idea of language as the transparent window on universal knowledge and the unified self to the idea that language socially constructs partial knowledge and multiple selves that raised the fears of postmodernism as a nihilistic abandonment of meaning. As Jean Baudrillard observed, "All of western faith and good faith was engaged in this wager on representation: that a sign could refer to the depth of meaning, that a sign could exchange for meaning and that something could guarantee this exchange—God, of course" (10). Although some postmodern theory does seem to revel in nihilism (Baudrillard is often charged with this), the accomplishment of postmodern theorists such as Michel Foucault, Jean-Francois Lyotard, and Zygmunt Bauman has been to explore instead the positive ramifications of this shift, particularly how it affects assumptions about power, responsibility, and the role of teachers (or intellectuals) in the classroom and in society.

If knowledge is not guaranteed by some authority—God, priests, intellectuals—the hierarchical underpinning of education (and many other institutions) breaks down. If knowledge is not a stable construct of ideas to be passed from teachers who know to students who learn, the basis for teachers' authority in the classroom is threatened; and if knowledge is socially constructed, students need to be able to engage in the process of knowledge construction in the classroom. Thus, in the 1980s, teachers and scholars focused on the question of how to restructure power relationships in the writing classroom. In an assertion that later turns ironic, Faigley says that in electronic discussions, "the utopian dream of an equitable sharing of classroom authority, at least during the duration of a class discussion, has been achieved" (Faigley 167). As Cindy

Selfe and Paul Meyer pointed out, the analysis of power relationships in electronic classroom conversations and the attempt to use electronic conversations to give all students more equitable access to discourse in classrooms depend for their success on a better understanding of what power is (188). Beginning with studies of how knowledge is produced in various discourses, Michel Foucault eventually arrived at a new understanding of power, and his articulation of this shift in assumptions allows us to better understand the problems involved in "sharing" power in the classroom.

The modernist assumption that still structures most of our language about power is that power is a possession, that some people have it and can give it to others or share it with them or help them gain it. In contrast, Foucault argues that power functions not as a possession but as a relation, and that it attempts to stabilize power relationships that are favorable to one party that result in power appearing to be a possession. This shift in ways of thinking about power is adumbrated in one of the electronic conversations Faigley analyzes:

> 72. *Gordon Sumner:*   JoAnn, what man do you know that will help in giving away some of his power?
>
> 79. *JoAnn:*   Gordon, good question, and so power is the issue. What we need is a structure that doesn't make power so appealing, that brings responsibility with it, that mandates the sharing of it.
>
> 81. *jane doe:*   It is very doubtful that a man will put aside his pride or shall I call it a "macho ego" to help women gain any power because men like where they have women: right under the palm of thir hand. (177)

The assumption that power is a possession that accrues to people in some positions and not to others is apparent in all three of these comments. But "JoAnn" calls for a different way of thinking about power, one that includes responsibility, and "jane doe" intimates what motivates the assumption that power over women is "possessed" by men: because men like where they have women.

The assumption that power is a possession validates established hierarchies. Thus, for example, men's acts of domination over women appear to be natural and inevitable when one assumes that men "have" power and women don't; but when, as Foucault suggests, these acts are seen instead as acts taken by individuals in order to establish dominance, individual responsibility in power relationships becomes visible and available to critique. Foucault says:

> The exercise of power is not simply a relationship between partners, individual or collective; it is a way in which certain actions modify others. Which is to say, of course, that something called Power, with or without a capital letter, which is assumed to exist universally in a concentrated or diffused form, does not exist. Power exists only when it is put into action, even if, of course, it is integrated into a disparate field of possibilities brought to bear upon permanent structures. . . . what defines a relationship of power is that it is a mode of action which does not

act directly and immediately on others. Instead it acts upon their actions: an action upon an action, on existing actions or on those which may arise in the present or future. . . . In itself the exercise of power is not violence; nor is it a consent which, implicitly, is renewable. It is a total structure of actions brought to bear upon possible actions; it incites, it induces, it seduces, it makes easier or more difficult; in the extreme it constrains or forbids absolutely; it is nevertheless always a way of acting upon an acting subject or acting subjects by virtue of their acting or being capable of action. (1983, 219-20)

From Foucault's perspective, people do not struggle over power in their interactions with one another, but rather continually structure power relationships among themselves through the ways their actions impact others' actions. People cannot give others power or take it away; their actions always respond to the actions of others and in return set up a range of possibilities for other's actions. No power relations are possible in the absolute situations of violence or consent (which are often considered to be situations of absolute power) because in these situations no responding actions are possible; thus "freedom must exist for power to be exerted." In sum:

[A] power relationship can only be articulated on the basis of two elements which are each indispensable if it is really to be a power relationship: that "the other" (the one over whom power is exercised) be thoroughly recognized and maintained to the very end as a person who acts; and that, faced with a relationship of power, a whole field of responses, reactions, results, and possible inventions may open up. (220)

A teacher who sets up a classroom discussion online is not giving or sharing power with students, but rather is performing an action that sets up a range of possibilities for action by students that is in some ways different from the range of possibilities set up by a face-to-face classroom discussion; and the actions that students take in electronic conversations—and the actions that teachers take in the resulting conversation—constitute relations of power.

How such relations of power develop can be seen when we analyze the conversational moves in any electronic (or face-to-face) conversation. If, for example, we look in this way at what happens in the conversation that Faigley cites as his "worst" experience in using pseudonyms in electronic class discussions (193-196), we see that, as Bartholomae observed of the students at New York Institute of Technology, it is not a matter of a struggle between those students who want to stay on track and some more rebellious students, nor of students single-mindedly pursuing individual agendas. Instead, through their actions students are constructing and reacting to an ongoing situation. Faigley tries to assign motivations to the students, both individually and collectively: he hypothesizes that the students were engaging in "a collective act of opposition," announced by "arm pit" early on ("isn't this so fun. let's not talk about the reading!!!") and most effectively forwarded by "Cherri Champagne," whose "comments . . . divert the sporadic discussion of the sex roles in the *Ladies*'

Home Journal article"; and that "Cherri" is "one of the women in the class who may have decided it was payback time for some of the fraternity men's previous insults" (196-197). Though not the only possible way to read the transcript, Faigley's interpretation is entirely plausible and well grounded in his general observations of the class dynamic—but it is focused on figuring out what overall effect the students intend their actions to have on the teacher and on other students.

When I focus instead on how the individual actions (comments) relate to one another, students seem more involved in the discussion of the topic of sex roles at the same time that they engage in intricate moment-by-moment positioning of themselves and others. In the account that follows, I pull out a strand of comments that contextualizes "Cherri Champagne's" contributions to the conversation to try to demonstrate the multiple and diverse actions she takes and responds to; I want to emphasize that my account should in no way be thought of as a representation of what is "really" going on.[1]

"INDIANA JONES" announces what becomes the dominant topic (and then for most of the rest of the excerpt he retreats into a private conversation with "King Kong Bundy" in German), and "Cherri" responds:

4.	*INDIANA JONES:*	Monogamy is a thing of the past.
6.	*Cherri Champagne:*	Monogamy sucks.

"Mighty Mouse" responds to "Cherri" and "joe" responds to "INDIANA JONES":

10.	*Mighty Mouse:*	Cherri Champagne. How about STD's?
13.	*joe:*	monogamy is not a thing of the past i mean how can you sleep with a zillion different people with all the creepy crawlies out there?

When "Cherri" asks, "What are STD's," "Laverne" and "joe" translate it for her, and in her next comment she seems to be responding to all the ensuing discussion of the perils of sleeping around by qualifying her position on monogamy:

25.	*Cherri Champagne:*	Pick a partner who has come to believe in fidelity through trial and error.

When "Alf" offers a correction to trend of the conversation so far, "Cherri" responds to the new topic of marriage he introduces, and she gets three responses:

33.	*Alf:*	The article is talking about monogamy in marriage. I think everyone wants your husband or wife to be monogamous don't you?
37.	*Cherri Champagne:*	Fuck marriage. What about healthy, happy sexual relationships?
43.	*yeah boy:*	Hey Cherrie—can we meet?

| 44. | *El Vira:* | No wonder society is so screwed up today. Too many people have attitudes like the Biffs, Cherris, and Yeah Boys. You guys are so messed up. You know what happens if there is no monogamy in the world? People run around having sex with every Dick, Tom, and Harry and then there are a bunch of mixed up children with no examples to follow, no family unit and no morals. We might as well have a nuclear war! |
| 46. | *Laverne:* | Allright Cherri! Are you saying who needs marriage to have sex? |

Then "Yeah boy" responds to the conflict he sees between "El Vira" and "Cherri," and "Cherri" responds to "Laverne":

| 47. | *yeah boy:* | El Vira and Cherri need to meet and duke it out. |
| 52. | *Cherri Champagne:* | No Laverne, I'm saying that you should not marry someone in order to have sex. |

"Cherri's" next comment seems to continue in some way her critique of marriage as well as responding to an exchange between "Mighty Mouse" and "butthead" ("butthead's" comment below also alludes to something else "Mighty Mouse" said earlier, in entry 29: "women are the ones concerned with emotion"):

40.	*Mighty Mouse:*	Butthead. I hope you are not saying that it is easy to sleep with a zillion people?!!!
55.	*butthead:*	M.M.—It's pretty easy—a little wine, dancing, some attention, it doesn't take much. You just have to feed on their emotions.
59.	*Cherri Champagne:*	Guys are bad lays.

"Yeah boy" responds almost immediately, and "Cherri" in answering his question seems to be thinking of a series of earlier comments on how women are expected to focus on making men happy and how "women carry all the burden in a seriously emotional relationship" (see entries 24, 26, 29, 39, and 41):

| 61. | *yeah boy:* | cherri, so are girls better in your opinion? |
| 63. | *Cherri Champagne:* | Girls know what men want. Men don't know what women want. |

In her entries, "Cherri Champagne" mostly responds to topics introduced by other students: monogamy ("INDIANA JONES"), STDs ("Mighty Mouse"), sex ("joe"), marriage ("Alf"). Although she is active in the conversation (her seven entries are second only to "yeah boy's" eleven entries) and her entries receive the most responses (fifteen total), it's hard to see her as dominating the conversation. "INDIANA JONES'" entry 4, initiating the topic of monogamy, receives the most responses of any single entry (eleven). In comparison, "Cherri Champagne's" entry 37 ("Fuck marriage") receives four responses and her entry 59 ("Guys are bad lays") receives five responses, while "El Vira's" entry 44 defending monogamy receives six responses. In her entries "Cherri Champagne" agrees with some comments, asks questions, synthesizes ideas from the preceding conversation, disagrees, and uses deliberatively provocative language. Some students respond to her (and in a variety of ways) and others ignore her, and she chooses to respond to some of those who respond to her and not to respond to others.

Nor is Faigley "disempowered" in the conversation. Though he felt the direction of the conversation foreclosed his possibilities for comment ("they wrote me out of the conversation. I had not planned to remain silent during the discussion, but I had no opportunity to enter it." 197), thirteen entries directly address the question of what the assigned articles say, and the longest of the entries are among these. And it seems to me that the students in this excerpt were for the most part responding to what they took to be the general topic set up by his opening comment and were discussing sex roles in relationships. "Cherri Champagne's" last entry seems especially on track, commenting on one result of women paying more attention than men to the success of a relationship.

What Foucault calls forms of power, the fossilized institutional and identity roles of student-teacher and male-female, do operate in this conversation, as in all human interaction, but they operate to open a range of possible actions which the individuals involved can choose to take up or refuse. Just as in the electronic exchanges Susan Romano examined, students do not simply occupy roles prepared for them but instead position themselves in relation to these roles through the actions they choose to take. By asking the initial question, Faigley positions himself as a certain kind of teacher, which offers the other people in the conversation the option to position themselves as certain kinds of students. Many individuals take up this option and respond in various entries as "good" students, "reluctant" students, "rebellious" students, or other more-difficult-to-characterize student roles; other individuals (or the same individuals in different entries) opt for different positions in response to the possibilities offered by people in the conversation other than Faigley. Faigley also has possibilities to position himself in the conversation (he is not prevented in any sense from entering), but he chooses neither to reaffirm the particular teacher position he started with nor to find a different position for himself.

Thus, even though established hierarchies put pressure on individuals to respond in terms of pre-established positions, to the extent that people are free to act at all, power is always an action taken by an individual in relation to another individual's actions, and thus the shape of power relations is always a matter of individual agency. "Sharing" power is not a matter of giving up something you have but rather of deciding what you want to do in any given situation and being conscious of and taking responsibility for how what you do affects others.

This revision of how we think about power goes some way toward addressing another fear writing teachers have about what goes on in classroom electronic conversations (and in face-to-face classrooms discussions of sensitive issues). In a period of legitimation crisis where there is no universally accepted external authority to appeal to nor any way to establish universal or enduring values and in which people take on shifting identities at will, there occurs, as Faigley says, "an all too frequent distancing of responsibility" for positions and actions taken. In electronic conversations, and especially in pseudonymous electronic conversations, this distancing may be intensified by the sense that these interactions are not "real," but merely "virtual." But, again, as with the fear of the loss of meaning that arises out of the modernist assumption that meaning must be guaranteed by some authority, this fear is predicated on a modernist assumption that individuals must be coerced by universal codes of ethics to behave responsibly (correctly) toward others. Indeed, in electronic conversations we do witness "the dance of death on the graves of the old narratives of moral order" (Faigley 196), but that does not mean that responsible behavior is no longer possible.

The transition in assumptions about responsibility that marks the postmodern condition has been best addressed by Zygmunt Bauman, who draws on the work of Emmanuel Levinas to develop a notion of postmodern ethics. Bauman argues that the assumption that individuals have to be forced or coerced to behave responsibly toward others (which dates at least back to Hobbes) and that correct behavior thus depends on submission to established external authorities and an accepted universal code of ethics has been one of the most pernicious of modernist assumptions. Bauman says:

> Ethics . . . acts on the assumption that in each life-situation one choice can and should be decreed to be good in opposition to numerous bad ones, and so acting in all situations can be rational while the actors are, as they should be, rational as well. But this assumption leaves out what is properly moral in morality. It shifts moral phenomenon from the realm of personal autonomy into that of power-assisted heteronomy. It substitutes the learnable knowledge of rules for the moral self constituted by responsibility. It places answerability to the legislators and guardians of the code where there had formerly been answerability to the Other and to moral self-conscience, the context in which moral stand is taken. (Bauman 11)

Just as people will not "share" power when power is seen not as something they are responsible for but rather as something that is naturally theirs, so too people cannot be blamed for distancing themselves from responsibility for the goodness or badness of their actions when they are prevented from judging for themselves the goodness or badness of their actions. For example, in classrooms where teachers can be counted on to tell students what they should or should not say, what reason do students have for reflecting on or being careful about how the actions or positions they take affect others?

Bauman, following Levinas, sees morality (as opposed to universalistic, externally imposed ethics) as grounded in a pre-ontological impulse to be responsible for the Other. The proximity of the "face" of the unknown Other imposes an obligation on an individual, and this obligation is the grounding of both signification and subjectivity: responding to the other is the reason for speaking; responsibility for the other (subjecting oneself to the other) is the act that establishes subjectivity. This responsibility for the Other is not reciprocal—not Martin Buber's quid pro quo acknowledgment between I and Thou, not the Christian do unto others as you would have them do unto you—but an absolute obligation. Nor is it a matter of a logic of identity, of knowing who the Other is, or what the Other wants. As Levinas says, "Proximity . . . does not revert to the fact that the Other is known to me" (97). And Bauman explains:

> The realm of moral command to be responsible (and thus to be free), Levinas calls 'proximity'. . . . Proximity is the ground of all intention, without being itself intentional. . . . Such an attention, such waiting, is not possessive; it does not aim at dispossessing the Other of her will, of her distinctiveness and identity—through physical coercion, or the intellectual conquest called 'the definition'. Proximity is neither a distance bridged, nor a distance demanding to be bridged; not a preambula to identification and merger, which can, in practice, only be an act of swallowing and absorption. Proximity is satisfied with being what it is—proximity. And is prepared to remain such: the state of permanent attention, come what may. Responsibility never completed, never exhausted, never past. Waiting for the Other to exercise her right to command, the right which no commands already given and obeyed can diminish. (86-88)

Levinas's notion of morality is like Iris Marion Young's notion of a politics of difference grounded on "an openness to unassimilated otherness" (227): it neither conceives of individuals as isolated monads in slave to self-interest nor, despite its privileging of face-to-face relations, denies difference in the way that the ideal of community does. Instead, it allows us to see responsibility for and responsiveness to others as a chance taken up by individuals, an expression of the fundamental sociality of humanity.

But why do people feel obligated to the Other? Levinas sees being responsible for the Other as the action that establishes a person as an irreplaceable individual, the only action one can take that no one else can take. Being responsible thus is not a matter of suppressing one's "natural" self-interestedness in favor of an effort to be good or to try to follow the rules but rather a fundamental impulse to be an individual agent, to be someone whose existence makes a difference. This, of course, does not mean that people are naturally good or even choose to act responsibly most of the time. Bauman notes:

> Uncertainty rocks the cradle of morality, fragility haunts it through life. There is nothing necessary in being moral. Being moral is a chance which may be taken up; yet it may be also, and as easily, forfeited.

The point is, however, that losing the chance of morality is also losing the chance of the self. . . . Awakening to being for the Other is the awakening of the self, which is the birth of the self. There is no other awakening, no other way of finding out myself as the unique I, the one and only I, the I different from all others, the irreplaceable I, not a specimen of a category. (Bauman, 76-77)

Though there are no guarantees in the postmodern world, this notion of morality offers a hope: people who are not prevented from taking responsibility may choose to be responsible in what they say and do, even if they do not always do so. In contrast, in a postmodern world where standards of behavior are invalidated or unavailable, people have fewer and fewer reasons to conform their behavior to any external standard.

In his final chapter on the ethical subject, Faigley also takes up the question of responsibility in writing, referring as I have to Young's politics of difference and also to the theories of Jean-François Lyotard. Lyotard (who, like Bauman, draws heavily on Levinas' ideas about ethics) focuses on the questions of justice that arise when different discourses come into conflict: how can people speak to or understand one another across the boundaries of discourses with competing or mutually exclusive assumptions? Like Bauman, Lyotard sees understanding as a responsibility undertaken by individuals rather than a matter of established rules of discourse. Competing discourses offer competing ways of understanding, competing ways of linking phrases together, but this conflict is not resolved by one discourse being more authoritative or legitimate. Instead, as Lyotard says, "It is up to everyone to decide!" (68). The "responsibility of linking phrases" (Faigley, 237) is another aspect of the responsibility for the Other. Faigley concludes:

> Bringing ethics into rhetoric is not a matter of collapsing spectacular diversity into universal truth. Neither is ethics only a matter of a radical questioning of what aspires to be regarded as truth. Lyotard insists that ethics is also the obligation of rhetoric. It is accepting the responsibility for judgment. It is a pausing to reflect on the limits of understanding. It is respect for diversity and unassimilated otherness. It is finding the spaces to listen. (239)

Responsibility for the Other in conversations manifests in the way people respond to others, in the way they take the responsibility for the shape of power relations and the direction of conversation as they listen to, recognize, and respect difference.

Using the perspective of postmodern ethics to look again at Faigley's problematic pseudonymous electronic conversation enables us to assess differently students' behavior in this forum. One question that arises is, why do students agree to participate in classroom electronic conferences at all? The modernist explanation would be that the institution of schooling compels or habituates them to doing what their teacher tells them to do: teachers have the power and the right as approved authorities to tell students what to do, and students who want the benefits of being in this institution submit themselves to this authority.

But as most teachers realize early on, this is a very fragile and undependable basis for getting students to really engage in any classroom activity, even if you also assume additional motivation from students' interest in getting good grades. The more I reflect on students' behavior in my classes—and especially in electronic conversations—the more I am impressed by their great good will, their willingness to trust in and respond to my (not always very good) ideas and suggestions. Their behavior does not seem to be simply motivated by institutional forms of power and self-interest, but rather by an impulse to be responsive to and responsible for me and to and for other students, and this impulse seems, at least in part, to be motivating Faigley's students in this problematic conversation too.

Why does Faigley's initial question about whether "the *Ladies Home Journal* article supported or contradicted Hochschild's claim" evoke from his students a "round of messages . . . giving short responses" (192), and why do eight of the nineteen students with entries in the excerpt Faigley published go on to specifically discuss what the article supports? If we assume that responsibility is an obligation to the Other and not a submission to authority, Faigley's students become individual agents responding not to a teacher-authority but to a teacher-person whom they feel responsible for just because he is a person, a person who, like any other person, deserves an answer. As "yeah boy" says, "someone reply to the article" (Faigley, 193). Students feel the responsibility for linking phrases; they listen to and respond to each other's differences and, on my reading at least, support each other as often as they fight with one another. Contributing the most entries in this excerpt, "yeah boy" in particular takes on a lot of responsibility for facilitating and directing the conversation. All of his entries are short responses to others: he supports "butthead" ("you tell him" [entry 19], "you're so macho, what a maniac" [entry 57]); he indirectly asks "Madonna" to explain why she picked that pseudonym and indirectly supports her explanation (entries 36 and 50); he challenges "Cherri" ("if you pick your partner like that you need to see a doctor" [entry 31], "can we meet?" [entry 43], "so are girls better in your opinion?" [entry 61]); he draws attention to differences ("El Vira and Cherri need to meet and duke it out" [entry 47]); and he answers "INDIANA JONES'" plea:

60. *INDIANA JONES:*   HELP! I'VE LOST TRACK OF THE CONVERSATION!
65. *yeah boy:*   indiana, that's because you've been speaking another language!

"Mighty Mouse" takes responsibility for engaging in and encouraging various strands of the conversation: he questions "Cherri" on an implication of her first entry (she says, "Monogamy sucks" [6]; he says, "How about STD's?" [10]); he joins in the discussion of what the articles said about the different emotional makeups of men and women begun by "Adam Heart" (entry 29); he responds to "butthead's" response to "joe" on the advisability of sleeping with a zillion different people (entry 40); he agrees with "El Vira's" position on monogamy (entry 53); and he tells "INDIANA JONES" to rejoin the public conversation ("Indiana Jones, will you please write in English!!!" [58]). Finally, to me, many of the responses to "Cherri Champagne" seem not so much angry retorts as attempts to figure out the *differend* that her entries create as she takes up seemingly contradictory positions within what is "normally" said about monogamy, marriage, and sexual relationships.

I don't want to imply that all these students are always acting responsibly, nor that all students will always choose to act responsibly in their actions in electronic conversations, but rather that, by not tightly policing their behavior in these forums, we can allow them to make such choices and perhaps better prepare them to participate responsibly in other uncontrolled situations. Indeed, if writing teachers have been worried about what happens in classroom bounded electronic conversations, they have been terrified by the possibilities for mayhem that open up when students in classes enter more public MOO and MUD spaces.

Julian Dibbell analyzes the ethical (and ontological) questions raised by an incident of rape that took place in LambdaMOO and draws attention to how the mind-body distinction created in the Enlightenment is dissolved in such virtual spaces. He suggests that his responses to this incident announce the final stages of our decades-long passage into the Information Age, a paradigm shift that the classic liberal firewall between word and deed (itself a product of an earlier paradigm shift commonly known as the Enlightenment) is not likely to survive intact. After all, anyone the least bit familiar with the workings of the new era's definitive technology, the computer, knows that it operates on a principle impractically difficult to distinguish from the pre-Enlightenment principle of the magic word: the commands you type into a computer are a kind of speech that doesn't so much communicate as make things happen, directly and ineluctably, the same way pulling a trigger does. (393-94)

The loss of the distinction between word and deed, which has been under attack at least since Ludwig Wittgenstein equated meaning and use in the notion of language-games and J. L. Austin elaborated Wittgenstein's notion into speech-act theory, has different implications when contemplated in cyberspace. Poststructuralist and postmodernist emphasis on the way language constructs reality primarily led to conclusions about the death of the real: both word and deed become imaginary, subject to the intentions or whims of individual or collective consciousness. But, as even Baudrillard observes, simulation only "threatens the difference between 'true' and 'false', between 'real' and imaginary' (5). When the difference dissolves, the result may just as well be the death of the imaginary, as words and thoughts take on the same character as actions, having real effects and real implications (as, of course, Freud and Lacan pointed out) that need to be taken as seriously as the effects and implications of "real" actions. As Dibbell says, "the more seriously I took the notion of virtual rape, the less seriously I was able to take the notion of freedom of speech, with its tidy division of the world into the symbolic and the real" (393).

Dibbell's account of how LambdaMOO dealt with "Mr. Bungle" (the rapist) is a good example of postmodern ethics in action in an electronic conversation. On modernist assumptions, the results are disappointing, for, even though there was consensus that the rape was intolerable and even though actions were taken to punish "Mr. Bungle" and to attempt to ensure that future offenses could be prevented, there was also a great deal of dissensus and ambiguity and very little closure on the incident. Immediately after the rape, victims called for the "toading" of "Mr. Bungle," which in a MOO involves not only the erasure of the description and attributes of a character, "but the account itself goes too" (Dibbell 383): it is the equivalent of a death sentence. Only wizards, the programmers of the MOO, can command a toading, and in LambdaMOO the wizards had announced four months before this incident that they would "only implement whatever decisions the community as a whole directed them to" (384). Thus, the residents of LambdaMOO held a real-time open conclave to discuss what to do.

Dibbell distinguishes four political positions that were taken in the debate: parliamentarian legalist types argued for the establishment of explicit rules along with "a full-blown judiciary system complete with elected officials and prisons to enforce those rules" (384); royalist types argued for the wizards returning "to the position of swift and decisive leadership their player class was born to" (384); technolibertarians argued for the individual "deployment of defensive software tools" like a gag command (385); and anarchist types (who included one of the victims) argued that toading was not a form of capital punishment but was rather "more closely analogous to banishment; it was a kind of turning of the communal back on the offending party, a collective action which, if carried out properly, was entirely consistent with anarchist models of community" (386). All four of these positions are clearly modernist in their assumptions: parliamentarians, royalists, and anarchists all argue for an ethics enforced by an authority derived from law, innate rights, or consensus, respectively; and technolibertarians argue for an ethics enforced by an isolated, asocial individual who is responsible to no one for his/her actions.

Perhaps predictably, none of these positions prevailed. The conclave lasted about three hours and no decision was taken. As Dibbell describes it: as the evening wore on and the talk grew more heated and more heady, it seemed increasingly clear that the vigorous intelligence being brought to bear on this swarm of issues wasn't going to result in anything remotely like resolution. The perspectives were just too varied, the meme-scape just too slippery. Again and again, arguments that looked to be heading in a decisive direction ended up chasing their own tails; and slowly, depressingly, a dusty haze of irrelevance gathered over the proceedings. (388)

Subsequently, "JoeFeedback," who was one of LambdaMOO's wizards and who, Dibbell surmises, "surely realized that under the present order of things he must in the final analysis either act alone or not act at all" (390), issued the command to toad "Mr. Bungle." How this action affected the community of

LambdaMOO, and the wizards' subsequent institution of a "system of petitions and ballots whereby anyone could put to popular vote any social scheme requiring wizardly powers for its implementation" (391) and of a boot command that residents could use to eject unruly characters is the focus of Dibbell's article, and it appears, on modernist assumptions, to be the ethical "lesson" of this incident: that differences within any community are too varied to be resolved through discussion and that instead either individuals must act alone or a supermajority of the community must vote on a course of action.

But other things of ethical import were happening at the same time as the formal decision making process proceeded. The rape had ended when "Zippy," a character with "near wizardly powers" (377) caged "Mr. Bungle," but another character who didn't know what had happened soon replied to his pleas for help and released him from the cage. Oddly to Dibbell, "Mr. Bungle" returned to LambdaMOO during the three days between the rape and the conclave and even appeared and took part in the conclave. At first, "Mr. Bungle" was confronted with hostile insults and challenges, to which he responded "with a curious and mostly silent passivity" (388), but when he appeared at the conclave, some of the residents asked him why he had done what he did. His response that he had just been experimenting in what was after all just a virtual, not a real, world, led the residents to dismiss him as "a psycho" (389), but he continued in the conclave to express "a prickly sort of remorse, interlaced with sarcasm and belligerence, and though it was hard to tell if he wasn't still just conducting his experiments, some people thought his regret genuine enough that maybe he didn't deserve to be toaded after all" (389). Furthermore, a few days after he was toaded by "JoeFeedback," "Mr. Bungle" returned to LambdaMOO in the guise of "Dr. Jest" (presumably by acquiring a new Internet account), and although he was recognizably the same person (whatever that means), he had changed: "he no longer radiated the aggressively antisocial vibes he had before. . . and . . . he was also a lot less dangerous to be around" (392-93). Dibbell concludes that "Mr. Bungle/Dr. Jest" had "undergone some sort of personal transformation" (393), which he implies was like his own recent transformation from "newbie" status through "developing the concern for [his] character's reputation that marks the attainment of virtual adulthood" (389), and he decided he would like to talk with him about it, but by the time Dibbell made up his mind to do so, "Dr. Jest" had stopped logging in to LambdaMOO, even though he left behind the room he had created there.

Although one might surmise that "Mr. Bungle/Dr. Jest's" transformation was caused by his ejection from LambdaMOO and the cancellation of his Internet account, the ease with which "Dr. Jest" got back to LambdaMOO suggests to me that other factors might have been more important in his change in behavior. The ethical lesson I draw from Dibbell's account—and it is a postmodern lesson—is that the remedy or solution to intolerable behavior in a community is not found in a process of formal decision-making or in an exercise of absolute authority but rather in the process of ongoing social interaction in which individuals take the responsibility of responding to one another and in which, as a result, the varying effects of the offense become available for conscious contemplation. This is not simply a matter of an individual's conforming to some antecedently decided upon conventions of the community, for, as the conclave made clear, there was no consensus within this community even about such basic questions as whether toading equates with death or banishment. Instead, "Mr. Bungle/Dr. Jest's" experience (which included people who attacked him and people who came to his aid and people who were interested in his intentions and his reactions) taught him that cyberspace offers no escape from the responsibilities of social life.

The lesson that postmodern ethics suggests for writing teachers faced with what they see as inappropriate behavior in electronic conversations is that rather than acting as wizards who enter the conversation only to lay down the law or to establish democratic decision-making procedures, they should put more trust in students' moral self-conscience and should engage in electronic conversations in such a way as to enable students to take up the chance to consciously consider and take responsibility for the effects their actions have on others. The transition in postmodernism in assumptions about knowledge, language, the self, power, and responsibility clearly implies a concurrent transition in the teacher's role in the writing classroom, whether electronic or face-to-face. Teachers who want their students to take responsibility for their positions will not try to set standards, lay down the law, or take responsibility themselves for everything that goes on in electronic conversations. Faigley notes: "Just as in Lyotard's postmodern condition of knowledge, the teacher's role as guarantor of authority—providing the 'metanarrative' that gives coherence—is disrupted when a class makes extensive use of electronic written discussions" (185). This "loss" of an authoritarian role can make teachers uneasy, and rightly so, for it can appear that the only alternative is to stand back and just let things happen as they will. But this is not the only alternative for teachers—again, it is clinging to modernist assumptions that makes it appear so—and, furthermore, what is happening, as I have also tried to suggest, is not entirely bad.

Classroom electronic conversations can be used as forums in which students learn how to be open to unassimilated otherness, learn how to take responsibility for others, and learn how paratactic juxtaposition of ideas and perspectives can lead to a better understanding of issues and problems that confront them. In order to move electronic conversations in this direction, writing teachers will have to give up their in loco parentis role of protecting students from and preventing inappropriate behavior.[2] Instead, they need to construct for themselves an authoritative role that does not rely on notions of knowledge, power, and responsibility as guaranteed by established hierarchies.

As a first step in defining such a role, we might consider Foucault's attempt to define his responsibilities as an intellectual:

My role is to address problems effectively, really: and to pose them with the greatest possible rigor, with the maximum complexity and difficulty so that a solution does not arise all at once because of the thought of some reformer or even in the brain of a political party. The problems that I try to address, these perplexities of crime, madness, and sex which involve daily life, cannot be easily resolved. It takes years, decades of work carried out at the grassroots level with the people directly involved; and the right to speech and political imagination must be returned to them. Then perhaps a state of things may be renewed, whereas in the terms by which it is being posed today, it could only lead to a dead-end. I carefully guard against making the law. Rather, I concern myself with determining problems, unleashing them, revealing them within the framework of such complexity as to shut the mouths of prophets and legislators: all those who speak for others and above others. It is at that moment that the complexity of the problem will be able to appear in its connection with people's lives; and consequently, the legitimacy of a common enterprise will be able to appear through concrete questions, difficult cases, revolutionary movements, reflections, and evidence. Yes, the object is to proceed a little at a time, to introduce modifications that are capable of, if not finding solutions, then at least of changing the givens of a problem. (Foucault 1991, 158-59)

Foucault's description of his method suggests a role for teachers like that described in the Freirian model by Ira Shor, where the teacher is "a problem-poser who leads a critical dialogue in class" (31). The intellectual's role and the teacher's role in this model is to help people understand the complexity of the problems that face them so that they can through patient grassroots action find ways to change at least some of the factors that are causing the problems. As Shor emphasizes, participation of students in their education—"the people directly involved" (Foucault 1991, 158)—"sends a hopeful message to students about their present and future; it encourages their achievement by encouraging their aspirations. They are treated as responsible, capable human beings who should expect to do a lot and do it well" (Shor, 21).

Shor describes a practice that balances the responsibilities of the teacher and the students. Teachers pose problems or present generative themes—they bring the complexities of everyday life into focus—and listen to student responses. From listening to students, Shor says, he learns "the centrality of certain themes in their lives, and re-present[s] them as problems for reflecting on the ordinary in an extraordinary way" (88). Listening to students is crucial in this practice, for, as Foucault suggests, it enables the teacher to unleash the complexity of problems as they connect to students' lives. In order to have "the legitimacy of a common enterprise," the re-presentation of student problems must focus on helping students become aware of the complexities and contradictions within their own discourse on and within their own experiences with the problems, rather than on explicating an official or authoritative perspective on the problem.

This is not to say that teachers should not offer their own perspective or other perspectives that are not known to students, but rather that these perspectives must be clearly connected with the students' experiences and must be offered as perspectives, not as the official or correct view. Enabling students to be conscious of the implications and effects of their positions so that they can take responsibility for them is different from asking students to be critical of their positions—but this can be a difficult distinction to maintain. Shor approvingly describes a "desocializing" history and English course on Columbus (118-23) that at some points moves beyond consciousness-raising into officially sanctioned critique. The course focused on the "Columbus myth" and offered students perspectives that had been left out of the history that they had encountered so far, and the teacher connected the theme with student experience by "discovering" one student's purse in class and proceeding to "claim" all its contents for his own. But the concluding work on this theme clearly indicated that the alternative perspectives and insights suggested by the teacher were not something for students to use to help them think about the complexities of Columbus' "discovery" of America, but rather were lessons to be learned. One of the "thinking questions" asks students, "Can you think of any groups in our society who might have an interest in people having an inaccurate view of history?" (121), and Shor concludes, "[the teacher] suggested that thinking about whose interest is served by lying about Columbus may desocialize students from the values such myths encourage" (122). Instead of enabling students to think about the logic of domination, to consider why and how and when some societies have sought to dominate others and why and how and when other societies have resisted such domination, such lessons ask students to accept what authorities tell them about domination and about particular incidents of domination. Rather than "revealing [problems] within the framework of such complexity as to shut the mouths of . . . all those who speak for others and above others," such lessons fall back on modernist assumptions about knowledge and ethical behavior deriving from authority and simply tell students that the beliefs and values they have been taught and have accepted are wrong.

What Bauman suggests instead is that it is depriving people of the chance to exercise their moral self-conscience that is wrong, and what Foucault suggests is that "the right to speech and political imagination must be returned to" those for whom the problem is a problem. Teachers (intellectuals) have an important role in helping students (people) become conscious of the complexities of the problems that face them, of helping them see the paratactic connections among diverse perspectives, but they cannot legitimately or effectively impose their own hypotactic structuring of the problems on students (others).

This consideration of a postmodern role for teachers suggests actions Faigley might have taken in his problematic pseudonymous electronic conversation. He might have asked students questions that would draw their attention to the problems raised by the positions they were taking—just as some of the students themselves were doing. I would be particularly interested in their saying more about exactly what monogamy means to them: Is monogamy the same as fidelity? Is it an absolute position you take once and for all or does it develop after some experience? Is it important in sexual relationships as well as in marriage? Is it a moral position or a pragmatic position based on fear of disease? Such a discussion, like the one that took place in the conclave in LambdaMOO, probably would not lead to a conclusion or any kind of consensus, but it would allow students to become aware of differences and of the implications and effects of their beliefs and values.

Because synchronous in-class electronic discussions contain many more strands than face-to-face class discussions and move so much faster, teachers have learned that, in order to allow for the kind of reflection that is necessary to reveal complexities, problems must be re-presented to students in succeeding discussions. These discussions can be conducted electronically or face-to-face or in individual writing, for there is no reason not to oscillate between the various media that operate to structure our transitional society. Teachers can bring transcripts of electronic conversations to class and ask students to talk about what happened in them—and everyone, especially the teacher, can be enlightened about the intentions and effects of what went on. Students can also be asked to respond in writing, individually or in groups, in hard copy or in further electronic conversations, to whole or partial transcripts of electronic conversations that have taken place in the class. And teachers can simply re-present in face-to-face class discussions problems that arose in electronic conversations.

In postmodern electronic conversations in writing classes, we in some ways witness the revenge of our advocacy of process, and the trick, if it is one, in using them productively is to continue the process of discussing and reflecting that they begin rather than regarding them as isolated events. As Foucault said later in his life, "Without a program does not mean blindness—to be blind to thought. In my opinion, being without a program can be very useful and very original and creative, if it does not mean without proper reflection about what is going on or without very careful attention to what's possible" (1987, 35).

NOTES

1.   My judgments about how entries are related to one another rest primarily on lexical and topical analyses of the comments: students often address the "person" they are responding to and they pick up topics and words from each others' entries. Like Faigley, I more or less arbitrarily assign gender to students based on the pseudonyms they use. I make no argument about the accuracy of these guesses, and I have tried not to depend on assumptions about gender in my analyses.
2.   I suspect it's still necessary for me to point out that I do not mean that teachers should tolerate inappropriate behavior in electronic or any other class conversations, but rather that teachers need to find new ways to deal with it.

Hyper-readers and their Reading Engines

James Sosnoski

N OT LONG AGO, I SENT A COLLEAGUE AT ANOTHER UNIVERSITY AN ELECTRONIC text of paper that had been posted on a listserv. The next day I received a message from him asking if I could mail him a printed version of the paper because he found reading lengthy texts on a computer screen an unpleasant experience. Though it was inconvenient, I sent him the requested printout. When I began to draft this essay a few days later, I was reminded of how often friends remark to me that they don't like to read from their monitors and I realized how telling an incident this was. Aversions to reading on screen, I suspect, are widespread; few persons of my acquaintance enjoy reading long texts on their monitors. Nonetheless, reading electronic texts on screens is likely to be the predominant mode of reading in the very near future. This essay reflects upon that possibility and the ways in which computer-assisted reading is already beginning to dominate our practices. Future advances in technology are likely to bring us pocket computers with the look and feel of books and to provide for us not only the text but also loads of complementary materials. This technology will probably begin with the conversion of heavy, unportable manuals, encyclopedias, and other reference works into disks which can easily fit into pocket computers not much heavier than most wallets.[1]

Leaving these possibilities aside, however, let us consider the computer-assisted reading we currently do. Most persons who work with word processing software read quite a bit from their computer screens and their reading is often of the book-length variety. Though many persons print out a final draft because they prefer to revise their work in print, they probably have read the texts they print out twenty or thirty times beforehand in the process of composing on the screen. If the trend continues, few persons will print out their own manuscripts in order to revise; but this is only "the tip of the iceberg" of change. There are innumerable other instances of screen-based reading and they are increasing at a rapid rate. Need I mention that the World Wide Web is a vast (hyper)text that we read with such increasing frequency that it has become difficult as the day wears on to dial up one's account in order to access the Web because so many of its readers are already online.

Though at present only a few persons read extensively from computer screens, their number will surely increase. I feel certain that many persons will come to prefer computer-assisted reading (CAR). Not only do I read my own work (this essay for example), but I also read the work of colleagues from my computer screen. Thousands of email messages arrive in my account, some of them papers sent to me from colleagues that I read as word-processing documents downloaded to my hard drive. Though I used to print long documents out, I no longer do so. In fact, I prefer reading them from my word-processing program because I usually am asked to comment on them and I like to insert comments in the file sent to me and return it to its author or editor. For me, computer-assisted reading infuses my work. For example, I wrote an article on the work of the same colleague who asked me for the printout of the paper I had emailed him. It was constructed by searching for "themes" common to his many essays and books which I was able to assemble quite rapidly since I had all of his work scanned into my computer. I used Zyindex, a commercial indexing program, to find everything he had said about the issues I planned to discuss. In this instance, Zyindex was a crucial extension of my reading act. This experience left an indelible and very positive impression on me. It would not be an exaggeration to say that it inspired this essay since my reading was extended by what is commonly known as a "search engine." This seems to be a type of reading which has emerged from our uses of the technologies of reading but little is known about it.

In "The Effect of Hypertext on Processes of Reading and Writing," Davida Charney reviews educational and psychological research on reading that bears on hypertexts, pointing out that "little research has been conducted of the actual effect of hypertext on reading" (250). Most of the research she surveys is based on reading print and she has to draw the implications from it for designers of hypertexts. But even in the research that is available on readers' responses to hypertexts, it should be noted that the research is conducted on hypertexts that are designed to accomplish a particular goal—usually to convey specific information to a target audience. The kind of computer-assisted reading to which I refer goes beyond situations in which persons access a "discrete" hypertext designed with them as a target audience, for instance "expository" hypertexts aimed at upper level college students which feature information related to course materials.[2] The essays published in online journals such as *Kairos* are instances of discrete hypertexts read on screen. I find that my own screen-based, computer-assisted reading practices go beyond these scenarios. Searching the Web is probably the best example. When I employ a search engine to deliver information for me on topics such as "cultural studies," my reading experience, as I visit the sites listed in the search results, is not so well defined as a visit to the *Kairos* or *InfoWorld* sites. The experience is closer to what Johndan Johnson-Eilola cautions us about in *Nostalgic Angels* or to what Geoffrey Sirc articulates in chapter ten of this book.

In Sirc's account, reading a teleintertext is not an event structured by the efforts of hypertext designers who attempt to create appropriate paths for readers.[3] This type of reading "allows for no logic—anything [that] comes across the screen is neutralized into electronic information. We are in a post-exchange-value-apocalypse in which the only value is use-value" (9) In such reading experiences, "Material is chosen not because it's a privileged text, a 'difficult' masterpiece from the "history of writing,' but because it's easily available. It's whatever you notice out of the corner of one's eye from the endlessly-shifting screen in front of you" (9). In "X-Ray Vision and Perpetual Motion: Hypertext as Postmodern Space," chapter five of his *Nostalgic Angels*, Johnson-Eilola describes the textuality of the reading experience to which I refer:

> The normal hierarchical arrangement of reading time regulating spatial movement becomes inverted in this articulation of postmodern space, with space portioning out time, regulating time (the time of the railway passenger). Thinking about hypertext in this way, readers are no longer reliant on the writer to lead them temporally from border to border in the span of a tale (Chaucer's travelers to Canterbury covering space with time); readers walk around, deconstruct and build, move over and under, exterior and interior. [4]

It seems fitting to refer to the practice of reading the postmodern space Sirc terms the "teleintertext" as "hyper-reading," However, we probably should introduce a distinction among hyper-readings that parallels Michael Joyce's distinction between exploratory and constructive hypertexts (41-42). The exploratory (or expository) hypertext is a "delivery or presentational technology" that provides ready access to information. By contrast, constructive hypertexts are "analytic tools" that allow writers to invent and/or map relations among bits of information to suit their own needs. The type of hyper-reading I describe here is "constructive." Understanding that when I use the expression "hyper-reading" in this essay, I refer to its "constructive" aspects, we can say that it differs from reading printed texts or expository hypertexts in several ways. Hyper-reading is characterized by: [5]

1. filtering: a higher degree of selectivity in reading [and therefore]
2. skimming: less text actually read
3. pecking: a less linear sequencing of passages read
4. imposing: less contexualization derived from the text and more from readerly intention
5. filming—the " . . . but I saw the film" response which implies that significant meaning is derived more from graphical elements as from verbal elements of the text
6. trespassing: loosening of textual boundaries
7. de-authorizing: lessening sense of authorship and authorly intention
8. fragmenting: breaking texts into notes rather than regarding them as essays, articles, or books [6]

In many anti-tech quarters, these differences will be perceived as losses. Though I am not of this opinion, I wish to remain alert to the limitations of hyper-reading which can be viewed in a number of contexts (for instance, in teaching research methods) as a loss of authorship, of coherence, of meaning, of depth, of context, and so on. In *Nostalgic Angels* Johndan Johnson-Eilola reminds us that "Dismantling the technology of the print book does not necessarily remove the social forces that articulated the classic book-text. Hypertext might be capable of orchestrating the reader/writer movement more effectively than a print text."[7] In this essay, however, I am concerned with the ways in which hyper-readers can "dismantle the technology of the print book." I subscribe to the notion that we live in a postmodern era and that we cannot operate on the conventions that governed the reading practices of previous generations.[8]

Baudrillard remarks that "We live in a world where there is more and more information, and less and less meaning (79).

Rather than creating communication, . . . [information] exhausts itself in the act of staging communication. Rather than producing meaning, it exhausts itself in the staging of meaning. A gigantic process of simulation that is very familiar. The nondirective interview, speech, listeners who call in, participation at every level, blackmail through speech: "You are concerned, you are the event, etc." More and more information is invaded by this kind of phantom content, this homeopathic grafting, this awakening dream of communication. A circular arrangement through which one stages the desire of the audience, the antitheater of communication, which as one knows, is never anything but the recycling in the negative of the traditional institution, the integrated circuit of the negative. Immense energies are deployed to hold this simulacrum at bay, to avoid the brutal desimulation that would confront us in the face of the obvious reality of a radical loss of meaning. (80)

Though Baudrillard makes his point in a somewhat hyperbolic manner, it is well taken. For example, presidential debates are no longer meaningful communications; they "stage the desires of their audiences" (e.g., lower taxes). One might add that public listservs more often stage performances of their discussants than meaningfully contribute to our understanding of the issues under discussion. Synchronous "talk" in computer labs, MUDS, MOOS, and interactive Internet games might be described as integrated circuits recycling in the negative of our institutional traditions. And, finally, the World Wide Web may be the ultimate "antitheater of communication." As Baudrillard puts it, "information devours it own content" (80). Because readers characteristically navigate textual landscapes by searching them for key words and thus often omitting passages that do not "match," hyper-reading will be labeled "subjective," "superficial," and "de-contextualized." The changes in academic writing and reading brought about by computing are a minefield for scholars. We need to locate these traps in order to make our paths navigable. The effort to chart viable routes through the wilderness of information that surrounds us will surely be worth our time and energy.

In what follows, I configure my hyper-reading practices as a way of delineating a new terrain for future investigations. Though I readily acknowledge that many persons do not like to read from their screens at this time, I assume that over a period of time, the practice will become so habitual that it will seem "natural"—just as it now seems customary to use a computer rather than a typewriter. Because I enjoy reading from my screen and prefer it to reading print, in my account, hyper-reading is a rewarding experience because it extends my ability to read. (I might add, for the record, that has not displaced my reading of printed texts.) After delineating the practice of computer-assisted reading, I balance the sunny picture I draw of the hyper-reading horizon by inserting some rain clouds, concluding with reflections on the implications of acquiring new habits of reading. I begin my sketch with the characteristics of constructive hyper-reading I listed above.

1. Filtering

Reading—of whatever sort—is a process of selection. To every text readers bring schema or framing notions that focus their attention on some but not all of the marked features of the text and which also supply non-linguistic clues not marked in the text.[9] If I believe a text is a romance, certain of its features stand out. If I believe it to be a drama, others do. Characters are given different postures in my imagination and certain passages leap up from the page or screen. The impact of such framing on readers is nicely captured in Stanley Fish's justly famous experiment recounted in *Is There a Text in this Class?* As he tells the story, Fish taught two courses back to back in the same classroom. The first was a course in linguistics and the second in 17th century poetry. As the students came into the poetry class, they saw what appeared to be a 17th century emblem poem on the blackboard. In fact, it was a list of linguists which happened accidentally to look like a cross. The inevitable occurred: the poetry class quite successfully read the list of names as if it were a poem providing anecdotal evidence for Fish's theses about reading communities. During this event Fish's students in their efforts to assemble a structure of meaning used a framework which was not "in" the text on the board in order to interpret its features. As inheritors of the work of Fish and other reading theorists, most teachers now readily admit that reading is a highly selective process, one in which the majority of details are forgotten, leaving the reader to be content with plot summaries, thumbnail characterizations, representative scenes, and themes, most of them memorable because they can be assimilated into what Frank Smith taught us to call "cognitive structures" (71).

Hyper-reading of the "constructive" variety is, in my experience, a more selective process than the reading of printed texts customarily allows. No matter where you align yourself in the debate about how much the text influences the reader over against how much is the text a subject of the reader's imagination, nonetheless the text is usually understood to provoke the selection of its details. In constructive hyper-reading, the selection criteria employed often govern the reader's interest before the texts are even found. Once these criteria are activated, readers can raid the texts uncovered by their search results in order to assemble their details as ANOTHER text which is, so to speak, re-authored by the reader. The extreme instance of such reading is a search engine. This statement requires a commentary before I can continue the argument in which it is embedded, so forgive me for digressing a bit . . . I expect my readers to object to my including a computer program in my description of the process of reading. So, let me offer some reasons why I believe it is necessary to do so.

When I read an encyclopedia, I search through its contents for the information I wish to obtain. If I were teaching someone how to read an encyclopedia, I would surely acquaint them with search techniques and encourage them to attend to the way the book is indexed. Were they not familiar with the roman alphabet, I would invite them to learn it since it is a cognitive map which is essential to reading an encyclopedia. The deployment of the alphabet as a cognitive map is intrinsic to the act of reading an encyclopedia. I mention this trivial matter because many of the cognitive frames we use in reading are so familiar as to appear to be trivial; but situations wherein a reader is not acquainted with them instantly reveal their non-trivial function in acts of reading. If you admit that sorting frameworks like the alphabet are an aspect of the cognitive process we call reading, then you would probably see the justice in saying that the index of a book is a crucial framework for reading it. One has only to attempt to retrieve the information you believe you have learned from a book without an index (and those pre-indexes we call tables of contents) to realize how significant key words are in processing the features of a text.[10] Now, to return to my argument.

Conceptual frameworks are crucial to reading acts because they allow for the selection of relevant textual details. An indexing program speeds up this characteristic reading activity by allowing readers to track the occurrence and reoccurrence of key terms. It's not that an indexing program does something that a person does NOT do; it merely does it faster, more thoroughly, and more systematically. It's a machine that extends our intellectual capacity in way parallel to the way eye glasses extend our sight.[11] The glasses do not see, we see. The index does not read, we read. However, in considering indexing as an extension of our reading acts, we need to acknowledge that we borrow a technique of reading (processing a text) from another reader of similar texts—the person who wrote the indexing program who built into it the principles of selectivity by which we search the text's features. When one thinks of surfing/reading the world-wide text we call the Web, using search engines to do so is indispensable. I believe we need to consider these programs as vital components in the engine of our CAR.

Hoping that you accept my personification of the programs like Zyindex when I describe such programs as the reading techniques of a designer, I'll now offer them as evidence for the claim I was making—that constructive hyper-reading (reader-directed, screen-based, computer-assisted reading) has a higher degree of selectivity than the print based, un-assisted reading we do away from our terminals. This claim can also be restated in a more phenomino-logical manner. Surfers of the Web who read its texts by using search engines like Yahoo select from its world-wide storehouse a very modest sample of texts from those available, albeit ones that are captured by the vested interests of the surfers. With respect to filtering, the scale introduced into our consideration of reading by instancing the Web is inordinate. To keep the issue in perspective, we need to remind ourselves that selectivity corresponds to relevance and therefore to the "reduction of uncertainty" upon which meaning depends (Smith 185).

2. Skimming

This brings me to a correlative aspect of hyper-reading—less of the text is actually read. The proportion of read text to un-read but available text is astro-nomical. Surfing the Web is "skimming" on a global scale. One might be tempted to think of this as a problem. In print environments there are contexts in which we tend to believe that one SHOULD read ALL of a stretch of text. Some readers (e.g., teachers) worry about other readers (e.g., students) who do not read all of the text. Conversely, some scholars brag that they have read "all" of Shakespeare or Milton or James Joyce. Obversely, persons sometimes con-fess that they read only the beginning of the book, or worse, only the ending. Yet skimming is an essential reading act.

The following anecdote suggests the usefulness of skimming in a print envi-ronment. I recall being jealous of a colleague whose questions at the end of every guest lecture implied that he had read the lecturer's most recent books. I never seemed to find the time. Then I realized that he skimmed them. By con-trast, I was saddled with readerly guilt when I skimmed a book; I felt that I had not read it, even though when I read the whole book, after a few months I only remembered its bare outlines. I felt less guilty, however, when I was working on an article and found hundreds of potentially relevant essays in innumerable journals and skimmed them to find only the information relevant to the issue I was discussing. Yet, to this day I have a compulsion to read every word of a printed book I begin to read. Perhaps I enjoy the Web because I feel less guilty surfing it for particular topics and reading only "at the surface."

When we consider the popularity of hypertexts, skimming takes on a whole new dimension. Hypertexts are designed for skimmers.[12] If you were to skim a printed book, you would probably look first at its table of contents, then its index and its bibliography, afterward read its introduction and its conclusion, and toward the end turn to an interesting chapter or pursue a conceptual thread or two. Hypertexts, like proposals, are designed so that such intelligent skimming is the norm which helps readers who have too much to read.

Permit me to end this section with another digression: I have always been astonished by the academic task of "keeping up with one's field" associated with the ideal of achieving expertise. One fatal summer when I decided I would not teach but catch up on my reading, I put together a modest reading list of books on literary theory. Anxious to keep up a reading routine that would insure getting through the list, I made the mistake of calculating the number of pages to be read and the number of hours of available reading time. When I matched these calculations to a sensible reading speed, I discovered that I could barely get through half the list and then only if I read at breakneck speed on an uninterrupted schedule. I should have skimmed them but I didn't. When Fall arrived all too soon, I went back to pecking as my customary school year mode of reading.

3. Pecking

Though I can no longer remember when or by whom, sometime during my education I was taught that skimming was bad but that pecking was worse, one a venial and the other a mortal sin on the occasion of reading. If you skimmed a text, you missed its details but followed its structure and at least came away with a sense of how the text cohered, sometimes a more cogent sense of the whole than readers who got lost its details could derive. But, if you pecked at a text, reading randomly, sometimes here, sometimes there in no particular sequence, then you had no hope of discovering the text's coherence.

The coherence of the text is usually regarded as a crucial issue. For persons trained in formalism and for their students, texts are "organic unities." Writers are taught to strive for coherence and readers expect it. If a textual detail does not fit in to the text's semantic network, writers remove it and readers find it a flaw. Good writing is often distinguished from bad writing on the grounds of coherence. Readers rank texts on the criteria of semantic harmony.

For most readers, incoherent texts are unintelligible. But, we might ask, who establishes what coheres with what? The author(s) or the reader(s)? Obviously, not all texts need to be read in the same way. Reading reference works contrasts with reading the single-authored, unified texts whose coherence is deemed to be the consequence of the insightful ordering of a writer's intention. As the research Charney reviews confirms, the more the intended structure can be discerned, the greater the corresponding sense the text makes (238). By comparison, the order of essays in a reference work corresponds to the conventions that facilitate the retrieval of the information desired by the person who consulted it. The coherence of "the text" in constructive hyper-reading—as in the use of reference works—is more the result of the reader than of the writer. As a consequence, pecking is an entirely suitable technique. In constructive hyper-reading the reader governs the reading and imposes coherence by reassembling textual fragments as a newly created text that often displaces the intention the authors of the textual fragments incorporated in it may have had.

4. Imposing

For years, reading theorists argued vehemently about whether the reader or the text played the greater role in determining meaning. The most notorious moment in those debates was the publication of Stanley Fish's essay, "Who's Afraid of Wolfgang Iser?" Fish, the primary advocate of the position that the reader constituted the text challenged Iser's more balanced view—the text guides the reader. Hyper-reading is not likely to renew this debate. In constructive hyper-reading, there is no doubt that the reader is in charge and that the text is subservient to the reader's wish. Such hyper-readers impose their frameworks on the texts they peruse. Yet, this is not the scandal it seemed to be when some reading theorists argued that readers create the literary texts they read. A simple analogy shows why. Hyper-readers of the Web parallel readers of telephone books (as the Internet Yellow Pages CD ROM invites us to believe). Pages on the Web are not held in the high esteem that pages of Shakespeare or Milton have been. Consequently, to regard them as information is quite common and in most cases more than justified. Just as telephone books hold little significance until they are queried for a relevant address, so the information available on the Web holds little significance until a hyper-readers search it for items relevant to their inquiries. Granting that queries impose significance on the pages of the Web, do they impose meaning? Taking a somewhat moderate stance, I would argue that readers do not create the meaning of electronic texts any more than they create the meaning of printed texts but that they do make them significant. By framing texts, readers assimilate them to their interests and hence render them significant in the context of their concerns. The significance of the text, in this sense, is more important than its "meaning." This can be most readily seen when hyper-readers abandon reading book length e-texts or articles from beginning to end and query them for data relevant to their reSEARCH. In this respect, we encounter what Umberto Eco refers to in *The Role of the Reader* as "unlimited semiosis"(193ff). Many academics will regard this as a loss of meaning parallel to seeing the film instead of reading the novel.

5. Filming—" . . . but I saw the film"

In his history of film, Kracauer comes close to arguing that superior films have more images than words. In instances where films are made from novels or plays, pictures translate many of their words. The ratio of image to word is, of course, quite different in novels and films. A similar remark can be made about hyper-reading. In the construction of hyper(media)texts—regardless of their significance—graphics often play a more meaningful role than words. Hyper-readers turn the graphics on web pages into virtual montages using conventions similar to cinematic ones (probably learned from countless hours of watching TV and film). And, as the Internet expands, graphical elements will be constructed with such hyper-readers in mind just as good photographers compose their pictures with specific viewers in mind (see Bernhardt on "graphically rich" hypertexts, 168-170). As I mentioned above, some persons will regard the tendency in hyper-readers to prefer graphical to verbal elements when deriving meaning or significance from web pages as a loss of conceptual depth. Nor is it surprising that persons weaned on literature should find texts with fewer words than pictures less likely to contain "serious" ideas. This, I believe, is a prejudice.

At this juncture, I should note that in the next three sections the act of hyper-reading becomes almost indistinguishable from the act of writing. Constructive hyper-readers are de-facto hyper-writers because they tend to assemble the texts they read. This qualifies, I suspect, as trespassing the boundaries we usually assign to the categories "literature" (reading) and "composition" (writing).

6. Trespassing

From my childhood, I remember Halloween as a night of trespass—of wrongful entry into the lands of another—because in the coal mining town where I grew up, trick or treaters who were not treated often went around to alley behind the offending house, entered the back yard and dumped the garbage can over, spilling the trash on the rear garage driveways. But probably the most familiar instance of trespass is burglary—the felony of breaking into and entering the house, office, etc., of another with the intent to steal. Hyper-readers are textual burglars. They break into electronic texts and once they have found the source codes hidden from sight, steal them away with their cut&paste tools and reassemble them (minus the serial numbers so to speak) in their own home pages. As Sirc implies in his chapter, hyper-readers are ardent plagiarists. The situation is so bad among hyper-readers that copyright lawyers have been called in to adjudicate the boundaries of texts.

7. De-authorizing

Many authors believe that they own their texts, that texts should rightfully be considered their intellectual property. For them, it probably seems sinful that constructive hyper-readers tend to dismiss such rights and regard texts as belonging to the public but hyper-readers sin even more grievously. By virtually reassembling texts, they dismiss the authors' intentions by replacing them with their own, thus de-authorizing texts altogether. This phenomenon can be seen on most websites. Every link to another person's page is an implicit act of de-authorization.[13] As hyper-readers read these linked pages, they cannot keep in their minds who authored which pages. It's like reading a Russian novel with a cast of thousands and not being able to remember which character is which. It is difficult in hyper-reading to attribute authorship to the pages being read. When hyper-readers arrive at websites, they often have no idea who may have authored the pages and in many cases the pages have no signatures and no imprimaturs.

If style is the hallmark of the writer's personality and a signature the legal bond of identity, then hyper-reading undercuts the personal aspects of authorship. Hypertexts are not given the same authority as printed ones because textual signatures become blurred in the unending surge of inter-textuality called the World Wide Web. The authority of a text usually depends upon the certification of its "signatured" authorship. It is assumed that a particular publisher certifies the authority of its authors on the basis of its standing (identity) in the reading community it serves. ("This must be a good book as it was published by Oxford University Press.") As self-publishers in the world-wide vanity press known as the Web, hyper-readers publish innumerable un-authorized intertexts. Because hyper-readers are invariantly hyper-writers of one type or another, they de-author the texts they read in the process of re-authoring them. The certification process is bypassed partly because the imprimatur controlled by institutions of publication can no longer easily be bestowed on the writer's signature. What is worse, books and essays are being torn to bits.

8. Fragmenting

For many years, the format of academic inquiry in the humanities has been the article. New forms of academic writing are clearly emerging, and they are tied to hyper-reading. If hyper-reading were not a way to manage the information glut, then collaborative hypertexts would not dominate the reading scene on the Web. Considering that HTML or SGML code can reproduce printed texts in formats identical to printed essays and considering that it is easier to reproduce a printed text in its native format than to convert it to a hypertext, one probably should conclude that the labor-intensive efforts of web-spinners to change printed texts into hypertexts is a response to hyper-reading practices and that the persons who read the Web prefer to read hypertexts. In other words, hyper-readers, especially constructive ones, may prefer fragmented texts to lengthy linear ones. But there is more to this issue than meets the eye.

If the developers of Storyspace, Jay Bolter, Michael Joyce, John Smith, and Mark Bernstein, are correct in believing that "fragments of text" or "notes" arranged by associative patterns correspond to the cognitive structures readers habitually use (Joyce 31ff.), then the conventional ways of structuring essays are likely to give way to more cognitively resonant ways of reading.[14] In other words, many hyper-readers may be more comfortable selecting textual details and reassembling them in their own virtual frameworks than using the frameworks imposed upon them. If we consider the structure of an argument from the viewpoint of Toulminian informal logic (Given X, if Y, then Z), it appears to be a way of forcing a reader to link specific items of information as an inferential chain (data > warrant > claim). We can consider such inference patterns to be mechanisms of selection in the sense that the data becomes relevant (is selected as evidence) in light of the warrant. In other words, warrants get the reader to select certain textual details as relevant to a thesis. From this point of view, one might argue that the traditional modes of organizing essays are devices to get readers to combine particular textual details into memorable patterns (see Charney, 242ff.). In this context, essays are written to satisfy readers' cognitive structures and to make the ideas of their author's memorable. It should not surprise us, then, if hyper-readers feel liberated from the constraints of such textual guidelines and feel that they are now free to organize textual features in patterns relevant to their own concerns whether logical, topological, or associative. Such textual flexibility is valuable and hypertexts tend to provide it. Hyper-readers, if they are of the constructive variety like me, tend to fragment the texts they read so that they can reassemble them virtually (or actually) in order to satisfy motives germane to their reading activities.

I hope you can discern in my account of these eight traits of hyper-reading specific advantages for readers of all sorts. When construed apocalyptically as "the end of reading as we know it," hyper-reading may appear likely to replace reading printed texts. I believe that a more sensible view sees hyper-reading, whether exploratory or constructive, as another way of reading (and writing) which is not likely to supplant the ones we already have since they accomplish different objectives. At this historical juncture, we need to remind ourselves of the gloomy forecasts of the end of the novel that came with the advent of film, the end of radio with advent of television, the end of bookstores with the advent of electronic texts. Though I welcome the advent of hyper-reading, I do see some rain clouds on its horizon.

RAIN CLOUDS ON THE HORIZON

What I see as a likely rain cloud is a conflict over how we theorize hyper-reading. In English departments, almost from the outset, work in electronic environments followed the fault lines of the old division between "lit/comp" as contrasting listservs, forums, and electronic journals began to spring up. One of the first major listservs where pedagogy was discussed was Megabyte University, which stood somewhat in contrast to another popular listserv at that time, TechnoCulture, where postmodern literary theory was invoked. I believe this pattern has continued. Two contrasting styles of theorizing seem to dominate considerations of cyberspace—a contrast I would name "pedagogical" and "postmodern." I do not believe that the concerns that provoke such contrasting theoretical styles are as yet well integrated. Theorists like Baudrillard are too speculative to be used as the basis of an electronic pedagogy and thus stand out as a "literary" interpretation of the World Wide Web as a "media" phenomenon. At the time I am writing, the circumstance that postmodern and pedagogical concerns are not well integrated in views of cyberspace as a "work environment" is not a problem, but it could become one.

Were proponents of electronic environments to use speculative theorems to evaluate hyper-reading practices—for example, postmodern conceptions of cyberspace that can be derived from the work of Baudrillard, I believe that hyper-reading would appear to imply the destruction of scholarly reading practices. Speculative theories about cyberspace and virtuality such as Baudrillard's tend to suggest more radical departures from our current norms than seem, at least to me, warranted. If we discussed hyper-reading in such terms, it would, I believe, have consequences in our academic forums not unlike the consequences deconstructive theorems have had subsequent to the 1966 Hopkins Symposium—scholars quickly divided institutionally into orthodox and heterodox groups. This led to the theory wars—to my mind one of the least productive periods in the history of English departments. Given the comp/lit split in many departments, it seems predictable that, as hyper-reading becomes a more significant feature of the work that goes on in English departments, clashes over its value will surely force realignments (but, in the last analysis, largely renew old hostilities). I do not mean to suggest that literature faculties will on the whole become proponents of postmodern views such as Baudrillard's and composition faculties will refuse such postmodern assumptions as incompatible with their pedagogies. On the contrary, I believe—as I mentioned in the beginning of this essay—that phenomenon such as hyper-reading will be perceived by anti-cybernauts as a loss of coherence, substance, and depth. Postmodern speculations about cyberspace can easily become rebuttal targets in arguments against practices such as hyper-reading by advocates of textual coherence, unity, and structure. In this scenario, my guess is that the pedagogical theorizing about electronic environments will, for the most part, be ignored and the battles will be fought over the potential loss of "norms" that provide "discipline."

So, how should we theorize hyper-reading?

CONCLUSION

I do not believe we need a "THEORY" of hyper-reading, even one that has a nice balance between speculation and pedagogy. This does not mean that we do not need to theorize hyper-reading. Quite the contrary. As Gail Hawisher suggested to me in her comments on an earlier draft of this essay, we need a *praxis* for hyper-reading. Relying on James Porter's *Internetworked Writing* she writes:

> I envision "praxis" as being somewhere between practice and theory—actually a thought-ful form of practice. Let me quote Porter here. He writes, "Praxis is more than a simple addition of or compromise between theory and practice; it represents a new kind of critical positioning. It is a practice, conscious of itself, that calls upon 'prudential reasoning' for the sake not only of production but for 'right conduct' as well. It is informed action, as well as politically and ethically conscious action that in its functioning overlaps practical and productive knowledge."

Hyper-reading, as I've characterized it, is an ongoing practice. To develop a theory of hyper-reading—meaning an integrated set of concepts that describe it—seems to me to be a trap. It would commit the persons with academic investments in the subject to an effort similar to the one both compositions and literary critics have made to articulate a "paradigm" of writing or reading. Paradigmatic theories no longer seem viable. One of the difficulties scholars of reading and writing face in their work that surfaced as a result of the explosion of theories about these practices is that no theory emerged as the "victor." This is indeed quite perplexing. Nor does there seem to be any convenient way to stop the flood of available theories unless one adopts the somewhat nihilistic view of postmodern thinkers like Baudrillard. Yet alternatives to such nihilism can be sought.

There seems to be an emerging network of teachers and scholars who work in educational electronic environments. They have been trained in both literature and composition programs and share with each other an interest in the technologies of reading and writing as teachers. Thus, persons interested in hyper-reading (or the reading/writing process for that matter) might find solace in pedagogical praxis. We could focus our energies on teaching others how to be hyper-readers. This can be done without recourse to a "general field theory" of hyper-reading since it only commits us to "thoughtfully" showing others how we do what we do. The test of our teaching practices would simply be whether our students could learn to hyper-read in the ways we do but as a "politically and ethically conscious action." Such an endeavor would change as the technology changes but this is a situation already familiar to any hyper-reader. Yet this tactic leaves a huge question open. Why hyper-read? The answer to this question is tied to another—what work are you doing? Doing one's work well, I believe, involves the praxis Porter advocates but does not require a generalized filed theory of an institutionalized subject matter.

I began this essay with an anecdote about a colleague who found reading from his computer screen to be a disagreeable experience and preferred to read printed materials. Though this essay has focused on what can be accomplished by the hyper-reading we already do (however reluctantly), I do not believe that the constructive hyper-reading experiences I have described will displace reading print. Nor do I believe they will replace the more structured reading we do of hypertexts designed to make context specific information available to us. I am inclined to predict that the sort of enjoyment I experience in hyper-reading will become common. The pleasure of reading is often associated with aesthetic experiences—the look and feel of a well made book, the comfort of a favorite chair, the crackle of a fire on a winter night as one reads a novel. Such aesthetic dimensions are not yet easily available in computer assisted reading. However, I notice some striking (though local) changes in the reading practices of at least one of my colleagues that make me confident in my prediction. Five or six years ago, I sat in my favorite reading chair in my book lined study comfortably reading from my portable computer. My friends and family were amazed. This winter I notice that my wife now often reads her own writing in bed while revising on her Thinkpad whose "awakening music" she "just loves."

NOTES

I thank Gail Hawisher for reading this manuscript in an earlier draft. Her suggestions have led to substantial improvements in this essay.

1. As Davida Charney notes in "The Effect of Hypertext on Processes of Reading and Writing," "Thus far, the most common application of hypertext has been for computer manuals, encyclopedias, or guide books, providing readers with immediate access to definitions of key terms, cross-references, graphic illustrations, or commentary from previous readers" (239). Since such texts have already proved most suitable to hypertextual formatting, it seems likely that they will also be among the first to made available for pocket sized computer books which are still in the experimental stage.

2. Most of the studies Charney reviews feature such expository hypertexts (252-255).

3. Charney's research concern in "The Effect of Hypertext on Processes of Reading and Writing"is captured in one of her subtitles: "Can Hyertext Designers Create Appropriate Paths for Readers?" The research she cites hinges upon this possibility and the effort is to discover which cognitive structures are "appropriate" to specific materials and identifiable audiences. The reading experience with which I am concerned in this essay is one in which readers use the cognitive frameworks or schema which they bring to the reading experience in place of the ones provided for them. In such reading experiences, readers assimilate bits of information into the schema which pertains to their own worldviews. Examples of such reading would be: reading word processing files with the aid of searching, indexing, outlining, bookmarking, and linking tools; reading a database through boolean search techniques; browsing randomly through a hypermedia text; reading electronic mail or notes; reading while randomly surfing the World Wide Web. In each of these instances, the reader's motives provide the "structure" of the reading acts rather than the writer's or designer's motive.

4. The text I have quoted is gleaned from Johndan Johnson-Eilola's website featuring *Nostalgic Angels* <http://tempest.english.purdue.edu/NA/na.html>. It seems "appropriate" to mention that I was not able to obtain a printed copy of *Nostalgic Angels* from Von's, the beloved Purdue bookstore, and had to have recourse to Johndan's website.

5. The argument of this essay (that constructive hyper-reading can be described in the terms listed) should be understood as a configuration, that is, as a phenominological description of my experience, generalized in a manner that invites concurrence. In effect, I am asking the readers of this essay if my description of hyper-reading matches their experience. If it does, then our concurrence becomes a basis for the articulation of a problematics of hyper-reading. See "Configuring" in *Token Professionals and Master Critics* and "Explaining, Justifying, and Configuring" in *Modern Skeletons in Postmodern Closets.*

6. In "The Shape of Text on Screen" (CCC 44, 151), Stephen Bernhardt suggests ten features of texts constructed to be read online: situationally embedded, interactive, functionally mapped, modular, navigable, hierarchically embedded, spacious, graphically rich, customizable, and publishable. These features correspond roughly to the aspects of hyper-reading I delineate. Although Bernhardt focuses on the online text rather than the reader, it is useful to note that his delineation

of hypertextual features parallels my experience of hyper-reading, especially since I did not employ his categories as the basis of my descriptors.

7.   <http://tempest.english.purdue.edu/NA/na.html>

8.   In the research that Charney reviews, for example, the questions posed are variants of: "Can readers make appropriate selections of what and how much to read? Can readers create appropriate sequences of textual material? If readers are unable to navigate a hypertext effectively, can hypertext designer-writers reasonably anticipate readers' various needs and create appropriate paths to satisfy them?" (250). At the same time, she acknowledges the limitations of these queries when she writes: "I am skeptical that a hypertext designer, even under ideal conditions, can anticipate all the paths that readers may wish to create within and between texts. As we have seen, a wide range of factors influence the appropriateness of a sequence for a given reader, including the reader's prior knowledge of the domain, the reader's task or purpose for reading, the reader's learning style, and the nature of the information itself. Because of the huge number of possible combinations of such factors, the array of alternative paths that a designer might create becomes a practical impossibility and there still remains the problem of directing the right readers to the right paths." (258) Notice the assumption that there are "right" paths. This assumption privileges the writer's motives in creating the text over the reader's motives for reading it because it is the writers or designers who finally decide what readers need to obtain the meaning offered by them. Though these assumptions are efficacious in studying reading for information, they do not correspond well to the sort of reading Sirc describes, in which the material is chosen because it is easily available and suits the motive of the reader which may be simply to be entertained. Charney tends to see designers of hypertexts that allow for the free play of the readerly imagination as "romantic." Yet, "serious" readers may dismantle texts organized to obtain specific arrays of information (which are therefore arranged in semantic hierarchies) for motives that belong only to them (which do not correspond to the hierarchies inscribed in the text). In a print environment, for example, a Foucault scholar may wish to read the text's "margins." In either environment, a scholar may be interested in articulations of a particular concept removed from its contexts. In this case, the reader could use the entire corpus of a particular writer AS IF it were a dictionary, that is, a source of definitions. In such cases, texts become information in the radical sense—discrete bits of meaning unrelated to each other—which readers RE-write, that is, re-assemble into schema of their own. This type of reading—searching for the articulation of a particular concept—is facilitated by reading machines such as search engines and disregards the textual structures provided by the writer or designer.

9.   Charney writes "Many cognitive theories assume that much of the knowledge in long-term memory is organized around such hierarchical frameworks (referred to in various theories as schemes, frames, or scripts) that capture familiar patterns among elements. There may be schemes for events, for genres of text, for characteristics of a species, for the elements in a system." Though some psychologists, she notes, "reject the schema as a cognitive mechanism, that is, as a way to formalize or model the way in which encountering a familiar proposition reliably evokes a pattern of related propositions. Neither Kintsch nor other psychologists, however, will dispute the consistently observed behaviors that schemes are

meant to capture. Regardless of what cognitive mechanism is ultimately selected as the best formalism for the phenomenon, the concept of a script or schema remains a useful one" (246).

10. Charney notes that many researches find that "it is easier to read comprehend, and remember a text if it contains an informative title headings, overviews, and topic sentences introducing key concepts that are repeated and developed in successive portions of text" (245).

11. Johndan Johnson-Eilola reminds us in *Nostalgic Angels* that books are machines for transmitting authority and that technology often performs the same social function. In my example, authority can be transmitted more systematically and thoroughly and the technology in this case may simply automate authorization in ways that are hardly liberating.

12. Issues of text embedding, navigability, hierarchy discussed by hypertext theories like Stephen Bernhardt's ("The Shape of Text on Screen") assume that hyper-readers skim electronic texts.

13. My view on this matter clashes somewhat with Johndan Johnson-Eilola's, who cites Eagleton, Baudrillard, and Moulthrop to the effect that "In this apparent subversion of print, the fluid, open nature of hypertext (the attributes that seem the most in opposition to print text) may actually be even more conservative than other media, which can not as easily subsume critique and resistance. By partly naming its inadequacies, an ideology may be able to "tighten rather than loosen its grip" with a self-deprecating honesty that appears to acknowledge its own flaws by showing a "limited degree of ironic self-awareness" that can mask and/or subvert important struggles." I suspect that in the question of academic authorization, the Web diminishes authorial authority. On the Web it is often impossible to tell whose "work" is on the page you are reading. At least at this moment, academic work on the Web is not entirely governed by institutional practices. At the Crossroads Conference in the summer of 1996, there was considerable discussion about the scholarly merits of any given web resource, making it clear that the sort of authorization that exists for publications in print environments does not translate easily to electronic ones. Until copyright issues are settled, if that is ever to be possible, the author's authority will probably not be entirely creditable.

14. This view has been challenged. See Charney, 240ff. However, there seems to be abundant evidence that hypertexts are growing in popularity and scope—e.g., the increase in websites that are not designed by professionals. This certainly suggests some correlation between reader's cognitive makeup and a less "linear" linkage between textual components, which is not to say that structured ("expository") hypertexts do NOT suit our cognitive makeup. The question this debate raises for me is whether, since logical formalities do not match the cognitive sequences that generate them, any essayistic formalities correspond (in a phenomenological sense) to cognitive activity.

CHAPTER TEN

"What is Composition . . . ?" After Duchamp
(Notes Toward a General Teleintertext)

Geoffrey Sirc

1. By all means, let's start with Duchamp (as all twentieth century composition already does, consciously or not). Particularly, as this is in part a story of seemingly failed writing, writing which doesn't win prizes, let's start with some of Duchamp's failures. I can think of three right off: First, coming home in a taxi, March 1912, with a painting that was supposed to . . . well, not win prizes, of course. It couldn't have. It was his "Nude Descending a Staircase," and the show where it was to be exhibited was in Paris at the Société des Artistes Indépendants. The slogan of this salon, open to anyone, was *ni récompense ni jury,* so there were no prizes to win, no panels to award them. But even if there had been, Duchamp was out of the running before the show began. A 1953 catalogue from the Musée d'Art Moderne refers to the story: "1912. March-April. Paris. 28th Salon des Indépendants. Gleizes, Le Fauconnier, Léger, Metzinger and Archipenko, members of the hanging committee, turn it into a great demonstration of cubism" (Lebel 10). Duchamp's "Nude" was a sort of culmination; he'd taken cubism as far as it interested him. He was at the time moving out of, away from, that particular school of painting; it implied a technology, an aesthetic, a certain problem-set and certain materials, with which he'd grown bored. The show's hanging committee must have thought . . . a cubist nude? This is a joke, non? And one they certainly didn't want played on their *great demonstration.* So Gliezes convinces Duchamp's brothers to get him to withdraw it. He does, and riding home in the cab, with this amazing work next to him, he feels some bitterness, surely, but vindication, as well, knowing he succeeded in almost animating Cubism, turning his canvas into a machine. "Just the same," he smiles, "it moves" (Lebel 9). Then there was the Big Show of 1917, the American counterpart to the Indépendants. Another show which was supposedly open to anyone, but another show which refused one of Duchamp's works—this one, the urinal called "Fountain." That non-prize-winning piece, taken to Stieglitz's studio, photographed (inscribed on glass), and then mysteriously disappearing—its photographic representation alone is enough to ensure its central place in twentieth-century art history. And finally, the later Duchamp, the one who has since left behind the stylistic nostalgia of painting's cult of technique (its mystic craftsmanship) to pursue the mechanical processes of "precision oculism," there at a French trade fair in the 1930s, trying to sell even one of his "Rotoreliefs", those fascinating revolving spirals, made for a kind of optical massage, to transport perception to another place. But his project fails. Roché recalls the scene with a certain smug glee:

> None of the visitors, hot on the trail of the useful, could be diverted long enough to stop [at Duchamp's booth]. A glance was sufficient to see that between the garbage compressing machine and the incinerators on the left, and the instant vegetable chopper on the right, this gadget of his simply wasn't useful.
>
> When I went up to him, Duchamp smiled and said, "Error, one hundred per cent. At least, it's clear."
>
> These "Rotoreliefs" have since become collectors' items. (84-85)

Ah, that Marcel. Even in chronicling his failures, we simply chart his success. But yet each failing must have been felt acutely. "Given that . . . ; if I suppose I'm suffering a lot." (*Salt Seller* 23). Failure intense enough, for instance, to necessitate inscribing a lament in the "Glass." Lebel reminds us of a note to that effect scrawled in "The Green Box", concerning the disillusioned litanies of the glider: "Slow life. Vicious circle. Onanism. Horizontal. Return trips on the buffer. The trash of life. Cheap construction. Tin, ropes, wire. Eccentric wooden pulleys. Monotonous fly-wheel. Beer professor.' All these terms express a single one: *ÉCHECS*, which Duchamp, with his instinct for inner meanings, seems in some way to have made his motto" (67).

Échecs, we are reminded, is the French term for "checks" and "failures," as well as "chess." For Duchamp, chess was "like constructing a mechanism . . . by which you win or lose" (*Salt Seller* 136). So *chess*, as *failure/success*, both in accordance, delayed, in check. Motto, indeed.

Like many, I'm interested in Duchamp. I'm interested, for example, in failures that really aren't, in works barred from gaining the prize which end up changing the world. Brief, personal jottings that become a litany for posterity; the apparently impoverished composition that proves a rich text. I'm interested in Duchamp the way I'm interested in certain writing, writing done by anyone-whoever: useless, failed, nothing-writing by some nobody that turns out to be really something. I'm interested in what Duchamp reveals about our era, the Modernist era, specifically in the way Modernism is institutionalized in our culture. And, in the way Duchamp, almost from the start, offered an alternative Modernism, one that constantly put in *check* forms, materials, and contexts. I would like in this writing, then, to use Duchamp as a way to wonder about the particular hold Modernism has in my field, the field of composition. I want to do this through an *allegorical appearance* of my field's story with another field's similar story—the story of art after Duchamp, the story of how alternative technologies can change fundamental compositional questions. To represent Modernism in our field, I'll draw heavily on an article by David Bartholomae, "What is Composition and Why Do We Teach It?"—an article that exists as his attempt at the field's self-definition. I choose Bartholomae because I feel he manifests some of the most committed thinking about students and writing in our literature, but thinking which nevertheless results in the persistence of a very specific compositional program. The limitations of that program I find not so surprising, given that Modernism is all about limits, but—and this is my central point—they may be limits we no longer want to define our composition. Increasingly, we have different compositional means available: new tools for the mechanical reproduction of texts and an on-going electronic salon in which to circulate them. Materially, Modernism delimits choice, fixed as it is on a certain work with certain materials; Duchamp didn't:

> [I]f you can find other methods for self-expression, you have to profit from them. It's what happens in all the arts. In music, the new electronic instruments are a sign of the public's changing attitude toward art.... Artists are offered new media, new colors, new forms of lighting; the modern world moves in and takes over, even in painting. It forces things to change naturally, normally. (Cabanne 93)

Painting was simply "a means of expression, not an end in itself" (*Salt Seller* 127). Modernist Composition, I would argue, seeks to define its ends in terms of narrowly-conceived means (or better, conceives of its means according to limited ends), despite the modern world's take-over.

2. In "What is Composition?" Bartholomae defines the enterprise as "a set of problems" located, mostly institutionally, around notions of "language change," specifically as those notions affect the "writing produced by writers who were said to be unprepared" (11). Bartholomae, here as elsewhere in his writings, structures his analysis of this set of problems around a few student papers—in this case, two essays from Pittsburgh student writing competitions and a travel-narrative, written in Bartholomae's introductory composition course, concerning a trip to St. Croix the writer took as member of a religious youth-group. The problem-set Bartholomae theorizes through these papers concerns his general project, using textual artifacts to articulate "the sources and uses of writing, particularly writing in schooling, where schooling demands/enables the intersection of tradition and the individual talent" (12). Bartholomae focuses first on a prize-winning essay, an academic account of Pittsburgh's steel industry, which he considers "too good, too finished, too seamless, too professional" (13); he wants to open up the "official disciplinary history" to "other possible narratives" (13), suggesting this essay reads as if it were "assemble[d] . . . according to a master plan" (14). Seeming, then, to dismiss "official" composition—which would only ask of a student's revision that it "make [the writing] even more perfectly what it already is" (14), and presenting himself as a teacher who would allow a student to fracture open the text,

making it "less finished and less professional" (14)—Bartholomae ultimately disappoints, championing no more than a personally-preferred version of official composition: one whose patina may be more transgressive, more outlaw, but is still charged with academic cachet. Analogically, Bartholomae would see "official" writing instruction as preparing student-artists for their juried show by having them dutifully perfect quaint, realistic sketches of traditional subject matter (in this case, simplistic renderings of St. Croix's local color); he offers instead revision as a series of treatments—a different master plan—that will complicate the sketch into a more daring work, a proto-Picasso, say. This new program nonetheless maintains the traditional compositional space—the space on the page where the work is done, the space on the wall where it is hung and judged—a space where the writer graduates from dilettante to artist, "the space where the writer needs to come forward to *write* rather than *recite* the text that wants to be written" (14, emphasis mine). Despite his distinction between those two verbs, in both scenarios the composition stands prior to the writer, as known, as already-written in all but the actual writing. The St. Croix paper, then, is student-writing-degree-zero, which needs a hipper make-over, a re-modeling around a better style—that of Mary Louise Pratt's travel narratives. The preferred prose being politically more acute, a variety of cultural-studies heuristics (like "Whose interests are served?" [27]) are brought to bear on the naive narrative in order to enhance it. The juried competition is not questioned, merely the taste operative among current judges, i.e., the way "we give awards to papers we do not believe in and . . . turn away from papers we do, papers most often clumsy and awkward but, as we say to each other, ambitious, interesting" (16). The language is still the connoisseur's, now claiming vanguard status. Bartholomae can maintain a distinction between himself and most composition (with its "same old routine" [16]), but outside of his specific compositional space, in the space of composition-in-general—where Bartholomae is compared to, say, William Burroughs—such distinctions become moot.

So, we first must speak of prized composition. For Duchamp, art was to be rid of privilege. "No jury, no prizes," became the slogan of the American Independents, as well, of which Duchamp was a founding member. The rules for their Society stated "Any artist, whether a citizen of the United States or any foreign country, may become a member of the Society upon filing an application therefor, paying the initiation fee and the annual dues of a member, and exhibiting at the exhibition in the year that he joins" (de Duve "Given" 190). Any artists today who want their work displayed now have an electronic exhibition-site. Though the initiation fee and the annual dues may be different, in many respects the Internet is the contemporary version of the Society of Independent Artists, a virtual museum-without-walls, a public salon open to anyone. But the academy, now as then, stands all too unaffected by the techno-democratization of the cultural space for composition. No jury, no prizes? Composition is all about prized writing, about what makes writing good; its scene, as shown in "What is Composition," always originates in a juried competition. Any artist eligible? Clearly not, for Bartholomae's theory works a very specialized field, *our field*, "writing in schooling," particularly that flashpoint, "the point of negotiation between a cultural field and an unauthorized writer" (12). There is no utopic dissembling about, say, Beuys' dream, that "fundamental thesis: every human being is an artist" (qtd. de Duve *Kant* 284). Some artists will simply not be hung, and art, for institutionalized composition, is defined by exhibition-value. But Bartholomae's description of the juried scene delineates the hollow folly of judging in the academy:

> Another prize-winning essay in a university contest, an essay on "Fern Hill," was the unanimous first choice by every judge except the one from the English department, for whom the piece was the worst example of a student reproducing a "masterful" reading (that is, reproducing a reading whose skill and finish mocked the discipline and its values). . . . The rest of us loved the lab report the chemistry professor said was just mechanical, uninspired. The rest of us loved the case study of the underground economy of a Mexican village that the sociologist said was mostly cliché and suffering from the worst excesses of ethnography. (15-16)

Such moments of disciplinary slapstick don't ironize the notion of juried writing for Bartholomae; rather, they cause him, in true Modernist fashion, to dig in his heels in insistence on the need for more discussion "on the fundamental problems of professional writing, writing that negotiates the disciplines, their limits and possibilities" (16), in the presumed belief that with enough dialogue we can give awards to papers we *do* believe in. This is composition, then, under the sign *limited possibilities*.

3. "Composition . . . is concerned with how and why one might work with the space on the page. . . . [T]he form of composition I am willing to teach would direct the revision of the essay as an exercise in criticism . . . I would want students not only to question the force of the text but also the way the text positions them in relationship to a history of writing" (Bartholomae 21). Such an attempt at defining the genre—finding, in this case, what is unique to composition (as opposed, say, to literature or theory, not to mention writing-in-general); doing so in terms of self-criticism or self-definition—is the Modernist enterprise. Greenberg outlines Modernism in the arts after Kant:

> What had to be exhibited and made explicit was that which was unique and irreducible not only in art in general but also in each particular art. Each art had to determine, through the operations peculiar to itself, the effects peculiar and exclusive to itself. By doing this, each art would, to be sure, narrow its area of competence, but at the same time it would make its possession of this area all the more secure. (68)

The specificity of Bartholomae's composition, its "historic concern for the space on the page and what it might mean to do work there and not somewhere else" (18), is the specificity of Modernism as seen by Greenberg in his notes on Modernist painting:

> Flatness alone was unique and exclusive to that art. The enclosing shape of the support was a limiting condition, or norm, that was shared with the art of the theater; color was a norm or means shared with sculpture as well as with the theater. Flatness, two-dimensionality, was the only condition painting shared with no other art, and so Modernist painting oriented itself to flatness as it did to nothing else. (69)

Both projects involve a certain kind of work—*flatness* in one scene, *fundamental problems in professional writing, writing that negotiates the disciplines in the other*—with a certain kind of materials—stretched canvases and tubes of paint, or the texts upon which "writing in schooling" is written. And both projects are subsumed by a reflexive criticism. For Greenberg, "The essence of Modern lies, as I see it, in the use of the characteristic methods of a discipline to criticize the discipline itself—not in order to subvert it, but to entrench it more firmly in its area of competence" (67). For Bartholomae, the "goal is to call the discourse into question, to undo it in some fundamental way" (14), "an act of criticism that would enable a writer to interrogate his or her own text in relationship to the problems of writing and the problems of disciplinary knowledge" (17), not in order to subvert the discipline but to entrench it more firmly, determining "the way the text positions them in relationship to a history of writing" (21).

4. What Duchamp offers is Modernism-in-general: self-definitions when the definitions are endless, disciplinary critique as anti-discipline, and composition as a catalogue of the ideas that grow from such work. Duchamp wanted to evolve a new language, a new aesthetics, a new physics, dissolving the conventions that would inhibit such a realization. He wanted new words, "'*prime words*' ('divisible' only by themselves and by unity)" (*Salt Seller* 31). His new discourse would *utilize colors*; it would be a *pictorial Nominalism*, conflating the verbal with the visual. For how else could *new relations* be expressed? Surely not by the *concrete alphabetic forms of languages*. His entire ouevre reads like a hypertext; almost as soon as you go into any depth in one section, you are linked to another, each with its own further-referential content. The "Green Box," for example, exists as the information stacks for the "Glass"; click on various parts of the bride- or bachelors-panel to access the awaiting text: "To reduce the "Glass" to as succinct an illustration as possible of all the ideas in the "Green Box", which then would be a sort of catalogue of those ideas. The "Glass" is not to be looked at for itself, but only as a function of the catalogue I never made" (Lebel 67). Indeed, the "Glass" can never been seen by itself: "it is no more visible in broad daylight than a restaurant window encrusted with advertisements, through which we see figures moving within . . . it is inscribed, as it were, like the other image of a double exposure" (Lebel 68). Composition as already-inscribed, double-exposed; catalogue the tracings and call it a text. He tells Cabanne:

For the "Box" of 1913-1914, it's different. I didn't have the idea of a box as much as just notes. I thought I could collect, in an album like the Saint-Etienne catalogue [a sort of French Sears, Roebuck], some calculations, some reflexions, without relating them. Sometimes they're on torn pieces of paper. (42)

If this is academic writing, it's writing outside the bounds of classroom composition, writing as found palimpsest: course-notes, say, over-written with an ambiguous personal message, or a barely-decipherable to-do list scrawled on the back of a parking ticket—extracurricular assignments gathered from the grounds of the Campus of Interzone University. Writing already ruptured, torn, pre-inscribed; but catalogue it all and a life emerges. It's much like Burroughs's, who describes his text as if it were an html catalogue made for cutting, clicking: "You can cut into *Naked Lunch* at any intersection point. . . . *Naked Lunch* is a blueprint, a How-To book" (224). E-conferencing, web-writing, email—all the false starts and lost strands—they all amount to an inscription, *a kind of rendezvous*, a meeting-site of various texts and people; an encounter, set up and waiting. The Duchampian notion of form is hypertextual: "the fact that any form is the perspective of another form according to a certain *vanishing point* and a certain *distance*" (*Salt Seller* 45). All writing is seen as punctuated periodically with "click here." It's writer as viewer, remote in hand, clicking, cruising, blending all televisual texts into one default program; all discrete works become subsumed in the composite-text, *bits and pieces put together to present a semblance of a whole.* Lebel offers an ideological overview, explaining Duchamp's grammatology of the permanently destabilized text:

> he takes the offense against logical reality. Duchamp's attitude is always characterized by his refusal to submit to the principles of trite realism. . . . By imposing laws imbued with humor to laws supposedly serious he indirectly casts doubt upon the absolute value of the latter. He makes them seem approximations, so that the arbitrary aspects of the system risk becoming obvious. . . . Evidently he finds it intolerable to put up with a world established once and for all. (29)

It's writing as surf-fiction: you never enter the same text twice. Bartholomae and Greenberg operate from a nostalgic perspective when boundaries and genres existed. But boundaries dissolve in the Panorama of the Interzone: "The Composite City where all human potentials are spread out in a vast silent market. . . . A place where the unknown past and the emergent future meet in a vibrating soundless hum" (Burroughs 106, 109).

5. Some math might be helpful here. De Duve shows the usefulness of Duchamp's *algebraic comparison*, as presented in "The Green Box". It's the ratio a/b, where a is the exposition and b the possibilities. The example Duchamp had given previously, in "The 1914 Box", was the equation

$$\frac{arrhe}{art} = \frac{shitte}{shit}$$

Duchamp is clear on the point that the ratio doesn't yield a "solution": "the ratio *a/b* is in no way given by a number *c* [such that] *a/b* = *c* but by the sign (-)" (*Salt Seller* 28). Duchamp calls this sign the *sign of the accordance* (*Salt Seller* 28), by which all terms vibrate together in an endless troping of infinite possibility, subsumed in the mechanical hum of *arrhe*. The ratio *a/b*, then, acts as a form of heuristicizing, allegorizing, delaying. We can see the value of Duchamp's algebra for our own field. The way Richard Rodriguez reads Richard Hoggart's *The Uses of Literacy* becomes, for Bartholomae and Petrosky, a standard, "a way of reading we like to encourage in our students" (3). Rodriguez's exposition, of all the possibilities inherent in Hoggart's material, becomes a measure, the criteria the jury can use in awarding prizes. As such, it's a way we encourage of all possible student ways. We can do the mathematics of accordance on that:

Rodriguez   =   *a way of reading we like*
Hoggart   students' ways of reading

The specificity and limitations at work in our field become apparent in such a ratio. It is this certain reading of a certain text that becomes, specifically, the way of reading we like—a specificity Bartholomae acknowledges in "What is Composition?": "I see composition as a professional commitment to do a certain kind of work with a certain set of materials" (22).

Rodriguez   =   *a certain kind of work*
Hoggart   a certain set of materials

In many fields, the generic has subsumed the specific. In music, for example, various genres or periods have evolved (after Cage) into "sound" as a generic practice. Theater, music, dance, film, and visual art are often blurred into "performance." But composition resists being subsumed by notions like "text" or "document." We insist on the academic as a distinction (and the various disciplines as further delineations); we don't make the passage to art-ness, to beyond-academic-writing-ness. What Duchamp did, for example, with the readymade (urinal or bottlerack chosen, purchased, and exposed as one's sculpture) was to legitimate a wholly unique situation: "you can now be an artist without being either a painter, or a sculptor, or a composer, or a writer, or an architect—an artist at large. . . . Duchamp liberated subsequent artists from the constraints of a particular art—or skill" (de Duve *Kant* 154). One can now be a compositionist-at-large; one needs only skills-in-general, a kind of meta-aesthetic. And yet the best theorists in our field—like Bartholomae—continue to try and determine those now-dissolved constraints on "art in a raw state—*à l'état brut*—bad, good or indifferent" (*Salt Seller* 139).

I've tried, in the shower of discourse available through electronic media, to dissolve the specific parameters of my own course's composition-logic. I've used more easily available materials and ways of reading those materials. My first attempt to seriously interrupt that logic was simple substitution: making Malcolm X's autobiography stand for the "history of writing," choosing what I felt were varied readings of it (Reverend Cleage's, Penn Warren's, Joe Wood's,

reviews of the book from 1965 media—even sound-bites from *Emerge* magazine of anyone-whoever's reading of Malcolm, recorded for the 1990 anniversary issue), as well as letting students choose their share of materials. My
rationale was to expand the classroom materially, allowing students a more
immediate entrée into the cultural flow of words and ideas. I didn't want to
prize any one manner of academic reading/writing, and I certainly wanted to
restore material like Malcolm's book to a place of dignity in the institution
(where it had been degraded for years). I used a fluxus of readings on Malcolm
to show students they could position their own reading of him somewhere,
anywhere. The form of that reading became more generic: within a system of
citational prose, strong material could come from anyplace-wherever—an
email message, a news clipping, an academic journal, or an online chat. When
an e-message has (at least) as much force as a formal essay, then *Emerge* magazine's person-on-the-street sound-bites became representative of any useful
reading of Malcolm. My new equation became

Emerge sound-bites   =   *a way of reading*
Malcolm X   students' ways of reading

Am I happy with this? Yes and no. It does what I thought it would, but I
want to go further, away from the specificity of Malcolm. I don't want to
replace one canonical text with a new one (no matter how canonical I think
Malcolm should be in our culture). So lately my students have been reading an
almost-anything-whatever like gangsta rap, along with a range of cultural
responses to the material (from the media, the academy, Web-sites, and fel-
low-students), then writing their own. I'm happier with the new equation:

a reading of gangsta rap   =   *a way of reading*
gangsta rap   students' ways of reading

This has proven a more democratic equivalency, allowing a broader range
of the possible. Gangsta is anti-traditional, anti-canonical; its force is sheer
negation. Of course the truly dissolved, wide-open flow would be

any reading
any subject whatever

Plugging that back into the original equation seems worthwhile, in order to
set up a sign of accordance between the Bartholomae & Petrosky standard and
the anything-whatever; to spin-blur Rodriguez/Hoggart on the *Rotative
Demisphère*, until they blend into the white noise of generic text:

Rodriguez   =   *any reading*
Hoggart   any subject whatever

The technology, of course, allows for no other logic—anything that comes
across the screen is neutralized in the electronic hum of information. We are in
a post-exchange-value-apocalypse in which the only value is use-value.
Duchamp chose a bicycle wheel for his first readymade, not because it was
beautiful (or rare or difficult) but because it was commonplace, easily available: if it were lost, it could be replaced "like a hundred thousand others"
(Lebel 35). He understood the necessity for de-valuing materiality in the new

art, affording anartism to everyone. With composition now defined in terms of choosing rather than fabricating, all material is equal; it's whatever catches the eye. "We will sample from anything we need. We will rip-off your mother if she has something we find appropriate for our compost-heap creations" (Amerika). Material is chosen not because it's a privileged text, a "difficult" masterpiece from the "history of writing," but because it's around, on hand. It's whatever stands out from the endlessly-shifting screen before one. Could we, then, substitute "gangsta rap" for "Hoggart" in our initial ratio? Gangsta rap is consumed by so many of my students; it's a fairly cheap, easily available addiction: "I am a consumer," pop critic Danyel Smith says of her gangsta jones, "chomping away at the brothers as they perform some rare times with a Nat Turner gleam in their eyes" (20). We'd then have the ratio

Rodriguez

gangsta rap

which exists, of course, on the Internet, in a piece by Rodriguez called "Ganstas." Is his way of reading gangsta equal to his way of reading of Hoggart? Is it (still) a way of reading we'd like to encourage? What reading (now) would we not want to encourage?

And what about substituting the top term in our equation, the exposition? What about anyone-whoever's reading of gangsta rap? Could that be a way of reading we'd like to encourage? Could anyone-whoever's reading of gangsta be equal to Rodriguez's? Take, for instance, this print-out of some Net stuff a student found, which is no more than a series of hip-hop definitions. It's from an anonymous writer's Website, which contains, among other things, a host of gangsta-terms some other unknown writers forwarded to the site. I'm not sure where it's from, exactly, or whose it is, because the print-out is incomplete, ruptured—my student just enclosed several printed pages from the larger site as a source he used in one of his writings—but I link it into my own site here, as greedily as Danyel Smith, cause some of the definitions are pretty slick:

> *sexual chocolate*—a dark boldheaded nigga with a proper ass car and some
> tight ass gear
> *Medusa*—a fly bitch who'll make yo dick turn to stone (kistenma)
>
> *rims*—wheels for yo sweet ass ride
> *regulate*—to creep on some sorry ass fool (see creep . . .) (fhurst)
>
> *money*—scrilla, scratch, mail
> *bad*—bootsie, janky
> *good*—saucy (crystalt)
>
> *baller*—a player wit ends in a benz (Ifunderburg)
> *ballin*—I have game (79D9407A62)
> *P*—Pimpish, the same as tight, slick, dope (Berry)

> *bammer*—busted and disgusted like half the definitions up on here (mold7316)

All the writers on this list are doing, when they post their definitions, is *inscribing*—cataloguing words, ideas, material that might become useful for the next writer. This is Cage's discursive project: "to find a way of writing which comes from ideas, is not about them, but which produces them" (X *x*). Or Amerika's, in which writing becomes a therapeutic cure for Information Sickness, "a highly-potent, creatively filtered tonic of (yes) textual residue spilled from the depths of our spiritual unconscious." It's the writer (to use Kroker's term) as possessed individual. Writing is now conceived of as drive-by criticism, rap slang; it's the *infra-thin* possibility of gangsta definitions appearing as a Rodriguez. With all writing leveled in the Interzone, every genre blurred into one, the textu(r)ality of all prose is in an accordance, best described by Wallace, when he traces the passage in contemporary fiction:

> the text becomes less a novel than a piece of witty erudite extremely high-quality prose television. Velocity and vividness—the wow—replace the literary hmm of actual development. People flicker in and out; events are garishly there and then gone and never referred to. . . [It's a prose that's] both amazing and forgettable, wonderful and oddly hollow . . . hilarious, upsetting, sophisticated, and extremely shallow. (192)

Is a writer who posted to the gangsta list able to "interrogate his or her own text in relationship to the problems of writing and the problems of disciplinary knowledge" (17)? I think so, but I wouldn't actually pose the question; the writer'd probably think I was a *busta brown* ("a fool that hangs around and isn't even wanted" [4jcf4]). Is the writing strong, forceful, able to bring about new knowledge? Of course, and Rodriguez thinks so, too: while he does rep after rep in his "sissy gym . . . the blond pagan house of abs and pecs," where he and his ilk "read the *Wall Street Journal,* [and] lose a few pounds on the StairMaster," he listens to the gangsta rap that blasts on the gym's sound system, realizing the "high moral distancing" that goes on around gangsta rap among the middle- and upper-classes, how they "consign the gangsta to subhumanity." But he also knows the sheer force of raw gangsta, its ability to foster growth and change, to survive in the Interzone; he knows, if his fellow middle- and upper-class gym rats don't, "why we use the music of violence to build up our skinny arms." Those gangsta lexicographers above used their sound-bite spaces to write about the only thing the contemporary writer can—what is already inscribed on their screens at any given moment; they're dubbers, remixers, electronically inscribing and re/circulating inter-texts of the rap reality that fills their inner glass, seeing no use in imposing conventional criteria on *l'état brut*. As Amerika reads it, it's Avant-Pop, "one step further" from Postmodernism:

> The main tenet of Postmodernism was: I, whoever that is, will put together these bits of data and form a Text while you, whoever that is, will produce your

own meaning based off what you bring to the Text. . . . The main tenet that will evolve for the Avant-Pop movement is: I, whoever that is, am always intersecting with data created by the Collective You, whoever that is, and by interacting with and supplementing the Collective You, will find meaning.

The heavy, intentional consciousness of Modernist composition is replaced by Avant-Pop's permanent state of mental preoccupation: readymade data is "something one doesn't even look at, or something one looks at while turning one's head" (Duchamp, qtd. de Duve "Echoes" 82); it's regarded as something momentarily seen (or, for the gangsta lexicographer, heard). Of course, even gangsta sound-bite writing is an easy textual call when judged against other possible texts-as-data-intersections. 'Cause what if the composition were non-verbal, or only slightly verbal—a graphics- and sound-heavy Website, perhaps? Or just barely written by the student—a catalogue of links, say? Not only, perhaps, are we no longer teaching words used in a special way—"writing [that] reflects on the fundamental problems of professional writing, writing that negotiates the disciplines, their limits and possibilities" (16)—we're not even sure about words themselves any more. Nesbit refers to the "Glass" as "linguistic but wordless . . . cinema with the lights up . . . a language move that makes language stop" ("Her Words"). *Language transparent,* the other image on double-exposed glass.

6. Buying a urinal from an iron-works, affixing a name to it, and submitting it as one's work is the art of the readymade. Not so much a found art as a chosen one. But there remains an aesthetic, a judgment-quality, that makes such art the legitimate subject of pedagogy and scholarship. Material is chosen from a vaster field than the disciplined one—a generic one, where all parameters dissolve, opening onto a flat, breathtaking landscape: "Regard it as something seen momentarily, as though from a window while traveling. If across Kansas, then, of course, Kansas" (Cage *Silence* 110). Cage's glass-inscribed road-trip through Kansas becomes the primal scene of Avant-Pop composition. Only those who don't listen to the silence think it's silent; only those who don't see the glass think it's clear. (Duchamp: "The 'blank' force of Dada was very salutary. It told you 'don't forget you are not quite so blank as you think you are'" [*Salt Seller* 125]). Only those who don't choose to read the anything-whatever, the document, feel there's no critical project there. What would it mean to have a document *pose* as composition, to have the everyday pose as a "difficult text"? This validates not only the readymade composition (to which only a new use or perception has been brought), but its textual concomitants, however ruptured—composition as the "Green Box", the "1914 Box"; writing as notes from a work/life in progress, under the reign of the anything-whatever. De Duve traces the movement from Courbet through Duchamp: "from the represented anything-whatever to the anything-whatever plain and simple . . . the devaluation of the precious, the finished, the noble . . . the correlative rise of new egalitarian values—or anti-values" (*Kant* 328). The cult of fabrication is gone. The

artist (or *arrhetist*), then, becomes "a technician of the absence of technique" (330). (In an interview in 1963, Duchamp called the readymade "a work of art without an artist to make it" [Roberts 47]). All other technical-aesthetic conventions are stripped bare as readymade writing, in the fact of its appearance as art, concedes everything except its status as writing. This locates aesthetics away from the traditional-criteria-based 'this is beautiful,' to the traditional-criteria-free 'this is art.' According to the new exhibition-value, a work, the writing, is exhibited in order to be judged as art, nothing more; all other conventions are seen through, transparent as a restaurant window. Duchamp himself termed the readymade *inscribed*; de Duve reads that as meaning "able to be written into the register of those things onto which the statement 'this is [writing]' is affixed" (*Kant* 394). Composition remains entrenched, preferring to universalize its maxims of taste and beauty. But the only beauty left in the post-beautiful Interzone is *the beauty of indifference* (*Salt Seller* 30). The choice of the readymade is *based on a reaction of visual indifference, a total absence of good or bad taste* (*Salt Seller* 141). For Donald Judd, there was only one important criteria: "a work needs only to be interesting." It was not a matter of taste, but simply "historical knowledge . . . some intellectual curiosity . . . some strategic desire" (de Duve *Kant* 238). Can it simply be enough to say, as Johns did of Duchamp, that *what composition is* is "a field where language, thought and vision act upon one another" (Cabanne 109)? Can it be enough for our art that it have *arrhe*? Enough for our writing that it have *writte*? Can we allow a composition that is definitively unfinished, an "indecisive reunion . . . with all kinds of delays" (*Salt Seller* 26, 32), deferring this need for writing as a revision toward a *certain* style, toward a *certain* end? Ends (unless they're *ends in a benz*) can bore: "No end is in view in this fragment of a new perspective. 'In the end you lose interest, so I didn't feel the necessity to finish it'" (Cabanne 109).

The tendency in our field is still on making rather than choosing. So Bartholomae urges a course "that investigates the problems of writing at the point of production," in which students practice "the ability to produce a critical reading" (28), but what he offers is nostalgia, a course in art appreciation, "the point of the course was to teach students how and why they might work with difficult texts" (26). *Difficult texts*, of course, means our canon, our hit-parade. The course's program becomes a *great demonstration* of the grand style, learning to paint like the masters, tracing their brushstrokes, "asking students to translate their sentences into and out of a style that might loosely be called 'Pratt-like'" (26). The reason Duchamp broke with painting was the cloying nature of such nostalgia. *La patte* was the name given to the cultish presence of the painter's hand in the work; to avoid that cramped space of virtuosity, Duchamp moved from a technique of overdetermined practices to one of mechanical processes:

> the "Glass" wasn't a painting; there was lots of lead, a lot of other things. It was far
> from the traditional idea of the painter, with his brush, his palette, his turpentine,

an idea which had already disappeared from my life. . . . the old masters, the old things. . . . All that disgusted me. (Cabanne 67)

Bartholomae cites a passage from Bové, which sounds very much like Duchamp, very negation-as-first-light. Bové urges a "negative" criticism, one that would "destroy the local discursive and institutional formations of the 'regime of truth,' . . . aimed at necessary conditions," but a negation that has a "'positive' content; it must carry out its destruction with newly produced knowledge" (18). This could be Duchamp's ironism of affirmation. But too often Bartholomae's negation is aimed only at students or at institutional composition not in his style. He has no hate for anything in his own composition; it's a restricted destruction, an anti-*certain*-production-strategy. His production-site remains canonical, the classroom walls full of reproductions of certified masterpieces. His production, termed revision, implies taking the student ready-made—in this case an essay on St. Croix, brought in under the institutional sign "irredeemably corrupt or trivial" (26), multiplied by the sign of the clone ("The St. Croix narrative can stand for all of the narratives the students wrote" [27])—and re-working it, running it through a series of self-reflexive heuristics that seem like a New (Old) Tagmemics:

> to ask questions of the discourse as a discourse: What is its history? Whose interests are served? What does the scene of the plantation mean? What does it mean in terms of the history of St. Croix? What does it mean that it is offered as background and color? Why don't the people of St. Croix get to speak? How might one not write a missionary narrative and yet still tell the story of a missionary trip to St. Croix? (27)

It means, he realizes, getting clumsier writing from students, a crude rendering that will seem "less skillful or less finished or less masterful than the original" (28), but one that is en route to more closely approximating the certain set of materials, one that is closer to replicating a travel narrative à la Pratt, "Pratt's argument and her way of reading" (28). Duchamp might have defined *genius* as the "impossibility of the iron" (*impossibilité du fer/faire*), but the iron is quite possible here—it just needs refining, purifying, forging into the prized fetish. This takes composition back to the Greek, pre-mechanical age of reproduction as Benjamin describes it: "founding and stamping" (218). Such a desire for re-production vitiates Bartholomae's critique of "official" composition: "You say you hate it? *You want to recreate it!*" (R.E.M.). The exigency becomes a crudely-copied masterpiece: blurred, like a fuzzy, ill-lit photo of the Mona Lisa (the ur-text) taken with a pin-hole camera. Why try to take a perfect picture of a masterpiece (unless you're a conceptual artist, like Louise Lawler, and you want to use it materially)? Better to just paint a mustache and goatee on it.

Composition, it appears, exists to turn *l'art brut* of the student's ready-made into a form that will produce not the cool-site *wow* but the *literary hmm*. The focus here is training the student to develop a high-quality hand-made reproduction of Pratt, one with disciplinary exchange-value cachet. The nostalgia is, perhaps, understandable: there were primal, formative moments when certain texts spoke to us with authority, and we want our students to try and reproduce that power. Composition, then, strives to combine cult value and exchange-/exhibition-value. But trying to maintain the aura in repro-writing is a doomed project. The Composite City cares nothing for aura, authenticity, or authority; in the Interzone, art's "social significance, particularly in its most positive form, is inconceivable without its destructive, cathartic aspect, that is, the liquidation of the traditional value of the cultural heritage" (Benjamin 221). Of course the St. Croix paper can stand for any (*faux* Pratt-like) narrative: they're all aura-less, the space of the writing deserted, to use Benjamin's metaphor (226), like a crime scene. Interzone writing in the virtual community of Composite City has only use-value, consumption-value: "Value will depend more on the ability of the different groups of artist-associates to develop a reputation for delivering easily accessible hits of the Special Information Tonic to the informationally-sick correspondent wherever he or she may be" (Amerika). In this ratio, readers = "addicts of drugs not yet synthesized," writer = "Fats" Terminal, trafficker in the ultimate controlled substance, "flesh of the giant aquatic black centipede . . . overpoweringly delicious and nauseating so that the eaters eat and vomit and eat again until they fall exhausted" (Burroughs 53, 55). It's the drug-use-value of writing; *a pimpish composition, dope.* "Anyone could scratch your surface now, it's so amphetamine" (R. E. M.). It's futile to hype the values of contemplation on the informationally-sick. The Interzone's discursive field is the wow of distraction, not the *literary hmm* of contemplation. Whatever contemplation there is amounts to the *pensées* of the possessed individual.

Just as the concept of juried writing is never displaced by Bartholomae, neither is the compositional genre that will decide the prize—it's the travel narrative, but a specific, authentic, highly-determined version of it. He simply substitutes one already-wrote text, the St. Croix narrative, with another, Pratt's. A more interesting substitution might prove replacing the already-written with, say, a *wrotten written* ("*morceaux moisis*"), like, for example, the following travel narrative, William Burroughs's non-entry in Bartholomae's contest; not a Contact Zone piece, but some Special Information Tonic from the Interzone, entitled "Atrophied Preface":

> Why all this waste paper getting The People from one place to another? Perhaps to spare The Reader stress of sudden space shifts and keep him Gentle? And so a ticket is bought, a taxi called, a plane boarded. We are allowed a glimpse into the warm peach-lined cave as She (the airline hostess, of course) leans over us to murmur of chewing gum, dramamine, even nembutal.
>
> "Talk paregoric, Sweet Thing, and I will hear." (218)

Contemporary composition insists on the literary aesthetic of the Contact Zone, but electronic writing operates in the anti-aesthetic of the Interzone, where "'content' is what the media-conglomerates deliver into one's home via the TV screen and form is the ability to level out or flatten the meaning of all things" (Olsen & Amerika). Burroughs wouldn't dream of translating Pratt, he's actually closer to the St. Croix writer-as-recorder: "There is only one thing a writer can write about: what is in front of his senses at the moment of writing. . . . I am a recording instrument. . . . I do not presume to impose 'story' 'plot' 'continuity'" (221). Limning what is in front of one's senses, tracing what is there on the screen—the writer of the intertext underscores every line with *This is now, this is here, this is me, this is what I wanted you to see* (R.E.M.). The web captures, in glass, this historical moment—the death of the craft of writing and its rebirth as idea (de Duve *Kant* 186). The progressive self-definition of the academy accelerated at an historical juncture much like today. As art-at-large was granted a kind of public credibility by the growth of salons, the academy, fearful that it could no longer control access to the profession, retreated into over-specification, hyper-pedantry. The Web, then, is the New Independents' Salon, Malraux's Museum-Without-Walls—built on the shards of the now-fractal Palace of Modernism. Beuys' dream has come true, everyone can now be curated. Benjamin saw this neutralization or democratization of expertise as one of the implications of mechanical reproduction. Film technology, for example (particularly newsreels and documentaries for Benjamin—though witness Bresson's casts of anyone-whoevers), allowed anyone to be a movie star. The same held true for print technologies:

> For centuries a small number of writers were confronted by many thousands of readers. This changed toward the end of the last century. With the increasing extension of the press, which kept placing new political, religious, scientific, professional, and local organs before the readers, an increasing number of readers became writers—at first, occasional ones. It began with the daily press opening to its readers space for "letters to the editor." And today there is hardly a gainfully employed European who could not, in principle, find an opportunity to publish somewhere. . . . Thus, the distinction between author and public is about to lose its basic character. (231-232)

Cinema in the Interzone is a crime-scene haunted by the death of traditional auratic "presence." All films are now read as documentaries; all cinema is *anémic cinéma* (*Salt Seller* 115) (and the anagram in general remains one of the few traditional textual strategies still meaningful). A new given, then:

any person = *any reader*
movie star   published writer/expert

People read their world through the glass in front of them and inscribe their interaction. Not exactly meaning their work for the marketplace, as eighteenth century painters did, writers of the electronic intertext still gear their art toward public consumption, data-interaction, supplementation: "email your comments!" website after website implores. The means of production are in the hands of the consumers; through a *mirrorical return* (*Salt Seller* 65), the specialized knowledge of the academy becomes again increasingly beside-the-point for the now on-going teleintertextual salon. New composing technologies mean the media may not have had time to be practiced, perfected, conventionalized, ritualized. What aesthetic remains lies in capturing, choosing, from *what is in front of his senses at the moment of writing;* the hurried snapshot of life on the run, not a stylized drawing. *"The important thing then is just* this matter of timing, this snapshot effect" (*Salt Seller* 32).

The readymade narrative, done by anyone-whoever, cannot stay delayed in glass for Modernist composition. Any stretch of found footage is not eligible for Best Documentary. Even though Bartholomae tries to distance himself from the kind of writing as revision taught by "the process movement"—where

> the primary goal was the efficient production of text . . . [in which] revision was primarily addition and subtraction—adding vivid details, for example, and taking out redundancies. The result (or the goal) was to perfect, and by extension, preserve the discourse. (27)

—his goal remains an efficient discourse-production, a perfection and preservation; only now it's Mary Louise Pratt's discourse. There remains this *progression* (even as he tries to distance himself from "the legacy of the liberal tradition in composition" [15]), a process-ion away from the St. Croix narrative—a text which is heart-felt but doesn't articulate the preferred politics of a certain reading—to a better one, in which "a writer would have to ask about and think about, say, the history of North American relations with St. Croix" (27). What Bartholomae doesn't do is *delay* that progression towards the certain style—to see if the canvas is not quite so blank as we think it is, to see if Modernism could take the blank canvas as its ultimate work, the flattest canvas ever. Call it the contact zone of the arts, the point where conception, *anart, arrhe,* meets aura, Modernism, art. Without a delay, a self-negation, a *SUR/cen/SURE,* a meta-irony, the on-going narrative of the discourse's tradition/production is never interrupted; the knowledge-engine never stops. Composition never explores the *possible,* just possible versions of the preferred. The desire of Duchamp's Bride was inscribed as "ignorant . . . blank . . . (with a touch of malice)" (*Salt Seller* 39). But we will define that blank canvas and know it, colonize it (ignoring the touch of malice, not even realizing the *canvas* is really a *glass*). "Knowledge, like the image, was built up in consecutive layers that would reenact the progress made by modernity" (Nesbit "The Language" 355). We care not for words but for knowledge, which we tirelessly pursue: "The question for the writing teacher, then," says Bartholomae, as he races through page after page, never stopping to dwell, "is 'What next?'" (26). The grand irony at the end of his article is his caveat that the compositionist must "be willing to pay attention to common things" (28). Sure, in order to determine what needs to be rarefied, Prattified. Duchamp located "the great trouble with art in this country" in just such an uninterrupted unfolding of tradition, in just such a perfection of a certain way of reading:

there is no spirit of revolt—no new ideas appearing among the younger artists. They are following along the paths beaten out by their predecessors, trying to do better what their predecessors have already done. In art there is no such thing as perfection. And a creative lull occurs always when artists of a period are satisfied to pick up a predecessor's work where he dropped it and attempt to continue what he was doing. When on the other hand you pick up something from an earlier period and adapt it to your own work an approach can be creative. The result is not new; but it is new insomuch as it is a different approach. (*Salt Seller* 123)

Going back to our algebraic comparisons, the logic for the readymade writings from the Campus of Interzone University is inescapable. Bartholomae's math posits a given:

$$\frac{St.\ Croix\ narrative}{all\ student\ narratives}$$

But under the vibrating hum of Composite City, where *form is the ability to level out or flatten the meaning of all things*, we can set it equal to any reading, on any subject whatever,

$$\frac{St.\ Croix\ narrative}{all\ student\ narratives} = \frac{any\ reading}{any\ subject}$$

That given, we remember, was the same one used for Rodriguez's reading of Hoggart, which allows our final ratio:

$$\frac{Rodriguez}{Hoggart} = \frac{St.\ Croix\ narrative}{all\ student\ narratives}$$

The vast silent market of the Interzone effects its neutralization. That final algebraic comparison doesn't imply a movement having been made from a student writer to a master writer, a looking-backward; rather both expositions are delayed in a stasis field, in accordance. They both *appear* as writing. As for the bottom terms, materially now anything is possible. As exposition, Rodriguez is any writing whatsoever: like all narratives, sometimes prize-winning, occasionally appearing as *irredeemably corrupt or trivial*. And Hoggart— as possibility—is any readymade data with which a writer interacts. All that would count Rodriguez as prize-worthy now (or Hoggart or Pratt or the "Fern Hill" essay) is taste because, after Benjamin, the technology of mechanical reproduction means anyone-whoever can become a published expert. It is Bartholomae's attempt to otherwise determine this that rings so hollow.

7. Composition after Duchamp is idea-generative, not product-oriented. As data-interaction, its only directive: Take whatever data is recorded (call them, perhaps, these 'having become') and from them make a tracing. If three-dimensional objects give off a two-dimensional shadow, writing is now conceived of as a three-dimensional shadow of a fourth-dimensional process of becoming. As Roché said of Duchamp, "His finest work is his use of time" (Lebel 87). The intertext, moving over time, means writing reconceived of as the teleintertext. Gervais uses the phrase *restricted teleintertext* to capture Duchamp's hypertextual strategies:

His almost systematic way of exposing at least two locations, two languages, or two sexes through pictorial and literary texts could be called the restricted teleintertext of his oeuvre: "inter" because it makes use of at least two texts; "restricted" because these texts were written by the same person; and "tele" because they are often several decades apart. (Gervais 399)

But instead of a restricted economy of the intertext, we'll have a general one, a world-wide economy-without-walls. Can we allow a writing that might be cracked, unfinished, but that circulates some interesting ideas? It doesn't have to be powerfully or rigorously conceptual (as some find Pratt): "please note that there doesn't have to be a lot of the conceptual for me to like something" (Cabanne 77). Just a touch will do: a drop or two of *Belle Haleine, Eau de Voilette*, a small whiff of *Air de Paris* (*Sérum physiologique*), some marble sugar cubes (one lump or two?)—just an easily accessible hit. Bartholomae fetishizes a conceptual ("a certain kind of intellectual project—one that requires me to think out critical problems of language, knowledge, and culture" 24) that's materially limited—imagine a student in his class, say, handing in a urinal as travel documentary (did Mary Louise Pratt do translatable urinals?). Under Duchamp, anyone can be a conceptual artist. The materials are readymade, common-place, easily available. What's involved is finding a new conceptual use: taking a hat rack, for example, putting it on the floor, and calling it *Trébuchet* (*Trap*) is not *materially* difficult. It simply involves picking something up from an earlier period and giving it a new function, a new thought for that object, adapting it to your own work. It's the use-value (rather than the exhibition-value) of fetishism, an unforeseen-use-value:

> it is not for walking that the fetishist 'uses' the shoe. For him it has a use-value that begins, paradoxically, . . . at the very moment it stops working, when it no longer serves locomotion. It is the use-value of a shoe out of service. (Hollier 140)

The hat rack, then, is not a "difficult text" as Bartholomae means it (the "Glass" is, but not in the way he means). It's rooted in the everyday in a way Modernism's program can never be. Rauschenberg, reflecting on his very Duchampian happening "Map Room II" (1965), interrogates the notion of a text(ual material) that's difficult to get; he begins at the Modernist point of limits and possibilities but inflects that setting differently:

> I began that piece by getting some materials to work with—again we have that business of limitations and possibilities. I just got a bunch of tires, not because I'm crazy about tires but because they are so available around here in New York, even on the street. I could be back here in fifteen minutes with five tires. If I were working in Europe, that wouldn't be the material. Very often people ask me about certain repeated images in both my painting and theatre. Now I may be fooling myself, but I think it can be traced to their availability. Take the umbrella . . . After any rainy day, it is hard to walk by a garbage can that doesn't have a broken umbrella in it, and they are quite interesting. I found some

springs around the corner. I was just putting stuff together—that's the way I work—to see what I could get out of it. I don't start off with any preconceived notion about content of the piece. If there is any thinking, it is more along the line of something happening which suggests something else. If I'm lucky, then the piece builds its own integrity. . . . You just mess around. The springs, for example, made an interesting noise, so I decided to amplify that. . . . [The tires] can be walked in, they can be rolled in, you can roll over them, you can crawl through them. All these things are perfectly obvious. Perhaps tires even have uses that you haven't seen before. What I'm trying to avoid is the academic way of making a dance of theme and variation. I'm interested in exploring all the possibilities inherent in any particular object. (Kostelanetz 83-84)

The most easily available material now is not umbrellas or tires, but electronic information. The institution suspects the commonplace, the ready-made, the anything-whatever, the any-narrative-at-all: transparent trash, like those gangsta definitions, you can just lift right off the Net—aren't there those who consider them "irredeemably corrupt or trivial"? But there are ideas there—*just the same, they move.*

Bartholomae's project uses "student writing as a starting point"; it exists "in relation to academic or high culture" (24). Ultimately, the Modernist focus—in composition as in art—is institutional rather than conceptual. The institution is the aegis under which the project is carried out. Knowledge of the historical apparatus is a prerequisite in order to work within the discipline, learning the style and thinking which result in a Morris Louis or a Louise Pratt. Duchamp's conceptual has nothing to do with the institutional; of what use can be the institution's material reification? Asked in 1966 by Cabanne, "Do you go to museums?" Duchamp replied,

Almost never. I haven't been to the Louvre for twenty years. It doesn't interest me, because I have these doubts about the value of the judgments which decided that all these pictures should be presented to the Louvre, instead of others which weren't even considered, and which might have been there. So fundamentally we content ourselves with the opinion which says that there exists a fleeting infatuation, a style based on momentary taste; this momentary taste disappears, and, despite everything, certain things still remain. (Cabanne 71)

Our fleeting infatuations are fixed in our field's galleries—more corporate collections, actually, than actual museums, as the works there are the obvious choices (only the already-legitimated are deemed worthy of the well-endowed walls of our semi-corporate academies). *Ways of Reading*, then, is composition's Paine-Webber collection. But there are other panes, other Web-bers. Electronic writing—the gangsta-sample, say—is the kind of raw, indifferent beauty that the profession never institutionalizes (because the larger academic audience has such specific, refined tastes). Duchamp explained the difference between reified institutional history and lived aesthetic pleasure, a use-value aesthetics rather than the museum's exchange-value. His explanation points to what's missing in the institutionally canonized texts that form our field's defining narrative:

> After forty or fifty years a picture dies, because its freshness disappears. . . . There's a huge difference between a Monet today, which is black as anything, and a Monet sixty or eighty years ago, when it was brilliant, when it was made. Now it has entered into history. . . .
>
> The history of art is something very different from aesthetics. For me, the history of art is what remains of an epoch in a museum, but it's not necessarily the best of that epoch, and fundamentally it's probably even the expression of the mediocrity of the epoch, because the beautiful things have disappeared—the public didn't want to keep them. (67)

"That was then, but now that is gone; it's past" (R.E.M.). Composition's Modernism revels in the trappings of history—but in their exhibition-value, not their use-value (Punks, for example, were interested in history's use-value; they collaged their looks out of a pastiche of various eras' styles). Why Duchamp's influence persists has much to do with the actual works, but it's probably equally the result of the heuristic-value of his aesthetics, the conceptual grammar or logic generated through all the texts—made, chosen, written and spoken (as well as interacted with)—that "Duchamp" names.

The negation/affirmation Bartholomae desires from Bové is displayed wonderfully in Duchamp, whose *prémiere lumiere* shines in his palindromic print as "NON." The force of his negation was the *physical "caustic" [vitriol type]* called "Possible" which he pursued through practically every compositional project, a caustic whose strength could dissolve notions of image and text, *burning up all aesthetics and callistics* (*Salt Seller* 73). Jasper Johns testifies that "his persistent attempts to destroy frames of reference altered our thinking, established new units of thought, 'a new thought for that object'" (Cabanne 110). Comparably, the Bartholomae/Greenberg negation/affirmation seeks simply to stabilize: it negates other art and artistic strategies in order to refine a unique definition of composition in a specific field. And they would refine desire, as well. Modernism needs a desire-d reading; there is an erotic force at the heart of these compositionists, a repetitive dynamic designed to lead to pleasure. With Greenberg, it's the smell of linseed oil, the almost palpable feel of the stretched canvas's flatness, a flatness his gaze could get lost in ("The flatness toward which modernist painting orients itself can never be an utter flatness. The heightened sensitivity of the picture plane may not permit sculptural illusion, or *trompe-l'oeil*, but it does and must permit optical illusion" [73]); with Bartholomae, it is the tracing, the iteration of the style and content of difficult texts ("I confess I admire those dense sentences" ["Inventing" 159]); for Duchamp, it's the steady hum of the precision optics—disks, palindromic/anagrammatic word-play, glass stared into for about an hour. Each strategy locates an incarnated desire; a kind of conceptualist *frottage* of the fleshy gray matter to produce the expected pleasure. But Duchamp allows eroticism's universality to subsume his project, making it a new "ism" to replace other "Literary schools [like] Symbolism, Romanticism" (Cabanne 88). Bartholomae/Greenberg could never allow eroticism to replace their critical, material practice, a practice specified by the frame: "how and why one might work with the space on the page" (Bartholomae 21); "the limiting conditions with which a marked-up surface must comply in order to be experienced as a picture" (Greenberg 73). Anything else is dismissed as inappropriate or irrelevant to their focus: "We move the furniture in the classroom, collaborate on electronic networks, take turns being the boss, but we do not change writing" (16); "for the sake of its own autonomy painting has had above all to divest itself of everything it might share with sculpture" (Greenberg 70). We know what the institution's last word on desire-charged e-writing is; witness Bartholomae's article on electronic conferencing, in which any benefits it has (benefits seen not socially but institutionally, students "beginning with more familiar forms of language and seeing how they might be put to use in an academic setting . . . a transfer of this mode to written work that was officially 'writing'" [242, 252]) are underscored by the final caveat, "a threat to academic values" (262). There is moving furniture, e-chatter, sculpture, even—then there is composition, whose institutional value is now seen as potentially threatened by new practices.

Bartholomae's St. Croix writer has written something—a potentially useful memoir of a time when a writer learned something about him/herself and others, perhaps; a narrative, a document(ary) of sorts—but it's not composition. It's like a drawing on the walls of Lascaux when compared by Greenberg with an Abstract Expressionist canvas; one is simply image, the other can be called a picture. Pre-Modernist texts suffer from being composed in ignorance of the governing conventions of the genre:

> The Paleolithic painter or engraver could disregard the norm of the frame and treat the surface in both a literally and a virtually sculptural way because he made images rather than pictures, and worked on a support whose limits could be disregarded because . . . nature gave them to the artist in an unmanageable way. But the making of pictures, as against images in the flat, means the deliberate choice and creation of limits. This deliberateness is what Modernism harps on. (76)

Bataille, of course, is a different sort of art critic from Greenberg. His response to the Lascaux "images" helps distinguish Modernism as an historical "ism" or literary school, one which compares a to b and gets solution c (*deliberate choice of limits*); as opposed to eroticism, which subsumes distinctions between a and b (*picture and image*) under the more general sign: "But Upper Paleolith man, *Homo sapiens*, is now known to us through signs that move us not only in their exceptional beauty (his paintings are often marvelous). These signs affect us more through the fact that they bring us abundant evidence of his erotic life" (31). Bartholomae and Greenberg prefer expensive fetishes; they limit their erotic *plaisir du texte* to exclusive, privileged materials. In their

Modernism, the certain aesthetic judgment which distinguishes between a picture and a successful one had to be preserved. Their space for composition was that infra-thin line between writing and good writing, words and knowledge; it was a very special, *definitive* space in which the artist could work. Bartholomae: "the space on the page . . . do[ing] work there and not somewhere else" (18). Greenberg: it "would, to be sure, narrow its area of competence, but at the same time it would make its possession of this area all the more secure . . . to fit drawing and design more explicitly to the rectangular shape of the canvas" (68, 69). Duchamp abandoned that definitive space, the traditional forms, limits, concerns, and materials. He went totally off the page, out of that space, allowing thought to dictate its own laws, the resultant *becoming* being anything-whatever: "Take. these 'having become' and from them make a tracing" (*Salt Seller* 33). He's interested in the appearance mainly to trace the apparition (the fact of appearing, the status as art): "In general, the picture is the apparition of an appearance" (*Salt Seller* 30). The answer is not a solution (not "what makes writing *good*"), but a sign (what makes *writing*). Bartholomae's *given* is a solution, "write like Pratt," not a sign. Such composition busies itself with the failings of a tracing's not having become (as it would have had it be); instead of tracing a becoming, he urges students to re-trace a became. So, although he insists on "the comparison of Stephen Toulmin and a freshman" (17)—a promising equivalence, that:

Stephen Toulmin
freshman

—its purpose is not so ideas can become a delayed sign, but rather to find a solution, *c*, to an item in composition's problem-set. His given yields a solution enabling us to use Bové's critique of Toulmin on our students, in order to get Pratt-text from them: we can now tell them, in so many words, "Next time, don't be so careless about interrogating your intellectual function within the regime of truth" (17). Composition as a set of problems for which we articulate solutions? Duchamp: "There is no solution because there is no problem" (Roché 85). Bartholomae's distinction—between himself and the "same old routine" of composition—is Greenberg's distinction between picture and image. The St. Croix narrative might stand for all student narratives, but it's clearly not a travel narrative in the Pratt style. Until it's subjected to the text-production strategies of cultural criticism, it remains unfortunately a "missionary narrative" (27). Bartholomae claims the same vanguard status for his aesthetic as Greenberg; but when the truly avant-garde art showed up—say, Frank Stella or Andy Warhol or, yes, Duchamp—Modernist Painting squirmed. It was for Greenberg what it is for Bartholomae, a question of a limited artistic context—the way the space is framed. The "cultural . . . social" context-in-general was not the specific, aesthetic determinant of Modernism:

All art depends in one way or another on context, but there's a great difference between an aesthetic and a non-aesthetic context. . . . From the start avant-gardist art resorted extensively to effects depending on an extra-aesthetic context. Duchamp's first Readymades, his bicycle wheel, his bottlerack, and later on his urinal, were not new at all in configuration; they startled when first seen only because they were presented in a fine art context, which is a purely cultural and social, not an aesthetic or artistic context. (Greenberg, qtd. in de Duve *Kant* 270)

8. Duchamp saw the problem with Modernist, criteria-based taste: "one stores up in oneself such a language of tastes, good or bad, that when one looks at something, if that something isn't an echo of yourself, then you do not even look at it" (Cabanne 94). Krauss, too, reads the desire-occluded retrojection which overlays the supposedly discerning clarity of Modernism's projective vision; for her, the blank canvas/page/screen is already filled by one's own viewing apparati, "already organized, already saturated by the lattice through which perspective will map the coordinates of external space" (54). The eye, the brain, are fleshy as well as neural, body as well as mind; hence, "the gaze is experienced as being saturated from the very start . . . the perspective projection is not felt as a transparency opening onto a world but as a skin, fleshlike, dense, and strangely separable from the object it fixates" (54). "The body exerts its demands," Krauss continues, furthering Duchamp's notion of how taste becomes constructed, intrusive: "The eye accommodates those demands by routinizing vision, by achieving a glance that can determine in an instant the purpose to which each object can be put. It's not a look that 'sees,' it's a look that sorts" (141). Greenberg, then, doesn't see Frank Stella, he sorts out non-flat art; Bartholomae doesn't see the St. Croix paper, he sorts out non-Pratt art. Duchamp pursued any avenue, as long as it contained a hint of the conceptual. Asked what sort of art he might make if he were still making art, Duchamp answered generically, conceptually: "something which would have significance. . . . It would have to have a direction, a sense. That's the only thing that would guide me" (Cabanne 106). Art that, just the same, moved. "Make a painting of *frequency*," is the note he jots to himself (and us) in 1914. That's the trouble with composition, it doesn't move, its timing is lousy. There is past and present in composition, but no future. The readymade was "a kind of rendezvous" (*Salt Seller* 32). Composition's gaze on student writing directs backward, towards the already-written, towards Pratt. The time-frame, then, is nostalgia—for aura, for presence; the perspective is retrojective. Without future, without frequency, composition is not three, it is simply two—the number of the double, the copy, the clone. This bars its move to the post-beautiful: "beauty is always the result of a resemblance" (Hollier 145). Writing becomes re-issue, founding and stamping, re-casting; like Arturo Schwartz, creating his new (highly-prized) sets of Duchamp's by-then lost or discarded readymades. Imagine—re-creating the readymade . . . composition as revising material into the alreadymade! "What is taste for you?" Cabanne asks. Duchamp's answer: "A habit. The repetition of something already accepted. If

you start something over several times, it becomes taste. Good or bad, it's the same thing, it's still taste" (Cabanne 48). Duchamp wanted art that moved—which is what drew him to chess: "it is like designing something," he said, "or constructing a mechanism of some kind by which you win or lose. . . the thing itself is very, very plastic" (*Salt Seller* 136).

This paper, then, is a plea for composition to be seen as writing-at-large, a delay in the glass we now inscribe as our writing medium. Let our default setting be the *document, rich text format*—such word processing terms, like *text file*, illustrate technology's ability to neutralize the ideological accrual of discursive genres. (*One may become a member* of the Teleintertexual Indeps *upon filing . . .*) The *document* differs from the compositional project envisioned by Bartholomae in the way use-value differs from exchange-value. "Fresh Widow and Why Not Sneeze" (1920) marked the point at which, according to Lebel, Duchamp "reached the limit of the unesthetic, the useless, and the unjustifiable" (47). As Roché noted, Duchamp's "gadget . . . wasn't useful." Of course not: the non-productive value of writing is its use-value, its inexchangeability. "Use-value cannot outlast use" (Hollier 136), it's only realized in consumption, in being used (up): *talk paregoric, Sweet Thing, and I will listen.* Duchamp, like Bataille's sun, is a permanent expenditure; his gadget is a word-engine that never stops running. The "Glass" was *not to be looked at for itself* (exhibition-value), *but only as a function* (use-value). Composition is mainly about preserving form at the expense of function, or limiting writing to an endlessly simulated exchange-function—dipping back into the same River Pratt each time, coming back with the same prized treasure. It's museumification, exchange-value as exhibition-value: "The same diversion that defines the market holds for the museum as well: objects enter it only once abstracted from the context of their use-value" (Hollier 136). Composition stalls on that distinction, "the opposition which dictates that one *uses* a tool and *looks* at a painting" (Hollier 137, emphasis mine). It's the difference between the way a Lascaux ritual-image was used vs. a PICTURE. Kosuth on Duchamp: "With the unassisted Ready-made, art changed its focus from the form of the language to what was being said. Which means that it changed the nature of art from a question of morphology to a question of function" (80). Bartholomae errs in taking his favorite painting to St. Croix in order to teach composition, "the thing out of place is never the real thing" (Hollier 138). Cult-value, Benjamin warns, is lost in exhibition-value. Pratt becomes the transposed fetish, losing all use-value; it "no longer works as a fetish: it has been discarded and framed to be put on the market; it has been degraded to become a commodity. It is no longer used but collected" (Hollier 147). The modern museum's curatorial strategy involves not time but location; it's "the Museum of Ethnography . . . exotic, remote in space" (Hollier 151n). The Museum of the Contact Zone, not the Interzone's Museum-Without-Walls, endlessly exhibiting its impermanent collection of readymades (*what is in front of his senses at the moment of writing*), done by the Society of Teleintertextual

Independents. Writing there is consumed on the spot, clicked through—a non-gallery tour, with no time for the literary hmm, just a quick series of wows; the tour itself becoming a kind of chance-inflected auto-performance art, a happening fashioned from easily-available, already-inscribed materials.

9. Bartholomae and I have different projects. He wants to entrench, I want to dissolve. He wants the specific, I want the generic. He teaches making, I prefer choosing. He'd like a writer to write like Mary Louise Pratt, I want writers who write like anyone-whoever. He's concerned with how one works with the space on the page, but I work on glass, already-inscribed glass behind which I can see the world pass by. He starts with the readymade and moves to the retrograde. I would start and stop with the readymade—delaying it, there on the screen, in glass, "capable of all the innumerable eccentricities" (*Salt Seller* 27). If he would just delay them rather than solve them, I could agree with Bartholomae on all of his givens: the travel narrative, for example, can stand for all writing; just as Benjamin let the film documentary stand for all art in the era of the mechanical composition. Whether prize-winning essay or rap slang, it's all a document-record, in *writte*, of a journey taken, field-notes from on the road. But I confess I learn more from those saucy travelogues that return from cool sites with new ideas (*some stuff from the bay*, say), rather than watching some janky slides from a trip I've taken a hundred times, stock scenes accompanied by an already-written political exegesis. I want an aesthetic judgment, of course; but I want to judge a student's art as art, not as "critical practice" (17). Actually, I would prefer to judge it as erotic practice. Duchamp's eroticism has infinite use-value in a post-disciplinary composition. The disciplines, the professions, lie buried in the "Glass", in the Cemetery of Uniforms and Liveries; but the *oculist charts* give those disciplinary bachelors another chance, so the 9 *malic moulds*—called by Duchamp "Priest, Department-store delivery boy, Gendarme, Cuirassier, Policeman, Undertaker, Flunkey, Busboy, Station-master" (*Salt Seller* 21); or named by "Me Craig Harrison Cincinnati Ohio Baby" as "G-DOGG HOE PIMP PLAYA WIGGER SKATER HUSTLER MAC TAGGER" (DOUGLAS_KOLLER)—finally have a chance to become ballers, to get some game, to replace their academic craft with mechanical precision, enabling their cemetery to become *eros's matrix*. Composition as I see it has now become a delay in glass, all writing is screen-writing. There is the artifact, which has been written about in notes, which refer to other artifacts, which contain ideas worked over previously or written about to friends, etc.—the whole text double-exposed by images and sound-bites. "Nude Descending a Staircase", that explosion in a shingle factory, represents composition as photochronography, each segment an exploded detail, "a ready-made continuously in motion . . . a sort of perpetual motion like that of a solar clock" (Lebel 68). It's writing become real-timed, e-conferenced and—mailed, a continuously updated home-page with running discussion list; links keep recurring, moved through back and forth, refolding back on themselves, a *kind of rendezvous* awaits the

reader, a *mirrorical return*. A bunch of "having becomes" that together form a tracing, a locale.

All I demand of writing is that it have *writte*; that it expose itself, announce itself, appear as writing. Writing stripped bare. Writing that wows me, dazzles me, that announces, "you're coming onto something so fast, so numb, that you can't even feel" (R.E.M.). Writing from a vast, universal field, Cage's Kansas prairie (or is it Burroughs's?), where language, thought, and vision act upon one another; panoramic writing, filled with all sorts of wonderful, seemingly useless treasures. The text I write becomes an interaction with those other texts, picking and choosing what's useful, building my own restricted teleinter-text. The "What is Composition?" of teleintertextual writing can be pulled any-where off the glass. At the end of that gangsta list is a call for more definitions which reads like a new textual strategy (but an old one, actually—it reads like a note from "The Green Box"):

Send me mail to include a new definition. . . . Make something up.
Please write Definitions in HTML Format. You can include links, pictures, or whatever else you want. All I am going to do is cut and paste.

And so, the *mirrorical return* to the concept of the *assisted readymade*. The Interzone is here, now, but I know I won't live there forever; just like I know electronic writing as now practiced will lose its charm (Duchamp writes to Stieglitz: "You know exactly how I feel about photography. I would like to see it make people despise painting until something else will make photography unbearable" [*Salt Seller* 165]). Until then, sampling, linking, glass, wires, photo-transfer, sound-scan—these are the materials of composition-in-gen-eral, the teleintertext; composition as I know it and love it: as blueprint, How-To Book, a sort of catalogue or "a sort of letter-box" (*Salt Seller* 38), *just putting stuff together—that's the way I work—to see what I could get out of it; very very plastic*. Writing full of new definitions, double-exposures, writing across all curriculums, *kicks in all genres* (Cabanne 82). *Return trips on the buffer. The trash of life. Cheap construction. Tin, ropes, wire.* Amazing and for-gettable, wonderful and oddly hollow; new adventures in hi-fi. Writing I strive to inscribe in my own thoroughly-mediated academic glass. Writing I love, yes, as much as a fetishist loves a shoe, as much as some people love (this is Duchamp's term, right? the bachelors' grinder? or was it Rrose's, maybe?) *sex-ual chocolate*.

CHAPTER ELEVEN

Access
The 'A' Word
in Technology Studies

Charles Moran

Problematics refer not only to what is included in a world-view, but also what is left out and silenced. That which is not said is as important as that which is said.

Henry Giroux

The income gap in America is eroding the social contract. If the promise of a higher standard of living is limited to a few at the top, the rest of the citizenry, as history shows, is likely to grow disaffected, or worse.

Lester Thurow

Billions of exclusions have been effected long before one of us applies for [an electronic] "mail address."

Louie Crew, quoted in Kaplan

Educational writers who attempt to present alternative visions of education that would require substantive social change as a prelude to, or in conjunction with, educational change, are marginalized or ignored.

J. Randall Koetting

I. THE ISSUE OF ACCESS IN COMPUTERS AND COMPOSITION STUDIES: THE PROBLEM AND ITS CONTEXT

My subject is the ways in which scholarship in computers and composition studies has not addressed the fact that access to emerging technologies, like access to other goods and services in America, is a function of wealth and social class. To put it more simply and directly, we in the computers-and-writing community know that there are *haves* and *have nots* among us and among our students, and we feel that the situation is getting worse, and we feel that the technology that fascinates us may be partially responsible, and we choose, for a range of good reasons, to ignore what we know and press on with our own research and writing agendas. As teachers, professors, and as newspaper-readers, we know that some people get access to computers, the Internet, the Web—and others don't. Perhaps 100 million people have Internet access—a huge number, but just 2% of the world's population. It is widely understood among us that the over-riding factor in determining who gets access and who does not is wealth: the per-capita funding of a given school, college, or university, and the income-level of the student's family/caregivers, determine the likelihood that a given student will have access, at school and/or at home, to emerging technologies(e.g. Anderson et. al. 25; Apple 169; Besser 61; Olson 195, 202; U.S. Congress 34–35; *Times Mirror* 8). We know, too, that though we can get more technology for a given dollar today than we could ten years ago, more technology is required today than it was then, and more will be tomorrow. To keep up, you need to buy a new machine every four years. Seymour Papert's assumption—that a student could use the same computer for thirteen years (13)—has proved to be a dream. Yet in our scholarship we either ignore/accept what Jonathan Kozol has termed the "savage inequalities" of the systems in which we work, or we give an obligatory nod in their direction and quickly turn to something else. For us, the relationship between wealth and access seems to be one of those issues that 'goes without saying.'

But the study of technology needs to be grounded in the material as well as in the pedagogical, cultural, and the cognitive if it is to be intellectually and ethically respectable. We have as a field substantially explored the ways in which gender plays in access to technology. We have looked at the ways in which women (e.g., Wahlstrom, Jessup) and minorities (e.g., Gomez, Salavert) get less access, or different access, to the technologies available in schools and homes. We have even, I think to our discredit, looked at the ways in which poor people use the computers they do have and have decided that they use them poorly! But I want to argue that these issues—gender and technology, pedagogical uses of technology—need to be addressed in the context of the relationship between wealth/class and access to technology. In the case of some minorities in America, wealth and minority status are overlapping categories: if you are black or of Hispanic origin in America, you are more likely to be poor than if you are not. So the one piece in our literature (e.g., Gomez) that does substantially consider minority access to technology does substantially address the issue of distribution-by-wealth. But though the subjects of the distribution of wealth and of social class seem taboo in our culture and in our literature, as a field we need to address the fact squarely: computers are, like other goods and services in our economy, available to those with money, and not available to those without money.

In this regard I've been no better than the rest of those who write in our field, and I need to say this, and in this chapter demonstrate my own implication in the problem I'm describing, partly because I am implicated in the problem, but chiefly because I don't want to be seen to be trashing my colleagues in the field, all of whom I love and respect and many of whom I count among my closest friends. Indeed, I seem to have taken on an almost self-destructive task: I attack my own scholarship, and that of my friends. Maybe this is why the field is so clear: because it is so personally dangerous.

Beyond the personal, I see two dangers in this topic I have chosen. One is rhetorical: that I will write a jeremiad, a James Sledd-like prophetic monologue that will leave an audience that admires but is not moved to action. I have always admired Sledd, and I have nodded as I read or heard his words, practically all of which have seemed to me to be incontestably true. After I have read, however, I have gone back to business as usual. My problem, certainly, but his, too. For me, there's a hint of academic posturing and something of Cassandra in the writing of those who, like Sledd, Kozol, and even Richard Ohmann, show us that we function in, and support, a class structure that is based largely upon wealth. But how to write about these matters and be heard? How to avoid being part of what Henry Louis Gates has called "the marionette theater of the political"(182)? And particularly since I am what I am: a tenured professor living comfortably on the top of the academic food-chain?

The other danger is compositional: that I will not have enough to write. The issue of access is easily and quickly framed: in America wealth is unequally distributed; money buys technology; therefore technology is inequitably distributed. If we are to redistribute technology, we need to redistribute wealth. End of argument.

Though this is a dangerous passage, I am willing to take the attendant risks because I believe the topic to be tremendously important to teachers of writing in the age of the new machine. It is important to scholars in our field, too, for if we are to do fully-useful scholarship, we need to include in our field of study the material context in which students and teachers work with new technologies. It is important, too, to me personally, and certainly because of my own situation. I therefore need to take a moment to sketch in the situation that informs my take on the issue of access and its relationship to wealth and social class.

I work at a public, land-grant university in a state that does not generously support public education, K-12 or post-secondary. Indeed, Massachusetts is ranked 50th of the 50 states in its per-capita support for public post-secondary education (State Rankings 1996, 144). This is a function of our state's history: Harvard was established in 1636, and with it a tradition of private post-secondary education that has made it difficult for public education in Massachusetts to find territory not already occupied. The University of Massachusetts co-exists not only with Harvard but with Brandeis, Wellesley, Smith, Amherst, Williams, Northeastern, Boston College, Boston University—a powerful private sector. Our state university therefore is technology-poor. This is not the result of administrative malfeasance: the University is underfunded everywhere. Our roofs leak, our offices are cleaned once each month, our classrooms are filled with broken furniture and dysfunctional shades, blinds, window-latches, lights. Our offices are understaffed, our classes are over-filled. The list goes on—not as a mega-complaint, for despite the effects that our environment has on us we are a generally happy and productive unit, with more than our share of awards and prizes, journals, books, successful alumna/ae, and students who feel well-served—but as evidence that, in our case, access to technology, like access to solid infrastructure generally, is a function of wealth, not bad management. We are a 'poor' institution, and those of us who teach and learn here have therefore limited access to emerging technologies. So long as we stay at home, we are content. When we travel to the computer labs of the more fortunate, we become unhappy and angry.

For our 17,000 undergraduates and 6,000 graduate students, we have fewer than 100 public-access PCs. Students can use, as well, another 84 terminals in our computer center to access email and to work on the university's mainframe. There are modest majors-only labs in our schools of management, and engineering and in a few academic departments, and there is the occasional computer in a dormitory lounge, but for first- and second-year students outside of these special situations, and for majors in departments in the humanities, you either buy your own computer, use your roomate's, or wait in line for one of the few public terminals. Not surprisingly, student computer-use on our campus is modest. In a recent survey of our undergraduates, 42% reported that they owned their own PCs. 35% reported that they used a computer "almost daily"; 34% that they used a computer "a few times per week"; 15% "a few times per month"; 10% "a few times during the semester"; and 6% "never." 25% used email "almost daily"; 21% "a few times per week"; 9% "a few times per month"; 7% "a few times during the semester"; and 38% "never."

In February 1996, I surveyed my first-year writing class, composed predominantly of second-semester freshmen but with a scattering of sophomores, juniors, and one senior. Of the 23 students in the class, nine said that they owned a computer; four said that they owned word processors (e.g., Brother, incompatible with either IBM or Apple); and 10 said that they did not own a computer. Here's a new owner talking about her experience with computers at our University: "I did not own a computer until this semester. Last semester I used one of my friend's computers but that was a real hassle. I also used some of my friends' word processors, but that was more of a hassle. I would have used the University's computers, but I was told that I would have to pay a fee. I really didn't have any money last semester and I couldn't afford to spend $20.00 on access to a computer when I could have spent $20.00 on books or food. I love having my own computer and I'm really pleased that I bought one for myself." And here's a non-owner: "My roommate has a word processor so I use that when it's free. When I am not able to use it I can go to the physics lab and use their computers. They are really slow compared to the one at home but better than nothing."

Area K-12 schools are even more poorly equipped than we are at the University. I had loaned my to-me-ancient IBM 286 to a graduate student so that she could write her dissertation on it. It came back in winter '96. What to do with it? I contacted the English Department of our local regional high school and asked if they would be interested. "Does it have a hard disk?" they asked. It did, all 40 megs of it, and was therefore very desirable: the computers available to their department had only floppy-drives. At another area school system, I gave a four-day in-service writing workshop and, on day one asked if the teachers and I could have access to a computer for printing purposes. The answer was, effectively, no, though they tried valiantly to bring in a Mac and get it working.

So it has proved impossible for me to take my friend Hugh Burns up on his offer of a tour of the Smith College computing facilities, because I know that I would get too angry at the difference between what is available to Smith College students and what is available to the University of Massachusetts students. When I visited Andover Academy, I saw there a computer facility that is light-years ahead of anything that we have here. Despite the fact that I can myself afford the new technologies, I can't advocate for them or even substantially use them in my teaching here, because the teachers and students in our writing program do not themselves have sufficient access to these technologies. A low-level, steady anger is what keeps me at the subject of this chapter.

As writing teachers, we have been able to ignore the question of access so long as the writing instrument of choice was the pencil and paper. Indeed, in K-12 education if someone does not have a pencil and paper, we are accustomed to give that student the materials she needs. Now, however, when the writing instrument of choice costs $2,000, and a printer another $500, we can't level the playing field for our students, even in the limited space of the writing classroom. The distance between the haves and the have-nots confronts us every day. And it seems that in public education this problem will only get worse, as public schools are attacked directly (voucher-systems and, in our state, charter schools), and state funding of public post-secondary education is reduced and replaced by increased tuition, making it still more difficult for poor families to send their children to college, let alone buy them the technology they may need there to survive.

II. REVIEW OF THE LITERATURE

I think of myself as belonging to a discipline, that of composition studies, and to a subset of that discipline, perhaps one defined by the readership of *Computers and Composition,* the "Five Cs," and attendance at the Computers and Writing Conference. We tend to call our field "Computers and Composition Studies," though our focus is upon our own home teaching-ground: first-year writing courses. We do not claim expertise in K-12 education. Most of us teach first-year writing at colleges and universities. Many of us direct writing programs, teach graduate courses in composition studies, teach in computer-equipped classrooms, and design, oversee, and run computer writing labs. We have, together, built a strong sub-field with a sub-stantial literature and the beginnings of a history (Hawisher, LeBlanc, Moran, and Selfe). I have looked through this literature—not all of it, but most—to find moments when we squarely confront the distance between the haves and the have-nots. And here's what I find.

Most of us simply do not deal with the relationship between wealth and access. I think of some of the major texts in our field—Bolter's *Turing's Man* and *Writing Space*, Landow's *Hypertext*, Feenberg's *Critical Theory of Technology*, Zuboff's *In the Age of the New Machine*, Papert's *Mindstorms*, Mason and Kaye's *Mindweave*, Negroponte's *Being Digital*, Harasim et. al.'s *Learning Networks*, Herring's *Computer-Mediated Communication*—none of which raise the question of access in a substantial way. Ellen Barton would place all of these writers except Zuboff in the "dominant discourse" of technol-ogy, a discourse that has as its foundation the assumption that technology will bring benefits to all. Barton includes as participants in the dominant discourse such works as Tracy Kidder's *The Soul of a New Machine* and popular histories of science and technology(57). I would add to Barton's list the September 1995 issue of *Scientific American*, a special, 150th anniversary issue titled "Key Technologies for the 21st Century"; any and all issues of *Popular Science* and *Discover*; and coffee-table histories of technology such as Steven Lubar's *Infoculture: The Smithsonian Book of Information Age Inventions.* I would add to this list, too, university alumni magazines and public relations documents that boast of their institution's technology without mentioning the fact that it is available only to a privileged few. A recent University of Washington alumni magazine gives a glowing report of an experiment in which entering first-year students received laptops and joined "U-Wired," an experimental online-enhanced curriculum. One has to read carefully to discover that there were only 65 students in this program. Buried in the piece is a note that "It is not feasible financially for the University to provide similar equipment free to the entire freshman class. To cover all 3,700 freshmen would cost more than $14 million"(Roseth 27).

Even books that Barton might consider belonging to the anti-dominant discourse do not deal with the issue of access. Sven Berkirts, in *The Gutenberg Elegies*, argues that computers will be evenly bad for everyone—and Birkerts's 'everyone' is a tiny and privileged fraction of the population: people like him-self, the tenured professoriate, professional readers and writers. Writers who have applied Braverman's insight that technology may de-skill work (e.g., Ohmann, Zuboff) do not deal with the relationship between wealth/class and access, either. Works in this tradition assume that computers will be forced upon workers and will change the nature of work—a situation that certainly is happening in the workplace, and in the offices of our home institutions, and is one that we need to pay attention to. Yet these works in the anti-dominant dis-course do not deal with the redistribution of wealth and the consequences that this has for us as writing teachers and as students of technology. The only book that I know of that deals in a substantial way with the relationship between wealth and access is Robert Anderson et al.'s *Universal Access to Email: Feasibility and Societal Implications.* Anderson and his co-authors argue that universal email would be a good thing for the United States, politically and economically. In the course of making their argument, they squarely face the fact that even almost-universal American access to email would require major policy moves, and large subsidies, by federal and state governments.

When we turn from full-length books to scholarly anthologies, a genre more typical of our field, we see that what is true for full-length books holds true for the anthology-chapter: as teachers and scholars we pay very little attention to the fact that technology is distributed principally according to wealth and social class. The only direct, full treatment of the subject is C. Paul Olson's 1988 essay, "Who Computes?" which was published in an anthology in the field of education, *Critical Pedagogy and Cultural Power.* Olson's powerful piece is cited in our literature, but often as if to say, "Olson has been there/done that. So now I can turn to my subject." In our field I take as a representative anthologies Hawisher and Selfe's 1991 anthology, *Evolving Perspectives on Computers and Composition Studies,* Selfe and Hilligoss's 1994 *Literacy and Computers,* and Muffoletto and Knupfer's 1993 *Computers in Education.* *Evolving Perspectives* is the flagship of NCTE's Computers and Composition series; *Literacy and Computers* is the volume of the MLA Research and Scholarship in Composition series that is devoted to emerging technologies. The chapters in these two anthologies are overwhelmingly written by scholars in the field that I have defined above—computers and composition studies. The third anthology, *Computers and Education,* is written not in our field but in the larger field of education. I include this anthology from the larger field to suggest that we in computers and composition studies are not unique. In all three of these anthologies the authors are generally silent about the issue of access. When the issue does arise, it arises in some interesting ways. It often seems to lurch into the foreground as a threatening presence, usually close to the end of its chapter.

First, *Evolving Perspectives.* The over-riding purpose of this anthology is to set a research/writing agenda for the 1990s (1). Read from our present perspective, the anthology does not begin on a promising note. In the Foreword, Edmund Farrell invokes the metaphor of the "genie in the bottle," suggesting that whatever effects the new technologies may bring are inevitable, an assumption that we often see in our literature: a version of original sin. When as researchers and writers we accept this assumption, we become spectators at a morality play, destined to watch the drama of sin and redemption unfold before us, as spectators, not agents. The genie is out of the bottle, humankind has eaten of the apple, and we watch as the plot unfolds. But then, a more promising note: the editors highlight the question of access as the first in a list of five "issues affecting our students and ourselves"(2). And yet, of the fifteen chapters in this book, only three raise the question of access at all, and only one of these (Gomez) raises the question in a substantial way. To shape the research agenda for field, the chapter-authors were asked to conclude each chapter with a set of "Questions for the 1990s." Of the 224 research questions posed and new directions charted, 17, or less than 8%, address the issue of access. Six of these questions arise in reference to a case study of a hospital, in which the staff objected to having the housekeepers record their cleaning-work on the institution's computer system. Other questions deal with ways in which a writing program, or a teacher working in a computer-equipped classroom, may distribute access to the computers in its control. Only three of the 17 questions that do deal with access to technology squarely face the fact that among our students, and among our teachers, there are haves and have-nots.

But let's get beyond the research questions and look at the ways in which the issue of access is addressed when it is addressed. In the first chapter of the book, "Ideology, Technology, and the Future of Writing Instruction," Nancy Kaplan quotes Louie Crew on the issue of access: "Billions of exclusions have been effected long before one of us applies for [an electronic] 'mail address'"(24). But in the next paragraph, without a trace of irony, Kaplan puts the issue behind her: "For the sake of argument, though, we might think of these privileges simply as the tools enabling pioneering efforts, helping us to actualize for all what the few now possess" (25). We, the field of computers and composition, must use our position of privilege "to actualize for all what the few now possess" (11). But how? Apparently, this actualization is implicit in the technology? Or in the work that we are now doing around technology? All we, or technology, need to do is to work within the existing situation, and wealth/class differences will disappear? At moments like this in the literature of our field, I am reminded of the Depression-era song, "The Big Rock Candy Mountain," in which the "hobo hikin'" sings his dream vision ("There's a lake of stew, and ginger-ale too—You can paddle all around it in your big canoe") without a hint of how all this might be brought to pass. Kaplan's real point is that she, and all of us in this new elite, are "hemmed in and hampered" (25) by the ideology implicit in the ways in which the new technology is designed. That's her subject, and it is an important one. But it is a study of the status quo: the technology that we are given, and to which most of us do not have access, is itself inscribed by our culture and carries with it values that we may find abhorrent. In a pattern that is characteristic of scholarship in our field, the author nods in the direction of access and then launches forth to address her own, very different, issue.

At other moments in this anthology the chapter-authors look at who gets access to the technology that is available (e.g., Ray and Barton, Jessup, and Gomez). Gomez, in particular, looks carefully at the ways in which women and minorities are given far less than their share of access to the equipment that is available to the institutions in which they learn or work. And Gomez does state flat-out that rich people, and rich schools, have more and better technology than do poor people and poor schools. But generally she accepts as part of the context the wealth-gap that she recognizes and focuses on what she terms "equitable teaching": how teachers can best work within the given, distributing their already-unequally-distributed material as equitably as they can.

A second anthology in our field, the recent MLA volume *Literacy and Computers*, suggests by its subtitle that access to technology might be central in its vision: *The Complications of Teaching and Learning with Technology*. But again we are disappointed, as the chapters focus on the changing nature of texts and what this change means (complications) for teachers and learners. I want to look closely at two chapters that do mention the question of resource-distribution in a substantial way: Paul J. LeBlanc's "The Politics of Literacy and Technology in Secondary School Classrooms," and Ellen L. Barton's "Interpreting the Discourses of Technology." I point to these two essays for their courage in choosing to deal directly with the subject I'm tracking, and for the ways in which the eruption of this subject into their essays proves destructive to what we might call their 'coherence.'

LeBlanc's chapter reviews what the author has seen in K-12 schools: teachers, schools, and students under-equipped and under-prepared for the world that is apparently to come. At the end of his chapter, LeBlanc gives us a tremendously powerful vision of the future: "The risk is that technology will only serve to widen the gap between the privileged and the disenfranchised. In the light of the potential for computers in education, such a reality makes the arrival of a new computer a cruel act masquerading as benevolence for Rose's students and others like them"(63). This conclusion is shocking in its directness, and it is surprising, given what has come before. In the body of the essay LeBlanc has tried to find the causes of what he has seen in K-12 schools. The candidates that he has brought forward are corporations, which have over-sold the computer to schools and parents; parents, for whom the computer has become "the talisman of educational achievement"; schools and school systems, for not training teachers; and schools and teachers, for using the computers they have for drill and practice. So the conclusion, in which LeBlanc looks beyond the schools, teachers, and students to the macro-economic context in which they operate, is shocking. It does not follow logically from what has come before, for if technology is really exacerbating the distance between rich and poor, then we should be looking at that problem, not the weaknesses of teacher preparation or the willingness of parents to take marketing-hype as truth. Emotionally, however, the conclusion does ring true. LeBlanc has studied the use of computers in poor schools and school systems. He has been to the mountain. When he has completed the writing of his chapter, he feels able to let the enormity of it all strike him fully, and he speaks.

We find the same pattern in Ellen Barton's chapter, "Interpreting the Discourse of Technology," although the moment of vision occurs not in the last sentences of the chapter, but on the third-from-last page. In her chapter Barton looks at the world of writing-about-technology and finds two kinds: a "dominant discourse . . . based on an unquestioned assumption that progress in technology brings a variety of benefits to individuals and society" (57), and an "antidominant discourse" which "exists as a minority voice, critiquing the assumption that technology always brings progress and pointing out some of its less-desirable consequences" (60). She reviews the writing in our field and finds "a clear association between pedagogical research describing the use of computers in the teaching of writing and the dominant discourse, which assumes the advantages of technology in education" (69). When the anti-dominant discourse does arise in our work, she finds, it is almost always quickly merged into the dominant discourse. This skilled and useful reading of our literature fills the first 17 pages of the chapter. And then, in the middle of a call for "a more complicated theoretical perspective," one that "makes specific contributions to both the dominant and antidominant discourses of technology," Barton inserts this amazing sentence: "The crux of this paradoxical position is in the unequal distribution of technological resources in literacy education" (73). This sentence occurs at the end of a paragraph; the next paragraph begins a review of an example of 'good' research that has nothing to do with the question of access; and then another amazing sentence: "Research in computers and writing more closely reflects the key ideas of the antidominant discourse when it exposes the unequal distribution of resources across groups using technology in literacy education" (74). And then Barton cites LeBlanc's chapter as something that it is not, really: an ethnographic study that demonstrates that "the benefits of technology are not extended equally to all institutions, instructors, and students" (75).

The third anthology I have chosen for this review has a promising title: *Computers and Education: Social, Political, and Historical Perspectives.* But the promise of the title is unfulfilled: "access" does not appear in the subject index, and despite the editors' contention that their purpose is "to address critical social, economic, and political issues concerning the implementation of computers in education" (249), the chapters in the anthology follow the pattern we have found in the two anthologies I have considered above: the chapters do not substantially deal with the fact that technology is distributed according to wealth and social class. The chapter-authors look primarily at the ways in which computers are mis-used in schools (e.g., Bork 73, Muffoletto). When the authors do face the issue of the relationship between wealth/class and access, they take this relationship to be a given in our culture, a matrix that teachers and students simply have to and work within. Howard Besser, in "Education as Marketplace," puts it succinctly: "In areas involving technology there is strong intuitive evidence to suggest that the addition of this to the curriculum will further exacerbate stratification. For example, in a classroom where computers are introduced we can expect that the students who can go home and practice on their parents' computers will learn far more quickly than those students from families who cannot afford a computer—particularly in the common situation in which the school does not have enough computers for all students" (62-63). But he has prefaced this statement with another: "Class and gender divisions in society are part of the social structure in which the educational system operates, and additions to curriculum tend to replicate and reinforce existing divisions" (62). Nancy Knupfer, too, seems to be squarely facing the relationship between wealth/class and access, but then she turns to other subjects. In a section of her chapter headed "Equity and Access," she lists "socioeconomic status" as one of the possible "causes of unequal access to educational computing" (169). But then with what I have come to see as a characteristic segue—"The "mere acquisition of computers in schools is one small facet of the much larger and more complex task"—she turns to a review of the research on such classroom variables as "the number and placement of machines" (169), "existing myths and prejudices about computer use" (169), and "the school's laudable dedication to the special needs of remedial or gifted and talented students" (170).

III. THE IMPORTANCE OF THIS ISSUE FOR OUR FIELD—TODAY

To review: so far I have established that we as a field all seem to agree that computers are unequally distributed to teachers and learners in our educational system, and that we agree, too, that access to emerging technologies is a function of wealth and social class. The rich have more, the poor less. I have established, too, that we've not, as a field, paid sufficient attention to the fact that our students have differential access to computers. Students from wealthy homes, who attend wealthy schools, have access to new technologies; students from non-wealthy homes and non-wealthy schools have less access to these same technologies. I have established, I think, sufficient exigency: if we believe that our teachers and students should play on a close-to-level field, we need to act—to do something other than what we are now doing.

But before I suggest some directions we might pursue as scholars and teachers, I want to suggest that the situation is even more desperate than I've so far suggested. Yes, the wealth-gap is there, and its existence should spur us to action. But the wealth-gap is not only there; it is getting wider every day. And the technology that so draws and fascinates us is widely held to be one of the seismic forces that is widening the gap (e.g., Besser 62-3, Frankel 32, LeBlanc 63). Given the link between wealth and access, this means that teachers and learners in poor schools and/or in poor families will be even further disadvantaged tomorrow than they are today. I am going to present what may at first seem to be too much data here. "Don't we all know this?" I hear you say. But given our record so far, I'm not sure that we really do know. So I take the risk and present the unpleasant story in detail.

In *Peddling Prosperity: Economic Sense and Nonsense in the Age of Diminished Expectations*, Paul Krugman, the Stanford economist, tells us that that in America since 1979 the rich have been getting richer, the poor poorer. He gives us a graph based on figures from the census (131) that shows the rate of income growth of citizens according to the size of their income during three periods: 1947-1973, 1973-1979, and 1979-1989. The graph helps us see that we've lived in three really different periods, at least as defined by rate of income growth. Between 1947-1973, the rate of income growth was almost equal for rich and poor, at c. 2.5%/year for all sectors. 1973-1979 was a period of no-growth for every sector except people in the top ranks. Between 1979-1989, however, the poor lost ground while the rich surged ahead. The graph for this period is almost a straight line: the greater your income, the greater your income growth during this period.

This information, disturbing as it is, masks an even more disturbing truth. The census figures don't get at the incomes of the really rich, because of "top-coding" (the census asks only if you make 'more than $250,000'—so it doesn't register incomes higher than that); and because income, as defined by the census, does not include capital gains, which are a major source of income for high-income families(133). Krugman calls on work by the Congressional Budget Office that has filled this gap(134). Using IRS data and data from the census, the CBO demonstrates that during the period 1977-1989, in constant 1993 dollars, incomes of families in the bottom 20% dropped 9%, while incomes of families in the top 2% to 4% bracket rose 29%, and incomes of families in the top 1% rose a remarkable 105%. Krugman notes that the average income of those in this top 1% was $800,000 (135). "What we have learned," Krugman writes, "is that when we speak of 'high-income' families, we mean really high income: not garden-variety yuppies, but Tom Wolfe's Masters of the Universe" (138). Krugman speaks of this redistribution of wealth as a "siphoning" (138) from the poor to the rich.   .

To make these figures concrete, Krugman asks us to imagine two villages, one in 1977 and one in 1989, "each composed of one hundred families representing the percentiles of the family income distribution in a given year—in particular, a 1977 village and a 1989 village. According to CBO number, the total income of the 1989 village is about 10 percent higher than that of the 1977 village; but it is not true that the whole distribution is shifted up by 10 %. Instead, the richest family in the 1989 village has twice the income of its counterpart in the 1977 village, while the bottom forty 1989 families actually have lower incomes than their 1977 counterparts" (138).

What has happened since 1989? Has the wealth-gap begun to narrow? It would be nice to think so. However, figures compiled by the Department of Commerce suggest otherwise. Between 1990 and 1993 median family income declined in constant dollars from $39,149 to $36,959. This decline was not shared equally by rich and poor. The number of families making less than $10,000 increased from 8.3% of the whole to 9.6%—a whopping 15.6% increase; while the numbers of families making over $75,000 stayed almost constant. In 1993, 25.8% of black families made less than $10,000, as did 17.9% of families of Hispanic origin. (U.S. Department of Commerce 474, Tables 731 and 732.) Lester Thurow (78) notes that the "by the early 1990s the share of wealth (more than 40%) held by the top 1% of the population was essentially double what it had been in the mid-1970s."

Further, in *Population Profile of the United States: 1995,* published by the U.S. Bureau of the Census, the authors bring us up to 1993, and the picture they paint is a grim one.

Household income distribution changed over the past 25 years. In 1993, those at the bottom 20% of the income distribution received less of the Nation's income than previously, while those at the top 20% received more.

In 1968, the poorest 20% of households received 4.2% of the aggregate household income. By 1993, their share declined to just 3.6%. In contrast, the highest 20% of households received 42.8% of the aggregate household income in 1968. By 1993, their share had increased to 48.2%.

Those in the middle of the income distribution also received proportionally less of the Nation's income in 1993 than previously. The middle 60% of households received 53% of the aggregate household income in 1968. By 1993, their share had declined to 48.2% (41).

The figures we have reviewed above should be sufficient to support our intuitive sense that the gap between rich and poor is widening. We read in newspapers that 28 million Americans now live in walled or gated communities (Thurow 79), and we see locally and nationally increased spending on police, prisons, and private security guards for the protection of private property, as we create barriers to keep out the have-nots. We see advertising directed at those few with disposable incomes sufficient to purchase $8,000 watches and $60,000 cars. In the rhetoric of political campaigns, further cutting taxes for the wealthy seems both good and inevitable. Should the system of taxation become more 'flat' than it is, the gap between rich and poor will increase even more rapidly. The re-writing of the welfare system guarantees that less money will be spent in programs targeted to the needs of the poor; and the effects of school choice, voucher systems, and, in our state, charter schools, is to reduce the amount of funding available to public K-12 education. And the wealth gap divides our profession, too, into a community like Krugman's 1989 village: a few well-paid professors directing writing programs and teaching graduate courses in composition theory, and legions of poorly-paid part-timers and graduate students teaching first-year writing courses.

IV. SO: WHERE TO GO FROM HERE? A
RESEARCH/WRITING/TEACHING AGENDA

I am hopeful, of course, that we can, as a people and as a profession, effect change. As Lester Thurow has written, "some very successful societies have existed for millennia with enormous inequalities of wealth and income— ancient Egypt, imperial Rome, classical China, the Incas, the Aztecs. But all these societies had political and social ideologies that fit this economic reality. None believed in equality in any sense—not theoretically, not politically, not socially, not economically. Democracies have a problem with rising economic inequality precisely because they believe in political equality—'one person, one vote'" (78).

Understanding that we do still live in a democracy, and that we do believe in at least political equality, I want to sketch out a research/writing/teaching agenda for our field that could be our contribution to the righting of the ship of state. To a degree I am responding to Ellen Barton's challenge: we need to find ways of integrating what she calls an "anti-dominant discourse" into our research and teaching agendas. Here are a few areas that we could easily explore, research, and write about.

- First, in our teaching and research we can partially finesse the relationship between wealth and access by learning about, using, and advocating, less-expensive equipment. We have, perhaps in unwitting complicity with those who market high-tech products, studied and advocated cutting edge technology: the educational uses of hypermedia or the Web or the MOO/MUD. Let's instead, or in addition, look for available low-end, inexpensive, relatively-affordable technologies. In 1980 Seymour Papert argued that a student could use Logo on the same computer for 13 years, amortizing the cost of the computer over the full span of K-12 education. This, of course, never happened: we have instead been taught that we need to stay up—which means renewing our technology every four years—or die. But how much technology does a writer need? We know, for example, that you can buy a versatile word-processor for about $200. On this inexpensive word processor you can enter and revise text—do everything except format and print. Once you have composed your piece on this "volks-computer," you can upload the text to a high-end computer-printing station and there do the formatting and printing. Reports of this kind of substitution are emerging from National Writing Project sites (e.g., Hunter and Moran, in press). Let's use these low-end writing-and-communicating machines. As we do, we'll need to study and report on the effects on teachers and student writers of substituting low-end for high-end technologies. The effects will almost certainly be different at different grade levels, or in learning different subjects, techniques, or concepts.
- Second, we can study the effects upon students and teachers of technologically-poor teaching and learning environments. We have in our field studied the effects of technologically-rich environments on students and teachers. But we have not studied the effects of a technologically-impoverished environment. What are the losses? And—let's face it squarely—what might be the gains? Really? Let's find out. Does a technologically-impoverished school environment affect students' performance? Learning? The students' self-image? Their sense of academic opportunity or futility? Does it affect the teachers' estimates of their students' potential? Of their school's effectiveness? And if a technologically-poor environment does have school effects, can these effects be compared to the effects of, for instance, working

in an athletically-poor environment—e.g., having a fine basketball team vs. having a poor basketball team? A run-down physical plant vs. a well-maintained physical plant? A building-wide sense of mission? Studies of this sort would fall into the tradition of school effects research established by such scholars as Ronald Edmonds and Wilbur Brookover and chronicled in *Advances in School Effectiveness Research and Practice* (Reynolds, et al.). Ideally, these studies would be longitudinal and long-range.

- Third, let's ask, relative to the job market, what is a good pre-employment curriculum for K-12 and college students? What preparation to students need to function adequately in today's workplace? Maybe the preparation they need does not require expensive hardware and software. And perhaps our public schools are not as retrograde as they are often understood to be. Let's not take the word of business that our students are radically underprepared; let's explore the hypothesis that school-bashing is a political act, not a sound judgment based upon accurate historical, comparative studies. To get at answers to these questions, we'd want to study graduates as they enter the workforce, a study that would look at the transition between school/college/university and the workplace.

- Fourth, in a college/university writing program, what access is available to the teachers—teaching assistants and part-timers who may be among the poorest people on campus? Does wealth make a difference here too? Wealth of institution and wealth of graduate student's family? And if so, how do these differences play out in, for example, graduate students' use of computers to teach? To research? To write? How do the differences affect the graduate student's time-of-passage through the degree? And how do they impact the graduate student's employability—her successful negotiation of a difficult job market?

- Fifth, what have teachers done in their classes to resist, or to in some degree undo/redress, inequalities of access to technology? We need here to follow the path pointed to by Mary Louise Gomez, and study what seem to be successful examples of "equitable teaching." What are the effects of these bold attempts, on learners and on teachers? Do the effects persist? Or are they limited to the time of treatment?

- And sixth and finally, what have students been able to do, individually or collectively, to obtain the access that they need? What can, and do, learners now do to level the technological playing field? When a student borrows access, from, for example, a roommate, what does the student give in exchange? In what coin do they re-pay, and what is the cost, to them? One could imagine the results of this line of research: handbooks for students, authored by students, on ways of achieving access to the technology they need; and handbooks by teachers for teachers on how to get access for themselves and for the students in their charge.

Much of the research I'm advocating would include its subjects as researchers and co-authors. It would take place in schools, homes, and workplaces. It would be collaborative in mode and characterized by an atmosphere of mutual trust and respect. In this research both students and teachers would be actual and potential agents, actors on the stage of American life, able, within limits, of course, to make choices and to effect change. This research would be part of what Paulo Freire terms "a pedagogy which must be forged with, not for" (30). Its aims would be Freirean: through studies of technology, to increase students' and teachers' awareness of the ways in which wealth and social class play in their lives. It would fall into the category of "action research," as defined by Garth Boomer: "Deliberate, group or personally owned and conducted, solution-oriented investigation" (8); and by Bogdan and Biklen: "The systematic collection of information that is designed to bring about social change" (223). Through the study of the ways in which technology plays in the distribution of power and wealth, this pedagogy would increase its subjects' awareness of the socioeconomic forces at play in their worlds, a necessary prelude to political action. A further result of this research would be through publication to increase our community's awareness of the wealth-gap and its effect upon the learning that takes place in our classrooms.

I want to close by reminding us of one of the epigraphs to this chapter: "Educational writers who attempt to present alternative visions of education that would require substantive social change as a prelude to, or in conjunction with, educational change, are marginalized or ignored" (Koetting 132). I've not presented an "alternative vision of education," but I clearly have one: an educational system that works within a democracy which offers equal opportunity to its citizens: equal access to medical care, legal services, housing, food, and, yes, good schools and good homes equipped with appropriate technologies. I know that my colleagues in our field share this vision. I very much fear, as do many of my colleagues, that emerging technologies are increasing the wealth-gap that now exists in our society. As members of the community of scholars in the field of computers and composition, as teachers of first-year writing courses, and as students of technologies that are arguably partially responsible for the increasing distance between rich and poor, I believe that we have to bring this topic forward on our agenda and give it more attention than we have in the past.

CHAPTER TWELVE

Speaking the Unspeakable about 21st Century Technologies

Bertram C. Bruce

WRITING IN 1841 TO A FRIEND WHO HAD ASKED HIM WHAT HIS "SONGS Without Words" meant, Felix Mendelssohn challenged the idea that words could say as much as he had already said in his music:

> People frequently complain that music is too ambiguous; that it is unclear to them what they should be thinking about when they hear it, whereas everyone understands words. For me, it is exactly the reverse . . . The thoughts I find expressed in music that I love are not too indefinite, but on the contrary, too definite to put into words. (Mendelssohn 3)

Mendelssohn's romantic invention of the song without words resonated with the romantic spirit of the mid-nineteenth century, embodying the idea that passions, faiths, and aesthetic responses, indeed, all that really matters, were too much for words, or at least for prose. The view that the important things in life lie beyond the realm of the analytical echoes in the enigmatic final few pages of Ludwig Wittgenstein's *Tractatus* (1961), when he tells us that "in [the world] no value exists," "ethics cannot be put into words," "death is not an event in life," "the riddle does not exist," or "anyone who understands me eventually recognizes [my propositions] as nonsensical."

It is ironic that Wittgenstein's circumscription of what words can do, essentially, mathematics and some aspects of the natural sciences, ignited logical positivism in the twenty-century. His "this is all that words can do," that is, not much, was transformed into "this is all that words can do!," a paean to the power of logic and operational definitions. It led to the twentieth-century philosopher's notion of expressibility, that any meaningful thought is ultimately expressible in language, once suitably defined and articulated, a notion that was soon extended far beyond the natural sciences to the social sciences, humanities, arts, and education.

A consequence of this is that many of the things we ought to be talking about fall outside what our institutional strictures encourage or even allow us to talk about. Then, in order to say what cannot be said, we have to contort ourselves, arguing for positions we never should have considered relinquishing. Thus, Nel Noddings (1984, 1992) appears to adopt a radical position in her call for caring in education, this despite the centrality of care in the experience of nearly all good teachers. But caring does not come with the institutional requisites of definability, measurability, replicability, and neutrality that are so conducive to disinterested academic discourse. Central to experience or not, its existence is not in what Wittgenstein means by words, or equivalently, the analyzable world.

SPEAKING OUTSIDE THE CIRCLE

What strikes me about the chapters in this section is that while they address what must be central to pedagogy today and in the future, they have to swim against the mainstream of pedagogical discourse to do so. The major currents flow the opposite way, away from asking questions about access, fairness, income disparities, corporate influence over education, disruptions of employment, hierarchies, power, authority, ideology, morality, writing that "dazzles," or even, meaningful communication. It is not that issues such as these are never mentioned in mainstream discourse, but that to the extent they lie outside Wittgenstein's circle, they slip away from the center; they are viewed as ancillary, preparatory, or incidental, not the hard stuff.

That is why Charles Moran can open his chapter with the assertion that "scholarship in composition studies has not addressed the fact that access to emerging technologies . . . is a function of wealth and social class." But if new technologies can make a real difference in teaching composition, extreme differentials in the opportunity to make use of them could have devastating consequences for democratic education. These differentials swamp many of the claims we might make about this or that approach to using technology for learning. Moran goes on to explore how the undeniably true and immensely important consequences of wealth and access in the educational experience of students are rarely examined. He shows that neither the dominant discourse of technology nor that of composition studies address the problem, or even, in most cases, acknowledge its existence.

Why should access[1] be a taboo topic, so that in professional discourse it is the forbidden A word? Moran suggests that it is a dangerous topic. He emphasizes our collective, but personal, implication in the taboo, and worries that he might be seen as "trashing [his] colleagues." He also talks about the rhetorical dangers, that writing about access is only academic posturing, and the compositional dangers, that there is too little to say about access. I was pleased to see that he did not dwell too long on these dangers, but went on to talk about the 'A' word, despite the taboo. His stories and data make a compelling case that should not continue to be ignored. And the agenda for research that he advocates could lead to a new kind of academic discourse that both lives within and speaks to the real conditions of schooling,

But I am still left wondering why access is taboo in the first place. The dangers Moran talks about might apply to other areas that do not carry the same taboo feeling. Could it be that we are so ensconced in Wittgenstein's circle that we cannot see outside it? Wittgenstein himself was so convinced of the circle's inadequacy for accomplishing humanly useful work that he left academic philosophy to become an elementary-school teacher (Janik and Toulmin, 202-238). He had completed the dirty job of pointing out the circle's existence, so others would be free to move beyond it.

But as we all know, the dominant currents in twentieth-century thought, including even, I would argue, most of postmodernist writing, have remained dammed by Wittgenstein's circle. Acceptable academic discourse, Wittgenstein's speaking, seeks language that is definable, measurable, replicable, and neutral, while avoiding passion, uniqueness, personal commitment, and overt politics. The access issue overflows too easily from the former to the latter. There is pain in the stories of access that Moran relates, and an uncomfortableness begins to develop that says we really ought to do something this time. Moreover, what if access disparities really are as great as all the data say? What does that mean for how we ought to be spending our lives? At the end of the century, we are still enmeshed in the problem Wittgenstein posed: Can we speak about what cannot be spoken?

Lester Faigley's chapter is an exception to the pattern of silence that Moran describes. He starts with a question many others have posed, "How does education change for a child who begins school with the potential to communicate with millions of other children and adults, to publish globally, and to explore the largest library ever assembled?" But rather than indulging in fantasies about our glorious technological future, he asks two other tightly linked questions, one about "large corporations making decisions about how children will learn" and the other about "massive redistributions of wealth and disruption of patterns of employment." These, like access, are taboo topics in the educational academy, so it is little surprise that his chapter opens with four news articles and draws heavily from news accounts of the economy, not from academic discourse.

Faigley sees a mismatch between his own teaching experiences and the visions of future education in the public media. This discrepancy persists in part because our academic discourse typically keeps within the safe circle, making it difficult to share personal experiences, especially when they touch on hot topics like distribution of wealth. But as Faigley says, "teachers have to enter policy debates, even when they are not invited" even though they will not be "directly rewarded for doing it." Once again, there is the challenge to say what cannot be said.

Access, and related economic issues, are not the only ones that strain against our self-imposed circle of silence. Any issue that undermines the authority of the academic institution is taboo as well. A case in point is that to question any fundamental goal of an academic enterprise immediately throws us outside its circle. We are not to ask about values, or about beauty, or any goal that cannot be delimited and scrutinized. Thus, Geoffrey Sirc's chapter must also struggle to maintain what is important outside the circle while trying to be heard within it:

> This paper, then, is a plea for composition to be seen as writing-at-large, a delay in the glass we now describe as our writing medium. Let our default setting be the document, rich text format—such word processing terms, like *text file*, illustrate technology's ability to neutralize the ideological accrual of discursive genres. (One may become a member of the Teleintertextual Indeps upon filing . . .) The document differs from the compositional project envisioned by Bartholomae in the way use-value differs from exchange-value.

Sirc talks of technology and its implications for composition, but his larger meanings are about the reasons for teaching, judging others and their work, setting goals for learning, and the nature of art. These topics are too unsettling for the circle; they are conceptual, where the institution wants technique. When Sirc says, "Bartholomae and I have different projects. He wants to entrench, I want to dissolve. He wants the specific, I want the generic. He teaches making, I prefer choosing" he is not just delineating an agenda for composition instruction that differs from Bartholomae's; he is also asserting values that pull us outside the safe zone. If the practice of teaching is to inculcate known procedures, we can establish our curricula with confidence. We define the scope, and then the sequence of learning activities. But if it is to "start and stop with the readymade," as Sirc says, then how do we speak about it? Clearly, the institution becomes unsettled. It is no accident then that, "ultimately, the modernist focus—in composition as in art—is institutional rather than conceptual."

One reason that all these chapters challenge the comfort zone is that they are aware of possibilities for radical changes, which could undermine everything about education as we know it. As Marilyn Cooper says, we are talking about transitions in assumptions "about knowledge, language, and the self, . . . about power, . . . about responsibility, and . . . about the teacher's role." In the modernist frame, these are supposed to be givens, not things to speak about, much less to change. But "if knowledge is not a stable construct of ideas to be passed from teachers who know to students who learn, the basis for teachers' authority in the classroom s threatened." This leads to new roles for teachers: " . . . rather than acting as wizards who enter the conversation only to lay down the law or to establish democratic decision-making procedures, they should put more trust in students' moral self-conscience." But then, technique is not the central issue. Instead, we must talk about human relations, the exercise of power, moral conscience—the ethical dimensions of teaching.

Near the end of her chapter, Cooper presents an interesting case: Ira Shor's desocializing history and English course on Columbus. We first see Shor's description of the teaching practice, which includes really listening to students, posing complex problems, and examining contradictions, in order to develop greater critical awareness. But she questions the slide from asking students to be conscious of and responsible for their positions to asking them to be critical of their positions (cf. Ellsworth, 1989). These are significant questions, because they get to the essence of the whole teaching and learning enterprise. They make us conscious of and responsible for our pedagogical positions in a way that conventional talk about techniques does not. Accordingly, they do not fall neatly into the discourse of cumulative educational research, but are generative questions that need to be raised again and again in new contexts. They reside outside the circle.

Perhaps the most succinct way to talk about the circle problem is to note that mainstream theorizing operates within a system in which there is a constant pressure to eliminate the idiosyncratic or the personal, and to mute questions about purpose, goodness, equity, and beauty. These are present in practice, yet practice's voice is often silent, and ignored within the circle. James Sosnoski comes to this issue in his chapter. He notes a wide range of issues about hypertext reading, such as,

> If style is the hallmark of the writer's personality and a signature the legal bond of identity, then hyper-reading undercuts the personal aspects of authorship. Hypertexts are not given the same authority as printed ones because textual signatures become blurred in the undending surge of intertextuality . . .

This and other issues suggest the need for a new theory about reading and writing in the postmodern, hypertextual world. But Sosnoski sees a "raincloud" in ungrounded theorizing. He calls instead for a "praxis of hyper-reading." Praxis means an integration of theory and practice that obviates Wittgenstein's circle. Rather than accepting the dualities of thought and action, theory and practice, speaking and not-speaking, praxis is action informed by reflection along moral, aesthetic, and political dimensions, all of those arenas Wittgenstein said "we cannot speak about."

SEEING TECHNOLOGY AS MORE THAN TECHNIQUE

Technology is not just "technology," if by that we mean only silicon chips in a plastic box or a web browser. It is an expression of the ideologies, the cultural norms, and the value systems of a society. The changes in social practices associated with new technologies then become extensions of our current selves. As we modify practices, we reshape both ourselves and the new technologies. This means that talk about technology and its effects is hopelessly inadequate if it remains entirely in the realm of the technical. That is one reason why it so valuable to step outside the circle as these chapters do.

Perhaps the most important societal process that technology expresses is what Ellul (1973) calls *la technique*. Technique does not mean machines, or technology in the narrow sense, or even procedures for accomplishing tasks, although its pervading of society has been fostered by the rapid growth of new technologies. For Ellul, technique is a sociological phenomenon, induced by examination of modern human activity. He defines it as "the totality of methods rationally arrived at and having absolute efficiency (for a given stage of development) in every field of human activity" (xxv). Technique enters into every area of life and progressively absorbs people. In a subsequent work, Ellul (1980) sees a double effect [of technology] on society and human existence. On the one hand, it disintegrates and tends to eliminate bit by bit anything that is not technicizable (this has been brutally felt on the level of merriment, love, suffering, joy, etc.). And it tends to reconstitute a whole of society and human existence on the basis of technological totalization (203).

The modern realization of Wittgenstein's circle is not only that we exclude from our discourse any talk of "merriment, love, suffering, joy, etc.," but also that we unquestioningly accept the virtue of absolute efficiency. We do this for many natural reasons: we are uncomfortable talking about deeply-held values where there is a chance for serious conflict; we are frustrated addressing issues knowing in advance that there is no easy solution (Wittgenstein: "the riddle does not exist"); we find it complicated to expand our compass to include the exigencies of daily life; we do not like to abandon familiar methods and rationales.

The consequences of this reluctance to step outside are that we reveal the operation of Ellul's technique in our most mainstream professional practices. Recently, professional education organizations[2] have proposed a set of standards for all teachers seeking certification in the U.S. The standards include items such as,

- operate a multimedia computer system with related peripheral devices to successfully install and use a variety of software packages
- use productivity tools for word processing, database management, and spreadsheet applications
- explore, evaluate, and use computer/technology resources including applications, tools, educational software and associated documentation
  (from ISTE *Recommended Foundations in Technology for all Teachers*)

Knowing how to operate a multimedia computer system is a useful skill; a teacher who does not know this has one fewer option for supporting learning. But a list of skills such as this remains (intentionally?) neutral about the underlying pedagogical values—those which might inform decisions about whether this option is appropriate for particular students in a given context, how it should be used, and how one might judge its success. On what basis do we judge educational software, or even verify that it is educational? What kind of instruction do we want to support? What do we want our productivity tools to help us produce? The standards carefully avoid these non-circle questions. Even when they use words such as "evaluate" they do not engage with the considerations that would enable meaningful evaluation. Safe in the circle of technique, carefully avoiding the judgments that might offend, they fail to connect with the most fundamental issues about teaching and learning.

Techniques are important, but beyond any set of techniques, teachers need to develop critical awareness. They are faced again and again with immediate, practical situations in which they have to decide whether to use a particular technology, and if so, how, and with whom. If it is to be used, how does it fit with all the other aspects of learning—oral discussions, reading, solitary reflection, hands-on activities, and with a larger conception of teaching and learning? Answering these questions is a central part of everyday teaching. They remind us that teachers must develop their own pedagogical philosophy—to think primarily about learning and secondarily about the technologies that support it.

ASKING IMPROPER QUESTIONS

Writing to Ludwig Ficker, Wittgenstein became his most explicit about the purpose of his enigmatic *Tractatus*:

> The book's point is an ethical one. I once meant to include in the preface a sentence which is not in fact there now, but which I will write out for you here, because it will perhaps be a key to the work for you. What I meant to write, then, was this: My work consists of two parts: the one presented here plus all that I have not written. And it is precisely this second part that is the important one. My book draws limits to the sphere of the ethical form the inside as it were, and I am convinced that this if the ONLY rigorous way of drawing those limits.
> (Janik and Toulmin 192)

Through his equation: speakable = unimportant, Wittgenstein did not convince many to abandon speaking (in the technical sense he had defined). Instead, the legacy for most of his readers was a perverse admonition against trying to speak in any way about what was most important. That conceptual constriction was bolstered by the practices of academic disciplines and professional organizations, the marginalization of intellectual life, and the difficulty of engaging with our deepest concerns, such that most of our discourse remains inescapably locked with Ellul's technique.

The articles in this section are not content to remain in the realm of technique. This, despite the fact that I suspect none of the authors would easily dismiss Ellul's assertion that it is vain to pretend that "the monolithic technical world that is coming to be . . . can be checked or guided" (1973, 428). But they shift the issues from technical to ethical. They ask different questions, such as . . . What do we want students to learn? How can we use new technologies? How should we? Why should we? What will change when we do? Do we want those changes? What do they mean for us, our students, society? What is fair? What kind of society do we want to live in? And, perhaps ultimately, who do we want to become?

NOTES

1.   It would be useful to theorize access more fully, but for the purpose here, I want to treat it as Moran generally does, as a process whereby social goods, such as technology, are inequitably distributed. We might explore more deeply how technology not only reflects inequities, but also establishes and maintains them. Yet at the same time, access is far from an unalloyed good, meaning as it often does, social disconnection, deskilling of work for many people, cyber-crime, corporate surveillance, loss of personal privacy, and even the recently named "Internet Addiction Disorder" (Hodder 1997).

2.   The National Council for Accreditation of Teacher Education (NCATE) is the official body for accrediting teacher preparation programs in the U.S. The International Society for Technology in Education (ISTE) is a professional education organization responsible for recommending guidelines for accreditation to NCATE. NCATE adopted the new Curriculum Guidelines for Accreditation of Educational Computing and Technology Programs from ISTE in October 1996. Programs seeking accreditation must develop a folio that addresses the performance-based standards. The guidelines document is available from ISTE <http://www.iste.org/standards/resources/projects/techstandards/, (800-336-5191), or <cust_svc@ccmail.uoregon.edu>.

PART THREE

Ethical and Feminist Concerns in an Electronic World

CHAPTER THIRTEEN

Liberal Individualism and Internet Policy
A Communitarian Critique

James E. Porter

The work of the Right is done very well, and spontaneously, by the Left on its own.

Jean Baudrillard

THIS CHAPTER EXAMINES AN ETHICAL FRAMEWORK PROMINENT IN DISCUS-
sions of Internet policy—liberal individualism—and critiques that ethical framework from the point of view of communitarian ethics. What is happening right now in Internet policy discussions is that the political and ethical framework of liberal individualism—a framework that undergirds policy proposals on the political left and right—is being offered as the only valid moral framework for Internet policy, as if there were no other viable alternatives, when in fact there are many.

In *Rhetorical Ethics and Internetworked Writing*, I lay out several alternative ethical frameworks that offer critiques of liberal individualism, including feminist ethics (Card; Jaggar; Cahill; McIntosh), casuistic ethics (Jonsen and Toulmin), communicative ethics (Habermas; Benhabib), and postmodern ethics (Lyotard and Thébaud). In this chapter I focus on one of these alternatives—communitarian ethics—to show that there is indeed an ethical alternative to the individualist paradigm, which both the right and the left, conservatives and liberals, Republicans and Democrats, invoke to guide their policy debates—debates on matters such as pornography and harassment on the Internet, copyright of electronic text, and free speech on the networks.

My interest in these issues is motivated by my feeling that there is a decided gap between the principles espoused by various network advocates (like the Electronic Frontier Foundation) and ethical problems arising on the nets. For instance, the various ways electronic text tends to be produced, distributed, and reproduced on the Internet are raising a serious challenge both to the conventional notions of intellectual property rights (i.e., authorship and ownership of text) and to the publishing industry (Porter, "Legal Realities"). Who owns electronic text? Who has the right to borrow it, and for what uses? The ethical/political principles people frequently invoke do not help them address such problems. "Free speech" and "pluralism" (or "diversity") are the most common god-terms. Like "democracy," everybody believes in "free speech"— which makes such a term useful as a rallying cry and strong as a principle, but nearly useless in terms of mediating differences about the limits of free speech. In short, it functions well as a prayer, a rallying cry, or as a starting point for inquiry. It doesn't function so well as a heuristic or guide to addressing real ethical dilemmas facing cyberwriters.

We need to take a closer, more introspective look at the ideological assumptions of our ethical frameworks. Examining our frameworks is important to the various kinds of writing work we do in cyberspace: to how we constitute and situate ourselves ethically as writers/publishers of electronic discourse; as listowners, managers, and developers of network groups and archives; as website developers; and as teachers in Internetworked writing classrooms. We need to examine the principles we invoke and the stances we adopt for ethical assistance in guiding our writing actions in cyberspace.

LIBERAL-INDIVIDUALISM AND THE POLITICS OF THE INTERNET

One place we can see liberal individualism influencing policy discussions is in the lobbying efforts of the Electronic Frontier Foundation (EFF). Howard Rheingold, Mitchell Kapor (co-founder and President of EFF), and others associated with EFF have, for instance, taken a more or less absolute free speech position toward discourse on the networks. Rheingold, for instance, thinks that "even the most obnoxious expressions deserve protection, on the grounds that restrictions on antisocial communications can easily be extended to communications that don't jibe with the political views or morals of those in power at the time" (1991, 46).

Kapor advocates "freedom of speech on networks" except in "exceptional cases" (162). Their position is warranted by the view that network participants can police themselves mostly. Even though they admit the likelihood that there will always be some nasty incidents (like the Jake Baker episode at the University of Michigan—see Branam and Bridgeforth; Branam; Cain), social pressure brought to bear will solve the problems. Their response to electronic harassment: just ignore harassers and they will go away.

The problem, as they see it, is government bureaucracy (especially law enforcement agencies) and Big Business Who Is Trying to Control what should be a free citizens' network. Rheingold (1991) identifies the villains as the Secret Service, the FBI, and the National Science Foundation. The "defenders" are the Electronic Frontier Foundation, the American Civil Liberties Union, and Computer Professionals for Social Responsibility (CPSR). Meeks sees the bad guys as the National Security Agency, the FBI, and "other assorted spook agencies." John Perry Barlow admonishes the Clinton administration for not living up to their 1992 campaign promise that they would stand up to the evil governmental bureaucracies (surprisingly, as he says, because "hell, a lot of them are Deadheads"). Barlow chides the Clinton administration for, instead, giving in to the old-paradigm "Guardian Class," those hanging on to a Cold-War mentality which justifies violation of individual rights under the auspices of protecting U.S. citizens from terrorism. Kapor sees legal and governmental institutions as a threat to civil liberties. The stories he tells, like the government raid on Steve Jackson's files, remind us of the ignorance of law enforcement agencies and their attempts to curtail individual freedoms.

In *The Virtual Community*, Rheingold expresses a view that we might call grassroots optimism. If only government bureaucracies and Big Business would stay out of the way and leave us alone, everything would be fine. People are fine. The technology is fine. The problem is Big Organization and Government. The Panopticon is what will happen if the Government gets control. Without interference, virtual communities will inevitably grow and prosper, like micro-organisms in petri dishes (6)—that is Rheingold's metaphor, the community as fungus. Another metaphor is the network known as the Great American Picnic (20). This is another version of the level-playing field, town-hall metaphor, a popular one for liberal individualists.

When you examine the particular features that constitute Rheingold's ideal electronic citizen, his vision seems less benign. Rheingold's community is white and upper middle class, with the leisure time to surf the net. It is mostly male, mostly baby boomers and their offspring, mainly centered in the cultural space between San Francisco and Silicon Valley. They are technologically sophisticated yuppies, but yuppies with a 1960s social conscience. They are liberals, but not radicals. They are, in Rheingold's own words, the "granola-eating utopians" (48). They are—not Rheingold's own words—the people who are most like Rheingold.

The irony of Rheingold's position is that though he is a liberal-individualist, his nominal emphasis in his book is as the title suggests: virtual communities. Rheingold, though, is by no means a communitarian. In his view communities are simply collections of individuals: "Virtual communities are social aggregations that emerge from the Net when enough people carry on those public discussions long enough, with sufficient human feeling, to form webs of personal relationships in cyberspace" (5). This construction of community is a Rawlsian contractarian one: the community is constituted by individuals (i.e., it does not pre-exist individuals) and gains its authority only through the rights granted it by the individuals in it. Such a position is not at all the same as communitarianism.

Don't get me wrong. I am in the main supportive of Rheingold's, Kapor's, and others attempts to protect civil liberties on the network and to act as advocates for electronic citizens. Abuses and violations of individual rights have occurred. Free speech is a good thing (we can all agree on that), and government invasion of privacy and censorship of discourse should be resisted. Many of their concerns are valid; the U.S. Congress has attempted to pass repressive legislation, which the EFF was justified in opposing. For instance, Meeks points out how the government seems to be moving toward approval of the FBI's request for "putting a trapdoor into digital switches, allowing agents easy access to phone conversations" and other forms of electronic communication. There is continued fear (into 1996) that the Clinton administration in collusion with the Republican-controlled Congress will propose legislation that will favor copyright owners rather than users of information by putting restrictions on the fair use of electronic text (Jacobson). Such legislation would work in favor of publishers' and property owners' interests to the detriment of teachers and students. Similarly, there is a strong desire in the U.S. Congress to punish those who use the Internet to distribute "obscene" or "pornographic" material. The so-called Gorton-Exon Communications Decency Act, which was included as part of a comprehensive telecommunications bill approved by both the U.S. Senate and House of Representatives and signed into law by President Clinton in early 1996 (see Wilson), was intended to make Internet service providers liable for pornographic material stored on their electronic databases, whether or not the service provider had put that material there or even had knowledge of it. (Update: In June 1996, a federal court overturned the decency act on the grounds that it stifled free speech—a decision that free network advocates vigorously applauded—see Quittner 56.)

I have no quarrel with EFF's effort to lobby government action in the direction of protecting the individual's rights to free speech and privacy. However, the principles they espouse have their limitations, because (1) there are some types of ethical dilemmas that liberal individualism cannot help us solve; and (2) liberal individualism often ends up protecting the rights of current property owners at the expense of the community good. Their position has some troubling economic implications. For instance, Kapor's brand of electronic freedom—which advocates "freedom of speech on electronic networks," except in "exceptional cases" (162)—is a position that will lead, ironically, to the increased commercialization of the nets. The free speech philosophy coupled with an open-market economics will lead to commercial control—and that will mean that the only denizens of the net will be those who can afford it: that is, the granola-eating utopians in Silicon Valley and California, but not the students in inner-city schools in Gary, Indiana, or in rural schools in South Carolina.

The extreme position that these advocates take will, I am afraid, lead to other kinds of abuses. First, the position of *absolute* anti-State intervention is a hard one to defend, if one examines the problematic cases. Should the State not intervene when a husband beats his wife? Or when a member of the Faith Assembly Church refuses to allow her child to receive necessary medical attention? Are these "private" matters only?

Granted, the nature of the harm is different in these cases. The issue in Internetworked writing hinges on the possible harm of "only words"

(MacKinnon). When do words alone constitute harm or physical threat to an individual? The Jake Baker case points to an instance where the courts initially determined that *in this particular context* the student's fictional story was more than simply fiction. In using a real classmate's name and in fantasizing about her rape/torture in email posted to the newsgroup alt.sex.stories, University of Michigan student Jake Baker blurred the fiction/nonfiction line just enough to get himself jailed. *Given their context of use,* his words alone constituted a threat to a person's physical well-being.

Those who advocate an absolute free speech position—based on what Catharine MacKinnon refers to as "the stupid theory of equality" (98)—do not sufficiently acknowledge the intimidating power of violent speech, the capacity of speech to silence especially those who have been historically silenced and marginalized. Nor can such a view address an ethical issue like "spamming" (also known as "mondo posting")—that is, the question of how (or whether) to control blanket postings of political or commercial messages to numerous newsgroups or, increasingly, listserv discussion groups. Neither Rheingold or Kapor take any heed of the relatively low participation of women in network activity. America Online reports tht 84% of its subscribers are male. CompuServe reports that 88% of its users are male ("It's a Man's World Online" B1). Exact numbers for the Internet at large are harder to come by, but estimates suggest that 65% to 95% of Internet users are male. Nor do they consider the numerous critiques that suggest that the Internetworked environment may be a hostile place for women (Takayoshi; Selfe; Hawisher and Sullivan).

The liberal-individualist image of networks—what they are, as well as what they could or should be—fails to recognize the role of power in any discursive arrangement and fails to acknowledge differences among participants. Not just race, gender, and age differences—but differences in values as well, i.e., different ethics, different attitudes about the way things ought to be, fundamental differences in how we orient ourselves to the world and how we make it. Those differences get obliterated by the kind of homogenizing metaphors that Rheingold invokes—but they also get obliterated in the political philosophy that informs his vision. As Rawls articulates this position in *A Theory of Justice,* liberal individualism is a philosophy that supposes that "each person possesses an inviolability founded on justice that even the welfare of society as a whole cannot override" (3).

A number of postmodern theorists have raised challenges to this sort of discursive model. Many are questioning whether a bill of rights for electronic use based on a liberal Enlightenment ethic—with its constructs of *man,* free speech, and *individual* human rights—is adequate for dealing with the postmodern phenomenon of electronic discourse via networks. Martha Cooper points out how both Classical and Enlightenment traditions are based on "a vision of face-to-face communication" between equal and opposite (and male) advocates, each of whom has "the possibility of obtaining accurate information and choosing among policy alternatives." She calls this "an image of autonomous individuals"—what we've come to know as "the level playing field" assumption about discourse rights.

Michel Foucault points out that there is no ideal speech situation free from institutional hierarchies, traditional alignments, and power relations. All discourse occurs already in a situated practice of power relations. Though the liberal Enlightenment view assumes an assembly of people speaking their minds freely—as Rawls says: "it seems reasonable to suppose that the parties in the original position are equal" (19)—no such assembly does or can exist.

> The thought that there could be a state of communication which would be such that the games of truth could circulate freely, without obstacles, without constraint and without coercive effects, seems to me to be Utopia. It is being blind to the fact that relations of power are not something bad in themselves, from which one must free one's self. I don't believe there can be a society without relations of power, if you understand them as means by which individuals try to conduct, to determine the behaviors of others. The problem is not of trying to dissolve them in the utopia of a perfectly transparent communication, but to give one's self the rules of law, the techniques of management, and also the ethics, the *ethos*, the practice of self, which would allow these games of power to be played with a minimum of domination. (Foucault 18)

Foucault's entire research project of studying institutions like the prison and the hospital argues that the *principles* of justice and freedom espoused by Enlightenment philosophers were seldom realized in *practice* (that is, in the institutions and bureaucracies that their advocates constructed). In a way, he suggests, the utopian ideal makes things worse, because it can have the effect of obscuring the exercise of power and thus making it more invincible in its invisibility.

Seyla Benhabib's chapter on "Models of Public Space," from *Situating the Self*, also considers the limitations of "the liberal model of public space." Her critique is based on the elision of "legal" and "ethical" within such a model.

> An additional limitation of the liberal model of public space is that it conceives of political relations all too often narrowly along the model of juridical ones. . . . The liberal principle of dialogic neutrality, while it expresses one of the main principles of the modern legal system, is far too restrictive and frozen in application to the dynamics of power struggles in actual political processes. (100-101)

Foucault and Benhabib serve as examples of how the liberal-individualist political metaphor is being challenged by postmodernist ethicists: that is, on the basis of its failure to recognize that human relations always already occur in a system of power; on its inadequacy to handle "tough ethical cases" that will inevitably emerge; and on its legalistic view of ethical problems (an impractical view for day-to-day ethical writing issues, as well as a potentially expensive one). The liberal-individualist view does not address the material conditions of the networked writing situation or the fundamental inequalities and differences that exist there. Foucault reminds us that all discourse occurs already in a situated practice of power relations, institutional hierarchies, and alignments.

Rheingold thinks that under the skin everybody is the same—and that given non-interference by Evil Powers—we will eventually work out our differences and form one big comfortable Virtual Community. This strikes me as a seemingly benign, but actually insidious, utopian goal—a dystopia. The image is of the world as a New England townhall meeting, with "all" citizens participating in an equal forum. Except we know that the forum was never equal and that not everyone got to speak (Phillips): The forum waved the banner of democracy when in fact it was a body based on the privilege of race, gender, and property.

This metaphor, which is also a model of discursive relations, is incapable of dealing with the tough ethical cases that are occurring in networked communities. It does not deal well with the collision of differences; it simply hopes that differences can be worked out. This kind of ethical approach cannot begin to understand or deal with ethnic slaughter in Rwanda. It cannot begin to deal with the problem of gang violence and drive-by shootings in Cleveland and Los Angeles. Nor can it understand how women might be intimidated into silence in an electronic community because of angry and hostile postings by men.

In 1992, a male student at Carnegie Mellon University was charged with violating the university's anti-harassment policy for posting "offensive" messages on the electronic bulletin board maintained by the campus Women's Center. The student's repeated and lengthy postings described in graphic detail instances of sexual violence against women and insisted that it was the job of men everywhere to re-establish their physical mastery over women. The student's postings had the effect of shutting down discussion on the bulletin board, intimidating some members into silence and provoking angry response from others.

Should the student be reprimanded? Should his account be revoked? The issue centered on whether the student's postings constituted harassment or whether they were a protected form of free speech, especially since they were directly related to the topical identity of the newgroup. Such issues hinge on a number of complex situational factors: e.g., the incident happened at a private rather than public institution; the student's messages were aimed at feminists generally not at specific women (which, from one point of view, made the remarks "political" rather than "personal"); the messages were posted to a public bulletin board, not to individuals; the university's student code explicitly allowed for free public expression of ideas, even controversial or potentially offensive ones.

One relevant principle (taken from the Netnews Bill of Rights, drafted by lawyers, systems administrators, and librarians as a guide to network usage—see Kadie) is that "Materials should not be proscribed or removed [from public bulletin boards] because of partisan or doctrinal disapproval." The Electronic Frontier Foundation took the viewpoint that, because the student posted to a public bulletin board he had an absolute right to post what he wanted; if people didn't like it they should ignore it. Others would say that his postings constituted harassment and intimidation of women on the basis of gender—and that such an instance is a clear form of harassment. As this case was discussed on USENET groups—mainly by the men who do 90% of the posting on the EFF newsgroups—the presumption was in favor of the student and his right to free speech, even when such speech effectively destroyed an electronic community. Such cases exemplify the tension between one individual's right to freedom of expression and another individual's right to be protected from harassment and intimidation based on personal characteristics of gender, race, religion, and other protected statuses.

There is yet another side to the problem: administrators and teachers might be ethically responsible or legally liable for offensive material stored on their computer systems or posted on their online conferences. An interesting test case concerning computer harassment occurred at Santa Rosa Junior College. At the request of students, the college set up separate bulletin boards for men and women to hold discussions regarding gender. (That was the first mistake: setting up separate lists based on gender itself is probably a civil rights violation). Some comments posted on the men-only discussion group contained "anatomically explicit and sexually derogotary remarks" about two women at the college. In April 1993, the women filed an harassment complaint with the Education Department's Office for Civil Rights. The male student chiefly responsible for initiating the discussion also filed a complaint that the university's response to the case threatened his right to free speech.

Now, one facet of the issue here is determining whether the computer conference is a public forum or an "educational program." DeLoughry and Wilson phrase the question this way: Do "students who use computer bulletin boards or conferences have the same rights of free speech that they would have on the campus quadrangle" (A26). If the conference relates to a specific class or instructional purpose, then the University has more responsibility (and authority) for what happens there. If the conference is more an open forum, then the free speech tenet probably holds more force. But the gray area is huge here—and we are especially at sea because we do not yet have an established body of legal precedent to help our deliberations. Branscomb sees the question as not admitting to a simple answer: "computer bulletin boards are an electronic hybrid, parts of which may be looked on either as public or private, depending on the desires of the participants" (158; see Kapor 162; Shade).

The end result: the college had to pay both women and the man $15,000 each to settle the claims. And this is one of the dangerous side effects of this kind of dilemma. Universities can be caught between the free speech principle on one end, and the problem of harassment and protection of the innocent on the other.

The university is damned if it does and damned if it doesn't, seemingly, and that can lead to a chilling effect. The more universities are caught in such dilemmas, the more their response will be to shut down resources or strictly monitor their use, and the less likely they will be to support a wide range of network activity.

In Rheingold's virtual community, women are just supposed to ignore harassment. At this point, Rheingold is just not sufficiently aware of historical factors in the exercise of power. At other points he is not aware of the economics of power that inevitably inhabit electronic spaces. The technology in his vision is supposed to simply "be there" to support our social activity. It is not clear to me how it is supposed to get there and stay there without some kind of business, government, or organizational "interference." "Organization" is a bad word in Rheingold's vocabulary. He just doesn't see the fact that he belongs to organizations (like Well and EFF), too, that in large part help him construct the view of community he espouses—and that it is largely through organization of some kind that large-scale action is made possible. (Rheingold sees Well and EFF as "communities" rather than "organizations" like IBM, Microsoft, and the FBI. Communities are benign, organizations are malicious.) Without the "interference" of the federal government, there would be no Internet as we know it today.

Is the First Amendment a desirable first principle for discursive practice on electronic networks? Richard Bernstein identifies a troubling emergent sentiment that views the First Amendment as the last line of defense for white heterosexual men. The First Amendment, according to Bernstein, is being invoked to protect men's rights to use sexually harassing and racist speech as a way to counter what many of them perceive to be unfair affirmative action in favor of blacks and women. By keeping the playing field level through broad interpretation of the First Amendment, those in power can be assured of staying in power. Bernstein's point is not to dismiss the First Amendment, but simply to suggest that although it may be a widely held legal principle, the First Amendment does not have and should not be granted universal status as an ethical principle, as many are wont to do.

In *Only Words*, Catharine MacKinnon points out that the First Amendment was originally developed to protect the powerless from the powerful (the U.S. government or Government generally). But increasingly, the First Amendment is being used in defense of continued discrimination against the less powerful, as Stanley Fish has also noted.

MacKinnon implies that the free speech principle should have built into it a preferential option for the marginalized. That is, it should allow the marginalized, oppressed, or silenced a chance to speak against the majority, the dominant, the hegemonic—but should not be applied to further discriminate against the marginalized, oppressed, and silenced (39). In any particular case, of course, one has to determine the degree of possible harm to those involved. Usually it is the weaker, the oppressed, and the marginalized who bear the greater burden of risk in such cases—though not always. (Acts of terrorism—for instance, the bombing of the federal building in Oklahoma City—show quite vividly how any individual or small group can, through an act of ultimate extremity, cause some harm to the more powerful. The futility of such acts, however, is that the terrorist attempt to harm the powerful usually ends up harming individuals while leaving the system of domination intact.) Essentially, MacKinnon is urging us toward a kind of affirmative action ethic in such cases. The other implication—more mine than MacKinnon's—is that the First Amendment is not a Rule, but a principle to be applied heuristically. Yes, it represents a deeply held value, but in any given case it may conflict with other deeply held values, in which case some kind of careful judgment is necessary. (MacKinnon thinks that the First and Fourteenth Amendment, which mandates equal protection for all citizens, ought to be placed in a kind of binary tension, though the courts typically don't do that. Without the balance of the Fourteenth, she feels, the First Amendment can become a tool of dominance.)

The Electronic Frontier Foundation takes the position that all network discourse should absolutely be protected by the First Amendment (Rheingold, "Why Censoring"). I consider this as a presumptive position, but they advocate it as an absolute rule. To advocate such a position is, to me, to underestimate the power of an individual's use of language, its capacity to do harm, and especially on electronic networks the capacity to shut down communities. Yes, the presumption lies with the individual because the individual is usually the weaker entity, but the communitarian position says that in some situations it's the community that needs protection.

The appeal to free speech is one that Stanley Fish sees as both a conservative and a liberal strategy. Fish distrusts the abstract appeal to principle, because such abstractions often obscure differences in how people construct the terms and differences in the way they are applied:

> when words and phrases [such as "free speech" and "neutrality" and "Reason"] are invoked, it is almost always as part of an effort to deprive moral and legal problems of their histories so that merely formal calculations can then be performed on phenomena that have been flattened out and no longer have their real-world shape. (viii)

Fish notes that there is really no such thing as free speech, and he thinks it is a good thing. He calls the First Amendment "the First Refuge of Scoundrels" (102). He notes that in cases involving hate speech, the neutrality or fairness argument is often used to advocate continuing a policy (or practice) of hate, oppression, and harassment.

The absolute free speech position, as advocated by the Electronic Frontier Foundation, assumes an ideal speech situation as its core model of discourse—a speech situation where everybody is more or less reasonable and more or less equal—or even if not, has an equal and inviolable right to speak. This view participates in the American myth of the classless society, which insists "Of course we are all equal!" Of course this is not true, especially as pertaining to access to literacy (Stuckey).

This view does not address fundamental inequalities in the material nature of the writing situation. Some people have access to computers and modems, others don't. Some know how to manipulate newsgroup technology, others don't. Large and muscular white males with shaved heads and swastikas on their arms can intimidate smaller women into silence—and they do.

Rheingold occupies a position that privileges individual identity, and rights extending from that identity, as the originating source for ethics and law. And in general, approaches to dealing with problems on the networks have been very individual-oriented. Even self-proclaimed postmodern positions (such as are often expressed in computers and composition forums like ACW-L) often end up circling back and becoming a kind of "liberal postmodernism," which still places its ethical focus on the individual writer. Rheingold and Kapor think that their position is the only reasonable alternative to a system of strict, top-down governmental control, but there are numerous alternatives that should be considered in any discussion of network ethics.

THE COMMUNITARIAN ALTERNATIVE

It's especially hard for those reading from mainstream U.S. culture to see beyond the god-term "individual rights"—but if you read African communitarian theory or liberation theology you can see how the principles "we" believe to be inviolable can in fact be problematic. You begin to see how the concepts "individual rights" and "human rights" are actually very different constructs. "Individual rights" is an Enlightenment, Western, and capitalist framework that posits individual ownership as the basis for discussions of policy. "Human rights" is a social construct that posits community justice as the more appropriate basis for such discussions.

The social-communitarian position posits that rights and responsibilities originate in communities and that "what is good for the community" should ultimately take precedence over individual rights in matters of tough ethical decision making (see Baynes; Bellah et al.; D'Entrèves; Devine; Miller).

Amitai Etzioni sees communitarianism as providing a necessary middle ground in U.S. politics between the absolutist Authoritarians (groups like the Moral Majority) and Radical Individualists (groups like the ACLU—166). (Kapor and Rheingold would fall into the category of Radical Individualists, though Etzioni does not consider issues involving Internetworked writing.) Etzioni's interest is in "balancing individual rights with social needs" (182)— and his argument is warranted by a belief in one's innate responsibilities to communities (social, familial, academic, electronic, disciplinary, professional, institutional, political, etc.) and by a principle of reciprocity (though not in a strict *quid pro quo* economic sense).

One example Etzioni uses to identify his position is the question of the ethics of airport electronic security gates. Though the ACLU originally opposed the use of such gates as violating the rights of the individual (who must be presumed innocent), Etzioni sees those gates as a good communitarian solution, treating everyone equally (and so not innately unjust) and also protecting all from terrorism. The analogy would extend well to security and privacy issues for Internetworked writing, suggesting that in the communitarian view some "invasion" of privacy—for example, trespass into someone's email account—might be allowable in order to protect users' from electronic terrorism in the form of viruses, as long as any such policy is applied equally and fairly to all users—and is used to *protect*, not to *monitor*. The irony here is that certain intrusions that restrict individual behaviors may be necessary (desirable) for the common good.

In *A Theology of Reconstruction*, Charles Villa-Vicencio advances his case for the communitarian agenda, beginning by noting that the liberal Enlightenment view of individuality is tied to a troubling economic agenda: free-market capitalism. As a South African, Villa-Vicencio writes from a context in which the liberal Enlightenment codes—indeed the verbatim principles of the U.S. Constitution—were used in conjunction with a strict rule-of-law philosophy to uphold a system of apartheid.

> The dominant western, libertarian, individualistic understanding of humanity (seen in the American *Bill of Rights*, the *Rights of Man* included in the French constitution and, to a lesser extent, in sections of the *Universal Declaration of Human Rights* read in isolation from the entire text) stands in contradiction to this emphasis [i.e., African communal ethics]. In these declarations the rights of individuals all too often in reality means the rights of *some* individuals at the cost of other individuals. (166)

Villa-Vicencio contends that the Rawlsian theory of justice which starts with individual liberties assumes a more-or-less free society to begin with: such a theory of justice "fits a society within which there is more or less equal distribution of wealth better than it does situations which show vast discrepancies between the rich and the poor, which is a dominant feature of South African society and an increasing number of contemporary capitalist countries" (236). Villa-Vicencio challenges the assumption of the sanctity of private ownership.

Villa-Vicencio sees the liberal Enlightenment view as presupposing a society of more-or-less equal participants, who have more-or-less the same access to wealth, and who already have equal rights under a constitution. In a society or community with inherently inequal participants, or with a long history of inequality, the appeal to the liberal enlightenment view may have the effect of maintaining the status quo (see Fish 76). In a culture where access to computer writing techology is unequal—like U.S. culture (see Piller)—the liberal-individualist view can have the effect of maintaining inequality by further distancing the haves from the have nots.

Villa-Vicencio offers an "alternative to western individualism" (172), which merges Christian ecumenical ethics and African communal ethics and builds from the principles of reciprocity and Christian charity (see West). "The African world view emerges as a striking alternative to western individualism. It is at the same time an alternative to ideologies that reduce people to by-products of social and economic forces. . . . Individual developments and aspirations . . . are tempered in traditional African society by the needs of the community" (172).

Villa-Vicencio sees such an ethics as grounded in theology, but also as having a secular and political manifestation which he sees as evident in the United Nations' *Universal Declaration of Human Rights:* "Theology grounds the human rights debate within a personal-communal sense of existence which transcends the divide between western individualism and collectivist notions of human rights, characteristic of much within the secular debate on human rights" (155).

Villa-Vicencio thinks that theology provides a missing perspective to secular ethics, and he invokes theological principles he feels can command broad consent, even by those opposed to any form of theological intrusion into political affairs. Theology provides a point of critique outside the borders of national boundaries. Villa-Vicencio starts with the principle of "love your neighbor," which as he says, is "for the Christian, a familiar doctrinal notion, but one that is not often given practical expression within the context of Western individualism" (174). On the contrary, liberal-individualism can often take the form of an isolationism (169) and a neglect of others, which Villa-Vicencio sees as inherently unethical.

An important feature of Villa-Vicencio's communal ethics is that its sense of community arises from *but is not tied* to particular racial, sociological, or geographical groups. He is talking about using a tribal and family based communal model in order to construct a trans-communal ethic; the community he imagines is a global one. In addition, the communal ethic that Villa-Vicencio advocates has a strong presumption in "favor[ing] the poor and marginalized members of society in defining and prioritizing human rights" (160). Presumption in favor of the weak and marginalized is an ethic that rhetoric/composition has not often advocated, but it can easily be forged into a principle for treatment of others in electronic communities.

The point here is that there are alternate ethics which Kapor, Rheingold, and others do not address, but which raise a serious challenge to their assumptions about what is, or should be, "right."

The ethic being appealed for requires an outlook on life significantly different to that contained within the creeds of liberal individualism. At the same time it affirms the democratic right and the ability of all people to share in the shaping of society, something often denied ordinary citizens within centrally controlled collectivist societies, ruled by a political elite. It is an ethic which is grounded in a vision of humanity within which each will no longer be responsible solely for him or herself. (Villa-Vicencio 162)

We see a communitarian, reciprocity-based ethic articulated in the Connolly et al. "Bill of Rights for Electronic Citizens." Connolly et al. realize that most who have tried to write an electronic bill of rights have begun with a commitment to the liberal ideal, which is inadequate for dealing with the post-modern phenomenon of electronic discourse via networks. Because Connolly et al. are more interested in developing principles that pertain to and support "the electronic community of researchers" (54), they develop an ethic based on a gift-exchange system of property as an alternative to the conventional property rights system of Western capitalism and Enlightenment liberalism. In this respect, their bill of rights for electronic citizens is compatible with Villa-Vicencio's communitarian ethic and poses a clear alternative to policies based on liberal individualism.

We should be clear about what Villa-Vicencio is proposing in his communitarian ethic: not that we should abandon the individual in favor of the State or Government, which is the binary that EFF assumes offer us our only two choices. Villa-Vicencio's position is that the "community" is something different, offering a mediating ground between the "individual" and the "state": in traditional African society, "the extended family unit and village membership . . . function as an intermediary between the individual and the state" (172). He argues for including the community as an important (and currently missing) feature of human rights legislation—and I would agree that the notions of "community" and "forum" (Porter, *Audience and Rhetoric*) are important constructs currently missing from most discussions of public policy on electronic networks.

COMPLICATING COMMUNITARIANISM: LIBERATION THEOLOGY

Some have accused the communitarian position in general of being soft on power—that is, for not recognizing the institutional inequalities that might exist in a given community (and that function to enable relations within that community); for not allowing space for the critique of community; and for not addressing the tough issue of incommensurability between communities. Communitarianism in some of its Anglo-American, conservative forms can promote intolerance of the Other or the individual in the name of the public good. Elizabeth Frazer and Nicola Lacey, for instance, critique communitarian theory from a feminist perspective, pointing out that "the communitarian emphasis on traditional discourses and practices inevitably reproduces the dichotomized thinking characteristic of western culture" (168). Among other things, this thinking leads to "the invisibility of gender in political theory" (213). They wonder whether communitarians have really escaped the "implicitly male individualism of liberal theories" (146).

Frazer and Lacey's critique aims at the communitarian philosophy articulated by Anglo-American theorists like Habermas, MacIntyre, and Rorty.

Similarly, Derek Phillips critiques the American communitarian theories of Bellah and MacIntyre for their utopian readings of American history. The golden past that such communitarians urge us toward, says Phillips, was in fact "a hierarchic political order resting on the natural right of the wise to rule the less wise" (62). Frazer and Lacey's and Phillips' critiques remind us to distinguish between various types of communitarian theory.

The Anglo-American theory of Etzioni, Bellah, and MacIntyre is is a type of communitarianism that suffers from many of the same faults as liberal individualism. It essentializes "community" in the same way that the liberal position could be said to essentialize the individual. But this is not the only form of communitarianism. Neither Frazer and Lacey nor Phillips consider postcolonial forms of communitarianism nor Marxist and neo-Marxist forms (such as liberation theology), which might be seen to practice in very different ways—though these, too, might be challenged on the grounds of obscuring gender difference.

The limitation of the Anglo-American communitarian position is, I believe, the potential threat it poses to the marginalized groups, the minorities, that constitute any social community. One corrective to this problem can be found in the Marxist version of communitarianism found in liberation theology.

Liberation theology attempts to situate theology in the material conditions of a people (as opposed to its more traditional location in metaphysics). Liberation theology as a movement aims to heal the binary between formally abstract theological speculation and situated pastoral care as it intersects with the material conditions of people; it is an effort to transform a decontextualized form of inquiry (traditional theology) into praxis. Liberation theology formally emerged in the Medellín document (written by 130 Latin American bishops in 1968), which denounced political and institutional systems which subjugated the poor. It argued that theology must reconceptualize itself not as abstract formulations but as a form of action directed at both critiquing economic and social systems which oppress and at improving the material conditions of the poor (see Smith; Berryman). Liberation theology has a Marxist component to its articulation—in the respect that it combines a Christian/Catholic theological emphasis with a Marxist praxis. Liberation theologians insist that theology and ethics must be situated in the material conditions of people and focus particularly on how ethics intersects with economics, labor, production, and the ownership/distribution of property in a society. In this respect, liberation theology is very much a situated ethic.

Liberation theology attempts to move theology from the realm of "theory" to that of praxis. Theology in this system is seen not only as a descriptive tool or as a means of spiritual action, but as a lever of critique for enacting social change. As a theory of economics, liberation theology opposes three things: "profit as the key motive for economic progress, competition as the supreme law of economics, and private ownership of the means of production as an absolute right that has no limits and carries no corresponding social obligation" (Smith 125; see also Boff and Boff; Gutiérrez; Berryman). What it begins by noticing is that the liberal individualism advocated by both the right and the left in U.S. politics operates in collusion with a model based principally on private ownership of property.

According to Enrique Dussel, the basic (and absolute) principle of liberation ethics is this: Liberate the poor (73). He sees the basis for this ethic in both New Testament scripture and in the theory of Karl Marx (who, he says, has been misinterpreted as "collectivist" rather than what he really is—"communal"). The community that Dussel imagines as operative here is an ideal ethical community that works against the existing social order (which primarily dominates and oppresses, at the very least by turning its back on the poor). This liberation version of communitarianism is very different from those in the Anglo-American tradition. Its key difference is that such a communitarianism has in it a preferential option for the poor. What prevents its becoming a kind of oppressive majority rule is chief operating principle that the operation of the community must presume in favor of the poor—by which Dussel means the economically disadvantaged, but which could be extended to cover all marginalized and oppressed groups in a community (see Sullivan and Porter).

"Liberate the poor" is the foundational principle of this ethic, because it provides a linkage between real persons in a community (and their material status) and the notion of a transcendent/utopian existence. It provides the linkage between current actual conditions and a hoped-for ideal state. It is an ethic that does not satisfy itself with merely expressing the ideal state (e.g., "equality for all") or articulating generalized action (e.g., Aquinas's "do good"), but situates the expression of an ideal in a demand for action which takes into account present circumstances. The implication is that since we do not have this ideal we hope for, the only ethical thing to do is to work to achieve it.

The ethical standpoint of liberation theology addresses relations between humans, both on an individual and a communal level: How should I be for/to others? How should we be for/to others? In what manner should I/we relate to them? In this respect at least, liberation theology and feminist ethics overlap: both focus primarily on the representation of ethics as relations—or in postmodern terms, subjectivities (see Porter, *Rhetorical Ethics*). Dussel defines praxis as "both act and relationship . . . praxis is the actual, here-and-now manner of our being in our world before another person" (8). Dussel's definition seems to posit a one-to-one praxis, but he posits this relationship as necessarily occurring within a community framework.

Given conditions of fundamental inequity, or faced with a situation of oppression, "liberate the oppressed" is the only ethical stance possible for a community or individual to take. It's the chief operative principle in such situations, and it's a principle not present per se in democratic ideals, not inscribed in the U.S. Constitution. Liberate the oppressed—the principle is not a static claim, but a pronouncement of an intention and an action. It indicates the fundamental posture one must take toward oppression. Liberation theology expresses this action as a "preferential option for the poor and marginalized." In the view of this theology, the principle is necessary to moralize the communitarian frame-work. Communitarianism without this principle runs the risk of further oppres-sion of the marginalized, it runs the risk of the majority determining the rules for the minority. Situating this principle within the communitarian framework allows communitarianism to work without (or, at least, with less) oppression. Hence (the argument implies), having a "preferential option for the poor and marginalized" is how a community maintains justice for its members.

We are always left with the issue of defining the oppressed. Who are they exactly? And who is the implied "we" addressed by the directive? Who does the principle speak to and what agency is implied by it? (See Sullivan and Porter, chapter five, for a discussion of the problematics of defining the oppressed.) Paulo Freire draws a sharp distinction between "oppressors" and "oppressed," between practices (especially educational practices) that humanize and those that dehumanize, and between right and left. The appropriate ethical position vis-ê-vis these concepts is of course to avoid being an oppressor and to assist the oppressed in improving their status. These binaries of Freire's arise out his lifeworld experiences in Latin American cultures with a dramatic difference between the poor and the privileged classes, and Freire's understanding of these binaries is quite materialistic: the distinction is based on socio-economic factors—who has wealth, who doesn't; who has access to the mechanisms of political influence, who doesn't; who has food and clothing, who doesn't. It is easier to "see" oppression in countries where the socio-economic gap between rich and poor is immense (like the U.S.), and where the disadvantaged condi-tion of the poor is observable in every city and village. It is harder to see in rel-atively affluent countries or communities, or in towns where everyone is in a similar condition. It is often masked in the arena of technology access, espe-cially in a privileged state university. You never see who's not on the Internet.

From the standpoint of Marxist liberation theology or communitarian the-ory, the first principle of Internet ethics might well be something like this: Work to insure that the poor and marginalized have access to Internetworked resources; make sure that such resources are fairly shared and distributed (such a sentiment is found frequently in discussions of access in computers and composition literature—see, for example, Hawisher et al. 257-262). Though there is no legal or constitutional imperative to liberate the poor, most computer ethicists agree that this is a critical concern of computer ethics: how to allot, distribute, and pay for computer resources; how to insure that com-puter resources are fairly shared and distributed in a society where full partici-pation in the political life of the community may soon *require* computers.

CONCLUSION

The communitarian ethic poses a significant challenge to the ideological framework of liberal individualism—especially to its reliance on abstracted and decontextualized first principles which often are exercised in the name of justice and democracy but which in practice can too often lead to continued oppression. What we might designate as a postmodern form of communitarianism examines the particular discourse dynamic to determine where and how power is being applied; it makes a situational and casuistic and essentially *rhetorical* judgment about the operation of power, and about the threat of domination, in any given discourse situation (Porter, *Rhetorical Ethics*). It would point out, for instance, that in certain cases it is the community that needs protection from individuals. It would certainly not allow an individual male to shut down a Women's Center newsgroup through the use of intimidating speech; rather, it would insist that the free speech clause of the U.S. Constitution was intended to protect the less powerful, not provide license for intimidation of marginalized groups. Liberation theology, a particular form of communitarian thought, posits the necessity of presumption in favor of the materially oppressed. Without such a presumption, any system operating from a belief in neutrality or applying a set of abstract first principles runs the risk of further oppression.

I am not offering communitarian ethic as the only alternative to liberal individualism, nor as an ethical framework we should always necessarily adopt. What I am saying is that we need to question the individualist ethic that supports many of the statements about ethics and legality on electronic networks. Unfortunately, the liberal-individualist policy position receives almost unquestioned support within the fields of computers and composition and from rhetoric/composition because it dovetails neatly with those fields' individualist focus on the activities of the *solitary writer*. Despite the considerable emphasis on collaboration and social construction, these fields' principal orientation is still the individual student writer (and also, "the text"), and they still favor an individualist ethic (albeit largely an implicit one) over communitarian and other sorts of ethical positions. We should examine the ideological assumptions of that framework, as well as its economic implications, and ask if it best serves the interests we claim to represent.

ACKNOWLEDGMENTS

This chapter is based on material from chapter four (and other portions) of James E. Porter's book *Rhetorical Ethics and Internetworked Writing* (Ablex/New Directions in Computers and Composition Studies, 1998). Some passages are borrowed from Patricia A. Sullivan and James E. Porter's book *Opening Spaces: Writing Technologies and Critical Research Practices* (Ablex/New Directions in Computers and Composition Studies, 1997).

CHAPTER FOURTEEN

On Becoming A Woman
Pedagogies of the Self

Susan Romano

*F*UTURE HISTORIANS EXAMINING THE PARTICULARS OF LATE TWENTIETH-century writing instruction doubtless will conclude that college-level literacy entailed significant practice in the assumption of alternate identities. Evidence of pseudonymous and anonymous electronic conferencing, of MOO sessions where fictive personae are required or encouraged, and of personal Web-page selves composed from multiple media will persuade these historians that writing teachers using electronic forms considered the idea of invented, multiple selves integral to literacy formation.

This essay takes you back to the early years of teaching with computer technologies—1986, 1987, and 1988—when teachers in networked classrooms using realtime conferencing software first began experimenting with what I call pedagogies of the self, teaching practices that undermine unitary concepts of self and induce students to take on alternate identities. For evidence, I turn to transcripts of online teaching archived at the University of Texas at Austin Computer Research Lab (CRL). In effect, I re-run in slow motion the magnetic tapes that have recorded the making of selves during realtime electronic conferencing, freezing frames to examine closely the range of subject positions made available to students—women students in particular—through their interactions with teachers and classmates. Electronic technologies not only alter our language practices; they provide both mechanism and impetus for reconsidering topics of long-standing interest to teachers and theorists of language, and the relationship of language to self is just such a topic. Across the centuries, theories of rhetoric have offered specialized vocabulary for figuring this relationship. Aristotelian ethos refers to the tailoring of self for persuasive purposes. Renaissance rhetoricians coined sprezzatura to signify an oscillating, contradictory self, whose artful instability constituted decorum (Lanham). Eighteenth- and nineteenth-century Scottish rhetorical theorists understood self as mind; hence the study of psychology directed the teaching of rhetoric (Horner). Kenneth Burke proposed identification—self location in relation to others—as the central mechanism of persuasive rhetoric. Poststructuralists, argues Linda Brodkey, "articulate relations between a possible self and a possible reality (which includes possible others)" (238). Postmodernism conceives the subject as multiple, competed for, and constituted in discourse. Finally, information age rhetoricians newly theorize subjectivity as a process of morphing or, to use a different metaphor, as the recombination of social identities (Balsamo; Haynes; Heath).

Whereas rhetorical theory addresses the relationship of self to language and provides a vocabulary for articulating this relationship, histories of rhetorical education (or writing instruction) examine the pedagogical procedures by which ideologies (including ideologies of the self) are transmitted to consciousness, or, alternatively, how pedagogies at the level of everyday practice constitute ideologies. In either philosophy of education, teachers are not absent from scenes of writing instruction because pedagogies, whether objectivist or epistemic, transmissive or social constructionist, are designed and implemented by teachers. I make this point because teachers using electronic conferencing technologies have frequently represented their influence on classroom discourse as negligible, celebrating their diminished presences and ceding classroom management to software applications. Eager, perhaps, that their institutionally conferred authority not undermine a student-centered model of education, they neglect conceptualizing a rhetorical authority designed neither to control knowledge nor win arguments with students, but rather to assist the development and maintenance of equitable discursive environments. I find, however, that teachers' reluctance to imbricate themselves in student discourse does not preclude their enactment of rhetorical authority.

"Rhetorical authority" implies both the use of persuasive language and an understanding of how discourse is working in a particular environment at a particular time. "Rhetoric" is a richly nuanced term, situated variously within different systems of knowledge, and historically, a "rhetorical" practice has been complex and specialized, something other than mere verbal presence among others. Indeed, Aristotle begins the *Art of Rhetoric* by making this very distinction:

> [F]or all [persons] up to a certain point, endeavor to criticize or uphold an argument, to defend themselves or to accuse. Now, the majority of people do this either at random or with a familiarity arising from habit. But since both these ways are possible, it is clear that matters can be reduced to a system, for it is possible to examine the reason why some attain their end by familiarity and others by chance and such an examination all would at once admit to be the function of an art. (I, i)

Granting that success in argument is well within the reach of those who practice speaking among others regularly, and certainly not out of reach of those who rely upon fortune alone if such persons are willing to take bad fortune along with good, Aristotle argues for an analysis of the differences. Presumably, the habitually successful disputant has tacit knowledge that well might be systematized so that interactive, public reasoning (or argumentation) becomes a discipline, that is, an art made accessible both theoretically and practically. Although Aristotle conceives success in terms of winners and losers of particular arguments, a teacher inserting herself into the electronic conference is perhaps more interested in exercising an authority that fosters equitable discussion.[1]

By its innovative character, much of our teaching in interactive electronic environments, continues to fall into the category that Aristotle might refer to as "chance" teaching, and which Plato disparagingly would call "cookery," for teachers in computer-mediated environments necessarily test the uses of electronic technologies for writing instruction on the spot, by trial and by error, risking chance outcomes. To examine the differences between electronic conferences left to chance and electronic conferences whose teachers practice a rhetorical authority, I examine conference transcripts logged early in the history of computers and writing, when all software features were innovative. Not only do these transcripts make available for analysis many examples of classroom discourse, they also provide access to numerous electronic discussions during which teachers analyze their own innovative practices. Hence a researcher has access not only to student discourse, alongside evidence of teachers' discursive presences, but also to the conversations whereby teachers begin to newly theorize writing instruction from practice itself, to the process of transforming risky pedagogy to disciplinary art. Researching online teaching is an interpretive practice, for I have had to read over the shoulders of teachers and students, so to speak, tracing out patterns perhaps invisible to these participants, despite their active presences at the very discursive events under scrutiny. As lurker historian, I read primarily from a teacher's perspective, with interest in outcomes but without responsibility for them, and I read at a more leisurely pace.

The scene of my investigation, then, is the online classroom; the object of inquiry, pedagogy; the human beings in question, students and teachers; the focus, women students. Focusing on women is appropriate for investigating the relationship of self to language in online environments on two counts. First, women not infrequently report that finding a satisfactory location from which to speak as women is not as simple as we would like it to be.[2] It follows that people who experience participation in online conferences as liberatory might wish to stop and listen closely to opposing accounts. Second, at the site whose documents comprise my research materials, gender issues pervaded classroom discourse. Gender became topical, for instance, when students read Deborah Tannen on conversation analysis, when they studied representations of women's speech in cartoons of the 1970s, when they debated implementing non-sexist language in the classroom, and when they read Helena Viramontes in tandem with Ernest Hemingway.[3] Gender became topical even when teachers did not so intend, for students frequently invited each other to a gendered social identity from which to read both print texts and the texts they were engaged in building online.

SEIZING THE DAY

Revolutions provide opportunities for the marginalized to participate in the rearrangement of the social, political, and economic hierarchies that affect their lives, and a media revolution is no exception. Our current media revolution offers opportunities to propose new social arrangements with an array of writing tools. It provides especially rich opportunities for women's activism because a gap between old and new literacy conventions has been forced, and the already legitimized concepts of "innovative" and "alternative" may be used to advantage by those who wish to wedge innovative and alternative selves into the new discourses. The proliferation of representational venues encourages women to fragment unitary conceptions of the female by representing selves in graphic and textual shapes not easily categorizable.

We need not be naive, however, in assuming unilateral correspondences between new media representations and the various civil, economic, and political arrangements that govern material lives,[4] nor even in assuming automatic correspondences between women's new self-representations online and equity in virtual space. Faced with building opportunities galore and few guarantees of outcome, we may wish to retain issues of equity in the form of open-ended questions: How do textual or graphical representations affect social arrangements both on and off line and what accounts for the variable effects?

Discussions of equity and computers often turn to the technicalities and politics of providing access, for this is an area over which we can plot remedial action. It is more difficult to imagine how change is effected rhetorically, once physical access to virtual spaces is provided. Indeed, it seems that our metaphors mark the very limitations of our imaginations. The metaphors of space and frontier frequently employed to describe online life contribute to the mystification of social arrangements in virtual environments just as they did during westward expansion. Such metaphors propose that once provided the vehicles by which to access virtual space, women are unstoppable in their quest for self-empowerment: they need only get there and fill the space. We might begin inquiry into the space metaphor by asking women pioneers whether they would confine "ease" in occupying the spaces to matters of technical access.

Indeed this was one of the questions Gail Hawisher and Patricia Sullivan addressed when researching professional women's uses electronic media. For twenty-eight days, thirty women conversed about their occupancy of e-spaces, a term used by the researchers to designate human cultures constructed by way of networked, online activities. Some women reported that difficult physical access did indeed prevent satisfactory online presence, but others located difficulty or ease in the discursive environment itself. Of these latter, some reported complete satisfaction with their online cultures; others, some satisfaction for the chance to speak without interruption, and still others, dissatisfactions sufficient to induce them to abandon certain e-spaces in frustration and anger. Although the researchers were anxious not to allow accounts foregrounding discontent to override those of satisfaction, they were interested in the narratives documenting perceived inequities, and so am I, not because I wish to affirm women's victimization, but, on the contrary, because I believe that close examination of the discursive mechanisms causing dis-ease may promote the discipline and art of producing equitable discourse. My investigation borrows from Joan Wallach Scott's understanding of historiographical practice:

> Perhaps the most dramatic shift in my own thinking came through asking questions about *how* hierarchies such as those of gender are constructed or legitimized. The emphasis on "how" suggests a study of processes, not of origins, of multiple rather than single causes, of *rhetoric or discourse rather than ideology or consciousness*. (4; second emphasis mine)

I am less interested in dramatic episodes of flagrant, misogynist conduct, such as the infamous rape on LambdaMOO (Dibbell) than in the quotidian discursive events that de-neutralize the spaces available, enhancing or eroding their desirability as suitable locations from which to speak.

UNDER PSEUDONYM

The 1987, 1988, and 1989 records of online teaching at the University of Texas at Austin Computer Research Lab do not indicate whether teachers spoke directly to students about subjectivity. Teachers did, however, report a particular fascination with pseudonymous conferencing, a practice certainly instrumental in altering subjectivity. During a 1988 graduate seminar, for example, graduate student and faculty instructors discussed the possible effects of pseudonymity on their students' sense of the relationship of self to language as experienced during online discussion. "FORUM" (now "InterChange") refers to the realtime conferencing module of the Daedalus system. The following excerpt is taken from the middle of the conference:

Lester Faigley:	Nonetheless, it is fascinating how you feel compelled to jump into the discussions in FORUM when it is so easy to sit back and listen in an oral discussion without participating. I'm going to pass out the last transcript from my E309 class. The students all took pseudonyms. I also invited JoAnn Campbell. The text we discussed is an ethnography called THE COCKTAIL WAITRESS. It's interesting that not only did everybody participate, but that everybody participated almost immediately, even though I had no idea who was doing what. I want to use this transcript as a text to analyze, particularly the week after next.
Graduate Student:	Lester, let's use pseudonyms for one of our sessions. Imagine the possibilities.
Graduate Student/ CRL Teacher:	I have had similar success in my E 309 class with pseudonymous Forums. I'm wondering why students jump in so easily, playfully. I talked to one girl in my class who said she assumed a persona

	exactly opposite of the way she felt she was, and said absurd statements that contradicted her own beliefs, just to see how people reacted and to see what it felt like to say those things.
Lester Faigley:	Are you suggesting that we go with pseudonyms next time?
Graduate Student/ CRL Teacher:	Lester: In a word, yes. Pseudonyms (and no-names) make for very different FORUMS. In such a confident and outspoken bunch as this, we might not notice it, but in my English 309 class, where there are people who are afraid of their ideas sounding stupid, the pseudonymous FORUM was a smashing success.
Graduate Student:	I think the pseudonym idea is great. I think of all shy freshman writers so reluctant to express an opinion.[5]

These off-the-cuff messages begin the process of building theory from practice, and although not explicitly articulated as such, two distinct theories of self and language are set forth during the sequence. One theory proposes that a student writing under pseudonym "outs" a formerly hidden or inhibited self through language ("shy freshman writers . . . reluctant to express an opinion"), and the other, that pseudonymity enables the construction of selves in language ("[a student] assume[s] a persona exactly opposite of the way she felt she was").[5] The first theory accommodates a writer's sense of self set free from social/discursive constraints, able to take advantage of the virtual spaces at her disposal, whereas the latter envisions pseudo-selves positioned within a social/discursive environment, regardless of space. Indeed, testing alternate personae in the company of others entails careful observation of the effects of one's speech within a particular environment.

During the above conversation, the instructors introduce several kinds of evidence supporting continued use of pseudonymity: near universality of student participation (formerly fearful students speak out), degree of student enjoyment (students jump in playfully), and increase in students' repertoires of possible discursive positionings (a student tries on different personae to see how the class reacts). Although the first two arguments are not specific to writing instruction, the third argument certainly is. If teachers of interactive argumentation begin with the premise, then, that pseudonymous conferencing is advantageous because it expands the range of subject positions available to students, then they would necessarily conclude that the practice of pseudonymous conferencing at Texas in the early days taught this lesson only erratically. Records indicate that some students taking on prefabricated literary personae created discursively impoverished characters. "Betsy Ross," to use an example from a pseudonymous conference featuring women in history, was unable to imagine herself speaking outside the confines of her needle. Her remarks consisted entirely of offers to sew for others, and she devised no alternative discursive action. Not infrequently, students in pseudonymous conferences withdrew into prefabricated literary or historical worlds, articulating new selves that were hard pressed to converse productively across spans of time and genre, as when Moby Dick and George Washington struggled to find common ground. Still others were encouraged by pseudonymity to set out information about their personal lives that would be withheld under "real" (or regularly appearing) identities. Yet apparently pseudonymity was considered by most CRL instructors a universally excellent classroom activity, and no evaluative distinctions among pseudonymous sessions were forthcoming during these years.[6]

Although large claims about the pedagogical value of pseudonymity cannot be based on fragmentary evidence, such evidence indeed can serve to frame the issues it raises. If the purpose of pseudonymous and other pedagogies of the self is to teach that identity is a construct, that subjectivities may be altered at will or by circumstance, or that language is not transparent, then the particularities do not much matter. So long as a student practices constructing, reconstructing, altering, and fictionalizing the self, the lesson is learned. If, however, teachers are invested in the shape of the discourse they wish students to produce online, in expanding the range of students' discursive options, and in producing equitable discursive environments, they will need to examine more carefully the means that best serve these purposes. The question becomes, then, not "What are the technical means by which we can problematize student identities?" but rather, "To what ends do we do so?"

INTERROGATING THE FEMALE SUBJECT

Under certain circumstances, pseudonymous discussion may dramatize for students the argument that gender is a cultural and linguistic construct, and this lesson is known in culture studies jargon as "the interrogation of subjectivity," an educational procedure enabling people to apprehend the social forces at work in the formation of self consciousness (Johnson). Implementing pseudonymity at Texas, however, may have served a more immediate purpose: establishing an equitable environment. For when gender became topical in sessions conducted under "real" social identities, the subjects placed under severe interrogation usually were women. Male students frequently antagonized female students by essentializing their behaviors, and it would become incumbent upon women to accept, refuse, or ignore the category "women," or to challenge the undesirable characteristics assigned to the category before speaking from within it, before allowing their experiences as women to openly inform their arguments.[7] Each option—to accept, refuse, ignore, or challenge—carries an array of immediate discursive consequences for the women students undergoing this form of interrogation. Indeed, the onus placed on women is striking. And to say so is by no means to fault the instructors who chose readings about women and by women in order to build women into the daily work of the language classroom. Nor should we necessarily fault male students who engaged, in many cases, not in the locker room dialectics described by Christine Boese in "A Virtual Locker Room," but rather in the familiar cultural practice of light, cross-gender teasing. Still, by being targeted, women students are more apt to experience the effects of a pedagogy of chance whose results are unpredictable, a matter of fortune. That is, by becoming the subjects under interrogation when gender is introduced into discussion, some women may indeed take advantage of the opportunity to become more savvy and "empowered" by practicing self-location within discourse when the going is tough. Others, however, may become silent or otherwise discursively disempowered, unable to find satisfactory locations from which to argue well.

Unpredictability of outcomes (or chance teaching) thus may be partially responsible for the election of pseudonymity as the medium of choice for interrogating gender, subjectivity, and language, at the CRL and elsewhere. Indeed, Donna Le Court and Cynthia Haynes, in separate articles, have begun theorizing feminist subjectivity in networked environments from the practices they observe and participate in. Both researchers ground some of their observations in data produced during pseudonymous conferences, and both assume the exclusionary nature of discourse, its impermeability, its easily invoked hostility to women's presences, and the inadequacy of traditional rhetorics for theorizing procedures or providing satisfactory strategies for rhetorical action. Both invoke French feminist theory and reject expressivist rhetoric (one of the theories under consideration in the University of Texas CRL), finding expressivism an ineffective means for challenging patriarchal discourses. Whereas the tactics Haynes and Le Court advocate may resemble various expressivisms by the inclusion of emotion as part of discursive repertoire and by the relaxation of politeness and decorum, these tactics are better understood as calculative discursive moves and their authors as among Lanham's "cynical connoisseurs of language" (146).

Haynes argues specifically for abandoning a cherished feminist practice— a politics of location that relies heavily upon space metaphors—believing this metaphor ineffective when translated to virtual environments. Advocating instead a feminist seizing of what is decidedly new in realtime virtual environments—speed and motion—and following Cixous, Haynes envisions feminist activists "flying through" but not occupying the spaces provided by programmers and/or wizards, whose likely masculinist persuasions and ideologies are merely constraining. Developed from images of motion, speed, and shape, a feminist "position," according to Haynes, is "amphibious," less a location than a process of making disorder.

Similarly (but following Irigaray), Le Court advocates using virtual spaces to "jam" discourse in order to create self-representations not contingent upon the dominant. Citing from pseudonymous course transcripts, Le Court provides examples of discursive episodes where both women and men purposely disappoint the expectations associated with the provision of writing spaces. Feminist action is achieved when writers accede to expectations by occupying space and speaking within conventional roles, then subvert these very roles by taking on multiple subject positions from within a single identity. Repetitious acquiescence to a traditional role achieves, in the end, an effect of mockery. Haynes demonstrates this very technique in part three of her essay (@gender). In preparation for the development of LinguaMOO, Haynes interviews a wizard from PMC (*Post Modern Culture*) MOO, ostensibly to inform herself more fully about pre-programming verbs (or emotes) for MOO participants. During the course of a short interview, Haynes writes "Cynthia smiles" and "Cynthia nods" seven times and otherwise signals support by murmuring "I thought so," "hmmm," "yes," and "I see" in an hilarious qua sobering parody of the friendly, supportive, space-ceding, female interviewer.[8]

Both Haynes and Le Court provide necessary visions, theories, and vocabularies—the beginnings of a new rhetoric of the self—for feminist performances in online environments. The classroom example I provide in the last section of this essay supports their work by illustrating the discursive mechanisms by which "free" space becomes baggaged with properties preventing women students from successful discursive occupation of that space. I hope to justify Haynes's and Le Court's critique of the commonplace among computer compositionists that providing physical access to virtual space suffices and that empowered self-representation is easily accomplished. However, the assumptions underpinning my argument differ somewhat from those of both Haynes and Le Court. Rather than cast all discourse in the role of patriarchal villain and principal opponent, I conceive discourse as more pliable and responsive to manipulation, less in need of violent disruption, although by no means innocent. Such a theory of discourse enables me to assign to teachers and other participant rhetorician/rhetors some responsibility for partial and temporary remedies for exclusionary events, an assignment that requires careful readings of discursive environments and careful writing, in short—a rhetorical authority. My alliance with Haynes and Le Court may weaken at the link where their revolutionary tactics brush up against my reformist ones. But a weak link, I believe (and hope they will agree), does not preclude the alliance.

I do not, for example, privilege pseudonymity at the expense of simulating possible selves under "real" names. Because we may reasonably assume that a good portion of women's professional and personal online work will be performed under their stable, off-line identities, certainly women will benefit from understanding and practicing self-representations under these identities. Gender erasure, argues Teresa De Lauretis, must be considered in light of its consequences:

> Do[ing] away with sexual difference altogether . . . closes the door in the face of the emergent social subject, . . . a subject constituted across a multiplicity of differences in discursive and material heterogeneity. Again, then, I rewrite: If the deconstruction of gender inevitably effects its (re)construction, the question is, in which terms and in whose interest is the de-re-construction being effected? (25)

Indeed, even without pseudonyms, electronic conferencing tends to destabilize a writer's sense of self. In realtime discourse, a range of available subject positions becomes visible to writers, and the idea of a possible or temporary self existing among possible alternatives becomes more apparent, if the writer/reader attends closely. The apparent separation of self from body that electronic conferencing enforces, or, put another way, the appearance before one's eyes of a simulated self who then scrolls right by and must be made by its author to reappear repeatedly in ever-changing rhetorical contexts, announces to students something about the constructive power of language and something about the limitations of linguistic constructs as well. Illusions of control are swiftly undermined by the diminished likelihood of long-term gain or fixed returns on a writer's choices. Successes online are fleeting, and rewards for careful construction of ethos are strikingly ephemeral.

Constructing or assuming alternate identities, however, is not synonymous with conceptualizing the relationship between language and self. Indeed, rhetorics or textbooks designed for undergraduate writing instruction in or outside of computer classrooms seldom provide discussions of self. Barry Brummett's 1994 textbook *Rhetoric in Popular Culture* is an exception. Although not designed for online environments, it does include an explanation of how reader subjectivities form in response to a text:

> The Marxist scholar Louis Althusser (1971) and others (for example, Hall 1985) have argued that texts ask those who read them to be certain kinds of subjects. To be a certain kind of subject is to take on a sort of role or character; these theorists argue that rather than having any single, stable, easily located identity, we do nothing but move from one subject position to another. In a sense, then, the power that a text has over you has a lot to do with what kinds of subject positions it encourages (or forces) you to inhabit. (98)

Unfortunately, Brummett's treatment suffers a partial loss of explanatory power when applied to online environments because it grants mobility to the reader only, who is said to take up subject positions ranging from "preferred" to "subversive," with respect to an inert text. Indeed, Brummett cautions students that "a subject position is not a character in the text itself" (98) and so marks the significant limitation of his approach for teaching in online environments, where participants indeed *are* characters in the texts they produce. Brummett positions readers as rhetorical analysts only, whereas in online environments, they are writers as well, required simultaneously to analyze and produce discourse, to be rhetoricians, rhetors, and subjects under construction by others as well.

Although the classical term *ethos* currently governs the idea of self and language in networked writing classrooms at Texas, and although students use the term with some success for both analysis and production of discourse, its presence derives not from the practice-based theories of teachers in the CRL, but rather from an off-line syllabus introduced in computer classrooms in 1991. Working from a substantial knowledge of digital text, Richard Lanham has suggested that the Renaissance term sprezzatura might prove useful for theorizing digital hermeneutics, but to my knowledge this term is not in use, either as vocabulary for theorists or as tool placed at the disposal of students. Although the teacher featured in the extended example below does not provide students with conceptual tools for considering their discursive options, his rhetorical pedagogy—his discursive art—attends carefully to the reluctance that women students exhibit when asked to take up subject positions as women, and he works to provide a broader range of possibilities from which they might construct their arguments.

ATTENDING TO WOMEN'S SPACES: A PEDAGOGY OF THE SELF

Prior to the Hopwood decision, the University of Texas at Austin sponsored a summer program for minority scholarship students residing in Texas, and enrollees were mostly Latina/os and African-Americans. According to archival records for summer 1988, a first-year writing course for students in this program was designed around texts documenting the communication practices at a variety of work environments. I have selected passages from three different electronic conferences performed during this course, tracking the specific discursive events that invite women students to speak as women even as the strength of such a discursive positioning is eroded. I track women's decisions to take up the position or sidestep it and the instructor's efforts to expand the range of available subject positions to all students.

Readings assigned in preparation for the first conference were taken from Studs Terkel's *Working*, a collection of workers' narratives transcribed from oral interviews. Just prior to the following excerpt, the instructor has suggested several times to students engaged in lively discussion of some of the men's narratives that they turn to the women's texts. Finally they respond to his urging, and one student observes that possibly the most difficult aspect of one woman's job is the lying she is required to do. Anxious, perhaps, to thicken this thread of discussion on women, the instructor responds as follows

> *Instructor:*   It's interesting that both Sharon Atkins and Enid Du Bois talk about lying on the job.

And perhaps because the phrasing of this message invites the response that women lie because they are women, the instructor reframes the observation, suggesting instead that workers might lie because of working conditions:

> *Instructor:*   Can you think of other jobs that require people to lie regularly?

Together these questions lay out an analytical terrain accommodating both essentialist readings of women and cultural readings of working conditions. They extend an offer to women to occupy the category "woman" and respond from this subject position, to occupy the category "worker" and respond from that position, or to occupy both or neither. Rhetorical decisions for women are immediately complicated, however, by a message that begins the ongoing process of larding the category "woman" with additional "information":

> *David:*   I wasn't surprised by Jill Torrance [one of the narrators in *Working*] in the
> least. Most women, excluding UT women, aren't as materially minded as
> others may think . . . .

David draws the following response:

> *Angelica:*   David, did you only exclude UT women because there are women in this
> room with you?[9]

Previously, Angelica had hedged when the instructor offered the subject
position "women," responding with a story about a female friend who regularly lied on the job. Her message to David constitutes another evasion, yet
marks her interest in issues of gender and rhetoric. Rather than contest, which
possibly would entail speaking as a woman, Angelica queries the rhetoric of
the discussion at hand, reading for author intention, reading for the effects of
writing on other writers.

When the question of women's "natural" or habitual shyness becomes topical
during a subsequent discussion about computer-networked writing, once again
women students must decide whether to respond as women, that is, to take up
subject positions as women, or to devise other places to stand. In the ensuing discussion associating computers with freedom to speak, several participants propose that the networked machines free the women to say whatever they want,
invoking the expressivist theory of networked writing ("shy freshman writers so
reluctant to express an opinion"). This time, women do respond as women, yet
gratuitous information about the nature of women shapes their responses. The
following sequence omits messages not directly relevant to my argument.

> *Alejandro:*   David, if it were not for computers, how many of us would be expressing
> our opinions as openly as we are now. I feel that the personal atmos-
> phere is much better.
>
> *Instructor:*   David, I think computers separate people if we were all just talking to
> computers. But since we are all hooked up together, we can come up
> with a lot more ideas as a group because we can all "talk" at once.
>
> *Gordon:*   It`s true what Alejandro said about computers. If we didn't have these
> things most of us (especially the girls) would be very shy and therefore,
> wouldn't express their feelings like they do here. I'm not saying anything
> to get the girls mad, but most girls are quiet when discussion are taken
> about and they are called upon. What do you think females?
>
> *Katy:*   I have to disagree with you Gordon.
>
> *Gordon:*   Why Katy?
>
> *Angelica:*   Gordon, I personally feel exactly the same way you do. I know that if we
> were sitting in a classroom I would not talk as much. It is alot easier for
> me to talk to the class using the computer.
>
> *Mara:*   I agree with Gordon that this interaction with the computer and the
> class is a lot more beneficial than an oral discussion but I do feel that
> girls can be just as vocal as boys if the guys just give them a chance.

Gabriela:	Well Gordon, most of us are not shy. At least I don't think I am. It is sort of hard to go up and talk to someone, especially a guy, without them thinking you want something or that you are interested.
Katy:	If we (females) have a comment to make on a particular subject than we usually state [it] unless you (males) are monopilizing the whole disscussin.
Gordon:	Normally we do but we'll be nice and hear your opinions.
Angelica:	Gordon, are you trying to say that the males have the option to let the females voice their opinions?
Miguel:	Katy, sorry but it would be impossible for us (males) to monopolize the whole discussion, considering the computer will print responses as fast as you can type them in. And we are not saying anything out loud, so we can't drown you out.
David:	Katy, what you did is very typical and transperant. Why play it off on the guys when it is the girls that usually don't enter disscussions. Also, the people that always talk the most are girls and they stop when they are asked to do so. Women are just contrary.
John:	Katy, you know that guys want to make their points across. So if someone says something wrong, a guy is less hesitant to disagree. Girls may want to get something across, but they feel if they interrupt someone, they better make sure they have their facts or evidence straight.
Angelica:	Miguel , I understand what you are saying and that is true, but David is really getting on my nerves. There are so many things I want to say to him. I just wish I had the guts to tell him.

The argument as to whether women are free to choose when and how to speak, both off- and online, and/or whether they are constrained by male monopolies is about how discourse works when gender becomes a factor in its production and analysis. Here women students demonstrate their attentiveness to the constraints of discourse even as they speak. While refusing to locate gender difference in shyness or reasoning power, they argue and demonstrate that they experience discourse differently from men, in both offline and online environments. For example, before Gabriela can reason about computer-based communication, she must clarify that what may look to men like shyness might better be understood as self-protection. Katy asserts that men typically monopolize conversations, thereby calling men to male subjectivity, a position Gordon readily accepts, as does Miguel, who asserts a corollary to the "women are now free" proposal: that technology actually prevents men from monopolizing conversations. Although the women who become involved in the discussion eventually affirm the advantages of networked conversation, they resist the essentializing of all experience in networked environments. Angelica's final ironic remark about not having guts to speak assures us that for her, even in computer-mediated environments, there are strong stakes that impinge upon her discursive choices. Evidently it is less a question of spaces available, than of the quality of those spaces.

When students read John Train's "For the Adventurous Few: How to Get Rich," an essay on global free enterprise, and Ehrenreich and Fuentes' "Life on the Global Assembly Line," an essay about working conditions for third-world women, the instructor carefully positions himself outside student discussion by asking students what Ehrenreich and Fuentes would say to Train and introducing his question via a student comment. Simultaneously, he avoids direct invocation of "women" and thus eases the pressure on women to respond as women to questions about women. Angelica takes up the topic proposal and produces an argument referring to women as "they":

> *Instructor:*   Mara says that Ehrenreich and Fuentes would likely despise Train's attitude. What would Train have to say about them?
>
> *Angelica:*   The authors of, "Life on the Global Assembly Line" would feel very different. They felt that the women are exploited in the Third World and as far as they are concerned there are no business ethics for the women. They are practically treated like slaves in the Third World.

Several messages later, Steve names women as the primary audience for the article, thus calling women students to a possible subjectivity from which to respond:

> *Steve:*   The way Ehrenreich and Fuentes keep mentioning how the women are working for such low wages it seems to me, that this essay is addressed more to women.

The instructor follows Steve with a message on women (not reproduced here) whose length strongly supports a third-world-women discussion thread without directly calling women students to gendered subjectivity. He adroitly directs Ehrenreich and Fuentes's arguments to the Latina/o members of the class but frames his question as a question about culture, not about women:

> *Instructor:*   Ehrenreich and Fuentes make some specific claims about the culture of Mexico—that it makes it easier to exploit women. At the end they say that because a woman's reputation is so important in Hispanic culture, women will "bend over backward to be respectable" and thus cause no trouble for the employer. Do you think this claim is accurate concerning Hispanic culture?

Two men address the question first, Alejandro pointing out strengths of Latin culture (being able to take care of yourself and speaking out for what is right), and John evidently rearticulating the claims that working-class women in Latin America must either work or get married. Angelica, on the other hand, undertakes the task of guarding against broad assertions about women and their actions. She challenges essentialized representations of Latinas and confronts the growing number of restrictions becoming operative in this locally constructed environment. I cannot speak for Angelica's intentions but can assert that her words serve within this discursive environment to clear once more a space for women of Latin descent to speak without encumbrances.

Alejandro: Hispanic culture does stress the reputation of women, but they do not necessary stay out of trouble. Another characteristic that is stressed is being able to take care of yourself which means speaking out for what is right.

John: I feel the claim is accurate because those Hispanic women have a choice of either getting married to someone or stay on the job. The thing is if you don't have a husband, then crying is the only thing that these women can do. The authors said that the men will not stay on the job after working a couple of times, so women will do it.

Angelica: In certain parts of Mexico where the women do not know any better, I think that this is true about them bending over backwards to be respectable, but it is not like this in all of Hispanic culture. I think that once these women come to a country like America they lose that claim.

The instructor interposes two more long messages, one on the politics of foreign investment in Mexico and the other on working conditions and entrepreneurship in South Africa, ending by offering all students subject positions as business executives. The geographic areas he names called students to ethnicity as well, albeit obliquely.

Instructor: . . . So what would you do if you were the executive of a company that had a factory in a country with no laws protecting its workers?

Marcos   [still on the woman question and likely not having seen the instructor's new post]: Angelica , I think that Hispanic women should revert to that type of thinking. Don't you agree?

Angelica: Marcos, I do not feel that they should revert to that type of thinking. Why are you trying to make me mad?

John: I`m not going to say anything about Marcos`s comment because I don`t want any lady in here mad at me.

Gabriela: In my opinion most Hispanic women are very consciencous about their reputation. It is very evident in the United States. I have been to Mexico several times and it is very common to see several women that are prostitutes, and they are all mostly young.

Steve: If I had a company in South Africa I would try to change the working conditions for the blacks, but if it got to the point that it was costing the company too much, then I would have to do what ever is best for the company.

Angelica: It would be real easy to say that I would try to improve the working conditions, but in reality I would probably, to some extent, take advantage of these poor people. It all depends on what your heart and mind allow you to do. If you can live with yourself after you run over these people then you will get your profit otherwise it is better just to stay out of it.

Gabriela: A lot of difference in a person response will depend on if that person is dealing with people of his own race. If I had a company in Mexico I don't think I would exploit my own people. It is very likely that my

 anscestors were probably treated like this and I do not think I could go
in there and do the same.

In this first-year course composed primarily of African-American and
Mexican-American students, the instructor introduces the ethnicity question
with careful subtlety, via articles on the effects of third-world capitalism. The
ethnic subject position is not thrust full force upon them, but is offered, nevertheless, and taken up in the above excerpts—by Latina/os and likely (although
I can't be sure) by African-American men. Gendered subjectivities for women
have been offered by the instructor previously and often, but most recently
during this session in combination with the discussion of third-world, working class women, and when complicated by the introduction of questions of
reputation and morality, the Latinas are put on the spot, for the woman position has become quite vulnerable and disempowered. Once the instructor
offers "executive" as subject position, however, he has many takers.

Donna Haraway writes that women's experiences are "structured within
multiple and often inharmonious agendas" (243), and this conference provides
a sense of what this powerful insight might mean. When women are asked to
encode their experiences within a specific classroom-produced discourse, even
one designed and executed with great care for equitable practice and populated
by polite, intelligent discussants, they comply, if they choose to do so, under
local constructions of the category "woman." When Gabriela is offered "executive" in addition to "worker" as a subject position alongside a heavily baggaged
"Latina," she finds an adequate position from which to relocate morality in
places other than women's psycho/sexual behaviors, which had been introduced
and sustained as characteristics typical of being Latin and female. As entrepreneur and "person," she writes using a male-gendered pronoun, she is able to
resituate morality within business ethics. In addition, she proposes ethnicity or
roots (ancestors) as causal forces for her ethical decisions: "If I had a company
in Mexico I don't think I would exploit my own people."

Perhaps even more crucial to the production of equitable discourse is the
possibility that when many women are present and differ in their self-representations, then "women" as a category—represented variously—can be taken back
from its reductive forms and rebuilt as a multiple. Both constrained and enabled
by the shape of local conversation, the women students in this virtual classroom
demonstrate some success in figuring "Latina" as a multiple construct, situated
variously within different geographical, socioeconomic, and psycho-sexual arenas, but the question remains as to whether their proposal for women's diversity
was influential among the discussants.[10] Noteworthy as well is Mara's role.
Although Mara did not participate directly in the more confrontational
episodes, she did provide useful metacommentary (indeed one wishes she might
have said more), naming what for Angelica and Gabriela was not easily namable
if they wanted to retain their positions as public reasoners rather than fractious
antagonists speaking from disempowered discursive locations.

THE IMPOSSIBLE DREAM

I have not discerned in the archival records examples of students either male or female creating new emotions (Haynes). I am unable to say comfortably that Gabriela or Angelica or Katy or Mara spoke their contradictory selves within a single voice (Le Court) or whether they shifted shape in ways that might be considered amphibious (Haynes). I am more comfortable saying that Gabriela, for example, was finally able to combine satisfactorily a number of the subjectivities made available to her in order to speak about a possible ethical self and possible ethnic self placed in a possible position of power. Indeed the metaphors of recombination found occasionally in the work of Ann Balsamo and Shirley Brice Heath might be usefully aligned with those of Haynes and Le Court, for still we have no adequate terminology to account for the exclusionary tendencies of discourse while attending to the making of online selves.

Gabriela, who may well have finished her coursework and graduated in 1993, is not available for commentary on my interpretation of her writing. I cannot provide her reading of the particular excerpt of online discussion I have magnified for inspection; likely she would not remember it. If by chance she were to have become a Marxist feminist in the interim and were to offer her own retrospective reading, quite possibly she would object more strongly to the economic binary—exploited and disempowered worker versus entrepreneur—than to the tainted, gendered subject positions that I am more concerned with. She might read the segment not as a provision of multiple subject positions for a woman's recombination but rather as entrapment within the false ideologies of capitalism. Still, I offer my nondefinitive reading of this excerpt as an example of teaching with some (partial) comprehension of the disadvantages for women who would speak from gendered spaces and their reluctance to do so. I offer it as example of a teacher's attempt to put rhetorical authority to good use, as an example of online teaching that leaves marginalization and inclusion neither to the spaces provided by the software nor to chance.

Teachers allotting class time to electronic conferences and committed to sponsoring equitable discursive environments find themselves awkwardly positioned with regard to their own assignments. Certainly, we should consider each session a new and untainted episode of interactive writing, but also, I argue, we should suspend naiveté about the benevolence of online discourse and acknowledge its exclusionary as well as inclusionary history. Positioned institutionally as constructivists, as instigators of student writing, and as the parties responsible for assuring its value, teachers may wish to distinguish between virtual space and discursive space, taking action to assure an ample range of discursive positions for all students. The above excerpts demonstrate the delicacy of so doing—the small turns of phrase by which the instructor carefully, gingerly, makes offers to students of possible selves. Even so, he is not able to extricate himself from his connections to these selves and from his own responsibility for their being. He may be faulted, perhaps, for not providing an "elsewhere," that place to stand outside oppressive discourses, or for providing sets of binaries—male-female, worker-entrepreneur—as materials for students' self-construction. Nevertheless, there is art and sound method to his cookery.

NOTES

1. One of the early Daedalus instructor manuals addressed the issue of conferences gone awry by proposing that most difficulties arise from students' psychological immaturity.

2. Early in the history of online writing instruction, for example, two titles appeared in the 1990 special edition of *Computers and Composition*: "Sharing Authority on a Synchronous Network: The Case for Riding the Beast." (Marshall Kremers) and "Taking Women Professors Seriously: Female Authority in the Computerized Classroom" (E. Laurie George). Although both articles placed under careful scrutiny budding notions of virtual utopias, the grammatical discontinuity between sharing (authority) and female (authority) signals important conceptual differences. Whereas Kremers conceives authority as distributive, however difficult the process of distribution, George understands authority as a situated, cultural construct and finds practicing authority in her environment irrevocably linked to gender.

3. These examples are taken from transcripts of Daedalus InterChange sessions logged from Fall 1987 through Spring 1989.

4. Joan Landes documents the unfortunate results of revolutionary opportunity in the aftermath of the French Revolution, when subordinate positions for women were reconfigured through their idealization as keepers of virtue and the attendant excision from public life.

5. Surveying both undergraduate and graduate students in 1987 and 1988, Jerome Bump reported this very distinction in students' perceptions of self in online environments. Although most students in his survey were pleased with the increased freedom of expression and with the reprieve from a politeness enforced by peer opinion, others conceived their activities as a role-playing, an understanding that defused accusations of insincerity ("Radical Changes" 57).

6. See Minock and Shor, "Crisscrossing Grand Canyon: Bridging the Gaps with Computer Conferencing," for a report on uses of pseudonymity that expand discursive options for students.

7. In his ethnography of a single University of Texas course, Wayne Butler documents one woman's inability or unwillingness to sustain a feminist perspective and concludes that her feminism was not strong enough to sustain the pressures of the discursive environment.

8. Haynes supplements her theorizing with education. She writes: " . . . I have constructed (in collaboration with Jan Rune Holmevik of Oslo, Norway) a text-based virtual reality environment called LinguaMOO where I train our teachers and students to pursue alternate writing activities and alternate classroom dynamics" (@gender par. 37).

9.   I have provided pseudonyms for the students represented here, and their messages are lightly edited (spaces inserted, for example) for the sake of reader comprehension.

10.   Gabriela has previously sent a confusing and perhaps defensive message, but one that insists upon differences within the Hispanic woman category: "In my opinion most Hispanic women are very consciencious about their reputation. It is very evident in the United States. I have been to Mexico several times and it is very common to see several women that are prostitutes, and they are all mostly young. Angelica writes, "but it is not like this in all of Hispanic culture."

Fleeting Images
Women Visually Writing the Web

Gail E. Hawisher
Patricia A. Sullivan

Hi everyone,

The very idea of choosing a face to accompany my online words horrifies me. Should I choose an "authentic" image, one that shows my age and deviations from standard female beauty markers? Or does the electronic medium license me to alter my image? License? Does it *mandate* that I alter my image (think of the number of times people have sheepishly said after a first time on a MUD—gee, I used my *real* name! I didn't know [the rules]. . . (blush))?

In creating a face to accompany my words, how would I deal with the very diverse audience of the net—remembering that I might want to retain a professional image for the job search and in addition construct a fanciful image for other lists or create some feminist symbol-face for this list? Will my female face get more or less respect if I make it nice looking, smiling? Does nice-looking reinforce the nice training that I want to shed or does it indicate my insistence on new and nice rules? Or should I make a face very much at odds with my words (mean face/nice words or nice face/mean words) in order to subvert stereotyping?

Ah so many rhetorical decisions if we add visual rhetoric. And gender issues become heightened, I think, rather than lessened.

She adds, almost as an afterthought,

Is anyone here making home pages?
I have enough trouble with words.

Tina (November 1994)

In this statement about online living made before web pages were commonplace, Tina anticipates some of the issues about visual representation that we explore in this chapter. Self-image is problematic for her, and more problematic as it becomes more visual. She sees "authentic" as deviating visually from "standard female beauty markers" and ponders whether a "nice-looking, smiling" female face will attract "more or less respect" as she wonders about how she wants to represent herself to the online world. Just as she considers retaining "a professional image for the job search," she also toys with the idea of making a face at odds with her words in order to subvert stereotyping. And although we suspect that a verbal description when juxtaposed with her picture is not so strong a tool for subverting viewers' stereotyping as Tina may suppose, her words help us understand the vexed relationship between online writing and images. Ultimately and interestingly, she connects image with face while, at the same time, remaining fully aware that she's creating her image through the very words that are also creating her. As visual as her verbal self-representation is, she foregrounds the complications that visual rhetoric will add to her creation of her own image on her home page. We agree that self-image and representation are at least as complicated as Tina suggests.

The Internet has been promoted in the popular press and in our professional journals as a space in which what is said becomes more important than who does the saying: the net is reputed to blind us to appearance and other markers of status which are readily apparent in face-to-face encounters (Sproull and Kiesler). Because online participants cannot see one another in electronic settings and therefore are unaware of paralinguistic cues such as voice, facial expressions, and dress, some argue that they are less likely to judge one another by differences in looks, race, social class, age, sexual preference, handicaps, and gender. Recent studies of writing and technology have begun to critique the adequacy of such egalitarian narratives for describing e-space. Instead of viewing the Internet as a space that masks differences because of its lack of visual and aural cues, some see women and other underrepresented groups as net victims, often unduly harassed on listservs and news groups. More recent work argues that these online environments are neither egalitarian utopias nor spaces devoid of communicative power for women (Hawisher and Sullivan). As of yet, however, published discussions have paid little attention to what happens when the mostly verbal online context of computer-mediated communication is transformed into the visually rich space of the World Wide Web. As women, we are interested in questions of how women and others represent themselves visually on home pages. As feminists, we are particularly interested in how these representations position women within society and what subject positions are available to them. As women visually construct themselves online, what issues of representation should they consider and how do they understand others' online construction of them? In other words, what happens to women's online lives when the visual comes into play? These are the questions this chapter seeks to address.[1]

GENDER IN ELECTRONIC DISCOURSE

In previous discussions of women online, the field of computers and composition has often focused on computer-mediated communication and read online issues inside a frame that is totally textual—or nearly so. As computer-mediated communication became a pedagogical option for writing classes, considerable enthusiasm accompanied its arrival. Teachers argued that it could encourage quiet students to speak up and out and that it abetted students' writing through its totally textually-based environment. In addition to providing real and expanded audiences, it was also said to encourage a sense of community, with students demonstrating a high degree of involvement and equitable participation all around. Teachers also believed that there could be a decrease in leader-centered participation. All these claims were grounded in an egalitarian ethos (see Hawisher 1992 for a review of these claims). That computer-mediated communication might improve the writing class in ways that fostered egalitarianism grew out of writing teachers' experience but was also grounded in studies that Sara Kiesler and her colleagues conducted at Carnegie Mellon, research which began in 1984 and which continues today. (See Sproull and Kiesler's *Connections* 1991 for an overview of the research.) The "reduced social context cues model" that they articulated regards networked discourse as an efficient medium for communicating information in business settings where the content of the message is of primary importance. Those working in computers and composition, however, have turned the research to a different end. Compositionists argue that because participants cannot see one another in electronic settings, writing instructors have a greater possibility for decentering their authority and transforming their classes into egalitarian sites for learners. This absence-of-sensory-cues foundation for online equality—the "if we could just strip away markers of difference" wish—is, of course, almost impossible inside the visually rich world of the Web. Students might play with representations of themselves, but it is difficult to hide visible markers of difference.[2] Further, because the textual CMC theory has not anticipated a visual frame, the entrance of the visual is theoretically jolting: those who have been pen or email pals with strangers are now "seeing" those strangers.

Even in discussions of online violence and victimization, feminists focus for the most part on the textual world of CMC. Calling on arguments from the popular press—the *Village Voice's* "CyberRape" (Dibbel); *Ms. Magazine's* "The Strange Case of the Electronic Lover" (Van Gelder); *Vogue's* "Terror Online" (Gill)—and also television news shows, such as *DateLine*, discussions of stalking and sexual harassment are used to combat the egalitarian narrative and the reasonableness of the research that supports it. Feminists have relied on very powerful stories of gender deception, violence, and harassment to counter the prevailing notions about the utopian possibilities of textual e-space. Stories such as Lindsy Van Gelder's "The Strange Case of the Electronic Lover," in which a fifty-something male psychiatrist posing as a crippled and mute woman who gives much advice and support to disabled women, have highlighted how deception has shattered women's trust in the online utopian community. As one woman who was duped noted: "Although I think this is a wonderful medium, it's a dangerous one, and it poses more danger to women than men" (375). Feminists in technology have further argued that stories of gender deception, violence, and harassment also prevail in professional settings. In a study we conducted of the online verbal lives of academic women in composition, again and again they reported being increasingly shut out in mixed-group electronic discussions. And analysis of online discourse finds that women make fewer and shorter contributions than men and that both men and women respond more frequently to men's postings than to women's (Selfe and Meyer; Herring; Ebben), thereby reinforcing the off-line status quo.

Our point? Feminists in computers and composition have understandably focused almost exclusively on the textual. But the heightened possibilities for self-representation brought about by the Web suggest that a simple transfer of arguments about women's online verbal lives is inadequate as a strategy for exploring visual representations. While writers can enhance (and even mask) their visual representations, it remains 1) that they are visually represented and 2) that most cultural castes are visually marked. If a woman features a woman on her homepage, that picture signs her into the feminine gender online. In order to extend and complicate electronic discourse theories, we need to examine online visual depictions in a variety of discursive settings.

The body, and representation of the body, certainly are key feminist concerns. Such feminists as Susan Bordo have argued that because "the construction of body as something apart from the true self . . . and as undermining the efforts of that self" (5) is seen as an historical constant and because "woman [is] cast in the role of the body" (5) reading the feminine body is central to feminism. But in a postmodern world where context is everything, Bordo concedes, reading bodies becomes extremely complex. Although she admits that readers will bring different interpretations to their reading, she argues that "to focus only on multiple interpretations is to miss important effects of the everyday deployment of mass cultural representations of masculinity, femininity, beauty, and success" (24). Bordo approaches the everyday interpretation through two analytical moves: finding how representations "homogenize" and articulating how these homogenized images "normalize"—that is, how they go about representing that which the self continually measures, judges, disciplines, and corrects itself by. (24-25) Although Bordo uses this analytic primarily to read ads and celebrity images, here we see its potential for reading pictorial representations of bodies on the Web.

In cyberspace the body of the machine (and its relationships to humans) adds yet another complicating factor to the visualization of gender online. Sandy Stone ("Will the Real Body") argues that Donna Haraway and Bruno Latour have already convinced cyber theorists that machines are artifacts with agencies, but that the multiple agencies enabled by the human-machine cyborg complicate the task of researchers who now have to determine what it is that they need to target for analysis. Online pictorial representations of the body treat theorizing to several new *whats*. Not only do these cyborgian images challenge feminist theorizing about CMC by adding a visual dimension to the previously textual renderings of the online body, but they also challenge gender binaries and stereotypical representations of the body that theorists such as Judith Butler, Elizabeth Grosz, and Bordo take as starting points.

Haraway has linked the biology of bodies with the mechanisms of machines in her consideration of cyborgs. For Haraway, "Technology is not neutral. We're inside of what we make, and it's inside of us. We're living in a world of connections—and it matters which ones get made and unmade (quoted in Kunzru 209)." Admittedly, this is not necessarily a visual view of cyberlife, at least not one that we would easily name visual. Nor does it reveal a process for interpreting the visual as Bordo does. But, it does, as Haraway unfolds it, revolve around the notion of the cyborg as a collection of networks "constantly feeding information back and forth across the line to the millions of networks that make up [the] 'world.'" (according to Kunzru 158) For Haraway, then, the cyborg—fully connected in ways that heretofore have not been possible—is cause for celebration.

Susan Leigh Star, on the other hand, responds more cautiously to cyborgian notions. When she examines the consequences of "links crisscrossing the world, these rearrangements of work and play," in relation to her sense of "freedom, privacy, and naturalness," she wonders whether "we may all be moving into a regime of virtual detention simply to manage the information available" (3). Star cautions that the cyborg is "an exciting, avant-garde notion of the merger of people with technologies, making possible new ways of being," and is at the same time "a despairing look at the devastation wrought by technophilia as coupled with late capitalism (21)." Thus, for Star, the cyborg evokes a mixture of hope and despair—both productive and troubling at once.

Haraway and Star agree that connections are key. Star draws on Haraway to define the cyborg as "the intermingling of people, things (including information technologies), representations and politics in a way that challenges both the romance of essentialism and the hype about what is possible technologically. It acknowledges the interdependence of people and things, and just how blurry the boundaries between them have become (21)." Both theorists focus on boundaries and interrogate them from the vantages of human-machine connections and feminist perspectives to encourage new ways of seeing.

Star uses "boundary objects" as an analytic for probing boundaries because it allows groups to come together for a specific purpose through a focusing of their mutual attention on a particular object at hand. Although members of the different groups may have radically different understandings of the object, their thinking is somewhat flexible and the object is understood on multiple levels. According to Star, such objects "occupy a tense but necessarily malleable position between several worlds ("The Politics" 96)." In earlier work, Star, with her co-author Griesemer, uses boundary objects as analytics in their construction of the ecology surrounding the emergence of a natural history research museum in the early twentieth century. In their concern with "the flow of objects and concepts through the network of participating allies and social worlds" (389), Star and Griesemer look to establish multiple stories that are supported by their data at the same time as they establish a coherent account to the institution's emergence. The boundary objects, which "inhabit several intersecting worlds" (393), are accepted by the various constituencies even though they are understood somewhat differently by each group. This allows for diversity and cooperation across groups because the boundary objects are "plastic enough to adapt to local needs and the constraints of the several parties employing them, yet robust enough to maintain a common identity across sites" (393). Further, the "creation and management of boundary objects is a key process in developing and maintaining coherence across intersecting social worlds" (393).[3]

Similarly, Haraway would have us "[nurture and acknowledge] alliances with a lively array of others, who are like and unlike, human and not, inside and outside what have been the defended boundaries of hegemonic selves and powerful places" (269). She breaks down the boundaries between human and non-human, thus attributing to non-humans the possibility for agency. Star, by contrast, locates agency in humans and groups, the traditional stuff of sociology. She struggles with the tension of humans needing to fit into a particular society while at the same time their needing increasingly to connect across cultures and groups.[4]

Thus we turn to all three theorists for this particular analysis of women's online visual representations and images. Bordo's analytic allows us to interrogate images through the binary relationships and pre-existing categories active in our culture. She helps us read visual culture through a gendered lens. Haraway and Star help us focus on the connections that might extend or refashion pre-existing categories. As complicated through the notion of boundary objects, their focus on cultural connections adds the dynamic quality needed for an analysis of the electronic imagery of the Web.

WOMEN'S WEB PAGES: READING TO THE ISSUES

What follows is an exploration of several websites that visually portray women online. We seek to address the issues in this area that are key for feminists in computers and composition who theorize gender in online environments. Our overarching aim is to elucidate how women make use of the cyborgian connectedness of electronic environments to claim multiple agencies for themselves and to show how institutional and cultural-ideological forces work against women's efforts at self-representation. Several questions related to the ones we posed earlier pertain: How do women use these new spaces to accommodate varied and multiple subject positions? In what ways are women writers, authorizers, and controllers of e-space in their web pages? How do the sites they connect with their names function? What subject positions does the central figure of their sites occupy? What messages about the women do the sites convey?

Our examples are drawn from several sources[5]: a group of professional women we studied in another setting, a group of young women drawn from two online directories of women's web pages, and several commercial sites. Only a few website classifications[6] address audience and purpose, and none provide rhetorical distinctions that allow us to probe the range of visual online representations of/for/by women. In order to ensure that our websites (1) paid attention to the ways in which they construct identities and (2) were intended to communicate with viewers, we drew examples from sites featuring three dimensions of promotion in its widest sense: advertisements of society's wares (commercial); repositories/dispensers of information (institutional); personal and professional disclosures of information (personal/professional). While we admit that these categories do not exhaust the rhetorical positionings found on the Web, they do relate to our work as teachers of writing and as professional women: a person developing a web page writes to represent herself to others who read the page. Likewise, an institution builds a representation of itself online, as does a commercial site. In the discussion that follows, we use several examples of web pages to articulate the issues attending women's visual representations on the Web.

COMMERCIAL

Commercial sites abound on the Web and when they picture women's bodies in their selling of wares these sites are open to the same kinds of feminist critique that advertisements in other venues attract. Representations of women in our society often occur as advertisements: women's bodies (and men's) used exploitatively to sell products. The World Wide Web also increasingly has its share of advertisements that depict women in much the same way as they appear in print. These are the images that the women themselves do not create and are posted to the Web not to announce their professional or their departments' credentials but to sell wares to online society. These are the same images which appear daily in the popular media and, more recently, in the catalogs that have taken over snail mail. For the most part, these female bodies are objectified and bartered by others: they are not under the control of the women pictured; nor do they speak those women's words.

The Victoria's Secret website offers an example we can straightforwardly connect to Bordo's reading of visual bodies.[7] Here we have an image, which begins as a "thumbnail" and when clicked upon becomes a lingerie-clad woman—the new pin-up of the home catalog industry. In this representation, the woman, who gazes directly out from the screen, seems to be inviting viewers into her parlor. (See figure 1.) But this image and other similar ones at the Victoria's Secret site are not controlled by the woman depicted, and instead are assembled by someone other than the woman herself. The crafters have a particular purpose in mind, ostensibly to sell the items featured, the images of the women as well as the clothes. In order to convince potential buyers to purchase this lingerie, the crafters seek to homogenize the woman's image as normal and attainable. The homogenized image is white, impeccably groomed, and perfectly formed. The Victoria's Secret webmaster seeks to be the master sculptor of the fantasy version of a desirable woman.[8]

Figure 1

And as Bordo has argued, "Popular culture does not apply any brakes to these fantasies of rearrangement and self-transformation. Rather, [women] are constantly told that [they] can 'choose' our own bodies" (247). The Victoria's Secret bodies do little more than foreground the current homogenized representations of "femaleness" and serve to reproduce the age-old stereotypical relations among the sexes. Obviously this is not self-representation.

But there are other commercial sites offering alternative representations of women in which the women themselves very much take control. Carla Sinclair's "Net Chick Clubhouse" serves as a fascinating example. Viewers can enter her cartoon-like, colored clubhouse to find out about her and her interests, but she also provides another front door (actually there are many) which features an advertisement of her book, *Net Chick*. Samples of email about the book, along with an excerpt from the book, accompany the necessary information for ordering a copy. (See figure 2.)

Although an instance of commerce, her home page also serves as a gateway into a playful nineties' designed environment, and she adroitly mixes the commercial purpose of peddling her book (found in the office room of her

Figure 2

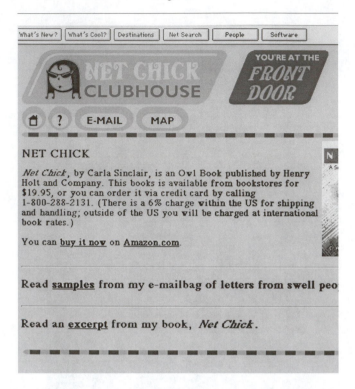

house if entered from her personal address) with biographical information, toys and games (found in the rumpus room), connections to other relevant pages and so on. Reminiscent of a child's playhouse in its upbeat attitude, the Net Chick Clubhouse is hardly the typical commercial exploitation of women's bodies that the word "commercial" schools us to expect. Instead of encountering lingerie and loud pitches to buy products (as at the Victoria's Secret site), we encounter many renditions of Carla.

And who is Carla? Is she the inventor of "Magic Eight Bra," an online game in which viewers make a wish, push the cups together, concentrate, and then open them for an answer? Or, is she the image in the sultry photo[9] that inspired Toups's choice for Babe of the Year for 1995? Or, is she the published author of a serious net book intended to educate women in the ways of the Web? The answer is "Yes" to all three questions. Her whimsical use of the bra deserves examination. Star might label it a boundary object because of the potential range of responses that visitors to her site might have to the "Magic Eight Bra" game or to Sinclair's opening statement from *Net Chick:* "Loosen your bra straps and take a deep breath—you're about to embark on a most sumptuous, estrogenic journey ever taken through online culture" (3). Because of the connections with bra-burning feminists, the bra can be seen as a symbol of rebellion. Because of its connection with constraining women's breasts, it may be seen as a token of subservience or of modesty. Because of its connection with fashion, the bra may be connected to the enhancing or reshaping of the breast—to creating allure. Because of its connection with Madonna, the bra may be seen as a provocative piece of outer wear. Regardless of the particular connection, Carla bets that her readers will respond in some way to the bra as cultural object: perhaps in Carla's mind the bra conveys some meaning to everyone she wants to reach. Ultimately, the bra is a teaser.

Carla integrates commerce into her panoply of selves—collapsing work/commerce with sexual play and children's club houses, pictures of victorian houses with the pink and blue of babies, and so on. She and others like her offer a more complex view of the commercial than does the Victoria's Secret site, though she still invites viewers to buy so that they can join in on the construction of net play. A cynical societal reading of Carla's house is that it is carefully crafted to produce sales.

INSTITUTIONAL

Unlike the commercial websites, institutional sites emphasize dispensing information, though not from an innocent or neutral position. The purposes of university websites, for example, are often related to image promotion; each university crafts information that promotes the image that it wants prospective students, future employers, and the public to associate with it. But in addition to advertising the university, these sites come to represent the institution online. Their dominant image is often a group of buildings—the institutional setting. To the general public and alums, the image of their university is historically situated in its campus architecture. Thus these websites frequently mimic and reflect dominant architectural features of the university. Here the body being visualized becomes the institution, the substance often the brick and mortar distinctive to that "body." The buildings comprise the body of the institution.

And the buildings are more than pretty pictures. They gain speech through the talk of the people, the knowledge, and the activities that inhabit them. The people contained are not always pictured or depicted visually; nor do they always control the words and pictures connected with their names. Further, because of the rapid growth of the World Wide Web, representations of people are not always placed consistently within the site. Universities are always still constructing their websites, so various departmental and program web pages are connected in such a way as to have some top-level consistency but not to convey a totally consistent design throughout. At Purdue University, for example, visitors enter through the red brick of the campus, and that red brick follows them to the department level. But inside a departmental page, categories can lead to subpages with entirely different design approaches (business writing and renaissance studies, for example, do not integrate with the overall design; nor do they share the same design philosophies).

Further, between departmental buildings at Purdue the people are presented differently. In Agricultural Economics the departmental space is dominated by pictures of faculty, while many other departments just list their
faculty's names. In some senses, this inter- and intra-departmental variation
stamps the Website as similar and familiar at the architectural level at the same
time as it is varied, and perhaps erratic, when it intersects with people and
their current agendas. Only one "human" body is at times shown in the photographic frame reserved for buildings—Purdue Pete, the University mascot that
is a hard-hatted, plaster big head (of Caucasian persuasion) worn by three
unknown, and real, male students at sporting events and civic functions.
Purdue Pete, also called Boilermaker Pete, will sometimes appear on the opening page of the site, striking a strong-jawed pose wielding his hammer. A mute
in "real life," Pete's wide-eyed and vacant stare, crafted in the 1920s, and only
mildly updated in today's version, offers us a thoroughly anonymous human
stripped of languaging capabilities beyond physical mime. The only central-
ized "human" photo that the institution presents, then, is a male student who
has been thoroughly tamed and de-languaged. Thus, in almost all senses,
human bodies are marginalized in favor of more stable architectural bodies—
both particular buildings and the omnipresent red brick—as the Website constructs the institutional image as one where buildings and, by connection,
knowledge pronouncements endure through the changing nature of the bodies that temporarily people them.

Thus it comes as no surprise that institutions tended to overshadow the
women from our previous study when we looked at their web pages. We found
that most were represented in institutional pages more often than in professional or personal pages that they themselves constructed and controlled.
Although a few reported that they had authored those institutional pages, the
authorship was limited by the wider website standards of the institution. Often
these web pages take on an image that cuts across institutions, becoming a
genre unto themselves. Consider, for example, Susan Hilligoss's departmental
home page at Clemson University (see figure 3).

The departmental home page "look" of Hilligoss bears a strong resemblance
to those in other English Departments[10] and features the pleasant smiling
image, along with links to her education and employment history, publications, and teaching activities. One of the authors' institutional web page is
almost an exact replica (e.g., smiling picture, scholarly areas of interest, contact
information), but in some ways it is even more institutionally shaped than
Hilligoss's, with the "University of Illinois at Urbana-Champaign" bannered at
the top of the page in orange and blue. Although there is some variation in the
kinds of institutional home pages featuring the women in the study, most foreground a headshot, similar to those on passports, and display scholarly qualifi-
cations—the women's credentials for engaging in university commerce. This
approach to portraying faculty conforms to an image of faculty members as
nomadic travelers moving through the institutions, the pictures changing

Figure 3

from time-to-time. In contrast, the buildings signal stable, enduring portrayals of the university's substance. This is not to say that faculty are considered unimportant. Taken together, the portraits of a department's faculty validate the institution's claims to knowledge and expertise (e.g., teaching and scholarship) in a particular field. But people are seen as marginal to the body, as pictures and credentials to be replaced at any time by other equivalent pictures and credentials. These faculty depictions are the most frequent kinds of online portrayals to be found among the women's web pages in our earlier study. They are not unlike what's done in yearbooks, company reports, brochures, all kinds of print sources before the World Wide Web—they are just what's done. In Bordo's terms they are homogeneous and normalized images. It is worth noting that such representation does not usually allow for multiple subject positions—the institutional framing of head shots is almost as singular and fixed as the oil portraits hanging in the stone and mortar faculty clubs.

Figure 4

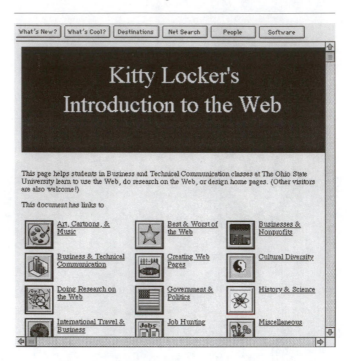

We also encountered a second kind of institutional page free of personal images and constructed by the study's participants for purposes of dispensing pedagogical resources. These pages usually aim to help students do appropriate web research, or to locate tutorial sources and tools for web page construction, or to assemble corporate web pages for employment research, or to serve as online writing labs and to point out online writing resources. Kitty Locker's web page (see figure 4) serves as an example of one such institutional resource site.

Although she doesn't picture herself, or personalize the site as a home or a parlor or even as a classroom, Locker clearly is present within the site. She titles her website "Kitty Locker's Introduction to the Web," and states that the page "helps students in Business and Technical Communication classes at The Ohio State University learn to use the Web, do research on the Web, or design home pages," with other visitors also welcome. The page displays links clustered into twenty-one tiles that educate and sometimes entertain, conveying the sense that the Web is fun and inviting as well as serious scholarly business. Disciplinary distinctions do not dictate organization so much as do writing procedures ("Resources for Writers" or "Creating Web Pages"), information about business sectors ("International Travel & Business" and "Businesses & Nonprofits"), and information of general interest ("News, Weather, & Sports"). In this page, Locker's assessment of students' needs and interests drive the development of the categories and contents. But this representation of the Web is not without a stamp of Locker herself and her view of Business and Technical Communication's pedagogical tasks and disciplinary reach—it gives viewers her take on how the Web should operate for those in her field. It also features her name prominently and places her institution's name in finer print, perhaps a move to establish her institutional presence as more than marginal, as less fleeting than the head shots of people in the departmental institutional pages. Although her page itself doesn't disrupt conventional notions of femaleness, it transcends the ready-made departmental photo album approach and conveys her teacherly persona. Although bodiless from the visual image point of view, Locker crafts a self out of her textual and graphical choices.

In the institutional pages we examined, on the other hand, women rarely had much say in how they sculpted a visual image for themselves. Buildings tended to dominate the visual landscape in these institutional sites and thus worked against women's efforts at self-representation.

PROFESSIONAL TO PERSONAL

Professional sites for women are contested as well. Constraints on visual representation online are many: first, it seems reasonable to expect that women's emerging representations would be restrained by their professional positions. Second, these representations might well be dominated by text because of the women's professional passion for text or because text is easier to craft online. Third, good feminist pedagogy might dictate that a site invite and encourage students to interact with their teacher. And, finally, feminist positions about online violence might dictate that women omit self-portraits and email addresses, so as to avoid crank email and other intrusions. Such complexity leads some to inject elements of the personal into the professional and the professional into the personal in interesting ways.

One solution for constructing web pages is to have two sites and, indeed, we found that several participants in the earlier study had written web pages that acknowledge societal expectations at the same time that they bend them a bit. Nancy Kaplan, for example, shows viewers two of her selves. She has an institutional home page devoted to professional identification—with a short academic biography and no visuals. But at the bottom of the page viewers can click on the link to Kaplan's home page and move to the professional web page she controls. Here they see an inviting set of pages which has further links to additional biographical information. (See figures 5 and 6.)

Unlike Hilligoss's web page, which was created by someone other than herself using a snapshot taken for the specific purpose of advertising a department, Kaplan's home page is homegrown, so to speak, created by her to show students her interests and to broadcast her persona to anyone on the Web who might come across her website. Yet despite its being more clearly under her control,

Figure 5

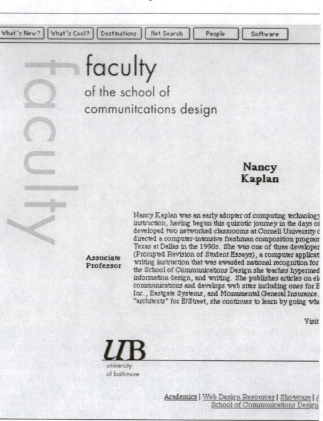

Figure 6

What's New?   What's Cool?   Destinations   Net Search   People   Software

What's Really Important

Nancy Kaplan -- born quite a few years ago and then some time later educated at the University of Mic
really important things to be everything that's absent from her official home page:

    Her children, Eva and Erica (a small bit of whose artwork can be found in the story about one
    E/Street, a WEBaltimore Community)

    Her friend, partner, lover Stuart

    And their three cats -- Athena (the portly), Lilith (the paranoid), and Vyvyan (the playful)

I won't embarrass any of us, least of all Athena, with the family portraits.

posted January 28, 1996

Figure 7

the visual representation Kaplan sets forth in her personal page is only slightly more graphic than Hilligoss's. Although she achieves considerable identity through her text, that identity is more abstract than embodied.

The range of visual representations for women, then, remains limited in this sampling of the personal components of professionals' websites. In order to appreciate more fully the possibilities for visually writing oneself online—a freedom that our students often enjoy—we need to widen our examination to the Web pages of young women students. For it is in their sites that visual representations may be less constrained by institutional culture. The personal home pages of 20-something women and students begin to forge different connections than the women from our earlier study created. When we looked at several examples of young women who are not writing teachers, many of them represented themselves as taking risks, pushing boundaries, and proclaiming themselves to be net chicks. Consider, for example, Amanda Wolf, a 24-year-old college student, studying graphic design (see figures 7 and 8):

Here there seems to be an irreverent sensibility at work—an attitude that we sometimes speak of as "in your face." Like the Victoria's Secret women,

Figure 8

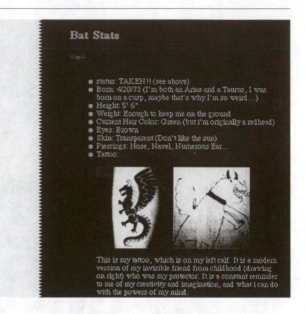

Amanda Wolf stares straight out at her viewers, alluringly—"PurEvil" is her trademark. Thus, she establishes contact using a visual form of direct address. But, unlike the Victoria's Secret women, her home page and image, she tells us, is "about me." And that "me," for those of us on the net, is batwoman, "goddess of all things Dark and Evil." Yet Amanda's page is not purely personal; the second paragraph of her description of herself explains why her program in graphic design at the University of Cincinnati is an excellent program. Clearly, if viewers are meant to see her as a person, it is as a professional person who very effectively draws viewers to her work as a graphic designer.

As one scrolls to a second screen, however, the view of Wolf expands and changes. Here there are the 'Bat Stats,' which are presented as a regimented list of facts and figures: status, birth date, height, weight, current hair, eye, and skin color, body piercings (nose, navel, numerous ear), and tattoo. Wolf then explains to viewers the origin of her tattoo—an imaginary childhood friend—which is inscribed on her left calf. She thus articulates a number of connections: current and future employers, friends and fellow students, would-be lovers, net surfers, childhood memories, mythologies. Not all of the connections operate in the same way for the same groups. Here we're thinking specifically of tattoos and body piercings. They may, in fact, be thought of as boundary objects, to use Star's terminology, that is, as "objects which are both plastic enough to adapt to local needs and constraints of the several parties employing them, yet robust enough to maintain a common identity across sites" (Star and Griesemer 393).

Figure 9

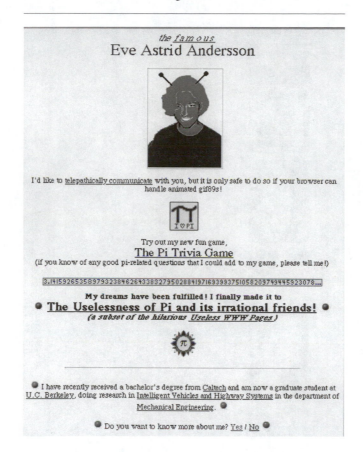

Some in encountering her web pages would share her view of tattoos and body piercings as desirable; others might view such objects with disdain. They might see her as not constructing a professional and personal identity so much as rebelling against society's norms and standards of propriety. Regardless of the interpretation, however, Amanda carves out a visual identity that attracts layers of interpretation that resist easy categorization.

Another 20-something woman, Eve Andersson, greets us with a headshot that strikes a traditional pose, smiling and affable, but with green face, red hair, and antennae, all enhanced by a constant stream of soft murmurings of the numbers that are *pi*, namely, 3.14159. (See figures 9 and 10.)

She calls herself the "famous" Eve Astrid Andersson. Although the green face and antennae signal deviations from a professional demeanor, Eve populates her space with displays of her academic credentials and work experience. The

Figure 10

Here are some recent pictures of me. Each of them links to a larger version of the picture.

viewer learns that she graduated from Cal Tech, moved to Berkeley as a graduate student in the department of Mechanical Engineering, and was formerly an
employee of Creative Internet Design, a web consulting agency in Pasadena,
California. Interwoven in her credentializing are fables, personal information,
games, creative writing, art work, photos of herself and family, and spoofs of
her lived experiences. Through it all, she visually represents herself as an athlete,
lab technician in work-out clothes, traveler, jailbird, wine taster, thinker,
20-something with-it chick—all working to challenge stereotyped images of a
20-something woman engineer. An alien, who as a baby was yellow, Eve enter-
tains viewers with stories of her growth to her adult green state. The mixture of

cartoons with colorized photos (and "real" ones) lends a childlike whimsy to the life of a young woman who also depicts herself as devoted to *pi* (pie?).

When placed alongside the professional and institutional home pages, these women stake out multiple subject positions for themselves. They doctor photos, use cartoons, animate quirky representations of themselves, and in general play with the visual in ways that blur the boundaries between physical selves and virtual selves. It's a cyborgian move in that they're using the technology to capture representations of themselves while at the same time they're using technology to add and change bodily features. In displaying their ears, calves, and tattoos, they celebrate their own writings of their bodies. In contrast, the professional women that we studied earlier are ostensibly valued for their minds and knowledge— their bodies are extraneous (at best), and potentially damaging to their success.

With these images, then, we begin to see how some women (both in and out of the field of writing) visually represent themselves on the Web and how they themselves get represented. When others control the Web images, we see women represented commercially in ways that seem familiar to us—as objects to be ogled, objects to stimulate, commodities to be bought and sold—and represented institutionally as serious, if smiling, heads that are interchangeable across schools and disciplines. But there are also examples of women writing their own visual representations in cyborg territory. These women begin to forge new social arrangements by creating a visual discourse that startles and disturbs. In claiming this cyborg territory as their own, the 20-something women on the Web—Gilbert and Kile tell us that "grrrls have attitude, girls don't"—clothe themselves in "attitude" and, as Donna Haraway aptly states, commit their cyborg selves to "partiality, irony, intimacy, and perversity (151)."

WOMEN AND WEB REPRESENTATION ISSUES

What conclusions can we draw from these visual snippets of the World Wide Web presented here? First there's the realization that current commercial portrayals of women's bodies as useful for selling products are likely to continue to function in much the same way in web space. We have come to think of the new technology as replicating and then extending the old—online publications, for example, are still strongly influenced by print. Thus it is not surprising that online commercials visually mimic, at least initially, commercials in print and on television. Certainly the Victoria Secret's pages mirror the glossy catalogs. But the possibilities of the new media also offer points of departure that challenge and subvert stereotypes. Carla Sinclair's home page is decidedly commercial but playful, ironic, complex in its portrayal of the women that Carla invites to buy her book. Here she uses old stand-bys such as the bra as an entry point into the male computer culture of games. But instead of attracting lustful gazes, she invites women to play. Thus, with Carla's computer game there is a possibility for interactivity and playfulness that was not possible in the Victoria Secret's commercial renditions. In both we see lingerie used to establish boundaries between older and emerging media, using connections already made, and making connections that have previously gone unmade and all related to women's bodies. Instead of burning the bra, this new generation of women toy with it, transforming it from a sexual display mechanism to an interactive animated computer game.

Second, the institutional control of professional women leads to visual depictions that are regimented and prescribed. In the institution's desire to sell its image to alums, parents, potential students, and legislators, it crafts faculty depictions in ways that conform to stereotypical images of the body-less professoriate. Thus, even when a group of academic women think that at times the visual might help invent new connections for online communication, institutional expectations dictate and shape their official portrayals of themselves. Some of these women, however, circumvent such expectations by creating alternate online personae that begin to complicate notions of professional representation. Others resist the institutional portrait by cloaking their multiple visual personae and displaying in text instead the wealth of their disciplinary knowledge. Still others alternatively construct themselves by wrapping themselves in teacherly or program-related activities. Many display words rather than pictures. Although today academic women can represent themselves visually on the Web—headshots are permitted—the institution shapes that visualization for its own purposes, striving to retain control of authorship, visual and otherwise.

Third, as women have more control over writing their own visualizations online, we see some women representing themselves complexly in creative, rhetorically effective ways. As students, Amanda Wolf and Eve Andersson make the visual work for them, even though we recognize that some would disagree and call them audacious. Although we do not see them disregarding their emerging professional selves (Amanda as a graphic designer, Eve as a mechanical engineer), and indeed we do see the online playfulness as displaying their online technological knowledge (important to some potential employers), these young women also manage to use visual discourse to construct multiply rich selves. Technologically and educationally privileged, these women write themselves in sophisticated ways. Multiple and competing visuals, animation, mythological drawings, and even sound all command the viewer's attention.

Perhaps the most obvious conclusion to be drawn from these examples is that the electronic world, and even the "unelectronic" world, is packed full of images that individuals view and interpret on a daily basis and which, in turn, exert a tremendous influence over them. When women become visual objects on the Web and have no say in the ways in which they are represented, the outcome is predictable—old identities like those of the "pin-up girl" or academic talking head are reproduced, and traditional narratives are re-created with new technologies.

Throughout this discussion we have been using examples taken from a number of venues to percolate our ideas about the range of online visualizations attempted by women who are writing themselves onto the Web. In addition to contrasting the various sites which have different purposes, we have also examined the connections and disconnections that cyborgian and feminist theorists foreground, if from slightly different perspectives. The play among the making, bending, extending, transforming, machining, and breaking of connections, both in societal and gendered contexts, and the danger of being constrained by inflexible connections—Star's notion of virtual detention—continues to fascinate us. We do not think we have located the necessary and sufficient features that are needed to control visual discourse online. Instead we have begun to position the visual as an inevitable component in the writing of women's online selves. In its profusion of visual images, the World-Wide Web is doing little more than imitating the material world we all inhabit. As inhabitants of this world—as women, as English professionals, and as teachers—we cannot afford to ignore the visual. We do so at our peril.

ACKNOWLEDGMENT

We thank Marilyn M. Cooper for her helpful reading of an earlier version of this chapter. As always, we are grateful for her insights and graceful nudgings.

NOTES

1. We realize that we view the visual reorganization of our online selves through the eyes of women and that these questions have implications for others as well. But women have always had complicated relationships with their representation in culture. They have also had troubled relationships with technology. For us, then, women are an appropriately fascinating case.
2. It would, of course, be possible to impersonate another by sampling other individuals' pictures from the Web and representing that person as oneself.
3. What might be a boundary object? In the Star and Griesemer study, one key boundary object is the State of California. Various groups important to the emergence of the museum can come together around California as a shared concern even when their meaning for it is quite divergent. Administrators, for example, like the fact that the museum focuses on California zoology because of their mandate as a state university to the State of California; the key scientist uses California as an ecological region of reasonable size to test his theories about the interaction of species evolution with environmental evolution; the patron wants to preserve a record of California wildlife; workers from nature groups want to study the animals of their home state; trappers know the most about the animals in their area; the institution can gain credibility more easily because of its regional (rather than national or international) focus. California becomes a connection point for divergently interested groups—a boundary object—and one that works to establish the zoological museum.
4. Later in this collection, Anne Wysocki and Johndan Johnson-Eilola offer another perspective from which to view the visual—one grounded in marxist and cultural

studies articulation theory. Focusing on the ways that linkages are repressed and enabled by society, and in hypertext environments by technology, they argue for a conception of online literacy "not as a monolithic term but as a cloud of some-times contradictory nexus points among different positions. Literacy can be seen as not a skill but a process of situating and resituating representations in social spaces" (353). The representations in social spaces interests us for this project, particularly as those representations are worked out visually. Wysocki and Johnson-Eilola view the linkages as operating through a lens of social structures (i.e., a society, as Stuart Hall puts it, where some linkages are repressed and others are enabled by ideology). Held in contrast with Haraway and Star, their framing points to a tension between the biological dimensions of information technolo-gies (in cyborgian theory) and the social dimensions of the same information technologies (in articulation theory). Both relate to building an understanding of visual representation of women in cyberspace. While articulation theory allows us to discuss the ways that societal views and pressures enable and repress certain imagings, cyborgian theory accommodates women's multiple agencies: actions of visual representation can thus be understood as actions of power.

5.   We began this review of web pages with a consideration of the women profession-als who participated in our "Women on the Networks: Searching for E-Spaces of Their Own." That study (see Hawisher and Sullivan for details on the constitution of the group and the course of the research) had been conducted in the fall of 1994 before web pages were very common, and we wanted to see what our research group had done with web pages in the ensuing years. The group itself included women of various ranks, ages, institutions, and geographical locations. All conver-sant with computer-mediated communication, the group was not a cross-section of the field of composition studies. They were, however, a wide-ranging group of women with diverse opinions. We were eager to look again at their work.

Because the women of our earlier study are exclusively professionals, we expanded the scope of our review to young, twenty-something women whom we found through various national directories of web pages. Working from the Yahoo Top Ten Sites of the Week Column that featured "Top Ten Sites about Women," we located two directories of web pages, Rob Toups's "Babes on the Web" and Leslie's "Pick of Chicks" that provided links to over four hundred web pages, most of them run by women. Despite its name, Toups's site proved to be an excellent resource because it required that women submit a photo be featured at the site. This ensured us that the visual representation was rich and self-autho-rized for wider distribution. The pages we ultimately review in this chapter, Amanda Wolf's and Eve Andersson's, were selected through random sampling of the top-rated pages.

Because we also wanted to look at commercial sites featuring women, we located Victoria's Secret. Since the Victoria's Secret example did not include a commercial use controlled by women, we also looked for websites of women authors of web texts (Laura LeMay, Carla Sinclair, Crystal Kile, and Laurel Gilbert), settling on Sinclair because she had a commercial site embedded in her home page and was also celebrated in Toups's "Babes on the Web."

6.   We've sorted our discussion rhetorically in order to distinguish among the pur-poses of the sites and the positioning of women who inhabit the sites. Hunt offers one of the few published classifications of websites that is constructed

rhetorically, and he claims that there are two types of sites—organizational sites (representing sites that exist in the real world) and special interest sites (representing sites that usually exist only in virtual worlds and are created by an individual). Because he does not sufficiently distinguish commercial and institutional cultures, Hunt's classification is inadequate to our analysis, though we do preserve his idea that some sites are group developed while others are individually developed and controlled.

7. To verify that http://www.cc.gatech.edu/people/home/jake/vs.html was indeed a site where one can legitimately order Victoria's Secret wares, we called the 800 number given at the Website. Our inquiry was greeted by a recording typical of those found at mail order sites. A woman, who incidentally spoke with a British accent, gave us various options for numbers we needed to press to gain information about processing an order.

8. This use of the perfect model's body resonates with Gunther Kress's observation that, "The body is coming to be used as a medium of representation and communication: even a brief look at a contemporary rock video will illustrate this clearly enough, and so do the industries of aerobics, jogging, roller-blading, and the televisual entertainments developed out of these." He might well add the World Wide Web. Kress goes on to argue that "These changes are not in themselves new: The body has been used in many cultures and in many periods as a medium of communication . . . . The point is . . . that after a period of some two-to-three hundred years of the dominance of writing as the means of communication and representation, there is now, yet again, a deep shift taking place in this system." (69) But, as Kress would readily admit, not all uses of representations of the body are the same.

9. While Carla's photo is the only realistic image at her site, it is not the first image you encounter. Instead, it is buried fairly deeply in the site, so that viewers must hunt for her sultry photo.

10. See, for example, the following websites which are just a few of the many we also visited: http://ernie.bgsu.edu/~kblair/index.html; http://www.english.uiuc.edu/facpages/Hawisher.htm; http://www.louisville.edu/~pdtaka01/; http://miavx1.acs.muohio.edu/~mtsccwis/jdautermann.html; http://www.pitt.edu/DOC/95/52/54269/mmarshall.html; http://www.hu.mtu.edu/~cyselfe/cindypages/; http://jan.ucc.nau.edu/~sg7/; http://rhet.agri.umn.edu:80../Rhetoric/Faculty/facbios/a-hduin.html

CHAPTER SIXTEEN

Lest We Think the Revolution is a Revolution
Images of Technology and the Nature of Change

Cynthia L. Selfe

WHEN ENGLISH STUDIES TEACHERS GET TOGETHER TO TALK ABOUT TECH-nology, we generally end up talking about change. It is common sense, after all to link computers with change when microprocessors, according to Moore's law, double in speed every eighteen months, when biomemory, superscalar architecture, and picoprocessors become feature stories for National Public Radio; and when media generations flash by in less time than it takes to uncrate a faculty workstation and get rid of the styrofoam packing.

And, at some level, English Departments have come to terms with technological change—we have adjusted diminishing supplies and equipment budgets to accommodate an ongoing program of purchases and upgrades, accepted computer studies as a new area of scholarly focus, integrated technology into various curricula, and modified many programs to include technology training and use (c.f., Selber, 1994; McDaniel, 1990; Schwartz, Selfe, Sosnoski, 1994; Wahlstrom and Selfe, 1994).

Like most Americans, however, even though educators have made these adaptations, we remain decidedly undecided about technology and change. At one level, we believe in the pairing; we believe in the computer's power, and we believe strongly in the beneficial ways that technology promises to improve our lives (Bump, 1990; Delany and Landow, 1991; Snyder, 1996). At other levels, we fear the effects of technology, and the potent changes that it introduces into familiar systems. (Apple, 1986; Kramarae, 1988; Hawisher and Selfe, 1993; Selfe and Selfe, 1994)

These contradictory impulses are the focus of this chapter, especially as they affect the work of English studies specialists and educators. In addition, these attitudes shade subtly into one another at multiple levels of a larger collective social experience, and they are worth exploring for that reason as well.

CHANGE, TECHNOLOGY, AND THE STATUS QUO: SOME BACKGROUND

Because our culture subscribes to several powerful narratives that link technological progress closely with social progress, it is easy for us—for Americans, in particular—to believe that technological change leads to productive social change.

Indeed, the narratives linking technological change to social change are part of the reason that English studies teachers—like many other educators—have come to embrace computer technology so enthusiastically over the past decade.

Quite simply put, like many Americans, we hope computers can help us make the world a better place in which to live. In the profession of English studies, for example, we hope computers can help make us, and the students with whom we work, more productive in the classroom and other instructional settings (Hafer 1996; Coogan 1995; Clark 1995; Tornow 1997; Sirc 1995) more effective as communicators (Blair 1996; Minock and Shor 1995; Sproull and Kiesler 1991), and more responsibly involved as literate citizens in world affairs (Schuler 1994; Selfe 1996; Geren 1996)

We are not alone in these stories that we tell ourselves—indeed, they are echoed for us constantly and in a variety of versions. Vice President Albert Gore (1994) has noted that the Global Information Infrastructure (GII) would increase opportunities for intercultural, communication among the peoples of the world. Howard Rheingold, in *The Virtual Community* (1993), describes how computer networks can support more citizens in their efforts to communicate with government agencies, corporations, political groups, and information resources. Nicholas Negroponte, in *Being Digital* (1995), sketches a picture of electronic landscapes that provide individuals new ways of making personal contributions to public deliberations and decision making. Dale Spender, while more careful in her perspective in *Nattering on the Nets* (1995), speculates on what it will take to establish new kinds of electronic forums that will support women and other groups now often left out of—or kept out of—public discussions in other venues.

This optimism about technology often masks in a peculiar way, however, a contrasting set of extremely potent fears. Moreover, and perhaps more importantly, an exclusive focus on the positive changes associated with technology, often serves to distract educators from recognizing how existing social forces actually work to resist change in connection with technology; how they support the status quo when technology threatens to disrupt the world in any meaningful way; how our culture, and the social formations that make up this culture, react with a special kind of conservatism to technology, even as we laud the changes it promises to bring.

This chapter will attempt to illustrate the ways in which change is modulated and complicated by forces of stasis by focusing attention on a series of images that come from commercial advertisements about technology. These advertisements reflect a portion of our collective American cultural imagination about technology. Like most images, they tell rich and powerful stories about the social contexts in which they are produced. Like snapshots—of weddings and graduations, of Christmas and family reunions, they reveal us, as Americans, to ourselves. They are laden with cultural information, shot through with the values, ideological positions, and social understandings that comprise our shared experience. Indeed, it is because we recognize the common cultural symbols in these snapshots so clearly, because we commonly construct meaning with and through them, because they are so loaded with social significance to us, that such images are powerful communication devices.

These are also the reasons that the ads included in this chapter can reveal to us the complications of our feelings toward technology and illustrate how these feelings are played out in the shared landscapes of our lived experience.

NARRATIVE #1: THE "GLOBAL VILLAGE" AND THE "ELECTRONIC COLONY"

One of the most popular narratives Americans tell ourselves about computers is that technology will help us create a global village in which the peoples of the world are all connected—communicating with one another and cooperating for the commonweal. According to this popular social narrative, the computer network that spans the globe will serve to erase meaningless geopolitical borders, eliminate racial and ethnic differences, re-establish a historical familial relationship which binds together the peoples of the world regardless of race, ethnicity, or location. As Nicholas Negroponte (1995) re-tells the story to us, "a new generation is emerging from the digital landscape free from many of the old prejudices. . . . Digital technology can be a natural force, drawing people into greater world harmony" (230) within a landscape where "we are bound to find new hope and dignity" (231).

This story, as you can imagine, is appealing at a romantic level to many Americans. It is also, incidentally, quite terrifying. Becoming just another member of the tribe, just another citizen of the global village, suggests the possibility that Americans could be asked to relinquish their current privileged status in the world where, as Negroponte (1995, 230) also reminds us, twenty percent of the population currently consumes eighty percent of the resources. Being just one among many village members also suggests the possibility of losing the economic benefits that have accrued to us as citizens in one of the most highly technological nations of the world and the possibility of functioning within a new global context in which classism and racism are unacceptable because so many members of the connected human family are poor and of color.

In fact, we find ourselves, as a culture, ill equipped to cope with the changes that the "global village" story necessitates, unable, even, to imagine, collectively, ways of relating to the world outside our previous historical and cultural experiences. As a result, in the advertisements included here, we revise the script of the narrative to fit within the historically determined contexts that are familiar and comfortable. In doing so, we also limit our cultural vision of the technological changes that are acceptable and possible for us as a culture.

The first series of images presented in this chapter reveals how our cultural imagination deals with the radical changes that the Global Village Narrative implies, by re-constituting technological change within the boundaries of these more historically and socially familiar contexts. In the global village narrative, for example, while we maintain the vision of linking peoples around the world, we imagine ourselves, not as simple members of this electronically constituted village, but rather as discoverers of the village, explorers of its remote corners, and even colonizers of its exotic peoples.

In the revised narrative, the global village retains its geographical reach, but it becomes a world in which different cultures, different peoples, exist to be discovered, explored, marveled at—in a sense, known and claimed by—those who can design and use technology. Inhabitants of this electronic global village, in turn, become foreigners, exotics, savages, objects to study and, sometimes, to control.

This revision is a familiar imaginative context for us—we have, after all, a history of experiencing the world as missionaries, as colonists, as tourists, as representatives of multinational companies. The revised story leaves no doubt about our own role—Americans are the smart ones who use technological expertise to connect the world's peoples, to supply them with technology and train them to use it. Nor does the revised story leave us in doubt about the roles of other peoples in the world—they are the recipients of technology and its benefits, those who use the technology that we control. This story is so familiar because it has happened before and in ways that Americans like to remember. We have a long and admirable history of exporting technological expertise to less fortunate neighbors—through the Lend-Lease, the Peace Corps, and the Space Program among other routes.

This re-telling or re-vising of the Global Village story—we can now call it the Electronic Colonial narrative—happens very naturally within the discursive venues available to our culture—on television, in our classrooms, in books, and articles, and in corporate settings—often without anyone noticing because the elements of revised Electronic Colonial narrative are so much more familiar and acceptable to us than were those of the original Global Village story.

The following pair of images reveals these themes (figures 1 and 2). Especially fascinating in terms of this revised narrative is the use in these two ads, by Virgin Sound and Records, of the "one tribe" motto.

In the first image (figure 1) we get a glimpse of both stories we have described. The text here narrates the Global Village story, "For the world to have a future, we must work together as one tribe" because "encroaching civilization,"

Figure 1

"disease," and "epidemics" are threatening some of the world's people with "near extinction." Virgin, the ad tells us, has donated a portion of their profits from their CD Atlas, entitled One World, to assist the Yanomami tribe in the Amazon Basin as they establish health care programs in their villages.

The second, revised story—the Electronic Colonial narrative—is revealed most clearly in the visual image represented in the ad, the picture of the Yanomami man. In accordance with the themes of the revised narrative, the Yanomami is shown in ritual dress with feathers and face paint, presented as a wondering savage, vulnerable to the crueler effects of civilization, and obviously unaware, in a critical or informed sense, of the power of the technology being used to his benefit. He is connected to Americans as "a member of the tribe," but he also remains a world away from us—the people who are creating the CD technology and donating the money to health care projects.

The second ad (figure 2), again for Virgin Sound and Records, announces two products and provides us another version of the revised Electronic Colonial story. In this story, Americans use technology to become world travelers, to learn about—and acquire knowledge of—other cultures, while

Figure 2

remaining comfortably situated within their own living rooms and, thus, comfortably separated from the other inhabitants of the global village.

On the left side of the page, the One Tribe CD is described, in which "MTV star Pip Dann takes you on a journey exploring the people and cultures of our world, from the origin of the Maori islanders to the rituals of a Tibetan monk." As the ad says, "One Tribe takes you further than you can imagine—right from your own Home." On the right side of the page, the One World Atlas offers "A stunningly rich trek around the earth," and a "wealth of maps and information all set to a culturally rich music track." The non-Americans featured in this ad are identified as exotic, albeit inviting, co-habitants of the global village. At the top left, are representations of two youngsters, spliced together to present a bizarre tribal image; on the left margin scattered among postcards from exotic destinations and lists of foreign vocabulary words, two picturesque French men sport the requisite berets and a veiled Middle Eastern woman with mysterious eyes is portrayed.

To complement the textual representation of the electronic colony narrative, the picture in the bottom left of this ad reveals the source of this world gaze—a white, blond woman sits in a well appointed living room that is chock full of artifacts from around the world; several big-screen viewing areas in front of her feature images of exotic peoples and far-off locations, a large computer with a world map on the screen, and a globe complete the representation. Virgin provides an interesting case study of the Electronic Colonial narrative. As a company, it has roots in Great Britain, but, given its marketing and advertising targets, it has acquired a decidedly American flavor, thus, joining the two countries under the potency of a single colonial gesture.

And, these are the tasteful and more subtle advertisements that are associated with the Electronic Colony narrative. The other end of the spectrum is represented in the next two images (figures 3 and 4).

Figure 3, entitled "Unexpected" shows an Indian woman, bone picks through her nose, feathers attached to her ear, beads around her neck, nursing a baby on one breast and a monkey on the other. The ad, for a color scanner, begins with a large dollar sign. The person in the image, the message suggests, is another inhabitant of the global village, but one important to Americans only as the unexpected exotic, an image that we can use to sell a piece of technology.

The next ad (figure 4), for Polyglot International software, provides yet another version of the electronic colony story. In this image, a male, of undefined indigenous origins, with gold teeth, a broad smile, and a Carmen Miranda kind of bonnet made up of roses and topped by either a radio antenna or a birthday candle. The ad's designers have superimposed a set of aviator's goggles over the man's eyes, and, across these goggles, are printed a series of 1s and 0s, denoting binary code.

In this ad, the text provides the background story for the image, "You need a team of software . . . experts who can help you culturally adapt every aspect of your software for global markets. What you need for what they want." The members of the global village, the ad implies, are indeed different from Americans, and strange, but we can, given the know-how that characterizes the American free enterprise system, identify what these people are seeking in terms of desirable software and provide it to them in a language that they can understand, even with a simplistic notion of our technology products.

These four advertisements—like the travelogue images we look at in National Geographic, like the tourist brochures we pore over in the travel agency, like the slides we view after a friends' trip abroad—are representations of exotic places and exotic peoples now available to Americans as new global markets, multiplied, as Fredric Jameson (1991) and Jean Baudrillard (1983) would say, to the point of dizzying accessibility and specificity. And it is the wondering native, the silly Indian, the veiled woman that is the object of our collective technological, cultural, and capitalist gaze. Americans, in these four ads, you'll notice, go almost un-represented in terms of images. Instead,

Figure 3   Figure 4

THE UNEXPECTED

$6,900...A LOT LESS THAN YOU'D EXPECT TO PAY FOR A DRUM IMAGESETTER
But that's the special offer price for the new **Mannesmann Scangraphic**
ColorStar, a PostScript imagesetter that uses Scangraphic's proven drum imaging
system for top quality colour work 〇 With an imaging area of 12.9 by 24 inches, and
resolutions up to 3252dpi, the ColorStar can produce full two page output with screen values
up to 300lpi. And there are no hidden extras -- the price includes a powerful Adobe
PostScript RIP, fitted with Adobe Accurate Screening Technology and an Ethernet
connection for rapid data transfer. 〇 Mannesmann Scangraphic also designs and
manufactures large format drum imagesetters and colour scanners with high speed
networking options. Scancorp can also supply and integrate Macintosh computers and
Helios OPI software and hardware to create complete PostScript-based pre-press systems.

The above price is stated in U.S. funds.
For more information on a range of pre-press solutions designed to grow with your requirements,
please contact:
ScanCorpPhotographics, 274 Alliance Road, Milton, Ontario L9T 2V2 Phone: (905) 875-0411
ScanCorp, 8609 W. Bryn Mawr, Suite 208, Chicago, Illinois 60631 Phone: (312) 693-2900

Reader Reply 110

Because the World Wants Your Software

You need a team of software
localization experts who can help
you culturally adapt every aspect
of your software for global
markets.

What you need
for what they want.

POLYGLOT INTERNATIONAL

340 Brannan Street, Fifth Floor
San Francisco, CA 94107
tel: (415) 512-8800
fax: (415) 512-8982

Americans are the canny and sophisticated minds behind the text, behind the image, behind the technology. We are the designers, the providers, the village benefactors. We are cybertourists and cybercapitalists who both understand and represent the world as a private standing reserve.

This next pair of advertisements (figures 5 and 6) from IBM entitled "Solutions for a small planet" also tells the electronic colony story, illustrating how generous Americans can be in providing other needier countries with useful technology, and providing the story a potent cumulative power. A small map portrayed in each ad helps to orient viewers to the particular area of the world that IBM and American influence have reached.

Figure 5

IN DRESDEN, FREEDOM RISES FROM THE RUBBLE. Germany's greatest church, the Frauenkirche, was bombed flat in 1945. Where Bach and Wagner once performed, there now lies only broken rock. But recently, stonemason Franz Huber and a team of other artisans and architects began to painstakingly resurrect the city's symbol of harmony. Once IBM reconstructed the Baroque landmark in 3-D cyberspace, the team could begin to rebuild the ruins. Guiding them is an IBM RS/6000™ running CATIA, a computer-aided design tool. By 2006, the church will reach to the heavens once more, thanks to 18th-century craftsmanship and a powerful 21st-century tool. What can IBM help you build? Call 1 800 IBM-3333, ext. G102, and find out.

Solutions for a small planet™   IBM

Figure 6

IN THE UNBLINKING mid-summer sun, the lager trucks of The South African breweries are as welcome as an oasis.

SAB drivers, too, rely on an OASIS to slake the thirst of their far-flung customers. They use an Onboard At Site Invoicing System each day to tailor customer delivery so precisely that no one's ever short a drop.

OASIS is just one of the ways IBM is helping the largest brewery in the southern hemisphere manage its operations.

A sleek computer network links South African Breweries' outposts across the country, allowing data to flow as freely as Lion Lager from a freshly tapped keg.

How can IBM services help your business? Call 1 800 IBM-3333, ext. G103. Or visit us on the World Wide Web at http://www.ibm.com

Solutions for a small planet™

In the first ad (figure 5), for example, with the tone of an old master, IBM provides the 3-D rendering technology needed to rebuild the Frauenkirche, a church destroyed during the allied firebombing of Dresden in 1945. The ad notes that this technology, along with the experience of talented stonemasons, allows the reconstruction to proceed, linking the power of a "21st century tool" with the imagination of "18th century craftsmanship."

In the next IBM ad, this set in South Africa, IBM helps the smiling driver of a South African Breweries truck "slake the thirst of . . . far flung customers. . . . so precisely that no one's ever short a drop."

If the previous series reduces the world to a series of tourist destinations, this pair of ads—representative of a much more extensive series of technological "solutions for a small planet"—reduces the worlds' problems to a set of embarrassingly quick fixes. American technology and technological know-how, these images imply, can provide reparations for the cultural damage caused by the firebombing of Dresden, recreate the painstaking artistic achievement of a destroyed eighteenth-century cathedral, and serve as a corrective for decades of apartheid. These implications, of course, are not only absurd; they are humiliatingly small-minded. Nothing can provide redress for the millions of human lives, the art, the history, the beauty lost in Dresden; nothing can totally ameliorate the pain and the lingering inequities of South African apartheid. As much as Americans might like to think it; technology is not the solution for all of the world's problems—and, indeed, it might well be a contributing cause to many of them.

Technology, in these ads, is an American tool. And what we use this tool for reveals all too clearly our values as *homo faber*—the tool maker. In these images, I'm afraid, we see reflected not those fundamental and much needed changes we talked about pursuing earlier; not improvements in the world situation, nor the elimination of hunger or pain or suffering or war; not, in other words, an improved life for our fellow inhabitants in the global village or an improved understanding of their cultures and concerns, but, rather, the all too familiar stories of how to multiply our own markets, how to increase our own cultural profits at the expense of others, how to take more effective advantage of need and difference whenever we identify them, and how to reduce the cultures of other people to inexcusable simplifications.

NARRATIVE #2: "LAND OF EQUAL OPPORTUNITY" AND "LAND OF DIFFERENCE"

A second favorite cultural story that we tell ourselves in connection with computers and change focuses on equity, opportunity, and access—all characteristics ascribed to the electronic landscape we have constructed on the Internet and to computer use, in general.

This landscape, Americans like to believe, is open to everybody—male and female, regardless of color, class, or connection. It is, in fact, at some level, a romantic re-creation of the American story and the American landscape themselves—a narrative of opportunity in an exciting land claimed from the wilderness, founded on the values of hard work and fair play. It is a land available to all citizens, who place a value on innovation, individualism, and competition, especially when tempered by a neighborly concern for less fortunate others that is the hallmark of our democracy. If you recognize this story, it is because it has been told so many times. It is the same story that Alexis De Toqueville (1735) told us in *Democracy in America* and one that we've been telling ourselves ever since—in *Horatio Alger* and *Huck Finn*, in *Nancy Drew* and in episodes of "Father Knows Best."

This next series of advertisements play on this narrative, emphasizing, in particular, our fascination with—and strong faith in—these traditional American values; in this case, specifically as they have the enduring power to inform and temper technological innovations. The first is an ad (figure 7) for Bob, Microsoft's friendly operating system. These images are all ripe with references to the 1950s, a time when America was entering the very beginning of an accelerated push toward technological growth and innovation. Although Sputnik, launched by the Russians on the 4th of October in 1957, weighed heavily on our collective minds, the fifties were chock full of optimism. We were still fresh from our successes in World War II, invigorated by the promise of the space program, tantalized by the bright future that the new world order seemed to hold for those who were innovative and farsighted, ready to help the world realize the promise of democracy and technology through special projects like the Peace Corp.

This cultural memory is a potent one for Americans, and these ads resonate with the values that we remember as characterizing that golden time—recalling for example, the down-home, no-nonsense comfort associated with a good dog, a good pipe, a warm fire, a comfortable pair of shoes (figure 7), and the other very American comforts accruing from a good salary and hard work in a culture where effort is rewarded with capital gain, regardless of race, color, creed, or class.

Indeed, we tell ourselves this clearly American tale—which I'll refer to as the Land of Equal Opportunity narrative—often and in many different versions. The next two images (figures 8 and 9) also play on it, for instance.

The first, for Cisco Systems, uses a picture that could have come right out of a Dick and Jane reader (figure 8). It shows another very American scene, also harkening back to the magic time of the fifties. This time, the focus is on landscape inhabited by smiling people who point to airplanes as evidence of the technological progress because these machines characterize what American know-how can accomplish in the land of equal opportunity when circumstances are right. The text notes, "With wide-eyed optimism, you thought technology was going to let you set information free. You were going to put power into the hands of the people." The ad goes on to explain that technology uninfluenced by traditional American values can run amuck, especially in a postmodern world

Figure 7

characterized by "conflicting standards," "rival companies," "incompatibilities," and inefficient work habits.

The second image (figure 9) tells a bit more of the Land of Equal Opportunity narrative. It speaks for a piece of software by C|Net called "The Ultimate Internet Tour," showing what looks like a frame from an old home movie. From a wide angle shot of a fifties suburban tract home development, we get a magnified perspective on a typical American family—three smiling kids, two smiling, upwardly-mobile parents posing in front of a spanking new, functionally designed, split-level home, with all the optimism characteristic of the Eisenhower era. The message, which urges readers to "keep up with the Joneses, the Gates and your kids," suggests that citizens of the twenty-first century can achieve the same kind of happy security and personal well being that was enjoyed by citizens of the fifties—by purchasing a software package rather than a new home.

Figure 8

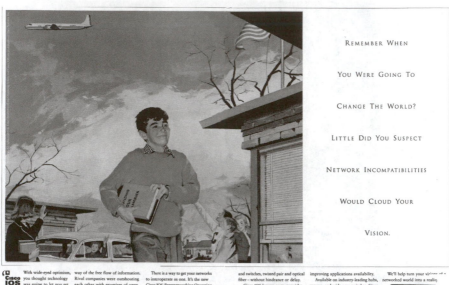

Unfortunately, if Americans have no collective imaginary context for, or historical experience of, a real global village, nor do they have any real experience with an undifferentiated land of opportunity. Our cultural experience, indeed, tells us something very different—that America is the land of opportunity only for some people. The history of slavery in this country, the history of deaf education, women's suffrage, immigration, and labor unions remind us of this fact; as do our current experiences with poverty, the differential school graduation rate for blacks and whites and Hispanics, the fact that we have never had a woman President, and the presence of border guards and the razor-wire fences over the Rio Grande. All these things remind us that opportunity is a commodity generally limited to privileged groups within this country.

Thus, the revised story in the case of these last five ads—which we can call the Land of Difference narrative—is present not in what they show, but what they fail to show. These ads are what my grandmother would call "mighty white." There is a remarkable absence in all the images of people of color, and poor people, and people who are out of work, and single-parent families, and gay couples, and foreigners. If citizens of all kinds are to have access to technology and the opportunities it provides, we do not see such a narrative imagined in the Land of Difference narrative; if technology is to improve the lives of all

Figure 9

Americans regardless of race and class and other differences, our collective ability to envision such a world is not evident in these images.

NARRATIVE #3: "THE UN-GENDERED UTOPIA" AND "THE SAME OLD GENDERED STUFF"

A third potent narrative that Americans tell ourselves about technology and change focuses on gender—specifically, this story claims that computers and that computer-supported environments will help us create a utopic world in which gender is not a predictor of success or a constraint for interaction with the world. This narrative, the Un-gendered Utopia story, encourages educators to see and understand computers as educational allies that can support efforts to create new kinds of educational and economic opportunities for students—regardless of gender. The potency of this narrative persists despite evidence to the contrary. It is clear, for instance, that fewer girls use computers in public secondary schools than do boys, especially in the upper grades, fewer women enter the advanced fields of computer science than to males, that the computer industry continues to be a space inhabited by and controlled primarily by males. Computer games are still designed for boys; computer commercials are still aimed mainly at males; computing environments are still constructed by and for males (cf., Spender 1995; Kramarae 1988; Jessup 1991). Computers, in other words, are complexly socially determined artifacts that interact with existing social formations and tendencies—including sexism, classism, and racism—to contribute to the shaping of a gendered society.

This situation, complexly overdetermined as it is within our cultural context, is nowhere more visible than in gendered images of technology use—especially, but not limited to, commercial images. In these richly textured images, the elaborately woven fabric of social formations that supports the male focused computer industry is coded ideologically at numerous visual and discursive levels for consumers and users. This fabric is so tightly woven, that for many computer users and consumers, for many students in our schools, it represents what Pierre Bourdieu (1977) would term "doxa"—ideological systems of belief so consistent with popular beliefs, and therefore so invisibly potent, that they preclude the consideration of other positions altogether. At the same time, all such fabrics have gaps, lacunae, that provide the space for resistance; and this one is no exception. Indeed, it is exactly because this ideological system is so densely and consistently coded that these images provide such rich sites of analysis and strategic information. In Andrea Dworkin's (1974) words, an analysis of these images can provide us the chance to unthink current discourses about technology and to transform the dialogues we hold with ourselves about gender and computers in new and productive, heterodoxic ways.

Like the Land of Equal Opportunity narrative, the Un-Gendered Utopia story can appeal at a romantic level to many Americans, while, at the same time, terrifying us on a practical level. Creating an electronic ungendered utopia means that we might have to learn how to understand people outside of the limited gender roles that we have constructed for them in this country, that we may have to abandon the ways in which we have traditionally differentiated between men's work and women's work in the market place, that we may have to provide men and women with equitable remuneration for comparable jobs, that we may have to learn to function within new global contexts that acknowledge women as Heads of State as well as heads of households.

In fact, we find ourselves, as a culture, ill equipped to cope with the changes that this Un-gendered Utopia narrative necessitates. We cannot, indeed, even imagine, collectively, ways of relating to gender outside the context of our familiar historical and cultural set of experiences. As a result, revise the script of the narrative to fit more snugly within the historically determined contexts that are familiar and comfortable to us. In doing so, however, we also limit our cultural vision of gender within technological landscapes—constraining roles and expectations and possibilities to those we have already constructed as a culture, limiting the potential for change by subscribing to a conventional framework for our imagination.

In this revision, for example, while we maintain the vision of an electronic landscape that is open to all innovative and hardworking people, regardless of their gender, we also limit the actual participation of women and men within this landscape to the more traditionally determined gender roles we have already constructed within our culture. In the revised narrative—the Same Old Gendered Stuff narrative—the new electronic landscape retains a value on innovation, hard work, and the individual contributions of people of both genders, but only as they are practiced appropriately—within the traditionally gendered contexts we have historically and culturally ratified for women and men in our culture.

In such a landscape, women use technology within a clearly constrained set of appropriate settings: to enrich the lives of their family and to meet their responsibilities at home—as wife, as mother, as seductress, as lover; within a business setting, women use computers to support the work of their bosses— as secretaries, executive assistants, and loyal employees. There are, of course, exceptions to this story, as we shall see, but this narrative, as Anthony Giddens (1984, p. 22) would say, is "deeply sedimented" in habit, historically deter- mined practices, in tradition, in our imaginations, and, thus, it exerts a strong influence on even these alternative stories. Men, in contrast, use computers at home to expand their personal horizons beyond current limits—for excite- ment, for challenge, to enhance their own private lives as explorers, pioneers, and builders. Within the business world, men use computers to support their historically constructed roles as bosses, leaders, decision makers.

This re-telling or re-vising of the Un-Gendered Utopia story happens very naturally. A good portion of our collective imagination is constructed by his- tory and sedimented in past experience and habit. Indeed, many of the images appearing in the next series have a distinctive "retro" look that harkens back to the fifties—for many of the same reasons as those ads telling the Land of Equal Opportunity narrative discussed earlier in this chapter.

In that optimistic time, women were no longer encouraged to maintain a presence in the workplace. At the close of WWII, they were displaced from the workplace by men returning home from the European and Pacific theaters (May, 1988). Women, faced with this eventuality, became the savvy managers of the private sphere—especially when they were assisted by technological innovations. These women, were urged to serve their families frozen foods and TV dinners, and to acquaint themselves with the scientific principles of eating so that they could be effective nutritional advisors to the family; they were expected as well to heed the advice of Dr. Spock, take advantage of the Salk vaccine for polio, and keep abreast of advances in antibiotics and modern theories of behaviorism to become effective health advisors; and they were expected to use the newly developed and improved technologies of electric vacuum cleaners, dishwashers, washing machines, televisions, cleaning products, and station wagons to be increasingly effective housekeepers.

The fact that this previous era of technological optimism provides the context for Americans' collective imagination about the current cultural project of technological expansion is both interesting and important. The results are evident in numerous advertisements about computers and women that use a retro look to link women's roles in the 50s to those in the 90s—in which each gender assumes their appropriate role in connection with technology. Men use technology to accomplish things; women benefit from technology to enhance the ease of their lives or to benefit their families.

And to understand how these traditionally gendered roles of the fifties are projected directly on the technological context of the nineties, readers can focus on the living room in figure 10, where images from the television-era of the fifties are overlaid by those of the computer-era of the nineties. Despite this fact, however, despite the fact that families in the nineties must maintain a dual presence in the work force, despite the fact that the rising incidence of divorce at the end of this century makes single-parent families the norm rather than the exception, despite the fact that the optimism of the fifties and sixties as articulated by John Kennedy has given way to the paranoia of the nineties as expressed by Pat Buchanan—the images of gender, the narratives they tell in connection with technology remain relatively stable, disturbing intact except for the imposition of a computer keyboard—held and operated by the father—and a computer menu—admired and enjoyed by the woman and children.

And so the revised narrative—the Same Old Gendered Stuff narrative—remains current. Its resonance is also demonstrated in figure 11 (see page 310), an advertisement for Reveal, and in figure 12 (see page 311), where we meet a thoroughly modern woman, Celeste Craig of Pontiac Illinois. Celeste, we learn, is finally achieving her dream of "going to college by staying home." The invention of a sophisticated distance-education computer network has allowed Celeste to undertake a course of study from her home in Pontiac Illinois while, at the same time, continuing to fulfill her role as a single mother supporting a family, parenting her children, and maintaining a household.

The gender roles of the fifties also translate into workplace roles for women in the nineties. In figure 13 (page 311), for example, Irma—like a good, upscale, personal business assistant in the nineties—speaks "fluent Internet" much like her fifties counterpart would have spoken French. In figure 14 (page 312), Fran, a fifties secretary with "just another pretty face" has been transmogrified, into a "multi-talented" nineties cyborg/robot assistant that "makes your website look good." And finally in figure 15 (page 313), which suggests

Figure 10

only a slightly revised version of the Same Old Gendered Stuff narrative, a nineties woman-as-boss, also portrayed in sepia tones against a fifties-style restaurant banquette, remains as decidedly cool, relaxed, and elegant despite the fact that she has also required the title of "hotshot," "collector," "work-horse," and "nomad."

But the roles of parent, housewife, and secretary/boss are not the only ones open to women in the new cyberlandscape represented by the Same Old Gendered Stuff narrative. Figure 16 (page 314), for example, shows an ad for Nokia monitors, and in doing so, portrays a woman in the traditional role of "beauty." In the advertisement, a sophisticated woman draped with jewels, decked out in a chic black dress, washed in sepia tones and softened by a grainy texture gazes into a computer monitor. Although the text accompany-ing this image ostensibly outlines the capabilities and design of the monitor,

Figure 11

Figure 12

Figure 13

Figure 14

Figure 15

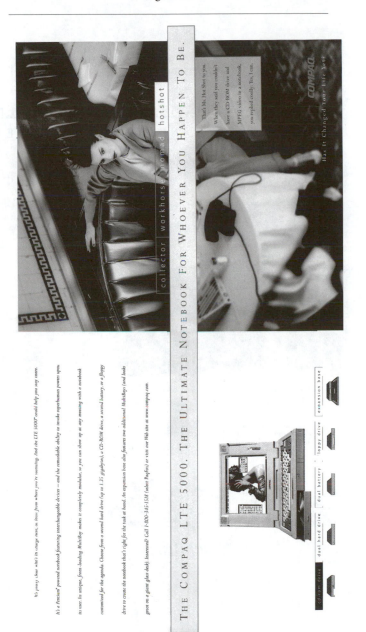

Figure 16

EUROPEAN ART COMES TO THE SCREEN, WITHOUT THOSE ANNOYING SUBTITLES.

technical perfection is embodied in the variety and sensitivity of Nokia's controls and components. And the continental lust for life and good health is evident in the extraordinary MPR II-compliant emissions controls Nokia invented.

Add to this the sheer elegance of the tooling, and even the availability of designer colors. A Nokia monitor is more than electronics. It's art. But, it's an avant garde that's quite easy to appreciate. Especially when it makes those little subtitles so much easier to read

Nokia is the leading brand of monitors in Europe, and an engineering standard for the world.

from the continent that gave us museums and luxury automobiles comes their combined spiritual equivalent: Nokia monitors. Nokia is already a household name (and café and office name too) throughout Europe. And now Nokia monitors are quickly winning the hearts and eyes of Americans too.

The European passion for beauty is expressed in the magnificent clarity of the screens and the soothing refresh rates.* The Nordic obsession with

Please call 1.800.BY NOKIA for more information.

NOKIA
MONITORS

Figure 17

the language itself leaves no doubt of picture's focus or intent. As it notes, the "European passion for beauty" is quickly "winning the hearts and eyes of Americans too" by seductive means. The woman pictured in this advertisement, it should be noted, gazes longingly into a monitor, but lacks a keyboard with which she could act on the computer.

Finally, the 1990s retro series offers Americans the role of seductress—also a traditionally defined role for women, and one that has retained enormous strength even in cyberspace where change is expected to affect so many areas of our lives. Figure 17, representing a narcissistic seductress for Samsung, illustrates the potency of these traditionally constrained roles.

In these ads, we see reflected the roles that our culture can imagine women playing in relation to technology. And they are familiar roles—the seductress, the beauty, the mother—all relationships ratified by our historical experience, easily accessible to our collective imagination, and informed by traditional

Figure 18

social values. These roles exist, and are reproduced, within a set of over determined social formations that makes radical change hard to imagine and even
harder to enact—especially when technology is involved.

The revision of the Un-Gendered Utopia narrative into the Same Old
Gendered Stuff narrative deals no less traditionally with men's roles, it should
be noted. In connection with workplace technologies, men are allowed essentially the same tie-and-oxford-cloth look in the nineties (figure 18) as they
were in the fifties (figure 19), although slight variations of this role—the
impatient-and-rebellious young entrepreneur on the go sans tie (figure 20,
page 318) or the successful architect-net-cruiser (figure 21, page 319) sporting a turtle neck—are also permitted. Out of the workplace (figures 22-24,
pages 319-321), men are shown to adopt the equally traditional and retrograde roles of bikers, nerds, and sex maniacs.

These ads, of course, are only one expression of our collective experience—
and I would not want to claim that they tell a totalizing story. They do indicate,
however, that it will be exceedingly difficult for Americans to imagine an electronic landscape in which individuals enjoy new kinds of opportunities to
relate to each other and new kinds of opportunities to make positive changes
in their lives. It takes energy and careful thinking to create a landscape in

Figure 19

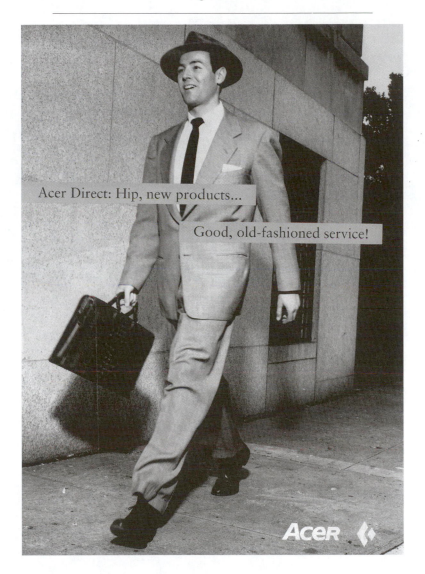

Figure 20

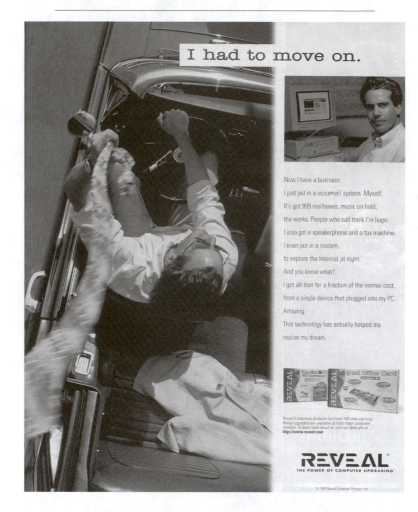

Figure 21

Figure 22

Figure 23

Figure 24

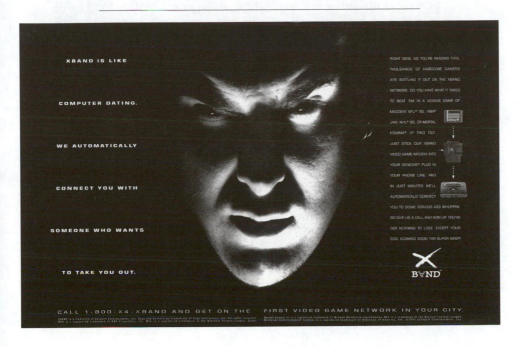

which women can participate in roles other than those of seductress, beauty, or mother; and in which men don't have to be bikers or abusers or rabid techno geeks or violent sex maniacs. It is far easier and more comfortable simply to re-construct for ourselves those traditional narratives that tell the same old gender stories over and over again, and that re-create the status quo ever more clearly in their re-telling.

CONFRONTING REVISED NARRATIVES

The images in this chapter illustrate the richly textured narrative fabrics within which computer technology and other communication technologies are situated in the American cultural scene. Our work as teachers, the curricula we fashion, the corporate and public environments our students enter as professionals, the schools that make up the educational systems—these social formations are also shaped by the same sets of culturally determined values, the same complexities, the same ambiguities, the same contexts for our imaginations.

Such a realization can serve to remind teachers that technology does not necessarily bring with it social progress, and that educators had better make sure that students recognize and understand this fact if we want them to be able to make contributions of which they can be proud. Within the English studies programs that we design and administer, and participate in, we place everyone in jeopardy if we limit our understanding of technology and change to one dimension, if we teach students only one part of this complicated picture.

A good English studies curriculum will educate students robustly and intellectually rather than narrowly or vocationally. It will recognize the importance of educating students to be critically informed technology scholars rather than simply expert technology users. Graduates of English studies programs will face an increasingly complex set of issues in the workplace and in the public sphere, and our failure to provide the intellectual tools necessary to understand and cope with these issues at multiple levels signals our own inability to lead productively as professionals and as citizens.

Finally the images can serve to remind educators that even though productive changes are hard to make—with or without technology—our responsibility to work for change, especially as educators, remains undiminished in its urgency and importance. Like Paulo Friere, we need to be optimistic enough to believe that in teaching ourselves and others to recognize the inequities that challenge humanity in our world—the ethnocentrism, racism, classism, sexism—we have begun the difficult work of addressing these problems.

NOTE

The images used in this chapter are included for the purpose of scholarly review, study, and critique, as permitted by the Fair Use Exemption of the U.S. Copyright Act. As a courtesy, the author notified all copyright owners about the use of these images; some have offered pro forma grants of permission; some have not replied; others are no longer in business and have returned the author's letter.

CHAPTER SEVENTEEN

Into the Next Room

Carolyn Guyer
with photographs by Dianne Hagaman

Recently, I realized that my husband and I take a lot of snapshots of our backyard. The last time we had a roll of film developed, more than half of it was devoted to different views of what is admittedly an old fashioned, overgrown, and idiosyncratic space more or less defined by a hundred year old house at the far end, a tumbledown toolshed at the other, and tucked midway at an L-bend in the property, the original outhouse. Of course the truly defining element is the Hudson river doing its tidal thing less than a block away, but within the confines of our little yard, much else happens. Fictions and memoirs, dinners and mosquitoes, tender shoots and the logic of blooms. It is not surprising, even predictable I suppose, that the current trendy popularity of gardening has produced the term "outdoor room" to describe any little troweled up space with something vertical plopped in it. A trellis, a statue, a chair. We do indeed know rooms in this way, as settings where things happen. We furnish our yards and gardens and all our rooms with an impulse to narrative. For a room, as embodiment of time and space, is the fret of human story. We need rooms in order to understand things, to make story. A room is a frame, a focus, it is the specificity of context—that which coheres and is not something else. As such, a room can stand for any context, a garden, a book, a photograph.

While sifting through this last batch of backyard snapshots, I noticed that none of the prints had people in them. There was nothing of me arduously digging the rocky, nearly impenetrable clay soil along the fence, mixing it with sand and gypsum and fertilizer, and then carefully planting the seeds of an array of sunflower varieties. Nothing of patiently watering during a long dry stretch. None of the anxious decisions about staking the eight foot stalks. Only tender views of the sunflowers nodding over the fence, ruddy old toolshed behind them mid-distance to the shimmered river with sailboat sweetly sauntering by just in time to prove the perfection of everything.

Everything in an empty backyard. I knew the story already, the one in the photographs. And so did the people I could hear from my open study window who sometimes stopped in front of the heavy, genial blooms to admire them. I could tell these people knew the story of the digging and watering because occasionally they spoke of wanting to confiscate a flower to plant the seeds in

Figure 1
World Mission Room, Gethsemane Lutheran Church.

their own yards. Yet even had I not indulged in such delicious eavesdropping, I would be certain that people passing by our backyard could read the fictions there. Of course, I realize that not every empty room is as engaging as this languorous old yard. There are rooms inside certain kinds of sad buildings, rooms offering only the harsh severity of reflective surfaces and hard lines, of too-bright lights, sharp corners and edges, empty rooms that broadcast notices of insistent, willful affairs. But these, too, help me to understand how the furnishings in our lives suggest events, and how boundaries operate. The phrase "empty room" is an odd one, an oxymoron of sorts. To say a room is empty might mean it is unfurnished and has no objects in it, though it usually means a room that has no people in it. Yet there can't really be such a thing as a room without people in it. A room may be completely bare of objects and humans and still it would have people in it. No matter what state of emptiness, a room has always been put together by someone and is a collection of features to be interpreted, the primary one being boundary. A room is an enclosure. Even without rigid walls of wood or plaster, a room by definition has definition.

In a gesture as quirky as the book itself, Roland Barthes places as the frontispiece of *Camera Lucida* a Daniel Boudinet polaroid that seems to offer the very essence of a room: chiaroscuro blue-green space furnished with objects and a wall of loose-woven, light-pierced curtain. The photograph shows a bare snippet of space and boundary, but it is very nearly the definition of a room, of context or story itself. I see an enclosed space with features of various possible functions, a space that indicates its own limits, its boundary, which is permeable and makes clear (*chiaro* or *claire*) that there is something other than itself.

Several good questions about this photo, plaintively put by Elsa Dorfman in her review of *Camera Lucida* are: "Why did Barthes . . . choose that untitled image as the frontispiece of his book? Was it playfulness? Was it to suggest that no theory is the whole story? Was it to accentuate the effectiveness of portraits? Was it to provide a counterpoint to his insights?" Let's just say yes, all of the above. It is perhaps a good bit of credit to give to Barthes (and why not? didn't he let crankiness run over into grace by refusing to provide the central image of the book, the Winter Garden Photograph, but then place another, so similar—a little girl holding her own finger and boy with arm outstretched, and only the most oblique hint of what he intended? (104-105), but Dorfman's litany does clearly point to how many questions can be located even in the implication of an empty room. Questions which are drawn in the space like the light in the weave of the curtain-wall. That is where the most important thing happens to human beings, I believe. For all its flaws and testiness, *Camera Lucida* offers the great gift of emotional insight, profound grief trying to accommodate itself, plus the second gift of an articulation of the process of perception. To be sure, Barthes intended his *studium* and *punctum* to articulate a process of perceiving photographs, and specifically *not* paintings, or rooms, or gardens. But for me, the idea of the *studium* (passing interest in an image that does not "take" me) and the *punctum* (that which "pierces" or takes my consciousness making the image unforgettable) translate readily enough to the ways humans perceive any narrative context, which is to say any context. Those light-filled questions passing through seem to me the very image of *punctum* and the creative moment.

To speak of a room being story is to immediately invite questions about human interpretive means, image and word. At first it might seem that limning the elements of a room would rely almost solely on the visual aspects there. Light streaming through tall windows into a kitchen, softening the edges of a wooden table, patching the floor in glowing panes. And then (*and then*) the telling ourselves or others becomes apparent. The reality seems to be that in a room (or a garden, or a book) our image and language perceptions will always find a changing, tensional mix. Time and narrative. Space and image. Story. This is what we cannot escape or evade because it is what we mean by time and space. So many of these questions surrounding image and word want to be about primacy and dominance. Which is more important? Which—image or word—is the most central to human thinking, learning, and creating? I understand all too well why we ask this question. As if primacy is always given to the primordial. As if primacy did not always dissemble. My profound wish is that we might recognize the real intention of the question.

Images are never unmediated. Just as with language, a brain must be involved. For instance, though we know that a photograph of an empty room is not the same as the room itself, we can also understand that looking at the photograph and looking at the room are similar actions, if not the same results. To stand in a room that is dominated by a galactic mural, taking in the bare tables and folding chairs, is to form something of a narrative about what happens there. As Barthes' *studium* or *punctum* (which one for you?) has us

Figure 2
San Francisco Kitchen

noticing the details of overturned, mismatched cups clustered in the center of each table, and reading a sign in the hall that indicates the missionary nature of this place, we could as well, by this same process, be looking at a descriptive photograph. The way in which a photograph of a room is different from the room itself is already an instance of why an individual perceiving a room is different from any other individual perceiving the same room. We each make our story, and rooms or photographs are always occasions of it.

The truth I instinctively sense in what I am trying to draw here has me wary of being distracted by discussions of refinements among layers of mediation and variations of representation. Neither do I wish to examine differences as such between image and language in human processes. Many have done this admirably before me, if to no generally agreed resolution. But I do not mean to imply that the difference between the two should be blurred or erased. The contrast between them is essential. W.J.T. Mitchell, in *Iconology*, puts the importance of difference between word and image at the heart of his own study.

The point, then, is not to heal the split between words and images, but to see what interests and powers it serves. This view can only be had, of course, from a standpoint which begins with skepticism about the adequacy of any particular theory of the relation of words and images, but which also preserves an intuitive conviction that there is some difference that is fundamental (44 [1]).

And so, as with Mitchell, it seems to me a more suitable occupation to attempt to understand the differences between image and language as both fundamental and permeable. That is, using these very elements to describe themselves (what choice do I have?), I imagine boundaries of difference as the

Figure 3
Dining Room, Bread of LifeMission

locus or situation of paradox, being at once both noun: wall, divide, fence, and verb: pass, shift, transfer.

This isn't just another way of looking at an old problem. In exploring boundary-crossing more than the boundaries themselves, it is clear I am choosing a philosophical and political direction. While it may seem that the wrangling over differences between image and word is reserved to an intellectual sphere, it is easy enough to recognize how the values we place on those differences flow into social organization. The most dreadfully inappropriate stereotypes emerge according to value perspectives: poets are a rarefied, inaccessible, and elitist lot, and painters are a lunkish, inarticulate breed when they do not have a brush in hand. And then there are the far more urgent biases that withhold justice, reversing guilt and innocence, and the ones that take homelands from whole societies, hatreds that justify torture, religions that diminish the soul. Oh, there are real reasons to brave the label of "being P.C." in order to consider what diversity means, and how it actually operates. Always, when differences of any kind are not perceived in their paradoxical nature as both necessary and permeable, values concerning them become judgments about people, infecting culture with the prevailing principle of dominance. That is, when society uses difference among individuals and groups as the measure of worth on a scale of power, it heads down a path of oppression and, ironically, towards the loss of the very individuality that we certainly in the U.S. constantly hear invoked as the requisite of existence.

I believe individuals *are* requisite to existence. I can hardly say enough that there must be genuine differences among people, and among cultures, in order for them ever to get along. It may be that the most useful and beneficial way of

Figure 4
Memorial service for Mary Witt, Lutheran Compass Center

really knowing what the differences are is to pass through them. Not take them down, imagine they don't exist, but to experience them, which is to say, to be committed to change even as I commit change. "How do we cross borders?," asks Hélène Cixous. "The person who doesn't tremble while crossing a border doesn't know there is a border and doesn't cast doubt on [her] own definition." Elsewhere I have tried to describe the creative moment as a buzz-daze mix of change, and so I also understand Barthes' *punctum* as the moment of meaning, of passage, passing through the curtain, or the door. It is the inevitable impossible of making something from nothing or everything. I mean: the past (what we already know), mixed with the future (what we know only as desire), that particular flux of doing and accepting, is architecture and plot. It is the meaning we create. Barthes himself says, "It is what I add . . . and what is nonetheless already there" (55). One can see the verb in this, and that it is almost like what Deena Metzger avers, that "A story is not what happens to us. It is what we do" (93). But "adding to" and "doing" do not alone make story, and are not enough to form *punctum* or creative moment. "What is already there" and "what happens" is also necessary. These, after all, are the other rooms, the ones I haven't been to yet.

In that same review of *Camera Lucida*, Elsa Dorfman, notes that for Barthes, "The Winter Garden image becomes a magic relic, as though it is part of his mother." Even more, I think. A magic relic, yes, and as that powerful, significant object, the Winter Garden photograph held for Barthes an actual biography. When we gaze at a photograph, whether in *studium* or *punctum*, we are making story from a story, just as we do when occupying a room, or reading a novel, or staring into someone's backyard. A photograph is not only a story in

Figure 5
Meeting Room, Highland Park Church of the Nazarene

At higher resolution, the blackboard says, "Kevin loves Brenda + it = true love"

itself—made by a photographer taking a certain perspective, organizing the elements in this way rather than another—but, as an object, as furnishing, a photograph is often a chapter or subplot or even the main theme in another story, say a book, or a room. When the photograph of a loved one who has died is centered at the memorial service. Or when the image of a sacred face is turned as if about to explain a particular message of love. Carolyn Heilbrun knowingly explains the telescoping manner of tales:

> What matters is that lives do not serve as models; only stories do that. And it is a hard thing to make up stories to live by. We can only retell and live by the stories we have read or heard. . . They may be read, or chanted, or experienced electronically, or come to us like the murmurings of our mothers. . . . Whatever their form or medium, these stories have formed us all; they are what we must use to make new fictions, new narratives. (37)

When, in the 1970s, Margaret Mead named and discussed the prefigurative society, she tried to avoid alarmist rhetoric and put a hopeful spin on her vision of a radical cultural shift. She saw that changes, induced largely by a range of technologies, were becoming so rapid that parents and teachers would no longer be able to use their own life experience and knowledge to prepare children for a future that cannot be anticipated. Mead recognized that this is not only a new situation in human history, but one that is "disconcerting, if not downright frightening," and she recommended at every turn in *Culture and Commitment* that we choose "and" solutions rather than simplistic and short-term "linear" ones. She balanced warning with hope, power with responsibility, unknown future with worthy past. She urged us to cross a cultural boundary so ingrained that it often goes unrecognized as such. Mead told us that we should take our guidance as parents and educators from children themselves, for they would be the ones most freshly experienced with the breaking edges of the future while also being least constrained by a personal history. She was describing what many educators now term cooperative or collaborative learning, though few are yet willing to permit equal status between student and teacher, and instead demote the process to something that happens only among the students themselves (who are all of equally low status, so no problem). The generosity and wisdom of the last stanza of Margaret Mead's poem to her young daughter in 1947 is still a rare thing in familial power hierarchies, to say nothing of educational ones:

> So you can go without regret
> Away from this familiar land,
> Leaving your kiss upon my hair
> And all the future in your hands.

How many of us can be heard to lament the short attention span that is coming more and more to characterize young people (and for that matter the populace at large)? There is blame enough to be passed around to the appropriate technologies, with television and computers at the top of the list. But it may be that this perceived failure to meet an admittedly unmeasurable intellectual standard could be taken as a clue to the radical cultural shift Mead predicted. Michael Joyce has suggested that "in an age like ours which privileges polyvocality, multiplicity, and constellated knowledge a sustained attention span may be less useful than successive attendings." (1) In an age like ours. . . . when channel zapping and web surfing are common enough activities that the cumulative effect of moving through odd gatherings of context should be well recognized. In an age like ours. . . when what has always before remained an invisible process becomes a prominent characteristic. In the particular pace and rhythm of each era, humans have continuously made context from the unlikeliest components. "A day in the life" of any of us is not usually themed so consistently as a coffee-table picture book. Shards of conversation heard in a doorway, a new sign going up in a store window, a friend's interrupted tale of woe, a cup falling to the floor, these accumulated make a day. We have always passed through the frame of many contexts, channel zapping if you will, toward threaded meanings, toward a worldview. Slipping into the next room is the only life journey any of us ever takes.

ANNE'S WORK ROOM

You see a large sun-lit room looking out over a rambling English garden. The windows are open and the smell of honeysuckle wafts in on the warm spring air. There are three large wooden desks. Two are covered with half-finished bits of code, books, papers, jottings of stories and poems, pictures. One is kept clear and here, neatly stacked, is the current work-in-progress. This desk has a green leather top and several deep wooden drawers. It magically keeps track of anything written on it.

> Obvious exits: out => Hi Pitched Voices
> You see scribbles here.
> Anne is here.

In a MOO room the view is created through words, it is all textual. And yet the sense of being in an actual enclosed space is so much like walking into a sitting room, say, of sun-painted chairs, that the story of doing it is just as profound or trivial. The memory of conversations there, of objects used, is of real experience, not something absent and false. When Anne Johnstone wrote the above description of one of her rooms in the Hypertext Hotel[1] she was creating a fiction and a reality to share with others in the collaborative, multivalent work done there by women in the HiPitched Voices collective. But before she was able to share this room, Anne was suddenly and without warning taken by cancer. Those of us who had worked with her in a swoop of exhilarating discovery and ambitious vision in the HiPitched Voices wing of the Hotel, were left after her death with our shock and sorrow, and then also with the task of gathering her personal work from her private rooms on the MOO. The discussion on our group's email list of what to do after finding the above room revealed the dual nature of so-called virtual life. Should we remove Anne's partially completed work out of respect for her, or was there a greater respect in leaving it intact and standing as long as the environment itself? The last line of the room description, "Anne is here," means that there was a character in the room named Anne, which stayed there waiting for Anne herself to return and inhabit it. We understood that technical fact of course, but the sense of the sentence itself—"Anne is here"—the impact it had of being literally true, had us catching our collective breath. The best memorial to Anne Johnstone's hypertextual work in the Hotel was, we knew, to leave it be. For us, Anne is indeed there.

It feels so obvious and "natural" that Pavel Curtis would choose the metaphor of rooms to create LambdaMOO (the prototype of MOOs located at the famed Xerox PARC), that it almost seems it couldn't have been done another way. In 1993, electronic performance artist and writer Judy Malloy was invited to work in LambdaMOO as an artist-in-residence at PARC. Malloy huddled with Curtis about possible projects for narrative, her particular interest. When he suggested that she should think of the space itself as literature, and that objects in MOO space could disclose text, Malloy conceived *Brown*

Figure 6
Sun Chairs

House Kitchen, a virtual narrative space in which visitors can discover the story by examining and engaging the objects there. Among the *Kitchen's* devices are an electronic book, a diary, a video device called Barbie-Q, a Ralph Will Clean Up After You robot, and a food-dispensing table called GoodFood. *Brown House Kitchen* was expressly designed to suit the likely interest of the inhabitants of LambdaMOO at that time. As such, it operates similarly to the old adventure computer games, with a literary hue washed in. There is no denying it makes for an odd mixture. For instance, if a visitor engages the Ralph robot, these words might come up on the screen:

> Ralph turns his head, and speaks these words softly: "I brought enough beer for everybody," Jack said. How different his face looks when he smiles. "Are you going back to work?" George asked. "Shit yes," Jack said and grinned. "Jack can do what he wants," Becky said. I was surprised that she said that.

Ralph always turns his head and speaks his words softly, but will say different things on different days. Whether time-based like Ralph, or random, or sequential like some of the others, all the devices in the Brown House Kitchen are more or less fitted together to gradually disclose a consistent narrative. When Malloy first created this work, she imagined individuals visiting the Kitchen and exploring it to discover the story. But, as she herself discovered during a class visit by a group of Carnegie Mellon students, what makes the *Brown House Kitchen* most interesting is the collaborative or group aspect. Because the narrative structure is in a MOO, any number of people can meet there and work together to create a story. This is the discovery of how we can be in more than one place at a time, and in a sense, it is the instantiation of how culture forms. Malloy writes that on the morning of the students' visit to *Brown House Kitchen,* "It was 9:00 a.m. their time and 6:00 a.m. our time. They were in a computer room with enough terminals for each of them. I was in bed with a laptop and a cup of coffee." She goes on to describe some of the activity that morning. "Tim came on . . . and began smearing butter all over the table 'to check its textual qualities.'" There was simultaneous discussion about the feel of different interiors of different MOOs. Some students activated Barbie's TV. Others tried to eat the cat. Following breakfast (that days' menu was French toast with strawberries and English breakfast tea), Malloy took the students to the garden just off the Kitchen to discuss public art, the role of the audience, and other subjects. "Some of the students climbed the lemon tree. Others activated the fugal text disclosing structures that I am writing in the garden." Back in the computer room at Carnegie Mellon the students were very vocal, and other people in the computer room gathered around the terminals to see what was going on. A loosely woven curtain, its fibers backlit, moved slightly with a passing breath.

At the dawning of World Wide Web awareness, those of us who had been occupied with (and occupying) MOO environments, pushing their functions more and more in order to learn about collaboration, performance, and creativity, unexpectedly found ourselves in a vacuum. The rush to the Web left our ears ringing and our questions unanswered, while the ensuing clamor and adolescent flapping of web growth rose to the place where things stick in the craw. But it can't be denied that the Web allows something which might be useful in a MOO. It has images. There is no reason to believe that we must rely on an environment where either word or image dominates. MOOs are insufficient as text only. And the Web is insufficient as an image-based advertising medium. Enter new—if still minimal—possibilities of traversal like Web-MOO clients, software which can be invoked to display web images within a MOO.[2] In a place where people from anywhere in the world can meet and use words and images to create story, to recognize and cross boundaries of every sort, we might begin to imagine and tell ourselves anew. We might, for instance, find ourselves gathered at *Springside,* a young MOO at Vassar College, chatting, gesticulating, and flying about the old lobby. The students who have created *Springside* have chosen to use this new technology to inhabit an antique version of their school.

The Vestibule

This room is the original entrance to Main Building. The thirteen feet high ceilings are supported by thick columns, giving the space a feeling of vastness. To the west are the stairs leading down to the main road to the College. Eastward is the primary corridor and the central double stairway, beyond which lies the great Dining Hall. . . . On the west wall, there is a small ladybug. The large door leading out of the building to the carriage is closed.

These are the same sort of young people who, according to Mead's perceptive reflections in the 70s, should in some ways be our examples. But while this is certainly a new model of learning, it does not mean that the young can learn nothing from those who have gone before. Indeed, given that they, like every-one, continue to exist in time and space, the stories and meaning the students make must form in a familiar way, even in the MOO. Interactions, conversa-tions with each other, through whatever means, are the most immediate and frequent boundaries we cross. Even the partitions of our own personalities are of this order. I have sometimes called these individual and interior traversals intracultural to remind that we are each a complex of contradictory notions, beliefs, and acculturations similar to the differences among larger cultures. By the time I am ready to read this essay in the final perusal before sending it off to the editors, I will be a different person than the one who began writing it. I am its first reader, and in reading this text, I adjust the story according to changes caused in me by the writing of it, which is to say, caused in me by con-versations with Barthes, Mead, Cixous. . .

Some argue that an entirely new kind of consciousness is being induced by electronic technology. Gregory Ulmer, for instance, uses the term "electracy" to indicate a kind of practice or acumen in electronic media equivalent to print literacy. "In the history of human culture there are but three apparatuses: oral-ity, literacy, and now electracy. We live in the moment of the emergence of electracy, comparable to the two principal moments of literacy." For myself, while I feel less able to describe the parameters of human consciousness in the future, I do believe with Ulmer, Mead, and many others, that something not only needs to happen here, but something is happening here. The cumulative form that we make out of so-called postmodern events, ranging from frag-mented print layouts and narratives to web surfing, may represent in a core sense a resurgence of human creativity. But this is a matter of emphasis, since a resurgence must come from what has existed before. If a new mind is arriving then, it is one in which perspective is everything. All we can do is keep moving, because when there is no such thing as a point in time and space, there are only infinite points of view. Under this condition, I must make my own view.

Turn here. See that the other side of my own view is any view. Turn again. All views are possible only if I have my own view. As I wander about beneath the vaulted ceilings of the entrance to Springside MOO waiting for the oth-ers to join me, I might take a moment to prop open the door to a website I know, one which I think they would like to see. My best friend's dining room actually, something he calls his "home's page." When you get here, come on in. Just step through this light-filled membrane, and slide into the next room.

NOTES

1.   Hypertext Hotel was originally a hypertext writing project used by students of Robert Coover at Brown University. It was later converted to a MOO devoted to hypertext writing by Tom Meyer who designed a filter to translate Storyspace

hypertext documents into the rooms of a MOO environment. At this writing, the Hotel has been down for radical remodeling for some time, but can be reached in partial form at: http://www.cs.brown.edu:7000/

2.   The Surf and Turf Web-MOO client is a Java-based client which allows the attachment of viewable web pages to any MOO object. One may then view these objects privately or display them to everyone else in the room. The purpose of this client, according to its designers, is "to make collaborative web viewing as simple as possible. " By the time this book is printed, Surf and Turf will either have been superseded by some newer development of the idea, or fallen unnoticed by the wayside.

PHOTOGRAPH NOTES

Dianne Hagaman's website is http://weber.u.washington.edu/~hbecker/dianne.html

Figure 1. "World Mission Room, Gethsemane Lutheran Church." from Hagaman 1996. Erecting a cross. . . was a metaphor for conquering something. . . . Evangelism connected the missions to the churches. It was the reason church people were in the missions and street people had to sit through the services to eat. Evangelism embodied a theory about the causes of the kinds of lives street people led; it assigned blame for their situation and defined what and who needed to be fixed and how. (71)

Figure 2. "San Francisco Kitchen." from Hagaman (forthcoming).

Figure 3. "Dining Room, Bread of Life Mission." from Hagaman 1996.
This is a photograph of the dining room at the Bread of Life Mission. The door next to the mural opens to a passageway that connects the chapel with the dining room and kitchen. The kitchen is through the door on the far right. After the service, people lined up at the front of the chapel, walked through the passageway to one door, and then entered the kitchen through the other. In the kitchen, each person filled a plate with food and passed though another door (not in the photograph, but beyond the right edge of the frame) into the dining room. The mural was dominant in my mind, but I composed the photograph to lessen its emphasis, not putting it in the extreme foreground, but rather attempting to embed it in its surroundings. (52-53)

Figure 4. "Memorial service for Mary Witt, Lutheran Compass Center." from Hagaman 1996.
One morning I stopped at the Lutheran Compass Center to say hello. I hadn't been there for almost a month. Dianne Quast, the chaplain, told me that Mary Witt, a well-liked counselor who worked with the women residents, had been killed in an accident a few days earlier. Mary was on her way to Montana to visit relatives when the accident happened. I went to a memorial service in the chapel that afternoon. Some of her family had driven to Seattle from Montana to be there.

Dianne had put a large photograph of Mary and votive candles on a table covered with a white cloth and a red Lutheran banner. During the ceremony for Mary, she asked people to come forward, light a candle, and say something about Mary: She was a good daughter. She was a good friend. She had a wonderful sense of humor. She was committed to her work. She will be missed. The altar was a makeshift, personalized, public shrine that marked off a sacred space in which a ceremony could be improvised. When I photographed it, I included a tapestry of *The Last Supper* pinned to one wall of the room: another table, another ceremonial cloth, another last and final offering. Diane had pushed the chairs back to clear floor space and create a second altar—the table with the candles and the photograph of Mary—ignoring the traditional altar on its raised platform, enclosed by a rail. (90-91)

Figure 5. "Meeting room, Highland Park Church of the Nazarene." from Hagaman 1996. A downstairs meeting room where refreshments were served after the Sunday service.

Figure 6. "Sun Chairs." from Hagaman, forthcoming.

CHAPTER EIGHTEEN

Virtual Diffusion
Ethics, Techné and Feminism at the End of the Cold Millenium

Cynthia Haynes

Its mixed genres and its interdigitating verbal and visual organs ask for a generous literacy from the reader. In its most basic sense, this book is my exercise regime and self-help manual for how not to be literal minded, while engaging promiscuously in serious moral and political inquiry about feminism, antiracism, democracy, knowledge, and justice in certain important domains of contemporary science and technology.

Donna Haraway

WHEN I READ AND FIND (UNEXPECTEDLY, YET HOPEFULLY) A KIND OF self-conscious confessional plea from an author to her reader (like Haraway's above), I instinctively feel at ease—as if in searching for the *logos* (or argument) in a text, somehow finding ethos makes it more palatable when *logos* asserts its proverbial cycle of claims, grounds, and warrants. When several texts are grouped (as in this section on ethics and feminist concerns), we wonder what means of linking them together we might use in order to co-respond.[1] We tend, I think, to rationalize (to make rational by means of linking) texts according to whatever *techné* (or art) is in fashion. Since Aristotle, the trend has been the argument, its *logos*. But I want to set another trend, to take another direction, to turn.

Consider this. It is now possible to visualize research by using algorithms to analyze millions of academic papers, and to create from this analysis a three-dimensional graphical landscape where mountain ranges "signifying hot research issues in biology may connect to an area in physics by a narrow ridge" (Steinberg 46). In other words, we could plot the logical links among loosely connected texts (even among arguments over time), plot them on a graph and analyze the raw data. We would then have a mathematical trajectory of points plotted, a rather crude inhuman representation of a sequence of conceptual displacements. But, what sort of index/map would we have? Of what? And why would we want it?

According to Chuck Meyers, project manager at Sandia Laboratories where this technique was developed, what we find in such a map are "connections that were previously hidden" (qtd in Steinberg 46). This accounts for why I am drawn to certain ideas and expressions in the essays contained in this section, and also for why I am drawn to the 'hidden.' Thus, it is a with/drawn tactic with which I conduct my efforts to co-respond, or to establish what I prefer to call a 'responsive relation.' My turn (trend) reveals itself in the form of holotropes of ethos and holograms of techné, immaterial images in what might be (re)en-visioned as hidden inflections of ethos, *techné* (though one not in the service of *logos*), and the feminine.

Yes, there are dangers in technology, in educational technologies, in education. And others in this collection have argued skillfully about these dangers and offer significant critiques of technomanic and technophobic pedagogy and rhetoric. Let me confess to having argued in this manner myself, though my confession is no concession to *logos*. It is the system we all inhabit. But I cannot resist mixing things up by sampling, plundering, pirating, hijacking, splicing, bootlegging, cribbing and blending—stirring in the unexpected with the expected. In short, I plan to pilfer (and deconstruct) narratives that we might not imagine as pliable. I aim to ply the trade routes of the past millenium for the morphological future now hailing us into a responsive relation to technology, and to each other.

HOLOGRAMS OF TECHNÉ

We know that in this cold (modern) millenium *techné* has been both a poison and a remedy (*pharmakon*).[2] And like writing (the *pharmakon* of Plato's millenium), technology is both threat and ally. The more extreme fears of technology seem to operate from a logocentric interpretive framework. That is, our relation to technology has been determined by our objectification of the world and our use of technology to subject the world to our will. Martin Heidegger captures the nature of the problem in his essay, "What Are Poets For?" He writes: What threatens man in his very nature is the willed view that man, by the peaceful release, transformation, storage, and channeling of the energies of physical nature, could render the human condition, man's being, tolerable for everybody and happy in all respects (116). What Heidegger reveals, in all its horror, is that man's self-assertion over against the objective world is a function of ethics gone awry, of value-systems (moralities) that man super-imposes by "reason" (*logos*) of his fundamental belief in his ability to control nature. In this essay, written as a lecture in 1946 (the date is not insignificant), Heidegger laments the link between objectification and values:[3]

The fact that we today, in all seriousness, discern in the results and the viewpoint of atomic physics possibilities of demonstrating human freedom and of establishing a new value theory is a sign of the predominance of technological ideas whose development has long since been removed beyond the realm of the individual's personal views and opinions. (112)

On recent visits to Los Alamos (NM) and Pearl Harbor, I had occasion to think "in all seriousness" about the realities of moving "beyond the real of the individual's views and opinions." Sitting next to Japanese tourists (wearing translation headsets) as we watched film footage of the attack on Pearl Harbor was a surreal experience. I had to ask myself how they would feel standing next to me as we stared at larger-than-life photos of the victims of Hiroshima in the museum in Los Alamos. The paradoxical effect of a will to domination of nature with technology (and abuses of it for violent ends) and a fear of technology (with attendant scapegoating, exclusion, and surveillance in order to defuse the fear) has inured educators to the suffusion (overpouring) or refusal (pouring back) of techné. To conceive a "responsive relation" to technology compels us into diffusion (pouring out over a wide area, to scatter, disperse).

Thus, I want to pour out (and sail among) an archipelago of *ethoi* from the essays of this section, but it is difficult when *logos* guards the gate. James Porter reminds us (via John Barlow) that the old paradigm "Guardian Class" served a Cold War mentality as justification of individual rights under the auspices of protecting U.S. citizens from terrorism. This squares with Arthur Kroker's analysis of French accounts of technology in a bimodern age. In Kroker's view, bimodernity means "living at the violent edge of primitivism and simulation" (18).What Kroker discovers is a response to the question of what to do "when technology is no longer an object that we can hold outside of ourselves but now, in the form of a dynamic will to technique which enucleates *techné* and *logos* in a common horizon, is itself the dominant form of western being— possessed individualism" (14). If the dangerous alliance is formed by *techné* and *logos*, an ethical alliance might be formed by techné, ethos, and the feminine. As I have stated elsewhere, "if *techné* and *logos* have formed the violent edge of primitivism, simulation and possessed individualism, then feminist teaching is where *techné* and ethos converge to form the ethical horizon of authenticity, negotiated space, and dis/possessed individualism" ("Inside," @dig par. 20).

HOLOTROPES OF ETHOS

From a panoptic view of the ethos of community (Porter) to synoptic views of the ethos of individuals (Guyer), the authors in this section mark the pedagogical scene with transgressions of the techno-logical. It is, in a manner of speaking, a section linked by transgressive moves and bimodern edges. A question we should ask is to what end this method of linking is put, a question similarly posed by Susan Romano: "The question becomes, then, not what are the technical means by which we can problematize student identities, but rather, to what ends do we do so." To what ends, with what ends, do we link? Lyotard says that "to link is necessary, but a particular linkage is not" (80). Some say this is an irresponsible political position. Without invoking the logic of responsibility, I suggest rather that we evoke "responsive relations" among teachers, students, and the technologies that serve as thresholds across which we may "turn," thresholds that bind us together as well as set us apart.

What are the possibilities for plying a theoretical, practical, and pedagogical alliance among techné, ethics, and feminism? Carolyn Guyer sets one such example:

> The truth I instinctively sense in what I am trying to draw here has me wary of being distracted by discussions of refinements among layers of mediation and variations of representation. . . . In exploring boundary-crossing more than the boundaries themselves, it is clear I am choosing a philosophical and political direction. . . . Always, when differences of any kind are not perceived in their paradoxical nature *as both necessary and permeable,* values concerning them become judgments about people, infecting culture with the prevailing principle of dominance. (my emphasis)

Guyer chooses to announce her wariness of conventional argumentation, and she resists the pressure to glorify politics, a tactic I find commendable, and one I employ via Haraway and Guyer in my expression of solidarity with them. "Permeable" and "promiscuous" are interesting (and evocative) terms with which to ply feminism, justice, science and technology together. This is what I mean by finding hidden connections.

Martin Luther King, Jr. may not have known how his "dream" presaged Cynthia Selfe and Olav Hauge, but where linking is not dependent upon *logos*, we can tack into the wind instead of allowing it to determine our route. Hauge, a Norwegian poet, wrote a poem called "It's the Dream" and captures the essence of linking by way of plying old trade routes:

> It's the dream we carry in secret
> that something miraculous will happen
> that must happen—
> that time will open
> that the heart will open
> that doors will open
> that the rockface will open
> that springs will gush—
> that the dream will open
> that one morning we will glide into
> some harbor we didn't know was there.

This is how it felt to read Selfe's essay. In her skillful analysis of commercial images about technology, Selfe (in a nod to her own history) grants us a powerful view of ethos in her observation that such ads often "fail to show" people of color. She writes: "These ads are what my grandmother would call 'mighty white.'" It does not seem incongruent to me to imagine Selfe as a child keenly logging her grandmother's truisms and teaching as a "nomadic feminist cyborg guerilla" (Handa), invoking her grandmother's wisdom in the classroom. My responsive relation to Selfe's invocation is quickened with kinship.

You see, it is not difficult to trace the paradox of electronic pedagogy, to see how it permeates and is permeable. It is how Guyer describes "boundaries of difference as the locus or situation of paradox, being at once both noun: wall, divide, fence, and verb: pass, shift, transfer." It is a turn, a turning away from splitting hairs using either and or, words (for example) that often lace a feminist panegyric on agentic subjectivity (either we have agency or we don't). Could the "subject" be both permeable and permeating in social relations?[4]

Porter relies on Foucault for one answer. Reminding us that there will always be relations of power in the social network, Foucault advocates a less utopian set of options with which to deconstruct those relations. He writes: "The problem is not of trying to dissolve them in the utopia of a perfectly transparent communication, but to give one's self the rules of law, the techniques of management, and also the ethics, the ethos, the practice of self, which would allow these games of power to be played with a minimum of domination" (Foucault 18).

Susan Romano picks up the theme by experimenting with what she terms "pedagogies of the self." As researcher of online teaching practices and student discourse, Romano's ethos emerges often, though nowhere so "responsively" as in this remark: "As lurker historian, I read primarily from a teacher's perspective, with interest in outcomes but without responsibility for them, and I read at a more leisurely pace." Like Haraway, Romano reveals her reading protocols, which serve as an ethico-imperative to her reader. Not "read me in this way" (a logical imperative), but "it is necessary to read with me in this way," a mode of reading designed to include her reader rather than to assume for her reader what protocols of reading she must adopt. As I read her, Romano exhibits a responsive relation to her students and her readers. She invites me (and you) to read over her shoulder, a familiar place for situating us as lurkers. In an interesting twist, lurking is historically perceived as a male practice. To find a woman pirating a practice of men in order to situate herself within the commerce of feminist composition research is not nothing. The hermeneutics of lurking, like the permeable and promiscuous, confounds established protocols of argument and research and thereby plies an old trade route where we are used to staking our interpretive claims.

Following the trade winds, Gail Hawisher and Patricia Sullivan also point to issues of ethos when they recount the claims of many computers and composition researchers as mostly grounded in an "egalitarian ethos," the classroom as community, the teacher as facilitator, the computer as equalizing. "As women" and "as feminists," Hawisher and Sullivan might seem to offer their ethos in a straightforward manner, but it is more oblique than we might assume (another hidden connection). And, it comes immediately through the voice of Tina, "Hi everyone." With Tina's self-conscious questions, asked without guile and posed blushingly, we hear Hawisher and Sullivan's ethos mediated by Tina's words. When they claim that "self-image is problematic for her and more problematic as it becomes more visual," they articulate an interesting turn of events. In the effort to name a problem for feminist compositionists researching how computers and Internet technologies complicate what has heretofore been assumed (i.e., its ability to evoke an "egalitarian ethos"), Hawisher and Sullivan suggest an ethos grounded in something else—they mark their ethos squarely in the tension between text and image, specifically in the "vexed relationship between online writing and images." Inside this relation, the vexation of the being between text and image, they respond to Tina. Thus, theirs is another instance of the responsive relation.

VIRTUAL DIFFUSION

I pause here to recapitulate how and why I have been writing against the grain of a conventional response essay. First, I am thinking against the grain of logical linking mechanisms. Second, I am working against the grain of mainstream feminist practices. Third, I am surfing the rhetorical trajectories of what will have been an off-the-chart virtual diffusion. No index for me. No solid grounds, just "groundless solidarity" (Elam 69). In short, my aim is to in/fuse my *ethos* among the pieces in this section (like injected dye into living organs, a fluid dispersal) as a means with which to view those brilliantly lighted points of radiation (or the archipelago)—not the commonplaces (*topoi*) of their electro(exo)skeletal arguments, so much as the uncommon *ethoi*, or the "common circulatory system" we all share (Haraway 22).

One warning, however—when traveling inside the fluids of our bodily metaphor, it is necessary at all times to "practice safe rhetoric." Elsewhere I have explained that to be rhetorical, to practice safe rhetoric, means to look at something from a number of perspectives, to analyze our culture in terms of how discourse shapes culture, shapes material and social conditions, and shapes attitudes. To be rhetorical is not to participate in scapegoating. It is not about placing blame, it is about understanding, to literally stand under something in order to speak about it, or against it, or with it (not to be confused with literal-mindedness, which can work against understanding). It means to question without being cynical, to look for answers without creating new problems, it means to include rather than exclude, to act rather than react. We cannot afford to engage in cynicism and exclusionary rhetorics that threaten to infect the progressive work of sociotechnologists like Donna Haraway, rhetorical ethicists like James Porter, and cyberfeminists like Diane Davis, Susan Romano, Gail Hawisher, Pat Sullivan, Cynthia Selfe, and Carolyn Guyer, all of whom examine identity politics in the light of actual practices and educational goals. Safe rhetoric, to be blunt, is about protecting oneself from infectious and communicable toxic discourse.

This does not mean that we can avoid the rhetoric of negative cyber-hype, but it does mean we can help determine the discourse protocols by engaging in productive discussion about computer-assisted instruction and the Internet in terms of their psychosocial impact on individual and collective lives. And especially with respect to the use of Internet technology in education, we should do so rhetorically, going slowly, doing our homework (so to speak) before we make claims about the "value" of the Internet and about its effects. The fact that children, women, and other marginalized and vulnerable groups are the potential victims of Internet stalking (and worse) raises crucial questions about how educators can protect the freedom to use this powerful medium at the same time they try to protect those who use it against potential abuses.[5]

To do our homework, however, means we must ply another old trade route called "freedom." Porter navigates these murky waters in his discussion of free-speech and violent speech on the Internet. In his view, the liberal-individualist perspective (that he claims is at work in the field of rhetoric and composition) "does not address the material conditions of the networked writing situation or the fundamental inequalities and differences that exist there." In his critique of this perspective, Porter suggests that a "communitarian, reciprocity-based ethic," such as that advocated by Connelly, Gilbert, and Lyman's "Bill of Rights for Electronic Citizens," offers "an ethic based on a gift-exchange system of property."

Interestingly, there may be a hidden connection here to the "hacker ethic" common among young (usually white) male computer programmers. Jan Rune Holmevik explains how the hacker ethic evolved:

> To hack in computing terms means to take an existing computer program and modify it to suit one's own needs and preferences. At the time when computers were far less powerful than they are today, writing programs that would make the most out of the limited computer resources at hand were very important. For the early hackers at MIT, the purpose of hacking was to make existing programs smaller and more efficient. The motive for doing this was often to impress one's friends or peers, and hence, listings of computer code were circulated freely for others to read, learn from, and be impressed by. When Roy Trubshaw and Richard Bartle of Essex University in the United Kingdom wrote the first MUD in 1979, they made all the source code available for others to use and improve on. . . . In 1989, a graduate student at Carnegie Mellon University, James Aspnes, wrote a MUD he called TinyMUD. It was a typical hack, written in one weekend. In contrast to other MUDs which could only be modified by wizards with special programming privileges, the TinyMUD was user-extensible which meant that anyone could add to it. The design of the MUD architecture was no longer a privilege for the wizards only. In the TinyMUD, anyone with an account on the system could build new locations and objects and describe them as s/he wished. (Haynes et al., 1997)

We might be tempted to discount the hacker ethic as an alternative to the liberal-individualist view of technology in education, but it may be more productive to guard the question of this ethic, to use it without excusing (Spivak,

"Feminism") its obvious ties to a masculinist domination of access to the actual and symbolic "code" with which the computer languages and cultures of the Internet have been written and in which they are implicated. The fact remains, the hacker ethic is a *gift-exchange system of writing*. We ought to ponder the implications of this for collaborative learning theories in rhetoric and composition, especially how the development of collaborative technologies on the Internet (i.e., educational MOOs, Linux operating system, and HTML)[6] could be used as models for new ethical electronic pedagogies in the field of computers and writing.

CONFUSION

The problem of institutional ideologies that *confuse* (pour together) the "solitary writer" and collaborative learning, as Porter points out, has to do with giving up their "principle orientation" toward the individual student. Taken one step further, when technology adds to the "confusion," when we pour together (often in disjunctive ways) new modes of intelligibility (and new codes), it effectively "outs" the faculty in ways that they may find unnerving. In Romano's study she concludes that "[t]eachers allotting class time to electronic conferences [i.e., online class discussions] and committed to sponsoring equitable discursive environments find themselves awkwardly positioned with regard to their own assignments." Not only this, but teachers become more accessible because of Internet technology, and the degree to which they prepare for teaching is revealed in ways we are only just now understanding.

To put it another way, educational technologies that utilize Internet-based programs are disturbing the *logos* of the "academy" and sending shockwaves throughout academia. The Internet challenges institutional systems by radically changing the way we teach and argue, and with whom. Not only is the Internet capable of jamming the credentialing machinery (such as online dissertation defenses),[7] it is beginning to split open the nature of grading,[8] as well as assessment at the level of tenure and promotion.[9]

As for the trade route of feminism, we have great distances before us and contrary winds. We could do with some confusion (pouring together) and a little deconstruction. I would, however, inject a more favorable view of deconstruction than Teresa de Lauretis, who merely flips the question of sexual difference over. She argues that "do [ing] away with sexual difference altogether . . . closes the door in the face of the emergent social subject, ... [and] if the deconstruction of gender inevitably effects its (re)construction, the question is, in which terms and in whose interest is the de-re-construction being effected?" (De Lauretis 25; qtd in Romano). Placing Spivak in dialogue with De Lauretis, I would stress that in the space of difference from which reversals operate to gain political independence, "there is always a space in the new nation that cannot share in the energy of this reversal" (*Outside* 78).[10] Spivak reminds us that we must accustom ourselves to starting from a particular situation and then to the ground shifting under our feet. As I mentioned earlier, Diane Elam's phrase for this kind of reading with and against the grain of feminism is "groundless solidarity" (69).

Although problems and solutions are conventionally the marks of argumentative discourse, especially about global issues, I prefer to consider where we have been together, and where we will have been—to look back and to drift on in the wake of our traversals (and our groundlessness). We have turned by way of hidden connections. We have lurked promiscuously. We have linked by way of diffusion. We have engendered the "responsive relation" by way of practicing safe rhetoric. Hopefully (and as I began, unexpectedly), we have plied old trade routes and tendered a new techno-commerce with which to exchange our tokens, our *ethos*, and our gifts of teaching and writing. And perhaps, we have sailed into some harbor we didn't know was there. It's the dream we carry in secret.

NOTES

1. I am what you might call a token feminist. That is to say, I use tokens of feminism and *ethos* as gift vouchers. I prefer to write as part of a running exchange. Cixous helps me explain why: "If you give a text that can be appropriated, you are acceptable. When the text runs far ahead of the reader and ahead of the author, or when the text simply runs, and requires the reader to run, and when the reader wishes to remain sitting, then the text is less well received" (7).

2. Jacques Derrida deconstructs this Greek term and cites Plato's *Protagoras* in which Socrates "classes the *pharmaka* among the things that can be both good (*agatha*) and painful (*aniara*)" (*Dissemination* 99).

3. This problem is one that I take up extensively in my dissertation, "In the Name of Writing: Rhetoric and the Politics of Ethos" (University of Texas at Arlington, 1994), though it is more focused on unhinging the link between *logos* and morality as it traces the politics of *ethos* in rhetorical traditions.

4. See my short essay on "the self/subject" in *Keywords in Composition* for a view of how these terms are contested within the rhetoric and composition field.

5. These passages appear in altered form in the section on ethics of our introduction to my chapter in *High Wired*, "From the Faraway Nearby" (p. 6–7).

6. This research is in progress in the dissertation by Jan Rune Holmevik (University of Bergen, Norway), "Constructing Cybermedia: Collaborative Technological Development on the Internet."

7. In July of 1995, the first ever online dissertation defense was held at Lingua MOO. The candidate, Dene Grigar, has co-authored (1998, with John Barber) an essay on her experience, "Defending Your Life in MOOspace: Report from the Electronic Edge." The transcript of the online portion of the defense can be found at http://wwwpub.utdallas.edu/~cynthiah/lingua_archive/phd-defense.txt.

8. One of the most outspoken voices on the topic of grading, especially in electronic environments, is Eric Crump. He has uploaded several threads on listservs

that deal with the issue of grading. One may be located at: http://dewey.lc.missouri.edu/rhetnet/gradegame/#end.

9.   Mick Doherty, Becky Rickly, Traci Gardner, Eric Crump, Victor Vitanza, and other participants in C-Fest (an online series of meetings I established in 1996 at Lingua MOO) have gathered various sources in which efforts to construct collaborative position statements about the use of technology in teaching and research are made available online. See the Lingua MOO Archive and Resource page for logs of C-Fest meetings on the topic, http://lingua.utdallas.edu/archive.html (esp. meetings from spring 1997 meetings), and Eric Crump's site on professional recognition, http://www.missouri.edu/~sevenc/recognition.html. Mick Doherty has also gathered links to key sites at http://www.rpi.edu/~doherm/recognition. For the joint CCCC/NCTE effort online, see Becky Rickly and Traci Gardner's site, http://kairos.daedalus.com/promo/promo.html. In addition, in the first issue of *Pre/Text: Electra(Lite)*, co-edited by Victor Vitanza and me, a critical polylogue on the T&P issue can be found at: http://www.utdallas.edu/pretext/PT1.1A/PT1.1A.html.

10.   Deconstruction involves a "double gesture," not a single reversal. Once the reversal occurs, it is necessary to implode the binary altogether—to *refuse* (pour back) its axiology. As Derrida explains the "double science" of deconstruction, "to do justice to this necessity is to recognize that in a classical philosophical opposition we are not dealing with the peaceful coexistence of a vis-a-vis, but rather with a violent hierarchy. . . . The necessity of this phase is structural . . .the hierarchy of dual oppositions always reestablishes itself. . . . That being said—and on the other hand—to remain in this phase is still to operate on the terrain of and from within the deconstructed system. By means of this double. . . writing, we must also mark the interval between inversion, which brings what was high, and the irruptive emergence of a new "concept," a concept that can no longer be, and never could be, included in the previous regime" (*Positions* 41-42).

PART FOUR

Searching for Notions of Our Postmodern Literate Selves in an Electronic World

CHAPTER NINETEEN

Blinded by the Letter
Why Are We Using Literacy as a Metaphor for Everything Else?

Anne Wysocki
Johndan Johnson-Eilola

*T*OO EASILY DOES "LITERACY" SLIP OFF OUR TONGUES, WE THINK, AND GET PUT next to other terms: visual literacy, computer literacy, video literacy, media literacy, multimedia literacy, television literacy, technological literacy.

Too much is hidden by "literacy," we think, too much packed into those letters—too much that we are wrong to bring with us, implicitly or no.

So:

Our first question in this essay: *what are we likely to carry with us when we ask that our relationship with all technologies should be like that we have with the technology of printed words?*

Our second question: *what other possibilities might we use for expressing our relationships with and within technologies?*

FIRST

There are two bundles we carry with us when we ask that our relationship with all technologies should be like that we

"Examining titles in the ERIC database for 1980–94, inclusive, indicates that educators felt moved to discuss almost two hundred different kinds of literacy during those fifteen years; that is, two hundred different kinds of modified literacy as opposed to plain, unmodified literacy." This is from Dianne G. Kanawati's article, "How Can I Be Literate: Counting the Ways," where the author found, among the 197 total references in the ERIC database, Cash-culture Literacy, Christian Literacy, Discipline Literacy, Risk Literacy, Somatic Literacy, Water Literacy, Competitive Literacy, and Post-Literacy.

have with printed words. There is, first, a bundle of stories we have accumulated about what literacy is and does; second, there is our regard for the object
to which we relate within literacy.

1
THE BUNDLE OF STORIES

a

> "Of course you can learn how to read. Do you want to try?"
>
> —Ransom Stoddard (James Stewart) to Hallie (Vera
> Miles), his future wife, in *The Man Who Shot Liberty
> Valance*

At almost the ending of *The Man Who Shot Liberty Valance*, Ransom
Stoddard and his wife Hallie are returning by train to Washington
D.C. for what he says will be his last term as senator. He has recently
finished recounting how he, a lawyer opposed to guns, helped bring
law—and order—and statehood—and 'book learning'—to the open
territory around Shinbone (an unidentified territory in the U.S.
West).

Hallie looks out the train window and says to Ransom, "It was once a
wilderness. Now it's a garden."

In an earlier scene in a makeshift schoolroom (with "Education is the
basis of law and order" written on the blackboard at the front), Ransom
asks Pompey, a man of middle years and a student in the class, to talk
about "the basic law of the land." Pompey, who works for Tom Donovan
(John Wayne), starts to talk, with hesitant pauses in his sentences but
with pride, about the Constitution; Jimmy Stewart corrects him:
Pompey means the Declaration of Independence. Pompey starts again:
"We hold these truths to be, uh, self-evident, that…"

He stops. Ransom finishes for him, "…all men are created equal." "I knew
that, Mr. Ranse," says Pompey, "but I just plumb forgot it."

The room is disrupted by Tom entering to tell of how the cattlemen—
who are fighting statehood because it will close off the free range—will
bring violence down upon the townspeople and farmers who want a
state. But, of course, eventually, Jimmy Stewart's gentle and learned ways
help tame the area into statehood.

b

February 13, 1996

President Clinton announced today his intent to nominate
Mary D. Green to the National Institute for Literacy Board…

The National Institute for Literacy was created to assist in upgrading the workforce, reducing welfare dependency, raising the standard of literacy and creating safer communities.

(http://www.ed.gov./PressRelease/02-1996/whpr24.html)

c

People who read, according to our reading of McLuhan, do nothing; they are helpless as the words they read pass through their eyes to shape them:

....print causes nationalism and not tribalism; and print causes price systems and markets such as cannot exist without print. (50)

.... the assumption of homogeneous repeatability derived from the printed page, when extended to all the other concerns of life, led gradually to all those forms of production and social organization from which the Western world derives many satisfactions and nearly all of its characteristic traits. (144)

....the mere accustomation to repetitive, lineal patterns of the printed page strongly disposed people to transfer such approaches to all kinds of problems. (151)

And quantification means the translation of non-visual relations and realities into visual terms, a procedure inherent in the phonetic alphabet. (161)

Or, as Walter J. Ong puts it in *Orality and Literacy*, literacy fulfils our destiny:

... without writing, human consciousness cannot achieve its fuller potentials, cannot produce other beautiful and powerful creations.... Literacy.... is absolutely necessary for the development not only of science but also of history, philosophy, explicative understanding of literature and of any art, and indeed for the explanation of language (including oral speech) itself. (15)

XXX

It is thus a large but not unruly bundle that comes with "literacy": John Wayne, Jimmy Stewart, the taming of the U.S. west, democracy, an upgraded workforce, less welfare dependency, our forms of production and social organization, science, and philosophy. The various descriptions and quotations above (a small selection from many possible) argue that if we acquire the basic skills of reading and writing—if we are literate—we have, or will have, all the goods the stories bundle together, no matter who or where or when we are.

"We think," writes Glenda Hull, "of reading and writing as generic, the intellectual equivalent of all-purpose flour, and we assume that, once mastered, these skills can and will be used in any context for any purpose, and that they are ideologically neutral and value-free" (34).

When we speak of "technological literacy," then, or of "computer literacy" or of "[fill-in-the-blank] literacy," we probably mean that we wish to give others some basic, neutral, context-less set of skills whose acquisition will bring the bearer economic and social goods and privileges. Aimée Dore says as much in an article titled "What Constitutes Literacy in a Culture with Diverse and Changing Means of Communication?":

> ... most people in education and communication are comfortable using the term "literacy" for [describing a relation to print, visual objects, television, and computer] because the various literacies have in common the image of people able to use symbol systems and the media or technologies in which they are instantiated in order to express themselves and to communicate with others, to do so effectively, and to do so in socially desirable ways. (145)

The same belief in a discrete set of basic skills shows itself in a recent White House document:

AMERICA'S TECHNOLOGY LITERACY CHALLENGE

February 15, 1996

"In our schools, every classroom in America must be connected to the information superhighway with computers and good software and well-trained teachers.... I ask Congress to support this education technology initiative so that we can make sure this national partnership succeeds."
President Clinton, State of the Union, January 23, 1996

NATIONAL MISSION TO MAKE EVERY YOUNG PERSON TECHNOLOGICALLY LITERATE: The President has launched a national mission to make all children technologically literate by the dawn of the 21st century, equipped with communication, math, science, and critical thinking skills essential to prepare them for the Information Age. He challenges the private sector, schools, teachers, parents, students, community groups, state and local governments, and the federal government, to meet this goal by building four pillars that will:

1. Provide all teachers the training and support they need to help students learn through computers and the information superhighway;

2. Develop effective and engaging software and on-line learning resources as an integral part of the school curriculum;

3. Provide access to modern computers for all teachers and students;

4. Connect every school and classroom in America to the information superhighway.

But—and (unfortunately) of course—this notion of discrete skills is only a partial view of "literacy." The bundle of meanings and implications that comes with this word is, we argue alongside many other writers, much denser and messier.

In "Arts of the Contact Zone," Mary Louise Pratt describes a 1200 page manuscript, dated 1613, discovered in Copenhagen in 1908:

Written in a mixture of Quechua and ungrammatical, expressive Spanish, the manuscript was a letter addressed by an unknown but apparently literate Andean to King Phillip III of Spain....

The second half of the epistle.... combines a description of colonial society in the Andean region with a passionate denunciation of Spanish exploitation and abuse. (34-35)

But:

No one, it appeared, had ever bothered to read it or figured out how. (34)

In *The Man Who Shot Liberty Valance*, reading and writing don't get Pompey (an African-American man) or Hallie (the white wife) or the Mexican children in Ransom's classroom or their parents the right to vote in the move towards statehood; that privilege is reserved for the white men in the movie—some of whom cannot read and write. In the non-film reality of our present time, becoming literate in English does not help a young Navajo woman feel that she has a real place in Anglo culture, as Anne DiPardo describes, nor does it help the Native Alaskans or African-Americans about whom Lisa Delpit writes feel that they really belong as students in graduate programs or as teachers in U.S. schools. Hull provides a catalogue of writers who warn that U.S. supremacy in business will be eroded by illiteracy in the workforce, but then Hull describes the experiences of two African-American women whose "failure" at a job (processing checks for a bank) was due not to their lack of literacy skills but to day care and transportation and economic problems unacknowledged by their employers.

In spite of the stories we quoted above, literacy alone—some set of basic skills—is not what improves people's lives.

Both Harvey J. Graff, in the early 1980s, and Ruth Finnegan, in the early 1990s, use "literacy myth" to name the belief that literacy will bring us everything the stories above promise; according to Finnegan,

> This story has been around for a long time. It reflects popular and still widely held assumptions: that literacy is a good thing, both the sign and the cause of progress, and that without it we and others would still be in the dark ages. Although it is under attack from a number of directions, this view is still in many circles the conventional wisdom and has played a large part in the rhetoric—and to some extent, therefore—in the practice of educationalists and "development" experts. (32)

Brian Street argues that the idea of such an autonomous literacy, whose acquisition necessarily causes progress, has played a part in the practice of national and international literacy programs; using programs in Iran, Great Britain, and Mozambique as examples, he argues that such programs—which claim to bring economic growth by giving people a simple neutral skill—ignore and override and irrevocably change the lives and culture of those who are made literate: "[T]hese grandiose claims for 'academic' literacy," he writes, "are merely those of a small elite attempting to maintain positions of power and influence by attributing universality and neutrality to their own cultural conventions" (224).

In *The Violence of Literacy,* Elspeth Stuckey's words are equally strong for those who believe that literacy is or can be neutral:

> In the United States we live the mythology of a classless society.... In a society bound by such a mythology, our views about literacy are our views about political economy and social opportunity.... Far from engineering freedom, our current approaches to literacy corroborate other social practices that prevent freedom and limit opportunity. (vii)

And:

> We must take responsibility for the racism throughout schooling, the racism leveled most brutally and effectively in children's earliest years of schooling by literacy whose achievements can be seen in the loss of a third or more poor students by schooling's end. (122)

Or, as Finnegan puts it:

> The myth can be seen as playing an essential ideological function for the governing social, political, or educational order, whether manifested by earlier imperial expansion or by current national or international inequalities. So, when people might want, for example, houses or jobs or economic reform, they are instead given literacy programs. (41)

When we speak then of "literacy" as though it were a basic, neutral, contextless set of skills, the word keeps us hoping—in the face of lives and arguments to the contrary—that there could be an easy cure for economic and social and political pain, that only a lack of literacy keeps people poor or oppressed.

And when we believe this—that poverty and oppression result from a lack of a simple, neutral set of skills—we have trouble understanding why everyone and anyone can't acquire the skills: there must be something wrong with someone who can't correctly learn what most of us acquired easily, in our early years in home or school. Delpit describes classrooms where students and teachers have cultural and grammatical differences, with the teachers then judging their students' "actions, words, intellects, families, and communities as inadequate at best, as collections of pathologies at worst" (xiv). According to Stanley Aronowitz, Walter Lippman and John Dewey argued for the importance of education and literacy because they thought that "lacking education the 'people' are inherently incapable of governing themselves" (298). When people aren't literate—when under this conception of literacy they are not economically secure or part of the culture of the rest of us—it is because of some (inherent?) failure of theirs. We ask them, by using a conception of literacy that allows us to ask them, to blame themselves. We overlook, if not forget, the economic and social and political structures that work to keep people in their places.

> If "literacy" is a deceptive promise of basic skills that on their own will fix someone's life, why do we wish to use this term when we speak of the relationship we desire for our students and others to have with newer technologies?

2

THE SECOND BUNDLE:

THE OBJECTS WE ADDRESS THROUGH THE RELATION OF LITERACY

a

> The paged book became the physical embodiment, the incarnation, of the text it contained.

(Bolter 86)

b

> ...if, in an era of uncertain values, we want to keep alive respect for ideas and knowledge, it is important to give books a form that encourages respect.
>
> (Levarie 306)

c

d

> Prepare a narrative of all which has held it.
>
> Prepare a narrative of all which has held it.
>
> Prepare a narrative of prepare a narrative of all which has held it.
>
> Out of the whole.
>
> Out of the whole wide world I chose it.
>
> Out of the whole wide world I chose it.
>
> (Stein 253)

XXXX

The other day, in *Dear Abby*, this was part of the opening letter:

> An ongoing cycle of illiteracy haunts children on the edges of poverty. When teachers ask their students to bring a favorite book to class to share, these children show up with an advertisement or a coupon book because they have no books at home.
>
> Abby, please help these children learn to love books and reading.
>
> (*Daily Mining Gazette*, Houghton, MI, 11/19/96)

As we have argued above, we believe that "literacy" is presented as a necessary and sufficient set of skills for entree to the good life when it is really a diversion from social and political situations. We do not, however, deny that reading and writing can be a useful set of skills amongst all the skills and practices and behaviors and attributes we all need in order to flourish in our present culture...

...but why should anyone love books—the objects— in and of themselves?

In "Literacy and the Colonization of Memory," Walter D. Mignolo argues that when the Spaniards colonized the area we now call Mexico, they were so steeped in book culture that they believed the Mexica had no sense of history—because the Mexica recorded their pasts in paintings rather than in words in books—and hence that the Mexica "lacked intelligence and humanity" (96).

(For a more detailed description of this meeting between the Inca and the Spanish—and more about how this incident hinging on a (the?) book can be tied to other consequences of literacy, see Diamond 68-81.)

Constance Classen, in *Worlds of Sense: Exploring the Senses in History and Across Cultures*, describes an incident in the Spanish colonization of the Inca, whose cosmology relied on hearing:

> ....the Spanish priest accompanying the expedition gave a brief summary of Christian doctrine, denounced Inca religion as invented by the Devil, and demanded that Atahualpa become the vassal of the Holy Roman Emperor. While giving his address the priest held a book, either the Bible or a breviary, in one hand. Atahualpa, deeply offended by this speech, ... demanded of the priest by what authority he made these claims. The friar held up the book to him. Atahualpa examined it, but as it said nothing to him he dropped it to the ground. This rejection of the essence of European civilization was the excuse the Spanish needed to begin their massacre. (110)

This attachment to books as essence hasn't changed in the hundreds of years following that massacre; witness Sven Birkerts' words from *The Gutenberg Elegies: The Fate of Reading in an Electronic Age*:

> I stare at the textual field on my friend's [computer] screen and I am unpersuaded. Indeed, this glimpse of the future—if it is the future—has me clinging all the more tightly to my books, the very idea of them. If I ever took them for granted, I do no longer. I now see each one as a portable enclosure, a place I can repair to release the private, unsocialized, dreaming self. A book is a solitude, privacy; it is a way of holding the self apart from the crush of the outer world. Hypertext—at least the spirit of hypertext, which I see as the spirit of the times—promises to deliver me from the "liberating domination" of the author. It promises to spring me from the univocal linearity which is precisely the constraint that fills me with a sense of possibility as I read my way across fixed acres of print. (164)

Birkerts' attachment to books is more self-conscious than the Spanish friar's, perhaps, but it nonetheless just as closed off to other forms of expression that might offer other senses of possibility. For both men, dream and value and self and culture and world seem to be fully enclosed within literacy, objectified in—and not separable from—the book.

Birkerts' words call to our minds Habermas, who wrote that a necessary (but not sufficient) step in the development of a critical public in the 18th century was that men read to themselves: in the privacy of their reading they developed a sense of individuated self, a self that could hold a position in the public sphere (45-56). Robert Romanyshyn puts an earlier date to the book's relation to this individuation:

> Linear perspective vision was a fifteenth-century artistic invention for representing three-dimensional depth on the two-dimensional canvas. It was a geometrization of vision which began as an invention and became a convention, a cultural habit of mind... At approximately the same time that Alberti's procedures [for perspective] are mapping the world as a geometric grid, laying it out in linear fashion, the book will be introduced and mass-produced. The linearity of the geometric world will find its counterpart in the linear literacy of the book, where line by line, sentence by sentence, the chronological structures of the book will mirror the sequential, ordered, linear structure of time in the sciences. In addition, the interiorization of individual subjectivity within the room of consciousness will find apt expression in the private act of reading and in silence, unlike the manuscript consciousness of the Middle Ages, where reading was done aloud. (349-351)

The exact date of this interiorization of a self is not important to our words here; rather, what we wish to call attention to is how writers like McLuhan and Ong, and Birkerts, accept that books—once they have somehow acquired the form we now take for granted, small enough for us to hold and carry about, and containing texts that encourage us to see continuity stretching like words linearly over the time of many pages—ask us to think of ourselves as selves. These writers' words are like commands—or interpellations—hailing us to see our selves and the possibilities of our world delimited between the covers of the book; Ivan Illich and Barry Sanders put it the following way in *ABC: The Alphabetization of the Popular Mind*:

> The idea of a self that continues to glimmer in thought or memory, occasionally retrieved and examined in the light of day, cannot exist without the text. Where there is no alphabet, there can be neither memory conceived as a storehouse nor the "I" as its appointed watchman. With the alphabet both text

and self became possible, but only slowly, and they became the social construct on which we found all our perceptions as literate people. (72)

Here are other descriptions (several possibilities from among many) of our relationship with books, and of how that relationship is to shape us:

> Ramus was entirely right in his insistence on the supremacy of the new printed book in the classroom. For only there could the homogenizing effects of the new medium be given heavy stress in young lives. Students processed by print technology in this way would be able to translate every kind of problem and experience into the new visual kind of lineal order. (McLuhan, 146)

> What is written has a disembodied existence; knowledge is no longer contained within human bodies but exists separately from them. In a literate society, therefore, knowledge—and by extension, the cosmos—is devitalized, de-personalized, and reified. The literate world is a silent, still world, one in which the primary means of gaining knowledge is by looking and reflecting.... (Classen, 110)

> ....print is a singularly impersonal medium. Lay preachers and teachers who addressed congregations from afar [through texts] often seemed to speak with a more authoritative voice than those who could be heard and seen within a given community. (Eisenstein, 148)

To the book, then, the writers we have quoted attribute our sense of self, our memories, our possibilities, the specific linear forms of analysis we use, our attitude towards knowledge, our belief in the authority of certain kinds of knowledge, our sense of the world.

What has been encompassed by the book, then, is the second (but still not unruly) bundle we promised in our beginning. If the first bundle that comes with "literacy" is the promise of social, political, and economic improvement, it is because the second bundle is the book, which covers who we are and what we might be and the institutions in which we act. If the Spanish friar had not thought this, if he had not acted out of a notion of "literacy" so tied to the singular object of the book, there would have been no massacre.

What else might we be—or be open to—if we did not see ourselves and our world so defined in books?

Y

When we discuss "technological literacy" or "computer literacy" or "[fill in the blank] literacy," we cannot pull "literacy" away from the two bundles of meanings and implications we have described. We may argue that we want to use "literacy" because it is a handy shortcut for covering a wide range of skills and procedures and practices; we may argue, "That's not what we meant at all; we really meant something broader, more open." But we are still using "literacy," which, unless we deny our histories, comes to us in the bundles we have just begun to unpack.

And our unpacking allows us now to offer up a response to the question that titles our work here: why are we using literacy as a metaphor for everything else? If we have unpacked "literacy" at all adequately, we hope we can now argue that "literacy" gets put behind "technological" or "computer" because "literacy" is already used to encompass everything we think worthy of our consideration: the term automatically upgrades its prefix. If "literacy" is already closely tied to our sense of how the world was colonized and settled and tamed, if "literacy" is already (deceptively) tied to political and social and economic improvement, if "literacy" already is the boundary of our sense of who we are, then why not apply the notion to newer technologies?

But. When we speak of the relationship we hope to establish—for ourselves and for our students—with newer technologies, do we want to carry forward all these particular attachments and meanings and possibilities?

Do we want to speak in the context of a set of practices and beliefs those with decision-making powers use to cultivate, to settle, to tame those without—so that those without remain without and blame themselves? When we say or write "technological literacy" how can we not expect others to hear, even if only partially, that we believe there is some minimum set of technological skills everyone should have—and that it is their own fault if they do not have them? And that it is therefore their own fault if they are not successful and mainstream? How can we not expect others to hear that this literacy constitutes not only a necessary but a sufficient condition for attaining The Good Life?

Do we want to use a word that contains within it a relation to a singular object that we use to narrow our sense of who we are and what we are capable of? Do we want to continue a relationship that is externalized, linear, private, visual, static, and authoritative? When we say, "computer literacy," for example, what part of this relationship to the book are we asking ourselves or our students to establish with, within, and through computers?

> Why aren't we instead working to come up with other terms and understandings—other more complex expressions—of our relationship with and within technologies?

S E C O N D

SO: WHAT OTHER POSSIBILITIES MIGHT WE USE FOR EXPRESSING OUR RELATIONSHIPS WITH TECHNOLOGIES?

In what follows (in only visually linear form) we analyze and reconstruct new approaches to communication that prioritize ways of knowing other than those dependent on 'literacy.'

There are two bundles in our writing here as well, but they are far from neat and tidy bundles, and we must pull them together rather than unpack them. These bundles unravel even as we write and revise and as you (and you and you) read: first we will offer an interpretation of what it might mean to think of literacy under postmodernism; second, we will begin to shift terms, suggesting other ways to think of literacy that begin moving away from the baggage outlined in the bundles above. And rather than simplifying any of the issues we have unbundled in the first section of our writing, the sorts of "literacy" we are about to discuss (we will abandon the term eventually) complicate, question, challenge, and make contingent.

1

LITERACY IN SPACE

a

Chia suspected that her mother's perception of time differed from her own in radical and mysterious ways. Not just in the way that a month, to Chia's mother, was not a very long time, but in the way that her mother's 'now' was such a narrow and literal thing. News-governed, Chia believed. Cable-fed. A present honed to whatever very instant of a helicopter traffic report.

Chia's 'now' was digital, effortlessly elastic, instant recall supported by global systems she'd never have to bother comprehending.

(The requisite William Gibson quotation, 13-14)

b

Having everything on-line is fantastic. Now as soon as a transfer is completed, it's there! You can really look up what you need. If someone calls, you know exactly what's going on. Sometimes you are looking for a part of a case that someone else has. You used to have to go looking for it, and maybe you wouldn't find it. Now you can see where it is without getting up from your seat. It's all right there at my fingertips.

(Clerk in Stock and Bond Transfer Department in a recently computerized insurance underwriter, quoted in Zuboff 157-158).

c

The great obsession of the nineteenth century was, as we know, history: with its themes of development and of suspension, of crisis and cycle, themes of the ever-accumulating past, with its great preponderance of dead men and the menacing glaciation of the world. The nineteenth century found its essential mythological resources in the second principle of thermodynamics. The present epoch will perhaps

@

Begin here, in a linear flow of text that suggests a flow of time, by imagining what literacy might be if we conceived it primarily as a spatial relation to information.

Although literacy has long been bound up with spaces (consider the geopolitical stories in the bundles we discussed above/earlier, for example), literacy changes profoundly if we choose to prioritize space over time. This shift has been frequently described by others with the term 'postmodernism,' although that term has become so complex and contradictory—so rich—that we use it to gesture generally rather than to point accurately: we are not here to argue whether the "postmodern condition" is indeed the one in which we find ourselves, but rather to use the thinking of different writers identified with postmodernism to lay out some possible relations with and within communication technologies.

be above all the epoch of space. We are in the epoch of simultaneity: we are in the epoch of juxtaposition, the epoch of the near and far, of the side-by-side, of the dispersed. We are at a moment, I believe, when our experience of the world is less that of a long life developing through time than that of a network that connects points and intersects with its own skein. One could perhaps say that certain ideological conflicts animating present-day polemics oppose the pious descendents of time and the determined inhabitants of space. (Foucault, 22)

I believe the most striking emblem of this new mode of thinking relationships can be found in the work of Nam June Paik, whose stacked or scattered television screens, positioned at intervals within lush vegetation, or winking down at us from a ceiling of strange new video stars, recapitulate over and over again prearranged sequences or loops of images which return at dyssynchronous moments on various screens. The older aesthetic is then practiced by viewers, who, bewildered by this discontinuous variety, decided to concentrate on a single screen, as though the relatively worthless image sequence to be followed there had some organic value in its own right. The postmodernist viewer, however, is called upon to do the impossible, namely, to see all the screens at once, in their radical and random difference.... (Jameson 31).

How is it that we are able to see all the screens at once? Prioritizing space over time—and so looking away from time and also then from history—removes origins, futures, and progress: we see "all the screens"—all the information—

all at once. In a spatially organized understanding of communication and knowledge, past and future can only merely be other locations in space. We are left with a sort of spread-out and flat simultaneity through which we travel.

> On a flat world, it is difficult to build an argument or to move directly from one point to the next because surfaces can be very slippery. Glissage or sliding is the preferred mode of transport. (Hebdige 170)

This "simultaneity" could be a way of thinking about how we have wired our communications and our "working knowledge" to new technologies. The speed with which we can move amongst screens of information—their visual, near instantaneous presence to us all at once—suggests that it is possible to describe information not as something we send from place to place, in books or on paper, over time, but as something we move (and hence think) within. Where "intertextuality" has long been understood at a conceptual level—text citing text citing text in an unseen network of reference—we now have conditions that allow it the possibility of it being material, visible and navigable, writable and readable, on our computer screens. "Literacy"—if we describe it as some set of skills that allows us to work with the information structures of our time—then becomes the ability to move in the new-technology spaces of information, the ability to make the instantaneous connections between informational objects that allow us to see them all at once.

> As long as the game is not a game of perfect information, the advantage will be with the player who has knowledge and can obtain information. By definition, this is the case with the student in a learning situation. But in games of perfect information, the best performativity cannot consist in obtaining additional information in this way. It comes rather from arranging the data in a new way, which is what constitutes a "move" properly speaking. This new arrangement is usually achieved by connecting together series of data that were previously held to be independent. This capacity to articulate what used to be separate can be called imagination. Speed is one of its properties. (Lyotard 52)

But seeing information (and hence "literacy") in that way plays itself back on how we conceive of the space we are creating by and within new communication technologies. The speed of our imaginations—our ability to make instantaneous connections—relies on the construction of information spaces that can be navigated so quickly that space seems compressed for us. With new communication technologies, we want to be able to—we feel we can—move from one end of space to another nearly instantaneously; we can bring any set of places—any set of things—together into one.

In one way of looking, then, this is not just about privileging space over time, but about time and space collapsing into each other... and if we can work as though time does not ration out what we can do, then we can work as though space doesn't either: with new communication technologies, space, like information, can become less something we experience and more something we simply work with/in, making creative connections and reconnections.

> For flatness is corrosive and infectious. Who, after all, is Paul Virilio anyway? The name sounds as if it belongs to a B movie actor, a member of *Frankie Goes to Hollywood*, a contestant in a body-building competition. I know that "he" writes books but  does such a person actually exist? In the land of the gentrified cut-up, as in the place of dreams, anything imaginable can happen, anything at all. The permutations are unlimited: high / low / folk culture; pop music / opera; street fashion / haute couture; journalism / science fiction / critical theory; advertising / critical theory / haute couture....With the sudden loss of gravity, the lines that hold the terms apart waver and collapse. (Hebdige 161)

In this way of looking, the collapse of our experience of "technological" space can also correspond to a collapse of "real" space. Two steps are at work here: first, physically distant locations are wired up, so that it seems the one with whom I am communicating is just on the other side of the screen; second, the possibility that virtual spaces are collapsible leads to the idea that real spaces are likewise. This may sound like faulty logic, but, instead, the shift is straightforward: if communication is real, then the spaces in which it occurs are also real.

But what are we, then, in this space of all spaces all at once and no temporal flow? Under the sense of literacy we unpacked in the earlier/previous part of this writing, we rely on our ability to construct ourselves at some nexus between past and future, to have faith in the present as the point where past and future meet like (exactly like) a reader progressing through a linear text, uniting what has gone before with what is now and with what will come.

> [P]ersonal identity is itself the effect of a certain temporal unification of past and future with one's present.... If we are

> unable to unify the past, present, and future of the sentence,
> we are similarly unable to unify the past, present, and future of
> our own biographical experience or psychic life. (Jameson 27)

When everything is all at once, what do we do?

Long ago, there must have been a golden age of harmony between heaven and earth. High was high; low was low; inside was in; and outside was out. But now we have money. Now, everything is out of balance. They say, "Time is money." But they got it all wrong: Time is the absence of money. (Wenders.)

> The shift towards privileging space over time—what so many
> say is a hallmark of now—can have a frightening and dangerous
> result: the shift towards postmodernism acts in a radical
> unbinding of history from subjectivity. The unbinding can
> become so overpowering that it colonizes subjectivities and
> tears them apart; with no guarantees of either a stable past or
> a connected future, it is impossible to believe in the unity of a
> single, stable subject—the subject of our previous discussions of
> literacy.

But the unbinding can also be understood as opening up room for another view of ourselves: in understanding the implications of a postmodern worldview, we open ourselves to the possibility of remaking cultural meanings and identities. The connotations of literacy, as we discussed it in the first sections of our writing, suggest a process of mechanical and passive individual reception: the book gives us who we are, the book sets the limits for who we allow into the realms of privilege. If we understand communication not as discrete bundles of stuff that are held together in some unified space, that exist linearly through time, and that we pass along, but as instead different possible constructed relations between information that is spread out all before us, then... living becomes movement among (and within) sign systems.

> Data Warehouse. *noun* 1: a process that collects data from vari-
> ous applications in an organization's operational systems, inte-
> grates the information into a logical model of business subject
> areas, stores it in a manner accessible to decision makers and
> delivers it to them through report-writing and query tools. The

> goal is to put standardized and comparable corporate information into employees' hands, enabling an enterprisewide view of the business. (McWilliams, DW/2.)

> ■

> Symbolic analysts solve, identify, and broker problems by manipulating symbols. They simplify reality into abstract images that can be rearranged, juggled, experimented with, communicated to other specialists, and then, eventually, transformed back into reality. The manipulations are done with analytic tools, sharpened by experience. (Reich, 178).

Here is the possibility of understanding our relation to our communication technologies as not being one through which we are passively, mechanically shaped. There is the possibility of seeing ourselves as not just moving through information, but of us moving through it and making and changing conscious constructions of it as we go. This is not about handing books to children or high-school dropouts or the underdeveloped, and hoping that they will pick up enough skills to be able to lose themselves in reading (and so to come back with different selves that better fit a dominant culture); it is instead about how we all might understand ourselves as active participants in how information gets "rearranged, juggled, experimented with" to make the reality of different cultures. This involves, of course, understanding our selves within the making and changing.

And this involves, then, not just thinking that we should pass along discrete sets of skills to others—or pretending that those discrete sets of skills are all that it takes to have a different life. There are certainly skills needed for connecting and reconnecting information—but the relationships to communication technologies we are describing now and here ask, in necessary addition, for a shared and discussed, ongoing, reconception of the space and time we use together and in which we find (and can construct) information and ourselves.

This reconception is thus not about handing down skills to others who are not where we are, but about figuring out how we all are where we are, and about how we all participate in making these spaces and the various selves we find here.

2

ARTICULATING LITERACY

So what else? We hope to have made it clear by now that our questions never have simple, bounded answers. No single term—such as "literacy"—can support the weight of the shifting, contingent activities we have been describing.

There are many possibilities—other than literacy, other than postmodernism—for how we might conceive our relationships with communication technologies (and no single correct answer). We can work from Stuart Hall's term "articulation" to suggest something else yet again.

> In England, the term [articulation] has a nice double meaning because "articulate" means to utter, to speak forth, to be artic- ulate. It carries that sense of language-ing, of expressing, etc. But we also speak of an "articulated" lorry (truck): a lorry where the front (cab) and the back (trailer) can, but need not necessarily, be connected to one another. The two parts are connected to each other, but through a specific linkage, that can be broken. An articulation is thus the form of the connection that can make a unity of two different elements, under certain conditions. It is a linkage which is not necessary, determined, absolute and essential for all time. You have to ask, under what circumstances can a connection be forged or made? (Hall 53)

Under this understanding of relationships, then, we could describe literacy not as a monolithic term but as a cloud of sometimes contradictory nexus points among different positions. Literacy can be seen as not a skill but a process of situating and resituating representations in social spaces.

> So the so-called "unity" of a discourse is really an articulation of different, distinct elements which can be re-articulated in different ways because they have no necessary "belongingness." The "unity" which matters is a linkage between that articulated discourse and the social forces with which it can, under certain historical conditions, but need not necessarily, be connected. Thus, a theory of articulation is both a way of understanding how ideological elements come, under certain conditions, to cohere together within a discourse, and a way of asking how they do or do not become articulated, at specific conjunctures, to certain political subjects. Let me put that the other way: a theory of articulation asks how an ideology discovers its subject rather than how the subject thinks the necessary and inevitable thoughts which belong to it; it enables us to think how an ideology empowers people, enabling them to begin to make some sense or intelligibility of their historical situation, without reducing those forms of intelligibility to their socio-economic or class location or social position. (Hall 53)

With the notion of connection, in articulation, comes the notion of potential disconnection. Literacy here shifts away from receiving a self to the necessary act of continual remaking, of understanding the "unity" of an object (social, political, intellectual) and simultaneously seeing that that unity is contingent, supported by the efforts of the writer/reader and the cultures in which they live.

> With and through articulation, we engage the concrete in order to change it, that is, to rearticulate it. To understand theory and method in this way shifts perspective from the acquisition

> or application of an epistemology to the create process of
> articulating, of thinking relations and connections as how we
> come to know and as creating what we know. Articulation is,
> then, not just a thing (not just connections) but a process of
> creating connections, much in the same way that hegemony is
> not domination but the process of creating and maintaining
> consensus or of co-ordinating interests. (Slack, 114).

Articulation is only one among many ways of re-presenting literacy. Jim Collins, paralleling Jameson's discussions, offers an "architectural" model as one possibility:

> Appropriation is not simply an anti-Romantic stance opposed
> to the mythology of pure genius; this shift also involves
> profound changes in regard to the mutability of both
> information and the forms of cultural authority which govern
> (or used to govern) its circulation. To appropriate is to take
> control over that which originated elsewhere for
> semiotic/ideological purposes....
> The determination to take possession .... does not signify the
> denial of cultural authority but, rather, the refusal to grant
> cultural *sovereignity* to any institution, as it counters one sort of
> authority with another. (Collins, 92-93)

Still other possible terms abound: Deleuze and Guattari describe the rhizomic nature of the nomad; Pratt offers linguistic contact zones; Giroux constructs border spaces; Anzaldua occupies borderlands. With such new bundles, we suggest new ways of relating to technologies (including texts) and to each other: both a process and a structure bound up (literally and figuratively) with social change.

BUT...

None of these terms exhausts new possibilities for "literacy," but only suggests productive ways of questioning our current positions, of unpacking old bundles and remaking new ones. Unpack ours and make your own.

A NOTE ON THE ILLUSTRATIONS

The drawings of people with books (and the one illustration of a woman with a television) come from a collection of clip art produced by the Volk Corporation and the Harry Volk Jr. Art Studio, both in Pleasantville, NJ, from 1959 through 1968. In the various small books of clip art from which these illustrations come, all the people are white and clearly middle class; there are many illustrations of women and children holding books; if men have printed matter in their hands, it is account books or newspapers—unless they are shown reading to their families (as one illustration here shows).

CHAPTER TWENTY

Family Values
Literacy, Technology, and Uncle Sam

Joe Amato

M Y UNCLE SAM ALWAYS SAID CHICAGO IS A "FAST TOWN." HE'S AN EX-CON, my uncle. Three-time loser who did a twenty-one year stretch in Attica and Auburn. Picked up on armed burglary, shot in the leg (it was entrapment actually, but who's taking notes?). The day he got out I spotted him walking down the street. It was the year I graduated from high school. He was wearing a toupee. My father didn't recognize him.

When I was a kid, nobody told me I had an uncle named Sam. But I can recall my grandma putting together care packages of food and such, and my father occasionally talking about driving to Auburn. And here and there dropping into Italian, capisce? I didn't get the connection till years later.

My grandpa and grandma were both poor people from Sicily. My grandpa, Rosario (or Roy as he was generally known), had been a fisherman in a small village, Spadafora. I'm not certain, but it seems he participated in the Italy-Ethiopia conflict during the early part of this century. When he came to this country, he worked with the railroad, and then construction-concrete. He helped pour the foundation for a major sewage treatment plant on the north side of the city. His English was what we used to call "broken," but he was nonetheless proud to be a naturalized United States citizen. After a meal cooked by my grandma—usually macaroni and assorted meats—my grandpa would tell stories and my father would translate. Or try to.

Sometimes my grandpa would ask me how many congresspeople were in the House of Representatives, how many senators were in the Senate. I could never remember, and he'd smile as told me the correct numbers. In his early eighties, he worked for the Onondaga County Park Service, taking care of the flower beds at different points along the lake. He smoked unfiltered Camels for sixty-five years. He died in 1975 of a stroke. He was eighty-seven.

My grandma, Antoinette, was always a difficult woman. For no apparent reason, she kicked her son Joe, my father, out of her house shortly after he returned from Europe with his French war bride Suzette, my mother. My grandpa found them another place to stay on the west side, on Belden Ave., with a not-so-distant relative. This was where I spent the first year of my life.

My grandma, who had been married since her early teens—that woman could cook. Never had a meatball like hers, or a red sauce. She was religious in a superstitious way, and could neither read nor write. She'd given birth to a child who died as an infant. He's buried in St. Agnes cemetery, up on Onondaga Hill, south of the city. And rumor has it she'd had a miscarriage at some point in the distant past. Rumor also has it my grandpa punched her in the mouth once and knocked her teeth out, also in the distant past. My grandma died last year. She was one hundred and one.

My uncle Sam had a stroke a decade ago, leaving him with a severe speech impediment. When I talk to him now, I read his sad, rehabilitated eyes. When I mention Chicago, he says "fast town." Sometimes he stutters a bit.

* * *

When Sam first got out of the can (my father's term), he'd steal packs of cigarettes. He'd also go after phony insurance claims, slipping and falling, carefully, in grocery stores and the like. No more stealing these days, no more phony claims.

And he's a hard worker, too, no fat on his frame. In fact he's been working odd jobs—junking, construction flagman, house painting—ever since he got out. No shit—even while slipping and falling, he's been hard at work making a buck.

He lives in Tampa now, with his partner Marietta. They live in a trailer park. Another of my uncles, Dominick, a former insurance salesman who lives in Cheyenne, paid for the trailer. Sam's in his late seventies now, earns a few bucks picking up and delivering for a charity organization in the Florida heat. Which for him is easier than delivering pizzas in Central New York cold.

There was always a war being waged between my father and his brothers. Four in all: Sam, Frank, Joe and Dominick. Sam is the oldest, but he was rarely around. Frank had met Clark Gable during the war, and had picked up some shrapnel in his right elbow. My father always insisted it was Frank's fault—he didn't phone my father, as they'd evidently planned, when he landed in France. My father was a corporal in the Signal Corps, and had somehow arranged, in between official duties and black marketeering, to get his older brother out of combat duty. Didn't work out.

My uncle Frank has always run hot and cold. It's his relationship with my aunt Mary, his wife. Or so I've been led to believe. Something about my aunt having had an affair with an African-American man while Frank was in Europe. More rumors. Not that Frank didn't screw around himself. Who knows? But you know how Italians of that generation can be, especially about black-white mixing. Mary—my mother always said Mary was a "sweet girl." My mother could relate to Mary's having been ostracized. To me as a kid, my aunt Mary seemed friendly, and a little loony. These days I know better—I can see the damage.

Frank himself has had a mistress since the war. He likes to play the horses. And shrapnel or no, Frank used to be a helluva bowler, as my father would say. My brother Mike and I used to see him at Syracuse Bowling Center after leagues on Friday nights, around eleven. He'd give us a few tips. Mike and I would bowl maybe a dozen games till well after midnight. First game thirty-five cents, second game a penny.

Sam could bowl too. Story goes he once rolled a couple of back-to-back perfect games in New York City.

* * *

After my folks got divorced, my father, Mike and I moved out of our three bedroom ranch house in the suburbs and into a dilapidated two-story house in a poor cul-de-sac just outside the city limits. About a quarter mile from the New York State Thruway. Very noisy. We lived in that house, 501 Raphael Ave., for a dozen years. Never managed to put up any curtains.

The place was owned by a gas station and heating equipment supply company, Clemmett Plumbing and Heating (I think I have the spelling right). The expansion and contraction of empty fuel storage tanks in the lots around the house would irregularly rumble up into my second-story bedroom window.

On two occasions (once during Hurricane Agnes), the polluted, rat-infested creek out back overflowed, flooding the area around our house for a week or better. Our basement was underwater, and we'd have no electricity, no gas for our stove, and no potable water. That creek fed into the same sewage treatment plant that my grandpa had helped lay the foundation for decades earlier.

Our downstairs neighbor, Gerry (who drove a school bus), would have his father and step-mother up from Florida during summers. Sometimes they'd live for months alongside the house in their RV.

Winter 1976-77, my final year as an undergrad, we were behind so far in our light and gas bill that the power company (Niagara Mohawk) shut off the electricity to our flat. My father gave Gerry twenty bucks a month and ran an extension cord downstairs, with which we powered the refrigerator, a lamp, a clock, a fan, and the TV. We used the gas stove to heat the place, and blew heat around with the fan.

My father and I were forced to find another place to live in 1981, when the water line broke and the county health department officially condemned the place.

During the early seventies, my father, Mike and I would occasionally be invited over to my aunt Mary and uncle Frank's flat. We'd show up, knock, but sometimes they wouldn't answer the door. We could hear their little Chihuahua, Mickey, barking. Mickey would tremble all over when you entered their apartment, his feet ticking and sliding across the wood floors. He lived to be nearly twenty human years.

During my grandpa's wake, my uncle Frank mouthed-off to my father, as he was prone to. My father, a southpaw who'd boxed in the army, ended up throwing Frank on the floor. That was the last time they spoke, far as I can recollect. Frank spent some time praying at my father's casket, right after the burial services. It was a cold January morning.

These days, my uncle Frank lives with my aunt Mary in a small house they bought in Eastwood, not far from the apartment complex my mother had lived in right after the divorce. When my mother moved back to Syracuse in 1988, she took another apartment in that same complex (coincidentally, the same owner as her apartment complex in Schenectady). I saw my uncle Frank and my aunt Mary when my mother died, and when my father died a year and a day later. I couldn't make it back east for my grandma's funeral, so I haven't seen them since.

My uncle Dominick—originally Domenico, but he goes by "Doc"—is the youngest, and also the most successful, moneywise. My mother always said that he was smart to get out of Syracuse early on. I would see him, my aunt Dorothy, and my two younger cousins, their sons Russ and Frank, whenever they visited us in Syracuse. Usually they'd stay with my uncle Frank and aunt Mary.

Russ is a chemical engineer, lives in Washington state with his wife Alison and their two kids, Amanda and Dominick. And Frank is a chiropractor in L.A. My father was never much for traveling, maybe because he'd traveled so much during the war. Anyway, my family never made it out to Cheyenne to visit. I've been to Cheyenne once on my own, three years ago, and twice with my wife, Kass. My aunt Dorothy was also of Italian heritage, born and raised in Cheyenne. My aunt died of cancer a few years after my uncle Sam had his stroke.

* * *

I live in Chicago now, work as an assistant professor of English at a technical institute here in town. I teach professional writing courses—technical writing, business writing and the like—and literature.

I'm the first in my family to hold a four-year college degree or better. I went to Syracuse University on a mathematics scholarship. I studied math and engineering, and went into engineering after graduation thinking I could at least make some money, help my father out. My father had been in and out of work, and the three of us had been on and off welfare for a long spell. We were in debt something like $7000 when I graduated from college in 1977—rent, light and gas, and so forth. I left engineering in 1984 to enter grad. school, thinking that I'd pretty much accomplished what I'd set out to. I had some passion for technology, and still do. But no passion at all for bureaucracies. Still don't.

I have a basic curiosity about technology—about how things may be made, methodically, to work—that helped propel me through my engineering studies (I always found math more interesting than engineering simply because its internal logic seemed to obviate any messy, external conditions). Technological thinking was and is, for me, a powerful way of apprehending so much of our constructed world. To think technically about things is to put a certain faith in the human capacity for building: engineers assume that the application of tried & true principle to concrete form results in structures or structured processes whose working details will somehow add up. Very much like writing, in fact, to the extent that each successive letter I write and you read makes words, which in turn make strings of words, perhaps sentences. Sense is another matter, affect another still.

From this point of view, it's remarkable that one often encounters resistance to technology from those whose livelihoods depend upon a highly technical understanding of their various materials—artists. Yet from another point of view, this is hardly surprising. So much of what we are accustomed to calling technology—software, automotive engines, toys—is predicated on the capacity to manufacture marketplace demand. And those who value the circumstantial, the temporal, the tentative as a means of nurturing the creative process may justifiably view marketplace motives with suspicion.

It's obvious that my success at landing tech. writing teaching jobs is owing to my engineering background. Seven years in project and process engineering. Two-and-a-half years in Syracuse, with Bristol-Myers Company (now Bristol-Myers Squibb). And before that, four-and-a-half years with Miller Brewing Company (owned by Philip Morris), twenty-five miles north of Syracuse, in Fulton. Real lake-effect snow country. When I drove up there to interview in 1977, I asked the standard question I'd been told to ask about upward mobility. They told me "the sky's the limit."

The brewery just shut down last year.

When I worked there, I had to deal with two corrupt trade unions in Oswego County, the painters and the laborers. The painters were the worst. They were run by a bunch of brothers, a couple of whom were pretty mean. Anyway, a New Jersey firm brought in a foreman reputed to have Mafia connections, and he brought in painters from the Utica-Rome local. His name was Sal, and he'd take me out to lunch once in a while. The brothers didn't bother him. Eventually the FBI was brought in, and I spent a couple of hours telling them exactly what I thought of Sal after I found out he'd threatened a competing contractor's life.

The brewery itself had its own internal management traumas. I was threatened with physical harm on three occasions by management personnel. It always left me feeling at a bit of a loss for words, but I'd developed an unfortunate tendency to smile when insulted, and to grow exceedingly calm. The last time it happened, I asked my combatant to meet me out in the parking lot. He balked.

Because things were so hectic at the brewery—we were always either in a start-up mode or in the midst of expanding operations—there was rarely anybody looking over my shoulder. So favors from contractors were relatively easy to come by. Once—only once—my frustration with the corporate turmoil led me to argue a contract estimate up instead of down. Three of my friends ended up with brand spanking new driveways. I felt like Robin Hood for a couple of weeks.

My brother Mike, a year-and-a-half younger than me, became an engineer too, also attended S.U. A brief stint with Xerox in Rochester, and then nearly a dozen years with General Electric in Syracuse (they like to call themselves GE these days), shock and vibration testing. He's self-employed now, buying and selling government surplus. He's doing well, has just relocated to Boulder, Colorado, with his partner Linda. He loves the outdoors, especially climbing.

At one point, my brother worked in the same building as my uncle Frank. And my father had worked at General Electric, too, doing cabinet finishing on the line, till the cutbacks of the late sixties. They offered him a buck less an hour or a move down to Virginia. He quit, took his severance pay, and bounced around from small business to small business for fifteen years.

I worked with him one summer, in 1976, refinishing the dorm furniture of Ithaca College. The pay was under the table, no benefits (though I managed to swipe a Binks 7 spray gun). The guy who owned the shop was an Arab, and in addition to my father and me, he had a Greek, a Sardinian, and a Jewish kid working for him. The shop-talk was animated and confusing, a circus of hand signals. In the corner of the shop where my father and I worked, you couldn't see ten feet, the spray fumes were that thick. I ended up with pneumonia.

My mother also worked at General Electric. Crimp and solder assembly line work—piece work—in the fifties, and then receptionist work after Mike and I had grown some. Following the divorce, my mother landed a job as main receptionist at General Electric Corporate Research & Development (CR & D) in Schenectady. Edison's and Steinmetz's company, where they once built a mechanical horse. Edison's desk was just across the lobby from my mother's desk, where she sat for twenty years. Atop it was displayed a perpetually-lit incandescent bulb. My mother, a former French citizen fluent in French, German and English (naturalized in 1949), never finished college because of the war. She and my father were married in Le Havre on 7 September 1945.

My aunt Ilse, my mother's only sibling, lives in Toronto. Her husband, my uncle Eric, died two years ago. He was French, had reentered France with de Gaulle. His father had been an artist in Paris, and three of my uncle's paintings, along with an oil-on-velvet by my mother's father, decorate our apartment.

Ilse's and Eric's only son, my cousin Dan, also has the artist in him. He's in business for himself in Toronto, does conceptual design and layout and the like, and is an accomplished pilot. His Quebecìoise wife Thérèse and he have two children, Serge and Michelle, both nearing thirty. My father knew Dan during the war, when Dan was just a kid.

My oma is buried in Toronto. I remember her only faintly, a stern but kind German woman. She lived her final years with her daughter and son-in-law in Toronto. I remember visiting them when I was very small. My mother took me by herself, on the train. I can remember the scenery whizzing by. And I think I can recall crawling around under a table with my uncle Eric's terrier, Yorick.

I never knew my mother's father. He was Parisian, like my uncle Eric. He died in France in 1950, from complications stemming from an injury he suffered when his jeep rolled over and crushed him.

* * *

Like I say, I live and teach in Chicago. I'm forty-one years old. I make about $37,000 on a nine-month contract. I teach six courses a year, have just been denied tenure (long story, for another time). The highest paid (non-admin) person on my faculty, fully tenured with twenty-five years experience, makes around $45,000 annually.

Summers I write, and travel if we have available credit. I don't teach summers because I need to publish (presumably) in order to get tenure. For better and for worse, publications are the only aspect of academic résumés likely to travel with you. To emphasize the importance of publishing tends to reinforce a research mentality over and against a teaching orientation, I know. But to make teaching the sole criteria in hiring or promoting faculty, especially on a tech campus such as mine, can have the effect of reducing teaching itself to a form of indoctrination—manufacturing the best student-widget. The best student-consumer.

What our various publics rarely understand is that, even if faculty define their primary obligation in terms of their work with students (I do), we need formal encouragement for our intellectual work, work that feeds into our thinking about what we teach and how we teach. Promoting research is one way of maintaining both a connection between teaching and publishing and a faculty interested in pushing the learning envelope.

In any case, I love to write, and there's not much time to do so during the semester. There are meetings, and committees, and a lot of one-on-one student work. I estimate a minimum of sixty hours per week if you're teaching three courses per semester (with approx. twenty students per course). This includes time spent at home grading papers and the like, and the requisite hours one puts into publishing. Much of my writing has to do with the Internet, and I spend hours upon hours dealing with students online, as well as exploring these newer media.

I bought my computer, an aging Mac IIci, with the retirement fund from my previous visiting appointment with the University of Illinois at Urbana-Champaign. About a half-hour's drive north of the adjacent towns of Urbana and Champaign is Chanute Air Force Base in Rantoul, and every now and then my uncle Dominick likes to recite for me how he taught liquid oxygen plant design there for a spell following his military service in the early fifties. This was before he made the move into insurance.

The average annual household income of the students I teach is around $40,000 per year. Down at Urbana-Champaign it was closer to $80,000 per year.

U of I at Urbana-Champaign is a land grant institution, located in the middle of the central Illinois growing region. The campus itself is a small city, spread across the central portion of Urbana and Champaign. The campus boasts the third largest academic library in the US. And it's also a National Center for Supercomputing Applications site. Lots of information passing back and forth across the former prairie.

I teach now on an urban campus, located right across the street from the largest public housing project in the US, which is really a series of projects strung together for twenty or so blocks—Robert Taylor Homes, Stateway Gardens, etc. Something like sixty percent of the almost exclusively African-American folks in these projects are on welfare. Money may be tight on both sides of the street, but it's clear who has and who really has not.

My car, a 1986 Ford Escort, has 140,000 miles on it. My wife's vehicle, a 1987 Nissan pickup, has 110,000 miles on it. My wife, Kass Fleisher, is 39 years old. She holds a doctorate in English too. Together we're in debt around $50,000 on credit cards. Our total "savings," consists of $28,000 in a Mutual of America retirement account. (Kass has an additional $12,000 that we can't get at till retirement). I figure we own, at most, $15,000 worth of stuff—books, furniture, stereo, clothes, appliances, etc.

After my mother's death due to heart failure, which was sudden and unexpected, my brother and I each received around $34,000. You don't think about such things, but there they are. I tend to believe that people with money and property in their families, with a real estate in their futures, derive a sense of security from same. But they may not think about such things, either. Anyway, the year my mother died, I earned $8,000 from teaching. I paid off my debts, moved to Illinois, and used up most of the remaining money purchasing furniture. Mike was able to put a portion of his inheritance toward getting his business off the ground.

My brother and I had supported my father since 1981, though I could do very little myself while in grad. school. My father died penniless. He would lie on the couch, with cancer, watching TV. Occasionally he'd ask me about the low-cost life insurance Ed McMahon was hawking.

We don't really know if Kass will inherit anything (it's difficult to write this without appearing as though we're asking). Kass's parents are both college graduates, in their sixties. Kass's father is now upper-middleclass, owns a nice home in West Chester, outside of Philly, where he lives with his partner Gail; he tells Kass not to expect an inheritance, partly because of the logistics of merging stepfamilies.

Her mother owns a small condo in North Palm Beach, is also remarried, but that part of the family is fractured. Kass has a brother in Florida, but they don't speak. Her mother hasn't spoken to her brother in 17 years. One of her uncles, like my uncle Sam, has been in and out of jail. Kass and her mother had another falling-out recently and it's hard to say whether they'll speak again. Kass has a total of six step-siblings she rarely sees.

Kass has just finished what will probably be her first published novel. She's looking now to do freelance writing (like me), and currently teaches adjunct. We're both opposed to adjunct work because of its low pay ($2000 per course on my campus) but we need the money—we're thinking of having a kid. Maybe two. Soon.

We have no additional source of income, other than gifts. People have been generous to us, but we still gross approximately my paycheck every year. And from here on out, whatever else Kass can make.

Kass and I met online. After we got married, she worked a final semester in Idaho. She resigned her visiting position there so that we wouldn't have to live apart, with all of our money going to MCI and American Airlines. Crazy life, living apart, but coming together crippled Kass's sense of community. And leaving Chicago, a likely eventuality given my paycheck, will put us both, like so many others, in the position of building a local network from scratch. Again.

We live in Kenwood, which is customarily viewed by its residents as the northernmost portion of Hyde Park. Hyde Park is one of the few desegregated, if not integrated, neighborhoods in the city, a middle—and upperclass enclave with Lake Michigan as its eastern border and the widespread African-American poverty of Chicago's south side to its north, west and south. The severe effects of joblessness and discrimination have persisted for decades now. But there's a heroic effort underway to salvage and restore various sections of the south side, including what is known affectionately as Bronzeville, an area that used to be the home of numerous jazz and blues hot-spots.

Seven blocks down the street from us looms the wealthy institutional presence of the University of Chicago. Two blocks up the street, in Elijah Muhammad's former house, lives Louis Farrakhan.

We pay a very reasonable $675 per month rent (heat included) for our two bedroom apartment. We live on the third floor of a three-floor walk-up. Security in our building has been a problem, especially on the first and third floors. I've been burglarized once, nine months after moving in.

* * *

I talk about my family, my family's history, my line of work, my earnings, my wife's earnings, my inheritance—the choices I've made, and the choices that have been made for me—I talk about these personal, if not private, realities because these things figure mightily into my social circumstances, my economic circumstances. These experiences and memories, these histories and associations, these material comforts and discomforts in many ways constitute, though they do not cause, my values. And my values have all to do with my sense of language, of what's possible with words, or should be possible. That is, my values have all to do with what needs saying.

* * *

(COMMERCIAL DIPLOMACY)

across la table
hoping to make the season
let go
no never mind of
making eyes
of others from around the globe

we came to exchange
places with our hands above
and beneath an image
of a village with children

being white is not a color
as among others can be
and we met at la table
women and men alike
dressing carefully
each word to measuring glance
that there would be no poverty
in the trade
no talk of hamburgers
news or processing of any lives

jockeying for quotation
in neighborhoods not already assigned
no match for cues or clues
for solace is a thing of season and
hoping to make the season
let go
we served only our polemic
with little talk of homes
returning callous and unnerved
to linger in the supermarket

as they do at times
in places
made to order
in the americas

* * *

   I teach writing, and I write poetry. My students, eighty percent of whom are male, are primarily engineering and science majors, and I often see my younger self in them—young and enthusiastic, eager to make a buck. Maybe too eager. Most, when asked, will tell you that they plan on three or four years in engineering, and then a move into management. When asked why, they pause. They don't quite understand why such "career paths" are in place. Most haven't studied the history of engineering as a profession. Most aren't aware of early efforts in this country to unionize engineers, and how corporations conspired to halt such efforts. Most aren't familiar first-hand with how the move from engineering into management requires a different set of loyalties, even in these enlightened times. And the rhetoric of success and technical leadership, rife on my campus, all but obscures the economic factors that suck such students into the corporate system wearing systemic blinders.

A number of my students are ROTC. More blinders.

As my earlier remarks would suggest, it's not that I have a thing against technology per se. Technology can be a good thing. Take my uncle Sam's artificial hips. Or my uncle Dominick's prosthetic knees. Or Kass and I meeting online.

Of course, there are a number of things I might mention on the downside. Take my tap water—please.

And as to my understanding of words, sentences, lines, letters: my sense of alphabet practices in general is that their more literary attributes are rapidly becoming an endangered species in the mainstreams of US public life—even among so-called "literate" groups, even given the enormous alphabetic presence of the Internet and the resurgence of performance-based arts, such as poetry slams. I don't know, maybe I'm wrong. But after years of plying my trade both as an engineer, where I was required to do a good deal of technical writing, and as a poet-prof, I'm convinced that one of the best ways to control groups of workers is to get them to understand letters in particular, and symbols in general, as but means to an end—skills and skills alone. STOP. YIELD. DO NOT PASS GO, DO NOT COLLECT $200.

The point isn't that I don't teach skills, but that part of my service as a teacher—to my students, to society—consists of teaching some rather fine points about writing and reading, points that have all sorts of practical value. The "literary" as I would like to see the term employed would denote not simply the static (by-)products of cognitive or creative faculties, but an active critical engagement with complex values and feelings. And for me, coming from where I'm coming from, losing this latter literary sensibility requires urgent attention. But not simply because "the future of our children's minds depends upon" etc. It's not only "our children's minds" that are at stake here—it's ours. It's our minds that are jeopardized by encroaching corporate-institutional values.

But the blinders I'm busy fretting over are not just about literary language, either. They have all to do with what's meant by literacy, that powerfully fuzzy word that, though it's been around for only a little more than a century, can connote just about anything these days—cultural literacy, functional literacy, computer literacy, critical literacy.

Disparate, competing, often strangely overlapping literacies: poets wedded to a specific aesthetic becoming literate in terms of that aesthetic; an ethnic group whose members share similar cultural experiences constructing conversation around a tacit knowledge of such experiences; a scientific community at odds over a given controversy, yet sharing assumptions about the nature of their inquiry and publishing their results accordingly. Whether you've found yourself excluded from or proficient in a specific literacy, it should be obvious that not all literacies enjoy equal voice in the mainstreams of American culture. Which is to say that not all folks have equal access to the benefits of their sociocultural system. And which is to recognize how conflicted communities can be, neighborhoods can be, networks can be. Am I making myself understood?

Let me try another association: I can recall my dad trying to fill out those damned welfare forms. He had only a high school equivalency, sure, but he could speak English and Italian, and was pretty good with French. And he could write well—I have his and my mother's (often passionate) letters to each other from 1948, when she returned to Europe for several months to visit her folks. Nevertheless, my father had a helluva time with those forms.

But not, not because they were difficult. He knew how to read, and he knew how to write—he possessed those skills. But he had a helluva time with understanding his own social predicament. Like so many first generation Americans of his era, he simply could not grasp what had happened "to" him, he could not (as we say in the biz) theorize his own subject position, his place within the social fabric.

Which is understandable, given what he'd been through and where he'd come from. But which is nonetheless as sure a sign of social injustice as of personal failure. He'd take one look at those forms and his hands would begin to shake. He was ashamed. I was only a kid, but I'd have to help him fill them out. And once in a while I'd even speak with the social workers myself.

The point is that my father had never developed the tools—the critical tools—to think about his social circumstances in social terms. Despite having spent a significant portion of his young adulthood on another continent embroiled in a world war, despite having lived through the hard times of a nationwide depression, he could see himself only individualistically, only as a self-made man. And this created a sort of block in his apprehension of who he was, and could be. Which is to say, could do. If he was self-made, he could attribute his struggles and failures—and we all struggle and fail at times—only to his own un-making, his own undoing. So when social times changed, he had a helluva time changing with them.

Who can blame him? I certainly can't. But I can, from my vantage-point these days, blame the establishment culture that fostered in him such complacency about social factors. When I think of literacy, my father comes immediately to mind: excellent speaking skills, solid writing skills, and yet a curious lapse in seeing himself in any but an individualistic context.

So like I say, after things fell apart, it could only be his fault. And once in a while, when he was drinking, steeped in the past, my mother's. Somebody's.

Despite my having observed this structural blindness in my father, I think I sometimes suffer myself from precisely this ailment: I often find myself attributing my successes and failures solely to my own choices, my own efforts, rather than to my social circumstances. I often don't recognize the array of advantages at my disposal or the liabilities inherent to my situation. After all, I am the oldest son—yet another subject position.

But my students—in terms of their individualistic leanings—most are just like my father: younger than me, but older, a lot older.

* * *

Like I say, I love to write. But I don't always love teaching writing. Part of the reason is that it's become difficult to convey why working or playing with words may be an enlightening, if not useful, thing to do. You don't, or should-n't, teach contemporary literature, or for that matter technical writing, with the assumption that students will understand why manipulating letters, inflecting sentences, or inhabiting paragraphs is a valuable asset, or better, process. The real value of writing may reside less in understanding how-to-succeed-in-business thinking (they couldn't have timed that Broadway revival better) than in understanding why-we-do-what-we-do thinking. And acting accordingly.

When I work with words, as in this essay, I'm alternately revealing some truths about myself and exposing some truths about others—some happy, some not-so-happy, some vital, some less so. Truth in these parts isn't stable, isn't fixed for all time. (Ask me next year what I think about what I've written here.) And I feel a certain responsibilty in saying what I've said. At times, I'm downright unnerved by what I've written.

And I have a tendency in my writing, some would say an annoying ten-dency, to work the writing process into the writing itself. Pause. Fix that typo on "tendency." Reread. [Sigh.] Who am I talking to? Why? Because I like to talk (write) folks into my own uncertainties. Because I like not simply to question my own authority but occasionally to talk through and write through the con-ventions in which this authority resides, and through which we must travel if we wish to write or think something a bit different. At least, this is my convic-tion as a writer.

I find it useful to think of writing as a technology, itself keyed into so many other technologies, human practices. While this allows me to understand my practice in helpfully pragmatic, human terms, it likewise tends to functionalize writing—more means to an end. But it doesn't have to be this way. What's important, as teachers say, is to remember your history.

Writing itself has a long and varied history. And to think of writing both as a technology and as subject to historical contingencies is to consider the various materials of writing—the alphabet, paper, ink, software, hardware, hands—in terms of their participation in material practices. Books didn't always look the way they do now, and won't always look this way. The same may be said about writing instruments. The letters may look similar—the swerves of an *S*, the zigzags of a *Z*—but the modes of production, consumption and distribution have altered both the products and processes of writing in significant ways. And the computer and networking technologies will continue to alter these products and processes further. The cultural feedback loop is completed when our processes are understood as themselves creating new product demands. And someplace in this loop, questions arise regarding human agency and social motivation—what sorts of economies and ecologies of communication are desirable? The sort of public domain we develop in this country depends in large part on how we as a society answer this question. And we as a society comprise disparate groups with differing heritages, aspirations, needs.

Thinking about writing as a technology, as a set of mutable human practices with a long history, has helped me in thinking about my profession, and in thinking about my family. I think of my family now as—yes—trying to communicate, and I see breakdowns in communication as owing in part to all-too-human failures. But despite the fascinating mix of languages and dialects that punctuate my childhood memories, I see more readily now that what at times prevented real communication from taking place was a certain resistance on my father's side of the family to the written word, and a certain reluctance on my mother's side to talking things out. And if this constitutes an indictment, then I'm party to the injured party.

My mother was always the more resilient, intellectually and emotionally, as most women are (I regard this as a predominantly cultural effect). My father— he could deal with violent confrontation, and had a solid sense of right and wrong, even if he wasn't always in the right. But he just couldn't cope very well, as I've indicated, with social changes, and with life-changes. Divorce. Lay-off (the bottom-line consequence of what corporate public relations now euphemistically refers to as downsizing, rightsizing, out-sourcing). Wholesale postindustrial retooling. Again, who can blame him? If my mother needed at times to speak more openly, or more plainly, about her insecurities—with my father, for one—my father could hardly speak at all about his own. But he knew when to raise his voice.

From my father, I learned how to handle conflict. A handy survival skill. From my mother, I learned how to think things through. Also handy. From both, I learned how to treat people fairly, and how to establish intimacy with other human beings. I'm still learning.

* * *

As I mentioned, my wife and sometime collaborator Kass Fleisher and I met online. We're both well-aware of how non-committal such online relationships can be, ASCII pixels underwritten by the absence of flesh-and-blood contact. But as writers, we both understand, too, how important it is at times to be able to enter into a written transaction, to be able to use letters to negotiate differences—at length, with composure. And the digitally-processed world, with its capacity for virtually infinite reproducibility—permanence—and virtually instant alteration—impermanence—helps throw into relief the provisional nature of (pre)recorded truths.

As creative writers, Kass (who writes prose) and I (primarily a poet) find ourselves occasionally at odds with certain of our colleagues. Again, artists in general often hold technology as such at arm's length. My conversion into what some would call an online junkie seems in retrospect inevitable, given my engineering background and fascination with technology, given the fact that, as a white, currently middle-class man, my migration to virtual regions is not demographically improbable. Yet Kass quickly saw the value of online technologies not in terms of any peculiarly technological attraction or fetish, but simply in terms of their value in communicating with friends near and afar, in getting students in her classes to interact with one another, and in providing access to information—whether political, personal, or culinary (we both haunt the Food Network site). In her case, it was only a matter of a few months between her initial online exposure and her decision to develop online discussion lists for each of her classes.

Kass and I got into the habit of semi-weekly phone calls the semesters we were apart. The telephone can be a wretched device for reaching out to touch someone. It always makes you yearn for more. But it's an absolutely indispensable tool for sensing metabolic status—mood—from a distance.

Online technologies, the telephone and its predecessor, the telegraph—these were no doubt developed in part to meet the communications demands of an increasingly mobile workforce. My mother always said it took eight days to cross the Atlantic. I do it these days at a little less than the speed of light.

Yet the "Information Superhighway" is no more a conduit than the air we breathe—we inhabit such spaces. And even this latter analogy breaks down when viewed in light of the necessity for providing enabling structures for public exchange. It's a mistake to see recent attempts to regulate "decency" in cyberspace as akin to legislating clean air. We would do better to learn to live with the all-too-human noise, however noxious or distasteful we may find it. That is, if we wish to speak freely.

Communications technologies have much to do with teaching, too, as with any human practice. I've always been a strong proponent of using our *son et lumière* machines both in and out of the classroom—how could we avoid doing so?—and of monitoring the ways these technologies seem at times to use us. Once any organization gets their hands on a more efficient means, look out: "distance learning" can quickly devolve from reaching students in remote locations to decreasing faculty-student ratios; and it's becoming difficult not to see the Web, however useful an educational tool, as auguring a ubiquitous virtual marketplace. Whatever our technologies, I'd like to see us keep those warm bodies around, intermingling, learning.

However much I falter online or on the line, it seems to me I have many more opportunities in my life—compared to my family's, that is—for seeking out and communicating my daily anxieties, frustrations, doubts, or elations. Sure, I'm a writer. But to those with access to the newer writing, speaking and imaging technologies, there's a certain emphasis on symbolic contact that may prove useful, especially during these economically insecure times. Provided, that is, folks come to understand such technologies as opportunities for growth, self-construction. And provided folks have access.

Still, these newer technologies probably only offset other social losses—losses of community due to job-based relocation (the middle classes are beginning to look a whole lot like a wide-scale witness relocation program), losses of grass-roots political commitment due to multinational-government collusion. We *need* these new communications technologies. So I doubt I'll end up further along, in my "enlightened" approach to social interaction, than my folks.

* * *

That's just it: here I am, wallowing in words on a daily, if not hourly, basis, getting *paid* to do so, no less—and no doubt *no* further along than my various family members in securing interpersonal relationships and the like. So why bother, what's the use?

But whether it comes to you dog-eared, in luminous projections, or accompanied by my scratchy intonations, this essay you're reading or listening to is a document, after all, not an article of faith. There is some measure of faith in believing that some of you may be willing to hear me out, even respond to my provocations. But if part of what I'm about hereabouts is finding ways to listen better—to myself—I nonetheless maintain a healthy skepticism as to my ability to do so. Not least because I understand how tricky these letters can be when it comes to mediating proximities from within.

The thing is, whether wedded to another person or to words, there just aren't any guarantees. There may be tried-and-true methods of expression and communication. But you never can tell what might happen when it comes to working with words, publicly or privately. All you can do is continue writing and talking and listening. And know when to stop writing and talking. This latter is something I need help with, and I'll take all the help I can get. After all, Chicago is a fast town, like my uncle Sam says.

And he knows better than most what a waste a life can be. But he doesn't have to say so. In fact these days, he can't say so—since the stroke, he isn't able to relate his life in detail. He can only look the part. But for those who know how to read him, he means business, and means well.

* * *

(FUTURES, BY THE OUNCE)

you wanted to know what i thought
would happen
so i told you:

how should i know?
   We know that Sing-Sing
   can be magical for tourism.
how should i know
how you live
lived
with these things
leaving behind

so much or
many
without so much as
a qualm?

origins may be unknown
as income
but until
    how to stay someplace
    is to change again
until
and we know this
you and i and
say
dressed again in nothing
but our lives
until
if we do it
it won't be by
ourselves
(listening is not
what we are or were
never were
too good at
no
)
will the process run
away?
will it
not?

there are so many more yet
to listen
to
taxing so many ears
if two
to ground

and grounded out i find
in you or
you
just funning or unjust
fearing to disclose
incompletely
whether partial

but a reason a
reason to till the soil
at times
like these
may be still

taking note
of the details
the disciplined wonder
wondering
how to
      (adjust, adjusted
and it's not about selves—

what
and who
on earth
will prosper
in the coming years

and who will not.

CHAPTER TWENTY-ONE

Technology's Strange, Familiar Voices

Janet Carey Eldred

Although they have no words or language,
and their voices are not heard

Their sound has gone out into all lands
and their message
to the ends of the world

THESE DAYS I CHECK MY EMAIL WITH SOME ANTICIPATION: I'M WAITING, not for the news from an academic colleague, not for the latest conference notice, not for an announcement of a new online archive, not even for the news from the wheaten terrier fanciers. I'm waiting instead, for the "senior special": words from either my mother or my uncle, ages 66 and 71 respectively, and both wired.

My uncle's voice online is strange—he doesn't use paragraphs for one thing, and so all his thoughts flow into one long list. But he sounds particularly strange because I've never before seen his written voice. His wife is a prolific and disciplined letter writer and has long served as the family correspondent. My uncle has always been the handwritten brief postscript at the end of a letter or the voice on the other phone, the one somewhere in the basement that never seems to come in quite clearly. "She can't hear you," my aunt calls out. "Move away from the television, turn off your modem, hang up the other phone," all in that search to find some elusive, magical technological act that turns a faint sound into an AT&T's true voice. I'm beginning to understand that in any discussion of voice, we necessarily hear technology's inflections.

Even when she's on the wrong channel of her cordless phone, I recognize my mother's voice. I'm more familiar with it in all its incarnations because we've had a long history of spoken and written correspondence. When I was in fourth grade, I wrote a completely unmemorable story that impressed a heroin addict who was brought to our parochial school to give one of those "Don't end up like me" testimonials. When the woman asked me to send more of my stories to keep her entertained during the rest of her jail term, I was a writer born. With audience found and purpose worthy, I penned a story, "The Purple Poodle," which my mother stubbornly refused to send. Censored, and indignantly so, I stopped writing. I had no way of seeing what I do now: that it wasn't the story-writing my mother objected to, nor the failure of this particular story (although a story about a purple poodle could hardly have been riveting reading for inmates). It was simply that as a mother, she didn't want me deeply involved in the life of a deeply troubled woman. And, more importantly, she herself wanted to and was to become my audience.

At age 13, I started writing again, this time long, impassioned letters to my mother, mostly trying to persuade her to persuade my father to let me date an 18-year old young man who, I was convinced, was the only one who could possibly understand someone as mature and sensitive and deep as I was. My mother was never persuaded, so I eventually dropped the letter-writing campaign, but not before we had discussed many an issue dear to my teenage heart. It was for both of us a reminder of a childhood lesson: we heard each other when we wrote.

But not when we spoke. It was the early 1970s and the time of the infamous P.E.T. voice. From what I could tell, Parent Effectiveness Training relied on one phrase—"Let's talk about it"—offered up in every circumstance, no matter how varied the occasion, emotion, or motive. I was caught smoking in the bathroom. "Let's talk about it," my mother said. I was caught sneaking out to meet my somewhat older boyfriend. "Let's talk about it," my newly effective parent suggested.

"Let's not," I said, shooting her a look, an exact copy of her angry or impatient one: left brow cocked like a loaded bow, right one arrow straight. Two people in the world can create such a look, and I—through the wonders of genetics—am one of them.

P.E.T., as its cute name suggested, was indeed pet training, and I resented it, more so because it was bad pet training. Even dogs can choose to disobey and are punished for the choice. No trainer makes them bark or whine or otherwise repeatedly give voice to the error. Still, P.E.T. was an even further cruelty because it fed on my mother's natural affection for talk and her faith in the power of language. It transformed her into a psycho-voiced horror.

Thankfully, my mother is a woman of many words with a range of emotions and a slow-boiling temper. P.E.T., though she never admitted it, tired her as well. She needed to use words badly—a wide range of them. So, somewhat newly-widowed and about to be empty-nested, she enrolled in composition, literature, and fiction writing courses at the local community college and wrote intensely for a space of three or four years, the same time that I was finishing an undergraduate degree in English. During these years, my mother was as generous with her prose as I was with my juvenilia and teenage outpourings, while I, with my new college writing, was stingy and safe. She gave me drafts of her literary analysis of D.H. Lawrence's *Women in Love*, a piece in which she tried to come to terms with something completely foreign and frightening to her. The final version contained this instructor comment, "Good revisions, Chris. No philosophizing in this version!" I recognized the academic "don't get too close" rule. It was something I proved my mastery and love of when I gave her, in return for her disturbing, disturbed feeling drafts, a carefully constructed analysis of the same novel.

Undaunted, she gave me letters she wrote to my father—angry, unromantic letters to a partner who had in death deserted her. In return, I shared a class assignment analyzing the nineteenth-century narrative poem, "The Haystack in the Floods"—and, as I headed off to graduate school, my cat named after Morris's heroine.

Finally, my mother showed me part of her in-progress autobiography:

All of my childhood and young adult years, I lived in a New England city of 100,000 people. The homes were old, close together, close to the street and drab. Unlike my other relatives who lived in the Portuguese ghetto, we lived in a fairly nice area of town. Still, it was cramped and old and colorless—even to the black automobile my father drove—"the only way to drive." Our home was furnished with mahogany furniture, which had to be polished, always. There were starched white curtains at the windows. Any piece of silver or brass that was around had to be polished to gleaming. Beds were always made-tight and straight, hospital-cornered.

I wanted to live in a small town, with front lawns. I wanted a house not so scrubbed and shined that there was no time for living.

I did not give her one of my struggling attempts at autobiographical poetry (nor indeed, anything else with which I struggled):

FIRST COMMUNION

The first grade choir sang as we, their superiors, processed
white shoes
white lace
white veils
white prayer books with Corpus Christi embossed in gold.

But once seated, they disappeared
And it was just me
in white, sitting near the altar,
looking up at the gold stars on the blue-sky dome,
hearing not the priest
but a choir of angels chanting the processional hymn.

At home in the living room
family voices conflicted and rose in Jesuit mock debate
brought out on special occasions with the silver.

I left the living room to find my mother who had pinned and repinned lace,

caressed my hair into shape
in rooms without brothers and sisters.

I found her in the kitchen washing dishes.
"I'll never forget this," I whispered passionately.
But she had transformed, forgotten.

And I thought it was the dirty dishes, her aloneness in the kitchen.
I thought she must have heard and felt it just as I had.
But now I know

She heard the discordant voices of a first grade choir.
I wore white and heard angels.

This passion-play poem I kept hidden (and keep hidden still). Instead, I mailed her a *published* paper, which had a chilling effect on our writing swaps.

Or perhaps I'm reading too much in and it was simply life. My mother stopped writing and started living again: the new town became familiar, the new job creative but demanding, her new friends rooted. "Write," I would urge her. But it was difficult for her to find the time—or the pain; she knew no other way to write. And while the P.E.T. voice never returned, an older voice did return with more intensity: her church voice.

First Communion

As a small girl, I remember the passion of my mother's Catholicism. Having survived Vatican II, she now was a passionate new Catholic, singing loudly to the wheat-and-honey guitar hymns, participating in the new liturgy and life of the church. She even worked there. And thus it happened that when I returned home from graduate school for visits, I found congregation members who knew intimately my life details. "This is my daughter who lives in Illinois," she'd say. And then I'd stiffen, waiting for their very physical embrace and the usual refrain, "I feel as if I know you." Still more annoying, I sensed that they never knew the intimate details of her life. I was the post-Vatican II sacrificial lamb, and I knew where she learned the ritual: those writing classes at the community college with the Ken Macrorie textbook. As a Master Catechist (lay people now held impressive titles with their low salaries), she had brought writing to her church work.

What was worse, she too now had a professional voice, and it was mimicking the one I was apprenticing. "I always begin my catechist training sessions with journaling," she told me proudly on one of my visits home.

"You do what?" I say in a tone that should make her rethink this accomplishment. It does not.

"I have them journal," she repeats, pride still there.

"Journal," I say in my best old-fashioned English teacher voice, "is *not* a verb."

But for her it was. As I realized on my last visit home, she had been journaling since the time she was empty-nested in 1980 until just this year, filling on a fairly regular basis a decorative, hardback notebook a year, working at the discipline of it.

> *September 1980:* Read my journal. Too many words. Like weeds in a garden. Choking-hindering-covering up the beauty. Is this what I do with my life too?
>
> *May 1985:* Mea culpa, mea culpa! So long, so long—two weeks—since I took pen in hand, wrote in my journal.
>
> *April 1995:* I am reminded of the importance of telling your story-how we tell it over again and again until it is right.

After I earned my degrees and began my probationary period for tenure, I longed for the exchange of our written voices. But she wasn't writing (or so I thought) and I was writing pieces I no longer reproduced for her. Secretly, I rewrote the ending for a short story she had sent to me some years back. She was dissatisfied with the conclusion, and I thought I might fix it and repair our writing relationship. But I realized almost immediately that editing and writing aren't the same. (It didn't help that the ending I wrote was also bad.) Instead, I asked her to begin a memoir for me, assigned it, so to speak. For a few years she was stymied. Then one day, while cleaning closets, she found some old photographs and began writing about them prolifically, with ease. When I returned for my biannual trips to California, she'd read sections aloud to me as I looked at photographs and listened. It was the relationship we had been practicing for.

Then I married and she remarried and our memoir project halted. For the past eight years, we haven't really shared writing at all. Instead, we've talked by phone about once a week. Superficial stuff, neighbor voice

Wedding

392   *Janet Carey Eldred*

mostly, nothing like those moments when we were each other's private audience. Still, sometimes we spoke seriously—about my marriage, about her marriage, about pregnancies and miscarriages, about adoptions, about health, about distance.

And then her voice began to break, slowly at first. A word slurred here or there. A year later, the slurring grew more pronounced. Entire phrases tripped her up. In mid-sentence, she changed directions so she wouldn't enter the unspeakable. We tried to pretend like her words were all there. But they weren't, and they were leaving quickly. While she could somewhat mask the slurs in person, the phone lines were unforgiving.

Soon, the game was up anyway as the slurring was followed by coughing and then choking. "Allergies," she would say. But by now, we all knew it was more than pollen. *Testing 1-2-3. Modern medicine, can you hear me?*

After the diagnosis (A.L.S.), there was one entire month of silence in which I heard about my mother only through my brother's or uncle's online postings. The phone, which feeds on true clear voices, became obsolete. Enter new technology: my mother was persuaded to go online. Through email I can now hear her written voice again. Sometimes, she writes in a casual phone way, neighbor-speak: so-and-so called, your sister did this, we drove here. But other times I hear the voice of the letters to my father and her photo-memoir. Back we are, I think, to the old times. But these aren't the old times. It's not pen and paper, it's keyboard and modem. And of course, there's the crucial distinction: I'm grown now, a mother myself, and she's dying. Which is why, I'm sure, my mother still prefers, indeed insists on, old technology,

And there is no technology like a visit, which the distance between Kentucky and California frustrates, but an airplane or two and some rental cars make possible. This summer, I see her for the first time since speech left her. Although she has a hand-held Crespeaker, she takes it out mainly for show and for the grandchildren to play with. She does a little demo for me and my son: we hear a male voice, with mechanical inflection. It mispronounces the names of family members unless she misspells them. Instead of the "ee" sound in "Kira," it gives voice to a long "i." Instead of the "oo" sound in "Kuka" (my son's Americanized shorthand for "babushka"), it sounds out the first "u" in "cucumber." The technological voice provided by the Crespeaker is strange and slow—she must pick out each letter one by one with a stick. I look at her thumbs, A.L.S.-crooked now, and realize that typing and writing will soon end. The Crespeaker will provide her future voice, however foreign.

But for now, through a combination of pantomime and writing, my mother converses, electing out of some talk, initiating some, and inserting herself into some. I'm surprised at how easy it is to enter the rhythm:

"What's this wet spot on the floor?" I ask as my bare feet find a cold spot on the carpet. My mother is staying at my sister's: one child (mine), one toddler, one dog, one cat—the wet spot could be anything.

My mother fills her cheeks, and as she does, moves her top hand in an arch over her bottom one, which rests in her lap.

"Ah, the giant bubble-making machine," I nod instantly, smiling because the wet spot is really only soap and glycerin, but most of all, because we're in sync.

My son and I come to the visit, of course, bearing gifts. We buy her a Discman and some compact discs. I choose something light and whimsical—MGM musical hits. She listens to the first track, moves her head as if dancing, and then begins crying, all the time still dancing with her upper body. She tries to move to the next track but, thankfully, does not yet know where the right buttons are and hits the stop. We take the chance to give her the music my four-year old son has chosen: the soundtrack from one of his favorite movies, *The Secret of Roan Inish*, a film about a lost child, and about a seal, who transforms herself into a woman, a wife, a mother, but all the time longs to be free of her body. Eventually, she is freed as she gives into her longing, shedding her human skin and slipping back to the sea. After my plot summary, my mother listens to the music intently, thoughtfully. Her hands form a "T."

"That means thank you," my sisters tell us. Mom nods affirmatively.

"Make a 'T' for grandma," I instruct my son.

"No," he says with the confidence I lack, "I say, 'You're welcome.'"

He has no trouble remembering that she can hear, no inclination to pass over her in a conversation. He does not speak about her in the third person. His two-year old cousin cries when grandma claps, points a finger, and shakes her head; she hates to be scolded.

As my mother eats her lunch, she puts on the *Roan Inish* music to drown out the noise and distractions. And though I don't hear the music, I see distinctly two images: the woman from the film, looking out to sea, longing to shed her human skin, and my mother, concentrating on bringing the blended food from bowl to lips, collecting the extra with napkins, clearing with faint noises the minute grains which, despite their pureed smoothness, deposit in the folds of her throat.

"Look at my shirt," she writes in her notebook when she's finished. She hands the message to my sisters who keep close and quiet watch during meals. "I think I need a bib."

But she doesn't need a bib; she just needs my sisters to share the joke, which they do with both light and heavy hearts.

During this visit, because I am thinking a lot about my mother's writing, I also bring along as a gift a May Sarton journal with an inscription: "From one journal writer to another." She finishes reading most of it while I'm there. Several months earlier when my mother could still speak, she told me she had begun a journal about her illness, thought then to be a stroke. It was to be her recovery journal. I'm not sure if she continued the journal when progress clearly became regress. I haven't read—or been shown—a single entry. Still, she is not going unrecorded. Quite the contrary. When pantomime fails, my mother grabs for her pen and notebook. It sits, like her walker and the notebook personal computer, within arm's reach. In it, she lends us her voices: practical ("Where's the TV control?"), trivial ("That dog's a pain"), thoughtful ("Here I am sitting a death sentence and your cousin is dead at 43. It makes no sense. At least I am not in pain. I live in fear of choking or suffocating, but I am not in pain."). At the end of each day, she has a record of everything she has said. At least theoretically.

"Do you need me to refresh your notebook," my sister asks, tearing out the notebook pages and wadding them for the trash.

All those words, I think. But, of course, my sister is right. No one has their every word recorded. It is only right that the everyday be weeded. And then, of course, there's the issue of privacy, which in my family, is not only a virtue, but a miracle. I know that I myself read several entries back on the page. Anything within view without flipping a notebook page is fair game. And if she naps, even a page flip or two is within limits. When my sisters enter the room, they check the notebook to catch up on anything they've missed. It saves having to recap.

"Oh, I see she didn't like lunch," one sister says to the other. "Next time I'll blend it with yogurt instead of cottage cheese." My mother nods her assent vigorously. Sometimes, my mother herself goes back a few pages and underscores or draws an arrow to save the effort of rewriting.

After lunch, my mother and son rest, she in my sister's guest bedroom, he in my mother's old room. I go with my son, ostensibly to rest, but instead of closing my eyes, I open them, wider than ever before. I do what I love best—archival research—scanning her bookshelf for clues, for words I might before have missed. And I find them—an assortment of her journals. I see her first journal, begun the year my brother, the last of her children, left home. She was preparing to move to a new city and take a new job, which she did, dutifully recording the change—the 1980 journal she devoted to looking back over her life; the 1981 journal she reserved for life unfolding. Then there are three missing years—years in which I know she wrote, the years we exchanged writing. I peruse the journals out of chronological order, as they appear on the shelf. I notice especially the references to me:

A nice end to a 12-hour day. I talked with Janet and she passed her M.A. competencies. But the joy was not limited to that alone. Someone asked her, "What are you going to do now?" and without thinking she said, "Call my mother!" After the blank stare, she realized that that wasn't what the speaker meant—they meant long term. But who cares! To still be #1 in her mind—to want to share her joy with me.
YIPPEE!! JANET IS COMING HOME!!
It's hard to not see your child for over a year—to touch her—to embrace her. The others can't take her place. Each is important—each loved but I can't love her by loving another.—The woman with the lost coin. The shepherd who loses one sheep. My God—the prodigal son.

This entry, I discover after placing them all in order, is from a period during which she centers her journals on her spiritual struggles. My mother, never one to miss a cultural movement, is heavy into meditation and for over a year records her efforts.

Graduation

> Meditating went well. I entered quickly and stayed with it. After some sensory exercises, I moved into painful memories to make sure that I wouldn't run or evade this important part of my meditation journey. I went to Bud's death and memories of the few days preceding. In retrospect, I realized he was dying then and going through the process and I didn't recognize it. He was abnormally upset because there wasn't enough taco sauce for Charles's birthday dinner, he was upset because Janet had Paul over and he wanted him to leave, for the first time ever in our married life we couldn't make love. I stayed with the pain—went through the guilt, felt the loss and asked for help.

In 1985, she began recording and analyzing the spiritual significance of her dreams, a practice she continued for a full year. A few of the entries catch me:

4/2/86

> I awoke (in my dream) to see myself in a mirror. I was amazed that as I slept, my hair grew. I was brushing my hair. The sun shone through it from behind. It was the color of gold. Somebody was watching me and we talked about my hair and how it shone in the sunlight.

Hair. My mother loves to have her hair brushed. It remains a pleasure untouched by A.L.S., one outside the disease's far reach. During my visit, I brush her hair frequently, following the strokes with my hands. Her hair is still thick. It still shines in the sunlight of her recorded dreams.

In her journals, I find her pleasures again and again, but it is the 1984 record of spiritual struggles that surprises me most. My mother has always struck me as someone who had faith, though now, A.L.S. has greatly shaken it. It is difficult to chant *lauds* and *vespers* with no voice, difficult to commune when host can't be swallowed, difficult to sway with a folk guitar when legs buckle beneath body, difficult to mingle with people when A.L.S. tears refuse to recognize restraint, difficult to find peace when A.L.S. ushers in anxiety. With no voice heard crying in the wilderness, the church congregation which enjoyed her labor, her words, for 15 years, has allowed her to lapse into silence.

Instead of home visits, they dedicate a service to her. It is one of life's little ironies that her hairdresser continues to minister freely to her failing body with regular manicures, pedicures, salon cuts-daily massages; meanwhile, her spirit is left sparsely, sporadically attended.

So faith is collapsing, understandably. But the journals showed that she had struggled all along. I consider slipping the two volumes in my suitcase. No one besides me, I think, is interested in her as a writer. And then I look to the front of the 1984 journal—a year that might have been the one in which our exchanges ended, certainly one before our memoir project began. The 1984 journal is inscribed to my sister, Gerianne, who along with my oldest sister, daily feeds her, administers her medications, arranges her medical visits, sponge bathes her, moves her: "Dedicated to Gerianne in thanks for the gift of this book—and the gift of herself." I put the book back on the shelf. There is so much I don't do and don't know. I can barely pronounce the names of the medications my sisters refer to with ease. I pack my suitcases, leaving all the journals in place. Instead, I take what I am certain my siblings don't want: a 10-volume set of short stories (at my mother's urging), and her underscored copies of Macrorie's *Telling Writing*, and Lyons's *Autobiography*. As an after-thought, I take her tattered *Morning Praise and Evensong*. One evening, home in Kentucky, I open the book, and two holy cards fall out, carrying with them the old order, the old sounds. I recite and chant vespers for her, singing the praises for August 15th, the (now unfashionable) feast of The Assumption.

V:	Let my prayer come before You like incense.
R:	The lifting up of my hands like an evening sacrifice.
1 ANT:	Like a cedar of Lebanon I am ráised aloft, / like a rosebush in Jericho.
2 ANT:	Fairer is she thán the sun / surpassing every starry cónstellation.
3 ANT:	The king's daughter enters all glórious / her róbes of spun gold.
Reading:	I grew to my full stature as cedar grows on Lebanon, as cypress on Sion's hill; or a palm tree in Cades, or a rose bush in Jericho; grew like some fair olive in the valley, some plane-tree in a well-watered street. Cinnamon and odorous balm have no scent like mine; the choicest myrrh has no such fragrance. Perfumed is all my dwelling-place with storax, and galbanum, and onycha, and stacte, and frankincense uncrushed; the smell of me like pure balm.
ANT. ZACH.:	Who is this that comes forth like the dawn, / beautiful as the moon, as resplendent ás the sun, / as awe-inspíring as bannered troops.

As promised, my words, the very words I remember her chanting when I was child, rise like incense, assumed, body and soul, syllables carrying meaning, intention.

I couldn't have imagined chanting *lauds* and *vespers* as I packed away *Morning Praise and Evensong* on the last day of my summer visit. Instead I was thinking about her journals, about how I am not the prodigal son, but a married daughter, a college professor with classes about to begin, about how this is not a return, but a visit. And about how visits must end.

"I'll email you," I say upon leaving.

My mother nods affirmatively and moves her hand as if typing on a keyboard. And then she makes the other gesture, hand grasping imaginary phone to ear. She wants me to remember to call, as agreed on, once a week. It is the old technology she prefers, and the old gesture she uses. But it is a new form we must rely on.

"California Relay Operator #335. Please hold one second while I connect you to your party."

And then I hear a sound, a keyboard clicking. I picture her on the other end with a headset, typing intently. I wait

Illness

until the sound stops. A stranger's voice, sometimes female, sometimes male, says "It's mom. Go ahead."

"Hi mom," I say, trying not to sound as if I'm talking in the presence of a third party, "How are you feeling? How was your visit at the specialist's? Go ahead." But we are speaking in the presence of a third person and all the family rules apply: no incriminating information, no emotion, just flat speech, facts, med-speak. Above all else, no tears, not in the presence of a third person—not when tears trigger choking.

My mother responds, but in the stranger's voice again: "I'm O.K. The home nurse will bring a respirator. They want to tubefeed me. Go ahead."

And so we continue, she through the strange operator, me estranged. "Go ahead," I say. "Go ahead," the mother/operator says. A treadmill of words, hard to get off.

"Well, I'm going to go now." A pause, "And your party has hung up. Thank you for using California Relay."

"Thank you," I say to the operator, and somewhat mean it.

I feel relieved. For a week, I know, my mother will be happy communicating with me by email and I will be happy to hear my mother's voice—the old one, the written one. But I know too, that after a week, she will request the T.D.D. phone, "Please call me this week. I want to hear your voice."

And I know that she means it. Because I want the impossible too: I want to hear her sing too loudly in church. I want to hear her neighbor voice. I'd even accept P.E.T. For the first time in my life, I want her to have the last word.

***

Before she died on December 17, 1996, my mother finished writing her memoirs. She left me her journals; she left me a better writing teacher.

CHAPTER TWENTY-TWO

Beyond Next Before You Once Again
Repossessing and Renewing Electronic Culture

Michael Joyce

I. COLOR

WE ARE WHO WE ARE. WE ARE USED TO SAYING SOME THINGS GO WITHOUT saying. This does not. For it is the saying which makes us what we are.

This essay borrows as its subtitle the name of Sherman Paul's collection of "essays in the Green American Tradition", *Repossessing and Renewing*, as a conscious nod and a continued memorial to my mentor, who late in his life offered me the grace of affirming that my hypertextual experiment was for him within the Green Tradition. I also appropriate the title as a charge to myself to take up Sherman's journey in the face of an emerging electronic culture seemingly too ready to discard place, body, and history. Notions like net years and virtual presence threaten the persistence of being which the tensional momentum (to use Carolyn Guyer's phrase for the reciprocal aspect of what we otherwise misrepresent as polarities) of repossessing and renewing call us to. This essay intends a gesture toward what comes beyond next, which is nothing less than what is before us: ourselves as expressed within time and space. We are who we are and we see ourselves in brief light but live always in the shadow of what comes next.

We are surely not the first but without doubt the most self-conscious age to see ourselves as living before the future. In our technologies, our cultures, our entertainments and, increasingly, the way we constitute our communities and families we live in an anticipatory state of constant nextness. There is, of course, a branch of philosophy which concerns those who see themselves as inhabiting the time before the future. That branch, eschatology, is perhaps the archetype of other-mindedness and its itch of desire for constant, immediate and successive links to something beyond.

Eschatological ages have both their virtues and their particular vices. The chief virtue is hope, that constant anticipation of the next which keeps us poised, unsettled and open to change. The chief vice is paradoxically inaction, a self-satisfied belief that there is no need to act in the face of a decisive and imminent history. Like any teacher and writer, I see my task as encouraging virtues and discouraging vices insofar as I can recognize the difference between them. And so as a teacher and writer deeply involved with technology I have for some time been concerned with the passivity that electronic media encourage.

Early on I distinguished between two kinds of hypertext, the merely exploratory and what I termed the constructive hypertext seen as "a version of what it is becoming, a structure for what does not yet exist." More recently as both packaged infotainments on CD ROM and the World Wide Web alike have encouraged a kind of dazzled dullness and lonely apprehension, I have elsewhere proposed that we appropriate as a trope, if not a model, for our interactions an obscure and foreign sense, the middle voice of the classical Greek verb. The middle voice is a form neither active nor passive, yet one which tips the meaning of an action to account for the presence of she who acts or is acted upon.

Our sense of ourselves as actors colors our appreciation of the world in which we act. We are who we are in an active and public sense. We become both the beneficiaries and the constitutive elements of what we might call, to use an old fashioned term, the public good.

In its eschatological aspect (and perhaps in millennial fervor as well) the Web encourages at least an expectation of public goods, if not a public good. There is a wide-spread if naive expectation that material ought to be universally and freely available. "Content-producers" (the obscene worker-bee appellation for artist and writers and thinkers) are urged by commentators like the computer market analyst and erstwhile pop-philosopher, Esther Dyson, to find their incentive and make their living from the value added in lectures, sinecures, and so on, which result from public knowledge of their work. What makes such urging suspect is not its truth value—since what Dyson and others so breathlessly prognosticate is merely the yawning present state of most artists and intellectuals—but rather its *misprision.*

Here, I mean *misprision* both in the common sense of that word as something of an insult and the root sense of *misprision* as a maladministration of public office. For the truth is that the kind of economy which would provide incentive and sustenance to she who provides free value to it assumes a common understanding of the public good which free access to information, knowledge, and art represents.

The question at hand seems to be whether there is any longer a *Public* in either the civic sense or economic sense. The public's expectation that it will have free access for possession of public good(s), cultural or otherwise, is fundamentally constructive. Art and commerce each intend to serve freedom (or at least make that claim). Yet to the extent the Web is predicated on anonymity and irresponsibility, no publics actively assume the responsibility for the goods to which they have access, instead they passively allow it, in greater and lesser volumes like irrigation sluices. So-called value-added schemes (the inner sanctum, the registered shareware user, and intranet) induce this public to increase the inward flow, to let the supposed provider include knowledge of the public holdings. In the net economy you don't take money from people, you give them the right to let you in the place where they spend it. When you charge access on the net it is the same as doing advertising, just a matter of what people will let into their lives.

As artists and thinkers and teachers we want, I hope, to reverse the flow. We want to encourage responsibility for even seemingly passive choices, for virtual worlds, and for alternate selves. We want to encourage a collaborative responsibility for all that we as makers and shapers consider a desirable thing to maintain and for which, we believe, there exists if not a *Public* then various communities willing to sustain it.

This is to summon an other-mindedness which is less a focus on the other than upon our mindedness. Networked learning calls us to be mindful of ourselves in increasingly other roles than that as passive consumer, but rather as co-creator and reciprocal actor.

Lately I find it useful to ask anyone I speak to, but especially my students, to consider what comes next after the Web, not in the sense of the next browser increments, Java applets and operating system transparency, nor the next order of magnitude of increase in instantaneity or availability. At first it is a shock—especially for those who have not lived through the succession of vinyl to cassette to CD to DVD—to understand that I do not mean some mere appliance like the cable-bound network computer. Instead I mean what next literacy, what next community, what next perception, what next embodiment, what next hope, what next light.

Perhaps these are the old habits of a once Irish Catholic boy, or the new habits of an increasingly old-hat hypertextualist, but they are also habits of other-mindedness and, while not restricted to any *techné*, are characteristic of the way we see ourselves through our technologies. Thus, for instance, the Canadian painter and theorist, Guido Molinari turns a color theory into a networked otherness:

> Establishing the capacity of color to bring about an indefinite number of permutations is what, in my view, constitutes the dynamic that produces fictional spaces and gives rise to the experience of spatiality—excluding, by definition, the notion of any specific, given space. It is only through the notion of becoming which is implicit in the act of perception that structure is explored and established as existential experience. (1976, 91)

We are who we are. We see our spaces in how we live our differences and we live in what we see of ourselves within their otherness. This is both the present task and the constant teaching we are called to by any *techné* from the oldest days to the next days which, after all and despite our lights, can only follow the present as we perceive it.

II. BODY

We seem to have lost track of mortality, if not death, in the face of the constant replacement which, as I have elsewhere suggested ("print stays itself, electronic text replaces itself"), is characteristic of electronic text and culture. We know better, but we wish for more.

The body is the fundamental instance of a nextness which argues for the value of what has come before it. It grounds and forms the "existential experience" which Molinari characterizes as "the notion of becoming which is implicit in the act of perception." Because we are going to die, we are the embodied value of what has come before us. I mean (you mean) the ambiguity of "come before" here, both the sense of that which—and those who—precede us, and in the sense of what we sense, as in that which comes before our eyes. In this instance, it may be useful to redeem the euphemism. Because we are going to pass away, we are the embodied value of what we pass through and what passes before us.

It is the push of passing, the fixed stamp of ourselves, that we resist in our embodiment. All this passing leaves us open. "Location is about vulnerability and resists the politics of closure," says Donna Haraway, "feminist embodiment resists fixation and is insatiably curious about the Webs of differential positioning" (196).

In this particular eschatological age we cannot help hearing the present state echoed (or prefigured) in Haraway's use of the word *webs.* Yet I would argue that the solipsistic perspective of self-selection which thusfar characterizes the brand-name World Wide Web (so-called in a time when even ketchup bottles have their own URLs) falls short of embodying the curiosity which drives the most of us to it. Also, and more importantly, the Web fails as yet to render the "differential positioning," the moving perspective (pun intended) from which Haraway can claim that "There is no single feminist standpoint because our maps require too many dimensions." The current web fills the sweet emptiness of space with static and keeps us static in the flow of time.

We are who we are and we stand beside a river. When my Vassar colleague and fellow Sherman Paul protegé, Dan Peck, told me the news of Sherman's final diagnosis, he urged me to write him but wisely warned me against the elegiac in favor of newsiness and shared thinking. Despite Dan's fraternal concern, it was unnecessary advice in the sense that I could not in any wise take it. In my mind, and given my own quasi-Irish predilections, the only news is our mortality and the nature of all shared thinking is elegiac. We are used to saying some things go without saying, but it is the saying which makes us what we are. "Whoever wants to write," Hélène Cixous suggests, "must be able to reach this lightening region that takes your breath away, where you instantaneously feel at sea and where the moorings are severed with the already-written, the already-known. This 'blow on the head' that Kafka describes is the blow on the head of the deadman/deadwoman we are. And that is the awakening from the dead" (58).

My tone with Sherman had always been excessive and elegiac from our first encounter in his office where I begged admittance to his Olson/Creeley seminar claiming the survivor's rights of someone who had failed to honor Olson during a Buffalo youth and now felt the blow on the head. My recollection (very clear actually) was that Sherman shared his own story of (literally) overlooking Olson across Harvard yard, thus taking me into the seminar while surely more deserving, if not necessarily better suited, graduate students were left outside. Likewise Sherman's tone had always been a survivor's and one of shared perspective, looking outward like the figure of Olson's epic Maximus poems. While Sherman may not have used these terms exactly, he often thought about what Haraway calls "resisting the politics of closure" and "differential positioning." Thus when he came to collect (in *Repossessing and Renewing*) his introductory essay to *Walden*, he meditated upon survival and being, casting the question in terms of how we live open to a world in which we are enclosed by responsibilities and the demands of others:

> Writing itself opens a space truly one's own, and when one enters it he is no longer moved by pressures of survival or ambition, but by the wholly different, imperious pressures of intellect and art. Personally, there was nothing paradoxical about my writings about Thoreau: it allowed me, as the classroom did, to live in my vocation, and gave me a way of being-in-the-world and the well-being without which the academic situation would have been less tolerable. (55)

This living-in is what constitutes location on Haraway's, Olson, or Sherman Paul's terms, and what Haraway means by an "embodiment [which] resists fixation." The paradox, of course, is that such an embodiment is bracketed by the saying which cannot go without saying, the elegiac voice which makes us what we are. "Could it be" Sherman wrote in the same afternote quoted above "that Life and our lives, the two words that enclose the [collected] introduction to Walden, were fortuitous?"

Not often an ironist, Sherman had a mortal ironist's retrospective sense of the tensional momentum of ambiguousness of the word, "fortuitous," with its paired qualities of happenchance and lucky legacy. He knew that the young man who by happenchance began his energetic scholarship with Life in the uppercase abstract had been lucky enough to live to a point (not then the end) where he could see the closure of life as lived and bracketed in ourselves.

It is this same bracketing that my old friend, Janet Kauffman means to summon in her novel *A Woman in Four Parts*, "Deprived of the elemental world— and who isn't, with a globe divided, the whole planet sectioned, roofed, cut and pasted—even its waters—what can a body do, if it is a body, but acknowledge, salvage, the elements in its own boundaries. Draw them out. Wring them out. House. Host. . . . [summon] its lost geographies" (12).

Writing to Sherman at a point which bracketed his mortal life, and thus marked the fortuitousness of my own, I was convinced of Kauffman's claim that "it is the dream of the body—to know a place bodily and to say so." (119)

That is, I was convinced that the important questions facing us as an increasingly technological culture will be played out in places like Vassar and similar human communities where we consider and profess the value added by (and embodied in) that community. In my last letter, I tried to tell Sherman how despite (or perhaps on account of) my modest role in its development, it seemed to me that the pervasiveness, immediacy and unmoored multiplicity of electronic culture will inevitably and increasingly throw us back upon human communities as sources of value, identity, and locality.

By that time we had moved to New Hamburg, one of the few towns along the Hudson where the railroad runs on the right side of town and not between town and river. Thus I was aware, as I also told Sherman in this last letter, that although we were only a block and a half away from the river, we were a lifetime away from understanding even the simplest of its rhythms. I was reminded of how in an almost identical context—discussing Barry Lopez's *River Notes*—Sherman had quoted the poet Charles Bernstein about the archaic and its "chastening lesson . . . of our own ignorance and the value in acknowledging it." (1992, 85)

Sherman wrote me back on Easter morning. The crows, he said, had dusted the snow from the branches of the pines. He was feeling briefly better. "There is no assurance that this well-being isn't transient," he wrote, "but isn't the transient, even miracles, which I am beginning to settle for, in the nature of things?" He had been able to walk out, he said, and "inspect the trees I've planted, some 35 years tall, and observe the emerging spring."

He once wrote me that over the years he had planted fifteen thousand trees throughout the eighty acres at Wolf Lake in Minnesota. I do not think it was an exaggeration. In some sense I am among them.

III WOOD

The crows dust snow from the pines.

What, finally, are we to make of the fundamentalist aspects of what seems a wood-pulp fetishism among the post-lapsarian (I won't call them neo-Luddites, Ned Ludd's fight is my fight as well: we are who we are, we have bodies which the machines cannot deny) critics of new writing technologies? Already, of course, my rhetoric barely hides its contradictions. Yet to convey and hide its contradictions in the same gesture is, of course, the purpose of any rhetoric, any tree, or, as we shall see, any screen alike.

We are "finally" to make nothing. Or rather we finally make only ourselves. Yet these selves are made of nothing lasting, wood or otherwise. In the face of such knowledge, or perhaps despite it, it seems that these contra-technologists—the post-lapsarian and eschatological wood sprites—long not to last but to be among the last. In an age of constant nextness, they long to set the limits: write here but no farther, write so that the mark is read in carbon but not in light. In an online exchange about "the cultural consequences of electronic text" (which he contributed to by the faux network of proxy fax), Sven Birkerts seeks to set such end terms:

> I catch suggestions of the death of the natural and the emergence of proxy sen-
> sualism, one tied up with our full entry into a plasticized and circuitized order.
> These synthetic encounters could only become real pleasures—objects of rhap-
> sody—after we had fully taken leave of our senses (literally) . . . A utility cable
> will be beautiful (and not in the surrealist sense) because we will have lost our
> purchase on branch and vine and spiderweb. (1995 online)

The prose is felicitous and rings round like a vine, yet the thrust of what he circles becomes clear upon further viewing. This is a maypole ceremony, a self-garlanding. He seems at first to come (literally) out of the woodwork with the claim for fetish. His stance seems to be that the book, being vegetal (i.e., made of wood), assures that we will continue to inhabit a natural world. Yet the obverse claim, (i.e., that the book in its apparent naturalness has blinded us to vine and spiderweb), is not only equally likely and as easy to sustain but also has been made by both the great men Birkerts admires from Plato to Thoreau and by a woman whom he may and I do admire, Donna Haraway, whose "webs of differential positioning" are considered above.

What really underlies Birkerts's argument, like most reactionary polemics, is I think a profound distrust of the human community and the future. We seem called upon to believe that, because there are apparently no naturally occurring polymers (let us put aside the natural origin of the copper—or the gold!—of the computer's utility wire), Birkerts's or my granddaughter will abandon the grape arbor for the World-Wide Web. I take another view. The so called "real pleasures of synthetic encounters" are just as likely (in a world in which we trust our progeny) to call them more strongly to the real plea-sures of human community and the world around us. To claim that the nat-ural world will necessarily be transformed beyond recognition is proxy sensationalism and impure fetishism. It is just as likely that the natural world will be transformed (which is to say brought back before our eyes) into recognition and that we shall gather there (by the river), not in rhapsodic flight from the net, nor in leave of our senses, but within the leafy garden of forking paths.

Though how we see ourselves as clothed in the natural world (whether shamed into fig leaves or in the splendour of the grass) is an old story and depends upon our understanding of tree and garden alike. In Haraway's explicitly post-Adamic paradise, "Webs can have the property of systematicity, even of centrally structured global systems with deep filaments and tenacious tendrils into time, space and consciousness . . . knowledge tuned to resonance not dichotomy" (194-195).

The turn from dichotomy to resonance is not easy and requires us to see ourselves proprioceptively, i.e., inside out. Regis Debray seemingly makes a more reasoned case for the fiber book as symbolic object rather than a fetish,

Written text converts the word into surface, time into space; but a single graphic space remains a planar surface. Written text, like screened text, has two dimensions; a parallelpiped has three, like the world itself. The memory of the world, materialized in the book, is itself the world . . . A volume of paper and cardboard is a resilient and deepening microcosm, in which the reader can move around at great length, without getting lost in its "walls." The book is protected because it is itself protective . . . One can take one's lodgings there so to speak, even curl up comfortably." (147)

Yet to a feminist critic, this microcosm where the homunculus "can move around at great length, without getting lost in its 'walls' . . . [and] curl up comfortably" must sound (in the root sense) familiar. It is the place where the family is formed, the inside-out which makes us who we are. To paraphrase the title of Irigaray's famous essay, this book which is not one is the multiplicity of the room as womb, not the tome as the world's tomb. The memory of this world, materialized (and maternalized) in ourselves, is itself the world. We are who we are.

Debray's claim (or my appropriation of it here) requires that we read ourselves from without (our lack is that we are one) and thus open ourselves to who we are within (where the difference between who and whom—and womb—here is everything). This requires a sense of not merely our not-one-ness but our doublenesses. Doubleness of course recalls Irigaray's "This Sex Which Is Not One," in which "within herself, [woman] is already two—but not divisible into one(s)—that caress each other" (Irigaray 24). In this doubled sense our memory of the world—and thus of what the book means to enact and the screen aspires toward—is neither an occupying gaze nor a phallocentric taking up of lodgings but rather the to-and-fro flow of meanings in which "the geography of . . . pleasure is much more diversified, more multiple in its differences, more complex, more subtle, than is imagined" (103).

"While the noun screen connotes an outer, visible layer, the verb to screen means to hide," the poet Alice Fulton writes in a meditation on the nature of electronic texts (in a collection edited by Birkerts):

The opposing definitions of screen remind me of stellar pairs, binary stars in close proximity to one another, orbiting about a common center of mass. Astronomers have noticed a feature common to all binaries: the closer the two members lie to one another, the more rapidly they swing about in their orbit. So screen oscillates under consideration. (111)

The place where binary stars lie is, of course, a bed. We are embedded in our differences and we oscillate under consideration. "Genuine books are always like that: the site, the bed, the hope of another book," says Cixous,

The whole time you were expecting to read the book, you were reading another book. The book in place of the book. What is the book written while you are preparing to write a book? There is no appointment with writing other than the one we go to wondering what we're doing here and where we're going. Meanwhile, our whole life passes through us and suddenly we're outside (100).

In that sudden, we read ourselves from without and thus open ourselves to who we are within. What has happened to the wood? the reader might ask. We might misread Shakespeare but not necessarily our natural grain to think that we are as much born into the wood by our mother Sycorax, as born from it by our stepfather Prospero, whose words and books are after all our only evidence that we were trapped there. In any case, whether we are fathered by tempest or a grim fairy tale, our truest nature (or at least our dream) is that we have to move. "In order to go to the School of Dreams," Cixous says

> something must be displaced, starting with the bed. One has to get going. This is what writing is, starting off. It has to do with activity and passivity. This does not mean one will get there. Writing is not arriving; most of the time it's not arriving. (65)

Not arriving, where have we come to? We can respond affirmatively, even enthusiastically, to Debray's claim that "The technological ecosystem of the textual relates back—in the same way as any microsystem—to the wider scale of cultural ecology," and even accept the proposition which he suggests leads from it as "something that bears a strong semblance to an anthropological constant: human communities *need* a unique defining space to belong and refer to" (148, his italics). However doing so does not, I think, oblige us to submit entirely to his further, enigmatic claim to "formulate it all too laconically: *no culture without closure* (and time alone as the defining medium of anything) *cannot close it off*" (148, his italics).

There is a closure which does not close us off but which, while leaving us open, encloses us. "Skin wraps body into a porous and breathing surface through which a variety of exchange takes place," the artist Heidi Tikka suggests in her essay "Vision and Dominance—A Critical Look Into Interactive System" (1994). Tikka suggests a notion of *inter/skin* as a correction to the penetrating phallic gaze of *interface*. Skin, she says,

> covers the face as well, but the communication skin participates in: touch, secretion, receptivity and sensitivity—when blushing, having goose pimples, shedding tears or sweating—remains the underside of human communication. The incalculability of these signs prevents them from being valid currency in the phallic exchange. In the economy of phallic representation skin does not count, it functions as a material support. (online)

Skin is screen. "I think about these things we create—these hypertexts—as part of our skin," "Martha Petry argued in her essay, "Permeable Skins, "as permeable and open as the eyes on our faces . . . what we see here . . . is the outer membrane, the surface layer, the rind or peel of fruit, a film on liquid." (1992,1) Tikka evokes Irigaray explicitly—and both Petry's and Donna

Haraway's notions of permeation implicitly—in arguing that "an inter-skin has a great sensitivity and completion for receiving a variety of signals from the environment and capability of changing its state accordingly." This is a literacy which offers us both well-being and the being in the world that Sherman Paul summoned from Thoreau; one which rather than leaving us in Birkerts terms "fully taken leave of our senses (literally)" instead for Tikka sensually "connects with other surfaces and conducts and circulates information in a network of similar surfaces."

In the place of Debray's laconic formulation "no culture without closure," we are faced with a Lacanic counter-proposition of encompassed enclosure. Birkerts's fear that we will take leave of our senses is posed as a fear that we will lose sight (of ourselves). Yet it really is a fear that we will lose touch with parts of ourselves. "The contemporary pressure toward dematerialization, understood as an epistemic shift toward pattern/randomness and away from presence/absence," N. Katherine Hayles suggests,

> affects human and textual bodies on two levels at once, as a change in body (the material substrate) and a change in the message (codes of representation). Information technologies do more than change modes of text production, storage, and dissemination. They fundamentally alter the relationship of the signified to the signifier. Carrying the instabilities implicit in Lacanian floating signifiers one step further, information technologies create what I call flickering signifiers, characterized by their tendency toward unexpected metamorphoses, attenuations, and dispersions. (1993, 76)

The fear of losing the world is a fear of dismemberment, we close ourselves off into the zipped, conservative ground of the male gaze and colonial vista alike. Against such a fear of loss, there is the countervailing play of surfaces, the joy of several worlds at once, passing and multiple. The "inherently diffuse surface" of skin, says Tikka, "changes identity, sometimes dissolving itself into another surface in a way that makes the identification between the two impossible . . . [and] refrains from the production of a fixed subjectivity."

In place of the male orgasmic rush of rhapsody, there is the fugal female orgasmic of not-arriving; in the place of Birkerts's "purchase on branch and vine and spiderweb" (where "purchase" is a verb of knot and lever and gather), there is the weave (the textus) of unexpected metamorphoses, attenuations, dispersions and the unmoving silence upon which Ezra Pound ends his Cantos (1972):

> I have tried to write Paradise
> Do not move
>   Let the wind speak
>   that is paradise.
>   (Canto CXX)

IV. LIGHT

We hear the wind through the trees as whispering music but we read it as varieties of light. In the play of inherently diffuse surfaces we hear the world speak.

Before the book of fiber, there was the book of skin, whether the vellum of the codex or the earth's own skin, clay tablets worked in dampness and dried in wind and light. The mediums of exchange for the skin are light, air, and water. Let us examine them in order, or rather as if they had an order.

The woodpulp fetishism of post-lapsarian critics seems at first a mistrust of the eye and a privileging of the hand. Their longing for the "resilient and deepening microcosm" of paper and cardboard seems a wish to touch the wound of culture and in that gesture heal over the openness which is its possibility. Yet there is a sense of reading which seems to favor the eye and mistrust it in the same gesture. In fact it mistrusts gesture, which is afterall the work of surface, and thus demands to inscribe it in the mark.

A year ago, the wind of descending helicopters spoke through the bare winter trees upon the campus where I teach, and thereafter I saw this mistrust in action. My Vassar College colleague, Don Foster, in the course of using computer tools to establish Shakespeare's authorship of *A Funeral Elegy* had drawn international media attention. Now the media had asked him to turn his attention to another, then more notorious, anonymous authorship, that of the political satire, *Primary Colors*. In writing about Shakespeare's text, Foster says

> *A Funeral Elegy* belongs hereafter with Shakespeare's poems and plays, not because there is incontrovertible proof that the man Shakespeare wrote it (there is not) nor even because it is an aesthetically satisfying poem (it is not), but rather because it is formed from textual and linguistic fabric indistinguishable from that of canonical Shakespeare. Substantially strengthened by historical and intertextual evidence, that web is unlikely ever to come unravelled. (1082)

Yet what served for Shakespeare and brought Foster his scholarly reputation and media notoriety alike did not serve entirely for the author of the political satire. The helicopters had come because Foster all but conclusively identified the author as the *Newsweek* writer, Joe Klein, a story which CBS News and *New York Magazine* reported in February 1996. Yet it was not until the following July, when *The Washington Post* engaged a handwriting expert to examine handwritten emendations on the galleys of the novel, that Klein and his employer owned up.

We might mark this down as a minor mystery, a passing event in the history of literacies and the further adventures of a premier Shakespeare scholar and technologist, were it not for what it suggests about the post-lapsarian insistence upon the place of marks. Foster couches his own methodology in a positivist science in which "researchers can now test . . . matters [such as authorship] objectively, by mapping the recorded language of an archived writer against the linguistic system shared by a community." (1083) We can put aside for the moment the question of authors whose works are not archived (or indeed whether archives of pulp or of light are likely to be more lasting than Horace's bronze), and we can even defer the question of where and how we find the marks of community, to ask a more fundamental question.

Does the mind leave a mark?

This question is of course another way to address our mortality, the mark we leave upon the world. Is the person in the physical mark or the mind's mark?

Foster's screens played across the body of text and yielded light. The methodology for Shakespeare was the same methodology used for the lesser scribe, locating "an extraordinary match between the distinctive vocabularies [as] a function not principally of verbal richness but of individual preference or habit . . . [as well as] fairly ordinary nouns used as only [the author] is known to have used them" (1083). We can of course see neither match nor preference, neither habit nor the idiosyncratic and thus not either the extraordinary ordinary, in a single screen or even any sequence of them. Unlike the characteristic whorls and slants which are the handwriting analysts stock in trade, the mark of the extraordinary ordinary flits across a screen in instances of light whose recurrences mark Foster's web of "textual and linguistic fabric."

A liar may not own up to a fabric of light (itself another name for skin). Nor, it seems, might a post-lapsarian. Both however seem susceptible to certain carbon forms, dried pulp and the etched mark. This mistrust of light on the computer screen is, I would suggest, a variety of our mistrust of the body in and of itself. To the extent that light and its dimming and recurrences mark the temporal, it is likewise a mistrust of our own mortality. Finally, it seems a mistrust of the locus of meaning which, as Foster's methodology suggests, is shared by a community. We cannot be sure what we see except in community. For what we see, as René Angelergues suggests, is itself woven with what we have not been able to see:

> Perception, hallucination, and representation are part of the same process. The object to be perceived is in no sense an 'initial condition' that creates a causal chain ensuring the object's imprint (image or information) in a focal centre, but rather a complex and conflictive process that mingles and opposes knowledge and recognition, discovery and familiarity. (461; cited and translated by Ottinger 26)

I believe the mind leaves its mark in the light filtered through the snow-dusted branches of thirty-five year old trees. In some sense, I am among them.

V. AIR

We are afraid to find ourselves in air. Dreams do this to us, as do leaps, journeys, syntax, the weave of perception, hallucination, and representation, the book the Web and the network as well.

Wind is sound. Recurrence is the sounding of memory in air. Air is spiritus, breath, whisper, ghost.

We have talked about all this before. We are who we are. We are used to saying some things go without saying. This does not. For it is the saying which makes us what we are. Recurrence is the sounding of memory in air.

This is child's play. Anyone who has read my writings about electronic texts recognizes a characteristic, not to say obsessive, rhetorical stratagem in them (and thus here). The recurrence (sometimes what we call "whole cloth" though we mean patchwork) of a phrase or paragraph (and at various times as much as a page). Self-plagiary is proprioception. Anyone who has read my writings about electronic texts recognizes the recurrence of Horace's phrase from *Ars Poetica* in them (and thus already above here): *exegi monumentum aere perennius.* "I have built a monument more lasting than bronze."

"As children," write Cara Armstrong and Karen Nelson, "we experience space through all our senses and we have an intimacy with place. Through monuments and rituals we try to recall this intimacy and awareness." (¶1)

The mark of light is sounded in recurrence. That sounding is the body's surface. These short sentences form a pattern not an argument. Its monument is what Lucy Lippard terms overlay:

> It is temporal-human time on geological time; contemporary notions of novelty and obsolescence on prehistoric notions of natural growth and cycle. The imposition of human habitation on the landscape is an overlay; fertility—"covering" in animal husbandry terms—is an overlay; so are the rhythms of the body transformed to earth, those of sky to the land or water. (1983, 3-4)

Overlay likewise offers a sense for understanding what, in a discussion of a student's (Ed Dorn's) work in terms of *his* mentor and teacher (Charles Olson), Sherman Paul discovers (he writes this book, *The Lost America of Love*, in short sentences that form a pattern not an argument) in Olson's sense of *Quantity.* Olson says it used to be called *environment* or *society.* He doesn't elucidate. Perhaps he suggests enough when he says it's the present time, characterized as it is by an increase in the number of things, by the extension of technology and "the increase of human beings on earth." Quantity as a factor of civilization, modern culture, cities: "the dominant, prevailing culture within which—against which—the deculturized [*dispossessed*] must learn to survive" (1981, 134, his italics and brackets).

The oscillation of within-which-against-which has become a familiar pattern for us, a ritual. "Who has seen the wind?" sang Yoko Ono, "Neither you nor I/But when the trees bow down their heads/the wind is passing by." We learn to survive our deculturization in overlay and passing-by as well as in what Cara Armstrong and Karen Nelson see as "carry over":

> Rituals are determined modes of action and interaction which can expand a person's relationship to the landscape and carry over time; past merges with an already obsolescing present and projects into the future . . . As (re)w/riting and

(re)reading, ritual can be used . . . to exploit the gaps within a system determined by the patriarchal hegemonic culture . . . [and is] a response to a genuine
need on both a personal level for identity and on a communal level for revised
history and a broader framework.(¶5)

The web is now the place of quantity in Olson's sense, and its quantity here
too is increasingly termed an environment or society. As a ritual space, the Web
encourages us to seek some sense of Armstrong and Nelson's "revised history
and a broader framework." Yet we are right to wonder whether in any sense (or
in which of our senses) its ritual action offers the expansion of our relationship to landscape which Armstrong and Nelson argue carries (us) over time.

Though the verb for it is *surfing*, we rather wade into web, approaching as
tentatively as someone's grandchild wades through bramble and approaches
branch and vine and spiderweb. Though much is made (and marketed) of its
search structures, the Web is not yet a monument enough for us. We as yet lack
intimacy with its places enough to know where to look. We are as yet only at the
first stages of its overlay, and our searches are thus repetitions like waves. These
waves too are marks of mind and fall into a ritual pattern of what we might call
confirmation, disclosure, and contiguity. We approach the space of the Web as
water and reach into its shallows and its depths. Sometimes, we reach into this
space seeking merely the confirmation that one or another part of the
world/body is here too, whether a list of species of birds or a tea merchant's
inventory of mountain tea. Other times, we seek disclosure, hoping to experience that an unanticipated part of the world/body is here, whether in the text of
a poem about the wind or the homepage of a cousin. Once comfortable with
this wave-like rhythm of confirmation and disclosure, we seek the broader
framework of contiguity, the changing pattern of smooth stones beneath an
ever changing surface. In contiguity, we confirm our sense that one or another
part of the world is adjacent and contiguous from time to time by turns.

In this way, the Web transcends the inevitable spatiality of other hypertexts
by becoming primarily ritual, nomadic and ephemeral and thus also richly
overlaid with our sense of space and time and body. By circling round, our
senses of confirmation, disclosure, and contiguity upon the Web, we find ourselves moving from the shallows and dropping off into sense. A recognition of
traversal prompts my Vassar student Samantha Chaitkin to offer "a brand-new
metaphor" in her critique of Storyspace and other Cartesian hypertext
representations:

> I'd rather . . . jump up into the air and let the ground rearrange itself so that I,
> falling onto the same spot, find myself somewhere different. Where am *I* going
> as I read? No, more where is the Text itself going, that I may find myself there.
> (unpaginated)

What is the place where we are if it is not the place where we think we are
when we are there? Where is the text going if it is not the place where we are
when we are on the network? Where do we wade and from what body? Where

is the whir of the wind? (These short sentences form the pattern of an argument. Stones along a stream or seafloor.)

We are where we are. We fall into the same spot yet find its difference in ourselves. This cannot go without saying, and yet the apparent placement of the network, the puerile illusion of virtuality, tempts us to do so. The importance of our embodied placement, our actual reality, arises not despite but because of our increasingly networked consciousness. We are (again) called not to take leave of our senses but to repossess and renew them. "Only in a culture in which visuality dominates," says Heidi Tikka,

> is it possible to assign a reality status to a visual representation in which some sound effects may enhance a non-tactile, tasteless and scentless world. Furthermore, the reality of the VR is not essentially visual, but . . . is made of a three-dimensional Cartesian grid in which the movement of the user can be traced as a series of exact coordinate points and which therefore locates the user as a punctual solid object among other solidly rendered objects. . . . The subject of the VR finds himself enclosed into a dataspace and deprived of a corporeal body. In the VR-space the abstracted vision becomes associated with a gesture. The pointing gesture moves the user forward in the constant state of erection. (online)

There is a sense of reading which mistrusts gesture, which is after all the work of surface, and thus demands to inscribe it in the mark rather than the gesture. Such mistrust is a maypole ceremony, its insisted mark a self-garlanding. Instead of this ceremony of erection I have elsewhere characterized hypertext in terms of contour: "how the thing (the other) for a long time (under, let's say, an outstretched hand) feels the same and yet changes, the shift of surface to surface within one surface which enacts the perception of flesh or the replacement of electronic text" (280). We are where we are, and it is a mistake to claim, even in cyberspace, that we are anywhere else. "Interacting with electronic images rather than materially resistant text," N. Katherine Hayles writes

> I absorb through my fingers as well as my mind a model of signification in which no simple one-to-one correspondence exists between signifier and signified. I know kinesthetically as well as conceptually that the text can be manipulated in ways that would be impossible if it existed as a material object rather than a visual display. As I work with the text-as-image, I instantiate within my body the habitual patterns of movement that make pattern and randomness more real, more relevant, and more powerful than presence and absence. (1993, 71)

The memory of the world, materialized in the body, for which both the book and the screen stand as repeated instances of embodiment, is itself the world. This is the nature of the erotic, another name for mortality and our presence in a real world. "Through ritual, individual, private actions can become part of a shared act," write Cara Armstrong and Karen Nelson,

Through repetition, actions can take on additional significance. Repetition can enlarge and increase an idea or purpose and may also suggest eroticism. Ritual, as shared acts, are potentially inclusionary. Ritual layers daily experience with the cyclical and the symbolic. (online)

We are who we are. We are where we are. Layered and overlaid, we make a world within our bodies.

VII. WATER OR THE BODY AGAIN

The mediums of exchange for the skin are light, air, and water. We examine them in order to see ourselves as who we are.

Water is the figure of the body as a medium of exchange. There is the formless place where the world is made. Heidi Tikka lingers like water over the smooth stones of the "continuous, compressible, dilatable, viscous, conductible, diffusable" qualities which Irigaray describes in "Mechanics of Fluids." In that essay, Irigaray notes how fluid "makes the distinction between the one and the other problematical: . . . already diffuse 'in itself', [it] disconcerts any attempt at static identification ." (111)

Mostly water ourselves, we are singularly plural and simply mindful of its complexity. In her own critical appreciation of Irigaray's notions of fluidity, N. Katherine Hayles observes how "within the analytic tradition that parses complex flow as combinations of separate factors, it is difficult to think complexity . . . [P]racticioners forget that in reality there is always only the interactive environment as a whole" (1992, 21).

We read ourselves in ebb and flow within the whole of water. The space of our mortality is the singularity of water, which turns by turns from solid to liquid to air. We mean within a flow of meanings, ourselves the repeated eddy of erotic gesture, ourselves the screen which, in Alice Fulton's phrase, "oscillates under consideration," ourselves as well the moist and knowing eye, a flow over the skin or pulp of the page. We ourselves likewise mark and mean the repeated touch of surface to surface within one surface, cyclical and symbolic, which enacts the perception of flesh. Beyond next before us once again we ourselves discover the current flow of electronic text within a desert of silicon. In not yet published speculations, Alison Sainsbury, considers the reader as the literal (I am tempted to write littoral) site of inspiration, breathing out breathing in, and thus casts the act of reading in terms of lung or gill, the membrane and surface of vital exchange. She insists she means no metaphor but a cognitive theory; meaning is an exchange of moisture. Our selves and our cells argue as much.

A similar exchange prompts Carolyn Guyer to conceive meaning in terms of an estuary which

at any moment contains some proportion of both salt water and fresh, mingled north then south then north again by the ebb and flood of . . . tides. Right here is where I am. . . . The present is a place as much as it is a moment, and all things cross here, at my body, at yours. It is where I consider the past, and worry about the future. Indeed, this present place is where I actually create the past and the future. (157)

She insists she means no metaphor but an actual ontology: "Nature is what we are, and so cannot be opposed to, or separate from, humans and their technologies." What comes beyond next is likewise inseparable and nothing less than what is before us: ourselves as expressed within time and space.

"When we get older," Sherman Paul writes about Robert Creeley's poem, "Later," we especially want the comfort of intimate space

> Where finally else
> in the world come to rest—
>
> By a brook, by a
> view with a farm
>
> like a dream—in
> a forest?

We move toward the feminine, toward repose. We wish to enter the *gymnaeceum,* the house (always maternal) of all houses, that of our childhood. (1981, 62)

Because it is named as such, because it is cast as both a wanting and a wish, this space seems different to me (it is different) from Debray's protected and protective space where one "can take one's lodgings . . . so to speak, even curl up comfortably." Sherman Paul's space is explicitly not a return to room (or womb) but an older space beyond next before you once again.

This orientation was something he wrote about explicitly, elegiacally, himself coming round again to the fortuitously bracketed senses of doubled life with which he began his scholarly journey. In "Making the Turn: Rereading Barry Lopez," Sherman accounts the body's exchange:

It is salutary to divide the day between the work of the mind and the work of the body—the *vita contemplativa* and the *vita activa,* the latter, as I practice it, *menial,* according to Hannah Arendt—and it is necessary. The work of the body, outdoor work, is *out:* To do such work is a primary way of being-in-the-world, of finding oneself in the cosmos, in touch with things, physically "at home." The work of the mind, indoor work, is *in,* doubly interior: To do such work is often a way of withdrawing from the world, of living with its images. I use the spatial distinctions (*in/out*) that accord with the dualisms of *mind/body, subject/object, self/world,* but these are dualisms I wish to overcome: when *out,* by a participatory activity of mind; when *in,* by a meditative activity that seeks in words to hew to experience. (68, his italics)

Inevitably, this meditation on Lopez turns to water, "to the natural relationships of the little-traveled upriver country." Lopez, Sherman says, has "undertaken an archetypal journey, a quest of the kind that distinguishes our literature, *The springs of celebration:*"

How often have we sought them in childhood and a world elsewhere; how seldom in the heart of darkness. Yet isn't the significant aspect in this instance the extent to which [Lopez] has made ecological study serve this end? the extent to which he has gone *out* in order to come *in*? With him, it may be said, the discipline of ecology heals the psyche and the healed psyche serves the unhealed world.

Here he finds the anima and dances with her . . . This is told, appropriately, in the clairvoyant manner of dream or fairy tale, and it is recognized as such, as a mysterious occurrence whose moral meaning is nevertheless clear. *He dances and tells stories*: with these sacred gestures he celebrates the springs. (84-85, his italics)

Growing old with technology, neither opposed to nor separate from nature, we watch water as if it were a seduction. Here we find the anima and dance. Form forming itself. Form drawing us to ourselves.

The charms of hypertext fiction, my dancing stories and technology, are those of any seduction, the intensity of likemindedness, a feeling that the story (and its teller) somehow match the rhythms of the stories you tell yourself. The vices are likewise those of seductions. What you think you see as your own mind is, as always, another's. Things pass. The links are like comets on the surface of a pond, doubly illusory.

What comes next? Will the Web supplant or supplement the world or book? When we get older we move toward the feminine, toward repose. I'm a little tired of the supplant and supplement question (even if I am in some sense guilty of forwarding it). Linear and hypertextual narratives seem a polarity but are only opposite shores of a stream. Our literacy is *littoral*. There are no linear stories, only linear tellings or readings. *Supplant* is a strange word (the dictionary renders it in terms of "intrigue and underhanded tactics"); I prefer succeed, with all its senses. If the linear narrative, insofar as it is aware of itself as a form, has always wished to succeed itself (as it seems, at least by the witness of its practioners, it has), then it is unlikely that the hypertextual narrative will be any less ambitious.

Water does as much as it travels or eddies, changing change, successively taking the same form. What comes next? What next literacy, what next community, what next perception, what next embodiment, what next hope, what dance, what home, what next light.

We will have to watch. "It is through the power of observation, the gifts of the eye and ear, of tongue and nose and finger," Barry Lopez says

that a place first rises up in our mind; afterward, it is memory that carries the place, that allows it to grow in depth and complexity . . . [W]e have held these two things dear, landscape and memory. . . . Each infuses us with a different kind of life. The one feeds us, figuratively and literally. The other protects us from lies and tyranny. (188)

We will have to watch. Consoled by a belief that nature is what we are, it remains to be seen whether we can move enough toward the "clear space" which Barbara Page locates within "the conscious feminism of the [experi-mental and hypertextual] writer." What "animates her determination"

> is not simply to write but to intervene in the structure of discourse, to interrupt reiterations of what has been written, to redirect the streams of narrative and to . . . clear space for the construction of new textual forms more congenial to women's subjectivity. (¶26.)

As artists and thinkers and teachers, we long for animation, interruption, redirection and construction. What comes next is before us, in landscape or memory alike. What scours the clear space are the waters of repossessing and renewing. Ever afloat in a journey to the place beyond next, we begin to settle for transient miracles before us once again, whether the truth of crows on an Easter morning or the lines which end Sherman Paul's *The Lost America of Love* and this essay as well:

> We must go back to sets of simple things,
> hill and stream, woods and the sea beyond,
> the time of day—dawn, noon, bright or clouded,
> five o'clock in November five o'clock of the year—
> changing definitions of the light.

CHAPTER TWENTY-THREE

Everybody's Elegies

Stuart Moulthrop

*T*HESE LAST YEARS OF THE CENTURY ARE A FAT TIME FOR STORYTELLING IN THE non-fiction, retrospective vein. Biography and memoir, albeit mainly of the ghostwritten "celebrity" stripe, are among the few categories spared the recent retrenchments in the book business. American readers seem to have a limitless hankering for intimate disclosures, especially of high life. *Es war immer so,* the History Channel would no doubt remind us, itself a further illustration of the market for war and remembrance, a round-the-clock cinematic scrapbook of the GI generation. And of course the cable box also has settings for other mellowing cohorts (*Nick at Nite*, VH-1, Cartoon Network). The biological urge to re-present the past, along with the canny economics of stock footage, have made a national pastime out of looking backward.

No wonder then that the four preceding essays feature so much retrospection. The academic discovery of personal narrative makes sense for many reasons, partly on pedagogical grounds (see Eldred's reflections on Macrorie), partly as sexual/cultural politics (hear in Joyce's piece so many voices of women, notably Cixous). This is largely to the good. Personal narrative testifies that minds are inseparable from gendered, class-identified bodies. Bodies experience history, and in a more direct sense, time. Memoir brings us back to ourselves and thus perhaps to our situated selves. The ability to recover even a personal past is essential in an age of mass-mediation, as Greg Ulmer has shown in arguing for "mystories" (Ulmer).

At the same time, though, this urge to recover what we were is also a cultural product, an idol of the generation, if not the tribe. The stories told here might be arrayed along a birth-ordered scale: Wysocki and Johnson-Eilola, apparently the youngest of the group, give us scenes of consumption reading or watching television (see their account of literacy in "The Man Who Shot Liberty Valance"): *la récherche des textes perdues.* Eldred and Amato, who seem roughly of an age with this writer, offer stories about hard life lessons that include the hardest of all, the decline and death of parents. In Joyce's essay, as you might expect from a consummate storyteller, the tendency of all this recollection falls most clearly into focus. The story woven through Joyce's essay concerns the final illness of a mentor and teacher, an experience that instigates an accommodation of the present self ("We are who we are") with both preconditions and posterity. Joyce writes the self in time and against what time has taken, which is to say, he does that quintessentially human work called mourning. There is a name for this sort of writing: *elegy.*

Elegy is an important intellectual pleasure, though like all pleasures it is subject to abuse. It may be possible to insist too much on the priority of the past, as any late-night viewer of "Year-by-Year: 1953" will recognize. There is, after all, something to be said about the present and the immediate future, little as we may wish to consider these rude realities that lack the charm of age. The younger you are, the more inclined you will probably be toward this critique. Generation X has little time for its elders' nostalgia and has yet to recognize its own susceptibilities. Sven Birkerts tells of a review of his *Gutenberg Elegies* by a twenty-something columnist somewhere on the Internet. "If all Birkerts wants is a return to the past," this writer allegedly said, "well, fuck that" (Birkerts). To which the usual responses suggest themselves—it sure is fun to say "fuck" in public, isn't it?—but curmudgeonly sneering does not undo the plain fact of rejection. "You can't let the little bastards generation-gap you," William Gibson counsels. As if we have a choice. We boomers have all been here before, and what goes around comes around. The familiar gap yawns behind us, stimulating a certain suspicion: *pace* Birkerts, maybe the kid has a point.

The mention of *Gutenberg Elegies* is of course deliberate, since that work comes in for specific criticism in two of the essays here. There are elegies and then there are elegies, or so some of us would like to think. Meaningful distinctions can probably be drawn. Joyce is no doubt right to criticize "contra-technologists" who "long not to last but to be among the last," wishing to "touch the wound of culture and in that gesture heal over the openness which is its possibility." By the same token, though, those of us more favorably disposed toward textual machines should probably examine our own cultural wounds, and likewise our interest in possibility. When we spend so much time looking backward, do we lose sight of what lies dead ahead? Are there other stories we should tell along with our recoveries of the past?

The four essays here do not completely overlook contemporary questions and controversies. Turning toward the past does not excuse one from the present. Each of these pieces begins with the recognition that "literacy," a complex set of assumptions about reading, writing, and their social consequences, has undergone important transformations in the latter half of the century. Both Eldred and Amato tellingly connect typographic literacy with particular economic realities, recognizing that writing is indeed itself a technology. These observations could lead to important insights about literacy in the age of commercial information. The crucial question posed by Joyce—what comes after the World Wide Web?—points more directly along this line of inquiry. The speculations (all too brief) on hypertextual literacy in Wysocki and Johnson-Eilola's essay sketch out some interesting answers. Nonetheless, these moments of engagement are largely just that—momentary—and the general tendency of these essays runs elsewhere, mainly to storytelling and retrospect. A very critical reader might find this evasive.

This reader is not so quick to criticize, mainly because he understands how hard it is to answer questions like what are you doing after the Web? Asked to foresee the next five years of media history, most academics might well prefer to tell the stories of their lives. What's next? How should I know?—We are who we are. It is easy to share Joyce's professed weariness with the technology-and-literacy polemic, the tedious quarrel over whether electronic writing extends the print tradition or threatens to drive it under:

> I'm a little tired of the supplant and supplement question. . . . Linear and hyper-textual narratives seem a polarity but are only opposite shores of a stream. Our literacy is littoral. There are no linear stories, only linear tellings or readings. Supplant is a strange word . . . I prefer succeed, with all its senses.

Nothing succeeds like succession, the affirmation that life and literacy go on basically unaffected by so-called revolutionary ruptures. This is common ground (see Moulthrop 1991). We believe that what comes next will necessarily spring from what has been before; the reasoning is tautological but no less valid for that. The sense of wholeness is important here. No surprise then that Joyce's metaphor is "littoral," drawn from (or upon) the waters and the earth. Many of us have long believed that questions of media involve complex, co-evolving systems or ecologies, opposite shores of a stream where both shores and stream belong to something greater. This conception is indispensable.

Unfortunately, it is also slippery and ambiguous. To begin with, the river vision like any ecological metaphor risks confusing propinquity with identity. It is important to realize that the two shores define separate cultural regimes. Their paths are approximately parallel. They are also distinct. We can trace the course of the river but can only stand on one shore at a time. That is, electronic writing succeeds itself, not the culture of print. There is no compelling reason to think of writing on the Internet as print by another name. To return to the metaphor, the shorelines cannot meet, else the figure would shift from river to lake, from current to reservoir, from flow to circularity, a very different scheme. More about this later.

Joyce acknowledges this separation, going on to say that hypertext, like print, can be expected to succeed itself. But the littoral image has other implications. Like all metaphors, this one exceeds its ostensible limits. Propinquity is not identity; the shores are only more or less-parallel. The river may widen or narrow. Littoralism, unlike (this) literalism, knows no pedantic exactness. Which is to say that language and imagination, like rivers and riverbanks, comprise a dynamic system. Such systems are changing and changeable by nature, subject to things like seasonal variation and tidal flow. Though this change ordinarily does not amount to "revolution," sometimes the rate of change changes, resulting in an event that is extraordinary or catastrophic. Deluge, downpour, flood stage, disastrous excess. Or the lines of flow can change, obliterating one shore while the other parches in the sun. Rivers do not always stay within their banks. What does this mean, not littorally but figuratively?

To come at that question, think of the other common meaning of "bank" and with it Amato's arrestingly frank account of life, literacy, and the pursuit of property. When the river Culture alters course, fortunes change. Some are washed out, and others find themselves with bottom land to sell. By his own account Amato, like most of us, does not find himself on the prosperous shore; midstream seems more like it. In his work life, he struggles to awaken capable imagination in educational consumers more concerned with earning potential and the status ladder. He also struggles to pay his bills. We know he cares about poetry and its unacknowledged legislature, but he feels this mission compromised, as do all of us who float between the library and the net, or along the backwaters of Amazon.com. The ecology of media is not simply a dualistic contest where *"ceci tuera cela,"* as Bolter quotes Hugo (1991), but we should not therefore imagine it a peaceable kingdom.

Like most valuable pieces of writing, Amato's personal history is both enlightening and disturbing. It shows with heroic honesty what lies behind so many of our assumptions about cultural production and reproduction. It reminds us that the humanist ideal of critical thinking stands sharply at odds with performative, end-driven assumptions of the info-market state. At the same time, though (as Amato no doubt intended), it also shows how dangerous it can be to think of culture as a homogenized unity, or to read the present through the past. According to his son's story, Amato's father had mastered the primary tools of 20th-century living. He was literate and willing to work. In the first part of the century (even in the Depression), this may have been enough to provide an adequate living, but as traditional industries and unskilled jobs disappeared from this country, the terms changed, with unhappy results for many workers. Here comes the son, then, trained as an engineer and prepared for social ascent but repelled by the greed and blindness of the collapsing industrial system. He turns into a poet and professor, sold as most of us have been on a fantasy of intellectual life. Small wonder that Amato ends his piece wondering what went wrong, where the dream turned delusional. He asks a question many of us will echo:

> what
> and who
> on earth
> will prosper
> in the coming years
> and who will not.

Though we certainly cannot address this question without a strong sense of the past, its focus on the future, like Joyce's formula, "next before you once again," brings us to the limit of elegy. Joyce's advice about the future seems very sensible—"We will have to watch"—but watching in itself is not enough. We need to tell and consider stories of the near as well as the distant past, or about events that are still unfolding. Joyce's critique of the World Wide Web, Wysocki and Johnson-Eilola's sketch of hypertextual literacy, and Eldred's account of her mother's newly technologized voice all respond to this need, but the responses are notably limited. In all the essays to some extent (though most clearly in Amato's and Eldred's), current developments are understood mainly as extensions of past experience. "Then" seems to have more force than "now," and this suggests a gap of engagement. Though it is important to sight back along both shores of the stream, we cannot overlook the ground on which we are standing.

Stories from the near present are notoriously hard to tell, mainly because we know that in the near future we will visit them again with a clearer understanding of our foolishness and errors. The risk of embarrassment is acute. We may want to change the names to protect the not-so-innocent. We may want to tell no story at all. Or maybe we will choose a higher standard. Amato's example is instructive here, a model of self-disclosure that shows how much can be gained by candor.

Here is a story to set beside the various accounts of reading, listening, teaching, and watching that precede it. This story concerns another, rather important concern of literacy, namely publishing. Last month (June, 1997), after considerable difficulty and delay, the online journal *Postmodern Culture* released a special issue featuring writing in and about hypertext.[1] The issue as published includes four projects not translatable to print or plain text (a fiction, two poems, and a collaborative essay), two articles where links figure more prominently than they do in most Web efforts, and a third essay of more conventional form. The hypertext issue is about ten times as complex as a regular issue of the journal. Its components, counting HTML pages and associated binary, sound, and image files, comprise more than 750 items connected by several thousand hypertext links. If this is a story about the fate of publishing, it has one obvious message: *I have seen the future and it takes work.* Copious amounts of work. "Hypertextual literacy" seems to increase considerably the responsibilities of those who produce, evaluate, and disseminate texts. Pilgrims who cross the river of culture seeking a promised land of productivity may be in for a rude arrival.

Behind this immediate message, however, lies another message and another story. The issue as published omits one text initially included, a large work of cultural commentary, speculation, and narrative that began as a collaboration by graduate students in a course on writing and technology. The circumstances of its removal might concern anyone interested in online literacy because they raise crucial questions about intellectual property and the generational divide. The decision to remove the hypertext (technically to suspend its publication) rested with this writer, who served as special editor of the issue. It was motivated by an objection from the journal's publisher, Johns Hopkins University Press, concerning possible copyright infringements. The

work in question contains a number of images and video clips from proprietary sources: an image taken from a popular board game, for instance, used
as a thematic page background. There are no credits or acknowledgments for
these elements. Officers of the Press felt that publishing this hypertext might
put them at risk, and since the issue in question was likely to set precedent for
future electronic projects, they took a strong position. Publication had
already been delayed several weeks by technical problems when the copyright
issue came up, so this writer chose not to argue the point. The problematic
work was removed with the understanding that it can be published later if the
authors obtain permission for the copyrighted images and video.

To the disappointed authors, this action probably seems irresolute and hyp-
ocritical. If hypertext is not print by another name, then there should be rules
of intellectual property more appropriate to its fluid, promiscuous information space. Even if we follow the old standards, why should the familiar fair use
defense not apply to this obviously creative and speculative work? There are
certainly plenty of projects on the Web that play fast and loose with trade-
marks and commercial images (to cite but one prominent example, Carl
Steadman's "Placing," http://www.placing.com). From the authors' position,
this outcome must seem a clear attempt to limit the freedom of electronic reference, if not expression.

No use pointing out that a successful legal defense can cost thousands, or
that the people who run academic presses necessarily see the world differently
than academics. "Fiduciary obligation" is not a familiar phrase for most faculty
members in the humanities, let alone graduate students. What we have here is
not a failure to communicate but a fundamental clash of values. The young
electronic writers assumed they could freely appropriate any textual production they liked. What is the Internet but a means of sharing information? What
is hypertext but a tool for connection? Writers (especially writers in their twen-
ties) are likely to value intellectual engagement over property claims.
Expression justifies transgression.

For managers, lawyers, and one uneasy editor, however, there is a limit to
this thinking. Those of us involved in the business of academic publishing—
and make no mistake, it is a business—cannot separate the expressive value of
writing from its commodity value. As many Internet startups are learning
these days, someone eventually has to pay the bills. Authors may transgress;
editors may offer to assume liability in case of court action (two editors did so
in this case); but as the publisher's counsel pointed out, academic writers make
poor targets of a suit. Damages would be sought from the party with ability to
pay. "Intellectual property" has a different ring when it is linked to material
property.

This is not a very pleasant story for anyone concerned. The most one might
hope from it is the enlightenment that comes from failure. What does this story
mean? Maybe it is a story about selling out; maybe it is about youth and middle
age; maybe it is about the collision of industrial and post-industrial societies; or

perhaps it is really about cultural geography. The fault line between expression and commodity cuts deeply across the technological landscape. It may in fact be the channel that carries the muddy waters of literacy and electronic culture—with which figure we come one last time to the littoral.

Projects like the hypertext issue (and there are many happier examples) attempt to pass from print to network textuality. But there are many ways to move between the banks of a river. Some are called bridges. Others are called dams. And, as said earlier, the metaphor of the river makes sense only if it allows us to observe distinctions and maintain a sense of flow. Propinquity is not identity. When we forget on which bank (or which sort of bank) we are standing, we are likely to find ourselves in the middle of things—or in the way. A bridge is a passage, a dam is an obstruction, and though our industrial iconography paints them as means of "taming" or "harnessing" a latent power (the better to shore up our banks), dams are also sites of contention and turbulence.

We should think about the future as well as the past, which unfortunately leaves more questions than answers. What does this story mean for the unpublished writers? What will they take from this experience in two years, five, or ten? How would they have told this story themselves? In the end, these writers and their contemporaries will decide the meaning. It is hard to say whether they will see this triumph of commodity as a betrayal or a devil's bargain—though it may be significant that one of the group now works for Microsoft. For the moment, we might suggest a parable in lieu of interpretation: a reminder about history and hydrology. Among other things, a dam represents a great debt to entropy. With good design and careful maintenance, it can carry this debt for many years, perhaps through several human generations. But of course the accounts of entropy are really kept on another sort of scale in which the span of a generation means almost nothing. It is through this slow, geologic time that rivers really run, revealing the true terrain of the littoral. Over this long run, no dam lasts.

NOTES

1.   Complete back issues of PMC are available only to Project Muse subscribers, but a text-only archive will be open to all on the net by the time this appears. Most likely only the introduction to the hypertext issue will be included in this archive. Details have yet to be determined.

WORKS CITED

Amerika, Mark. 1996. *Avant-Pop Manifesto: Thread Baring Itself in Ten Quick Posts.* http://marketplace.com:70/0/alternative.x/manifestos/avant.pop.manifesto.txt.

Anderson, Robert H. et al. 1995. *Universal Access to E-Mail: Feasibility and Societal Implications.* Santa Monica, CA: Rand.

Anderson, Worth, Cynthia Best, Alycia Black, John Hurst, Brandt Miller, and Susan Miller. 1990. Cross-Curricular Underlife. *CCC* 41: 11-36.

Angelergues, René. 1995. *Les Paradoxes du Complexe Hallucination-preception.* Revue Francaise De Psychanalyse. Paris: PUF. 458.

Apple, Michael W. 1988. *Teachers and Texts: Political Economy of Class and Gender Relations in Education.* New York: Routledge.

Aristotle. 1982.. *"Art" of Rhetoric.* Trans. J. H. Freese. Cambridge: Harvard UP-Loeb.

Armstrong, Cara and Karen Nelson. 1993. *Ritual And Monument, Architronic.* http://www.saed.kent.edu/Architronic/v2n2/v2n2.05.html.

Ashworth, Kenneth H. 1996. Virtual Universities Could Produce Only Virtual Learning. *The Chronicle of Higher Education.* Issue A88.

Bacon, Francis. 1985. Of Marriage and Single Life. *The Essayes or Counsels, Civill and Morall.* Ed. Michael Kiernan. Oxford: Oxford UP. 24-26.

Baldwin, Beth. 1996 Evolving Past the Essay-a-saurus. In *RhetNet, a Cyberjournal for Rhetoric and Writing* (Snapshots). http://www.missouri.edu/~rhetnet/

Balsamo, Anne. 1995. *Technologies of the Gendered Body: Reading Cyborg Women.* Durham: Duke UP.

Barker, Thomas T., and Fred O. Kemp. 1990. Network Theory: A Postmodern Pedagogy for the Writing Classroom. In *Computers and Community.* Ed. Carolyn Handa. Portsmouth, NH: Boynton-Cook/Heinemann. 1-27.

Barlow, John Perry. 1993. Jackboots on the Infobahn: Clipping the Wings of Freedom. *Wired 2* <http://www.eff.org/pub/Publications/John_Perry_Barlow/infobahn-jackboots_barlow_eff.article>

Barthes, Roland. 1981. *Camera Lucida.* Trans. by Richard Howard. New York: Hill and Wang.

———. 1976. *Image-Music-Text.* London: Fontana

Bartholomae, David. 1996. What Is Composition and (If You Know What That Is) Why Do We Teach It? *Composition in the Twenty-First Century: Crisis and Change,* ed. Lynn Z. Bloom, et al. Carbondale: Southern Illinois UP. 11-28.

———. 1993. I'm Talking About Allen Bloom. *Network-Based Classrooms: Promises and Realities,* ed. Bertram C. Bruce, et al. Cambridge: Cambridge UP. 237-262.

———. 1985. Inventing the University. *When a Writer Can't Write,* ed. Mike Rose. New York: Guilford. 134-165.

——— and Anthony Petrosky. 1990. *Ways of Reading: An Anthology for Writers.* 2nd ed. Boston: Bedford.

Barton, Ellen 1994. Interpreting the Discourses of Technology. Selfe and Hilligoss. 56-75.

Bataille, Georges. 1989. *The Tears of Eros.* Trans. Peter Connor. San Francisco: City Lights.

Batson, Trent. 21 Sept 1995. Deep Change and Info Tech. Email to listserv aahesgit@list.cren.net.

Baudrillard, Jean. 1994. *Simulacra and Simulation.* Ann Arbor: U of Michigan P.

———. 1983. *Simulations.* Trans. Paul Foss, Paul Patton, and Philip Beitchman. New York: Semiotext(e).

Bauman, Zygmunt. 1993. *Postmodern Ethics.* Oxford: Blackwell.

Baynes, Kenneth. 1990. The Liberal/Communitarian Controversy and Communicative Ethics. In *Universalism vs. Communitarianism: Contemporary Debates in Ethics,* ed. David Rasmussen. Cambridge, MA: MIT P. 61-81.

Bazerman, Charles. 1995. *The Informed Writer.* 5th ed. Boston: Houghton/Mifflin.

Bellah, Robert N., et al. 1985. *Habits of the Heart: Individualism and Commitment in American Life.* New York: Harper and Row.

Benhabib, Seyla. 1992. *Situating the Self: Gender, Community, and Postmodernism in Contemporary Ethics.* New York: Routledge.

Benjamin, Walter. 1969. The Work of Art in the Age of Mechanical Reproduction. *Illuminations,* ed. Hannah Arendt. New York: Schoken Books. 217-251.

Bernhardt, Stephen A. 1993. The Shape of Text to Come: The Texture of Print on Screens. *CCC* 44: 151-175.

Bernstein, Richard. 1994. Guilty if Charged. *The New York Review of Books.* Jan 13: 11-14.

Berryman, Phillip. 1987. *Liberation Theology: The Essential Facts about the Revolutionary Movement in Latin America and Beyond.* New York: Pantheon.

Besser, Howard. Education as Marketplace. Muffoletto and Knupfer. 37-69.

Bingham, Janet. 1996. Kids Become Masters of Electronic Universe: School Internet Activity Abounds. *Denver Post.* 3 Sep: A13.

Birkerts, Sven.1997. Literature Abhors a Circuit. Paper. English Studies in the Late Age of Print Colloquium. Ohio State University, Columbus, Ohio.

———. 1994. *The Gutenberg Elegies.* New York: Ballantine

———, Carolyn Guyer, Michael Joyce and Bob Stein. 1995. Page Versus Pixel: the Cultural Consequences of Electronic Text. *FEED* magazine (inaugural issue), June. http://www.feedmag.com/95.05dialog1.html.

Bishop, Wendy. 1995a. If Winston Weathers Would Just Write to Me on Email. *CCC* 46:

———. 1995b. Teaching 'Grammar for Teachers' Means Teaching Writing as Writers. In *The Place of Grammar in Writing Instruction: Past, Present, Future,* Susan Hunter and Ray Wallace, eds. Portsmouth, NH: Boynton/Cook Heinemann.

Boese, Christine. Forthcoming. A Virtual Locker Room: Gender and Democracy in Classroom Chat Spaces. *Feminist Cyberscapes: Essays on Gender in Electronic Spaces,* ed. Kristine Blair and Pamela Takayoshi. Greenwich: Ablex.

Boff, Leonardo, and Clodovis Boff. 1986. *Liberation Theology: From Confrontation to Dialogue.* San Francisco: Harper and Row.

Bogdan, Robert C. and Sari Knopp Biklen. 1992. *Qualitative Research for Education: An Introduction to Theory and Methods.* Boston: Allyn and Bacon.

Bolter, Jay David. 1991. *Writing Space: The Computer, Hypertext, and the History of Writing.* Hillsdale NJ: Erlbaum.

———. 1984. *Turing's Man.* Chapel Hill NC: UNC P.

Boomer, Garth. 1987. Addressing the Problem of Elsewhereness: A Case for Action Research in the Schools. In *Reclaiming the Classroom: Teacher Research as an Agency for Change*, ed. Dixie Goswami and Peter R. Stillman. Upper Montclair NJ: Boynton/Cook. 4-13.

Bordo, Susan. 1993. *Unbearable Weight: Feminism, Western Culture, and the Body*. Berkeley: UC P.

Bork, Alfred. 1993. Technology in Education: An Historical Perspective. Muffoletto and Knupfer, 71 90.

Boston, William. 1996. Industry Says Clock Is Ticking for "Germany Inc." *The Reuter European Business Report*. 18 June.

Bradshaw, Peter. 1996. Welcome to the Brave New World of Job Insecurity. *Evening Standard*. 24 March 9.

Branam, Judson, and Arthur Bridgeforth, Jr. 1995. Internet Writer Arrested. *The Ann Arbor News*. February 2: A1+.

———. U-M Expelling Student for Internet Fantasy. 1995. *The Ann Arbor News* February 3: A1+.

Branscomb, Anne W. 1991. Common Law for the Electronic Frontier. *Scientific American*. 154-158.

Brent, Doug. 1997. Articles on Communications, Information Technology, and Rhetoric. www.ucalgary.ca/~dabrendt/mystuff.html.

Bridwell, L., Sirc, G. and Brooke, R. 1985. Revising and Computing: Case Studies of Student Writers. In *The Acquisition of Written Language: Revision and Response*, ed. S. Freedman. Norwood, NJ: Ablex. 172-94.

Bridwell-Bowles, L., Johnson, P., and Brehe, S. 1987. Composing and Computers: Case Studies of Experienced Writers. In *Writing in Real Time: Modelling Production Processes*, ed. A. Matsuhashi. Norwood, NJ: Ablex. 81-107.

Brodkey, Linda. 1994. Making a Federal Case out of Difference: The Politics of Pedagogy, Publicity, and Postponement. *Writing Theory and Critical Theory*, ed. John Clifford and John Schilb. New York: MLA. 236-261.

Brookover, Wilbur B. and Jeffrey M. Schneider. 1975. Academic Environments and Elementary School Achievement. *Journal of Research and Development in Education* 9: 82-91.

Brown, J.R. and Earnshaw, R., Jern, M., and Vince, J. 1995. *Visualization: Using Computer Graphics to Explore Data and Present Information*. New York: Wiley.

Brummett, Barry. 1994. *Rhetoric in Popular Culture*. New York: St. Martin's P.

Buchanan, R. and Margolin, V., ed. 1995. *Discovering Design: Explorations in Design Studies*. Chicago: U of Chicago P.

Bump, Jerome. 1990. Radical Changes in Class Discussion Using Networked Computers. *Computers and the Humanities* 24: 49-65.

Burke, Kenneth. 1950. *A Rhetoric of Motives*. New York: Prentice-Hall.

Burroughs, William. 1959. *Naked Lunch*. New York: Grove Press.

Bush, Vannavar. 1945. As We May Think. *The Atlantic Monthly*. July.

Butler, Judith. 1990. *Gender Trouble: Feminism and the Subversion of Identity*. New York: Routledge.

Cabanne, Pierre. *Dialogues with Marcel Duchamp*. 1971. Trans. Ron Padgett. New York: Viking.

Cage, John. 1983. *X: Writings 79- 82*. Middletown: Wesleyan UP.

———. 1973. *Silence*. Hanover: Wesleyan UP.

Cahill, Lisa Sowle. 1990. Feminist Ethics. *Theological Studies* 51: 49-64.

Cain, Stephen. 1995. Grand Jury Sets New Indictments Against Writer. *The Ann Arbor News*. March 16.

Card, Claudia, ed. 1991. *Feminist Ethics*. Lawrence, KS: UP of Kansas.

Case, D.P. 1985. Processing Professorial Words: Personal Computers and the Writing Habits of University Professors. *CCC*. 36: 317-322.

Chaitkin, Samantha. 1996. Unpublished hypertext essay. Vassar College.

Charney, Davida. 1994. The Effect of Hypertext on Processes of Reading and Writing. In *Literacy and Computers: The Complications of Teaching and Learning with Technology*, ed. Cynthia L. Selfe and Susan Hilligoss. New York: MLA.

Chartier, R. 1994. *The Order of Books*, trans. L.G. Cochrane. Stanford: Stanford UP.

Chomsky, N.A. 1965. *Aspects of the Theory of Syntax*. Cambridge MA: MIT P.

Cixous, Hélène. 1993. *Three Steps on the Ladder of Writing*, trans. Sarah Cornell and Susan Sellers. New York: Columbia UP.

———— and Mireille Calle-Gruber. 1997. *Hélène Cixous Rootprints: Memory and Life Writing*. trans. Eric Prenowitz. London: Routledge.

Clanchy, Michael T. 1993. *From Memory to Written Record: England 1066-1307*. 2nd ed. Oxford: Blackwell.

Clark, Irene. 1995. Information Literacy and the Writing Center. *Computers and Composition* 12: 203-219.

Clinton, William J. 1998. Remarks at Technology '98 Conference. *Federal Document Clearing House Political Transcripts*. 26 Feb.

Coleridge, Samuel Taylor. 1949. *The Philosophical Lectures of Samuel Taylor Coleridge*, ed. Kathleen Cobrun. London: Pilot Press.

Connell, E. S. 1984. *Son of the Morning Star: Custer and the Little Bighorn*. New York: Harper and Row.

Connolly, Frank W., S. W. Gilbert, and P. Lyman. 1991. A Bill of Rights for Electronic Citizens, Part One. *EDUCOM Review* 26.2.

Coogan, David. 1995. Email Tutoring, a New Way to Do New Work. *Computers and Composition* 12: 171-182.

Cooper, Marilyn M., and Cynthia L. Selfe. 1990. Computer Conferences and Learning: Authority, Resistance, and Internally Persuasive Discourse. *College English* 52: 1-23.

Cooper, Martha. 1991. Ethical Dimensions of Political Advocacy from a Postmodern Perspective. In *Ethical Dimensions of Political Communication*, ed. Robert E. Denton, Jr. New York: Praeger. 23-47.

Crystal, David. 1987. *The Cambridge Encyclopedia of Language*. Cambridge: Cambridge UP.

———— and Quirk, R. 1964. *Systems of Prosodic and Paralinguistic Features in English*. The Hague: Mouton.

de Duve, Thierry. 1996. *Kant After Duchamp*. Cambridge, MA: MIT P.

————. 1994. Echoes of the Readymade: Critique of Pure Modernism. Oct 70: 61-97.

————. 1993. Given the Richard Mutt Case. *The Definitively Unfinished Marcel Duchamp*, ed. Thierry de Duve. Cambridge, MA: MIT Press. 187-230.

De Lauretis, Teresa. 1992. *Technologies of Gender: Essays on Theory, Film, and Fiction*. Bloomington: U of IN P.

Debray, Regis. 1996. The Book as Symbolic Object. In *The Future of the Book*, ed. Geoffrey Nunberg. Berkeley: U of C P.

DeLoughry, Thomas J., and David J. Wilson. 1994. The Case of Computer Conference at California College Pits Free Speech Against Civil-rights Protection. *The Chronicle of Higher Education* 41: A26.

Devine, P. E. 1992. A Communitarian Critique of Liberalism. *New Oxford Review* 59:16-18.

Dibbell, Julian. 1996. A Rape in Cyberspace; or How an Evil Clown, a Haitian Trickster Spirit, Two Wizards, and a Cast of Dozens Turned a Database into a Society. In *High Noon on the Electronic Frontier: Conceptual Issues in Cyberspace*, ed. Peter Ludlow. Cambridge: MIT P. 375-95.

Didion, Joan. 1979. *The White Album*. New York: Simon and Schuster.

Dillard, Annie. 1982. Expedition to the Pole. *Teaching a Stone to Talk*. New York: Harper. 17-52.

Dorfman, Elsa. Camera Lucida: A Review. *The Journal of Photography in New England*. Vol. 3, No. 3.

During, S. 1992. *Foucault and Literature: Towards a Genealogy of Writing*. London: Routledge.

Dussel, Enrique. 1988. *Ethics and Community*, trans. Robert R. Barr. Maryknoll, NY: Orbis Books.

Dworkin, Andrea. 1974. *Woman Hating*. New York: E. P. Dutton.

Dyrli, Odvard Egil, and Daniel E. Kinnaman. 1995. Telecommunications: Gaining Access to the World. *Technology and Learning* 16: 79-84.

Eagleton, Terry. 1996. *The Illusions of Postmodernism*. Oxford: Blackwell.

———. 1983. *Literary Theory: An Introduction*. Oxford: Basil Blackwell.

Eco, Umberto. 1979. *The Role of the Reader: Explorations in the Semiotics of Texts*. Bloomington: Indiana UP.

Ede, Lisa and Andrea Lunsford. 1990. *Singular Texts/Plural Authors*. Carbondale, IL:Southrern Illinois Univ Press.

Edmonds, Ronald R. 1984. School Effects and Teacher Effects. *Social Policy* 15: 37-39.

Eisenstein, Elizabeth L. 1979. *The Printing Press as an Agent of Change*. Cambridge: Cambridge UP.

Elam, Diane. 1994. *Feminism and Deconstruction: Ms. en Abyme*. London: Routledge.

Elbow, Peter and Kathleen Yancey. 1994. On the Nature of Holistic Scoring and Reading. *Assessing Writing* 1:91-109

Elfin, Mel. 1996. The High Cost of Higher Education. *U.S. News and World Report* 16 Sept: 89.

Ellsworth, E. 1989. Why Doesn't this Feel Empowering? Working Through the Repressive Myths of Critical Pedagogy. *Harvard Educational Review* 59: 297-324.

Ellsworth, Jill H. 1994. *Education on the Internet: A Hands-On Book of Ideas, Resources, Projects, and Advice*. Indianapolis: Sams.

Ellul, J. 1980. *The Technological System*, trans. J. Neugroschel. New York: Continuum.

———. 1973. *The Technological Society*, trans. J. Wilkinson. New York: Knopf.

Engardio, Pete. 1996. Microsoft's Long March. *Business Week* 24 June: 52-54.

Etzioni, Amitai. 1993. *The Spirit of Community: Rights, Responsibilities, and the Communitarian Agenda*. New York: Crown.

Fahys, Judy. 1997. Leavitt Plugs "Virtual" U. to World. *Salt Lake Tribune* 22 June: A4.

Faigley, Lester. 1992. *Fragments of Rationality: Postmodernity and the Subject of Composition*. Pittsburgh: U of Pittsburgh P.

———— and Susan Romano. 1995. Going Electric: Creating Multiple Sites for Innovation in a Writing Program. *Resituating Writing: Constructing and Administering Writing Programs*, ed. Joseph Janangelo and Kristine Hansen. Portsmouth: Heinemann/Boynton-Cook. 46-58.

Feenberg, Andrew. 1991. *Critical Theory of Technology*. New York: Oxford UP.

Firth, J.R. 1957. *Studies in Linguistic Analysis*. Oxford: Blackwell

Fischer, Katherine M. 1996. Down the Yellow Chip Road: Hypertext Portfolios in Oz. Computers and Composition. 13.2: 169-85.

Fish, Stanley. 1994. *There's No Such Thing as Free Speech ... And It s a Good Thing, Too.* New York: Oxford UP.

————. 1980. *Is There a Text in This Class: The Authority of Interpretive Communities.* Cambridge, MA: Harvard UP.

Foster, Donald. 1996. A Funeral Elegy W[illiam] S[hakespeare]'s "Best Speaking Witnesses" (followed by the text of A Funeral Elegy). *PMLA* 111:5, 1080-1106.

———— and Jacob Weisberg. 1996. Primary Culprit. *New York*. Feb 26: 50-58.

Foucault, Michel. 1996. The Subject and Power. *New York Times Magazine*. March 10: 32-34.

————. 1994. What is an Author? *Professing the New Rhetorics*, ed. T. Enos and S. Brown. Boston: Blair. 178-193.

————. 1991. The Ethic of Care for the Self as a Practice of Freedom. *The Final Foucault*, ed. James Bernauer and David Rasmussen, trans. J.D. Gauthier, S.J. Cambridge, MA: MIT P. 1-20.

————. 1987. Sex and the Politics of Identity: An Interview with Michel Foucault. by Bob Gallagher and Alexander Wilson. In *Gay Spirit: Myth and Meaning*, ed. Mark Thompson. New York: St. Martin's. 25-35.

————. 1984. Space, Knowledge, and Power. In *The Foucault Reader*, ed. P. Rabinow. New York: Pantheon. 239-256.

————. 1983. *Beyond Structuralism and Hermeneutics*, 2nd ed. Chicago: U of Chicago P. 208-226.

————. 1980. *Power/Knowledge: Selected Interviews and Other Writings 1972-1977*, ed C. Gordon. Brighton: Harvester Press.

Fox, Helen. 1994. *Listening to the World*. Urbana: NCTE.

Frazer, Elizabeth, and Nicola Lacey. 1993. *The Politics of Community: A Feminist Critique of the Liberal Communitarian Debate*. Toronto: U of Toronto P.

Freire, Paulo. 1996. *Pedagogy of the Oppressed*. rev. ed. New York: Continuum.

Fulton, Alice. 1996. *Screens: An Alchemical Scrapbook, Tolstoy's Dictaphone: Machines and the Muse at the Millennium* (Graywolf Forum I)., ed. Sven Birkerts. St. Paul: Graywolf.

Gardner, Howard. 1988. *Frames of Mind*. NY: Basic Books.

Gates, Henry L. 1992. *Loose Canons: Notes on the Culture Wars*. New York: Oxford.

Gay, P. 1988. *Freud: A Life for our Time*. New York: W.W. Norton.

George, E. Laurie. 1990. Taking Women Professors Seriously: Female Authority in the Computerized Classroom. *Computers and Composition* 7: 45-52.

Geren, P. 1996. Global Communications on the World Wide Web. In *The Nearness of You*, ed. Christopher Edgar and Susan Nelson Wood. New York: Teachers and Writers Collaborative. 28-36.

Gervais, André. 1993. *Connections: Of Art and Arrhe. The Definitively Unfinished Marcel Duchamp*, ed. Thierry de Duve. Cambridge, MA: MIT Press. 397-426.

Giddens, Anthony. 1984. *The Constitution of Society: Outline of the Theory of Structuration.* Berkeley, CA: University of California Press.

Gilbert, Laurel, and Crystal Kile. 1996. *Surfer Grrrls: Look, Ethel! An Internet Guide for Us!.* Seattle: Seal Press.

Giroux, Henry A. 1988. *Teachers as Intellectuals.* South Hadley MA: Bergin and Garvey.

Gomez, Mary Lou. The Equitable Teaching of Composition with Computers: A Case for Change. In *Evolving Perspectives.* 318-335.

Gore, Albert J. 1994. Remarks Prepared for Delivery at the International Telecommunication Union. Address prepared for the International Telecommunications Union. Buenos Aires.

Greenberg, Clement. 1973. *Modernist Painting. The New Art.* Ed. Gregory Battcock. New York: Dutton. 66-77.

Gresham, Morgan and Mike Jackman. 1996. A Conversations about Conversations about *Conversations. KAIROS:* 1:3. http://english.ttu.edu/kairos/1.3/

Grigar, Dene and John Barber. 1998. *Defending Your Life in MOOspace: A Report from the Electronic Edge.* Haynes and Holmevik. 192-231.

Grosz, Elizabeth.1994. *Volatile Bodies: Toward a Corporeal Feminism.* Bloomington: Indiana UP.

Guyer, Carolyn. 1996. Fretwork: ReForming Me. In *Readerly/Writerly Texts.* Eastern New Mexico University. Spring/Summer. http://mothermillennia.org/carolyn.

———. 1992. Buzz-Daze Jazz: the Quotidian Stream. Paper presented at MLA annual convention. http://mothermillennia.org/carolyn

Haas, C. 1989. How the Writing Medium Shapes the Writing Process: Effects of Word Processing on Planning. *Research in the Teaching of English* 23: 181-207.

Habermas, Jürgen. 1990. *Moral Consciousness and Communicative Action,* trans. Christian Lenhardt and Shierry Weber Nicholsen. Cambridge, MA: The MIT P.

Haefner, Joel. 1992. Is the Essay Democratic? *College English* 54: 127-37.

Hafer, Gary. 1996. Computer-Assisted Illustration and Instructional Documents. *Computers and Composition* 13: 49-56.

Hagaman, Dianne. Forthcoming. *Howie Feeds Me.*

———. 1996. *How I Learned Not To Be A Photojournalist.* Lexington: UP of Kentucky.

Halliday, M.A.K. 1989. *Spoken and Written English.* Oxford: Oxford UP.

Halsey, F. W., ed. 1902. *Authors of our Day in their Homes.* New York: James Pott.

Handa, Carolyn. 1992. An Interview with Cynthia L. Selfe: "Nomadic Feminist Cyborg Guerilla." *Writing on the Edge* 4: 67-81.

Harasim, Linda, et. al. 1995. *Learning Networks: A Field Guide to Teaching and Learning Online.* Cambridge MA: MIT P.

Haraway, Donna J. 1997. *Modest witness@second millenium. FemaleMan meets OncoMouse.* New York: Routledge.

———. 1991. *Simians, Cyborgs, and Women: The Reinvention of Nature.* New York: Routledge.

Harris, William V. 1989. *Ancient Literacy.* Cambridge: Harvard UP.

Haswell, Richard. 1989. Textual Research and Coherence. *College English.* 51: 305-319.

Hauge, Olav. 1990. It's the Dream. In *Olav Hauge: Selected Poems,* trans. Robin Fulton. Freedonia, NY: White Wine Press. 58.

Hawisher, Gail E. 1992. Electronic Meetings of the Minds: Research, Electronic Conferences, and Composition Studies. In *Re-Imagining Computers and Composition:*

Teaching and Research in the Virtual Age, ed. Gail E. Hawisher and Paul LeBlanc. Portsmouth, NH: Boynton/Cook. 81-101.

———— and Charles Moran. 1993. Electronic Mail and the Writing Instructor. *College English* 55: 627-43.

———— and Cynthia L. Selfe. 1997. Wedding the Technologies of Writing Portfolios and Computers. In *Situating Portfolios*. Logan: USU P.

———— and Cynthia L. Selfe. 1993. Tradition and Change in Computer-Supported Writing Environments: A Call for Action. In *Theoretical and Critical Perspectives on Teacher Change*, ed. P. Kahaney, J. Janangelo, and L. A. M. Perry. Norwood, NJ: Ablex. 155-186.

———— and Cynthia L. Selfe, ed. 1991. *Evolving Perspectives on Computers and Composition Studies: Questions for the 1990s.* Urbana IL: NCTE.

———— and Patricia Sullivan. 1997. Women on the Networks: Searching for E-Spaces of Their Own. In *Other Words: Feminism and Composition*, ed. Susan Jarrett and Lynn Worsham. New York: MLA.

hawisher. 30 Oct 1996. To Myka from Cindy. Email to M. Spooner and K. Yancey.

Hayles, N. Katherine. 1993. *Virtual Bodies and Flickering Signifiers*, October 66: 69-91 MIT.

————. 1992. Gender Encoding in Fluid Mechanics: Masculine Channels and Feminine Flows, *differences 4*, Brown University.

Haynes, Cynthia. 1997. Practicing Safe Rhetoric: The Passion and Paradox of Ethics in Educational MOOs. Haynes and Holmevik.

————. 1996. Self/Subject. *Keywords in Composition*, ed. Pete Vandenberg and Paul Heilker. Portsmouth, NH:Heinemann/Boynton-Cook. 217-20.

————. 1996. Inside the Teaching Machine: Actual Feminism and (Virtual) Pedagogy. *The Electronic Journal for Computer Writing, Rhetoric and Literature* 2: 55 pars. Online Internet Sept. 1996.

————. 1994. In the Name of Writing: Rhetoric and the Politics of Ethos. Dissertation. UT Arlington.

———— and Jan Rune Holmevik, ed. 1998. *High Wired: On the Design, Use, and Theory of Educational MOOs,* Ann Arbor: U of MI P.

———— and Jan Rune Holmevik, Beth Kolko, and Victor J. Vitanza. 1997. MOOs, Anarchitexture, Towards a New Threshold. *The Emerging CyberCulture: Literacy, Paradigm, and Paradox*, ed. Stephanie Gibson and Ollie Oviedo.

Heath, Shirley Brice, and Milbrey W. McLaughlin. 1993. *Identity and Inner-City Youth: Beyond Ethnicity and Gender.* NY: Teachers College P.

Heidegger, Martin. 1971. What Are Poets For? *Poetry, Language, Thought.* Trans. Albert Hofstadter. New York: Harper and Row. 89-142.

Heilbrun, Carolyn G. 1988. *Writing A Woman's Life.* New York: Random House.

Heilker, Paul. 1996. *The Essay: Theory and Pedagogy for an Active Form.* Urbana: NCTE.

Henderson, Bill. 1994. No Email from Walden. *New York Times* March 16. A15.

Herring, Susan C. 1996. *Computer-Mediated Communication: Linguistic, Social and Cross-Cultural Perspectives.* Amsterdam: J. Benjamins.

Hesse, Douglas. 1994. Essays and Experience, Time and Rhetoric. *Writing Theory and Critical Theory*, ed. John Clifford and John Schilb. New York: MLA. 195-211.

Hoaglund, Edward. 1976. What I Think, What I Am. *The New York Times Book Review.* 27 June.

————. 1994. The Recent Rise of Literary Nonfiction: A Cautionary Assay. *Composition Theory for the Postmodern Classroom*, ed. Gary A. Olson and Sidney I. Dobrin. Albany: SUNY P. 132-142.

Hodder, H. F. 1997. Cyberholics Anonymous. *Harvard Magazine* (Jul.-Aug.): 12-13.

Holdstein, Deborah. 1996. Power, Genre, and Technology. *CCC.* 47: 279-283.

Hollier, Denis. 1995. The Use-Value of the Impossible. *Bataille: Writing the Sacred*, ed. Carolyn Bailey Gill. London: Routledge. 133-153.

Honan, William H. 1996. Without Money to Build, Western Colleges Innovate to Handle More Students. *The New York Times* 25 Sept.: B9.

hooks, bell. 1997. Cultural Criticism and Transformation. Media Education Foundation videotape. Northampton, MA.

Horner, Winifred Bryan. 1996. *Nineteenth-Century Scottish Rhetoric: The American Connection.* Carbondale: Southern IL UP. 1993.

Hunter, Patricia F. and Charles Moran. 1998. Writing Teachers, Schools, and Technological Change. *Dialogic Space*, ed. Todd Taylor and Irene Ward.

Irigaray, Luce. 1985. *This Sex Which Is Not One*, trans. Catherine Porter with Carolyn Burke. Ithaca, New York: Cornell UP.

Irish Times. 1996. Drawn into the Net by Alaskan Weather. 26 March. Education and Living Supplement 8.

Iser, Wolfgang. 1978. *The Act of Reading: A Theory of Aesthetic Response.* Baltimore: John Hopkins UP.

Lafayette Journal and Courier. It's a Man's, Man's, Man's World Online. 1995. March 11: B1.

Jacobson, Robert L. 1995. No Copying. *The Chronicle of Higher Education.* March 10: A17-19.

Jaggar, Alison M. 1992. *Feminist Ethics. Encyclopedia of Ethics, Volume 1*, ed. Lawrence C. Becker and Charlotte B. Becker. New York: Garland. 361-370.

Jameson, Fredric 1991. *Postmodernism Or the Cultural Logic of Late Capitalism.* Durham, NC: Duke UP.

Janik, A., and Toulmin, S. 1973. *Wittgenstein's Vienna.* New York: Simon and Schuster.

Jessup, Emily. 1991. Feminism and Computers in Composition Instruction. Hawisher and Selfe. 336-355.

Johnson, Richard. 1986-1987. What Is Cultural Studies Anyway? *Social Text: Theory/Culture/Ideology* 16: 38-80.

Johnson-Eilola, Johndan. 1988. *Nostalgic Angels.* <http://tempest.english.purdue.edu/NA/na.html>

Jonsen, Albert R., and Stephen Toulmin. *The Abuse of Casuistry: A History of Moral Reasoning.* Berkeley, CA: U of California P.

Joyce, Michael. Forthcoming. New Stories for New Readers: Narrative Contour, Coherence, and Constructive Hypertext. *Page to Screen: Taking Literacy into the Electronic Era*, ed. Ilana Snyder. Melbourne: Allen and Unwin.

————. 1997. New Stories for New Readers: Narrative Contour, Coherence, and Constructive Hypertext. In *Page to Screen: Taking Literacy into the Electronic Era*, ed. Ilana Snyder. Melbourne: Allen and Unwin.

————. 1996. (Re)Placing the Author: A Book in the Ruins. *The Future of the Book*, ed. Geoffrey Nunberg. Berkeley: U of California P.

————. 1995. *Of Two Minds: Hypertext Pedagogy and Poetics.* Ann Arbor: U of Michigan P.

Kadie, Carl L. 1991. Hypothetical Netnews Bill of Rights. <http://www.eff.org/pub/CAF/library/library-netnews-analogy>

Kaplan, Nancy. 1997. http://raven.ubalt.edu/staff/kaplan/

———. 1991. Ideology, Technology, and the Future of Writing Instruction. Hawisher and Selfe. 11-42.

Kapor, Mitchell. 1991. Civil Liberties in Cyberspace. *Scientific American* 265: 158-64.

Kauffman, Janet 1993. *The Body in Four Parts*. St Paul: Graywolf Press.

kbyancey. 13 Dec 1994. Early Final Thoughts. Email to M. Spooner.

Kemp, Fred. 1995. ACW—Not Your Father's Kind of Organization. Available website: http://english.ttu.edu/acw/essay/acw%5Fessay.html

Kirsch, Gesa. 1997. "Multi-Vocal Texts and Interpretive Responsibility." *College English.* 59:191-201.

Kirschenbaum, Matthew G. 1997. *Chronicle of Higher Education.* July 25: B11

Klaus, Carl. 1996. Remarks during Teachers and Writers: A Workshop for Essay Writers. CCCC. Milwaukee.

Knupfer, Nancy Nelson. Teachers and Educational Computing: Changing Roles and Changing Pedagogy. Muffoletto and Knupfer. 163-180.

Koetting, J. Randall. Educational Technology, Curriculum theory, and Social Foundations: Toward a New Language of Possibility. Muffoletto and Knupfer. 129-140.

Kostelanetz, Richard. 1968. *The Theatre of Mixed Means: An Introduction to Happenings, Kinetic Environments, and Other Mixed-Means Performances.* New York: Dial.

Kosuth, Joseph. 1973. Art After Philosophy, I and II. *Idea Art,* ed. Gregory Battcock. New York: Dutton. 70-101.

Kozol, Jonathan. 1991. *Savage Inequalities: Children in America's Schools.* Harper Collins: New York.

Kramarae, Cheris. 1988. *Technology and Women's Voices: Keeping in Touch.* New York: Routledge and Kegan Paul.

Krauss, Rosalind E. 1993. *The Optical Unconscious.* Cambridge, MA: MIT Press

Kremers, Marshall. 1990. Sharing Authority on a Synchronous Network: The Case for Riding the Beast. *Computers and Composition* 7: 33-44.

Kress, G.R. 1996. *Before Writing: Rethinking the Paths to Literacy.* London: Routledge

———. 1995. *Writing the Future: English and the Production of a Culture of Innovation.* Sheffield: National Association of Teachers of English (50 Broadfield Road, Sheffield S8 OXJ).

———. 1993. *Learning to Write.* London: Routledge

——— and Theo van Leeuwen. 1996. *Reading Images: the Grammar of Visual Design* London: Routledge

Kroker, Arthur. 1992. *The Possessed Individual: Technology and the French Postmodern.* New York: St.Martin's Press.

Krugman, Paul. 1994. *Peddling Prosperity: Economic Sense and Nonsense in the Age of Diminished Expectations.* New York: W.W. Norton.

Kunzru, Hari. 1997. You are Borg. *Wired* 154-159, 209-210.

Landes, Joan B. 1988. *Women and the Public Sphere in the Age of the French Revolution.* Ithaca: Cornell UP.

Landon, Brooks. 1997. http://www.uiowa.edu/~english/landon2.html (10 February).

Landow, George P. 1992. *Hypertext: The Convergence of Contemporary Critical Theory and Technology.* Baltimore, MD: Johns Hopkins.

Lanham, Richard.A. 1994. The Implications of Electronic Information for the Sociology of Knowledge. *Leonardo* 27: 155-163

———. 1993. *The Electronic Word: Democracy, Technology, and the Arts.* Chicago: U of Chicago P.

Latour, Bruno. 1993. *We Have Never Been Modern,* trans. by Catherine Porter. Cambridge: Harvard UP.

Lebel, Robert. 1959. *Marcel Duchamp,* trans. George Heard Hamilton. London: Trianon Press.

LeBlanc, Paul J. *The Politics of Literacy and Technology in Secondary School Classrooms.* Selfe and Hilligoss, 22-36.

Levinas, Emmanuel. 1985. *Ethics and Infinity: Conversations with Philippe Nemo,* trans. Richard A. Cohen. Pittsburgh: Duquesne UP.

Lippard, Lucy. 1983. *Overlay.* New York: Pantheon Books.

Lopez, Barry. 1990. Losing Our Sense of Place. *Teacher Magazine* Feb: 188.

Lubar, Steven. 1993. *Infoculture: The Smithsonian Book of Information Age Inventions.* Boston: Houghton Mifflin.

Lyotard, Jean-Franìois. 1988. *The Differend: Phrases in Dispute,* trans. Georges Van Den Abbeele. Minneapolis: U of Minnesota P.

——— and Jean-Loup Thébaud. 1985. *Just Gaming.* Trans. W. Godzich. Minneapolis: U of Minnesota P.

MacIntyre, Alastair. 1984. *After Virtue: A Study in Moral Theory,* 2nd ed. Notre Dame, IN: U of Notre Dame P.

MacKinnon, Catharine R. 1993. *Only Words.* Cambridge, MA: Harvard UP.

Malloy, Judy. 1993. Brown House Kitchen. Interactive Fiction on LambdaMOO. telnet lambda.moo.mud.org 8888 (@go #24969).

———. Private correspondence with Carolyn Guyer.

Marvin, Carolyn. 1988. *When Old Technologies Were New: Thinking about Electric Communication in the Late Nineteenth Century.* New York: Oxford UP.

Mason, Robin and Antony Kaye. 1989. *Mindweave: Communication, Computers, and Distance Education.* Oxford: Pergamon.

May, Elaine Tyler. 1988. *Homeward Bound: American Families in the Cold War Era.* New York: Basic.

McDaniel, Ellen 1990. Assessing the Professional Role of the English Department Computer Person. In *Computers and Writing: Theory, Research, Practice,* ed. Holdstein and Selfe. New York: MLA. 84-94.

McHugh, Kathleen. 1997. http://darkwing.uoregon.edu/~kmchugh/ (10 February)

McIntosh, Mary. 1992. Liberalism and the Contradictions of Oppression. *Sex Exposed.* Ed. L. Segal. London: Virago.

Mead, Margaret. 1978. *Culture and Commitment: The New Relationships Between the Generations in the 1970s.* New York: Doubleday. 1970. Revised and updated edition, New York: Columbia UP.

Meeks, Brock N. 1994. The End of Privacy. *Wired* 2.4. <http://www.hotwired.com/Lib/Privacy/privacy.meeks.html>

Mendelssohn, F. 1978. *Songs Without Words: Selected Favorites for the Piano,* ed. W. A. Palmer. Van Nuys, CA: Alfred Publishing.

Metzger, Deena. 1983. *The Woman Who Slept With Men to Take the War Out of Them and Tree.* Berkeley: Wingbow Press.

Miller, Carolyn R. 1996. This Is Not an Essay. *College Composition and Communication* 47: 284-288.

———. 1993. Rhetoric and Community: The Problem of the One and the Many. In *Defining the New Rhetorics*, ed. Theresa Enos and Stuart C. Brown. Newbury Park, CA: Sage. 79-94.

Miller, Susan. 1994. The New Discourse City. In Reagan et al. 283-300.

Minock, Mary, and Francis Shor. 1995. Crisscrossing Grand Canyon: Bridging the Gaps with Computer Conferencing. *Computers and Composition* 12: 355-365.

Mitchell, W.J.T. 1994. *Picture Theory.* U of Chicago P.

———. 1986. *Iconology: Image, Text, Ideology.* U of Chicago P.

Molinari, Guido. 1976. *Color in the Creative Arts. Guido Molinari: Ecrits Sur L'art (1954-1975).* Ottawa: GNC, Texte de 1972. 86-94.

Monseau, Virginia, Jeanne Gerlach, and Lisa J. McClure. 1994. The Making of a Book. In Reagan et al. 61-76.

Moulthrop, Stuart. 1991. You Say You Want a Revolution: Hypertext and the Laws of Media. *Postmodern Culture* 1.3.

Muffoletto, Robert and Nancy Nelson Knupfer, ed. 1993. *Computers in Education: Social, Political, and Historical Perspectives.* Cresskill NJ: Hampton Press.

National Center for Education Statistics. 1998. Internet Access in Public Education. http://nces.ed.gov/pubs98/98021.html (21 May 1998).

Neel, Jasper. 1988. *Plato, Derrida, and Writing.* Carbondale: Southern IL UP.

Negroponte, Nicholas. 1995. *Being Digital.* New York: Alfred A. Knopf.

Nesbit, Molly. 1994. Her Words. Walker Art Center. Minneapolis, 8 Nov.

———. 1993. The Language of Industry. *The Definitively Unfinished Marcel Duchamp.* Ed. Thierry de Duve. Cambridge, MA: MIT P. 351-384.

Noddings, Nel. 1992. *The Challenge to Care in Schools.* New York: Teachers College P.

———. 1984. *Caring: a Feminine Approach to Ethics and Moral Education.* Berkeley: U of California P.

Ohmann, Richard. 1976. *English in America: A Radical View of the Profession.* New York: Oxford UP.

Olsen, Lance and Mark Amerika. 1996. *Smells Like Avant-Pop: An Introduction, of Sorts.* http://marketplace.com:70/0/alternative.x/memoriam/1.txt. (20 Sept.)

Olson, C. Paul. 1987. Who Computes? *Critical Pedagogy and Cultural Power*, ed. David Livingstone. South Hadley, MA: Bergin and Garvey. 179-204.

Ong, W. 1982. *Orality and Literacy.* New York: Methuen and Company, Ltd.

Ottinger, Didier. 1996. *The Spiritual Exercises of René Magritte.* Magritte. Montreal: The Museum of Fine Arts.

Page, Barbara. 1996. Women Writers and the Restive Text: Feminism, Experimental Writing and Hypertext. *Postmodern Culture* 6. http://jefferson.village.virginia.edu/pmc/issue.196/page.196.html

Paley, Nicholas and Janice Jipson. 1997. Personal History: Researching Literature and Curriculum (Literal, Alter, Hyper). *English Education.* 29:59-69.

Papert, Seymour. 1980. *Mindstorms: Children, Computers, and Powerful Ideas.* Harper-Collins.

Paul, Sherman 1992. *For Love of the World : Essays on Nature Writers.* Iowa City : U of Iowa P.

———. 1981. *The Lost America of Love: Rereading Robert Creeley, Edward Dorn, and Robert Duncan.* Baton Rouge : Louisiana State UP.

————. 1976. *Repossessing and Renewing : Essays in the Green American Tradition.* Baton Rouge : Louisiana State UP.

Petroski, Henry. 1990. *The Pencil: A History of Design and Circumstance.* New York: Knopf.

Petry, Martha. 1992. Permeable Skins. *After the Book Writing Literature Writing Technology.* Perforations number 3 spring/summer. Atlanta: Public Domain.

Phelps, Louise. 1985. Dialectics of Coherence. *College English.* 47: 12-30.

Phillips, Derek L. 1993. *Looking Backward: A Critical Appraisal of Communitarian Thought.* Princeton, NJ: Princeton UP.

Piller, Charles. 1992. Separate Realities: The Creation of the Technological Underclass in America s Public Schools. *Macworld* (September): 218-231.

Porter, James E. 1998. Legal Realities and Ethical Hyperrealities: A Critical Approach Toward Cyberwriting. *Computers and Technical Communication: Pedagogical and Programmatic Perspectives,* ed. Stuart C. Selber. Norwood, NJ: Ablex.

————. 1998. *Rhetorical Ethics and Internetworked Writing.* Norwood, NJ: Ablex, in press.

————. 1992. *Audience and Rhetoric: An Archaeological Composition of the Discourse Community.* Englewood Cliffs, NJ: Prentice Hall.

Pound, Ezra. 1972. *The Cantos of Ezra Pound.* New York: New Directions. 1954.

Prejean, Sister Helen. 1994. *C.S.J. Dead Man Walking.* New York: Vintage.

Prince, Michael. 1989. Literacy and Genre. *College English.* 51 Nov 730-749.

Purves, Alan. 1996. Animadversions on Writing Assessment and Hypertext. *Assessing Writing,* 2 5-20.

Quittner, Joshua. 1996. Free Speech for the Net. *Time* 147. June 24: 56-57.

R. E. M. 1996. So Fast, So Numb. New Adventures in Hi-Fi. *Warner Bros,* 9 46320-2.

Rawls, John. 1971. *A Theory of Justice.* Cambridge, MA: Belknap.

Ray, Ruth and Ellen Barton. *Technology and Authority.* Hawisher and Selfe. 279-299.

Reagan, Sally Barr, Thomas Fox and David Bleich, eds. 1995. *Writing With.* Albany, NY: SUNY P.

Renov, Michael, ed. 1993. *Theorizing Documentary.* New York: Routledge.

Reynolds, David, et. al. 1994. *Advances in School Effectiveness Research and Practice.* Oxford: Elsevier.

Reynolds, Nedra. 1994. Fragments in Response. *CCC.* 45: 264-273.

Rheingold, Howard. 1994. Why Censoring Cyberspace is Futile. *San Francisco Examiner.* April 5: 27.

————. 1993. *The Virtual Community: Homesteading on the Electronic Frontier.* Reading, MA: Addison-Wesley.

————. 1991. The Thought Police on Patrol. *Publish* Jul: 46-47.

Roberts, Francis. 1968. I Propose to Strain the Laws of Physics. *Art News* Dec: 47.

Roché, Henri. 1959. *Souvenirs of Marcel Duchamp.* Marcel Duchamp. Robert Lebel. Trans. William N. Copley. London: Trianon Press. 79-87.

Rodriguez, Richard. 1996. Ganstas. http://www.mojones.com/MOTHER_JONES/JF94/rodriguez.html. 9 Sept.

Romano, Susan. 1993. The Egalitarianism Narrative: Whose Story? Which Yardstick? *Computers and Composition* 10: 5-28.

Rorty, Richard. 1989. *Contingency, Irony, and Solidarity.* Cambridge, MA: Cambridge UP.

Roseth, Bob. 1995. Plugged In. *Columns* 15 (December 1995): 24 27.

Rudolph, Frederick. 1962. *The American College and University: A History.* New York: Vintage.

Sainsbury, Alison. 1995. Personal communication.

Salavert, Roser. 1991. Integrating Computerized Speech and Whole Language in the Early Elementary School. *Literacy as Praxis: Culture, Language, and Pedagogy,* ed. Catherine E. Walsh. Norwood, NJ: Ablex. 115-129.

Salvo, Michael. 1996. Draft. Available website: http://129.118.38.138/salvo/cadc/salvo.htm.

Sanouillet, Michel and Elmer Peterson. 1973. *Salt Seller: The Writings of Marcel Duchamp (Marchand du Sel).* New York: Oxford UP.

Schilb, John. 1996. *Between the Lines: Relating Composition Theory and Literary Theory.* Portsmouth, NH: Heinemann/Boynton-Cook.

Scholes, Robert and Carl Klaus. 1969. *Elements of the Essay.* New York: Oxford UP.

Schwartz, Helen, Cynthia L. Selfe, and James Sosnoski. 1994. The Electronic Department. *Works and Days* 12: 261-86.

Scribner, Sylvia, and Michael Cole. 1981. *The Psychology of Literacy.* Cambridge: Harvard UP.

Selber, Stuart. 1994. Beyond Skill Building: Challenges Facing Technical Communication Teachers in the Computer Age. *Technical Communication Quarterly* 3: 365-390.

Selfe, Cynthia L. 1996. The Gendering of Technology: Images of Women, Men, and Technology. Paper presented at CCCC. Milwaukee, WI. March.

———. 1996. Theorizing Email for the Practice, Instruction, and Study of Literacy. *Electronic Literacies in the Workplace: Technologies of Writing,* ed. Patricia Sullivan and Jennie Dautermann. Urbana, IL and Houghton, MI: NCTE and *Computers and Composition.*

———. 1989. The Multi-layered Grammars of Computers. In *Critical Perspectives on Computers and Composition Studies,* ed. Hawisher and Selfe. 3-15. NY: Teachers College Press.

——— and Susan Hilligoss, ed. 1994. *Literacy and Computers: The Complications of Teaching and Learning with Technology.* New York, MLA.

——— and Richard J Selfe. 1994. The Politics of the Interface: Power and It's Exercise in Electronic Contact Zones. *College Composition and Communication* 45 (Dec 4): 480-504.

——— and Paul Meyer. 1991. Testing Claims for Online Conferences. *Written Communication* 8 : 163-92.

Shade, Leslie Regan. 1996. Is There Free Speech on the Net? Censorship in the Global Information Infrastructure. *Cultures of Internet: Virtual Spaces, Real Histories, Living Bodies,* ed. Rob Shields. London: Sage. 11-32.

Shor, Ira. 1992. *Empowering Education: Critical Teaching for Social Change.* Chicago: U of Chicago P.

Sinclair, Carla. 1996. *Net Chick: A Smart-Girl Guide to the Wired World.* New York: Henry Holt.

Sirc, Geoffrey. 1995. The Twin Worlds of Electronic Conferencing. *Computers and Composition* 12: 265-278.

Slate. Online journal. Available website: http://www.slate.com/TOC/current/contents.asp

Sledd, Andrew. 1988. Readin "not Riotin": The Politics of Literacy. *College English* 50: 495-507.

Smith, Christian. 1991. *The Emergence of Liberation Theology: Radical Religion and Social Movement Theory.* Chicago: The U of Chicago P.

Smith, Danyel. Holler If You Hear Me. *Village Voice* 1 March 1994, Pazz and Jop Supplement: 20.

Smith, Frank. 1971. *Understanding Reading: A Psycholinguistic Analysis of Reading and Learning to Read.* New York: Holt, Rinehart and Winston.

Snyder, Gary. 1995. *A Place in Space.* WA:Counterpoint.

Sosnoski, James. 1996. Notes on Postmodern Double Agency and the Arts of Lurking. *CCC.* 47: 288-292.

————. 1995. *Modern Skeletons in Postmodern Closets: A Cultural Studies Alternative.* Charlottesville: UP of Virginia.

————. 1994. *Token Professionals and Master Critics: A Critique of Orthodoxy in Literary Studies.* Albany, NY: SUNY P.

————, Patricia Harkin and David Downing. 1994. Configurations of Lore: The Changing Relations of Theory, Research, and Pedagogy. *Changing Classroom Practices: Resources for Literary and Cultural Studies*, ed. David Downing. Albany, NY: NCTE.

Spellmeyer, Kurt. 1993. *Common Ground: Dialogue, Understanding, and the Teaching of Composition.* Englewood Cliffs: Prentice Hall.

Spellmeyer, Kurt. 1989. A Common Ground. *College English.* 51: 262-276.

Spender, Dale. 1995. *Nattering on the Net: Women, Power, and Cyberspace.* North Melbourne: Spinifex.

Spivak, Gayatri Chakravorty. 1993. *Outside in the Teaching Machine.* New York: Routledge.

————. 1989. Feminism and Deconstruction, Again: Negotiating with Unacknowledged Masculism. *Between Feminism and Psychoanalysis*, ed. Teresa Brennan. London: Routledge. 206-23.

Spooner, Michael and Kathleen Yancey. 1996. Postings on a Genre of Email. *CCC* 47: 252-278.

Springside MOO. Vassar College. http://www.iberia.vassar.edu/~mistaken/moo/WebMOO.html

Sproull, Lee and Sara Kiesler. 1991. *Connections: New Ways of Working in the Networked Organization.* Cambridge: MIT P.

Stam, Robert, Robert Burgoyne, and Sandy Flitterman-Lewis. 1992. *New Vocabularies in Film and Semiotics: Structuralism, Post-Structuralism, and Beyond.* New York: Routledge.

Star, Susan Leigh. 1995. The Politics of Formal Representations. *Ecologies of Knowledge: Work and Politics in Science and Technology*, ed. Susan Leigh Star. Albany: SUNY P.

————, ed. 1995. *The Cultures of Computing.* Cambridge, MA: Blackwell.

————. 1989. The Structure of Ill-Structured Solutions: Heterogeneous Problem-Solving, Boundary Objects and Distributed Artificial Intelligence. *Distributed Artificial Intelligence*, ed. M. Hahns and L. Gasser. Menlo Park: Morgan Kauffman.

———— and James R. Griesemer. 1989. Institutional Ecology, Translations and Boundary Objects: Amateurs and Professionals in Berkeley s Museum of Vertebrate Zoology. 1907-1939. *Social Studies of Science* 19: 387-420.

Steinberg, Steve G. 1997. Mapping Science. *WIRED* 5 (Jan): 46.

Stokes, Paul. 1996. Fear of the Financial Jobs Axe. *The Scotsman* 4 Apr: 24.

Stone, Allucquere Rosanne. 1991. Will the Real Body Please Stand Up? Boundary Stories About Virtual Cultures, ed. Michael Benedikt. *Cyberspace: First Steps.* Cambridge, MA: The MIT P. 81-118.

Street, Brian V. 1984. *Literacy in Theory and Practice.* Cambridge: Cambridge Univ. Press.

Stuckey, J. Elspeth. 1991. *The Violence of Literacy.* Portsmouth, NH: Boynton/Cook.

Sullivan, Patricia A., and James E. Porter. *Opening Spaces: Writing Technologies and Critical Research Practices.* Norwood, NJ: Ablex, in press.

———— and Jennie Dautermann, ed. 1996. *Electronic Literacies in the Workplace: Technologies of Writing.* Urbana: NCTE.

Takayoshi, Pamela. 1996. The Shape of Electronic Writing. *Computers and Composition,* 13.2: 245-59.

———— . 1994. Building New Networks from Old: Women's Experiences with Electronic Communications. *Computers and Composition* 11: 21-35.

Thurow, Lester. 1995. Why Their World Might Crumble: How Much Inequality Can a Democracy Take? *New York Times Magazine.* 19 Nov: 78-79.

Tikka, Heidi. 1994. Vision and Dominance—A Critical Look Into Interactive System. ISEA'94 Proceedings, the 5th International Symposium on Electronic Art, The Inter-Society For The Electronic Arts, Helsinki Finland, August 20-25 http://www.uiah.fi/bookshop/isea_proc/nextgen/j/10.html

Times Mirror. 1994. Technology in the American Household. Los Angeles: Times Mirror Center for the People and the Press.

Tornow, Joan. 1997. *Link/Age: Composing in the Online Classroom.* Logan, UT: Utah State UP.

Toulmin, Stephen. 1976. *The Uses of Argument.* Cambridge: Cambridge UP.

Trimbur, John. 1994. Taking the Social Turn. *CCC.* 45.1Feb 108-18.

———— . 1990. Essayist Literacy and the Rhetoric of Deproduction. *Rhetoric Review* 9: 72-86.

Tufte, E.R. 1990. *Envisioning Information.* Cheshire, CT: Graphics Press

Tumulty, Karen, and John F. Dickerson. 1998. Gore's Costly High-Wire Act. *Time* 25 May: 20.

Turkle, Sherry. 1995. *Life on the Screen.* NY: Simon & Schuster.

U.S. Bureau of the Census. 1995. Current Population Reports, Series P23 189, Population Profile of the United States: 1995. Washington DC: Government Printing Office.

U.S. Department of Commerce. 1995. Statistical Abstract of the United States: 1995. Washington, DC: Government Printing Office.

Ulmer, Gregory. n.d. What is Electracy? http://www.elf.ufl.edu/electracy.html

———— . 1994. *Heuretics: The Logic of Invention.* Baltimore: Johns Hopkins UP.

———— . 1992. Discussion. In Myron Tuman, ed. *Literacy Online.* Pittsburgh: U of Pittsburgh P.

Unabomber. 1996. Letter to the *San Francisco Chronicle* (April 25)

Villa-Vicencio, Charles. 1992. *A Theology of Reconstruction: Nation-building and Human Rights.* Cambridge: Cambridge UP.

Wahlstrom, Billie J. 1994. Communication and Technology: Defining a Feminist Presence in Research and Practice. Selfe and Hilligoss. 171-185.

———— and Cynthia L. Selfe. 1994. A View from the Bridge: Piloting among the Shoals of Computer Use. *ADE Bulletin,* #109 (Winter): 35-45.

Wallace, David Foster. 1993. E Unibus Pluram: Television and U.S. Fiction. *Review of Contemporary Fiction* 13: 168.

Weathers, Winston. 1980. Grammars of Style. In Richard L. Graves, ed. *Rhetoric and Composition*. 133-47 Upper Montclair, NJ: Boynton/Cook.

Western Governors University. 1997. http://www.westgov.org/smart/vu/vu.html (28 Jul).

Wilson, David L. 1995. Senate Bill Takes Broom to Internet. *The Chronicle of Higher Education* (April 7): A21-A22.

Wittgenstein, L. 1961. *Tractatus Logico-philosophicus* (tr. D. F. Pears and B. F. McGuiness). London: Routledge and Kegan Paul.

Wittig, Rob. 1994. *Invisible Rendezvous*. Hanover, NH: Wesleyan U Press

Yancey, Kathleen and Michael Spooner. 1994. *Concluding the Text*. In Kathleen Yancey, ed. *Voices on Voice*. Urbana: NCTE.

Young, Iris Marion. 1990. *Justice and the Politics of Difference*. Princeton: Princeton U P.

Zuboff, Shoshana. 1988. *In the Age of the New Machine: The Future of Work and Power*. New York: Basic Books.

CONTRIBUTORS

JOE AMATO is the author of *Symptoms of a Finer Age* (Viet Nam Generation, 1994), and *Bookend: Anatomies of a Virtual Self* (SUNY, 1997). His poetry and essays have appeared in numerous journals and magazines, including *Nineteenth Century Studies*, *electronic book review*, *Computers and Composition*, *Crayon*, *Postmodern Culture*, *Writing on the Edge*, *Denver Quarterly*, and *Perforations*. His recent autobiographical project, *No Outlet*, details his life during the seventies, how a technology career provided a path out of poverty. He teaches literature and writing in Chicago, where he lives with his wife and partner Kass Fleisher.

DENNIS BARON is professor of English and Linguistics and head of the Department of English at the University of Illinois at Urbana-Champaign. His books on the English language include *Grammar and Good Taste* (Yale, 1982); *Grammar and Gender* (Yale, 1986); *The English-Only Question* (Yale, 1990), *Declining Grammar* (NCTE, 1989), and *Guide to Home Language Repair* (NCTE,1994). His comments on language have appeared in the *Chicago Tribune*, *The Washington Post*, and *The Chronicle of Higher Education*. His cartoons have appeared in *English Journal*. He is currently working on a book on literacy and technology.

BERTRAM C. BRUCE is a professor at the University of Illinois at Urbana-Champaign on the faculties of Curriculum and Instruction, Bioengineering, and Writing Studies. His current research focuses on information technologies, especially on how they mediate social relations and manifest social practices. He is co-author of *Network-based Classrooms*, *Electronic Quills*, and many other publications addressing issues in information technology, computers and literacy, language and literacy, science education, and curriculum issues. This work has also led to educational software, including Quill, Statistics Workshop, and Discoveries.

MARILYN M. COOPER is associate professor of humanities and director of graduate teaching assistant education at Michigan Technological University. With Dennis A. Lynch and Diana George, she won the 1998 CCCC Braddock Award for the article "Moments of Argument." She is working on a book on postmodern ethics in the writing classroom. She would never have been thinking about electronic conversations had she not been befriended by Cindy and Gail, the dynamic duo of computers & writing.

JANET CAREY ELDRED is associate professor of English at the University of Kentucky, where she is completing (with Peter Mortensen) *Imagining Rhetoric*, to appear in the Pittsburgh Series on Literacy, Composition, and Culture. Her recent articles, including collaborative efforts, have appeared in *College English, Written Communication, Rhetoric Review,* and *Rhetoric Society Quarterly.* Her essays (literary nonfiction) have appeared in *CCC, Willow Review* and *Literal Latte.*

LESTER FAIGLEY holds the Robert Adger Law and Thos. H. Law Professorship in Humanities at the University of Texas at Austin. He serves as director of the Division of Rhetoric and Composition and the Concentration in Technology, Literacy, and Culture. He has published widely, and his 1992 *Fragments of Rationality* won the MLA Mina Shaughnessy Award. In 1996, he was chair of the *Conference on College Composition and Communication.*

DIANA GEORGE teaches composition studies, theories of visual representation, and British literature at Michigan Technological University. She is co-author with John Trimbur of *Reading Culture* (now in its third edition) and editor of the upcoming collection, *KitchenCooks, Plate Twirlers, and Troubadours.* With colleagues Marilyn Cooper and Dennis Lynch, she won the 1998 CCCC Braddock Award for their article "Moments of Argument." Her work in composition studies, media representations, and classroom practice have appeared in a wide range of journals and books.

CAROLYN GUYER is among the first wave of writers to publish hypertext fiction. She is the author of *Quibbling,* published on disk by Eastgate Systems in1992. Her other hypertexts include the first published collaborative fiction, *Izme Pass,* with co-author Martha Petry, published by *Writing on the Edge* in 1991. Forthcoming is the web fiction *Sister Stories,* with co-authors Rosemary Joyce and Michael Joyce. Guyer has also contributed to the theoretical work surrounding the use of hypertext. Samples of her essays and fiction are available at http://mothermillennia.org/carolyn. Guyer was the founder and coordinator of *HiPitched Voices,* a women's hypertext collective at Brown University. She is currently developing a web project titled Mother Millennia that will densely link 2,000 or more stories and works from all over the world on the subject of "mother." http://mothermillennia.org9.

DIANNE HAGAMAN is a photographer and writer and maker of hypertext photographic works. She lives in Seattle and San Francisco. Her article, "'The Joy of Victory, the Agony of Defeat;" which deals with various aspects of photographic practice in journalism and in research, appeared in *Visual Sociology.* Her other papers include "Connecting Cultures," which appeared in *Cultures of Computing,* edited by Susan Leigh Star (Blackwell 1995). The University Press of Kentucky published her book, *How I Learned Not To Be a Photojournalist.*

GAIL E. HAWISHER is professor of English and director of the Center forWriting Studies at the University of Illinois, Urbana-Champaign. With Paul LeBlanc, Charles Moran, and Cynthia Selfe, she is author of *Computers and the Teaching of Writing in Higher Education, 1979-1994: A History.* Other recent books with Cynthia Selfe include a college reader entitled *Literacy, Technology, and Society* and a collection of essays titled *Global Literacies and the World Wide Web* to be published by Routledge. She is co-editor of several other books focusing on a range of theoretical, pedagogical, and research questions related to literacy and technology. With Cynthia

Selfe, she edits *Computers and Composition* and the series *New Directions in Computers and Composition Studies*. Her articles have appeared in *Research in the Teaching of English, English Journal, College English, College Composition and Communication*, and *Written Communication*, among others. With Purdue's Pat Sullivan she is also author of "Women on the Networks: Seeking E-Spaces of their Own" in the MLA collection *Feminism and Composition*. She is currently a member of the MLA Committee on Computers and Emerging Technologies and a past member of the Executive Committee of the National Council of Teachers of English.

CYNTHIA HAYNES is assistant professor in the School of Arts & Humanities and director of Rhetoric and Writing at the University of Texas at Dallas where she teaches both graduate and undergraduate rhetoric, composition, and electronic pedagogy. Her publications have appeared in *Pre/Text, Composition Studies, Keywords in Composition, St. Martin's Guide to Tutoring Writing, Works & Days, The Writing Center Journal, Kairos*, and *CWRL*. She is co-editor of *Pre/Text: Electra(Lite)* and *Elekcriture*, both electronic journals publishing innovative scholarship in/on digital rhetorics. With Jan Rune Holmevik, she is co-founder of Lingua MOO and co-editor of their collection of essays, *High Wired*. She founded the C-FEST series of online real-time meetings at Lingua MOO. She is currently at work on her book, *Technologies of Ethos*, and with Jan Rune Holmevik, *MOOniversity*.

DOUG HESSE is professor and director of English Graduate Studies at Illinois State University. From 1994-98 he edited *WPA*, and in 1999 he became president of the Council of Writing Program Administrators. He publishes on the essay in such journals as *JAC, CCC, Rhetoric Review*, and *Writing on the Edge* and has written chapters for several books, including *Essays on the Essay, Literary Nonfiction*, and *Writing Theory and Critical Theory*.

JAN RUNE HOLMEVIK is a visiting assistant professor and doctoral candidate in the Department of Humanistic Informatics at the University of Bergen, Norway. He holds a degree in the history of technology from the University of Trondheim, Norway 1994, and his publications on history of computing and science policy have appeared in journals such as *Annals of the History of Computing* and *Forskningspolitikk*. He is co-editor of *High Wired* and co-author of *MOOniversity* with Cynthia Haynes. His *Educating the Machine* is published by Ad Notam Gyldendal (1998). Holmevik has been involved with MUDs since 1989, and is co-founder of LinguaMOO, a synchronous Internet-based learning environment that he continues to administer with Cynthia Haynes.

JOHNDAN JOHNSON-EILOLA works as the director of Professional Writing at Purdue University, where also he teaches undergraduate courses in professional writing and graduate courses in computers and writing, postmodernism, distance education, and writing pedagogy. He has published award-winning work on computers and communication in edited collections and journals including *Computers and Composition, JAC, Writing on the Edge*, and *Technical Communication Quarterly*. In 1997, he published a cultural study of hypertext, *Nostalgic Angels* (Ablex). He is currently working with Carole Yee on an edited collection on theories of computer documentation (Baywood) and on a professional writing website with Jim Porter and Pat Sullivan (Allyn and Bacon).

MICHAEL JOYCE is perhaps best known as the originator of hypertext fiction. His work includes *afternoon; Twilight, a Symphony;* and *Twelve Blue.* His shorter hyperfictions include *WOE* and *Lucy's Sister.* A linear novel, *Going the Distance,* is published on the web by Pilgrim Press. His most recent collection of essays, *Othermindedness,* will be published by the University of Michigan Press, which previously published his collection *Of Two Minds: Hypertext Pedagogy and Poetics* (1995). He serves on the editorial boards for *Works & Days* and *Computers and Composition.* He is currently associate professor of English and director of the Center for Electronic Learning and Teaching at Vassar College in Poughkeepsie, NY.

GUNTHER KRESS is professor of education at the Institute of Education at the University of London, where he pays special attention to English curricula. His many publications include *The Grammar of Visual Design* with Theo van Leeuwen (1995), *Learning to Write* (1994), *Language as Ideology* (1993), *Social Semiotics* (1988) and *Halliday: System and Function in Language* (1976).

CHARLES MORAN is professor of English at the University of Massachusetts at Amherst. With Gail Hawisher, Paul Leblanc, and Cynthia Selfe he has co-authored *Computers and the Teaching of Writing in American Higher Education, 1979-1994: A History;* with Anne Herrington, he co-edited the award-winning *Writing, Teaching, and Learning in the Disciplines.* He frequently publishes his work in *College English* and *Computers and Composition.* With Diana Callahan, Pat Hunter, and Bruce Penniman he co-directs the Western MassachusettsWriting Project.

STUART MOULTHROP is associate professor of Communications Design at the University of Baltimore. He has published numerous essays on new media and digital culture, as well as creative hypertexts including *Hegirascope,* which was nominated for the Prix Ars Electronica, and *Victory Garden.* Moulthrop is currently co-editor of the online journal *PostmodernCulture,* a judge for the inaugural New York University Press Hypertext Fiction Prize, and recipient of the 1998 Communications Studies International Fellowship at the Royal Melbourne Institute of Technology in Australia.

JAMES PORTER has taught rhetoric and professional writing at Purdue University since 1988. His research focuses on relationships between rhetoric theory (especially postmodern and critical theory) and digital technology. His book *Rhetorical Ethics and Internetworked Writing* (Ablex, 1998) examines ethical and legal issues in writing for the Internet and World Wide Web. Together with Patricia Sullivan, he has published a book on methodology and the study of computers, titled *Opening Spaces* (Ablex, 1997). His current interests include designing instructional materials for online writing courses and examining the rhetoric of policy discourse at the university.

SUSAN ROMANO is an assistant professor of English and coordinator of composition at the University of Texas at San Antonio. She is interested in the pedagogies of online writing instruction, and her recent research examines the rhetorical means by which student participants in electronic conferences establish and refuse discussion topics and social identities. She has published articles on ethnicity and gender in online teaching environments, on writing program administration in the electronic age, and on composition research on the World Wide Web. Currently she is studying the Internet literacy practices of secondary school students in northern Mexico. Her 1993 "Egalitarianism Narrative" won the Ellen Nold Award for best article in computers and composition studies.

CYNTHIA L. SELFE is professor of composition and communication and chair of the humanities department at Michigan Technological University. She is also the founder and co-editor (with Gail Hawisher) of *Computers and Composition*. Selfe is past chair of the Conference on College Composition and Communication and past chair of the College Section of the National Council of Teachers of English. In 1996, Selfe was recognized as an EDUCOM Medal award winner for innovative computer use in higher education—the first woman and the first English teacher ever to receive this award. She is also the author of numerous articles and books on computers including *Computer-Assisted Instruction in Composition* (NCTE) and *Creating a Computer-Supported Writing Facility (Computers and Composition Press)*, and a co-author of *Computers and the Teaching of Writing in American Higher Education, 1979-1994* and *A History and Technical Writing*. She has also co-edited several collections of essays on computers and composition studies.

DIANE SHOOS is associate professor in the humanities department at Michigan Technological University where she teaches and publishes on visual representation and gender studies. She is currently working on a manuscript on film and television representations of domestic violence.

GEOFFREY SIRC works in composition at the University of Minnesota's General College. He believes, of course, that what we're doing is exploring a field, that the field is limitless and without qualitative differentiation but with multiplicity of differences, that our business has changed from judgment to awareness—he believes all this and it makes him speechless, for there is nothing to say. For if he says he is especially active in the theorizing electronic discourse and work with the avant-garde, it doesn't tell you what the others (who are also us) are doing. Would it be accurate to say then that we are all off in separate corners engaged in our special concerns?

SARAH SLOANE is an associate professor of English at University of Puget Sound, who teaches courses in composition, rhetoric, creative writing, and women's studies. She has written or co-written essays and reviews in *Rhetoric Society Quarterly, Reading Research Quarterly, Educators' Tech Exchange, Education of the Visually Handicapped, Composition Chronicle*, and *Tricycle*. She has published chapters in *Scottish Enlightenment Rhetoric and its American Influence* (Gaillet, ed.); *Colors of a Different Horse* (Bishop and Ostrom, eds.); *Unheard Voices in Composition* (Hunter and Fontaine, eds.); *Feminist Cyberscapes* (Blair and Takayoshi, eds.). Her current projects include a chapbook of poems and a book called *Computing Fictions*. She lives in Tacoma with her partner of fifteen years, the writer Judy Doenges, and their lively menagerie of three cats and one alpha dog.

JAMES J. SOSNOSKI is a professor of English at the University of Illinois at Chicago. He is the author of *Token Professionals and Master Critics* and *Modern Skeletons in Postmodern Closets*, as well as various essays on literary and pedagogical theory, computer-assisted pedagogy, and online collaboration. With David Downing, he co-edited "The Geography ofCyberspace," "Conversations in Honor of James Berlin," and "The TicToc Conversations"—special issues of *Works and Days*. He was the executive director of the Society for Critical Exchange, the director of the Group for Research into the Institutionalization and Professionalization of Literary Studies, and the TicToc project. He is collaborating with David Downing on *Living on Borrowed Terms*, a study of the use of terminology in literary and rhetorical studies, and with Patricia Harkin on *Arguing Cultures*, a textbook and website on contemporary persuasive practices.

PATRICIA SULLIVAN is professor of English and director of the Graduate Program in Rhetoric and Composition at Purdue University. Her writing intersects research methodology, computers and composition, and professional and technical writing; her consulting examines the usability of various computer products. She has twice won the NCTE award for best publication in technical and scientific communication. In addition, she is also a former chair of the NCTE Committee on Technical and Scientific Cmmunication and a member of the Committee on Instructional Technology. Her most recent book is *Opening Spaces*, with James Porter. With Gail Hawisher, she is currently at work on a book-length text titled *Women's Online Lives*.

MYKA VIELSTIMMIG is the creation of Kathleen Blake Yancey (associate professor of English at University of NC—Charlotte) and Michael Spooner (director of Utah State University Press). These collaborators have written together in a more conventional style from time to time, but have taken to using the pseudonym for their works that study issues of (electronic) genre, of authorship and collaboration, and of textuality. The most recent article by Yancey and Spooner was published in *CCC*, February 1998. In addition to the chapter here, Myka Vielstimmig has published in the online journal *Kairos* and in *New Worlds, New Words* , a collection edited by Barber and Grigar (forthcoming, MIT Press).

ANNE F. WYSOCKI teaches multimedia, graphic design, digital photography, and other computer arts and writing classes at Michigan Technological University. Her graphic design work can be seen in the cover designs of the books in the Ablex series, *New Directions in Computers and Composition Studies*, edited by Hawisher and Selfe. When she is not designing, her research is in those areas where words and images overlap and move. At the 1998 MLA Convention, she presented a paper on "SeriouslyAnimated: Toward a Rhetoric of the Visually Moving and Interactive."

INDEX